LEARNING ABOUT THE EARTH

Tide Pools

by Colleen Sexton

BELLWETHER MEDIA • MINNEAPOLIS

Note to Librarians, Teachers, and Parents:

Blastoff! Readers are carefully developed by literacy experts and combine standards-based content with developmentally appropriate text.

Level 1 provides the most support through repetition of high-frequency words, light text, predictable sentence patterns, and strong visual support.

Level 2 offers early readers a bit more challenge through varied simple sentences, increased text load, and less repetition of high-frequency words.

Level 3 advances early-fluent readers toward fluency through increased text and concept load, less reliance on visuals, longer sentences, and more literary language.

Level 4 builds reading stamina by providing more text per page, increased use of punctuation, greater variation in sentence patterns, and increasingly challenging vocabulary.

Level 5 encourages children to move from "learning to read" to "reading to learn" by providing even more text, varied writing styles, and less familiar topics.

Whichever book is right for your reader, Blastoff! Readers are the perfect books to build confidence and encourage a love of reading that will last a lifetime!

This edition first published in 2011 by Bellwether Media, Inc.

No part of this publication may be reproduced in whole or in part without written permission of the publisher. For information regarding permission, write to Bellwether Media, Inc., Attention: Permissions Department, 5357 Penn Avenue South, Minneapolis, MN 55419.

Library of Congress Cataloging-in-Publication Data
Sexton, Colleen A., 1967–
  Tide pools / by Colleen Sexton.
    p. cm. – (Blastoff! readers. Learning about the earth)
  Includes bibliographical references and index.
  Summary: "Simple text and full-color photographs introduce beginning readers to the characteristics and geographical locations of tide pools. Developed by literacy experts for students in kindergarten through third grade"–Provided by publisher.
  ISBN 978-0-531-26037-1 (paperback : alk. paper)
  1. Tide pool ecology–Juvenile literature. 2. Tide pools–Juvenile literature. I. Title.
  QH541.5.S35S47 2009
  577.69'9–dc22   2008013326

Printed in the United States of America.   010111   1185

Contents

Tide pools form on rocky shores by the ocean.

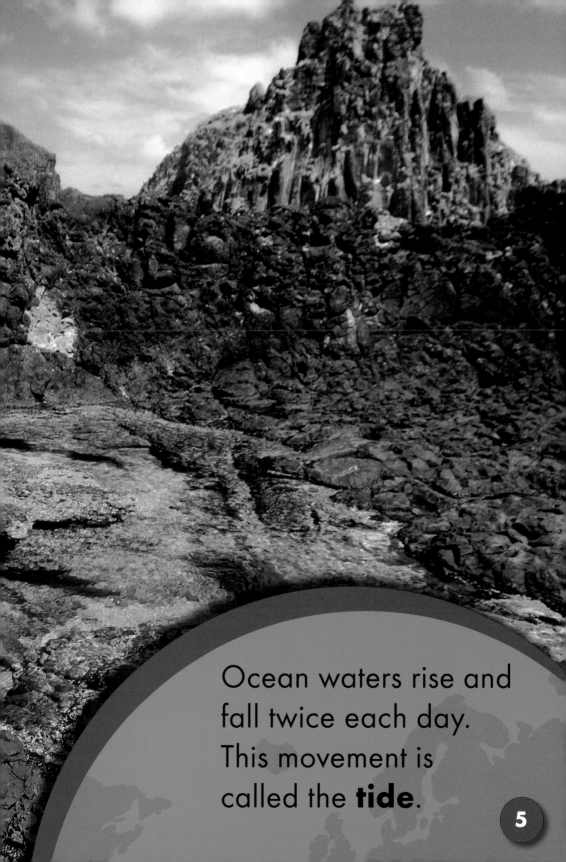

Ocean waters rise and fall twice each day. This movement is called the **tide**.

5

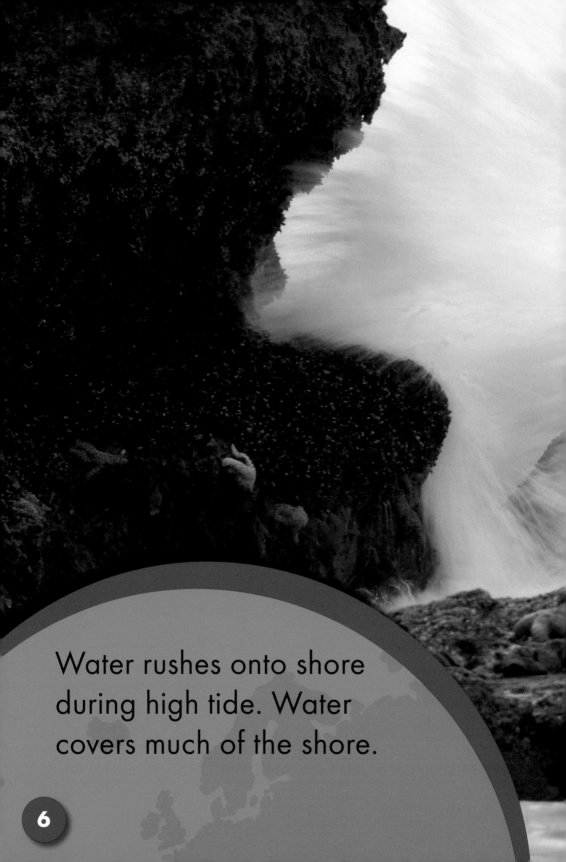

Water rushes onto shore during high tide. Water covers much of the shore.

Water moves away from shore during low tide. The shore becomes part of the land again.

Sometimes water stays on the shore at low tide. It fills **hollows** in the rocks. These hollows become tide pools.

Tide pools that are high on the shore are usually small and **shallow**. Tide pools that are closer to the water can be large and deep.

Tide pools are full of life. Some plants and animals wash in and out with the tide. Others live there all the time.

Tide pools can be dangerous places to live. A strong wave can carry away or crush plants and animals. However, some have found ways to stay safe in a tide pool.

Kelp, Irish moss, and other **seaweed** stick to rocks with a **holdfast**. A holdfast keeps the seaweed from washing away.

Some animals grab hold of rocks.
Sea stars use suckers on their tube
feet to hold on to rocks. Snails
hang on with their one big foot.

Other animals stay safe from waves in other ways. Shrimp and small fish hide in cracks in the rocks. Sea urchins squeeze their prickly bodies between rocks.

Mussels make thick, sticky threads that attach them to rocks. Crabs crawl under thick, wet seaweed.

During low tide, the sun's heat can dry up tide pools. Animals must find ways to stay wet.

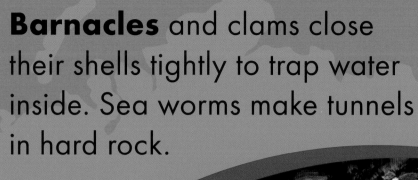

Barnacles and clams close their shells tightly to trap water inside. Sea worms make tunnels in hard rock.

Sea anemones pull in their wet **tentacles** to keep them from drying in the air.

Many tide pool animals breathe **oxygen** in the water. They need oxygen to live. During low tide, animals can use up nearly all of the oxygen in the water.

High tide brings fresh oxygen to the tide pool. It also brings food. Millions of tiny, clear creatures called **plankton** drift in on the tide.

The plankton are a feast for many of the hungry tide pool animals!

Glossary

barnacle—an ocean animal with a hard shell that attaches itself to clams, rocks, ships, and even whales; a barnacle stays where it is attached for its whole life.

holdfast—a rootlike body part that holds some types of seaweed to rocks and other hard surfaces

hollow—an empty space; a place where the ground is lower than other land around it.

oxygen—a gas that animals need to survive

plankton—tiny creatures that float in the ocean and are food for other animals; plankton are too small to be seen with the naked eye.

seaweed—a type of algae that grows in the ocean

shallow—not deep

tentacles—the long, thin arms of some sea animals

tide—the regular rise and fall of ocean waters; water rises at high tide and lowers at low tide.

To Learn More

AT THE LIBRARY
Brenner, Barbara. *One Small Place by the Sea*. New York: HarperCollins, 2004.

Halpern, Monica. *All About Tide Pools*. Washington, D.C.: National Geographic, 2007.

Hodgkins, Fran. *Between the Tides*. Camden, Maine: Down East Books, 2007.

ON THE WEB
Learning more about tide pools is as easy as 1, 2, 3.

1. Go to www.factsurfer.com

2. Enter "tide pools" into search box.

3. Click the "Surf" button and you will see a list of related web sites.

With factsurfer.com, finding more information is just a click away.

Index

The images in this book are reproduced through the courtesy of: Chris Cheadle / age fotostock, front cover, pp. 8-9; Andre Seale / age fotostock, pp. 4-5; rollie rodriguez / Alamy, p. 6; Michael Howell / Alamy, p. 7; George Grall / Getty Images, pp. 10, 14-15, 20-21; Visual&Written SL / Alamy, pp. 12, 13; Mark Conlin / V&W / imagequestmarine.com, p. 16; Carly Rose Hennigan, p. 17; Georgette Douwma / Getty Images, p. 18.

The Caribbean Islands

The Caribbean Islands

Helmut Blume

Translated by
Johannes Maczewski and Ann Norton

Longman

Longman Group Limited
London

Associated companies, branches and representatives
throughout the world

© *Georg Westermann Verlag 1968*
This translation © Longman Group Limited 1974

First published as *Die Westindischen Inseln* 1968
This translation first published 1974

Second impression and first paperback edition 1976

ISBN 0 582 48574 6

Printed in Great Britain by
Lowe & Brydone (Printers) Ltd., Thetford, Norfolk

Contents

Maps

Diagrams

Tables

Illustrations

Preface

The Caribbean Islands are most rewarding for geographical research for two main reasons: first, they offer in a relatively limited space an extremely wide variety of physical factors and second, the cultural landscape is strongly diversified in the various regions. Tempting as it is for the geographer, a comparative study of this colourful archipelago is impeded by the differing amount of research which has been done in the various parts. Indeed, the variations in official statistics resulting from national fragmentation and the limited possibilities for travel and field work caused by sometimes tense political situations presented obstacles for obtaining a general survey of this Middle American sub-region. The author was prompted to deal with this region from the geographical point of view, because until now a geography of the Caribbean Islands did not exist in the German language.

The views expressed in this book are based both on personal acquaintance with most of the Caribbean Islands and on an extensive knowledge of the literature. The results of special research in physical as well as cultural geography undertaken by the author in various islands have been published already. Maps, diagrams and illustrations are by the author if not otherwise stated.

The manuscript was finished in late 1966; it contains, however, several supplements which take into account the developments of 1967. It was not possible to deal in this book with the material published in 1967. This only appears as an appendix in the bibliography.

Authorities and private individuals, librarians and archivists, not only in the Caribbean Islands but also in Amsterdam, London, Madrid, Paris, and Seville, greatly assisted me during my field work and in obtaining statistics and publications. I received essential information and important comments during countless conversations with persons of many different classes, races and nationalities. I am greatly indebted to all those who offered their help but whom to name at this place is impossible. I am grateful to Dr E. Ehlers and H.-D. Haas for assisting me in the proof reading.

Last but not least I want to thank the Deutsche Forschungsgemein-schaft which made possible my visits to the Caribbean Islands and the print-ing of this book, and secondly, the Westermann publishing house for its great patience regarding the illustration of this book with maps, diagrams and illustrations.

I dedicate this book to my wife Ilse.

Tübingen   Helmut Blume
Autumn 1968

Geographical research of the present time

Until very recently geographical research work in the Caribbean has been carried out almost exclusively by European and North American scientists. Among the institutions which have concerned themselves especially with the geography of the islands, and which stand out in this field, are the Geographical Institutes of McGill University in Montreal, and the University of California in Berkeley, and the Centre d'Études de Géographie Tropicale of the University of Bordeaux, each of which has published numerous works on the subject. In addition, individual scientists from the above countries, from Germany and Great Britain, and also more recently from the Soviet Union and Czechoslovakia, have made valuable contributions to Caribbean geography. Reference should be made here to the bibliography which follows, in particular also to the Supplement 1967–70.

Within the Caribbean Islands geographical study has primarily been concentrated on Cuba. Cuba is also the only island in the area which has produced a modern thematic atlas (*Atlas Nacional de Cuba*, Habana 1970), the result of many years of systematic research work carried out together by Cuban and Soviet geographers. Elsewhere in the Caribbean area the founding in 1965 of the Geographical Institute of the University of Puerto Rico in Río Piedras, and shortly after the founding of the Institute of Geography at the University of the West Indies in Mona, Jamaica represent real milestones in the establishment of geographical education and exploration.

Scope for geographical research work in the Caribbean area is constantly expanding owing to the wide variety of topics for study. There are few aspects of geographical research, either from physical, cultural or social points of view, which could not be taken up in some part or other of the area. In spite of this, geographical research is still in its early stages. Because of their extraordinary range of geographical complexities, the Caribbean Islands offer the geographer an apparently inexhaustible field of study.

In view of this it is commendable that the Geographical Institute at the University of the West Indies is publishing for the first time in 1971 an informative periodical *The Caribbean Geographer*. This publication will promote contact between all geographers doing work in and on the Caribbean Islands, and will keep them informed of the current research work being done by both institutions and individuals. As in other subjects, greater cooperation in the field of geography will doubtless be of value in the future.

Note on the English text

The content of the text in the English edition has remained practically unchanged from that of the German version. However, in order to make allowances for the frequent changes in the world of the Caribbean Islands, as far as possible more recent figures on the development of the economy and the official estimate of population in Cuba for the year 1966 have been used. Furthermore, the text concerning the CARIFTA has been extended and a small section on geographical research of the present time added. The Bibliography has been enlarged with a supplement giving details of publications relevant to the geography of the area which appeared between 1967 and 1970.

The writer wishes to express his gratitude to the Longman publishing group for its promotion of an English version. Further he wishes to thank Mr Johannes Maczewski and Miss Ann Norton in Kingston, Jamaica, for the care they exhibited in the painstaking work of translation; Mrs R. Wilson in Edinburgh for going over the translation and for reading the proofs; and finally he thanks Dr H. D. Haas for his help in compiling more recent figures regarding the economy.

Tübingen, October 1971   Helmut Blume

Part 1
General Survey

1

The Caribbean island chain in Middle America[1]

The Caribbean islands: their geographical position in space and through time

The term 'Caribbean Islands' is here used to describe the chain of Middle American islands which extends from North to South America, separating the American Mediterranean from the Atlantic Ocean. For western historical reasons these islands are commonly referred to as 'the West Indies'. The Caribbean Sea and the Gulf of Mexico together make up the American Mediterranean: in oceanography the term 'Central American Sea' has been proposed by Wüst (1963) because its hydrological management differs greatly from that of the Old World Mediterranean.

The meaning of the term 'West Indies' has changed repeatedly, and while German, and to some extent English speakers continue to use it, though not consistently, the use of the term 'Caribbean' has come into favour in general today, as applied to the whole archipelago. 'Caribbean Islands' in particular refer to the chain of islands within the arc; this terminology is followed in this book, except in contexts where historical considerations make 'West Indies' more appropriate.

The Spaniards termed all territories which were reached by going west from Europe and which they discovered and conquered as the 'West Indies'. This was to stress their different position relative to the territories which the Portuguese discovered in the east and which were called the East Indies. In the same way that the term 'East Indies' designated countries far from each other in South and South-East Asia, the term 'West Indies' at first related to the American continent as well as to the offshore islands. When the Spaniards ceased to refer to their increasingly differentiated colonial empire in the New World by the term 'West Indies' the British and the French, when they themselves became colonial powers in America, continued to use it in its original Spanish meaning. During the first period of colonization

[1] Middle America covers the following areas:
Central American States of Guatemala, Salvador, Honduras, British Honduras, Nicaragua, Costa Rica, Panama, and Mexico, and all the Caribbean Islands.

the British even thought of their possessions in North America as part of the West Indies, and as late as the end of the eighteenth century there was talk of 'two Indias'. With time the English language definition of the term became more precise. It referred mainly to the colonies among the Middle American islands, and sometimes included the colonies on the Middle and South American mainland. Today the term 'West Indies' is often still used by the British to mean the British islands in Middle America as well as British Honduras (soon to be renamed Belize) and Guyana, the former being an independent member of the British Commonwealth since 1964 and the latter having become independent in 1966.

The term 'West Indies' is sometimes appropriate from a historical point of view. But as far as geography is concerned it is unsatisfactory, and in this book the term 'Caribbean Islands' is used, to include all the Middle American islands, regardless of whether they used to belong, or still belong, to Spain, France, Britain or the Netherlands, and including the Antilles and the Bahamas.[1] In American and English (cf. Wilgus), French (cf. E. Révert), and Spanish (cf. G. Arciniegas) linguistic usage the term 'Caribbean' includes all countries surrounding the Caribbean Sea: the so-called 'West Indies', the North of South America, where Venezuela and Colombia are border states to the Caribbean Sea, and the various nations of the Central American mainland.

Position, subdivision and size

The Caribbean Islands are scattered over a distance of about 4000 km extending east in a wide arc from Cape San Antonio at the western tip of Cuba to Aruba. They represent a subdivision of Middle America and form a belt, generally speaking, parallel to the Central American continental bridge from north-west to south-east, between 85° and 59° 30′W and between 32° 30′ and 7°N. The islands cover an area of 233872 sq km, about the size of the Federal Republic of Germany, and make up 8·6 per cent of the Middle American area. In the north-west, the large islands of Cuba, Hispaniola, and Puerto Rico are aligned from WNW to ESE. North of them, extending in roughly the same direction, are the Bahama Islands, and to the south of Cuba lies Jamaica. To the east of Puerto Rico, the Virgin Islands are the first links in a chain of small islands which runs in a southerly direction as far as Trinidad near the north coast of South America and then continues in a more open pattern to the west as far as Aruba, off the Venezuelan coast.

The usual subdivision of the islands in use since their discovery and conquest by the Spaniards, is based on their position and size. Three groups of islands are easily recognized: the large islands of Cuba, Hispaniola, Puerto Rico, and Jamaica are jointly called the Greater Antilles; the chain of small islands from the Virgin Islands to Aruba is known as the Lesser

[1] The Commonwealth of the Bahamas became independent in July 1973.

Antilles; and the numerous islands north of the Greater Antilles form the Bahama Islands. Only the Lesser Antilles allow a further subdivision. The north–south part of the island chain has always been called the 'Islands to the Windward', and the chain of islands running from east to west off the South American north coast from Margarita to Aruba the 'Islands to the Leeward'.

About nine-tenths of the total area covered by the islands comes under the Greater Antilles, while the last tenth is almost equally divided among the Lesser Antilles and the Bahamas (Table 1).

Table 1.   The Caribbean island groups: area and population, 1960

	Size		*Population*		*Density of population (persons*
	sq km	*%*	*(1000)*	*%*	*per sq km)*
Greater Antilles	207 968	88·9	17 227	87·8	83
Lesser Antilles	14 078	6·0	22 357	11·6	161
Islands to the Windward	12 007	5·1	2 089	10·3	167
Islands to the Leeward	2 071	0·9	268	1·3	127
Bahama Islands (incl. Turks and Caicos Islands)	11 826	5·1	113	0·6	10
The Caribbean islands (total)	233 872	100·0	19 697	100·0	84

Source:
Statistisches Jahrbuch für die Bundesrepublik Deutschland, Stuttgart und Mainz, 1964;
The Statesman's Year Book 1964, London and New York, 1964;
Academia de Ciencias de Cuba; *Area de Cuba*, Habana, 1965.

Names of the islands and island groups

Almost all the islands were discovered and named by Columbus. The Lesser Antilles have retained their Columban names in spite of their eventful history. This is surprising because these islands were colonized very late by north-west European nations and not by the Spaniards. The Bahamas and the Greater Antilles are no longer called by their Columban names. In the case of the Bahamas this is not surprising since the Spaniards did not stay there for long. Although they were at the centre of the Spanish colonial empire, some of the islands of the Greater Antilles, such as Cuba and Jamaica, assumed the names in use among the indigenous Indians who soon afterwards became extinct. The Indian name Haiti was reintroduced in 1804 when the newly founded Negro republic chose it as its name. Before that, the second largest island of the Antilles was usually referred to by the

Spanish name, Santo Domingo (after the name of its capital, founded in 1496), as well as by the French version, Saint Domingue. Both names referred either to the Spanish part, or to the French part of the island, as well as to the island as a whole which had been called La Española by Columbus. During the nineteenth century the name Haiti was added to the older name Santo Domingo, and was used synonymously and applied to the entire island. Today these inconsistencies in the name are being eliminated by the increasing use of the name Hispaniola, which is the latinized version of La Española and which can be traced back to 1493. The American Geographical Society has accepted this name. Of the three possible names, Santo Domingo, Haiti, and Hispaniola, the last is preferred here. As to the island of Puerto Rico, the name San Juan de Bautista which Columbus gave to the island, survives in the name of its capital, while the name Puerto Rico, given to the city when it was founded, today refers to the island.

The names of the three groups of islands have different origins. Bahamas is an Amerindian name and the word Antilles is derived from the legendary island Antilia which was believed (before Columbus's journeys) to lie somewhere between Europe and Asia.

The division of the Lesser Antilles into the two groups of 'Islands to the Windward' and 'Islands to the Leeward' has been in use since the early times of Spanish colonization and was adopted by the Spanish, French, Dutch, and German languages:

The meridional chain of islands (from the Virgin Islands in the north to Trinidad in the south)	Islas de Barlovento Iles au Vent Bovenwindse Eilanden Inseln über dem Winde
The islands off the South American mainland (from Margarita in the east to Aruba in the west)	Islas de Sotavento Iles sous le Vent Benedenwindse Eilanden Inseln unter dem Winde

These names express the position of the islands in relation to the prevailing easterly Trade Wind. In fact, both of these groups of islands are affected by the trade winds, but the early seafarers knew that the trade winds brought rain to only one of these groups. Therefore they called the humid islands, the 'Islands to the Windward', and the arid islands, the 'Islands to the Leeward'.

Confusion over the nomenclature of the Lesser Antilles exists because the English language also makes the distinction in this region between Windward and Leeward Islands, but without meaning the same thing as the Spanish, French, Dutch, and German languages. The British divided their possessions within the meridional chain of the Lesser Antilles (the 'Islands to the Windward') into the Leeward Islands in the north and the Windward Islands in the south. But these are purely administrative units, as can be

5

seen by the fact that in 1940 the island of Dominica left the Leeward group and joined the Windward group. So the paradox arises that the Dutch possessions, officially called Bovenwindse Eilanden, are situated among British possessions, which are also officially called Leeward Islands. We shall therefore use the terms 'Islands to the Windward' and 'Islands to the Leeward' in their traditional meaning since Spanish colonial rule and use the terms Leeward and Windward Islands only for the British administrative units within the group of 'Islands to the Windward'.

An island bridge between the continents?

The Caribbean islands have been called a bridge between North and South America. Certainly, a chain of islands lies between these two continents and some islands are not far from the mainland coast. The shortest distances between the islands and the mainland amount to some 20 km across the Boca de la Sierpe and the Boca del Dragón from Trinidad to the South American coast and only 80 km across the Florida Strait from Bimini, the westernmost island of the Bahamas, to the North American mainland. The Florida Strait is 180 km wide between the mainland coast of Florida and the large Caribbean island of Cuba, and the Yucatán Channel between Cuba and the Middle American mainland is 210 km wide. The distances between the individual Islands to the Windward are usually so small that on a small-scale map the islands resemble a string of pearls. Indeed, the islands in this part of the Caribbean are so very close that one can see from one island the coastline of the next island with the naked eye. From a plane it is often possible to see more than two islands at the same time.

Nevertheless, it would be wrong to describe the Caribbean islands as a bridge between continents. At present not even the Central American mainland is a land bridge between North and South America as far as traffic is concerned. Far less do the islands possess the character of a bridge. Communication between them has always been bad, and still is; factors resulting from physical disunity are much too strong. Thus they are not a bridge: they are simply a chain of islands between the two continents, made up of a multitude of individual parts separated by distances of various lengths.

2

Topography and structure

Distribution of terrestrial topography

Caribbean topography is extremely varied. Three islands of the Greater Antilles (Hispaniola, Jamaiça, Puerto Rico) exhibit a distinctly mountainous character, while the surface features of the fourth (Cuba) are dominated by extensive lowland plains. Among the Lesser Antilles, the Islands to the Windward may be divided into two groups: an outer chain of low-lying islands (from Anguilla to Barbados), and an inner chain of mountainous islands (from Saba to Grenada). Finally, the Islands to the Leeward are hilly or mountainous, accordant with the relief of the nearby mainland coast of Venezuela.

Hispaniola exhibits the greatest amplitude of relief: the Pico Duarte in the Cordillera Central reaches 3175 m and the surface of the nearby Enriquillo Depression descends to a depth of 40 m below sea-level. In other islands as well, the mountains rise to considerable heights: the Blue Mountain Peak in Jamaica reaches 2257 m, El Yunque in Puerto Rico, 1065 m, and Pico Turquino in the Sierra Maestra in the south of Cuba 1972 m. In Hispaniola these peaks are situated in long mountain ranges which are separated from each other by longitudinal depressions. All mountains and longitudinal depressions extend roughly in a west to east direction. Extensive plains of less than 100 m above sea-level are to be found only in Cuba.

The greatest heights among the chain of Islands to the Windward are represented by Soufrière (1467 m) in Guadeloupe and Montagne Pelée (1397 m) in Martinique. A linear pattern of mountain ranges, like that in the Greater Antilles, is not found in the Islands to the Windward, but is present in the Northern Range of Trinidad, near the Venezuelan coast, where El Tucuche reaches 937 m, and in the Islands to the Leeward which rise to 920 m with the Cerro de San Juan in Margarita.

Distribution of submarine topography

The magnitude of Caribbean relief, which has great altitudinal variations

7

within very short distances, becomes even more strongly accentuated when the distribution of submarine topography is also taken into consideration. The mountain system of the Middle American islands then appears as one of the most majestic of mountain ranges displaying an absolute range in height of up to 12 500 m.

An extended narrow depression runs parallel to the outer side of the Antillean arc from mid Cuba to the Tobago Basin between the southern Islands to the Windward and the Barbados ridge. Its basal parts have a depth of 8540 m in the Puerto Rico Trench and descend to minus 9219 m in the Milwaukee Trough. The Puerto Rico Trench continues westward through the Windward Passage between Cuba and Hispaniola towards the Cayman Trench in the Caribbean Sea.

Inside the Antillean arc the Caribbean Sea is divided into several basins of deep water. The Beata Ridge, stretching from Hispaniola in the NNE–SSW direction, separates the western Colombian from the eastern Venezuelan basin. The Aves Ridge, running from north to south, separates off the Grenada basin adjacent to the inner edge of the arc of Islands to the Windward. The Nicaragua Ridge (Pedro and Rosalind Banks), stretching WSW–ENE, forms the northern boundary of the Colombian basin. Parallel to it is the Cayman Trench (Bartlett Trough) which reaches a depth of 7250 m only 30 km off the Cuban coast. North of this trench lies the Cayman Ridge (Cayman Islands, Misteriosa and Rosario Banks), also aligned in a WSW–ENE direction, and beyond this ridge lies the Yucatán Basin. The sea depths in the southern basins are mainly between 4000 and 5000 m; in the northern, except in the Cayman Trench, they lie between 3500 and 4500 m. Subdued relief prevails.

Major relief forms and geological structure

The Cayman Trench and the adjoining ridges in the northern Caribbean Sea follow the same direction as the mountains and depressions of the Greater Antilles. All these belong to the jumbled young structures that divide up the American Cordillera system which developed from Alpine folding. The faultblock mountains of the Cordilleras, originating in North America, continue along the Cayman and Nicaragua Ridges in the Caribbean Sea, proceeding from the Middle American mainland as far as the mountain ranges of the Greater Antilles. Eastwards, they extend to the Anegada Trench (depths of up to 4500 m) to the east of the Virgin Islands. Geologically, therefore, the Virgin Islands belong to the Greater Antilles. The northern branch of the Middle American fault block mountains extends from Guatemala and British Honduras across the Cayman Ridge to the Cuban Sierra Maestra and then on across the north-western peninsula of Hispaniola into the Cordillera Central of that island. The southern branch runs from northern Honduras along the Nicaraguan Ridge and the Blue Mountains of Jamaica into the south-western peninsula of Hispaniola.

The curving of the North American Cordilleras in a west to east direction in Middle America has its parallel in northern South America where this continent's mountain ranges also turn in a west to east direction. The Cordilleras of western South America continue not only into the Venezuelan coastal regions, but also into the mountains of Trinidad and the Islands to the Leeward.

The relief of the Antillean faultblock mountains is neither the result of Alpine folding in Late Cretaceous nor Early Tertiary, but of Late Tertiary tectonic fracturing which caused some faultblocks to rise and others to sink, some in parts well below sea-level. These post-uplift structural movements began during the Pliocene, lasted through the Pleistocene and are still in effect today. This is shown in the raising by several hundred metres of Pleistocene marine deposits and in the frequent terrestrial earthquakes and submarine earthquakes of the present time.

Large faultlines distinctively stamp the appearance of the landscape. The faults generally follow the Alpine fold structures of the Late Cretaceous and Early Tertiary orogeny. Therefore, the faultblock depressions in Hispaniola, which appear topographically as longitudinal depressions, are situated in a synclinorium, and the mountains between in an anticlinorium. In detail, however, one can recognize a considerable divergence in the course of the faultlines and the old fold structures. Usually the faults intersect the folds at an acute angle, and in some places a still greater divergence is to be noted. For instance, a wide belt of fold structures of the Cordillera Central in Hispaniola, running mostly WNW–ESE, turns sharply in a southerly direction. This is even more true in the instance of the Sierra de Baoruco in the same island, whose old fold structures running in a southeasterly direction, form the eastern part of the southern Cordillera which runs WNW–ESE. The distinct fault scarp forming the northern boundary of the Enriquillo Trench truncates the fold structures. On the whole, the presentday relief is largely independent of the structures of the Alpine orogeny and is clearly determined by post-orogenic faulting.

As in the Central American mainland bridge, the gap between the North American and South American Cordillera system in the West Indies is occupied by a chain of volcanoes. They are present in the young volcanic mountainous islands of the inner island arc of the Islands to the Windward, while in the low-lying islands of the outer arc Middle and Late Tertiary limestone overlies older volcanic deposits. Volcanism in the Islands to the Windward, which was begun by the Antilles orogeny, dates from Early Tertiary and has continued to the present time. The tectonic period to which the Islands to the Windward belong is not quite clear. J. Butterlin has listed many of the theories of the mountain-building of the West Indies. They differ mainly in the interpretation of the structural history of the Islands to the Windward. Adjacent to the faultblock mountains of the Greater Antilles, with their bold relief and their distinct fault scarps, lies an orogenic foreland, a topographically monotonous region of lowland plains,

9

consisting of low-lying horizontal limestone plateaux. Like the peninsula of Florida in North America and the peninsula of Yucatán in the Middle American mainland, most of Cuba and the Bahama Islands on the northern side of the Caribbean faultblock belong to this landform grouping.

As a result three different categories of relief of structural origin may be distinguished (Map 5): (1) the faultblock mountains usually with a large amount of local relief; (2) the volcanic mountains, again with a large amount of local relief, but less bold; and (3) the low and uniform limestone plateaux, often found within the orogenic foreland and, in small pockets, within the fold mountains themselves. Category 1 includes the islands of the Greater Antilles (although only a small part of Cuba), the Islands to the Leeward, and Trinidad and Tobago; category 2 includes the mountainous islands in the inner arc of the Islands to the Windward; and category 3 represents the greater part of Cuba, the islands in the outer arc of the Islands to the Windward and the Bahama Islands.

Earthquakes, volcanism, and the distribution of gravity anomalies

Earthquake epicentres are found throughout the entire Antillean arc and on the adjacent sea floors. Very strong submarine earthquakes occur at the edges of the Cayman Trench; earthquakes also achieve high degrees of intensity in the area of the faultblock depressions of the Greater Antilles. Cities in the Antilles have been repeatedly destroyed by earthquakes. Recent volcanism is restricted to the inner arc of the Islands to the Windward, but during the initial and widespread mountain building there was volcanic activity and also, until the Miocene era, the subsequent volcanism affected the entire area of the Antilles. In most of the Islands to the Windward volcanism ceased after the Tertiary. Only Montagne Pelée in Martinique and the volcanoes called Soufrière in Guadeloupe and St Vincent have been active during recent decades. The eruption of Montagne Pelée in 1902 led to enormous destruction. The formation of solfataras has been observed, mainly in St Lucia.

Earthquakes and volcanism point to the instability of the earth's crust in the Caribbean area. This instability is characterized by strong post-orogenic movements, and by the distribution of gravity anomalies. While a rather balanced and uniform distribution exists in the Caribbean Sea with only a small area of positive anomalies, a narrow belt of strongly negative gravity anomalies runs along the outer front of the Antilles from Cuba to Trinidad and further on to the north of Aruba. The gravity anomalies reach the extreme negative value of -346 milligals in the Puerto Rico Trench. This considerable anomaly seems to point to an exceptional thinning of the earth's crust and heavy sedimentation resulting from turbidity currents in the Puerto Rico Trench.

3
Oceanography

Surface water

Temperature and salinity

The high temperature of the surface water in the sea area around the Caribbean islands which results in heat loss into the atmosphere, is of great significance to the climate. During the warmest month the water temperature everywhere amounts to 28·3°C–28·9°C; during the coldest month the temperature falls to 23·9°C around the Bahamas and to 25·6°C around the Greater Antilles and the Islands to the Leeward; in the seas enclosed by the Islands to the Windward, the water retains a higher temperature. In general, seasonal changes in the temperature of sea water are minimal; they amount to a maximum of 4·4°C around the Bahamas, 2·7°C–3·3°C around the Greater Antilles and the Islands to the Leeward, and only about 2°C in the centre of the Caribbean Sea.

Since the temperature leads to a high degree of evaporation, the surface water contains a high proportion of salt. However, salinity is well below that of the Old World Mediterranean, because the exchange of water between the Atlantic Ocean and the Caribbean Sea is fifteen times as high as it is in the Mediterranean. Compared with the North Atlantic, the Caribbean Sea has much higher seasonal variations in salinity, from 35·9 per thousand during the winter to 35·2 per thousand during the summer (Wüst). This is to be attributed to the varying precipitation during the dry winter and the wet summer. The centre of the Caribbean Sea receives only 100–150 mm of precipitation from December to May, but 300–400 mm between June and November (Möller). The decrease in salinity at the surface of the Caribbean Sea during the summer rainy season is also caused by a higher water inflow from rivers (exact data not yet available).

Currents

Currents at the surface of the Caribbean Sea are primarily the outcome of the earth's atmospheric circulation; the topographical factors are only a

11

secondary cause (cf. p. 8). The entire region is characterized by a strong surface current resulting from its position in the trade wind area. Between about 28°N and the South American north coast, the westward flowing North Equatorial Current strikes the West Indian islands on a broad front. Its southern part near the coast which is directed more to the north-east is called the Guyana Current (Map 1).

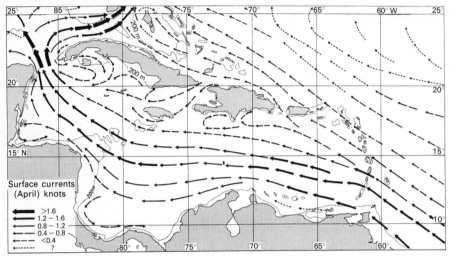

Map 1. Surface currents in the Caribbean Sea, April (after Wüst).

The greater part of the North Equatorial Current and the Guyana Current continues westward through the Caribbean Sea as the Caribbean Current beyond the Islands to the Windward. The speed of the Caribbean Current varies considerably according to seasons. It amounts to 1·2 to 1·6 knots during April, and 0·8 to 1·2 knots during October, and is highest during the dry winter season when the trade winds blow most strongly. The decrease in speed during summer results from the more northerly position of the Inter-Tropical Front which in its turn causes the cessation of the trade winds.

The surface current, turning towards the narrows of the Yucatán Channel, gains greater speeds (maximum 2·5 knots during April) as the north flowing Yucatán Current. The Yucatán Current, which bifurcates in the Gulf of Mexico, continues as the Florida Current attaining a very high maximum speed of 3·7 knots during April in the Florida Strait. It is the source of the Atlantic Gulf Stream.

The existence of strong currents in the Caribbean, influenced by the trade winds, led to the establishment of certain sea routes during the time of sailing ships. While there were several passages into the Caribbean Sea through the Islands to the Windward, the Florida Strait was the only outlet into the Atlantic Ocean (cf. p. 65).

Within the area of uniform surface currents in the seas around the Caribbean islands several countercurrents and eddies result from the distribution of land and sea and from the topography of the sea floor. These are
especially noticeable at the end of winter (April). An eastward counter-
current is then characteristic along Hispaniola's south coast and along the
south coast of the Cuban Oriente. An eddy with a clockwise rotation sometimes develops on the south coast of western Cuba.

Tidal currents hardly exist in the Caribbean Sea. The tidal range along
the shores of the Caribbean islands amounts to only 0·20–0·40 m.

Distribution of warm and cold water

The annual changes in temperature and salinity are perceptible only to a
depth of 100 m. Further down the temperature falls quickly to about
7°–8°C at 600 m, and then more slowly to about 5°C at 1000 m, until it
reaches slightly more than 4°C at a depth of 2000 m and hardly falls any
further down to the sea floor. As regards temperature zones, one may distinguish between an upper warm water layer and a much more extensive
lower layer of cold water.

In the warm water layer, salinity reaches a maximum of 36·6 per thousand
at a depth of 150 m. The water in this layer near to the surface comes mainly
from subtropical regions in the North Atlantic as a subtropical under-
current, and to a lesser extent from the subtropical regions of the South
Atlantic by means of the deep reaching Guyana Current which moves
through the Caribbean Sea via the islands in almost the same direction as
the surface currents. The subtropical deep sea water which flows into the
Caribbean Sea at a depth of 150 m along both sides of St Lucia is noticeable

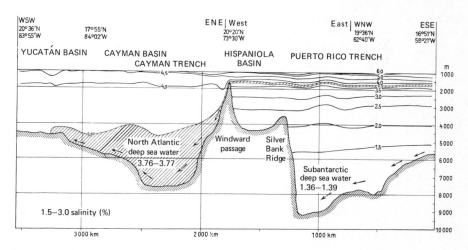

Fig. 1. The flow of North Atlantic deep sea water through the Windward Passage
(simplified from Wüst).

13

as far west as Jamaica and must be seen, after the surface Caribbean Current, as the second source of the Gulf Stream.

Within the cold water layer two bottom currents can be traced according to their different oxygen contents. An intermediate layer at a depth of between 700 and 850 m, characterized by a minimum oxygen content, carries subantarctic water into the Caribbean Sea through the passages on both sides of St Lucia. Its oxygen content is only slowly reduced by mixing and it can be traced as far west as the Yucatán Channel. The second bottom current flows between about 1500 and 2500 m. It consists of North Atlantic water from the Greenland region and flows into the Caribbean Sea mainly through the 1625 m deep Windward Passage (Fig. 1). Far less water flows in through the 2300 m deep Anegada Passage because of its narrowness. Beyond these passages the North Atlantic water sinks and fills the lower parts of the secondary basins of the Caribbean Sea. Obviously it is not replaced as regularly as the water in the upper layers, because mixing at depth is irregular. This can be seen by the annual changes in the proportion of salt in the North Atlantic deep sea water on the floor of the Caribbean Sea. Presumably, one main reason for the irregular influx from the North Atlantic is the limited depth of these underwater passages; depending on their depth, the North Atlantic cold water currents either can or cannot flow along these passages between the islands.

Observations of the currents, at the surface and at various depths, prove that the entire water volume of the Caribbean Sea is constantly being renewed, while in the Old World Mediterranean the deep water of the basins is not fed by the Atlantic. The topographical division of the American Mediterranean into several basins, its incomplete seclusion from the Atlantic by the islands, because of the different depths of their various passages, and finally, the global position of the Caribbean Sea in the tropics, therefore, cause water characteristics and circulation, which are quite unlike those of the Old World Mediterranean.

4

Climate

Climatic elements

The climate of the Caribbean islands is determined by their position in the tropics, by their insular position surrounded by water whose temperature never falls below 25°C and by their relief.

Temperature

The high temperatures result from the low latitude. At sea-level the average temperature throughout the year is over 25°C everywhere; it rises slowly towards the equator, from 25·1°C in the Bahamas to 26·7°C in Curaçao. Simultaneously, the difference in temperature between the coldest and the hottest months decreases from 6·2°C in the Bahamas to 2·3°C in Curaçao. Seasonal differences are therefore hardly, if at all, determined by temperature. Temperatures in the islands do not vary according to a seasonal climate, but a daily climate (Fig. 2).

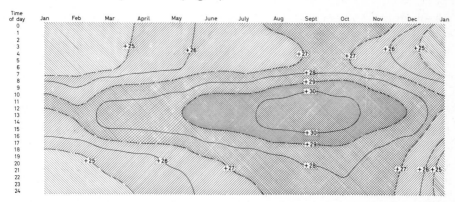

Fig. 2. Daily temperature changes in Willemstad, Curaçao.

The daily variation in temperature in the Caribbean islands averages 8°C; there are, however, considerable differences according to time and region.

15

Temperature reaches its minimum immediately before sunrise, which is generally about 6 o'clock, because of the uniform length of day. First, the temperature quickly rises several degrees, then more slowly, until it reaches its maximum when the sun is in its zenith position. It is obvious that during the heat of midday people should try to avoid being in the open. The buildings in the cities hardly cast shadows into the sunlit streets. The temperature falls rather quickly during the afternoon and more slowly during the night when the walls continue to radiate back their stored heat for a long time.

Very extreme temperatures are non-existent in the Caribbean islands. For instance, the average maximum temperature in Pointe-à-Pitre in Guadeloupe amounts to 29·6°C, the average minimum temperature is 21·2°C; 32·6°C was recorded as the highest absolute temperature and 13·0°C was the lowest. Temperature maxima and minima depend on the islands' latitude and humidity. Greater humidity and a position nearer to the equator cause more balanced temperatures. There is no place in the Caribbean islands where the average maximum exceeds 36°C or the average minimum falls below 12°C.

In the mountainous islands one may distinguish various temperature zones according to altitude since there is an average decrease in temperature of 0·6°C/100 m with height. As in the South and Middle American mainland, the lowest zone, up to a height of about 900 m, is called the *tierra caliente* has an average temperature throughout the year of over 21°C; the next temperature zone is the *tierra templada* (21°C–16°C); the highest zone, with a height of about 2000 m and above, is the *tierra fría* (<16°C). Only the mountains in the Greater Antilles are high enough to be in the tierra fría zone.

Atmospheric pressure and winds

Mean monthly atmospheric pressure varies regularly. During the winter months higher pressure reflects the strong influence of the subtropical anticyclone, but during the summer months lower pressure reflects its weaker influence. Between June and August there is a secondary maximum in atmospheric pressure. On the whole, differences in atmospheric pressure are not great. Monthly averages differ between 1009 and 1012 mb in the Islands to the Leeward, between 1012 and 1018 mb in the Greater Antilles, and between 1014 and 1020 mb in the Bahamas. These data express the mid-position of the Caribbean islands between the equatorial region of low pressure and the subtropical belt of high pressure. It is this pressure gradient between the subtropical and equatorial latitudes that produces the trade winds. Observations in the open sea show that, throughout the entire Caribbean region, the trade winds blow steadily throughout the year from easterly directions, without any daily deviations worth mentioning. Above the trade winds which blow at the earth's surface, the antitrade winds blow from westerly directions at varying heights during the year. Wind roses compiled from data measured at observatories on the leeward sides of the large islands do not register the regular air flow of the trade winds since the rhythm is replaced here by the daily rhythm of land and sea breezes. The high trail of smoke from the Kingston cement factory demonstrates most clearly how, on the leeward side of Jamaica, the land breeze is superseded by the sea breeze during the morning. The wind shearing of many of the trees on the windward sides of all Caribbean islands, and everywhere in the Islands to the Leeward, illustrates the force and the prevalence of the trade winds. Trade winds and local winds blow everywhere in the Caribbean and make the high temperatures easy to endure.

Atmospheric humidity and cloudiness

Relative humidity is high in the Caribbean area. It shows greater daily variations than seasonal and reaches its peak of more than 90 per cent everywhere at about sunrise. This results in the formation of a large amount of dew and in the development of misty veils particularly in the mangrove swamps. Rising day temperatures cause a decrease in relative humidity, nowhere falling below 50 per cent and usually not below 70 per cent. Because of the high relative humidity, even in dry islands, the air seldom achieves the distinctive transparency of the subtropical arid regions. The stifling heat, caused by the high humidity, is felt especially during times when the airflow decreases or during periods of lull.

The air masses above the Caribbean have a high relative humidity throughout the year because of their long journey westward across the Atlantic Ocean. They are in a state of latent instability which causes the formation of banks of cumulus. During the winter their upper parts indicate the very distinct trade wind inversion, i.e. the borderline between the lower humid, and the upper dry, air masses. This inversion occurs at a height of 1500 to 1800 m during winter, and during summer, if it exists at all, between 3000 and 6000 m. Cumulus clouds develop during the morning as the temperature rises. Relief also has a strong influence, as even the smallest differences in elevation lead to the formation of clouds and precipitation when the unstable, humid air masses rise. Usually the mountains are cloud-covered by 10 o'clock in the morning. Cloud formation reaches its maximum by early afternoon when each island has its own cloud layer, cumulus above small islands, cumulonimbus clouds above large islands. For instance, in Guadeloupe clouds may extend down to 800 m or 300 m above sea-level according to weather conditions. In islands with alternating plains and mountains, as in Trinidad and Cuba, the mountains sometimes remain cloudless while cumulonimbus clouds hover above the plains. This is caused by the katabatic flow of air down mountain slopes beneath the unstable air above the plains. Over the sea cloud formation is active, especially during the night, and reaches its maximum immediately before daybreak. Windward shores are seldom cloudless during the night, in contrast to leeward shores.

17

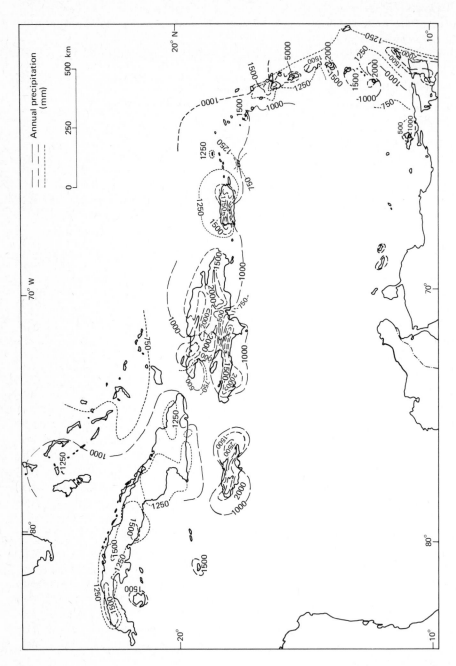

Map 2. Annual precipitation in the Caribbean area.

Precipitation (Map 2)

Atmospheric instability causes heavy precipitation, generally in the form of short and violent showers. During the dry season in Guadeloupe the average amount of precipitation per hour is 5·5 mm, during the rainy season 8·5 mm. The following figures demonstrate the intensity of summer precipitation: in Fort-de-France (Martinique) 77 mm of rain fell within one hour on 13 September 1958, 220 mm within 5 hours; 12 mm of rain poured down within 8 minutes in St Barthélemy. Showers during the dry season can also be rather violent: in Nassau (Bahamas) 67 mm of rain fell within 42 minutes on 14 December 1946. These showers set in suddenly, accompanied by strong gusts; it then rains very heavily and the water thunders on to the roofs. Country roads and city streets are transformed into torrents which deposit piles of red mud, according to regional conditions. Traffic comes to a standstill, as visibility is down to zero. Streets are deserted while everybody tries to find a shelter where he can wait for the rain to stop. After a short time the sun shines again. Its parching heat quickly draws the dampness out of the ground and a whitish haze rises. After intervals of varying duration—minutes, hours, days or weeks according to weather conditions—the next downpour bursts.

The amount of annual precipitation varies considerably, not only from island to island, but also in the same island. It averages between less than 500 mm and more than 9000 mm and depends very much on topographic conditions. Mountainous islands receive more precipitation than flat islands. For instance, the Bahamas receive less precipitation than the Greater Antilles, low-lying Cuba less than mountainous Jamaica, the islands in the outer arc of the Islands to the Windward less than the islands in the inner arc with their volcanic mountains.

Annual precipitation increases rapidly with altitude over very short distances. For instance, on the east side of Guadeloupe precipitation increases from 2061 to 4414 mm with an increase in height of 230 m (20 and 250 m respectively above sea-level) over a distance of only 6 km. Annual precipitation also depends very much on the topography in the low-lying islands. In addition, the amount of precipitation differs greatly on the windward and leeward sides of the islands, that is on the slopes which either face the trade winds or are turned away from them (Table 4). In low-lying islands the difference is not as striking as it is in mountainous islands, where the windward coast receives more precipitation than the leeward. The difference is greater at higher altitudes because there is a greater increase in precipitation with height on the windward than on the leeward side. Only at very high altitudes does this difference decrease until it finally disappears.

There is only one important exception to these features in the distribution of orographic rainfall: the low precipitation in the Islands to the Leeward. In earlier days the dryness of these islands and of the Venezuelan coast was attributed, not very convincingly, to the cool, upwelling waters. Only

19

Bahama Islands

Nassau,
New Providence

Grand Turk,
Turks Islands

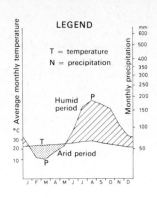

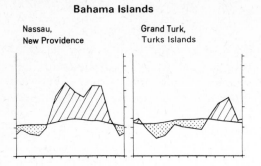

Cuba

Nueva Gerona,
Isle of Pines

Habana

Camagüey

Santiago de Cuba

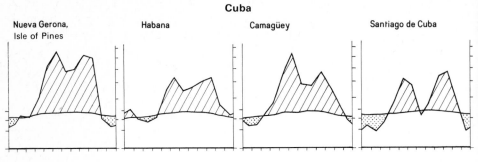

Hispaniola

Haiti

Dominican Republic

Limbé
(West of Cap-Haitien)

Port-au-Prince

Santo Domingo'

Azua

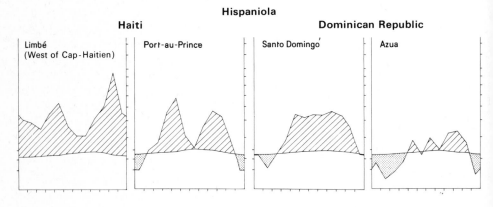

Jamaica

Puerto Rico

Port Antonio

Kingston

Humacao

Ponce

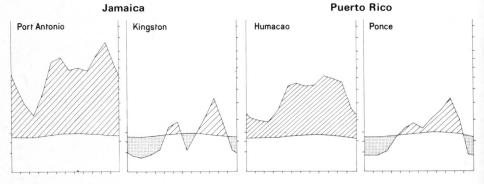

20

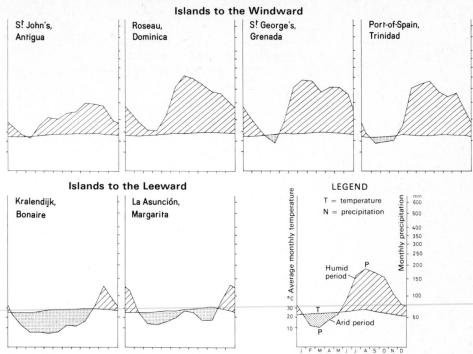

Fig. 3 Temperature-precipitation graphs.
Supplementary Data for the climatic graphs.

	Altitude above OD in m	Average annual precipitation (N) in mm	Average annual temperature (T) in °C
Nassau, New Providence	4	1185	25·1
Grand Turk, Turk Islands	4	750	26·3
Nueva Gerona, Isle of Pines	60	1751	25·4
Habana	24	1223	25·2
Camagüey	107	1421	25·3
Santiago de Cuba	35	1109	25·9
Limbé	45	2062	25·0
Port-au-Prince	37	1371	26·1
Santo Domingo	18	1393	25·8
Azua	81	735	26·3
Port Antonio	3	3328	26·5
Kingston	7	732	26·3
Humacao	30	2121	25·1
Ponce	24	909	25·9
St John's, Antigua	24	1251	26·0
Roseau, Dominica	8	1928	26·8
St George's, Grenada	155	1839	26·0
Port-of-Spain, Trinidad	40	1606	25·1
Kralendijk, Bonaire	3	512	26·7
La Asunción, Margarita	30	701	26·9

21

recently was it possible to prove that during the summer the trade winds accelerate in the area of the Islands to the Leeward because at this time there is a steeper gradient between the relatively high pressure over the Caribbean Sea and the low pressure area over the heated northern part of South America. The resulting gradient causes a descending airflow at altitudes of up to 6 km and reduces the effectiveness of the trade winds, which at that time produce precipitation in all the rest of the islands. This also explains why minimum precipitation occurs during summer in the Islands to the Leeward, the time of maximum precipitation in all the other Caribbean islands.

The amount of annual precipitation varies considerably. These differences are very great in both the very humid and the very dry regions of the Caribbean; in the dry islands, however, divergence from the average annual precipitation is very common and droughts are frequent. Drought has to be reckoned with even in areas where average annual precipitation is adequate.

Throughout the Caribbean one can distinguish between periods of little and great precipitation, usually called the dry and rainy seasons. In spite of various deviations in detail, one can distinguish between the following types of rain distribution (Fig. 3):

1. Summer rainy season (May/June–October/November)
    (*a*) with one rainfall maximum (e.g. Roseau, Dominica);
    (*b*) with two rainfall maxima: (i) during a single rainy spell (e.g. Nassau, Bahamas); (ii) during two rainy spells; the two rainfall maxima are separated by a time of relative dryness (Veranillo). Such a double rainy season occurs in places where precipitation is relatively low, and it is therefore not really an independent type of seasonal rain distribution (e.g. Kingston, Jamaica);

2. Winter rainy season (November to January/February). Two rainfall maxima occur: one during the rainy season, another during the dry season (e.g. La Asunción, Margarita).

The winter rainy season is restricted to the Islands to the Leeward. The summer rainy season, occurring in almost the whole Caribbean area, differs because of the occurrence of either two rainy spells or one. The latter is experienced in leeward locations in the inner arc of the Islands to the Windward, from St Kitts in the north to St Lucia in the south. Two rainfall maxima occur also on the windward sides of these islands. Rainy seasons with two rainy spells are therefore not restricted to the Greater Antilles and Trinidad, as has been believed, but are typical for all the islands. The double rainy season is causally related to the changes in atmospheric pressure. Precipitation is triggered only during times of low pressure, when the subtropical anticyclone shifts to the north. This happens twice during summer.

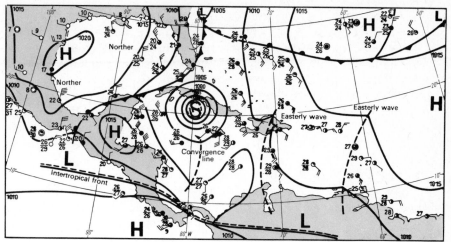

Map 3. Weather conditions in the Caribbean, 9 September 1932.

Weather conditions (Map 3)

The trade winds determine the weather in the Caribbean throughout the year. A seasonal rhythm is produced by the summer rainy season with very active cloud formation, heavy showers and long spells of sunny weather, and by the winter rainy season when cloud development is reduced, fewer showers occur and precipitation is lower.

The heavy precipitation of summer occurs during the period when the subtropical anticyclone and the Inter-Tropical Convergence zone (ITC) shift to the north, but it is not connected with the ITC. The ITC reaches Central America and the extreme south-west of the Caribbean Sea, but not the Caribbean islands. Only Trinidad and the southern Islands to the Windward might have precipitation caused by the northward shift of the ITC. The heavy precipitation during summer is in fact caused by troughs of low pressure superimposed upon the trade wind system known as easterly waves, which occur only when the subtropical anticyclone shifts north. These troughs interrupt the flow of the trade winds for a short while. Furthermore, summer precipitation is intensified by the incomplete formation of the trade wind inversion which disturbs the unstable, humid air masses to produce convectional rain.

During winter, however, convectional rain is greatly reduced by the formation of the trade wind inversions at low altitudes. The orographic effect of the mountains is fully effective, and the dry season is therefore not absolutely without precipitation. In addition to orographic rainfall caused by relief differences, winter precipitation develops as a result of weak disturbances which cross the Islands to the Windward from east to west along with the trade wind air stream.

Disturbances during winter, together with easterly waves during summer,

23

both of which intensify precipitation, are elements of the trade wind system, although during these spells the trade winds change their direction or cease for a short while. Cold waves from the north during winter, and hurricanes during summer, represent very effective and, with regional variations, longer disruptions of the trade wind system. Cold waves from North America are experienced after the passage of a depression. They reach Cuba and Jamaica, sometimes the Greater Antilles in the east and the Islands to the Leeward, perhaps even Trinidad, and they are accompanied by widespread heavy rain. Only the Islands to the Windward are spared these cold waves.

During summer, from June to November, hurricanes sometimes disrupt the trade wind system. These tropical hurricanes apparently develop from easterly waves. Their build-up, especially at the beginning and at the end of the hurricane season, occurs in the western part of the Caribbean Sea, at other times mainly over the Atlantic and east of the Islands to the Windward. The hurricanes, with diameters of 600 to 800 km, take a westward course across the Caribbean area causing extensive destruction in the islands every year. The hurricanes of the first mentioned group, after they have swung away to the north-east, mainly affect Cuba and the Bahamas, whilst those of the second group affect the Islands to the Windward and the Greater Antilles. Only Trinidad and the Islands to the Leeward are safe from these destructive hurricanes, because the Coriolis force decreases rapidly towards the equator (Map 4). Hurricanes may cause continuous heavy rains. For instance, Silver Hill in the north-eastern part of Jamaica received 3428 mm of rain in seven days caused by a hurricane in November 1909; 728 mm is the most known to have fallen in one day.

Year-round good weather with intermittent rainy spells, which are more frequent and violent in summer, is associated with the trade wind system. It is interrupted by the following weather conditions which lead to increased precipitation:

During summer

1. easterly waves of the trade winds: in all the Caribbean islands except in the Islands to the Leeward;
2. the intertropical front, after having shifted to the north: Trinidad and the rest of the southern Islands to the Windward;
3. hurricanes: in all the Islands, except Trinidad and the Islands to the Leeward.

During winter

1. weak disturbances: in the Islands to the Windward as far west as Puerto Rico;
2. cold waves from the north: in the Greater Antilles, the Islands to the Leeward and, perhaps, Trinidad.

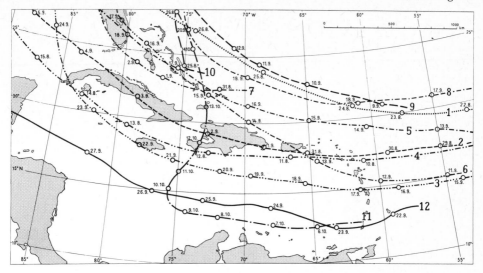

Map 4 Tracks of catastrophic hurricanes in the Caribbean (after Tannehill).

Climatic regions

Because of their latitudinal position all the Caribbean islands belong to the Tropical summer rainfall zone, according to Flohn's genetic classification of climatic types. This zone is characterized by the dominance, according to seasons, of either the equatorial westerly winds bringing summer rain, or the tropical trade winds from the east.

The basis for a climatic subdivision of the area can only be humidity. An essential characteristic of the latitudinal climatic division is seen in the differing degrees of humidity which result from dynamic factors and which set the Islands to the Leeward apart from all the other islands. The Islands to the Leeward are markedly arid, while all the other islands are mainly humid. This latitudinal climatic division is clearly seen in the generic climatic classifications. According to Köppen's classification the Islands to the Leeward have a BW climate, the Islands to the Windward Af, and the Greater Antilles and the Bahamas an Aw climate.

If the moisture index of De Martonne/Lauer is used as the basis, as in Troll's classification of climates, a detailed division is possible. The whole scale of thermic-hygric[1] climates, from the arid climate with only three humid months to the perhumid climate with twelve humid months, is present in the Caribbean islands.

---

[1] i.e. classified according to the relationship between temperature and precipitation, using a moisture index to measure 'precipitation efficiency' (e.g. Thornthwaite, 1955). The terms perhumid, humid, subhumid, semi-arid and arid have this connotation throughout the text. (Translator's note.)

25

Table 2.   Distribution of thermic-hygric climates at sea-level

Island group	Number of humid months	Climatic type
Bahama Islands	4–6	tropical climate with seasonal rainfall
Greater Antilles	3–12	tropical arid climate; tropical climate with seasonal rainfall; tropical moist climate with summer rainfall; tropical wet climate
Islands to the Windward	4–9	tropical climate with seasonal rainfall; tropical moist climate with summer rainfall
Islands to the Leeward	3	tropical arid climate

A great variety of thermic-hygric climates at sea-level can be observed in the Islands to the Windward and especially in the Greater Antilles. This is mainly because of the great variation in local relief of these island groups: in the mountainous islands there are distinct climatic differences at sea-level depending on their exposure, i.e. windward slopes are more humid than leeward. The influence of aspect is also noticed at higher altitudes. Moisture increases everywhere with height above sea-level but greater humidity occurs at a lower altitude on the windward side than on the leeward. For instance, in the Islands to the Windward the perhumid region begins 200 m lower on windward than on leeward slopes; in the Greater Antilles the difference in level may be as much as 2500 m (Hispaniola).

Thus, because of their varied dynamics, topography, and exposure the Caribbean islands exhibit a multitude of climatic variations. The range of different climates in one island increases with the variety of relief. Since the transition from the more arid to the more humid thermic-hygric climates takes place within a short distance, both horizontal and vertical, the close proximity in a small area of several climatic types is another characteristic. Table 4 shows the different sea-level and vertical divisions of thermic-hygric climates in the various island groups, together with the climatic climax vegetation forms (cf. p. 41, Table 3).

5
Landforms

Structural relief types

The landforms within the three major types of relief (cf. p. 10 and Map 5) distinguished by topographical and structural criteria, vary greatly with different rock materials and varying rock stratification, and also because of great differences in the amount of local relief.

Faultblock mountains

Low magnitude of relief at high altitudes within faultblock mountains and 'gipfelflurs' which are numerous even in areas of mature dissection point to a former level of planation. Subdued relief is preserved mainly at higher altitudes in the Cordillera Central and the Sierra de Baoruco in Hispaniola. The recent orogeny explains their relatively slight destruction by erosive forces. In all the Caribbean faultblock mountains several levels of planation can be reconstructed from the many erosion surface fragments (cf. p. 31). They suggest that the mountains experienced uplift in different stages. The benches, often splendidly developed in transverse valleys, also demonstrate the recent uplift of the mountain ranges.

Where the faultblock mountains consist of igneous rocks and of crystalline or folded sedimentary rocks, they have a dense drainage network and, as a result, a distinctly dome-shaped relief; e.g. the Central Cordillera in Puerto Rico. Apart from these forms of basal rock complexes, most of the sedimentary highlands are limestone plateaux, whose main features are an open drainage network and karst topography: e.g. the north-west Haitian upland region. Wherever the sedimentary cover strata overlie undisturbed the basal rock complexes they form distinct landform boundaries: e.g. the abrupt edge of the Lares limestones in Puerto Rico, and the coral limestones in Barbados.

Volcanic mountains

Volcanic mountains are restricted to the inner arc of the Islands to the

Windward. Both these and the faultblock mountains have in common a high degree of local relief and therefore a strongly dissected and dome-shaped topography. In areas of older volcanism no superimposed formations are preserved. In areas of young volcanism many volcanic domes and plugs stand out in the landscape, most beautifully developed in the dacitic lava domes of the Pitons in St Lucia (Plate 24) and in the Pitons de Carbet in Martinique. But conically shaped composite volcanoes with extensive craters are also found; like Soufrière in St Vincent and Quill in St Eustatius (Plate 26).

Low-lying limestone plateaux

The low-lying limestone plateaux with their more or less distinct karst topography possess much less variety of landforms than the two relief types mentioned above. Frequently they are partly dissected marine abrasion platforms of Pleistocene age which have been uplifted by recent tectonic activity. Genetically they correspond to the sometimes extensive submarine platforms which fringe the islands at differing depths. In contrast, the vast plains of Cuba, which are underlain usually by igneous rocks, are erosion surfaces formed by subaerial denudation. These erosion surfaces with isolated monadnocks are most distinct in the Cuban province of Camagüey. Recent uplift has caused a steplike division of these erosion surfaces, but with a much smaller vertical interval than in the faultblock mountains; they are dissected by rivers and must be termed fossil landforms.

Degradational processes

Weathering

The prevailing moist, warm climate of the Caribbean means that chemical weathering plays a more important role than physical weathering.

Deeply penetrating rock decomposition is very common in subhumid and humid areas. Brightly coloured laterites occur on the remnants of erosion surfaces in the faultblock mountains and also along all roads cut in the slopes of Tertiary volcanoes. At higher altitudes, with their low temperatures and in dry areas, these lateritic soils with a dominance of kaolinite in their clay fraction are fossil features. For instance, in the dry Dutch Islands to the Leeward, the lateritic soils of the limestone plateaux are fossil relics from one or several moist pluvial eras. In other dry areas, however, the common dark-grey soils with a dominance of montmorillonite in their clay fraction are products of the present climatic conditions, as are the red earths and lateritic soils at low altitudes in humid or subhumid areas.

In addition to strong chemical weathering, physical weathering by hydration is of great importance. It is not only active in dry regions, e.g. in the depressions formed of diorite in Aruba (Wilhelmy), but also in the rocks

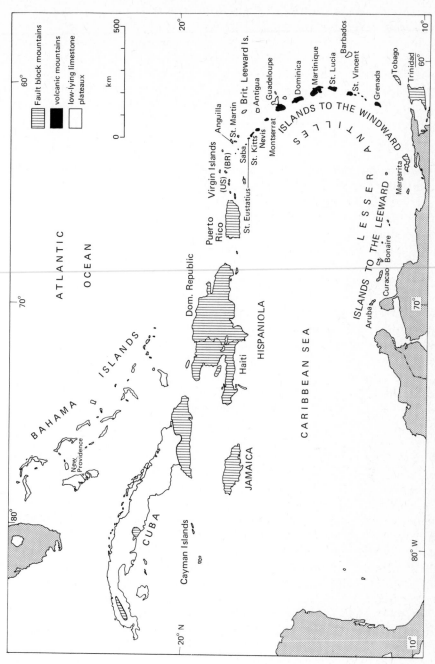

Map 5. Major structural relief types in the Caribbean islands.

Fault block mountains

volcanic mountains

low-lying limestone plateaux

km

0   500

60°

70°

80°

20°

ATLANTIC

OCEAN

BAHAMA ISLANDS

New Providence

CUBA

Cayman Islands

JAMAICA

Dom. Republic

Haiti

HISPANIOLA

Puerto Rico

Virgin Islands (US) (BR)

St. Eustatius

Anguilla

St. Martin

Saba

St. Kitts

Nevis

Montserrat

Antigua

Guadeloupe

Brit. Leeward Is.

Dominica

Martinique

St. Lucia

Barbados

St. Vincent

Grenada

Tobago

Trinidad

ISLANDS TO THE WINDWARD

LESSER ANTILLES

ISLANDS TO THE LEEWARD

Margarita

Bonaire

Curaçao

Aruba

CARIBBEAN SEA

10°

20° N

80° W

70°

10°

20°

60°

of subhumid regions, e.g. in the monadnocks of the Haitian Plaine du Nord. It is also active in perhumid regions; rock formations are jointed and weathering results in the diorite boulders in the Puerto Rican Central Cordillera or in the Cuban Sierra Maestra, for example. Physical weathering is by no means restricted to dry regions and to mountainous areas at higher altitudes. Wherever erosional processes are active, in humid or subhumid regions, their effects are considerable. Their most effective results can be seen where rock has been extensively cut back along scarps within cuesta topography.

Denudation

Degradational processes are much stronger in the faultblock and volcanic mountains than in the low-lying limestone plateaux. This is the result of much greater local relief and the consequently higher rainfall in both the former types of relief. The degradational processes, denudation and erosion, show considerable seasonal variation according to the annual rhythm of precipitation. Denudation always occurs after heavy precipitation and can be directly observed. For instance, extensive rock slides occur along the coral terraces in Barbados, and large slips occur on steep slopes of volcanoes and within the basal rock complexes, even where they are forest-covered. Monroe refers to the high degree of degradation caused by landslips of this kind in the humid mountain area of Puerto Rico. Again and again mountain roads in the Antilles are made impassable by landslips during the rainy season. Because the leached soils quickly receive new mineral nutritive substances after such soil movements, owing to active chemical weathering, the peasant population in mountainous areas prefers to cultivate steep slopes. Their cultivation in forest clearings made by burning assists denudation. Destruction of the forest cover at middle altitudes, e.g. in the mountains of Puerto Rico, Jamaica, and especially Hispaniola, has led to such extensive soil erosion that the eroded slopes with their steadily expanding, branching gully networks present a terrifying example of a destroyed area where cultivation is no longer possible.

The mountains of the Caribbean islands do not reach levels where periglacial activity takes place. The boulder fields (Weyl, 1940) in the Dominican Cordillera Central, the highest massif in the islands, have to be interpreted as examples of the lowering of temperatures during the Pleistocene era which was restricted to the highest altitudes of Caribbean mountains. Rock wasting is also observed in arid regions where heavy showers are characteristic. Often soil erosion is more distinct and more disastrous in its effect than in humid mountain regions whether through natural or manmade processes. Even gently inclined slopes are often dissected by deep ravines, e.g. in the dry longitudinal valleys in Hispaniola.

Erosion

The intensity of river action, erosion and aggradation, shows similar seasonal variation and differences according to the type of structural relief as rock wasting. There are only a few large rivers: Cuba and Hispaniola, being the largest islands, have the longest rivers. Because of the topography and resulting regional differences in climate only a few of these rivers are diareic, that is, their entire course lies within humid regions. Most Caribbean rivers, however, are endoreic, that is, they run from a humid into a (semi-)arid region to form inland drainage. Their discharge varies considerably according to the season. Only in times of flood can most rivers break through the bars which seal off their mouths from the open sea during low water periods. Among the areic rivers only the larger ones have a regularly recurring flow, while the smaller rivers only flow intermittently. The coefficient of runoff, especially in dry regions, is low because of high evaporation. As a result extensive alluvial cones, consisting of coarse materials, fringe the mountainous areas and are especially impressive in the dry, longitudinal depressions of Hispaniola. The smaller the rivers, the greater and the briefer are the fluctuations in their flow of water. Fords, impassable immediately after showers, are usually passable again within a few hours. The waters of the rivers are muddy during rainy seasons, and even the sea waters off the river mouths then acquire a brownish colour because of sediment load.

In areas with great local relief downcutting is especially active. Where the gradient decreases in the longitudinal profile of the valleys, accumulation also occurs in wide mountain valleys. Aggradation prevails in plains, some of which are mainly built from river deposits, e.g. the plains of the Cauto and Nipe in Cuba, and the Yaque del Norte and Yuna in Hispaniola, where rivers usually meander between levees in their lower course. Several depositional plains are presently being dissected by headward erosion because of recent uplift.

Geomorphological features

Erosion surfaces

The erosion surfaces in faultblock mountains have been partly uplifted to an altitude where the climatic conditions for further active development no longer exists. But even in areas where these conditions do exist active erosional forces are largely destroying the subdued relief—a result of recent tectonic activity. Weyl (1966) states accurately that the most impressive feature of the surface configuration in the Antillean faultblock mountains is the contrast between the subdued relief at high altitudes and the deeply incised, narrow and often terraced valleys. Thick layers of lateritic soil are usually preserved only in high altitude areas of subdued relief which are undisturbed by erosion.

The dry Islands to the Leeward also possess exhumed erosion surfaces covered by lateritic soils. There they indicate a more humid climate in the

31

past, e.g. periods of greater rainfall during the Pleistocene. In addition to these laterite formations, other geomorphological facts point to a formerly humid climate in the Islands to the Leeward: the development of cuestas through springline erosion (cf. p. 34), the dendritic pattern of dry valleys, the fossil dripstone formations and the fossil vertebrates in the caves and crevices of the limestone plateaux.

The varying heights of the exhumed erosion surfaces allow one to recognize the different tectonic uplift of the islands or their subregions. Although it has not yet been possible to correlate all the erosion surfaces of the various islands, one can give the heights of Mio-Pliocene planation surfaces with a degree of certainty. For instance, they occur at:

2500 m in the Cordillera Central in Hispaniola (Weyl),
700–800 m in the Central Cordillera in Puerto Rico (Meyerhoff) and in the
          Escambray mountains (Sierra de Trinidad) in Cuba (Rutten),
300–400 m in the Cuban Sierra de los Organos (Rutten, ˙Massip,
          Lehmann),
180–280 m (Miocene) ⎫ in the mountainous country of Matanzas, Cuba,
40–100 m (Pliocene) ⎭ (Duclos),
150–160 m in Marie Galante (Lasserre).

The formation of erosion surfaces in the Caribbean islands had not been restricted to the Tertiary. Duclos described Pleistocene erosion surfaces in Cuba, and Lasserre in Grande Terre (Guadeloupe). These surfaces lie only a few decametres above sea-level and have been partly dissected by river erosion. They must also be considered as fossil features.

Active formation of erosion surfaces is only found to a limited extent, which is understandable, when one considers the tectonic instability of these islands. Varying rock types and conditions in low-lying areas near the coast where one could expect the formation of erosion surfaces, are not favourable for their formation since the karst topography, mainly of young limestone, hinders sheet erosion. Sheet erosion, however, is recognized as an essential precondition for the formation of erosion surfaces in tropical areas with seasonal rainfall. But lateral erosion by floods at the margin of limestone areas may lead to the formation of areas of planation. This type of planation process is occurring at the present time at about sea-level along the coastal plain of Abymes in Guadeloupe (Blume). Erosional processes, initiated by sheet floods, can best be observed in the eastern region of the humid coastal plain in north Puerto Rico which is usually flooded after heavy rain. Another area where the first stages of erosion surface formation can be clearly noticed is the area near the coast of the Scotland District in Barbados.

Erosion surface development, which is to be expected in the islands in the marginal tropics with seasonal rainfall, is only active, therefore, in low-lying areas near to the coast where there are favourable climatic, structural and geological conditions. It does not occur in areas with great local relief or in arid regions since these do not provide the necessary structural and/or climatic preconditions. The numerous erosion surfaces, therefore, developed at low altitudes either during times of tectonic inactivity or, in arid regions, under climatic conditions which were more humid than at present; most of them are definitely fossil formations.

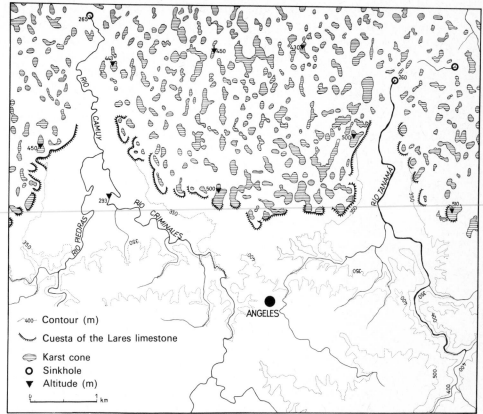

Map 6. The cuesta scarp of the Lares limestone looking towards the erosion surfaces in the Central Cordillera (east of Lares, Puerto Rico).

Cuestas

Cuestas (escarpments caused by structure) are to be found in all thermic-hygric Caribbean island climate types. They depend on the alternating stratification of permeable, resistant layers with impermeable, less resistant layers. Within the perhumid regions lie parts of the Barbadian coral limestone cuesta (Map 79), and also the Oligocene limestone cuesta between Lares 0·5–3 m, and Utuado in north-west Puerto Rico (Map 6) which has been dissolved into limestone haystack hills and faces the basal rock complexes of the Central Cordillera. The cuesta in the Cuban mountainous region of Matanzas lies in a semi-humid area; and the coral limestone cuesta in Bonaire is in a dry region (Map 87).

The mechanism of headward erosion, occurring along cuestas, varies according to climatic conditions. The different ways in which the cuesta edges are eroded in humid or subhumid climates, are to be observed along the Pleistocene coral limestone cuesta in Barbados which extends from humid to almost semi-arid regions. The strong headward erosion of the entire cuesta is seen in the numerous beheaded valleys of the limestone plateau: the floors of these valleys form wind gaps along the scarp edge. The cuesta in the humid region, like the cuesta between Lares and Utuado in Puerto Rico, is greatly indented as a result of active springline erosion. In the subhumid region, however, the escarpment is relatively straight, like the scarp in the mountainous area of Matanzas. There, the many rocky steps, caused by landslips, apparently reduce the effectiveness of springline erosion. These rocky steps, very extensive in places, seem to be responsible for the straightness of the cuesta in the subhumid areas of Barbados (Plate 27). On the scarp slope and at the bottom of the coral limestone cuesta in the arid island of Bonaire sheet erosion can be seen to be the only active erosional force at present. This undoubtedly results in a lowering of the scarp slope gradient. The features of the Bonaire cuesta, however, consist of an indented course caused by springline erosion, and detritus, scattered along the slope and at the foot of the scarp, i.e. they consist of formations similar to those developed under the humid and subhumid conditions of the Barbados cuesta. This is not to be explained by the present dry climatic conditions; on the contrary, it indicates a more humid climate in the past (pluvial phases, i.e. periods of greater rainfall during the Pleistocene), the existence of which is also suggested by various other phenomena (cf. p. 32).

Karst*

Karst phenomena are widespread in the Caribbean islands. Dinaric karst, featuring dolines, and cone karst (*Kegelkarst*) appear side by side, the latter in form of limestone cones (*Kalkkegel*, mornes) and haystack hills (*Kalktürme*, mogotes) with deeply entrenched hollows (*Hohlformen*, cockpits). Dinaric karst formations are much more common (Maps 49, 79). Lehmann who worked in the Caribbean area and especially in the Cuban Sierra de los Organos discovered that cone karst is restricted to tropical regions (Fig. 6 and Plate 2).

In addition to Cuba, there are various impressive cone karst formations in Hispaniola, especially in the region of Haitises south of the lower Río Yuna (Map 7); other areas are the peninsula of Samaná and the slopes of the Cordillera Septentrional south-west of Gaspar Hernández. The Cockpit Country in the north-western part of Jamaica (Map 33 and Plate 7) is an

---

* Commonly used English translations or equivalents of German or Slavic terms are used where possible. The foreign term is italicized and appears in brackets before local terms the first time the term is used. Where there is no English equivalent the foreign term is explained in footnotes. For further details the reader is referred to W. H. Monroe, *A Glossary of Karst Terminology*, Washington, 1970.

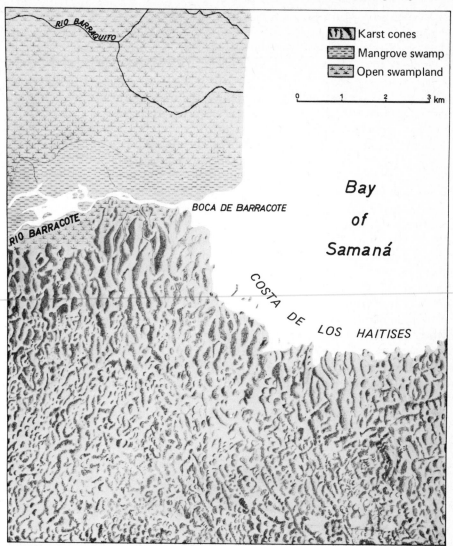

Map 7. The cone karst area of Los Haitises, south of the Bay of Samaná, Hispaniola.

extensive cone karst area, and Puerto Rico possesses cone karst in various limestone formations in its north-western regions (Map 60). Whereas the Greater Antilles have numerous cone karst areas, the islands to the Windward have only one, in Grande Terre, Guadeloupe (Map 72).

When the dispersed cone karst regions are compared, it can be seen that three basic requirements exist for the development of cone karst: a high, soluble $CaCO_3$ concentration in the limestone, a warm and moist climate, and finally, the development of karst plains (*Karstrandebene*) with a high water table which allows lateral undercutting by solution at the margins of

35

the limestone. This type of karst plain, which serves as a major drainage channel, and inland poljes in limestone areas, called Interior Valleys in Jamaica, are common features in Caribbean cone karst areas.

A cone karst region is developing today in Grande Terre. Lateral chemical weathering has eroded the dinaric karst formations of a limestone plateau—a Late Pleistocene coastal plain in origin—into various limestone cones. Cone karst, therefore, is not necessarily a type of relief which dates back to the beginning of karst development in humid and subhumid areas. It develops when all three above-mentioned conditions are fulfilled.

All Caribbean cone karst areas exhibit formations which Corbel defines as the end stages of karst development in moist tropical areas and for which he postulates a continuous development since the limestone was exposed. The Caribbean cone karst formations are much younger, however, especially in Puerto Rico where, according to Gerstenhauer, they date back to the Quaternary. They seem to be even younger in Guadeloupe, where they have developed only since the Late Pleistocene rise in sea-level and the formation of a coastal plain (Blume). The Caribbean area demonstrates, in these cases, that the formation of cone karst can occur very rapidly.

Dinaric karst in Barbados (Map 79), formed within the Pleistocene coral limestone region and displaying numerous caves and many underground water courses, is at a surprisingly advanced stage in spite of its comparative youthfulness. This can only be explained by the high solubility of limestone in a tropical climate. Its formation in the semi-arid area in Barbados suggests a more humid climate in the past which may be explained by this island's higher elevation above sea-level during colder eras resulting in more precipitation. A change of climate is not necessarily involved.

Coasts

There are many different types of coasts in the Caribbean islands. Erosional features are important along some parts of the cliffed coasts of all the islands (Plate 25); depositional features prevail along coasts where offshore bars form lagoons and along dune coasts (Plate 29). Some parts of the small islands have only become continuous land through depositional processes and have been built up gradually by the infilling of lagoons behind offshore sand bars, as in the case of the island of St Martin (Map 68). There exist both delta coasts and partly submerged coastal plains. The first type is clearly exemplified by the Cuban Cauto delta; the latter is characterized by the circular Bolsa Bays in Cuba with their narrow outlets to the sea which are very similar to the Bocas in the Dutch Islands to the Leeward (Maps 87, 88, 89). The deeply indented south coast of Grenada (Map 78), with its valleys flooded by the sea, strongly resembles a ria coast, although Valentin's definition of a ria as an 'old drowned fold bay coast' cannot be applied at all to the coast of this volcanic island.

As the Caribbean islands are situated in tropical waters their coasts are lined with numerous mangroves and coral reefs. The mangrove, above all its *Rhizophora* variety with the characteristic stilt roots (cf. p. 45), is restricted to shallow waters along the coast and it encourages the process of sedimentation, especially in lagoons. Mangrove swamps extend over wide areas in Cuba, Guadeloupe and Trinidad. These amphibious scrub forests are very difficult to penetrate.

Coral islands, built from coral limestone and coral sand, constitute the Bahama Archipelago in the continental shelf area of the Bahama Bank. The other Caribbean islands are sometimes adjoined by quite extensive fringing reefs. These fringing reefs, formed by about forty species of reef building corals, exhibit a distinct zoning parallel to the coast. The north coast of Jamaica (according to Coreau), for instance, is fringed by a barrier reef more than 100 m in width and built, mainly at a depth of 7–15 m, of massive pillars of the coral species *Montastraea annularis* and *Acropora cervicornis*. This reef is followed by the pinnacle reef, about 100–180 m in width. It is distinct from the fringing-reef from which it is separated by the buttress zone which is situated at a depth of 1–10 m and built, among others, from *Agaricia agaricites* and *Acropora palmata*; this is followed, at a depth of 0·5–6 m by the palmata zone with its branching colonies of *Acropora palmata*. Then the pinnacle reef is followed, at a depth of 0·5–3 m by the reef flat, often covered by a detrital mound and then by the back reef, which descends steeply into the lagoon, which is 2–15 m deep and covered by coral sand and silt. Beyond the 10–300 m wide lagoon the coral sand slowly rises forming the beach. On the beaches lime precipitates from ground water often cause the formation of beach rock which quickly hardens in the air. The zoning of the fringing reefs is very distinct, especially from the air, with the surf at the reef crest and with the different movements and colours of the water inside and outside the reef ridge.

Many Pleistocene coral reef limestones along the coasts of the islands have a system of ascending marine abrasion terraces and steep cliffs (Plate 32) with numerous wave-cut notches. These terraces reach the highest altitudes in the plateau of Bombardopolis in north-west Hispaniola where a sequence of 28 marine terraces have developed up to a height of 640 m above sea-level (Woodring, Butterlin). Evidence of recent tectonic movements and eustatic changes in the sea-level is found in these terraces. As the tectonic forces have been very strong and varying from island to island, it is extremely difficult to differentiate between the tectonic and the eustatic forces, as Alexander and Buisonjé have tried to do in the case of the Dutch Islands to the Leeward. Although such surveys also exist for coastal regions in Cuba (Duclos), Hispaniola (Barrett), Puerto Rico (Kaye), and Barbados (Price), the above-mentioned difficulties make it practically impossible to correlate the marine terraces of the various islands.

The development of relief, and past climates

Some geomorphological features in the Caribbean cannot be interpreted as having been formed at the present time but must have had their origins in the past. If the types of relief which developed under differing circumstances in the past and present are termed 'development of relief' (Büdel) they can be divided into two groups; (1) development of relief, which has originated because of changing tectonic conditions, and (2) development of relief which has come about because of changes in climate. The best examples of the first mentioned group, that of tectonic development of relief, are the old formations of subdued relief in the faultblock mountains of the Greater Antilles and their valleys, deeply entrenched because of strong renewed erosional processes. Changes in climate need not be postulated in order to explain this relief development.

Examples of the group mentioned under (2), development of relief by climatic changes, are found especially in the geomorphology features of the dry Islands to the Leeward which form part of the dry region along the north coast of South America. Examining this area's geomorphology one can clearly prove a more humid climate during the Pleistocene with one or several wetter periods. Another example of the climatic type of development of relief, i.e. a change of erosional processes because of a change in climate, is the existence of Pleistocene periglacial formations in the mountain regions of Hispaniola which point to a lower upper limit of the tropical mountain climate during cold eras than at present. Apart from these cases, however, the study of the development of relief by climatic changes has not so far produced any proof of recent climatic changes in the Caribbean islands. Lasserre points to the continuity of climatic conditions in Guadeloupe, and Lehmann, considering the development of the cone karst in the Antilles, also stresses the uniformity of climatic conditions through geological time.

On the whole, however, one has to assume different climatic conditions in the Caribbean area during the Pleistocene: a decrease in temperature during the colder Pleistocene, even in the tierra caliente, is very probable, taking into account the results of the research on sedimentary pelagic foraminifera at the bottom of the Caribbean Sea. According to these, the surface temperature of the water in the Caribbean Sea has varied by about 6°C within the last 280 000 years, between 23°C during the cold eras and 29°C in the post-glacial climatic optimum (Emiliani, Schott, Zobel). Also indicating different climatic conditions during the Pleistocene is the fact that in the Caribbean islands the slightest variation in altitude has an extremely strong effect on the amount of annual precipitation. Therefore, the lowering of the sea-level by about 90 m during the cold eras must have caused considerably higher rainfall in the trade wind region of the humid islands combined with a noticeably higher degree of humidity, because of slightly lower temperatures, and more effective erosional processes.

It is therefore obvious that the Pleistocene climate in the Caribbean area did not correspond to present conditions, as it was more humid during the cold eras. Yet its basic character, the seasonal precipitation of the marginal tropics, was preserved. This is proved by the continuous formation of erosion surfaces in suitable areas during the Pleistocene and the present (cf. p. 32). When considering the climatic changes during the Pleistocene, therefore, it is still relevant to present and past formations to retain the classification above, which differentiates between climatic and tectonic development of relief. This classification will probably have to be improved and modified in the future when more data are available.

6

Flora and fauna

General survey of the flora

The flora of the islands belongs to the Caribbean neotropical group which includes a very large number of species. The local names for plants in the area, including cultivated plants, differ not only in the Spanish, French and English languages but also between islands, sometimes even on one island. The large number of indigenous plants is very characteristic, especially in the Islands to the Windward which because of their higher altitudes may justly be called oceanic islands from a floristic point of view. Whereas only 12 per cent of the tree varieties are indigenous in the dry forest which covers the lower altitudes of these islands, this proportion increases with height above sea-level: 42 per cent in the evergreen rain forest, and 52 per cent in the elfin woodland (Beard).

Neotropical plants dominate the Caribbean flora but they often form colonies together with holarctic elements. While the Islands to the Windward are almost completely void of northern species, the Greater Antilles do possess examples of holarctic flora (*Pinus* and *Quercus* species) which expanded at high altitudes in these islands during the Pleistocene cold eras just as they did in the mountains of the Middle American mainland. Less numerous are elements of subantarctic flora at high altitudes in the West Indian mountains (e.g. *Podocarpus* and *Weinmannia*). In addition to the large number of examples of holarctic flora, neotropical examples also grow in the highest regions of the Greater Antilles.

Because of their relatively high percentage of holarctic flora, Cuba, Hispaniola and the Bahamas constitute a separate floristic region within the area: another group is formed by the Islands to the Windward and Puerto Rico, among which only Trinidad is distinctive because of its close ties to South American flora.

Climatic plant formations in the Tierra caliente

Human activities, which started with Amerindian cultivations in pre-

40

Columban times, have considerably changed the Caribbean flora. Both the European plantation economy with its high demand for wood, especially for the sugar boiling-houses, and the peasant shifting agriculture, especially in the mountains, have much graver consequences. Extensive forest areas were changed into cultivated land, and the original plant colonies in the tierra caliente and tierra templada were often replaced by secondary communities. The great range of climatic conditions produces an extremely varied flora. A larger number of different types of vegetation grow within the tierra caliente (Table 3), which includes a greater part of the area than the tierra templada and tierra fria, than in the mountain regions, since it is only in the tierra caliente that the entire range of humidity from three up to twelve humid months, is found (index De Martonne/Lauer).

Table 3.   Climatic vegetation forms in the Caribbean tierra caliente

	per humid	*humid*		*semi-humid*			*semi-arid*			*arid*
Number of rainy months	12	11	10	9	8	7	6	5	4	3
arid months (Index De Martonne/ Lauer)	0		1	2	3	4	5	6	7	8	9
Climates (after Troll/Paffen)	tropical wet climate			tropical moist climate with summer rainfall			tropical climate with seasonal rainfall			tropical arid climate
annual precipitation	>2000 mm			2000– 1250 mm			1250– 750 mm			750–300 mm
Vegetation forms after Lauer/Troll	tropical rain forest			semi- evergreen seasonal forest			tropical deciduous forest			dry woodland
after Beard	rain forest			semi- evergreen seasonal forest			deciduous seasonal forest			
after Stehlé	forêt hygrophile			forêt mésophile			forêt xérophile			

Tropical evergreen rain forests

Tropical evergreen forests are only to be found in areas with more than 2000 mm of precipitation and with more than ten humid months in the year. In the Greater Antilles this type of forest grows in low-lying moist windward areas; in the Lesser Antilles it grows only at a height of several hundred metres above the semi-evergreen seasonal forest zone. With increasing and, according to the island, at varying heights above the sea, the rain forest changes into the evergreen montane forest. In the Islands to the Windward with their high precipitation the evergreen rain forest borders the montane elfin woodland at an altitude of only 500–600 m.

The tropical rain forest exhibits a storeylike arrangement. The upper storey—the tree top canopy—spreads at a height of about 40 m above the ground. Below a middle and lower tree section is the herbaceous plant section, with ferns predominating. The forest is evergreen since even trees of the same type lose their leaves at different times. These dense and extremely damp forests, the earth beneath them only slightly penetrated by the sun's rays, give an impression of luxuriant growth of a multitude of lianas and epiphytes, usually ferns near the ground, orchidaceae and bromeliaceae at higher sections. The luxuriant growth easily obscures the fact that soil nutrients are lacking. All the nutrients the vegetation needs are stored in the living plants and in the plant materials not yet decomposed. When an area is deforested the soil nutrients are leached out and it is soon exhausted. This encourages a pattern of shifting peasant agriculture. The secondary forest growing on eroded soils does not grow as luxuriously as does the primeval forest.

The tropical evergreen rain forests in the Caribbean islands are rich in species. Areas with one species dominating and forming a continuous tree top canopy exist only in the *Morea excelsa* forests in Trinidad. The floristic composition of these forests varies considerably between the Greater Antilles and the Islands to the Windward. In the upper tree section of the forest in the latter group of islands the *Sloanea* (Elaeoarpaceae), furnished with mighty buttress roots, and the *Canarium* (Burseraceae) are so numerous that this formation is called the Dacryodes-Sloanea-Colony (Beard). In the upper tree section of the tropical rain forests in the Greater Antilles, however, the main plants are the *Psidium* (Myrtaceae) and the ficus species (Moraceae). Also, tree ferns are much more common at higher altitudes in the tropical evergreen rain forests in the Islands to the Windward than in the Greater Antilles. Both the *Licania* (Chrysobalanaceae) and the indigenous *Oxythece pallida* (Sapotaceae) are especially characteristic of these islands.

Areas with a precipitation of 1250 to 2000 mm and seven to nine humid months in the year are covered by **semi-evergreen seasonal forests**. Trees in these forests lose their leaves during the dry season. This is true for at least three-fifths of the species in the upper tree section. Therefore, semi-evergreen seasonal forests look rather bare during the dry season. In the Islands to the Windward they adjoin the lower tree line of the tropical evergreen rain forest; in the Islands to the Leeward they occupy the regions above the tropical deciduous seasonal forest; and in the Greater Antilles they cover the areas which extend at various altitudes between the tropical deciduous seasonal forest and the semi-evergreen montane forest or the evergreen montane forest.

Only two storeys can be recognized in the semi-evergreen seasonal forest which has been even more decimated by man than the rain forest. From its wide variety of tree species several individual trees emerge to form the upper storey of this mixed forest, as for instance, the *Ceiba pentandra* (Bombacaceae) the *Cedrela* (Meliaceae), and especially the pinnatifid Leguminosae, which become more numerous with increasing dryness. The epiphytes are represented by Bromeliaceae, Orchidaceae and also, though much less numerous than in rain forests, by ferns. *Inga* and *Hymenaea* (both are Leguminosae) are especially numerous in the upper tree section.

Tropical deciduous forest

The tropical deciduous seasonal forest grows in areas with less than 1250 mm of precipitation and five to seven humid months in the year. It covers extensive low-lying regions in the Greater Antilles and in the Islands to the Windward; in the Islands to the Leeward it replaces the thorn and succulent woodlands upslope. The trees grow to a height of slightly more than 10 m, and the tree cover is rather open. The shrub region contains several thorny species, and bromelia species and opuntiae grow on the ground. Lianas and epiphytes are rare and both lichen and moss, abundant in semi-evergreen and rain forests, are practically non-existent. In many places the tropical deciduous seasonal forest appears as an almost impenetrable thicket, green and fresh during the rainy season, bare and dusty during the dry season. While some trees have adjusted to the dry season by losing their leaves, others have tiny and tenacious leaves which shine like leather or are ciliated and which curl to protect themselves against the heat of the sun. In addition to succulent leaves and trunks, the xerophytic aspect of this dry forest is underlined by the fact that various species contain aromatic substances and quick-drying oils. Most common among the trees are the *Bursera* (Burseraceae) and *Pisonia* (Nyctaginaceae). Evergreen shrub forest grows in limestone regions especially in the outer arc of the Islands to the Windward and in the Islands to the Leeward. Stehlé compares the habitat of this shrub forest with the mediterranean Garrigue.

Thorn and succulent forest

This type grows in the driest areas which receive less than 750 mm of precipitation and have only three to four humid months. Thorn woodland is dominant in regions with more than 500 mm of rainfall, and cactus scrub

43

in regions with less than 500 mm of rainfall. This type of vegetation has greatly expanded as a result of excessive grazing; it is prevalent in the Islands to the Leeward, it exists in low-lying limestone areas in the Islands to the Windward and in the Bahamas, and is to be found on the leeward sides of the Greater Antilles, especially in the dry sections of the longitudinal valleys in Hispaniola. Very common in the thorn woodland are Leguminosae: *Acacia*, *Caesalpina*, *Prosopis*, *Pithecolobium*, and *Haematoxylon campechianum* which was imported from the Middle American mainland. There is a great variety of oddly shaped cacti. The spines of the columnar, the spherical and the candelabra-shaped cacti, and the agaves as well as the thorn trees make these thickets almost impenetrable.

Edaphic plant formations in the Tierra caliente

The climatic plant formations, described above, are not present everywhere in the tierra caliente. In various places particular soil conditions produce different plant colonies which are termed edaphic plant formations. The most common edaphic plant formation is the savanna in subhumid and semi-arid regions; it is grassland with many different types of grass and cyperaceae. It extends, especially in Cuba, into areas with waterlogged, clayey soils, but also onto sandy soils, usually resting on serpentinite. The high percentage of indigenous species proves that this is a natural plant colony. These open grasslands, called sabána by the Arawak aborigines, cover about one third of Cuba which is about the same area as in pre-Columban times (Waibel). Because of the lack of soil nutrients they are not cultivable. Trees grow either separately or in loosely dispersed groups. The savannas are divided into three types according to their stand of trees. *Pinus caribaea*, *Pinus tropicalis* and *Quercus virginiana* are dominant in the pine-oak savanna; in the palm tree savanna, the best example of which is found in the Cuban Camagüey province, the palm tree species *Sabal*, *Coccothrinax* and *Copernicia* dominate. Outside Cuba, e.g. in the middle part of the Cibao in Hispaniola, savannas with *Curatella* (Dilleniaceae) and *Byrsonima* (Malpighiaceae) are very common. Because of their dispersed stands of trees these savannas are sometimes called 'orchard savannas'. 'Water savannas' exist in Trinidad. These have forest islands usually made up of palm trees, and therefore strongly resemble the Llanos in the Orinoco region.

Other edaphic plant formations in the subhumid regions of the tierra caliente are the pine forests of the Greater Antilles. For instance, coniferous forests with *Pinus tropicalis* and *Pinus caribaea*, which form colonies with *Quercus virginiana* and possess a rich shrub section, grow on soils weathered from sandstone and lateritic serpentinite in western Cuba. The Cuban island of Pinos is named after these pine forests. The Cuban pine forests with their many holarctic elements correspond to the areas with *Pinus occidentalis* in Hispaniola which are, however, more common in the tierra templada, and which seem to have expanded only as a result of shifting cultivation in low-lying regions cleared by burning (cf. p. 215).

Almost undisturbed by man, another edaphic plant formation has developed on the inaccessible and steep limestone haystack hills (mogotes) in the subhumid cone-karst areas. These areas are very dry because of the permeability of limestone, and therefore succulent trunks and leaves are very common (e.g. Bombacaceae and Cactaceae). These woods, examined by Lötschert in the Cuban Sierra de los Organos, are very dense in spite of the dryness of the sort found on the mogotes, and contain many indigenous species. The forests in swamp areas and along river banks, which are very common in the Greater and Lesser Antilles but which display greatly differing floristic compositions, are also edaphic plant formations. So are the rather uniformly developed grass, shrub and bush types of vegetation along the coasts of all the islands, and the beach thickets where the evergreen and broad-leafed *Coccoloba uvifera* (Polygonaceae) which sometimes grows to a height of several metres is clearly dominant.

Mangrove trees, which are restricted to coastal areas with shallow water (cf. p. 37), are also rather uniformly developed. Usually this edaphic plant formation constitutes only a narrow fringing tract along the coast and displays a regular arrangement. The outer belt is formed by the *Rhizophora mangle* (Rhizophoraceae) with their characteristic stilt roots, bordered by the belt of *Avicennia nitida* (Verbenaceae) which are furnished with asparagus-like pneumatophores and which prefer areas with less flooding. Further inland the *Laguncularia racemosa* (Combretaceae) appear and, finally, the *Conocarpus erecta* (Combretaceae) which possess no aerial roots and also grow on non-flooded ground. This sequence of mangrove vegetation can be clearly identified in the lagoons of the Islands to the Windward.

Plant formations in mountain regions

In the Caribbean mountains humid or perhumid conditions are often found even in the tierra caliente since precipitation increases rapidly with altitude. Annual precipitation in humid mountain regions exceeds 2 m and may rise to a maximum of 10 m. As a result evergreen montane forests and, upslope, elfin woodland are the plant formations in these regions.

The tropical rain forest changes into the lower montane forest at very different altitudes. On the leeward slopes of the Cuban Sierra Maestra and of the Jamaican Blue Mountains the lower montane forest rises to about 1500 m, but on the windward slopes to only about 500 m. The lower montane forest corresponds in its general appearance with the tropical rain forest in great part, but its floristic composition changes with increasing altitude with tree ferns (*Hemitelia, Cyathea*) becoming much more common. Elfin woodland which is also evergreen borders the lower montane forest upslope. Its floristic composition is characterized by a high proportion of indigenous species and varies greatly in different islands. Several species,

45

e.g. *Magnolia* and *Prunus occidentalis*, which belong to the holarctic flora and present in the Greater Antilles, do not exist in the Islands to the Windward. *Micropholis* (Sapotaceae), *Richeria* (Euphorbiaceae), and *Podocarpus* (Coniferae) are especially common types of trees. Sometimes twisted trees reach heights of only 15–18 m and are thickly covered with epiphytes among which ferns are dominant. Moss forms dense clumps on branches which often hang down like garlands. Tree ferns are very common in the Islands to the Windward, especially in areas where the primeval forests have been destroyed by deforestation. Dense thickets of mountain bamboo (*Chusquea*, Gramineae), a secondary plant formation, coat the mountain slopes of Martinique, Puerto Rico, and other islands. Palm trees form an impressive cover on the steep slopes, especially in the Puerto Rican Sierra de Luquillo where the *Euterpe globosa* species predominates. Elfin woodlands grow in the tierra templada at the highest altitudes of the Islands to the Windward in the form of gnarled, stunted trees. The trees, e.g. *Charianthus* (Melastomaceae) and *Didymopanax* (Araliaceae), have a maximum height of 7 m; they become stunted because of the strong winds and are thickly coated with epiphytes.

Moorlands

Sphagnum moorlands exist in the mountainous regions of the Islands to the Windward. The rock surfaces of the woodless and very exposed peak regions of these islands show a heavy growth of lichen and moss, e.g. on Soufrière in Guadeloupe at an altitude of more than 1400 m. Ferns and particularly lobelias (*Lobelia cirsiifolia*, Lobeliaceae), which only appear at much higher altitudes on the mainland, grow here. It has not yet been discovered whether the lack of trees in the highest regions of the Islands to the Leeward is a natural phenomenon (Stehlé), or whether it has to be seen as one stage in the development of elfin woodland (Beard).

Pinewoods, instead of the semi-evergreen montane forests, are found in the subhumid regions of the tierra templada and tierra fría in Cuba and Hispaniola. In the mountains of Hispaniola they contain the *Pinus occidentalis* mainly (Plate 11) and the characteristic knee-high grass species of *Danthonia* and *Agrostis* (both are Gramineae). In parts the pines reach a height of 45 m and a trunk diameter of more than 1 m. In Cuba, the *Pinus occidentalis* grows in relatively dry areas in the mountainous regions of the western Sierra Maestra, and the *Pinus cubensis* on laterite soils in the mountains of the eastern Oriente.

Vegetational/geographical zones

The distribution of climatic plant formations closely reflects the differences of the Caribbean climate. It is dependent on three factors (cf. p. 26): (1) the variations in humidity resulting from changing factors which set the Islands to the Leeward apart from all the other islands; (2) the orographic increase in humidity and the simultaneous decrease in temperature with increasing altitude above sea-level; and (3) the difference in humidity caused by exposure either to windward or to leeward.

The first factor results in the predominance of thorn and cactus forest and dry forest in the Islands to the Leeward. In all the other islands the dominant vegetation types are those which require a higher degree of humidity, except when the topography, exposure, or other edaphic factors do not give these conditions, and there is, instead, aridity.

An increase in humidity with altitude is noticeable in all islands with marked differences in relief. For instance, one may recognize the different altitudinal zones from thorn and cactus woodland, to tropical deciduous forest, and up to semi-evergreen seasonal forest in the Islands to the Leeward (Margarita). In the Islands to the Windward the zonal sequence is from semi-evergreen seasonal forest and tropical rain forest up to montane forest, elfin woodland and stunted elfin woodland and in some treeless peak regions to moss, lichen and Lobelia colonies. Several of the Islands to the Windward display the complete range, from thorn and cactus forest to stunted elfin woodland. The Greater Antilles exhibit two types of succession in relation to increasing altitude: from tropical rain forest to elfin woodland, and from thorn and cactus forest through semi-evergreen seasonal and lower montane forest to elfin woodland.

These differences in the vertical zoning of vegetation types exist both in the Greater Antilles and in the Islands to the Windward. They are caused by factor (3) above: the difference in humidity on slopes facing to windward or to leeward (cf. p. 26). Vegetation types which require a higher degree of humidity reach further down on the windward slopes of the mountains than on the leeward slopes.

The schematic representation (Table 4) of the distribution of Caribbean vegetation shows the enormous variety of plant formations in the tierra caliente. Furthermore, it shows that hand in hand with an increase in altitude goes a decrease in the number of different plant formations because of the increasing similarity in the amount of humidity of thermic-hygric climates, until, at last, only one type of vegetation is found in the highest regions. And finally, the survey shows the considerably wider vertical extent of plant formations in the Greater Antilles. This results from the greater differences in relief and from higher elevation of the mountains. Therefore, only the Greater Antilles, especially Hispaniola, resemble the situation in the Middle American mainland as far as the zoning of vegetation is concerned.

Cultivated plants

Cultivation in the Caribbean islands is restricted mainly to the tierra caliente. Even if the lower regions of the tierra templada in the mountains of the Greater Antilles are cultivated, the type does not differ from the culti-

Table 4.   Distribution of vegetation zones in the Caribbean islands
(number of rainy months in brackets)

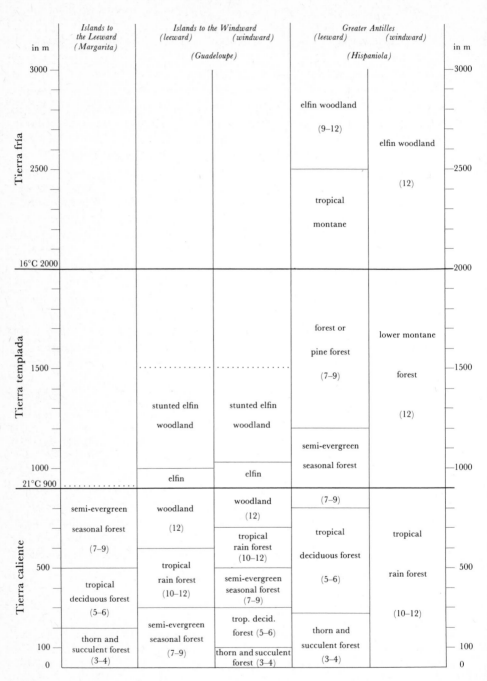

48

Table 5.   The most important cultivated plants in the Caribbean islands

climatic vegetation forms and thermic-hygric climates	cultivated plants	origin[1]
(a) cultivation for export		
tropical rain or montane forest (10–12 rainy months)	ginger, *Zingiber officinale* (Zingiberaceae)	(*y A*)
	coffee, *Coffea arabica* (Rubiaceae)	(*y Af*)
	cocoa, *Theobroma Cacao* (Sterculiaceae)	(*o*)
	coconut, *Cocos nucifera* (Palmae)	(*y A*)
	nutmeg, *Myristica fragans* (Myristicaceae)	(*y A*)
	banana, *Musa sapientum* (Musaceae)	(*y A*)
	vanilla, *Vanilla pompona* (Orchidaceae)	(*o*)
	lime, *Citrus aurantifolia* (Rutaceae)	(*o?*)
semi-evergreen seasonal forest (7–9 rainy months)	pineapple, *Ananas sativus* (Bromeliaceae)	(*o*)
	cotton, *Gossypium barbadense* (Malvaceae)	(*o*)
	pimento, *Pimenta dioica* (Myrtaceae)	(*o*)
	arrowroot, *Maranta arundinacea* (Marantaceae)	(*o*)
	tobacco, *Nicotiana Tabacum* (Solaneae)	(*o*)
	sugar cane, *Saccharum officinarum* (Gramineae)	(*y A*)
tropical deciduous forest (5–6 rainy months)	mainly sugar cane and bananas with irrigation	
thorn and succulent forest (3–4 rainy months)	sisal, *Agave sisalana* (Amaryllidiaceae)	(*y Am*)
	henequén, *Agave fourcroydes* (Amaryllidiaceae)	(*y Am*)
	mainly sugar cane and bananas with irrigation	
(b) cultivation for the domestic market		
tubers	sweet potato, *Ipomoea Batatas* (Convolvulaceae)	(*y A*)
	malanga, *Xanthosoma sagittifolium* (Araceae)	(*o*)
	manioc, *Manihot utilissima* (Euphorbiaceae)	(*o*)
	taro, *Colocasia esculenta* (Araceae)	(*y A*)
	yams, *Dioscorea* div. spec. (Dioscoreaceae)	(*y A*)
grain and pulse	peanut, *Arachis Hypogaea* (Papilionaceae)	(*y Am*)
	maize, *Zea Mays* (Gramineae)	(*o*)
	rice, *Oryza sativa* (Gramineae)	(*y A*)
	beans, *Phaseolus* (Papilionaceae)	(*o*)
	Indian bush pea, *Cajanus indicus* (Papilionaceae)	(*y A*)
fruit trees	avocado, *Persea gratissima* (Lauraceae)	(*o*)
	bread fruit, *Artocarpus communis* (Moraceae)	(*y A*)
	mango, *Mangifera indica* (Anacardiaceae)	(*y A*)
	plantain, *Musa paradisiaca* (Musaceae)	(*y A*)
	papaya, *Carica Papaya* (Caricaceae)	(*y Am*)

[1] (*o*) indigenous to the pre-Columban Caribbean islands; (*y*) imported from *A* Asia, *Af* Africa, *Am* American mainland.

vation in the higher regions of the tierra caliente with regard to cultivated plants and types of enterprise. This applies to both export-orientated cultivation (coffee) and to the peasant subsistence economy. There are only a few mountainous regions where non-tropical cultivated plants are grown (vegetables, lettuces), e.g. in the upland basin of Constanza in the Dominican Cordillera Central at a height of 1200 m, in the Kenscoff region above Port-au-Prince (at 1500 m), and in the Matouba region in Guadeloupe (at 700–800 m).

Quality of a product for export is much more dependent on the degree of humidity than is cultivation for local consumption. Cultivated plants, grown as export produce, grow particularly well in certain specific types of hygric-thermic climate, and can be classified with certain climatic vegetation types (Table 5a), although several cultivated plants are not strictly confined to one particular type of climate. For instance, the coconut tree grows in both humid and subhumid coastal regions (Plate 29). Most important, sugar cane and bananas are also cultivated in semi-arid and even in arid regions with the help of irrigation, e.g. in the western part of Cibao in Hispaniola. Sugar cane, which belongs to the subhumid region in its climatic requirements, is the most important cultivated plant within the export-orientated agriculture of the Caribbean.

Cultivated plants supplying the domestic market are grown in all the areas where the different climatic vegetation types are found, especially, though, in the areas of semi-evergreen and rain forests. Their cultivation in semi-arid and arid regions depends on natural or artificial irrigation. Among the cultivated plants which are listed in Table 5b only rice is extensively cultivated with irrigation in arid regions.

In contrast to the Middle American mainland north of the Nicaragua depression, the most important cultivated plant in the Caribbean is manioc, which was imported from South America by the Arawaks and Caribs before Columbus arrived. The Caribbean archipelago therefore belonged to the tropical American manioc belt, although maize was not unknown; on the other hand, the greater part of the Middle American mainland belonged to the maize belt (Sapper). Within a subsistence economy the peasant continued to cultivate tuberous plants such as sweet potato, malanga and manioc, and also maize and beans, which the Amerindians used to cultivate. Since then, however, Caribbean peasant agriculture has been enriched by the importation of various cultivated plants such as different tubers, cereals, pulses and various fruit trees. Some of the imported plants represent relatively recent innovations into the cultivated landscape. For instance, the breadfruit tree was only brought to the Antilles from southeast Asia in 1793. Today it is a characteristic feature of peasant agriculture in all the islands.

Most of the plants cultivated for export are not indigenous. The plants with the highest export value, such as sugar cane, bananas, coffee and many others, were imported from the Old World tropical regions. Sugar cane was introduced so early that its cultivation was characteristic of the coastal regions near Santo Domingo in Hispaniola by the beginning of the sixteenth century.

Land fauna

The Caribbean fauna is extremely poor when compared with the Middle American mainland. Only Trinidad differs in this respect because of its nearness to the mainland and because of its land connection to the mainland which existed until about 8000 years ago. The nineteenth century German naturalist H. Gundlach, contributed greatly towards the knowledge of the fauna in the Greater Antilles, especially in Cuba. The distribution pattern of the native vertebrates (*Vertebrata*) and the mammals (*Mammalia*) reflects the geographical distribution of the Caribbean fauna.

The only mammals are insectivores (*Insectivora*), rodents (*Rodentia*), and bats (*Chiroptera*). The insectivores are represented only by *Solenodon* and *Nesophontes*. More numerous are the rodents living either in brackish and fresh water (e.g. *Trichechus manatus*) or on land (e.g. *Capromys pilorides*). The peasant population hunts the latter group for meat, and also the rabbit-like Agoutidae in the Islands to the Windward. The bats show the greatest diversity. Bats which live on insects, fruit and fish are very numerous in all the islands. Trinidad itself possesses sixty-two species of bats. A bat research laboratory was started in this island after eighty-nine people died in the 1930s from bites received from vampire bats (Desmodontidae) infected with hydrophobia, and after large losses of cattle for the same reason. Trinidad possesses larger animals of different genera in addition to the above genera of vertebrates. The edentates (Edentata) are represented by the sloth and the ant-eater. Predators (Carnivora) are: the tiger-cat (*Felis pardalis*), the pine marten (*Mustela barbara*), the racoon (*Procyon*), and two species of howling monkeys (*Alouata*).

Amphibious animals are also rare in the Caribbean area. Among the thirty frog and toad genera only one frog genus (*Eleutherodactylus*) is represented on all islands. The reptile fauna is more versatile. In contrast to the Middle American mainland there are more lizards than snakes. For instance, Cuba possesses forty-six lizard genera but only fourteen snake genera; only one snake is poisonous, the Fer-de-Lance (*Bothrops caribbaeus* and *Bothrops lanceolatus*, Crotalidae) living in Martinique and St Lucia. Trinidad, however, possesses many snakes among which are the boa and several poisonous species. Crocodiles are represented by two indigenous species only in Cuba. Freshwater fish are not numerous. Only Trinidad has rivers abounding in fish.

A multitude of species can be found if one looks at the bird kingdom. Many mainland species are missing but, on the other hand, numerous indigenous species exist. In Cuba 340 bird species are known, among which 54 are indigenous. Several migrants from North America hibernate

51

in Caribbean islands, e.g. the wood warbler (*Dendroica*). The many bird species are very useful in destroying insects and larvae. This is especially well illustrated by the small white *Ardeola ibis* which only immigrated from the Old World in 1952. This bird, which picks vermin from the hide, can always be observed near cattle. The many species of parrots (Psittacidae) and of humming birds (Trochilidae) are distinctive in their colourful plumage. Aquatic birds usually appear in flocks, e.g. the red ibis (*Eudocimus ruber*) in the extensive mangrove swamps in Trinidad. The long-legged red flamingoes (*Phosenicopterus ruber*) come to the island of Bonaire in such quantities that the island is sometimes called 'Flamingo Island'.

Comparison of the fauna of the small island of Trinidad, which is relatively abundant in animals, with the fauna of the larger island of Cuba, which has relatively few animals, shows that the fauna of the islands, including the Greater Antilles, is poorer than might be expected from their size. Leaving out Trinidad one can say: the more extensive the area of an island, the greater the number of species of one genus and of the fauna in its entirety. For instance, Cuba possesses seventy-five species of amphibious animals and reptiles, Puerto Rico has forty, and Montserrat nine. The fauna in different islands varies considerably, but the links between the various islands are closer than those with the mainland. From the point of view of fauna all Caribbean islands, with the exception of Trinidad, are oceanic islands because of the small number of vertebrates; from the point of view of flora, however, this classification applies only to the Islands to the Windward.

There is no doubt that the fauna immigrated from the mainland, but it is not clear how this happened nor by which routes. According to Darlington South and North American elements among fauna are supposed to have reached the Antilles via Central America. An expansion across former land connections is thought impossible because the impoverished Caribbean island fauna is oceanic in its character. Recently, the theory has been put forward by Simpson that the mammalian fauna originated chiefly in South America and reached the islands quite by chance, being carried by air and water currents: during the Miocene and Pliocene from the mouth of the Río Magdalena to Jamaica and Cuba and from there to the rest of the Greater Antilles; and from the mouth of the Orinoco to Trinidad and the Islands to the Windward during a time not yet known. Rouse (cf. p. 56) uses a modified version of this theory to describe the expansion of mesolithic Amerindian cultures in the Antilles. Simpson endeavours to explain by this theory both the destitution of the mammalian fauna in the area and the differences between the Greater Antilles and the Islands to the Windward.

Sea fauna

The Caribbean sea fauna far surpasses the land fauna in its diversity. This is especially true in regard to the littoral fauna. Large stretches along the shores of the islands are characterized by the structures of reef-building corals (cf. p. 37). These structures are biotope formations where various types of animals and plants create a very characteristic colony. The fauna of these coral reefs is marked by a multitude of foraminifera, sea urchins, crabs, mussels, oysters, and fish (e.g. the colourful Chaetodontidae). Among the snails the *Strombus gigas*, sometimes called the seafarer snail, is distinctive for its size; its meat is delicious and its shell can be found on any beach. Of economic importance are the pearl banks off the island of Margarita and the sponges, above all the *Hippospongia canaliculata*, which are especially numerous along the shores of Cuba and the Bahamas. The sand beaches and even more the mangrove lagoons are practically perforated by vast quantities of sand crabs. Oysters and fish (Gobiidae) also live in mangrove areas. Countless turtles (*Chelonida mydas*) used to deposit their eggs in the sand beaches of the Caribbean, especially in the Cayman Islands. Today only a few are left. Their meat is much superior to that of the turtle *Eretmochelys imbricata* which is only consumed locally. The *Caretta caretta* is hunted because of its shining shell. Also of particular economic importance are crustaceous animals, shrimps and prawns (e.g. *Pencus*) and lobsters (Palinuridae).

Although the littoral fauna possesses a very high percentage of indigenous species it corresponds closely to the littoral fauna of the Pacific shores in tropical America. This indicates the existence of a connection between the Atlantic and Pacific Ocean in the Central American region in the recent geologic past (Ekman, Kraus).

Among the hundreds of fish genera and species[1] of both the oceanic and the continental pelagic fauna in the Caribbean the following are of particular importance for consumption: the tunny (Thunnidae), the bonito (Katsuwonidae), the mackerel (Scombridae), the sword-fish (Xiphidae), the snapper (Lutjanidae), and the dolphin (Coryphaenidae). All of these appear in different species and are very numerous, also the balao (Hemiramphidae), the flying fish (Exocoetidae) which constitutes the main portion of the fish caught by the Barbadian fishing fleet, the many species of the Carangidae, the sawfish (Pristidae), and many others. There exist more than twenty species of sharks (Carchariidae and Carcharhinidae) of which the skin, meat and liver are used. Among the predatory fishes two types can become dangerous to man: the blue shark and the *Sphyraena barracuda*.

Up to the present the abundance of fish in the Caribbean has been insufficiently exploited. The development of a fishing industry has been planned and partly realized by the territories adjacent to the Caribbean Sea. Research on fish resources, spawning habits and migrations has been carried out by the Marine Laboratory in Miami, by the Caribbean Marine

[1] 866 species of fish exist in Cuban waters (Núñez Jiménez).

Biological Institute in Curaçao, and by the Instituto de la Pesca in Cuba, among others. Almost all the territories adjacent to the American Mediterranean are participating in the United Nations Caribbean Fisheries Project which started in 1967. An increase in the amount of fish landed from the Caribbean Sea is of great importance since these territories spend about US $50 million annually for importing fresh and dried fish.

7

The aborigines

The number of inhabitants in the Caribbean islands at the time of their discovery has been estimated recently at 200 000 (Kroeber), while according to the conquistadores several million Indians were supposed to have crowded into them.

Three Amerindian ethnic groups existed at the end of the fifteenth century. The most numerous was the group of insular Arawaks (Tainos) who inhabited the Greater Antilles, the Bahamas, and the Islands to the Leeward. In the Islands to the Windward lived the Caribs, and in the westernmost part of Cuba and also in the south-west peninsula of Hispaniola lived the Ciboney.

The Ciboney who settled along the coast were fishermen; in the interior they were hunters and gatherers. The insular Arawaks, superior to the Ciboney, made their living from agriculture. There is no doubt that Arawaks forced the Ciboney to retreat to less favourable inland areas. From the conformity of the spoken Arawak language in the various islands Rouse concluded that the expansion of the Arawak people occurred only a short time before Columbus's arrival. The Caribs were also agriculturalists, but in contrast to the Arawaks they were a warlike people; they raided the Arawak villages in the Greater Antilles and either killed or took the men captive for later use in cannibalistic rites. The term 'cannibal' is derived from the Spanish name for the Caribs, 'Caribal'. It seems that only a few generations before the discovery of America the Caribs ventured into the Islands to the Windward, coming from the South American mainland, and subjugated the Arawak population of this region. During their invasions they killed the Arawak men. The descendants of the Arawak women and the Caribs spoke the Arawak language; for this reason the Carib language was not spoken in the Antilles in Columbus's time, but was confined to the mainland.

Two important migration waves are recognizable when viewing the ethnic differentiation of the pre-Columban population. Both started out from the South American mainland and were directed towards the Caribbean islands. The Carib wave, the last of the two, was still in full progress,

55

when Columbus appeared on the scene. The expansion of the Arawaks and the Caribs was possible because both Amerindian peoples were skilled seafarers. Huge canoes, manned by up to eighty men, were used by the Arawaks who were not familiar with the art of sailing. The Caribs also used large dugouts for their expeditions. Arawak trade across the sea seems to have been quite considerable. Trinidad and Margarita, at least, must be considered as having been important trading bases for both the insular and the mainland Arawaks during pre-Columban times. Communication with Central and North America seems to have been minimal.

The pre-Columban population of the Caribbean islands did not achieve as high a culture as did the upland population of the Middle American mainland, either materially or spiritually. Nevertheless the conquistadores were very much impressed by the carefully cultivated areas of the Amerindians. Of the plants cultivated by the insular Arawaks manioc (cf. p. 50) was the most important crop. Like sweet potatoes and malanga it was planted in 'montones' (Lovén), earth mounds spaced equidistantly.

The culture of the insular Arawaks in Hispaniola was the most advanced. On that island five caciques existed. In Cuba Arawaks from Hispaniola seem to have exercised a feudal rule over an older Arawak population. The Arawaks, whose pottery was of a high standard, settled in populous villages, all of which had a spacious square. These squares were rectangular or oval in their layout and surrounded by stones. They were used for ball games, and around them stood wooden sanctuaries where gods were worshipped. Effigies of gods were carved into some of the rocks surrounding the square. Neither the group of insular Arawaks in the Bahamas, called Lucay, nor the mainland Arawaks achieved the high standard of culture attained by the Arawaks living in the Greater Antilles, especially those in Hispaniola.

Recent research has helped greatly to clarify the history of Amerindian migration to the Caribbean islands. Evidently the settlement of the islands did not occur before the Amerindian mesolithic, a stage of culture which corresponds to the Old World mesolithic. These were fishing cultures, similar to the European Kjökkenmöddinger, to be traced in the Islands to the Leeward and in the Greater Antilles, but not in the Islands to the Windward. The distribution of a variety of Amerindian mesolithic cultures over the Greater Antilles as well as their differing relationships to corresponding cultures on the mainland shows great diversity. This observation leads Rouse to believe that the mesolithic population could not have come to the Caribbean islands in one or several waves of immigration. Instead, winds and currents drove solitary groups in their boats from various places on the Venezuelan coast to the Greater Antilles quite by chance, similar to the way Simpson envisaged mammals had spread over the islands (cf. p. 52).

The presence of the Ciboney in Cuba and Hispaniola proves that the transition to the Amerindian neolithic, marked by agriculture and ceramic art, had not begun in all the islands when Columbus arrived. Numerous excavations during the last two decades now enable the construction of a

Table 6. Chronology of Mesolithic and Neolithic cultures in the Caribbean (after Rouse, simplified)

AD	Cuba west	Cuba centre	Hispaniola Haiti	Hispaniola Dom. Rep.	Puerto Rico (west)	Virgin Islands	St Lucia	Grenada	Trinidad	Margarita	AD
1500			Carrier	Boca Chica	Capa	Magens Bay	Fannis –?–?–?–?– Choc –?–?–?–	–?–?–?–?– Savanna Suazey –?–?–?–	Bontour	Playa Guacuco	1500
		Bani									
1000	Cayo Redondo		Meillac		Ostiones	Salt River	Massacré	Wester-Hall	Erin		1000
			Macady	Anadel			Trou-Massée	Salt Pond		El Agua	
500			Couri		Cuevas	Coral Bay-Longford	?	Pearls	Palo Seco		500
					Hacienda Grande			Black Point Beach	Cedros	Punta Gorda	
					Maria La Cruz						
0						Krum Bay					0
500	Guayabo Blanco		Cabaret						Ortoire		500
1000											1000
1500										Manicuare	1500
				Marban							
2000											2000
3000											3000
4000										Cubagua	4000
BC 5000											BC 5000

——————— = separating Mesolithic from Neolithic

–?–?–?–?–?–?–?–?– = separating Arawak from Carib

chronology of the Amerindian mesolithic and neolithic cultures. The first is based on artifacts, the latter on ceramic styles. Lately, the new carbon-14 method of dating has allowed a more exact dating, and a tentative chronology of Amerindian cultures in the Caribbean islands has been compiled which is shown in a simplified form in Table 6. It shows clearly that the Islands to the Leeward experienced the advance of the insular Arawaks and the corresponding retreat of the mesolithic Ciboney much earlier than the Greater Antilles. It also shows the time of the Arawaks' westward drive into the Greater Antilles, from the Virgin Islands in the east to Central Cuba in the west, as well as the early Arawak colonization of the Islands to the Windward. But so far the transition from Arawak to Carib colonization in the Islands to the Windward is not clearly recognizable. It has to be correlated with the transition either to the Choc or the Fannis ceramics (St Lucia), that is either about A.D. 1000 or 1250.

8

History of discovery, political and economic development

Spanish voyages of discovery and *conquista*

The 'West Indies' appeared on the European horizon in the wake of the first voyage of Christopher Columbus. The Genoese Cristoforo Columbo (Cristóbal Colón) took possession of the newly discovered shores for the Spanish Crown. On 12 October 1492 he set foot on American soil in the island of Guanahani (San Salvador, Watling Island) which belongs to the Bahamas. In commemoration of this event, the Día de la Raza has been made a public holiday in nearly all countries of Latin America.

Anyone who has seen the *Santa Maria* in the harbour of Barcelona, a copy of one of the three sailing ships Columbus used during his first voyage, will sense the daring of the man who ventured into the unknown space of the Atlantic Ocean in such a nutshell. Columbus discovered America while he was searching for a new route to the spice countries in Asia. Even on his deathbed, after four voyages to Middle America, he still believed that he had discovered the eastern shores of Asia. The name 'Indians', given to the American natives, and the term 'West Indies', designating the Middle American island chain, still bear witness to that erroneous belief.

Because European trade with the east was made difficult by Turkish interference, different routes to reach the spice countries in Asia had to be found. Columbus was able to take the chance of the westerly crossing of the Atlantic Ocean because the compass had by then been known to sailors for some decades and, most important, because he was convinced of the spherical shape of the earth. This theory was taught by Toscanelli, a cosmographer from Florence, with whom Columbus was in contact. Toscanelli designed the first world map which showed Asia in the west and Europe in the east. He followed the ancient geographers, though, having allowed too short a distance between these two continents. Ranke once observed that 'at no time has a phenomenal error produced a more phenomenal discovery'[1]. No belittling of Columbus's achievement is intended by saying that America

[1] Ranke, L. v., *Weltgeschichte*, Vol. 9, 2, p. 129, Leipzig 1888.

would have soon been discovered by Portuguese sailors even without Columbus. In 1487 Bartholomew Dias rounded the Cape of Good Hope; and on later voyages to India along this route Portuguese sailors reached the eastern shores of South America, driven off their course by the trade winds. The first to land there was Cabral who set foot on South American soil on 1 May 1500.

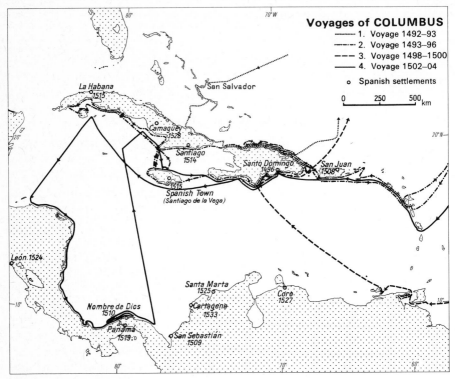

Map 8. The voyages of Columbus, and early Spanish cities in the 'West Indies'.

Columbus went on four voyages to America (Map 8). After he left the Canary island of Gomera to cross the Atlantic Ocean in a westerly direction for the first time, the north-east trade winds drove him to Guanahani in thirty-seven days. In autumn of 1962 nine daring Spaniards decided to relive the Columban adventure. On 10 October they started out from the Canary Islands in a westward direction and set sail in *Nina II*, a replica of the caravel Columbus used on his first voyage to America. The caravel went missing and caused a large-scale search, and on 30 November it was spotted from the air about 800 miles east of Puerto Rico. It did not dock at San Salvador until 25 December 1962, after a voyage of seventy-seven days. From Guanahani Columbus sailed to the north coast of Cuba, via Rum Cay and Long Island, the eastern part of which he then explored. He continued along the north coast of Hispaniola, but had to start his homebound voyage from there in January 1493 after his flag-ship *Santa Maria* ran ashore and had to be abandoned. The following passages are taken from the log book of Columbus. They mirror his impressions and his sentiments during his landings in Guanahani and Cuba (see E. G. Jacob):

12th October: . . . At 2 o'clock in the morning the land appeared, at a distance of about 8 nautical miles. . . . We hove to and waited for daylight. . . . There we soon saw naked natives. A landscape was revealed to our eyes with lush green trees, many streams, and fruits of different types. . . . Immediately there gathered many people of the island. In order that they might develop a friendly attitude towards us, and because I knew that they were a people who could better be freed and converted to our Holy Faith by love than by force, I gave to some of them red caps and glass beads, which they hung on their necks, and other things of slight value, in which they took much pleasure. . . . They came swimming to our ships and brought us parrots and cotton thread in skeins and darts and many other things which they exchanged for the things we gave them, such as glass beads and little bells . . . .

13th October: . . . I was very attentive and worked hard to discover whether there was any gold in the area. I saw that some of the men had pierced their noses and had put a piece of gold through it. By signs I could understand that one had to go to the south to meet a king who had great vessels of gold and possessed many gold pieces . . . .

14th October: . . . In order to find a place where I could build a small fortress I went reconnoitring today and discovered a peninsula . . . which, by a few days' labour, could be transformed into an island. I do not think, though, that this would be necessary, because these people are very unskilled in arms, as Your Highness will see personally from the seven that I caused to be taken in order to carry them to Spain where they are to learn our language before we bring them back here. If Your Highness should order them all to be taken to Castile or held captive on their own island this could easily be done, for with some 50 men they could all be subjugated and made to do all one wishes.

17th October: . . . On all these days since I have been in India it has rained more or less. Your Highness may believe that this land belongs to the most fertile countries and in regard to climate to the temperate regions of the world.

28th October (off Cuba): . . . I have never seen a more beautiful place: trees all along the river, beautiful and green, and different from ours, with flowers and fruits each according to their kind, and with countless little birds singing very sweetly. There were great numbers of palms, of a different kind from those in Guinea and Spain, of a middling height, and the trunk without any bark, and with large leaves which the natives use to thatch their houses. The land was very flat. . . . That island is the most beautiful that eyes have ever seen, full of very good harbours and deep rivers . . . I dare to suppose that the mighty ships of the Grand Khan come here, and that from here to the mainland is a journey of only 10 days . . . .

His second voyage (1493–6) led Columbus first to Dominica. He turned north and discovered numerous islands belonging to the Lesser Antilles, e.g. Marie Galante, Guadeloupe, Montserrat, Nevis, St Kitts, St Martin, and St Croix. He sailed along the south coast of Puerto Rico, reached Jamaica and Cuba after visiting Hispaniola's north coast, explored the south coasts of these three islands, and returned to Spain via the Lesser Antilles. He had discovered twenty large and over forty small islands. The third voyage (1498–1500) took Columbus to Trinidad, Margarita, and to the neighbouring coastline of South America. On his fourth voyage (1502–04) he came to Martinique, and later on he thoroughly explored the Central American coastline. For the first time this fourth voyage was aimed at finding a westward passage to India (many following expeditions were to have the same objective).

The result of Columbus's voyages was the knowledge of the existence of the Caribbean chain of islands. The island character of Cuba was not definitely proved until Sebastian de Ocampo circumnavigated the island in 1508 (Table 7). Columbus's voyages also initiated numerous expeditions which, within a few decades, led to the conquest of all Central America and Mexico, using Spanish settlements in what were known to them as the West Indies as their base.

Table 7.   The most important voyages of discovery in the Caribbean

Bahamas, Greater Antilles, Islands to the Windward	Islands to the Leeward
1492/3 Columbus's first voyage: Bahama Islands; eastern Cuba; Hispaniola's north coast	1498/1500 Columbus's third voyage: Trinidad; Gulf of Paria; Margarita
1493/6 Columbus's second voyage: Dominica and Islands to the Windward north of Dominica; south coasts of Puerto Rico, Hispaniola and Cuba; shores of Jamaica	1499 Alonso de Hojeda and Juan de la Cosa: Margarita and shores of Venezuela
1508 Sebastián de Ocampo: circumnavigation of Cuba	1500 Cristóbal Guerra and Per Alonso Niño: pearl-oyster banks of Margarita and of neighbouring islands; shores of Venezuela
1513 Juan Ponce de León: Bahama Islands; Florida	

Because of the success of the Conquista all Central America became an area of Spanish colonization. The main incentives for the Spanish Conquista were not only the search for gold, silver, pearls, and slaves, but also the crusading spirit which was just as strong and which had arisen in Spain during the wars against the Arabs. These wars had only ended in 1492 with the fall of Granada.

The conquistadores were characterized by 'a curious mixture of God and profit, of religion and rapacity' (Friederici i, 311). Their greed led them to commit many crimes, and their treatment of the native population was a mockery of Christian morality. And yet, most of these men were eager to evangelize. Most of them joined the voyages at their own risk and expense, fighting both for their own benefit and for God and the Spanish Crown. Their achievements, their courage, toughness and stamina through all the hardships, which at that time were involved in any trip to the tropics, laid the foundations for the subsequent Spanish colonization.

The islands under Spanish rule

By the middle of the sixteenth century all countries adjacent to the Caribbean Sea had become Spanish possessions, and the era of the conquista had ended. Santo Domingo, founded in 1496, became the administrative centre of the 'Spanish Indies' during the first period. Columbus was appointed viceroy of the Spanish Indies without ever taking up this post. In 1526 the audiencia of Santo Domingo was established with Hispaniola, the other islands of the Antilles, and even with the mainland coast (*tierra firme*) under its jurisdiction. This was changed when the viceroyalty of New Spain, with its capital Mexico, was founded in 1535 and when the viceroyalty of Peru, with its capital Lima, was established in 1542. The audiencia of Santo Domingo to which the north coast of South America and the Antilles belonged for a time, and the administrative district of Guatemala which extended over most of Central America, were put under the jurisdiction of the viceroy of New Spain. New Spain then included by far the greater part of Middle America, and later even the Spanish possessions in North America. At first only the eastern part of Peru and the Isthmus of Panama belonged to the viceroyalty of Peru and, after 1739, to the newly founded viceroyalty of Nueva Granada with its capital Santa Fé de Bogotá.

The changes in the administration of the Spanish colonial empire in the middle of the sixteenth century clearly indicate the shifting of its main activities from the Antilles to the mainland—to the uplands of the former Indian realms of the Aztecs in Mexico and the Incas in Peru, which were very wealthy because of their precious metals. During the time of the conquista the Caribbean islands served as stepping stones for all Spanish expeditions to the mainland. During the colonial period their main function was merely to safeguard the shipping routes between the American mainland and Europe.

The transition from the conquista to the colonial period began with the founding of various cities which, because of a royal decree in 1513, were mostly built in a grid-pattern. The oldest city in America, founded by the brother of Columbus, Bartholomaeus Columbus, is Santo Domingo de Guzman in Hispaniola. On the neighbouring large island of Cuba early city foundations were Santiago de Cuba (1514) and Habana (1515). Some of the early settlements had to be abandoned but most of them lasted and became prosperous. Colonial penetration started out from the cities which became the administrative, cultural and economic centres and the strongholds of Spanish colonial rule.

All Middle America was nominally under Spanish rule at the middle of the sixteenth century; in reality, however, Spanish colonization in the Caribbean was restricted to the Greater Antilles. The warlike Caribs and the economic worthlessness of the Islands to the Windward prevented the Spaniards from establishing themselves there. As was the custom during the reconquista in the old country, so in the colonies was landed property given to the soldiers at the end of the conquista (*repartimiento*) with the difference of conveying to the landowner, together with the land, the natives living on it for use as labour in agriculture and mining. This feudal system of enfeoffment, introduced by Columbus, was called the *encomienda* system. It led to reckless exploitation, enslavement, and drastic reduction of the native population within a few years. A royal decree, issued in 1512, declared the right of each landowner to demand tributes from the Amerindians. At the same time it obliged the proprietors to treat the natives well, to protect them, and to engage a priest to teach them the Christian belief. These regulations were not observed in practice. The Amerindians were forced into hard labour, and often landowners took possession of the *ejidos*, the land in the vicinity of the villages where the natives were to be settled in groups (*reducciones*) which the 1512 decree ordered to be given to the Amerindians for their common use. Bartolomé de Las Casas, a priest of the Order of St Dominic, challenged the inhuman exploitation and enslavement of the Amerindians, with the result that in 1542 new regulations explicitly stated the freedom of the Amerindians and stated that they were not to be forced to work for the landowner throughout the year. These laws came too late for the Amerindians in the Greater Antilles. The native population there had been exterminated by that time, and Negro slaves had to be imported as labourers. However, these new laws probably saved the mainland Amerindians from extinction.

The Spaniards took much care in spreading their imported domestic animals and plants. On his second voyage Columbus brought seed and animals. Horses, donkeys, and horned cattle were shipped to America. Among the imported cultivated plants, sugar cane and coffee were to become very important in later days. On the whole, though, the Spaniards did very little to further agriculture in their colonies. Peasant settlements were almost non-existent. They introduced a plantation economy to the

Antilles, but during the Spanish era it did not really flourish anywhere. Large-scale agricultural enterprises were usually based on extensive pastures. Mining was of no importance. By contrast to the Antilles, where precious metals were very rare, Mexico possessed great wealth of gold and especially of silver. Huge quantities were shipped from there as well as from Peru home to the old country via the Caribbean.

Spanish colonial economic policy was based on the principles of mercantilism. Primarily, colonies were objects of exploitation and at the same time markets for home products. From the beginning all traffic to, and all trade with, the colonies were monopolized by the home government which delegated the respective rights to the government-owned Casa de Contratación, founded in 1503 in Seville. Without its consent no ship, no person, and no goods were to leave Spain for America. During the first period Seville handled the entire traffic to and from America. When its own port facilities could no longer meet the rising volume of trade it was joined by Cádiz, to which centre the Casa de Contratación was finally transferred in 1717.

During the first decades of Spanish colonial rule all ships leaving Seville sailed for Santo Domingo; and then other ports in the colonies were supplied from there. Following the conquest of Mexico and Peru, Santo Domingo became less important since ships with destinations in these countries no longer called at Santo Domingo. Spanish caravels, galleons and brigs only started to sail in convoys because of the growing danger of being attacked by ships of north-west European nations. Convoys coming from Spain split in the region of the Lesser Antilles. One group sailed to Porto Bello (former Nombre de Diós) on the Isthmus of Panama. It followed a route leading between Trinidad and Tobago, then along the South American mainland coast via Cartagena, which was later the starting point of the return voyage. Porto Bello on the Atlantic and Panamá on the Pacific side of the Isthmus were the two most important trading centres for goods to and from Peru and the La Plata region. The second group followed a route along the coasts of the islands of the Greater Antilles and through the Yucatán Channel to Veracruz. This port was not only the emporium for Mexican goods, but also for goods from the Philippines which were brought via Acapulco on the Mexican Pacific coast. Both ship formations reunited during summer in the beautiful and easily defended natural harbour of Habana in Cuba, then left together for Spain carrying with them the riches of Mexico and Peru. Since the Florida Strait proved to be the best sailing route from the American Mediterranean into the Atlantic Ocean, Habana logically became the point of departure for home-bound voyages. Besides, Habana commanded the western approach to the Florida Strait. This timetable and these commercial routes between Spain and its American colonies took into account not only physical factors such as air and water currents in the American Mediterranean, but also military considerations.

The necessity of observing prescribed trading routes; the state monopoly of exploiting and transporting the New World wealth; and the very important fact that the various areas adjacent to the Caribbean Sea were relatively sparsely populated: these were the essential preconditions for the successful invasion of Middle America, which was purely Spanish until the middle of the sixteenth century, by north-west European powers.

The founding of colonies by north-west European nations

The north-west European nations gained Caribbean footholds mainly in three stages. French privateers, or corsairs, turned their attention to the American Mediterranean following an incident in 1523 when part of the Mexican loot sent by Cortes to Charles V was captured off the Azores by Jean Fleury. After 1536 their numbers increased as a result of the Treaty of Lyon according to which the French Crown forbade them to attack Portuguese shipping between Africa and Europe. The Bahama Islands then became their most important strongholds. From here they attacked Spanish shipping through the Mona and the Windward Passages, and the Florida Strait in particular, which was vital to Spain. There was also illicit but peaceful trading between merchants of the north-west European nations and Spanish possessions in Middle America. Between 1562 and 1568, for example, John Hawkins made four voyages to the Caribbean; an early stage of the European–African–West Indian triangular trade. For the most part, however, this first stage of English and French penetration into the Spanish colonial empire (1536–1609) was characterized by armed raids on Spanish shipping and harbours, carried out by the corsairs (privateers). Raids on Santiago de Cuba in 1554 and on Habana in 1555 caused a great stir in Spain. Defensive steps had to be taken, such as the more rigid organization of the convoy system and the fortification of the harbours which were most important for Spanish American trade: Cartagena, San Juan de Puerto Rico, Santo Domingo, Santiago de Cuba and, above all, Habana. To ensure safe routes to the mainland ports which were so important to Spain now became one of the functions of the Greater Antilles.

That Spain did not succeed in keeping the American Mediterranean as a *mare clausum*, wholly under its control, was mainly due to Francis Drake. After completing several successful trading and raiding voyages, Drake left England in 1585 with more than twenty ships. He did not, however, achieve his aim of effectively challenging the Spanish monopoly. Nevertheless, his capture and destruction of Santo Domingo and Cartagena weakened the Spaniards considerably. In spite of this, the Spaniards were able to defeat a large English fleet, under the command of Drake and Hawkins, off San Juan de Puerto Rico and again near Porto Bello. In the Treaties of London (1604) and Antwerp (1609) England and the newly independent Netherlands recognized Spanish hegemony over all the American territories which were effectively occupied by Spain. But they did not recognize Spanish rights over territories which only nominally belonged to Spain. This qualification clearly indicated the intentions of these nations to find other means of invading Middle America.

The second phase of north-west European intrusion (1609–97) is characterized by the founding of colonies in the islands of the Lesser Antilles not settled by the Spaniards, as well as by the activities of the filibusters against the Spaniards. The Dutch had become the greatest naval and commercial power in Europe. Their main interest was directed towards the East Indies, but they were also very active in the 'West Indies'. It is true to say that the English and French established colonies encouraged by the strength of the Dutch West India Company's fleet, founded in 1621. In 1628 Piet Heyn proved the superior strength of the Dutch naval force when he intercepted the Spanish silver fleet off Matanzas Bay in Cuba. The Dutch, after conquering Brazil and settling in West Africa and Guyana, claimed only small islands around the Caribbean Sea. Between 1630 and 1640 they claimed Curaçao, Aruba, and Bonaire off South America, and St Eustatius, St Martin, and Saba in the northern region of the Islands to the Windward. Curaçao and St Eustatius, being free ports, became the most important commercial centres. Almost the entire trade of the Spanish *tierra firme* was in the hands of the Dutch. In the Peace of Westphalia, 1648, the Dutch possessions were recognized by the Spaniards.

After failures in Guyana the English founded their first colony in 1624 in St Christopher (St Kitts). In the same year Barbados became an English colony, followed by Nevis in 1628 and Antigua and Montserrat in 1632. Attempts to settle in the larger islands to the south failed at first because of the resistance offered by the Caribs. France had a colony in St Kitts by 1624. Settlements in Martinique and Guadeloupe were established only after Richelieu had founded the Compagnie des Isles d'Amérique. In contrast to the Spanish colonies and in contrast also to the Dutch trading stations, English and French settlements were planned from the outset as areas for development. At first Dutch traders supplied the necessary provisions, but the English Navigation Ordinance (1651) and Colbert's Compagnie des Indes Occidentales (1664), both following the principles of mercantilism, were a heavy blow to their trading position. After 1652 several wars were fought in the Caribbean area between the Netherlands, France and England, each within changing hostile groupings, with the result that the Dutch position was so weakened that in 1674 the Dutch West India Company went bankrupt. Different European nations appeared on the scene, founding or at least planning to found colonies: in 1671 Denmark acquired the Virgin Islands; St Barthélemy was in Swedish hands for a short time; and Brandenburg founded the ephemeral Brandenburg–Amerikanische Kompagnie. But only England and France succeeded in establishing themselves firmly in a large number of islands. After claiming the Islands to the Windward and the Bahamas, Great Britain captured Jamaica in 1655, and France took over the western part of Hispaniola in 1665. In the Treaty of Rijswijk in 1697 Spain recognized the newly acquired British and French colonial possessions. This event saw the end of the era during which the north-west European nations were founding colonies in the Middle American islands.

During the seventeenth-century period of colonization, the filibusters and buccaneers continued the fight of the corsairs begun in the sixteenth century against Spanish shipping and harbours. In the Greater Antilles, especially in Hispaniola, men living outside Spanish jurisdiction were called buccaneers. They lived from hunting herds of wild pigs and horned cattle, the meat of which was cured in strips by smoking them over a slow fire on boucans. The smoked meat was then sold to passing ships, mainly to filibusters. The name 'filibuster' is derived from the term for their light and fast ships (flibot, flyboat). During the various wars these lawless pirates, living only from plundering, were a welcome tool in the hands of the British, the French and the Dutch. Even in years of peace these nations approved of their raids, as is seen by the splendid reception given in 1671 to the British filibuster Henry Morgan when he returned to Jamaica after successful undertakings against Cartagena and the Isthmus of Panama. Port Royal in Jamaica became the stronghold for British filibusters, while the island of Tortuga off the north-west coast of Hispaniola served as stronghold for the French. The French occupation of West Hispaniola started out from Tortuga and other filibuster harbours along the coast of that island. Hardly any Spanish settlement along the rim of the American Mediterranean was spared from being plundered by the filibusters at least once. Only the economic development of their islands, which had begun in the late seventeenth century, made the British and French governments stop the activities of the filibusters. This was finally and effectively done after the Treaty of Rijswijk (1697).

The great conflicts between Great Britain and France which characterize the third stage of north-west European intrusion, during the eighteenth century (1697–1814), were caused mainly by the enormous economic boom experienced by their island colonies. They had developed into 'sugar islands'. The sugar plantation economy was dependent on slave labour and this completely changed the islands' social structure (Plate 1). Wars among colonial powers during the eighteenth century usually had as their issue the possession of these islands, which were very valuable to their mother-countries. Many islands changed hands several times. Nevertheless, the Treaties of Aachen (1748), Versailles (1783), Amiens (1802), and Paris (1814) brought only a few territorial secessions, if any. Only the Treaty of Paris in 1763 led to extensive territorial exchanges, in favour of Great Britain which showed its superiority in the Caribbean during the Seven Years War. This superiority was due to the fact that Great Britain, in contrast to France, possessed naval bases, both equipped with dockyards, in Port Royal, Jamaica, and in English Harbour, Antigua.

The Treaty of Paris (1814) consolidated the European colonial posses-sions: Spain retained all mainland areas except a small coastal strip in the Gulf of Honduras. Of the 'West Indies' it kept the islands of Cuba and Puerto Rico. Santo Domingo, the eastern part of Hispaniola, was returned to Spain, after being in French hands for a short period and after it had been occupied by the army of Haitian freedom fighters. France had lost its most valuable colony, Saint-Domingue (the western part of Hispaniola), through a slave rebellion, which led to the proclamation of the independent Negro Republic of Haiti in 1804. Martinique and Guadeloupe as well as the small islands of St Barthélemy and St Martin (northern part) remained in French hands. Great Britain gained most. It now possessed Jamaica and most of the Islands to the Windward: Trinidad, Tobago, Grenada, St Vin-cent, St Lucia, Dominica, Barbados, St Kitts, Nevis, Montserrat, Antigua, Barbuda, Anguilla, and several of the Virgin Islands. The Netherlands kept their possessions: Aruba, Curaçao, Bonaire as well as St Eustatius, St Martin (southern part), and Saba. The three largest Virgin Islands St Thomas, St Croix, and St John belonged to Denmark.

Following the example set by Mexico and the Spanish colonies in South America, Santo Domingo proclaimed its independence in 1821, only to be annexed for the second time by the neighbouring Negro Republic of Haiti the following year. In 1844 independence was again granted to the Domini-can Republic, but because of the continued danger of Haitian invasion it asked for Spanish protection and rule in 1861. In 1865 the Dominican Republic finally became independent.

The last Spanish possessions in Middle America, Cuba and Puerto Rico, remained Spanish colonies until 1898.

Economic development in the colonial period

The economic development of the West Indian colonies did not follow a single pattern. Yet, there is one essential common chacteristic: the develop-ment of the plantation economy. It is still in operation today (cf. pp. 78, 86, 105).

Spain had introduced the plantation economy to its West Indian colonies by the beginning of the sixteenth century. This economy was based on sugar cane farming (p. 219). But because of economic stagnation in the Spanish West Indies, the plantation economy did not flourish until 1815 when the government of Madrid issued the Cedula de Gracias, thereby abandoning the principles of mercantilism. Until the nineteenth century the former Spanish colonies used their land mainly for pasture, while for the British and French islands this was the heyday of the colonial sugar plantation economy, founded on slave labour.

The British and French possessions were not plantation islands when they were first colonized. The importation of sugar cane brought about the

69

plantation economy, and at the same time caused the abrupt end of peasant farming. Sugar production in the Islands to the Windward (first in Barbados between 1640 and 1650) was started by Portuguese Jews who emigrated from Brazil. Within a few decades most of the British and French islands were cultivating sugar cane on plantations. This method of cultivation flourished during the eighteenth century, especially in St Domingue (cf. p. 22).

The colonial sugar plantations were considerably smaller than the large-scale enterprises of today. This is especially true of the plantations in the Islands to the Windward, where only a small acreage of flat land, suitable for plantation cultivation, was available. Farms were of an average size of not more than 50 hectares (farms in the Greater Antilles usually were around 500 ha), the majority of them being family enterprises. On large-scale farms the system of absentee landlords developed during the eighteenth century: the owner returned to live in his own country and left his enterprise in charge of an overseer.

Colonial sugar plantations were located near the coast with road connections to the nearest harbour. Just as today, a very unbalanced economy of large-scale enterprises, cultivating only sugar cane, grew up on the coastal plains at that time. The mountainous interior of the islands became refuge areas for peasant settlers as well as for escaped slaves. Parts of the interior were taken into coffee plantations and other parts remained relatively uninhabited.

An essential characteristic of the colonial sugar plantation was the fact that the sugar producer was both cultivator and manufacturer. At first the crushing mills used to be turned by a mule or an ox, a method which is still in use in parts of Haiti. Later, windmills were used whose ruins add a special touch to the present landscape of many islands. Waterwheels were rare. Next to the crushing mill stood the boiling house where the cane juice crystallized to raw brown sugar (Plate 1).

Monoculture dominated the plantations, but the entire farmland was not used for sugar cultivation (Map 73) and grazing lands were extensive. Stock animals were necessary for transporting cane, therefore each plantation was dependent on having enough livestock to guarantee a steady, uninterrupted supply of cane for the mills during harvest time. The wooded areas on a plantation were not completely cleared in order to leave an adequate source of wood both for building purposes and for the furnaces of boiling houses. Part of the farmland was used for cultivating basic food, and in several areas the custom developed of giving plots of land to slaves to cultivate for themselves. This enabled plantation owners to reduce food imports, and the right was granted to slaves to sell their own produce. According to their size, some plantations owned less than a hundred slaves, others several hundreds and in extreme cases up to several thousand. Primitive tools were used for farmwork. Because of the abundance of labour, ploughs and other time-saving equipment were not in use.

The settlement pattern of colonial plantation areas was characterized by villagelike concentrations adjacent to the plantation houses (Map 73). At first, plantation houses were simple wooden structures on a stone base, later they were impressive buildings. With their spacious encircling verandas they were very suitable for the tropical climate. Near to the plantation house lay the sugar factory and the other farm buildings; adjacent to them were the slave quarters, consisting of small rectangular wooden huts, like those still used by rural Negro populations in the British and French islands, and finally the house belonging to the overseer.

The importation of Negro slaves, necessary for establishing and maintaining a plantation, completely changed the population structure in the islands. The population grew rapidly in each island, and in most islands Negroes outnumbered the white population. The white population also decreased in many regions because white peasants migrated from these areas. Since the death rate was high, the natural increase of the slave population was low. In 1820 only 340 000 slaves lived in Jamaica, although 800 000 slaves had been brought to the island between 1690 and 1820 (Augelli).

Next to the importation of slaves, the import of food was essential to the colonial plantation economy. Imports consisted mainly of cheap dry saltfish brought from New England for the slaves, and of high quality food and alcoholic liquors from Europe for the planter aristocracy. In addition, the economy of the islands depended on the industrial products of their respective homelands for sugar factory machinery. A considerable volume of trade developed, supplying slaves from West Africa to the North American colonies of England and France and the West Indian colonies. This became known as the triangular trade. The colonial plantation economy thus offered many incentives to European shipping, trade and industry, but the basis of all these lucrative enterprises was sugar production.

This plantation economy did not come to an end until the first half of the nineteenth century. A Negro revolt caused its sudden end in St Domingue. In all the other British and French West Indian colonies, the abolition of slavery, competition with beet sugar, and the end of exclusive control of the European market by Caribbean sugar led to crises which resulted in the disappearance of sugar cane cultivation from all marginal areas. It survived only in areas where, in spite of the increasing marketing difficulties, relief, climate and transport facilities proved to be favourable. In all other areas sugar cane was replaced by different crops and former plantations were divided into peasant smallholdings.

Wherever sugar cane cultivation survived, the plantation system changed considerably. This was not only because paid farmhands had to replace slaves; the gradually increasing concentration of ownership also became characteristic, caused by the introduction of power mills which increased the capacity of sugar factories. The majority of colonial plantations were no longer viable. Sugar production could only become economic and survive (Map 11) if several plantations amalgamated to supply cane to one enlarged central sugar factory. One result of all this was the creation of the sugar cane latifundium in the second half of the nineteenth century (cf. p. 87), not only in the British and French West Indies but also in the Spanish West Indies where the classic colonial plantation economy had never been introduced.

United States influence in the Caribbean

In the early nineteenth century the United States of America bought Louisiana and Florida and thereby came to abut on to the American Mediterranean. When they expanded to the Pacific coast a few decades later the Americans became greatly interested in building a canal in Nicaragua or Panama to shorten the sea route from their Atlantic to their Pacific coast. The Monroe Doctrine, announced in 1823 immediately following the proclamation of independence by the Latin American countries, shows the growing power of the USA. This doctrine stated, among other things, that in future there should neither be new European colonies in America nor should there be European intervention in American territories. Initially it was aimed at protecting young American nations against intervention by European powers; but soon it served as the justification for US expansion into Middle America. Intervention in unstable Middle American countries was necessary, according to the US interpretation, whenever there was the danger of European interference which would be adverse to US interests.

US expansion in Middle America was characterized by the acquisition of territories. Just as typical, though, was the economic expansion which brought about the economic and political dependence of many Middle American territories and led to several military interventions. The construction of the Panama Canal served mainly the military interests of the USA, and only secondly those of world maritime trade. When the canal was opened the USA were eager to get complete control of the American Mediterranean in order to protect the canal and the sea routes leading to it, possibly by turning it into the mare clausum it used to be 400 years earlier during Spanish colonial rule.

US expansion in Middle America could be carried out without serious confrontation with European great powers firstly because further British expansion was checked by the Clayton-Bulwer Agreement from 1850, and secondly because European colonies in the Caribbean lost much of their economic value during the nineteenth century. The abolition of slavery and especially the competition from beet sugar ended the monopoly of cane sugar production.

When the US occupied the former Spanish West Indian colonies in 1898 they gained large territories: Cuba for a short period and Puerto Rico permanently. During the nineteenth century US interest in Cuba became obvious in their offer to buy it from Spain and in their active support of the Cuban struggle for independence. After revolts in 1823 and 1849 a ten-year conflict between Spanish armed forces and revolutionaries began in 1868. But Spain maintained its control over the island and was able to suppress another revolt started by José Martí who was a member of a Cuban exile government in the USA and who landed in Cuba in 1895. In 1898 the battleship *Maine* was sent to Habana to protect US citizens. After it exploded for unknown reasons, and after Spain rejected a US ultimatum to leave the island, American forces landed in Cuba and together with the Cuban freedom fighters defeated the Spanish. By the Treaty of Paris in 1898 Spain had to disclaim Cuba and Puerto Rico and thereby lost its last colonies in Middle America. Cuba was granted its sovereignty in 1902 after four years of American occupation. However, the so-called Platt Amendment gave the USA a right to intervene (renounced in 1934) and the right to build naval bases. During the following period Cuba's economy became increasingly dependent on the USA. Puerto Rico experienced American military administration until 1917, before receiving the status of a US territory.

There were many armed conflicts during the US expansion into the Spanish West Indies. But in 1917 the US employed peaceful means to expand their territorial possessions in the Caribbean: they bought the Danish Virgin Islands St Thomas, St Croix and St John for the price of US $25 million.

The Caribbean islands became the objects of US intervention, as did Central America and Mexico. US forces occupied Haiti for twenty years (1915–35). The USA had taken control of the revenue of the Dominican Republic by 1907, and they occupied the country from 1916 to 1922.

The Platt Amendment of the Cuban constitution; the colonial administration of Puerto Rico (in spite of its independent status which Spain had granted to it before the US occupation in 1897); and, last but not least, the interventions in Mexico and Central America and in Caribbean territories were the most obvious signs of US policy of expansion into Middle America. They were resented by Latin America generally, not only by the territories concerned. Growing economic dependence on their superior great neighbour in the north contributed another reason for resenting 'imperialismo yanqui'. US economic and technological aid within the framework of the Good Neighbour Policy (since 1933) and the Alliance for Progress (since 1961) have not changed this attitude, since these policies are seen as a way of exercising an influence on Caribbean and Latin American territories which is not very different from direct intervention.

US expansion into Middle America and the building of naval bases in Cuba, Puerto Rico, and St Thomas enabled them to obtain control of the American Mediterranean. This position was further strengthened during the Second World War. By an agreement in 1941 the British Government conceded to the US the right to build bases in several British West Indian territories. In addition to the old military bases in Cuba (Guantánamo), Puerto Rico and St Thomas, the USA today possess naval and air bases in Trinidad, St Lucia, Antigua and in the Bahamas. Before the Second World War military bases in the Caribbean served exclusively to protect US presence in Middle America. Since then, the former and the more recent US military bases in the area serve to protect the entire western hemisphere. They constitute only one part of the arrangements made by the USA towards building up a defensive system which is to encompass all America.

Although only small parts of Middle America are in North American hands the USA still controls the whole of the American Mediterranean because of their unquestioned superiority within the western hemisphere. The events in 1959 in Cuba, the nearest and largest Caribbean island off the US coast, endangered the strong position of the USA in Middle America. The Cuban revolution under Fidel Castro (cf. p. 165 f), finally successful on 1 January 1959 after two years of civil war, resulted in a USSR-inspired administration of this island. After the traditional economic and political ties with the USA were completely broken off, the Caribbean area and the USA themselves were threatened militarily in the summer of 1962 by the presence of Soviet jet bombers and the installation of inter-mediate-range missiles on Soviet bases in Cuba. Forced by a partial US blockade of Cuba this Cuban-Russian enterprise had to be cancelled in November 1962.

The Cuban blockade, which was successful in removing the immediate threat to the US military position in the Caribbean, was not the only direct intervention by the USA in recent years. In 1965 US forces landed in Santo Domingo to intervene in the Dominican Civil War, thereby demon-strating to the whole world that the USA still consider the Caribbean islands to be within their sphere of influence.

Present political organization

The political fragmentation of the Caribbean islands (Map 9 and Table 8) arises out of the European struggle for one of the earth's wealthiest colonial regions, a struggle that lasted for centuries; it also reflects US expansion and the present decolonization drive. Although the entire group of islands belonged to Spain, at least nominally, during the sixteenth century, no Spanish colonies remain today. The small Danish islands were also given up by their mother-country. France forfeited 91 per cent of its West Indian colonies gained during the seventeenth century when it had to give up the western part of Hispaniola; and Great Britain lost 53 per cent of its posses-sions in the Caribbean gained during the same period when Jamaica, Trinidad and Tobago became independent. Only the Netherlands have succeeded in retaining up to the present the tiny islands which they

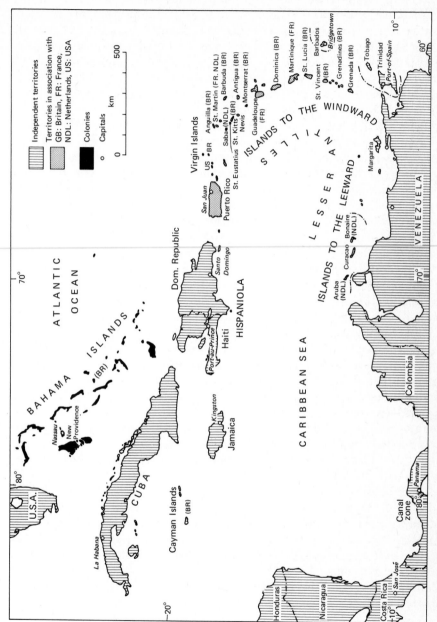

Map 9. Political organization of the Caribbean islands, 1968.

occupied in the seventeenth century. During recent years the colonial status of most of the European possessions has been replaced by various kinds of association. Among the nations with associated territories only the USA has made territorial gains: in 1898 at the end of the Spanish-American war, in 1903 and in 1917 respectively.

The new political order of the twentieth century developed as follows. In 1917 the USA purchased the Danish Virgin Islands, after which there were no territorial changes or alterations in colonial status until after the Second World War. In 1946 the French islands of Martinique and Guadeloupe (with adjoining islands) each became a French Overseas *Département*. In 1952 Puerto Rico acquired the status of a US-associated territory, designated the Commonwealth of Puerto Rico. Since 1954 the Dutch Antilles have constituted an autonomous part of the Netherlands. In 1958 Barbados, the British Windward and Leeward Islands (except the Virgin Islands) together with Jamaica and Trinidad and Tobago came together as the West Indies Federation. This problematic political integration uniting widely dispersed islands disintegrated again in 1961 with the withdrawal of its two largest members, Jamaica and Trinidad and Tobago. Full independence was granted to both these former British colonies in 1962. Years of negotiations over the political status of the rest of the British West Indian colonies followed before Barbados received complete sovereignty in 1966. The following island territories shed their colonial status in February 1967: the Leeward Islands of Antigua-Barbuda, and St Kitts–Nevis–Anguilla, and the Windward Islands of Dominica, St Lucia, and Grenada. They became associated autonomous territories with the right to renounce, at any time, their association with Great Britain and proclaim their full independence. The integration of these islands into the Commonwealth of the Caribbean Associated States is planned; but the traditionally strong political ties of former British territories (including Guyana which has been independent since 1966) to Britain are being replaced by closer relations with Canada, largely on an economic basis (cf. p. 104). These relations have developed to the extent that the Canadian Commonwealth Caribbean Conference of July 1966 expressed the view that it represented the launching of a new political block.

In 1972, seven independent territories occupy 87·9 per cent of the Caribbean area, and 6·8 per cent is made up of states associated either with European nations or the USA (Table 8). Colonial possessions make up 5·3 per cent of the whole area. Only British possessions retain colonial status: the Bahama Islands, the Turks and Caicos Islands, the Cayman Islands, and, among the Leeward Islands, the Virgin Islands and Montserrat.

9

Population and social structure

The age structure of the population of the Caribbean islands differs considerably from that of European industrial nations. For instance, because of the high birth rate the population pyramid of the Dominican Republic has a much wider base than those of industrial nations. The percentage in older age groups falls rapidly in the Dominican Republic, while it changes only slightly up to the middle-aged groups in industrial nations. In the Dominican Republic 44·6 per cent of the population are under fifteen years of age, against 22·9 per cent in the Federal Republic of Germany (West Germany) (24·1 per cent in United Kingdom). 64·6 per cent of the population in the Dominican Republic are under twenty-five years old (West Germany: 39·2 per cent), (UK: 38·6 per cent) and only 2·9 per cent over sixty-five (West Germany: 9·7 per cent), (UK: 12·9 per cent).

The Caribbean Islands have a population of about 19·7 million (1960): 87·8 per cent live in the Greater Antilles, 11·6 per cent in the Lesser Antilles, and 0·6 per cent in the Bahamas (Table 1). The density of population (Map 10) is very irregular: 161 persons per sq km in the Lesser Antilles, 81 persons per sq km in the Greater Antilles, and 9 persons per sq km in the Bahamas. Within groups of islands the density of population varies considerably from one island to another (Table 8). Barbados has the highest density with 540 persons per sq km; most of the other Islands to the Windward are also overpopulated to varying degrees. Among the Greater Antilles Haiti, Jamaica, and Puerto Rico must be considered overpopulated. Because of the high birth rate and the rapidly decreasing death rate the problem of overpopulation has become alarmingly serious in many of the islands. Among the larger territories only Cuba and the Dominican Republic have a relatively low density of population; the only uninhabited islands are in the Bahama archipelago.

Strong regional differences between the Caribbean populations are not only seen in population densities. The affiliation of the various islands to the former colonial areas of European nations is demonstrated by their speaking Spanish, English, or French (the latter two languages are clearly distinguished from their mother tongue by African elements). Some islands illustrate past changes in their affiliation in that their inhabitants do not speak the language of the nation with which they are associated at the present, but that of the former colonial power. For instance, the language in the British islands of Grenada and St Lucia is French, and in the French island of St Martin it is English. Only one new language has developed: Papiamento (cf. p. 376) in the Dutch Islands to the Leeward.

The Caribbean islands may be divided into three different cultural areas according to their linguistic differentiation. The Spanish area, including Cuba, the Dominican Republic, Puerto Rico, and Margarita, makes up 73·0 per cent of the land and 61·8 per cent of the population; the French area comprises 13·3 per cent of the land and 21·6 per cent of the population; and the English area 13·3 per cent of the land and 15·6 per cent of the population.

Most important of all is the heterogeneity of the racial structure of the population. This is very marked, even if one does not take into consideration small groups such as the Chinese or the Lebanese or, in the Greater Antilles, the Asian Indians (Table 9). The Greater Antilles differ greatly from the Lesser Antilles and the Bahamas, since in the latter the negroid element is predominant. The Negro population outnumbers other ethnic groups mainly in the areas of the slave-dependent sugar plantation economy of the eighteenth century in the British and French West Indies, i.e. in most islands of the Lesser Antilles and, among the Greater Antilles, Jamaica and Haiti (cf. p. 69).

Not only do the Caribbean islands as a whole have a racially heterogeneous population, but so does each of the islands. Islands with racial homogeneity are the exception, like the small French island of Désirade inhabited by a white population, or the small Islands to the Windward with a Negro population. Islands with a high percentage of their population white are Cuba (73 per cent) and Puerto Rico (80 per cent); islands with a very low percentage white are Jamaica, Haiti, and the Islands to the Windward where the percentage of white people is usually well below 5 per cent. Table 9 shows a surprisingly small number of mulattoes. This is to be explained by the fact that people of mixed race with either a rather fair or dark complexion are listed as either white or black in official statistics. The racial structure of Trinidad is different from that of other islands, since only here do Asian Indians (40 per cent) challenge the Negro predominance (53 per cent). Indians (Amerindians) and mestizos live only in the Islands to the Leeward (Margarita and Aruba).

Closely related to the racially heterogeneous character of the population is their social and cultural pluralism. Even a casual glance reveals that the European and African heritage are no equal partners in the cultural scene. It is equally obvious that the European way of life among the upper classes in various islands, may be differentiated according to their affiliation with either Spanish, English, or French culture. The social gap between the

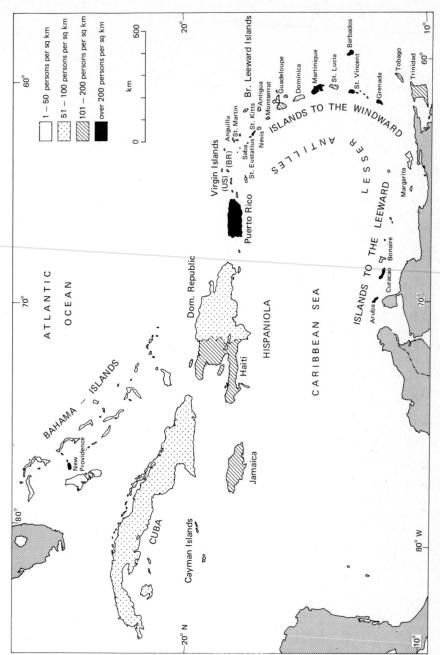

Map 10. Density of population, 1960.

Table 8. Caribbean territories: Size and population 1960 (the political pattern reflects the situation in 1967)

	size		population		density of population
	sq km	*%*	*1000*	*%*	*pers./sq km*
independent territories					
Cuba	110 922	47·4	6 743	34·2	61
Dominican Republic	48 734	20·8	3 014	15·3	61
Haiti	27 750	11·9	3 505	17·8	126
Jamaica	11 424	4·9	1 607	8·2	143
Trinidad and Tobago	5 128	2·2	826	4·2	161
Margarita (Venezuelan)	1 150	0·5	76	0·4	66
Barbados	430	0·2	232	1·2	540
Total	205 538	87·9	16 003	81·3	78
associated with the US					
Puerto Rico	8 897	3·8	2 350	11·9	270
US Virgin Islands	344	0·1	32	0·2	93
Total	9 241	3·9	2 382	12·1	258
French overseas départements					
Guadeloupe	1 729	0·7	275	1·4	155
Martinique	1 080	0·5	267	1·4	247
Total	2 809	1·2	542	2·8	193
Netherlands Antilles					
Bovenwindse Eilanden	68	—	4	—	54
Benedenwindse Eilanden	921	0·4	192	1·0	209
Total	989	0·4	196	1·0	198
associated with Great Britain					
among the Leeward Islands (St Kitts–Nevis–Anguilla, Antigua, Barbuda)	843	0·4	111	0·6	132
among the Windward Islands (Dominica, St Lucia, St Vincent, Grenada)	2 127	0·9	320	1·6	151
Total	2 970	1·3	431	2·2	145
British Colonies					
Cayman Islands	241	0·1	8	—	32
Bahama Islands	11 396	4·9	107	0·5	9
Turks and Caicos Islands	430	0·2	6	—	13
among the Leeward Islands (British Virgin Islands, Montserrat)	258	0·1	19	0·1	74
Total	12 325	5·3	140	0·6	11
The Caribbean Islands (total)	233 872	100·0	19 694	100·0	84

Sources:
Statistisches Jahrbuch für die Bundesrepublik Deutschland, Stuttgart und Mainz 1964; *The Statesman's Year-Book 1964*, London and New York 1964; *The West Indies and Caribbean Year-Book 1964*, London, New York, Ottawa 1964; Academia de Ciencias de Cuba: *Area de Cuba*, Habana 1965.

Table 9.   The racial structure of the population of the Caribbean
islands, 1960*

	Caribbean Islands (total)		Greater Antilles		Lesser Antilles		Bahamas	
	1000	%	*1000*	%	*1000*	%	*1000*	%
Whites	7 800	39·6	7 700	44·6	80	3·4	23	20
Negroes	7 800	39·6	6 000	34·8	1 720	73·2	90	80
Mulattoes	3 670	18·6	3 550	20·6	120	5·1	—	—
Asian Indians	350	1·8	—	—	350	14·9	—	—
Indians and Mestizos	80	0·4	—	—	80	3·4	—	—
Total	19 700	100·0	17 250	100·0	2 350	100·0	113	100

* approximate figures

small, wealthy upper class and the destitute masses of the lower class
assumes abysmal proportions. The social hierarchy in most of the islands
lacks a middle class almost completely. The inflexibility which distinguishes
this unsound social structure is the heritage of Spanish colonial feudalism
as well as of the British and French plantation system. At present the social
differences are being reduced in countries where industrialization has
begun: Cuba, Jamaica, Puerto Rico, Trinidad, Curaçao, and Aruba. The
change in the social structure is closely connected with the process of
decolonization in Jamaica and Trinidad. But most of the islands have
retained their traditional social structure, which differs in each island and
reflects the racial structure of its population. The various racial groups have
developed multiple ways of coexistence. Hoetink speaks of a 'segregated
coexistence' among the various races in the Caribbean. Several small
islands exist where, in spite of their racial heterogeneity, there is no social
hierarchy based on racial differences. For instance, the white population in
Désirade and Saba live completely separated from the black population
without either group possessing a socially more advanced status, and both
groups form a classless society, as Lowenthal (1960) points out correctly.
But 'segregated coexistence' is also found in islands where the social and
racial differentiations of the population are closely related. This happens in
islands with a small white minority, that is in almost all the islands of the
Lesser Antilles, but also in Haiti where mulattoes represent the elite. An
actual colour bar like the one which still exists in the south of the USA, does
not exist, but there are various invisible barriers, and it is virtually impossible to advance socially into the upper class. Racial coexistence has
assumed different aspects in islands with Negro minorities, e.g. in former
Spanish possessions, especially in Cuba and Puerto Rico. There the social

and racial structure of the population is not interrelated, and the upper class hardly differs from the rest of the population as regards racial factors. In general it is possible for the coloured population there to ascend the social ladder, though this is possible only after interbreeding and after adopting the European way of life.

A fairer complexion is still the essential condition for high social prestige among the Negro population throughout the islands. The shade of complexion plays an important role in the choice of friends or husbands. This racial prejudice, together with the regional differentiation in the distribution, language, and race of the population, is a direct heritage of colonial times when a small white minority developed the plantation system.

The majority of the Caribbean population lives in rural areas. This is true for all islands. The settlement pattern in agricultural areas shows a clear, regular division. Village-type settlements dominate within the plantation areas where the compact and systematically planned quarters for workers adjoin the industrial plants of the plantations, as slave quarters used to during the times of the early plantation economy. In contrast to this, dispersed settlement characterizes the irregular, small-scale mixed farming areas, with an extremely scattered distribution of dwellings in parts. In peasant farming areas village-type settlements as well as dispersed settlements are found; the latter mainly in mountainous areas, especially in districts of shifting cultivation where clearings are made by burning.

The prevailing rural house type in the Spanish islands is the so-called bohío (Plate 3), which seems to originate from the Arawaks (as does the name). In rural areas of Cuba, Puerto Rico and the Dominican Republic these small, rectangular huts are ubiquitous. They are built from boards, thatched with palm leaves, and usually rest on uprights. The kitchen is in an extra wooden hut at the rear of the living quarters. The rural houses in the British and French islands with their predominantly Negro population do not show the same uniformity, even though they all have a rectangular layout. There are many variations in building materials and construction plans. For instance, there are distinct differences in the wooden structure of houses in Barbados and Guadeloupe; and in Haiti the walls of the huts are often made of wattle and daub and then lime-washed.

Urban settlements are similar in the Spanish, French, and British islands in so far as their layout usually exhibits a grid pattern. Exceptions are rare; if they do occur it is because of topographical factors. Another common feature among urban settlements is their coastal position: without exception the capital of each island is also its most important port. The majority of cities are situated on the leeward side of the islands where they are protected against trade winds. Exceptions are found when there are extensive inlets on the windward side which have been used for a long time because they are excellent natural harbours, as in the case of Habana and San Juan. Only the larger islands have cities in the interior, usually much less important than the seaports. Cities in the interior are centres of the food industry where agricultural products are processed; but seaports have in addition industrial plants for consumer goods which depend on imports. This is especially true of the few centres with capital goods industries which are highly port-orientated.

The layout and function of the individual cities are very similar. Their architecture, however, exhibits important differences. This is particularly obvious in the city centres where the architectural style of public buildings as well as of private homes clearly shows the respective influence of either Spanish, French, or English culture. The area of the Lesser Antilles, where, in addition, Dutch and Danish influences determine the urban landscape most impressively, is a good illustration of these differences in close proximity. Trinidad with its high percentage of Indians offers townscapes which are strongly influenced by South Asian culture (Plates 5, 13, 22, 30, 33).

There are 14 cities with populations of more than 100 000 in the Caribbean islands (Table 10), all of them in the Greater Antilles. Cuba has seven, three of which make up the conurbation of Greater Habana. Puerto Rico accounts for three; all the other territories have only one, which is at the same time the capital and largest port.

Table 10. Cities with a population of over 100 000*

Habana, Cuba (1966)	946 000 inhabitants
Marianao, Cuba (1966)	455 000 ,,
San Juan, Puerto Rico (1970)	445 000 ,,
Kingston, Jamaica (1960)	377 000 ,,
Santo Domingo, Dom. Rep. (1960)	367 000 ,,
Santiago de Cuba (1966)	248 000 ,,
San Miguel del Padrón, Cuba (1966)	156 000 ,,
Bayamón, Puerto Rico (1970)	148 000 ,,
Camagüey, Cuba (1966)	142 000 ,,
Port-au-Prince, Haiti (1950)	136 000 ,,
Ponce, Puerto Rico (1970)	126 000 ,,
Santa Clara, Cuba (1966)	115 000 ,,
Guantánamo, Cuba (1966)	102 000 ,,
Holguín, Cuba (1966)	102 000 ,,

* Figures for population size are in accordance with the latest census. More recent figures (estimated) are given in the respective regional sections.

The urban population constitutes a share of slightly more than 40 per cent of the total only in Cuba and Puerto Rico, the two islands where the industrialization process is most advanced. In contrast with this is Haiti with an urban population of only 7 per cent. The proportion of urban and rural population in most of the other islands is somewhere between these two extreme figures. Relative to their economic development the majority of islands have too high a percentage of urban population. This high percentage has come about because of a rural exodus which has no economic basis, such as there is in industrialized nations. Many townspeople cannot find work and are therefore forced to live in slums. In the past the Spanish islands contrasted with others in the Caribbean in having a much higher percentage of city dwellers. This was peculiar to the Spaniards who based their colonization on urban settlements. At the present time, this contrast in the percentage of the city dwellers is being increasingly reduced by the rural exodus and industrialization in all the Caribbean islands.

10

Agricultural regions, agricultural systems, and agrarian social structure

The agricultural regions of the Caribbean Islands exhibit a great variety (shown for the former British Islands to the Windward in Fig. 4) in their market orientation[1] (*Produktionsziel*), farm size and farming system, dominant crop or crop combination (*Wirtschaftsflächenbild*), and field and settlement patterns; however, some common characteristics are present. If one defines agricultural regions as extensive agricultural areas which are characterized by a uniform market orientation one may distinguish between those concerned with monoculture and those concerned with polyculture; that is to say, the agricultural landscape is characterized by either uniform or mixed cultivation. Pastures represent a third type of agricultural region. A secondary distinctive feature is the dominant crop. This allows the landscapes associated with monoculture to be grouped into those of sugar cane, tobacco, etc.; and the landscapes associated with polyculture into those of tree and ground crops.

Each of these agricultural regions, homogeneous with regard to their market orientation, shows a distinct physiognomic subdivision according to the predominance of either small- or large-scale farms. The agricultural system may vary considerably in all agricultural regions, even when all farms have the same market orientation. This results in a great variety in the patterns of crop cultivations, fields and settlements. Any agricultural region despite an overall uniform appearance may be divided into two sections according to Waibel's definition of agricultural systems. The following classification therefore succeeds in encompassing the great variations in the appearance of the Caribbean agricultural landscape. It is valid both for the past (p. 69 f) and the present (Table 11).

This classification of the agricultural regions differs greatly from the one proposed by Credner,[2] since it tries to describe the divisions exactly by

[1] i.e. whether producing for the domestic and/or export market and/or for agricultural processing industries.
[2] Credner (1943) identified the following agricultural regions in the Greater Antilles: areas of sugar plantations, of tobacco cultivation, of coffee cultivation, of banana cultivation, of cocoa cultivation, of sisal cultivation, of peasant farming, and of pastoral farming.

taking into consideration their market orientation, structure of ownership, and the differences in technical and functional structure resulting from the latter.

Table 11.   Agricultural landscapes and systems in the Caribbean islands

agricultural landscape	large-scale farming system	small-scale farming system
landscape associated with monoculture	bananas	
	cotton	
	coffee	
	cocoa	
	coconut	
	sisal	
	tobacco	
	sugar cane	
landscape associated with polyculture	tree crops	
	ground crops	
		irregular, multi-crop cultivation by peasants
landscape associated with pastoral economy	extensive pasture	
	intensive pasture	

Two of these agricultural regions seem to be especially characteristic since they are most common in the Caribbean Islands: the agricultural region associated with sugar cane monoculture is dominant within the large-scale agricultural system (Map 11, Plates 6, 17, 30); next in importance is the agricultural region associated with polyculture within the small-scale agricultural system of irregular multicropping by peasants (Map 12, Plate 23). The description of the various islands deals with the differences in the pattern of crop cultivation, fields, and settlements within these two contrasting types of agriculture. The description of sugar cane monoculture by large-scale enterprises in the Cuban province of Camagüey (cf. p. 139), and the description of irregular multicropping by peasants in the Jamaican Central Range (cf. p. 189) may be referred to as examples.

The modern large-scale system of sugar cane monoculture generally occupies areas, where climate, topography, soil, and transport are espe-

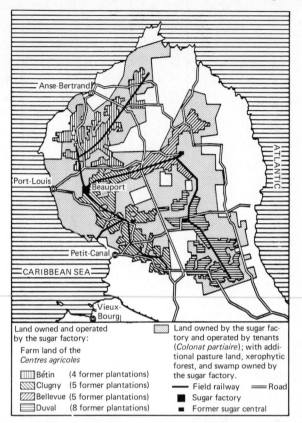

Map 11. Beauport (Grande Terre, Guadeloupe): an example of a sugar-producing enterprise within the large-scale farming system (after Lasserre).

cially suitable for sugar cultivation. In Cuba, the Dominican Republic, and Puerto Rico much larger areas are occupied by this type of agriculture today than in the past. These are the Spanish territories where sugar cane cultivation has only developed since the nineteenth century. In Jamaica, however, in Haiti, and in the Islands to the Windward in particular, this type of agriculture was far more extensive in the past than it is now. These islands constitute the former British and French areas and have a pre-dominantly Negro population. They are the former 'sugar islands', where the plantation economy based on slave labour was at its height by the eighteenth century. In some areas this type of agriculture and enterprise has survived, but in most areas it disappeared as a result of the crisis in the sugar industry. In the islands mentioned above the sugar cane monoculture has usually been replaced by peasant cultivation. The small-scale farming system based on irregular multicropping by peasants has therefore come to make up a large proportion of the agricultural area in the British and French islands.

87

Agricultural regions

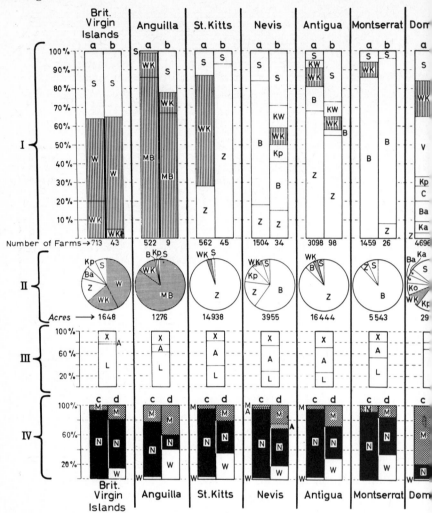

Fig. 4. Cultivated area and land ownership in the British Islands to the Windward.

I Percentage classification of small- and large-scale farms according to the predominant cultivation.
Striped: Cultivation for special or local demand. *White:* Export Crops.

a small-scale farms (1–50 acres)	Z sugar cane	C citrus	MB maize, millet, beans
b middle- and large-scale farms (>50 acres)	B cotton	Kc coconut	WK root crops and tropical tubers (cassava, sweet potato, yams, malanga)
	Ko cocoa	M nutmeg	
	Ka coffee	V vanilla	
	Ba banana	P arrowroot	
			W pasture
			S other crops

II Percentage classification of cultivated area (arable land and tree crops).

III Classification of farm managers of small-scale farms according to their professions, in percentages.
Size of farms 1–100 acres (0·4–40 ha). The statistics do not allow for the sizes of farms in categories I, III and IV to correspond exactly. Principal professions of the farm managers of small-scale farms: L = landowner; A = farm labourer; X = worker employed etc. outside agriculture (generally seasonal worker).

88

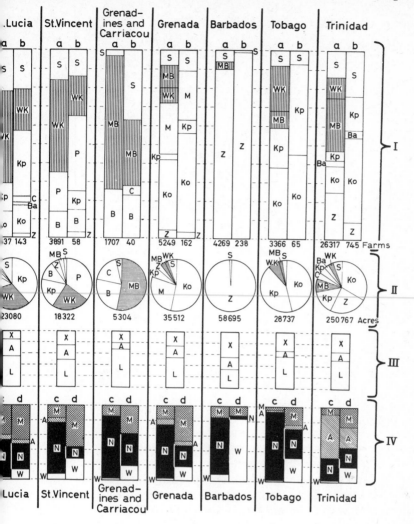

IV Racial classification of farm managers of small- and large-scale farms, in percentages:

c = small-scale farms (1–100 acres)
d = large-scale farms (>100 acres) (See note for III)
A = asiatic
M = mixed race
N = negro
W = white

In all agricultural regions, irrespective of the prevalence of mono- or polyculture, large-scale farming occupies the areas with the most suitable soil, with the most favourable relief, and with the best transport conditions. Small-scale farming is practised where the land gets steeper, the soil less fertile, and the terrain less accessible (Map 13). In the lower-lying islands the two farming systems usually penetrate one another's territory according to the features of the terrain, whereas in mountainous

89

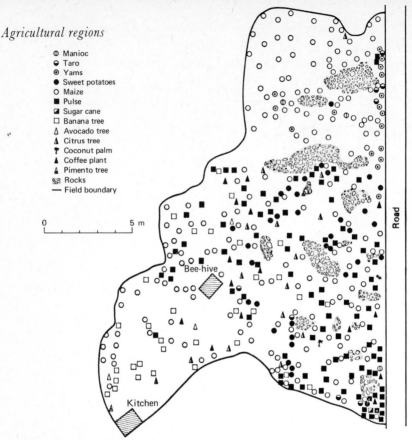

Agricultural regions

① Manioc
◒ Taro
◎ Yams
● Sweet potatoes
○ Maize
■ Pulse
◪ Sugar cane
□ Banana tree
△ Avocado tree
▲ Citrus tree
🍗 Coconut palm
▲ Coffee plant
▲ Pimento tree
▨ Rocks
— Field boundary

0   5 m

Bee-hive

Kitchen

Road

Map 12. Crop pattern within the small-scale farming system of irregular polyculture, near Christiana, Jamaica (after Innis).

islands they are generally separated according to altitude.

The agricultural regions have emerged mainly in response to the variations in physical features and to world market conditions. Different crops are suitable for arid and humid areas respectively, and also for different altitudes in the mountains. Different farm sizes lead to different patterns in the two agricultural systems which appear in all agricultural regions. A survey of the structure of land ownership therefore provides the key to understanding the different character of agricultural systems in the islands.

The classification of farms into size groups (Table 12[1]) shows the pre-

[1] Classification of farms into size groups has to be based on statistics which differ greatly between the various islands. According to their respective planimetry the threshold value in Table 12 between small-scale and medium-sized farms lies between 20–25 ha, between medium-sized and large-scale farms between 80–100 ha. There is no doubt that this division, which treats uniformly very different Caribbean islands, cannot always do justice to the sociological aspect of agrarian enterprises nor to their economic importance. For instance, in Barbados farms of less than 4 ha (10 acres) are counted as small-scale farms (peasant farms) and all other enterprises as large-scale farms (estates). A considerable number of the latter, however, appear as small-scale farms in Table 12.

Table 12. The Caribbean islands: farm size and important features of agrarian social structure

	I	*II*	*III*	*IV A*	*IV B*	*V*	*VI*
a2		Barbados	Grenada Jamaica	Dom. Rep.	St Lucia	Anguilla	
b1	St Kitts		Tobago	Puerto Rico Dominica Trinidad			
b2		*Antigua* *Montserrat* *Martinique*	*Nevis* *St Vincent*			*Guadeloupe*	*Haiti*
c1			Cuba				

Legend: small farms < 20 ha[1]; medium-sized farms 20–100 ha; large-scale farms > 100 ha;

I > 90%[2] large-scale farms
II > 66% large-scale farms,
   < 10% medium-sized farms
III > 50% large-scale farms
IV A 33–50% large-scale farms,
   33–50% small farms, large-scale farms dominant;
   > 15% medium-sized farms
   B 33–50% large-scale farms,
   33–50% small farms, small farms dominant

V > 50% small farms
VI > 90% small farms
a smaller sizes (100–200 ha) dominate within the system of large land-holdings
b larger sizes (> 200 ha) dominate within the system of large land-holdings
c like b, but state-owned
1 percentage of very small farms (< 2 ha) below 10%
2 percentage of very small farms over 10%

Italicized names of islands signify a combination of the agrarian social structure's negative features (cf. p. 93).

dominance of large-scale and small-scale farms as against medium-sized farms. The differences in farm size are reflected in the type of enterprise. Small-scale enterprises are generally peasant farms cultivated without outside help. In the British and French West Indian islands these are, with only a few exceptions, Negro peasant farms which have been established since the mid nineteenth century after the abolition of slavery. In the Spanish West Indies, where there were no early slave-based sugar plantations, the peasant farms, originating in colonial times, are cultivated by the white population. The Guajiro in Cuba, the Conuquero in Santo Domingo and the Jíbaro in Puerto Rico already existed in colonial times. Medium-sized farms, which constitute 15 per cent of the area under cultivation only in the Spanish islands, are also family enterprises, though they depend on outside help. Finally, the large-scale enterprises have grown to their present size by

[1] According to available statistics slightly differing threshold values had to be taken as a basis for the division (Blume 1961, p. 76/7).
[2] Percentages of the farm land.

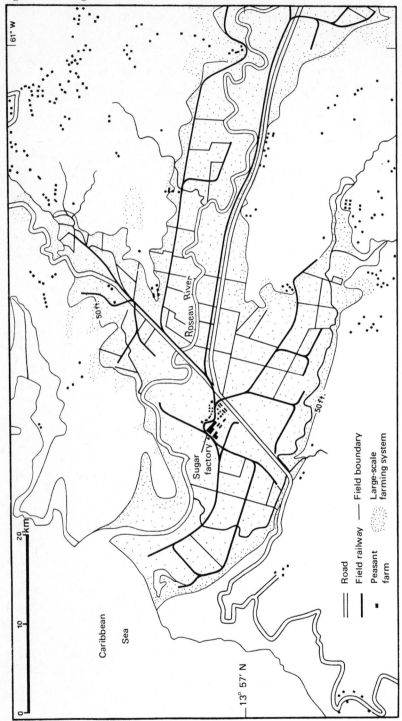

Map 13. Distribution of the two farming systems: large-scale and small-scale farms in the Roseau Valley, St Lucia.

means of property concentration. This has happened very recently in all the Caribbean islands, but during the eighteenth century the slave-based plantations only developed in the British and French colonies. Contrasting with the traditional plantations, the newly created plantations are larger in size and cultivation is separate from industrial processing. Formerly, these two activities were both done by one enterprise, which seems to Waibel to be an essential characteristic of the traditional plantation.

Table 12 and Map 14 indicate that all the islands fall within a scale between St Kitts at one end, where more than 90 per cent of the cultivated area is farmed by large-scale enterprises, and Haiti at the other end, where more than 90 per cent of the land is in the hands of small-scale enterprises. Large-scale enterprises clearly predominate in the cultivable areas. This rough classification of farms according to their size can be made more accurate by taking into consideration certain aspects of the agrarian society. This has been done in Table 12 and Map 14. Less extensive, less important large-scale enterprises, usually family property, may be distinguished from those which are more extensive and which are the property of private companies or, as in Puerto Rico and especially in Cuba after the Revolution, are state-owned. On a few islands very small smallholdings occupy a high proportion of the farmland. Very small smallholdings, which have a size of less than 2 ha and are therefore not viable, have developed as a result of subdivision of property. Extremely large latifundia, whether privately or state-owned, as well as extreme fragmentation of property into very small small-holdings must both be considered as negative characteristics within the structure of land ownership. One of these characteristics is present in every Caribbean island. Wherever they both exist the agrarian social structure must be seen as exceptionally weak. This is the case in the islands which are listed in the horizontal column b2 of Table 12. On all these islands, which belong either to the French or the British sphere, there is a very marked contrast between the agricultural systems of large-scale and small-scale enterprises. This is further emphasized by the fact that the small-scale farming systems of the British and French islands, represented by Negro peasant farms, have developed, almost without exception, a pattern of irregular mixed cultivation. The equivalent in the Spanish islands is usually polyculture with tree and ground crops.

Map 14. Types of agrarian social structure.

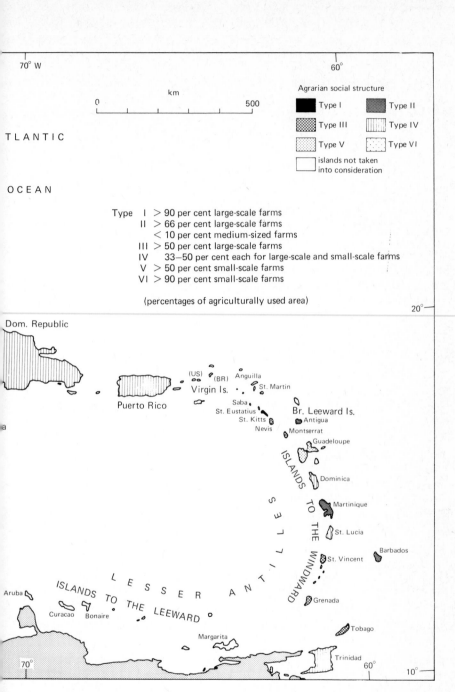

70° W
60°

km

0   500

Agrarian social structure

- Type I
- Type II
- Type III
- Type IV
- Type V
- Type VI
- islands not taken into consideration

A T L A N T I C

O C E A N

Type   I > 90 per cent large-scale farms
        II > 66 per cent large-scale farms
           < 10 per cent medium-sized farms
        III > 50 per cent large-scale farms
        IV 33–50 per cent each for large-scale and small-scale farms
        V > 50 per cent small-scale farms
        VI > 90 per cent small-scale farms

(percentages of agriculturally used area)

20°

Dom. Republic

(US)
(BR) Anguilla
Virgin Is.   St. Martin
Puerto Rico   Saba
                  St. Eustatius   Br. Leeward Is.
                  St. Kitts   Antigua
                  Nevis   Montserrat
                                   Guadeloupe

L E S S E R   A N T I L L E S

ISLANDS TO THE WINDWARD
                                 Dominica

                                 Martinique

                                 St. Lucia

                                              Barbados
                                 St. Vincent

L E S S E R   A N T I L L E S

ISLANDS TO THE LEEWARD

Aruba
Curacao   Bonaire
                                 Grenada

                                              Tobago

        Margarita

70°   Trinidad
                              60°
                                              10°

11

The economy and international trade relations

The Caribbean islands had a foreign trade balance in 1966 of about US $8·4 thousand million[1] (Table 13). This is a small amount in comparison with the Federal Republic of Germany (US $38·2 thousand million) which corresponds in area to these islands, but has three times as many inhabitants and possesses a different economic structure, being an industrial nation.

Table 13. Volume of foreign trade, 1966

I Island or group of islands	Exports mill. US $	%	Imports mill. US $	%	Total mill. US $	%	US $ per person 1961	1966
Bahamas	23	0·6	140	2·9	163	1·9	401	1141
Cuba	593	16·5	926	19·1	1519	18·0	233	195
Jamaica	198	5·5	286	5·9	484	5·7	242	260
Haiti	38	1·0	36	0·7	74	0·9	19	16
Dominican Republic	137	3·8	161	3·3	298	3·5	70	83
Puerto Rico	1321	36·7	1811	37·4	3132	37·1	680	1160
US Virgin Islands	56	1·6	138	2·9	194	2·3	2000	3811
British Leeward Islands	9	0·2	27	0·6	36	0·4	26	247
Guadeloupe	139	3·9	57	1·2	196	2·3	52	628
Martinique	46	1·3	93	1·9	139	1·7	78	434
British Windward Islands	40	1·1	82	1·7	122	1·5	134	347
Barbados	36	1·0	68	1·4	104	1·2	310	416
Trinidad and Tobago	265	10·1	392	8·1	757	9·0	826	772
Dutch Antilles	600	16·7	625	12·9	1225	14·5	7239	5833
Caribbean Islands	3601	100·0	4842	100·0	8443	100·0	321	364

[1] The share of the Bahamas is 1·9 per cent, the Lesser Antilles 32·9 per cent, and the Greater Antilles 65·2 per cent. The share of the Lesser Antilles is remarkably high considering their size and population. It is to be explained by the import and export of petroleum by Trinidad and the Dutch Antilles. The value of foreign trade per capita of the population in these islands amounts to as high as US $772 and $5833 respectively. The respective figures for the Greater Antilles are not nearly as high (e.g. $16 in Haiti, and $83 in the Dominican Republic; cf. Table 13).

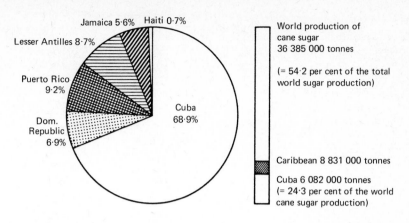

Fig. 5. Sugar production in the Caribbean islands, 1965.

Most of the islands contribute raw materials to the world market; they always have done. Sugar is still the most important item within the agricultural sector (Fig. 5) and ranks first (by a wide margin) by export value in Cuba, St Kitts, Antigua, Guadeloupe, Martinique, and Barbados. All the other islands have developed a more versatile export-orientated pattern of agriculture. For instance, sugar cane monoculture is no longer as common as it was in the past. Bananas, coffee, and cocoa have been added as important export crops. Although most islands, especially the smaller ones, specialize in agriculture, their contribution to the world market is not restricted to the above agricultural products. Minerals are exported, especially bauxite, which ranks first in Jamaica by export value; and in addition Caribbean trade is further diversified by petroleum exports from Trinidad and the Dutch Antilles. Only Puerto Rico has manufactured goods as its main export, and recently Jamaica and Trinidad started to export manufactured goods in small amounts (Map 15).

Food imports are extraordinarily high in all the islands, even where agriculture is the main occupation, since what is cultivated for the domestic market is not nearly sufficient. Consumer goods also have to be imported in large quantities, because only a few islands have succeeded in establishing a consumer goods industry.

It is obvious that the economic structure and foreign trade in the Caribbean islands is no longer as unbalanced as it was in the past. The most important changes are the diversification of agriculture and the increase in mining and industrialization, very strongly developed in some islands, but in others not at all. At the present time, regional differentiation in economic structure and foreign trade is becoming increasingly evident.

Important changes have also occurred since the Second World War with regard to international trade relations. Details about the direction of foreign trade will be given when the islands are dealt with individually. For the whole group it is correct to say (Table 14) that trade with West

97

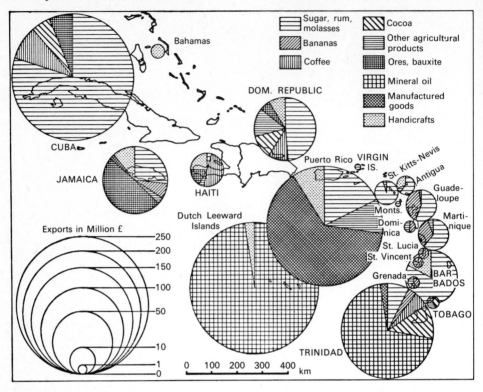

Map 15. Caribbean island exports (after Niddrie).

Table 14. Caribbean islands: Direction of foreign trade, 1966

	Exports mill. US		Imports mill. US		Total mill. US	
	$	%	$	%	$	%
Central America	138	3·9	97	2·1	235	2·9
South America	52	1·5	708	15·4	760	9·4
North America	1947	55·2	2012	43·8	3959	48·7
EEC	171	4·8	333	7·3	504	6·2
EFTA	346	9·8	321	7·0	667	8·2
Communist block countries	482	13·7	762	16·6	1244	15·3
Others	393	11·1	360	7·8	753	9·3
Total	3529	100·0	4593	100·0	8122	100·0

Sources:
Based on: *United Nations Yearbook of International Trade Statistics;* without the Bahamas, Leeward and Windward Islands and Martinique which only contribute 3·8 per cent to the foreign trade of the Caribbean islands (Table 13).

European nations (the former colonial homelands) is decreasing greatly. North American countries, especially the USA, are increasingly taking their place as trading partners. But the increase in the balance of trade with the USA does not compensate for the trade decrease which the islands suffered as a result of the changes in Cuba's foreign trade relations. Communist East European countries, which played no part in Caribbean trade until 1959, and outside Cuba still do not today, in 1966 attracted not less than 15·3 per cent of the Caribbean islands' foreign trade; West Europe took only 14·4 per cent[1].

It is peculiar that trade between Caribbean islands is practically non-existent, in spite of increasingly divergent economic structures. This has always been so; transport connections existed with the respective home country, but not with the neighbouring island. For instance, mail from Trinidad to Jamaica went via London until shortly before the Second World War. Only air traffic has improved transport conditions between the islands and proved to be an essential factor in the formation of the West Indies Federation. In addition, air traffic is a basic essential for the very active tourist industry (Map 16). The islands have developed into one of the most important tourist areas in the tropics. The volume of tourism is increasing steadily, and the traditional high seasons are becoming less and less distinct. More and more tourists, almost exclusively North Americans, visit the tropical Caribbean islands during the summer, attracted by greatly reduced prices. Recently, advertising campaigns for holidays have even reached Europe.

An extensive network of air routes connects the islands. Most of them are served by scheduled flights. Air traffic is increasing rapidly each year (Maps 17 and 18). Decisive changes in air traffic took place when the formerly intensive connections between Cuba and the USA were cancelled. Nevertheless, the best connections from the islands are still those to the USA, and the links are stronger today than ever before.

The present sluggishness of trade between the islands corresponds closely to what used to be the situation in Central American countries, where trade relations only improved when there was greater integration through the formation of a common market and of a customs union. Within a few years trading between the Central American Common Market territories has risen rapidly and imports from overseas have dropped remarkably. This economic association, which has proved very stimulating to the Central American countries, has not yet been imitated by the Caribbean islands, whose leaders might well find this move towards integration, and the resulting increase in internal exchange of goods worth studying.

The Caribbean Free Trade Agreement (CARIFTA), which came into force on 1 May 1968 after long negotiations, must count as a first step towards economic integration. Antigua, Barbados, Guyana as well as

---

[1] EEC (mainly France): 6·2 per cent; EFTA (mainly Great Britain): 8·2 per cent.

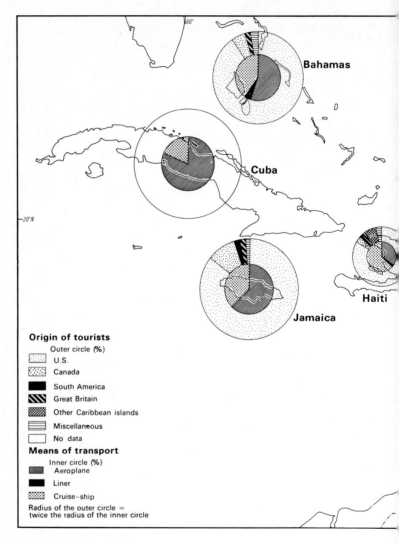

Map 16. Tourism, 1959.

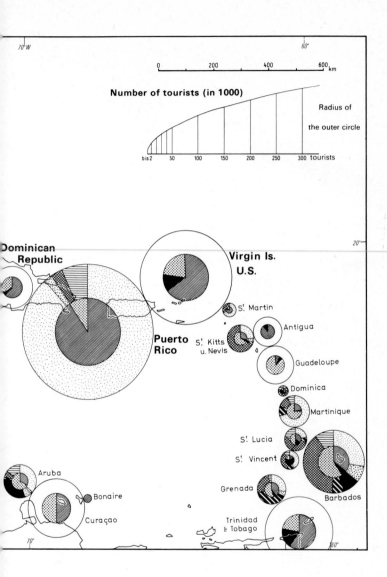

Number of tourists (in 1000)

0   200   400   600 km

Radius of
the outer circle

bis 2   50   100   150   200   250   300 tourists

Dominican
Republic

Virgin Is.
U.S.

S! Martin

Puerto
Rico

S! Kitts
u. Nevis

Antigua

Guadeloupe

Dominica

Martinique

S! Lucia

S! Vincent

Aruba

Bonaire

Grenada

Barbados

Curaçao

Trinidad
& Tobago

101

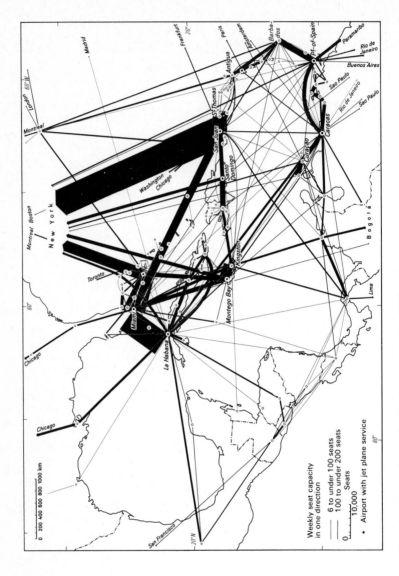

Map 17. Air traffic in the Caribbean Islands, 1960.

Trinidad and Tobago were the founding states of CARIFTA. In 1968
CARIFTA was joined by Jamaica and most of the islands belonging to the
Leeward and Windward groups, which were at one time British and which
had founded, in 1967, an Eastern Caribbean Common Market (ECCM).
CARITFA's aims are the development and diversification of trade among
its member states through simultaneous abolition of customs duties and
rates. The broadening of trade within the Caribbean should benefit the
economic development of all member states in an harmonious manner.

In a study, which shows quite clearly the difficulties involved in the
inception of economic cooperation between those Caribbean islands which

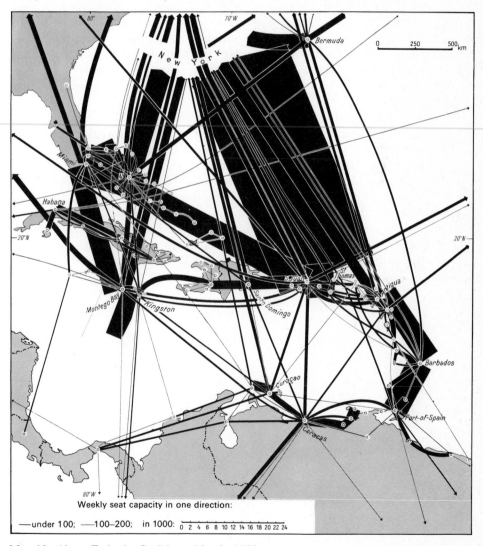

Map 18. Air traffic in the Caribbean islands, 1966.

103

were previously under British rule, Mulchansingh comes to the conclusion that the economy of the individual islands has the capacity to expand, both in the agrarian as well as industrial sector, despite their overwhelmingly similar production performance. What is lacking is an operational market system and above all the extension of traffic links between islands.

The reason for CARIFTA not having had the same results as the Central American Common Market certainly lies in the special conditions that prevail in the area, in its island character, in the varying extent and achievements of economic development, and also in the deeprooted individuality and consequent national rivalries. It is certain that the future of the economy of the islands can only be assured if, quite apart from the free trade agreement of today, a union of economies is reached. There can be hardly any doubt that such an economic union worth striving for in the future should incorporate not only the present members of CARIFTA but all the Caribbean islands. However, for the time being an extensive economic union of this sort is difficult to imagine in face of the present political situation.

The proposal to form a common market among the former British West Indies caused long discussions at the Canadian Commonwealth Caribbean Conference in 1966. Canada has developed into an increasingly important trading partner for the former British islands. It even has trade preferences with these islands, especially for the import of Caribbean sugar, and is contributing more and more economic aid for development purposes. In future negotiations, dealing with the economic integration of Caribbean Commonwealth territories, Canada will certainly play a mediating and leading role. The Canadian government is trying to fill the gap which developed in the Caribbean as a result of decreasing British interest in the wake of decolonization.

12

The position of the Caribbean islands
in the New World

Although the countries of mainland Middle America belong culturally to Latin America, this is not true of the Caribbean archipelago. The Spanish cultural area is the largest in the group, but of equal importance are the French and British areas. The usual division of the New World into Latin and Anglo America is not applicable to the cultural-geographical situation of the Caribbean since it belongs neither to Latin nor to Anglo America. The French cultural area might be considered part of 'Latin America' at the most, but not as part of Spanish Latin-America.

In respect of culture and social structure it is possible to recognize a subregion within the New World which has been called 'Plantation America' or 'Afro-America'[1]. It is the area of present or former plantation economies (cf. p. 69) which extends between the southern states of the USA and Brazil, and where a high percentage of Negro population results from the former plantation economies. This area is not a coherent region. The Caribbean islands could be considered as forming its centre. Here the first plantations of the New World were established. Surveying the islands separately reveals, however, that some of their cultural-geographical characteristics do not seem to fit into the picture of 'Plantation America'. For instance, islands such as Saba and Iles des Saintes never experienced the plantation economy. These islands are inhabited by a poor white population which was able to retreat from the plantation system, as did the 'poor whites' of the southern United States, and which is analogous to various other groups: the Conuqueros, Guajiros and Jíbaros in the Spanish West Indies, and the Petits Habitants in Martinique and the Red Legs in Barbados, in the French and British islands respectively. One should not question the uniformity of the Caribbean cultural area, which is basically determined by plantation economy, on these grounds[2]. Instead, one should

---

[1] Wagley (in Rubin, 1960) divides the New World into 'Plantation America, Euro-America, Indo-America'.

[2] This is done for instance by J. Y. and D. L. Keur in their treatise about the Dutch Islands to the Windward where only a few characteristics of the plantation economy are to be found.

consider three characteristics as being essential for the definition of 'Plantation America' and, thus, the Caribbean islands: the juxtaposition of peasant farms and plantations, the racial heterogeneity of the area, and the rigid social structure, characterized by distinct class differences.

If the Caribbean islands are indeed to be interpreted as being a part of the larger New World area of 'Plantation America' one has to stress at the same time the unique characteristics of the subregion, which differs from other subregions of 'Plantation America'. Perhaps one should interpret the great variety of cultural-geographical aspects and the many variations on basically the same physical themes as making up the distinctive cultural-geographical individuality of the islands.

The division of the islands into those with Spanish cultural influences on the one hand, and those islands with British and French based cultures on the other, is more profound than the clear linguistic-cultural differences among the chain of islands may at first suggest. It has already been shown that racial heterogeneity, which can be detected in Caribbean areas of different cultural backgrounds, is to be attributed to the different patterns of economic development in colonial times. The areas of the first slave-based plantation economies were situated exclusively in the British and French West Indies, not in the Spanish territories. Only in the late nineteenth century did the Spanish area become increasingly characterized by the modern plantation economy, when US capital poured in and cultivation and processing were mechanized. At the same time the British and French areas also developed the mechanized modern plantation economy, which is always accompanied by a strong concentration of property. Again many parts of the British and French areas experienced the transition from plantation economy to peasant farming at the same time. The juxtaposition of old and new plantation areas with marked differences in the racial structure of their populations but with a rather uniform social structure, and the co-existence of old and new areas of peasant farming with regional differentiation between islands are very characteristic features. Recently the many cultural-geographical differences were again increased by an important event: 47 per cent of the territory and 34 per cent of the population came under a communist regime as a result of Cuba's adoption of Soviet methods.

The Caribbean islands, which represent a clearly defined large area, can be viewed as a basically homogeneous area within 'Plantation America', in spite of their many cultural-geographical differences. Present problems and future objectives are largely identical in all the islands.

Present problems and future aspects

Agrarian problems

The colonial heritage is a heavy burden for the Caribbean islands. The unhealthy social structure in agricultural areas; the reluctance of the rural population to work as wage labourers and their unprogressive attitude towards the economy in general; and finally, the colonial or at least semi-colonial economic structure, which is still present even in independent countries, all have to be viewed as a heavy and restrictive burden inherited from colonial times (cf. p. 69). There are still some islands which can be labelled as true plantation islands as in the times of the 'classic' sugar plantation economy, since large landholdings are completely dominant. Islands with a large number of peasant farms are in the minority. Where peasant farms exist they are usually small, very often just smallholdings. Their operators, whether they are owners or tenants, often cannot support their families from the output of their farms alone and therefore have to look for additional means of income. These opportunities are very rare, however, and are available only during certain seasons, particularly where monocultural agriculture still prevails.

A reform of land ownership seems to be an urgent necessity in almost all the Caribbean islands. The problems of agrarian reform in Cuba, Jamaica, the Dominican Republic, and Puerto Rico will be dealt with in the regional part of this book. A comparison of the measures taken within the framework of agrarian reform in these islands reveals that 'socialization', as it was applied in Cuba, did bring about the end of private large landholdings, which led to an improvement of the farm labourers' social conditions. But for economic reasons the system of large-scale enterprises was not abandoned. Reforms in Puerto Rico, Jamaica, and the Dominican Republic show how important it is to take into account both agrarian social conditions and national economic considerations.

There is no doubt that a healthy farm labour force is the prerequisite for a sound agrarian social structure. Peasant farms have proved their ability to produce both for the local market and for export. Labour intensive export-orientated crops such as tobacco are particularly suitable for peasant farming, and even bananas have proved to be very suited to small-scale production. It seems that sugar cane can be cultivated profitably only by large-scale enterprises, since it employs a considerable amount of capital. The export of agricultural products which is, and possibly always will be, a necessity for the Caribbean islands, would not necessarily suffer a decrease in the event of the reform of the agrarian social structure, provided this reform is executed carefully and small-scale farming is assisted during the first stages.

In the British West Indies agricultural settlement programmes often failed, because the peasant farms established were too small in size. This shows that when small-scale farms are created they should be of a reasonable size, the farmers must be taught modern methods of cultivation, marketing must be organized, and the problem of the lack of available capital for the farmers must be overcome, if the newly established enterprises are to be viable and profitable. Lack of capital is the main obstacle preventing farmers from applying progressive methods in farming; exploitive farming

107

and lower yields per acre than on the plantations are the results and have to be prevented. To understand the reason for the farmers' lack of initiative one must realize that any economic progress by one of the farmers tempts his envious neighbours to steal part of his crop, besides leading to social boycotting. Obviously very far ranging measures, suited to the particular situation, have to be taken, aiming among other things at altering the rural population's obsolete attitudes towards the economy.

The improvement of the agrarian structure is an urgent necessity in many islands, especially in the overpopulated British and French islands. Since no other natural resources exist, agriculture will certainly remain the foundation of their economy. Not only does the rural social structure leave much to be desired in these islands, but so also does the orientation of agriculture, since monoculture is still widely practised. In these instances the crop is very vulnerable to the irregularities of weather as well as to diseases, and the life of the whole population is solely dependent on the prices on the world market for the export product in question. An important aim, therefore, is to reduce any imbalance in the economy. The transition from monoculture to polyculture could mean a decrease in profitability for some farms, especially for the export-orientated plantations. In the long run, however, it will have the effect of creating greater immunity to crises, of achieving a sounder national economy, and of turning away from a colonial or semi-colonial economic structure.

Population

Most Caribbean islands are overpopulated and, with the rapid growth of their population, this creates a serious problem. At least in theory there are several possibilities of meeting this problem: emigration, birth control, and industrialization. In earlier times many itinerant workers moved from one island to another. Cuba used to employ seasonal workers from Haiti and the Lesser Antilles. This is no longer the case. The Dutch Islands to the Windward and Trinidad employed workers from other islands in the early stages of their industrialization, but no longer do so. The refusal of the 'rich' islands, Jamaica and Trinidad, to give their consent to unrestricted immigration from the 'poor' islands was instrumental in destroying the West Indies Federation. Thinking of the British islands one could conceive of a wave of emigrants to the mainland colonies of Honduras and Guyana, but they do not welcome Negroes. These territories did not join the West Indies Federation in order to prevent the possibility of immigration. Emigration to the European homelands is difficult today and does not provide a sufficient outlet for population pressure. Recently, only Jamaica and Puerto Rico have registered a large number of emigrants. Industrialization in the overpopulated island of Puerto Rico resulted in the desired improvement of living standards only because it went hand in hand with a high rate of emigration. In Jamaica, on the other hand, emigration and industrialization were not high enough to cut down unemployment effectively, nor to raise noticeably the standard of living. Birth control has been strongly encouraged in Barbados and Puerto Rico, but so far only Puerto Rico has experienced small results and not before living standards had been raised. In general one has to admit that neither emigration nor birth control can solve the problem of overpopulation in the Caribbean islands.

Industrialization

With the exception of oil in Trinidad, bauxite in Jamaica and Hispaniola, and iron-ore and other minerals in Cuba, industrialization cannot be based upon local raw materials or on the local market, but only on the abundant local labour supply as in the case of Puerto Rico. Industrialization in Puerto Rico was started on this basis, and the methods applied there are now being imitated by Jamaica and Trinidad. Without doubt the pace and diversity of industrial development in Puerto Rico has benefited from favourable preconditions absent in all other islands. Nevertheless, Puerto Rico might supply the pattern on which to base new industrial development programmes in other islands, unless of course, these islands are so small and remote that industrialization is out of the question anyway. It will develop in other islands in a less spectacular manner than in Puerto Rico. The example of Cuba after the Revolution shows that industrialization does not have the desired effect if it is pushed forward too rapidly. On the other hand, several of the islands have very recently learned the lesson that to neglect agriculture whilst industrializing is not to their advantage.

Tourism

In many small islands industrialization will presumably never be economically feasible. The only alternative presenting itself to these islands is the tourist industry which has increased rapidly throughout the Caribbean each year since the Second World War. Each island, even the smallest and most remote, is eager to take part in the tourist boom (cf. p. 99). Wherever a growing tourist industry serves to widen the economic base it may be called positive; but the tourist industry is always of questionable value when traditional branches of the economy are neglected because of it. After all, the tourist industry, which is completely dependent on economic conditions in the USA, is a branch of the economy and therefore as unbalanced and vulnerable to crises as monoculture used to be.

The economic future of the islands depends on how completely the colonial heritage with its many negative attributes can be discarded. Puerto Rico and Cuba are trying, admittedly in very different ways, to overcome traditional problems such as poverty, hunger, and unemployment. Solving the same problems, and especially the one of social differences, is just as urgent in the other republics or dependencies. At present, the outlook for improving the conditions in the small and overpopulated Leeward Islands and in the Republic of Haiti is dim. The 1965 civil war in the Dominican Republic, which lasted several months, showed among other things that the Caribbean islands are far from economic and political stability. To achieve this stability is an urgent task. The future will show whether other islands will see the Cuban solution as providing the pattern for improving their own internal economies. Any radical step taken to improve the grievances outlined above will certainly put the Caribbean archipelago into the spotlight of world politics, as was the case during the revolutions in Cuba and the Dominican Republic.

PART II

13

The Bahama Islands

South-east of Florida and almost parallel to the Cuban coastline the Bahama Islands extend over more than 1000 km. The Bahama group consists of more than 2000 cays and about 700 islands of various sizes with an overall area of 11 826 sq km (including the Turks and Caicos Islands).

The climatic conditions are determined by the islands' position on the equatorial side of the subtropical high pressure belt, and by the regularity of the trade winds which lead to a mild winter season. These climatic conditions are the foundation of the recent economic development of the Bahamas brought about by tourism. Proximity to the North American mainland and jet age traffic explain the positive results of a rather costly and intensive publicity campaign in the USA and Canada. The number of tourists rose from 45 000 in 1950 to 605 000 in 1964, and 1 072 000 in 1968.[1]

Proximity to the mainland brought various economic advantages to the Bahamas in earlier times. At the end of the American War of Independence (1783) when British Loyalists and their slaves immigrated, the size of the white population doubled and the number of Negroes trebled. Cotton cultivation by the Loyalists caused a temporary boom in agriculture. During the American Civil War in the mid nineteenth century the Bahamas profited by transporting contraband to the mainland, and in the 1920s they profited from smuggling alcohol during the American prohibition era. However, the Bahamas did not in the past experience any economic development which was based on their physical features.

The Bahama Islands represent the highest elevations of the Bahama Banks which lie only 20 m below sea-level and which at their edges descend steeply to great depths. Various channels with depths of up to 2000 m dissect the area (Florida Strait, Tongue of the Ocean, Exuma Sound, and many others). These channels are not submarine canyons, neither can their steep slopes be seen as cliffs. They are interpreted as Tertiary fossil coral reefs by Newell. The young coral reefs which have

---

[1] The number of American tourists visiting the Bahamas doubled by 1963 after Cuba lost its position as a tourist attraction (1959: 264 000 tourists).

112

developed on the windward side of the banks since the Pleistocene, are not widely distributed.

Like the banks themselves, the cays and islands are built from oolitic limestone and hardened calcareous sand with a thickness of up to 4500 m. According to Illing the calcareous sand on the banks is formed primarily from precipitated aragonite from the sea water and is not, as was previously assumed, limestone detritus. This precipitation and deposition occurs chiefly on the marginal zones of the banks where relatively cool water is carried into the deep channels by tidal currents and it results in a relative raising of the bank edges. Therefore, the previous interpretation of the Bahama Banks as atoll formations is no longer tenable. The strong tidal currents and the many cays which are partly submerged below sea-level complicate local navigation. During the past few decades the shipping routes have altered considerably because land emerged from the sea, e.g. in the region of the Turks and Caicos Islands. The raised marine terraces and cliffs, as well as the limestone and clay deposits in island basins, indicate repeated alterations of sea-level caused both by structural forces and eustatic alterations of the water level.

Some shores are rocky, especially here and there along the east coasts where there are steep cliffs. In many bays, however, there are wide stretches of pure calcareous sand. The beautiful sandy beaches and the clear, multicoloured waters fascinate every tourist and compensate for the otherwise rather dull scenery. All the islands are extremely flat and rise only a few decametres above sea-level, exceptionally to about 100 m. Their surfaces present karst topography; fluvial erosion features do not exist. Weathered earth may be found only in patches in karst depression hollows. Both this and the relative aridity (six to eight arid months) therefore present very unfavourable conditions for agriculture.

Extensive salt marshes cover most of the low-lying basins, and mangrove grows along large parts of the low coastlines. Mainly bare rocks and cactus plants are found in the eastern islands which receive less rainfall (Grand Turk, 750 mm). On the inner islands the primeval forests were destroyed and secondary vegetation, mostly bush, has taken its place. A programme of reafforestation has been started recently. Forests can be found only on the western islands of Grand Bahama, Abaco and Andros which receive higher precipitation (New Providence, 1185 mm). These forests contain mainly the long-needled pine (*Pinus caribaea*) and, together with the dispersed deciduous woods which supply mainly mahogany and dyewoods, they have been economically utilized only recently.

Europe only became aware of the Bahamas after Columbus had landed on San Salvador (Guanahani, Watlings Island) on 12 October 1492. The Spaniards exterminated the Lucayer, a branch of the Tainos people (insular Arawaks). About 40 000 Amerindian slaves are supposed to have been brought to Hispaniola by the Spaniards. No Spanish settlements were established in the Bahamas, as these islands were of no economic value. There are thus no traces of the Amerindian or Spanish era. Later the islands became hiding-places for British buccaneers. The position of the islands was very favourable for them since all Spanish ships had to pass the Florida Strait for navigational reasons on their homebound voyage from the Antilles to Europe. The first Bahama Island to be settled was New Providence, which the British, coming from Bermuda, took possession of in 1656. New Providence is one of the smaller of the twenty islands of the archipelago inhabited today. It has an excellent natural harbour in the north-east, protected by the offshore Paradise Island. Nassau, the Bahama Islands' capital, was founded there. All other islands are called Out Islands because of the position of New Providence at their centre. Several Out Islands, including the Caicos Islands, were only settled in the eighteenth century by British Loyalists. The Turks and Caicos Islands were annexed to Jamaica from 1873 until 1962, when they became an independent British crown colony, under the administration controlled by the Bahamas' Governor. The Islands' constitution is now under review, since the Bahamas' independence in mid-1973, and they will probably remain as a separate British dependency within the Commonwealth.

At present the Bahama Islands have a population of 137 144 including the 5716 inhabitants of the Turks and Caicos Islands (Table 15). About 80 per cent are Negroes. Nassau, as the capital, has strongly attracted the population of the Out Islands. Its percentage of the entire population rose from 46 per cent to 63 per cent between 1931 and 1963. This may be explained by the fact that only New Providence has transport links with the outside world and that so far only this island has experienced economic growth. For a few years now the government has been trying to include the Out Islands in the economic progress. This will probably restrain the present exodus from the Out Islands.

Agriculture plays only a minor role in the economy of the Bahamas. The Loyalists introduced cotton cultivation mainly to Abaco, Long Island, and the Caicos Islands. After a few decades, though, this stopped because of soil exhaustion, insect pests, and the abolition of slavery (1834). Renewed efforts at cotton cultivation have failed. Sisal cultivation was successful only for a short while. Today it only supplies the local weaving industry with the exception of the Caicos Islands where sisal represents part of their

Small-scale peasant cultivation has replaced the former plantations in the Bahama Islands. Negro peasants cultivate the Indian bush-pea and beans for their own consumption on small fields which lie dispersed in bush and forest areas. Often one may find papayas, bananas, mango and avocado trees standing side by side on not very well cared for parcels of land. The fields can only be cultivated during the summer rainy season and at various times the yield suffers from drought since irrigation is not possible. Peasants living on islands not too far from New Providence supply Nassau with increasing quantities of fruit and vegetables which grow in the tropical and temperate climate. A few plantations produce very small quantities of

Table 15. The Bahama Islands: Size and population, 1963

	Size sq km	Population	Density of population (persons per sq km)
New Providence	155	80 907	522
Out Islands			
Andros	4 135	7 461	2
Abaco and Cays	2 006	6 490	3
Inagua	1 446	1 240	1
Grand Bahama	1 126	8 230	7
Eleuthera	424	7 247	17
Cat Island	412	3 131	8
Long Island	335	4 176	12
Acklins	310	1 217	4
Exuma and Cays	258	3 440	13
Mayaguana	248	707	3
Crooked Island	196	766	4
San Salvador	155	968	6
Bimini Islands and Cat Cay	22	1 652	75
Ragged Island	13	371	29
Harbour Island	4	997	249
Spanish Wells	1	849	849
Others	150	1 579	11
Bahamas (total)	11 396	131 428	12

tomatoes, onions, cucumbers, okra, pineapples and citrus fruits for export, e.g. near Marsh Harbour in Abaco and near Mastic in Andros. The export of fresh tomatoes and cucumbers amounted to about 3·5 per cent of the total value of exports in 1967. The relative underdevelopment of agriculture results partly from transport difficulties. Recently small canning factories were built in far-off islands to process the market-orientated agricultural produce. Two modern beef farms in Eleuthera supply dairy products to Nassau. Nevertheless, the very small agricultural output necessitates the import of large quantities of food.

The fishing industry is more profitable than agriculture. The waters of the Bahama Banks abound in fish and attract many tourists who enjoy game fishing. The local populations of Abaco, Grand Bahama and Harbour Island (north-east of Eleuthera) in particular fish these regions with small boats. The catch mainly supplies the local demand but some fresh and frozen fish, particularly crayfish, is exported to Florida. Nassau is the main fishing harbour and possesses a freezing-plant. The Caicos Islands also export frozen crayfish to Florida. Crayfish exports amount to 4 per cent of the total value of export in the Bahamas and to 92 per cent in the Caicos

Islands. Turtles, once the basis for the shell industry, have greatly decreased in numbers; and the sponge-fishery which was once very important, especially in Andros, ceased to exist when the banks experienced an insect pest in 1938. Not until 1956 could this industry be revived to a small extent. Mussels are consumed by the local population, and the shells are exported to Florida as tourist souvenirs. The Turks and Caicos Islands export the dried meat of a large sea snail (*Strombus gigas*) to Haiti, the annual quantities of which sometimes equal the Haitian meat imports.

The semi-arid islands to the east achieve economic importance because of their salt production. Salt exports amount to 6 per cent of the entire value of exports from the Turks and Caicos Islands, and the salt which is produced in Inagua makes up 12·5 per cent of the exports from the Bahamas (Table 16). Salt is produced by the evaporation of sea water in artificial basins. The output falls considerably in more humid years, particularly when a hurricane touches the islands. Even before the Caicos Islands were finally settled in 1783 the inhabitants of the Bermudas came each year between March and November to collect the salt from the basins which were built by them.

Timber from the pine forests of the western islands is the most valuable item after cement and rum production among Bahamian exports (17 per cent of the entire exports). In earlier times timber was exported to Great Britain mainly for the mines; today, three companies supply timber to the US paper industry. Timber, mainly from the deciduous forests, but also from the pine forests, is also being used by the recently established furniture industry in New Providence and for shipbuilding which has an old tradition in Andros and Abaco.

Although raw materials and cheap power are insufficient in the Bahamas the Government Development Board seeks to establish industrial enter-

Table 16. Exports from the Bahamas and the Turks and Caicos Islands, 1968

| | Bahamas | | | Turks and Caicos Islands | |
	£	%		£	%
Cement	7 719 107	36·5	Crayfish	58 115	92·1
Rum	4 644 544	21·9	Salt	3 796	6·0
Timber	3 629 076	17·2	Murails and		
Salt	2 647 582	12·5	shells	1 222	1·9
Fresh tomatoes			Total exports	63 133	
and cucumbers*	negligible	—	Total imports	442 793	
Crayfish	852 229	4·0			
Total exports	21 144 235				
Total imports	73 494 790				

* 1967 still £463 125 = 3·5 per cent.

prises. To achieve this aim a harbour has been built on the south-west coast of Grand Bahama where freighters of all sizes can berth (Freeport Harbour); it includes the biggest fuel bunker in the western hemisphere which can serve up to 160 vessels per month. During its second year of existence more fuel was tanked on board there than by all the harbours in Florida together. In addition, an area of 20 000 ha has been provided for industrial plants. The government offers almost complete exemption from taxation to enterprises until the year 2054. By 1960 160 licences had been issued to industrial and commercial enterprises. One of the first major industrial plants has been a cement factory which went into operation in 1964; a plant for manufacturing electrical appliances is soon to follow. It seems as if this project in the Bahamas which has been judged very critically by US industrialists will be successful. Cheap local labour and exemption from taxes counterbalance the relatively high transport costs.

The Bahamas government collects neither real estate nor income nor property taxes. Two results may be observed. Hundreds of companies from the USA, Britain and Canada do business in the Bahamas. In Nassau it is not unusual to find on one building the signs of dozens of companies all of them taking advantage of tax exemptions by establishing a branch office. Secondly, numerous wealthy North Americans have acquired real estate, recently also in the Out Islands. The prices of real estate have risen drastically within a short period of time.

Economic development since 1950, which coincided with the explosive expansion of tourism, affected only New Providence during its first stages (Map 19). Between 1953 and 1960 six new hotels joined the older buildings with their worldwide reputation. North American bank managers have built exclusive colonies of houses complete with golf-course, yachting harbour and clubhouse, such as Coral Club House in the south coast and Lyford Cay on the west. Later on land speculation also affected the Out Islands. For instance, A. Wenner-Gren invested US $11 million for a yachting club and a luxury hotel on Andros; he acquired an area of 40 000 ha and is now selling part of it as building sites. On Eleuthera there is now a similar situation. Hotels and yachting clubs have also been built on Bimini which houses the Lerner Marine Laboratory, on Abaco, Cat Cay, Eleuthera, Exuma, and especially on Grand Bahama.

At least some of the Out Islands have experienced an unprecedented economic growth. Tourism, forestry, agriculture and industries are being developed and result in much improved transport conditions. Today, most of the Out Islands have their own airport and highways. Air services connect the various islands better than ever before (Map 20). New Providence airport, where all types of aircraft can land, ranks third in volume among all the Caribbean island airports. Both the number of tourists and other economic developments have resulted in excellent transport connections between the Bahamas and the outside world. However, most of the

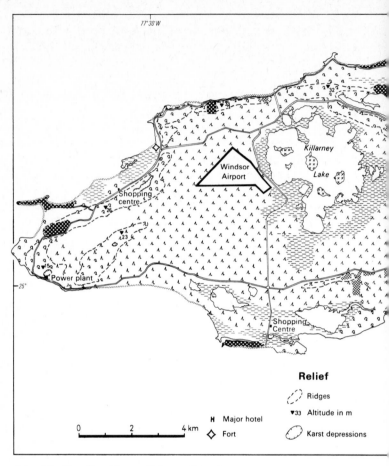

Map 19. New Providence, Bahama Islands.

economic and transport connections of this British crown colony are with the neighbouring mainland of North America and not with its homeland, as before. Mainly US citizens are investing in the Bahamas, and the tourists are almost exclusively North Americans.

The wealthy visitor who for a long time used to come to Nassau during winter is now seeking the exclusiveness of the Out Islands or is going to another remote island in the Caribbean. Nassau has become a place of mass tourism. Reduced hotel rates during summer have eliminated the former seasonal character of tourism. Nassau has become a bigger tourist centre than any other city in the islands. In the centre of the city, especially along Bay Street, which is the main shopping area, one tourist shop follows another. Cheap articles may be found which suit the taste of the average American tourist, as well as many exquisite import goods from all over the world. The older large hotels are also situated in the centre, and along

118

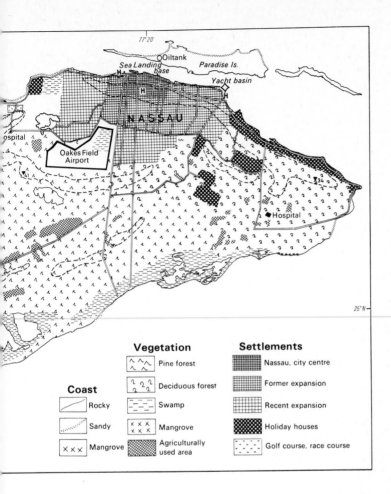

Bay Street streams an endless throng of adventure-seeking Americans, dressed in holiday clothing and contrasting strongly with the carefully preserved British colonial type of architecture. This past which is still present, at least in the buildings of this rapidly expanding city, is an additional impulse for Americans to take the one-hour flight from Florida to Nassau for a short visit to the Bahamas. Nassau tourists are mainly short-time visitors. Usually they spend as much money as the visitors who stay slightly longer so that they are the most sought after guests; their presence has turned Nassau into an overcommercialized tourist 'paradise'.

119

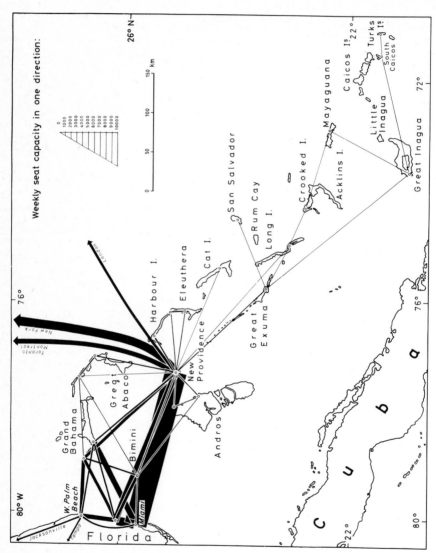

Map 20. Air traffic in the Bahamas, 1964.

120

The Greater Antilles

14
Cuba

Cuba is the largest of the Caribbean islands. It occupies a special position among the Central American islands in various respects. Its size of 110 922 sq km[1] makes up almost half the entire Caribbean island area, and the predominance of flat country distinguishes it noticeably from the other rather mountainous islands of the Antilles. Cuba and several islands of the Bahama archipelago have proximity to the North American mainland in common, but for Cuba this has had a quite different and unparalleled economic and political effect compared with other Caribbean islands: no other (not counting the US territories) had closer economic ties to the USA than Cuba, and today no other island has fewer contacts with the USA than Cuba after the Revolution of 1 January 1959. Cuba was called the 'sugar island' for a few decades because of its enormous production of cane sugar. This volume of production has only been achieved by sugar cane monoculture during the twentieth century—a time when the Islands to the Windward and Haiti, the most important sugar producers of the eighteenth century, have long ceased cultivating sugar cane exclusively. The recent growth of sugar production in Cuba, which is closely linked with the influx of US capital, caused both the social and the economic structure of this island to deteriorate even more than during colonial times. To change both has been the aim of the 1959 Revolution. World politics focused on Cuba when sovietization followed this Revolution.

Physical geography

Cuba extends for about 1200 km in length and is only 32 to 145 km in width. The distances to the neighbouring islands of the Antilles (77 km to Hispaniola, 140 km to Jamaica) are less than those to the North or Middle

[1] The previously accepted Cuban area of 114 524 sq km was corrected by an ordnance survey carried out after the Revolution: cf. Academia de Ciencias de Cuba. Area de Cuba, Habana, 1965.

American mainland. The island rises above a flat basal platform of varying width which has the topographic features of a flooded erosion surface. This platform descends steeply to great sea depths on all sides. Its marginal regions are characterized by strings of islands built from coral limestone or calcareous sand: the Los Colorados and Járdines del Rey in the north, the Járdines de la Reina in the south and, flanking the 3061 sq km large island of Pinos on both sides, the Los Canárreos. This multitude of islands, numbering about 1600, together with numerous reefs and sand banks, complicates the access by sea to several coastal regions of the main island.

Cuba's coastline has a length of 3500 km. There are steeply rising shores in the north, whilst the south coast is mostly flat and covered by mangroves. There are numerous excellent harbours, most of them wide, circular bays which extend far into the interior with only a narrow access. Habana, Nipe, Guantánamo, Santiago, and Cienfuegos are the most important of these so-called bolsas. The many harbours together with the relatively narrow width of the island are an advantage for the export of sugar. As many as twenty-three harbours are used for the export of sugar; nowhere do the distances between them and the sugar factories amount to more than slightly over 70 km.

Among the many factors which contributed to the development of sugar cane monoculture the topography played an important role. Cuba is basically a flat country. Extensive plains favour a modern, mechanized type of farming and only in these areas did sugar cane monoculture and latifundia develop. Almost a quarter of the island's surface is occupied by mountainous regions which do not form a coherent area but consist of dispersed ranges. Peasant farming is to be found in these areas with sugar cultivation playing no role at all.

The low-lying plains hardly reach heights of 100 m and are very uniform in the province of Camagüey. They are mostly limestone and exhibit various karst formations, e.g. sinkholes and dolines. Black and red clayey residual soils cover great parts of these limestone plains among which the deep and relatively light red Matanzas loam is the most famous: it is supposed to be the best possible soil for sugar cane cultivation. Wherever the plains are formed of different materials sugar cane cultivation decreases or disappears. This is the case in the Camagüey plains in the regions of peridotite-serpentinite rocks where the character of the cultural landscape changes completely: intensively cultivated sugar cane areas are replaced by extensive pasture lands with short-grass, palm trees and bush. On the sandy residual soils in the plains of Pinar del Río in the western part of the island sugar cane cultivation is also absent.

The highest mountains are found at either end of Cuba. In the western province of Pinar del Río the Sierra Guaniguanico rises to a height of 728 m. Among the elongated subregions the Sierra de los Organos is especially distinct on account of its scenery. Characteristic landmarks are the bizarrely shaped, steep limestone mountains with many caves. They are usually in a cone or haystack-like form, rising from flat valleys of great width. Their local name 'mogotes' has entered geomorphological nomenclature, designating end formations of tropical cone karst. The mountains at the south-eastern end of the island rise to higher altitudes. The Pico Turquino in the Sierra Maestra, running west–east, reaches 1972 m,[1] and the Cayman Trench descends to more than 7 000 m below sea-level at a distance of only 30 km off the coast. These impressive differences in relief give expression to the recent and continuing movements of the earth's crust as illustrated by repeated earthquakes. Earth movements can also be inferred from the high altitude of extensive flat regions which are remnants of Mio-Pliocene erosion surfaces, as well as from the sequence of Pleistocene marine terraces which are beautifully developed along several stretches of the coast. The Sierra Maestra is covered by dense forests and is separated from the Sierra de Nipe and from the mountain region of Baracoa by the wide Valle Central in the east. All these southern mountains are very important to Cuba because of their mineral deposits. Manganese ore, iron ore with a concentration of nickel, and copper ore are mined in these mountains and are the basis for the heavy industry which is planned and partly realized in the regions of Habana, Santiago, and the Bay of Nipe. The smaller and isolated mountain ranges of the Sierras de Trinidad-Sancti Spíritus rise to an altitude of up to 1156 m in the centre of the island; they have been called the Escambray Mountains since the Revolution. Magnificent karst formations have developed in their limestone areas. Coffee is the main crop in all Cuban mountains; the quantity, however, has decreased greatly since the nineteenth century.

Another essential precondition for the development of sugar cane monoculture in Cuba, in addition to the configuration of the island and its coast, its topography and soil, is the climate. The climate in Cuba is very favourable to sugar cane farming as regards temperature and rainfall. Cuba, being the northernmost island of the Antilles, is subject to winter cold waves from North America. Nevertheless, temperatures below freezing point do not occur as they do along the US Gulf coast where they affect the sugar crop. For many years Habana has not experienced temperatures below 12°C, and the average temperature of the warmest and coldest month respectively is 28°C and 22°C, and the annual average temperature is 25·2°C. High temperatures and a small annual temperature variation together with the amount and seasonal distribution of precipitation favour sugar cane cultivation. Annual precipitation everywhere in the plains is between 1000 and 1500 mm. With the latitudinal position of Cuba a winter dry season alternates with a summer rainy season, each season having one rainfall maximum. This type of climate with seasonal rainfall, in the marginal zone of the tropics (Aw according to Köppen's climatic classification), is especially favourable for the cultivation of sugar cane.

[1] New survey; previously noted height: 2 005 m.

Because of the size and the subdued relief of the island extensive regions enjoy a constant average humidity of seven to nine humid months. Only the mountain ranges may experience twelve humid months (Map 21). Arid districts, as they occur in the leeward plains of the mountainous islands, do not exist except in the easternmost parts. In general, this island experiences the effects of leeward and windward positions only in the extreme Oriente. As a result, sugar cane is cultivated everywhere without irrigation. Nevertheless, a large-scale system of irrigation has been planned by the revolutionary government. Only the mountains receive rainfall during the winter season and are therefore not threatened by drought. Sometimes the sugar cane cultivations, especially in western regions, are endangered by hurricanes which usually occur in late summer or early autumn. Not only is extensive damage caused by the violent winds; even more serious is the resulting high rainfall and the consequent flooding of great parts of the Cuban plains. The short Cuban rivers also flood their surrounding districts following violent convectional rains during summer. Only a drainage system in the flat country has enabled effective cultivation. The Institute of Hydrology founded in 1962 has begun to examine the water economy of the Cuban rivers and its best utilization for agricultural and industrial purposes. The construction of a network of meteorological stations, started in 1959, and the establishment of an Institute of Soil Science serve the same aim.

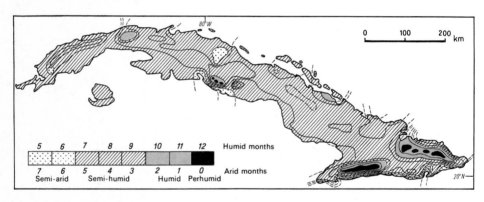

Map 21. Cuba: isohygromenes (index Reichel's).

The primary forest cover of the Cuban plains has disappeared for various reasons: the early beef farming, the supply of wood to the sugar boiling houses during the nineteenth century, the expansion of the area under sugar cane cultivation in the twentieth century, and the production of charcoal. Mountain forests have decreased because of the establishment of coffee plantations and because of clearing by peasants. Today only 11 per cent of Cuba is forest land. Tropical rain forest covers the moist northern slopes of the Sierra Maestra and especially the mountainous districts of Baracoa, and extensive forests containing the long-needled pine

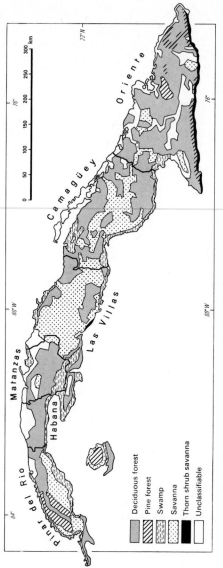

Map 22. Cuba: the original flora (adapted from Waibel).

Deciduous forest
Pine forest
Swamp
Savanna
Thorn shrub savanna
Unclassifiable

Pinar del Rio
Habana
Matanzas
Las Villas
Camagüey
Oriente

are preserved in the mountains of the Pinar del Río province, on the Isle of Pines and in the Sierra de Nipe. The plains were not uniformly forested at the time of discovery. Numerous *Sabána* placenames indicate the existence of open country in various regions. The Amerindian word *Sabána* designates treeless land (cf. p. 44). When Waibel undertook to ascertain the original flora (Map 22) on the basis of placenames he recognized that the vegetation of the plains was not distributed according to climatic, but exclusively to soil conditions, as the sugar cane cultivations are today. Grassland appeared everywhere in the deciduous woods of the Cuban plains where the soil was poor, for example in the areas of serpentinite. This grassland contained short grass with thorny scrub, palm trees and pines. Even today these areas with varying floristic formations are hostile to field crops and of hardly any value to beef farming. They are still covered by short grasses interspersed with groups of palm trees, less often with pine trees, and give a special character to the scenery which impresses every traveller. In addition to these savannas in various areas of the island, and in addition to the montane forests and to the thorn and cactus forests in the semi-arid regions of the mountain slopes along the south-east coast, there are extensive swamp areas which set bounds to the expansion of sugar cane farming.

Population and settlement

At the time of its discovery by the Spaniards Cuba was inhabited by an estimated 500 000 Amerindians (island Arawaks = Tainos) who had developed an agricultural economy. More recent estimates reduce the figure to 80 000–100 000. Less numerous and more ancient peoples were the Ciboney and the Guanahatabey, the former being fishermen, the latter gatherers and hunters. The Tainos had pushed them to the extreme western regions of Cuba. Forced labour and imported diseases reduced the number of Amerindians to a few thousand within the first two decades after discovery. In order to obtain labourers the Spaniards started to import Negroes in 1513. Cuban ethnic types and Cuban culture have developed from the transplanting and combination of both Spanish and African people and cultural elements; whereas the nations on the Latin American mainland are based on Spanish and Amerindian foundations.

In contrast to most of the Caribbean islands the white population in Cuba predominates (73 per cent). Negroes constitute 12 per cent, mulattoes 15 per cent, and Chinese less than 0·5 per cent of the population. This has not always been so. The white element dominated from the beginning of the Spanish colonization until the end of the eighteenth century; in 1841, however, Negroes dominated the Cuban population with 60 per cent. The large increase in Negroes during the early nineteenth century resulted from the expanding sugar cane cultivation at that time. The immigration of labourers from Spain and the Canary Islands was so high, following the abolition of slavery in 1845, that by the end of the nineteenth

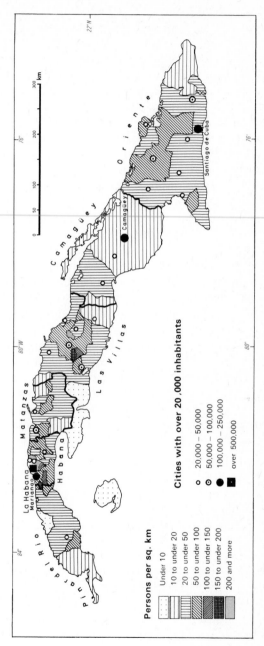

Map 23. Cuba: density of population, 1953.

century the percentage of the white population was twice as high as that of the Negroes. During the first three decades of this century about 700 000 Spaniards and 300 000 Negroes from Haiti and Jamaica migrated to Cuba. Since then immigration has been insignificant. Between 1841 and 1943 the population rose from 1 to 4·8 million and to an estimated 7·8 million in 1966. The birth rate (1964) is 33·9 per thousand and the death rate 7 per thousand. About 300 000 Cubans have left their island since the Revolution in 1959.

Cuba's population density is 68 persons per sq km (1966) which is much less than in most of the Caribbean islands. The distribution of the population is very uneven (Map 23). The plains, especially in the province of Camagüey, are thinly populated. Twenty per cent of the entire population is concentrated in and around Habana, and in the agricultural areas also the Cuban population is largely urbanized. The number of townships has increased greatly during this century and the large cities in particular have expanded greatly. At the beginning of this century cities were found mainly in the western regions of Cuba. By 1930 numerous new towns had been founded and the existing towns were expanding in the central and eastern parts of the island, both on the coast and in the interior. Until 1930 the urbanization process was controlled mainly by the extending railway network resulting from the ever-increasing area under sugar cane cultivation. Later on it was mainly associated with the road building projects. The latter is especially true for the districts surrounding Habana, but also for the entire island whose whole area became accessible in 1931 when the construction of the Carretera Central, a wide all-weather road, was completed.

Cuba's well-established, highly urbanized population does not result from industrialization. The island has always been and still is an agricultural country. The high percentage of city dwellers is partly explained by the fact that a great part of the rural population was forced to settle in towns during the wars of liberation. Nevertheless, it is probably not incorrect to interpret the early urbanization in Cuba as the heritage of Spanish colonization which was based on urban settlements.

Regional divisions

Cuba is divided into the major historical regions of Occidente, Las Villas, Camagüey, and Oriente (Map 24).

Occidente

The Cuban Occidente extends from Cape San Antonio eastwards beyond the Peninsula of Zapata. The backbone of its western part, roughly comprising the province of Pinar del Río, is formed by the **Sierra Guaniguanico** with its two extended chains, the Sierra de los Organos and the Sierra del Rosario. While the scenery of the latter Sierra exhibits a multitude of

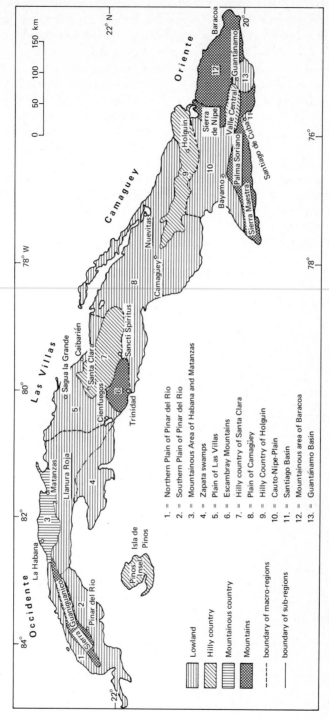

Map 24. Cuba: regions.

Lowland
Hilly country
Mountainous country
Mountains
------- boundary of macro-regions
——— boundary of sub-regions

1. = Northern Plain of Pinar del Rio
2. = Southern Plain of Pinar del Rio
3. = Mountainous Area of Habana and Matanzas
4. = Zapata swamps
5. = Plain of Las Villas
6. = Escambray Mountains
7. = Hilly country of Santa Clara
8. = Plain of Camagüey
9. = Hilly Country of Holguin
10. = Cauto-Nipe-Plain
11. = Santiago Basin
12. = Mountainous area of Baracoa
13. = Guantánamo Basin

knolls formed of different rock materials, steep limestone cones tower in the former (Fig. 6 and Plate 2). The Valle de Viñales is known throughout Cuba for the unique beauty of its scenery. In the surrounding districts H. Lehmann examined the development of tropical cone karst formations and contributed essential material to explain the genesis of karst haystack hills (*Karsttürme*, mogotes), karst hollows (*Karsthohlformen*, hoyos), and karst margin plains (*Karstrandebene*, poljes). The revolutionary government has built a *centro turístico* with several hotels and restaurants near Viñales with its impressive views of the Sierra de los Organos and of the cultural landscape of the Valle de Viñales where peasants grow tobacco mainly. Numerous mineral springs are associated with the fault lines along which the recent uplifting of the mountains occurred. San Vicente and San Diego de los Baños are much-frequented mineral baths. Xerophytic types of vegetation grow on the limestone mountains, and the mountainous areas in the western Occidente are covered by extensive forests with pine and oak trees (*Pinus tropicalis*, *Pinus caribaea*, and *Quercus virginiana*). They are used mainly for charcoal production, and even today herds of pigs are driven into the oak forests to feed on the acorns.

The most important economic regions of the western Occidente are located in the plains of **Pinar del Río** on either side of the Sierra Guani-

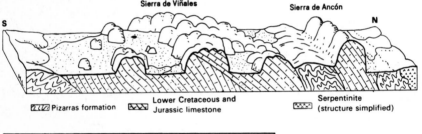

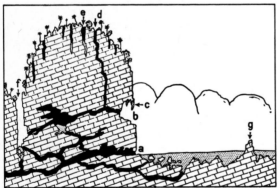

Fig. 6 Cuba: cone karst formations in the Sierra de los Organos (after H. Lehmann).
    (*a*) Block diagram of the Sierra de los Organos (on the left the Vivales karst margin plains.
    (*b*) Cross-section of a karst cone in the Sierra de los Organos.

guanico. They constitute the area of Vuelta Abajo and Semivuelta where the world-famous Havana tobacco is produced. Mainly white peasants have cultivated various types of tobacco on sandy and clayey soils on the lower mountain slopes and the adjacent plains since colonial times. This tobacco is said to be the best in the world. The small-scale fields require almost horticultural care. The great demand in the world market for quality tobacco has helped the small but very efficient farms in the Vuelta Abajo and Semivuelta to maintain their position against the expanding sugar cane latifundia in the Cuban plains. The guajiros (farmers with small land holdings) cultivate their lands, of an average size of 10 ha, either on a family basis or with the help of a few peones (farm labourers). The small thatched farm buildings, usually built from white-washed timber or clay (Plate 3), lie amidst the vegas (fields bearing tobacco); near to them grow some bananas, several fruit trees and some vegetables for the farmers' own use. Adjacent to the living quarters one often finds a large shed for tobacco drying; sometimes these sheds are built right on the parcelled tobacco fields. Solitary royal palms give a special note to the otherwise rather uniform cultural landscape. Another variation of the landscape is to be observed during the winter dry season when white gauze is fixed to high poles to protect the most valuable tobacco plants against the parching heat of the sun from a cloudless sky. Only in the south-west of Pinar del Río do vast fields and huge tobacco sheds indicate that the vegueros (peasants) have been replaced by large-scale farms. American capital was used by the Cuban Land Tobacco Co. only in the tobacco plantations of the Vuelta Abajo. One of the first state-owned enterprises, the Pancho Pérez farm, was built on this company's land after the 1959 expropriation. Vuelta Abajo and Semivuelta are the most important areas under tobacco cultivation in Cuba with an area of about 28 000 ha and a tobacco production of 20 000 tonnes. The tobacco is not processed locally but in the industrial plants of Habana.

In addition to tobacco cultivation increasing importance is being achieved by rice and cotton farming in the plains south of the Sierra Guaniguanico. In addition, nine state-owned latifundia (granjas estatales) in the western Occidente produce 4 per cent of the Cuban sugar crop. Taking the sugar cane area near Mariel on the north coast as an example, R. Platt has shown how the originally circular landed properties, dating from Spanish colonial times, often overlapped and how the land had to be redistributed as a result of the developing sugar cane cultivation (Map 28). Even today one can clearly recognize from the air, almost everywhere in Cuba, the circular boundaries of the former hatos (beef-farming enterprises) and corrales (sheep-farming enterprises).

The copper mines near Matahambre north-west of Pinar del Río represent the only mining industry in the western Occidente. Before the Revolution the only industrial plant was a large cement factory in Mariel; today it has been joined by a power plant based on mineral oil. The chemical plant 'Patricio Lumumba' in Santa Lucía (Pinar del Río) is one of the largest factories built after the Revolution.

The economic centre of the western Occidente is the busy provincial capital, Pinar del Río (pop. 58 000) with good transport connections to Habana by rail and road being the terminus of the Carretera Central. The number of urban settlements in the small-farming area of the western Occidente is considerably higher than anywhere else in Cuba.

The **mountainous area of Habana and Matanzas** constitutes the greatest part of central Occidente. The limestone has been eroded into cuesta topography. Longitudinal valleys, like the Valle del Yumurí west of Matanzas, extend in the direction of the strike of breached anticlines. The limestone at their centres has been eroded away, and the present land surface consists of serpentinite. The cuestas are sometimes cut through by narrow transverse valleys and from both sides open into the wide longitudinal valleys.

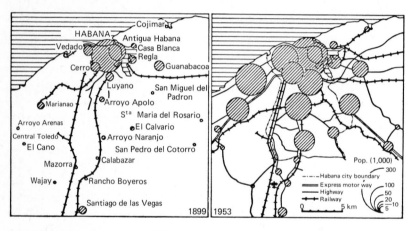

Map 25. Cuba: the growth of Habana, (after Dyer).

The capital of Cuba is located in the western region of the mountainous area of Habana and Matanzas. The international metropolis of Habana is the largest city in Cuba and in the Caribbean islands. In 1953 the city had a population of 788 000, the metropolitan area about 1·2 million, i.e. one quarter of the entire Cuban population (Map 25). The population of Habana had risen to an estimated 1 946 000 in 1966. The city was first founded in 1515 on the south coast, not far from the present town of Batabanó. Then it was moved to the north coast, first to the mouth of the Almendares and finally, in 1519, to the Bay of Habana. This large bolsa-bay, protected by its narrow access, has been the reason for the growth of Habana. In 1553 the governor of the Spanish colony moved to Habana from Santiago. After French corsairs sacked and destroyed the town in 1555 the Spaniards rebuilt it as the best fortified port in the Caribbean islands. Up to the present day three forts guard the 200 m wide and one kilometre long passage into the inlet which has an area of over 20 sq km: the sixteenth-century Castillo del Morro, the large Fortaleza de la Cabaña on the east side and the Castillo de la Punta on the west side of the passage. This protected and excellent natural harbour served as the pivot of the Spanish convoy system: all ships from Spain to the Caribbean, Mexico and Colombia assembled here each year during the summer in order to set out together for the homebound voyage to Europe. The city had long since grown beyond its walls when they were pulled down in 1863. The population had risen to 160 000 by 1850. Old Habana (Map 26), the city within the former walls, occupies the tip of the peninsula which juts out from the west between the bay and the open sea. Two- and three-storey buildings fringe the narrow streets which form an almost completely regular grid pattern. These streets used to be flooded by crowds of people and cars until the suburb of Vedado developed into the main shopping area in the 1950s. Today the old town is rather peaceful. The cathedral, the Plaza and the palace of the former governor are beautiful examples of Spanish colonial architecture. The railway station, extensive car parks, monumental buildings, e.g. the Capitol, which is an imitation of the US building and at present the seat of the Academia de Ciencias, and the presidential palace are located just outside the former city walls.

At the end of the nineteenth century the urban area covered the entire peninsula up to a point west of the Bay of Atares. Various suburbs extended towards the south, south-west and west. Habana expanded along these directions during the twentieth century (Map 27). Numerous suburbs were built and almost everywhere the streets were laid out in a grid pattern in spite of the hilly land surface. The modern city has been built in an open pattern, parks and recreation areas are dispersed in the residential areas. About 90 per cent of the villas in the formerly privileged residential area of Miramar were deserted by their owners who emigrated. They are occupied nowadays by students. Industrial plants and large residential areas for workers developed mainly in the suburb of Luyanó south-west of the bay. The city expanded towards the south-east following the construction of the Carretera Central. The water of the bay and its inlet, uncrossed by any bridge, has long prevented the urbanization of the eastern districts. The new road tunnel under the passage between Morro and Cabaña stimulated the growth of Habana even beyond the bay. There the revolutionary government built the satellite city of Habana del Este which consists mainly of multistorey apartment blocks.

The character of the city changed decisively shortly after the Second World War when a new shopping centre, which was soon to become a rival of the old town, was built in the previously residential western suburb of Vedado. At present it represents the real city centre. The heaviest traffic was formerly to be found in the Obispo Street in the old town; today it is found in the Calle 23 in Vedado (Plate 4). Here, mainly in its lower section

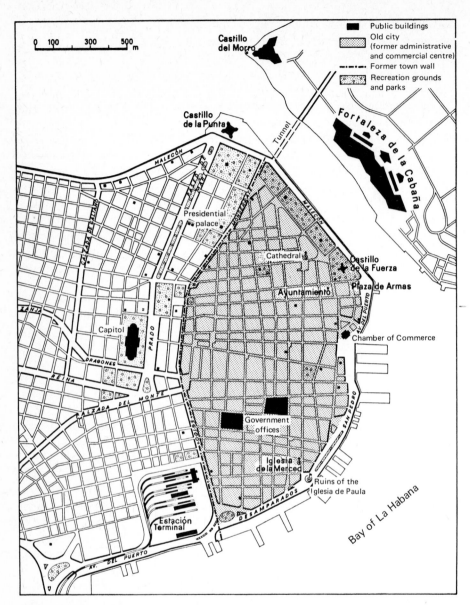

Map 26. Cuba: Old Habana.

'La Rampa', multistorey commercial buildings and hotels stand side by side, the 'Habana Libre', formerly the 'Habana Hilton', among them. Following the North American pattern modern multilaned highways have been built, for example from the airport, in Rancho Boyeros, north to the large Plaza de la República adjacent to which stand several buildings of the revolutionary government. In its centre rises the monument to the national

134

hero José Martí. A world-famous boulevard, the surf-sprayed Avenida Malecón, leads from the Castillo de la Punta all the way to Vedado along the coastline. Habana's urban area has very good bus services which are only surpassed in the Caribbean islands by San Juan in Puerto Rico. Both the inner and outer districts are served by a tight network of frequent bus connections which have their centre in a modern and generously built bus terminal on the Avenida de la Independencia. These excellent transport facilities have greatly stimulated the growth of settlements near Habana. For instance, Marianao (pop. 455 000) a satellite city to Habana, has grown to the second largest city in Cuba and almost forms a single urban area with the capital. San Miguel del Padrón (pop. 156 000) is the largest of the remaining five neighbouring cities belonging to Greater Habana (Map 25).

The present position of Habana with its excessive concentration of population is the result of its many functions, past and present. For many years Habana represented the most important military base in the Spanish West Indies, and since 1553 it has been the administrative centre of Cuba. Habana is the centre of the home and export trade and is also the commercial and financial centre. More than 80 per cent of Cuban imports pass through Habana, but only 25 per cent of the exports are shipped from there, because sugar is exported from various other ports. In 1963 Habana harbour handled only 137 800 tonnes of exports, but 2·3 million tonnes of imports. For a long time Habana was the only site of Cuban manufacturing plants. Today its diversity of industrial plants is unparalleled in Cuba. Various plants, such as those of the food, beverages and tobacco industries, the finishing, and the consumer goods industries, which are chiefly port-orientated, have joined the traditional processing and manufacturing industries such as the sugar and cigar industries. No heavy industry existed before the Revolution except for the petroleum refineries. Now an iron foundry (in Guanabacoa) and various machine factories have been added. Numerous new factories have been built following the Revolution, e.g. large-scale enterprises of the pharmaceutical and plastics-processing industries. In addition, Habana has always been very active as the scientific and cultural centre of the island. Its university, founded in 1721, is the most important in Cuba. The proximity to the North American mainland meant that, before the Revolution, Habana was the city with the largest number of tourists in the Caribbean: 300 000 tourists arrived in 1958, by air from Miami and by train and automobile ferries from Key West. Habana lost its traditional function as a tourist centre after the 1959 Revolution. However, the big hotels, all of them state-owned, are not idle. They are now occupied by advisers and specialists from Communist East European countries together with their families, sometimes for periods of several months.

Agriculture in the districts surrounding Habana has specialized mainly in supplying the urban market. The intensively cultivated and irrigated area in the plain of Güines south-east of the city, noted especially by

135

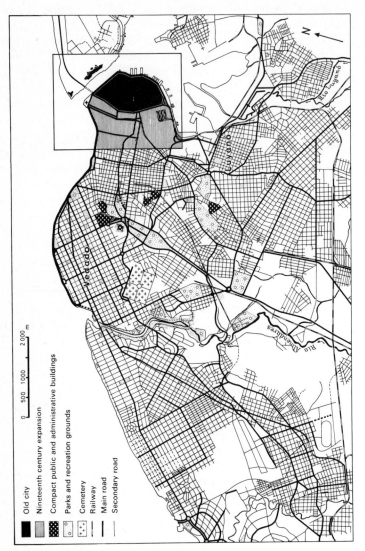

Map 27. Habana, street map.

Old city

Nineteenth century expansion

Compact public and administrative buildings

Parks and recreation grounds

Cemetery

Railway

Main road

Secondary road

0 500 1000 2 000 m

A. v. Humboldt, is called the Huerta de la Habana. Numerous industrial enterprises are located on the periphery of the capital, e.g. the large Ariguanaba textile plant in Bauta and the post-revolutionary textile complex 'Alquitex' in Alquízar which employs 1400 workers.

South of the mountainous area of Habana and Matanzas and further to the east of the province of Matanzas the **Llanura Roja** extends from coast to coast. This plain, which is also called Llanura de Colón in the Matanzas province, has the most fertile soils in Cuba. The yields from the red-coloured Matanzas loam are outstanding. Sugar cane farming in Cuba started here, and the whole plain was under sugar cane by the nineteenth century. This pattern has not yet changed. Latifundia (*granjas estatales*) produce 20 per cent of the entire Cuban sugar crop in the provinces of Habana and Matanzas. The rather uniform scenery is everywhere dominated by sugar cane; only the chimneys of sugar factories, the bold upright royal palms and the emergent crowns of Ceiba trees are distinct landmarks. Before the construction of the Roque drainage canal extensive parts of this plain used to be flooded during the rainy season. The western district of the Llanura Roja is used by peasants for tobacco cultivation, not in a mono-culture, however, as in the Vuelta Abajo but together with fruit and vegetables for the urban market of Habana. While henequén cultivation is to be found in the hinterlands of the cities of Matanzas and Cárdenas, rice farming has expanded in the southern Llanura Roja towards the Zapata swamps.

The provincial capital of Matanzas (pop. 81 000) possesses an excellent natural harbour used for the export of sugar from nine sugar factories. The construction of a free port favoured industrial development even before the Revolution. In addition to the manufacturing of artificial silk and shoes, chemical and petrochemical industries have recently been established on the western side of the bay. The town is served by a frequent rail service, and one can travel to Matanzas by car from Habana using either the Carretera Central or the scenic road which passes through the north coast resorts such as Guanabo and Jibacoa. From Matanzas a highway leads to the famous beach of Veradero with its many hotels and holiday cottages 30 km to the east on the narrow Hicacos peninsula. Before the Revolution direct flights linked Miami and Veradero. Cárdenas, an export harbour for sugar, lies 20 km away. A paper factory using bagasse and a light metal industry have been established there.

The **peninsula of Zapata** belongs to the Occidente as well. It has the largest swamp area in Cuba with two indigenous types of crocodiles (*Crocodilus rhombifer* and *americanus*) and is a paradise for birds. A mangrove belt many kilometres in depth fringes the flat shores of the peninsula where hard working *carboneros* (charcoal burners) produce charcoal. Vast mangrove woods also extend through the interior from the Bay of Broa to the Bay of Pigs which became known in 1961 because of an unsuccessful invasion attempt by exiled Cubans. Towards the interior the mangrove swamps change into extensive marshy districts.

Beyond the Batabanó Gulf, which belongs to the epicontinental region off the south coast of the Occidente, lies the **Isle of Pines** named after its large pine forests. When Cuba gained its independence it was still undecided whether this island would become Cuban or US territory. This explains the relatively large number of American immigrants who cultivated citrus and especially grapefruit in the north of the island. They supplied the US market and were successful at first, but high transport charges because of transhipment in Batabanó and Habana made their plantations uneconomical. Their decline was completed even before the Revolution set a final end to these American plantations in 1959. Nueva Gerona, the largest town on the island, is the base of an active fishing industry, and possesses a fish canning plant like its sister port Batabanó on Cuba itself. The shallow waters of the Batabanó Gulf abound in fish and crustaceae. In addition, the Isle of Pines has flight connections with Habana and is one of the most frequent tourist centres in Cuba.

Las Villas

The full width of the eastern plain of the Occidente continues into Las Villas, and along the north coast the plain of Las Villas extends as a narrow tract to the plain of Camagüey. The **plain of Las Villas** differs from the Llanura Roja in the Occidente in so far as the red-coloured Matanzas clay occurs in only a few of its districts. Grey and dark coloured clayey and also rocky residual limestone soils alternate in an irregular pattern. As a result the soil conditions are not as favourable for sugar cane cultivation as they are in the Llanura Roja. Nevertheless, the plain of Las Villas is characterized by this crop. Fifty large estates (*granjas estatales*) supply 21 per cent of the Cuban sugar produce and export via Caibarién on the north coast and especially via Cienfuegos (pop. 89 000) which is located on a large bolsa-bay in the south. The northern port of Sagua la Grande on the mouth of a river has a salt-pan and a chemical industrial plant.

The **hilly country of Santa Clara**, bordered by the plain of Las Villas to the west and north, rarely rises above 200 m. It is an extended dome shaped anticline in the centre of the island. The serpentinite massif, which is mixed with extrusive rock, is overlain in its northern region by limestone materials which dip slightly northwards and which either form cuestas or chains of isolated mogotes. The soils vary according to their rock base. Sugar cane is cultivated on the clayey residual soils of the serpentinite, tobacco on sandy soils. The latter crop characterizes the agricultural landscape. The hilly country of Santa Clara produces as much tobacco as the western Occidente. However, the produce of this tobacco area, known as *Remidios*, is of a lower quality. Only the tobacco cultivated in the Manicaragua basin reaches the quality of the Vuelta Abajo tobacco. Cultivation is carried out by peasants in a multicrop system. In addition to tobacco, beans, maize, and tropical tubers are the most important plants produced for the domestic market. Tobacco cultivation in the *Remidios* originated during colonial times. It was developed by colonists who fled Jamaica when it was taken over by the British and who settled near Santa Clara, founded in 1689. Santa Clara (pop. 115 000) is the capital of Las Villas which is the most diversified province in Cuba with regard to agriculture. Due to its central position and excellent transport connections by rail and road it has recently experienced a remarkable growth. This is demonstrated by numerous modern buildings among which are the Universidad Central Marta Abreu and a new light metallurgical plant manufacturing kitchen utensils. Santa Clara is definitely the most important town in Central Cuba.

South of the hilly country of Santa Clara rise the **Escambray Mountains** delimited on all sides by fault lines. They represent the only mountain range in Central Cuba and are subdivided into the Sierra de Trinidad and the Sierra de Sancti Spíritus. Gold mines existed in these mountains in colonial times. Diorite and crystalline limestone form their dome-shaped heights from which short yet high discharge rivers flow in all directions. Among these the Río Hanabanilla is especially well known for its series of waterfalls which the revolutionary government have harnessed for the first hydroelectric power station in Cuba. Karst cones with numerous caves create picturesque scenery especially in the karst regions of the Sierra de Trinidad. The mountains receive heavy precipitation. Small coffee plantations formerly cultivated on lease are dispersed through the humid montane forests. On the southern side of this range lies the peaceful city of Trinidad (pop. 20 000) founded in 1514. Its little houses, the grid pattern displayed by its streets, and the many architectural treasures from the early period of colonialism, create the atmosphere of an old Spanish colonial settlement. Sancti Spíritus (pop. 49 000), however, has quite a different atmosphere although of the same age. It is located near the plain of Camagüey where the Escambray Mountains border the hilly country of Santa Clara. As it is now served by the Carretera Central, it has grown rapidly in recent years. The production of evaporated milk and cheese indicates the proximity of this town to the plain of Camagüey where dairy farms are numerous.

Camagüey

The **plain of Camagüey** extends over a vast area. Wide stretches along the coast are completely flat with clayey residual limestone soils. In the region of the diorite-serpentinite massifs towards the centre of the island the plain becomes slightly hilly. Low-lying cuestas or rugged karst cones with numerous caves indicate the transitional zone between the limestone and the underlying serpentinite. When looking at the cultural geography, the landscape has two contrasting regions—the central part where dairy farms are dominant and the marginal regions which are completely dominated by sugar cane cultivation.

139

Whereas in the Occidente and Las Villas sugar cane has been cultivated since the nineteenth century, it was only introduced to Camagüey during the present century. In order to acquire the land for profitable cane farming vast forests were burnt in the plain of Camagüey during the period when the sugar industry experienced its boom following the First World War. There are only twenty-four *granjas estatales* producing sugar in Camagüey which is fewer than in other regions. The sugar yield is greater, however, amounting to 26 per cent of the entire Cuban production. The state-owned sugar plantations in Camagüey are modern, over-large enterprises, resembling in this respect the typical sugar latifundia in Camagüey before 1960 which were then unusually big. The influence of American capital was stronger in these regions, where sugar cane farming began only after political independence had been achieved, than it was in other cane districts. The majority of the sugar factories were US owned before their expropriation.

The areas under sugar cane cultivation have unique features which are characteristic, to a greater or less extent, not only of Cuba but of all the sugar-producing Caribbean islands. The rectangular and uniformly cultivated cane fields, divided by the tracks of the field railway, cover vast areas. The Cuban cane area is interspersed with fallow pastures which are grazed by hundreds of beef cattle as long as the neighbouring fields yield cane from the same ratoons, i.e. eight to twelve years. Then the land is used in a rotating pattern. The tall chimneys of the sugar factories are visible in the plains from a great distance. Tool sheds, bagasse stacks, the track system and the processing and administrative buildings belong to the plantation complex. In addition there are the so-called *bateys*, the living quarters for labourers, with a school, a hospital, and a grocery store which was formerly run by the plantation and which is today a *tienda del pueblo* (shop for the people). The proprietors of the sugar cane latifundia used to cultivate one part of their land under their own administration (*caña de administración*), the rest was distributed among *colonos* (tenants) who received areas of various sizes and whose state of dependence on the main sugar factory also varied greatly. The ploughing of the fields has been done by machines for a long time; the cane cutting, however, is still done by hand, using a machete, in Cuba and throughout the Caribbean. The cane is then transported on carts drawn by oxen or tractors to the field railways where cranes handle the reloading. The combination of beef and sugar cane farming in one enterprise is explained by the high demand for draught animals. In 1963, when labour was in short supply, the Cuban government ordered cane-cutting machines from the Soviet Union. These were tentatively put into operation during the 1964 harvest.

The summer rainy season, while the cane is growing, is a dead season for sugar cane cultivation. The crop is harvested in the winter dry season beginning in December or January, filling the land with bustling activity. Large numbers of seasonal workers are brought from the towns to work in the fields or factories. Previously, many migrant workers came to Cuba from Haiti and Jamaica for the cane harvest. The sugar factories then operate day and night, and the cutting of the cane is organized so that the factories receive the required amounts of cane in a continuous flow.

The largest sugar factories in Cuba are the Ciro Redondo (formerly Morón) in north-west Camagüey and Antonio Guiteras (formerly Delicias) in the northern part of Oriente. They produce an annual average of more than one million sacks of sugar (325 Span. lb each[1]). Camagüey exports is sugar produce mainly via the port of Nuevitas (pop. 16 000) on a north coast bolsa-bay where a cement factory and light-metal industry have developed recently. This port handles more of the sugar export (1963: 521 000 tonnes) than any other port in Cuba. This is not only because of the large sugar production of the Camagüey plain, but also because there are only a few ports along this part of the Cuban coast, which is relatively inaccessible because of the many offshore islands and reefs.

The interior plains of the Camagüey region consist mainly of pastureland and barren savannas. *Hatos* (beef farms) have been, and still are, the characteristic enterprise although the aim of production has changed. In earlier times hides were produced, then the production of meat and the supply of draught animals became more important. Because of the recent improvement in transport facilities milk production has now been added. As in the early days, there still exist unfenced pastures, e.g. on the island of Cayo Romano off the north coast of Camagüey. This 'kingdom of the *vaquero*' (cowboy, gaucho) included more than half of the Camagüey plains only half a century ago. Modern and intensively cultivated dairy farms, with fenced meadows (*potreros*) of improved grassland have replaced the older and extensive hatos. Imported breeds of cattle, e.g. Zebu, Santa Gertrudis and Holstein, have resulted in an increase in meat and milk production. The plain of Camagüey has always been the leading beef-farming region in Cuba. Its cattle population of 1·1 million head amounts to 27 per cent of all the cattle in Cuba. But there are still valueless savanna regions on the sterile soils. Wiry short grasses, bush (mainly *Byrsonima crassifolia*) and palm trees (*Sabal, Copernicia* and *Coccothrinax*), sometimes *Ceiba* trees or kalebasse (*Crescentia cujete*) are the most common members of these plant colonies. Larger districts of barren land are called *marabu* since they are covered by an impenetrable thicket of the exuberantly growing leguminous plants of the same name (*Caillea glomerata*).

The provincial capital of Camagüey (pop. 142 000) was founded in 1514 and is today the largest city in the interior of Cuba. It has developed greatly since the construction of the railway rescued it from its isolation in the dairy farm region of the central plain of Camagüey. The production of evaporated milk, of butter and cheese, the processing of leather, the manufacture of sausages, preserved meat and smoked meat is based on the livestock farming

---

[1] 1 libra (lb) = 460 grammes; 1 million sacks of sugar = 149 500 tonnes.

in the surrounding districts. The town has the largest railway works in Cuba, and the railway and Carretera Central offer excellent rail and road connections. Camagüey airport was the only one, besides Habana, to have international flights after the Revolution. The older parts of the town with their narrow and irregularly winding streets depart from the usually systematic layout of Spanish colonial settlements. Numerous churches and public buildings as well as the spacious patios of private homes are interesting examples of the Spanish-colonial type of architecture.

The **hilly country of Holguín**, stretching WNW–ESE in the centre of the island between Camagüey and the Nipe Bay, is mostly pastureland on residual serpentinite soils interspersed with some barren short grass savannas. More fertile land is only to be found in the east of the Oriente province near the busy town of Holguín (pop. 102 000) where bananas, beans, maize and oranges are intensively cultivated. The metamorphic and igneous rocks in the hills west of Holguín and also near the provincial capital in the central region of the Camagüey plain contain rich deposits of chromiferous minerals which have been exploited for the last four decades.

Oriente

South of the hilly country of Holguín where the island narrows between the Gulf of Guacayanabo and the Bay of Nipe the **Cauto-Nipe-Plain** extends west–east across the island. It is crossed by the most important river in Cuba, the Río Cauto, 254 km in length, and its many tributaries. It rises in the Sierra Maestra and its course, with well-developed meanders, flows into the Gulf of Guacayanabo forming a vast mangrove delta. The Cauto plain rises slightly towards the east. Its watershed towards the Bay of Nipe lies near Alto Cedro. The Cauto and Nipe rivers, with their respective tributaries, have built the extensive plain. The cultural landscape is dominated by sugar cane and dairy farming. The sugar cane enterprises in the Cauto-Nipe-Plain are among the largest in Cuba: 27 per cent of the Cuban sugar produced is supplied by forty large estates in the Oriente province, of which the majority are situated in the Cauto-Nipe-Plain. As in the Camagüey plain, sugar cane cultivation developed mainly in the twentieth century and, as in the Camagüey plain, cultivation, until 1960, was controlled to a great extent by the USA. Employees of the United Fruit Co. or of the West Indian Sugar Company were able to travel from coast to coast over the Cauto-Nipe-Plain without leaving the land belonging to their respective companies. Extensive areas along the lower Cauto have recently been used for rice cultivation. The urban centre is the old town of Bayamo, a favourite place for many Cubans. During the first decades of Spanish colonial rule this town gained great wealth by trading illegally with ships of West European nations. Because of its many historic buildings it was declared a Monumento Nacional. In the Bay of Guacanayabo lies Manzanillo where the revolutionary government have built a shipyard and which has developed into an important fishing port.

East of the Cauto-Nipe-Plain and south of the Bay of Nipe rises the **Sierra de Nipe**, a serpentinite massif with altitudes of up to 1000 m. Extensive erosion surfaces occur within this Sierra and its lower parts are fringed with limestone. High-lying plains are covered by pine forests of *Pinus cubensis*. The Sierra de Nipe is of economic importance because of its rich ore deposits, mainly iron ore with nickel. This lateritic ore, in plateaux with a greatly decomposed serpentinite cover, was exploited by surface mining by US companies until 1960. Large mechanical loading installations in Felton were used to ship the iron ore to the USA, and the nickel ore was enriched in a modern dressing plant in Nicaro, an export port for ore, also on the Bay of Nipe. Modern American residential blocks of houses were built in both places.

Bordering the Sierra de Nipe on the east extends the **mountainous area of Baracoa** which, so far, has hardly been opened for traffic. Like the Sierra de Nipe and the Sierra Maestra this area belongs to the Cretaceous-Tertiary faultblock mountains of the Greater Antilles. Low amplitude relief at various altitudes indicates the recent uplift of these mountains. The coastline is bordered by a sequence of uplifted marine abrasion platforms. The fifth and highest platform lies near Cape Maisí at an altitude of 480 m. The western part of the mountainous area, the forest region of the Sierra del Cristal, is the only national park in Cuba and is up to 1143 m high. Near Sagua de Tánamo further to the east chromiferous minerals are mined. A nickel and cobalt dressing plant was built on the Moa Bay to process the lateritic ores from the Cuchillas de Toar (cf. p. 156) where they are deposited on serpentinite bedrock and can be mined on the surface. This dressing plant and those on the Nipe Bay, all of which were built by US companies and nationalized after the Revolution, were the first steps towards a heavy industry in Cuba.

The northern slopes of the mountain range face the trade winds and have a perhumid climate. The slopes are covered with tropical rain forests and, above those, with evergreen lower montane forests and with pine forests at the highest altitudes. Bananas, cocoa and mainly coffee are cultivated, especially in the fertile Toa valley in the hinterland of the town of Baracoa (pop. 13 000). Baracoa, founded in 1512, is the oldest Cuban settlement. It was originally intended to be the capital but its secluded position made this impossible. Until 1960 no road connections existed and it could be reached only by plane or boat. The south coast on the leeward side of the mountain range is covered by a narrow tract of thorn and succulent forest. Cacti and thorn scrub are characteristic scenery of this arid part of the country. At an altitude of about 500 m this definitely xerophytic type of vegetation changes into evergreen rain forest at the eastern end of Cuba near Cape Maisí.

Between the Sierra de Nipe and the mountainous area of Baracoa to the north and the Sierra Maestra to the south lies the **Valle Central**. It borders the Cauto-Nipe-Plain on the west and the Guantánamo Basin on the east. Extending west–east, this hilly area, which rises only to about

200 m, forms a structural depression partly filled with the detrital material from neighbouring mountains and partly with limestone bedrock in many other places. It is a wide structural basin between the northern and southern mountains. The Carretera Central and the railway from Bayamo in the Cauto plain follow the Valle Central and serve Palma Soriano (pop. 48 000), which lies at the centre of the valley's western region. Cultivation of coffee and cocoa mainly in the vicinity of Alto Songo and Palma Soriano, and of maize, tubers, oranges and also sugar cane indicate the diversified agricultural production in the Valle Central. It has additional wealth in its manganese ore deposits near El Cristo. During the Second World War these ores were heavily exploited by US companies.

The most distinct subregion of the Oriente is the **Sierra Maestra** bordered by longitudinal fault lines which are still active today. Its central core is formed of various volcanic rocks surrounded by a limestone belt. Being 250 km long and about 30 km wide, the Sierra Maestra extends from Cape Cruz in the west to the Guantánamo Basin in the east. It is divided into a larger western and a smaller eastern part by the Santiago Basin. Several parallel mountain ranges constitute this Sierra, e.g. the Cordillera del Turquino in the west reaching an altitude of 1972 m, and the Gran Piedra reaching 1250 m. Only the eastern region of the Sierra Maestra is easily accessible since the recent construction of a tourist centre very close to the huge boulder (Gran Piedra) containing volcanic breccia. It is served by an asphalt road. Short rivers, with many waterfalls and full of water, have cut deep transverse valleys into the range and destroyed, to a great extent, the subdued Tertiary relief at various altitudes. As is the case along the coastline of the mountainous area of Baracoa, the uplifted marine terraces along the southern foot of the Sierra Maestra indicate recent movements of the earth's crust. Copper, iron, manganese and chromiferous ore deposits are to be found in the Sierra Maestra.

A compact forest covers the steep Sierra Maestra slopes. The northern slopes are wet from the foothills upward because of their position facing the north-east trade winds; the southern slopes, however, are perhumid only at heights of 900 m and above. Accordingly, the vegetation on either side differs at various altitudes. Pines, mainly *Pinus occidentalis*, and juniper grow in the western Sierra Maestra from heights of 1300 m upwards. Dispersed along the sides of the wet northern slopes in edaphically dry areas are numerous small and secluded settlements. Coffee cultivation was much more intensive during the nineteenth century than it is today. In various places peasants have cleared the forests by burning. They cultivate mainly bananas and tropical tubers in small fields. The number of these *precaristas* (squatters) who settled on land not owned by them is very high. Within the framework of recent agrarian reform after the Revolution many of them received titles. The southern slopes and the arid coastal region have very few settlements. During the nineteenth century several coffee plantations, which were cultivated by French refugees from St Domingue, existed along the south side of the Gran Piedra at heights of 200 m and more. The revolutionary government rebuilt the living quarters and farm buildings of the former La Isabelica plantation as a museum. The steep slopes are being afforested to a large extent. In 1956 Fidel Castro landed on the lonely coast of the western Sierra Maestra south-west of Niquero. For two years he and his comrades used the inaccessible mountain forests of the Sierra Maestra as hiding-places from which he eventually succeeded in carrying through his revolution.

Between the Sierra Maestra to the west and the mountainous area of Baracoa to the east and extending to the south coast, lies the large Basin of Guantánamo representing the continuation of the Valle Central towards the east; 30 km to the west, surrounded by the Sierra Maestra, lies the smaller, semicircular Basin of Santiago de Cuba. The **Basins of Santiago and Guantánamo** are tectonic structural depressions. In the central region of each basin, the sea reaches far into the interior. Serious earthquakes have repeatedly caused heavy damage and, in Santiago, a large number of casualties. Both basins, on the leeward side of the mountains, have a semi-arid climate. Large quantities of salt can therefore be collected on the shores of Guantánamo Bay. The basins differ considerably regarding their cultural geography. The very dry part of the Bay of Guantánamo, near the coast, is still occupied by an important US naval base. Towards the interior, at the head of the bay, lies an intensively cultivated area with sugar cane in the basin (valle) and with coffee, cocoa and banana farms in the surrounding regions (monte). As in the other mountain areas of the Oriente, most of the coffee cultivations were established by French refugees from Haiti in the early nineteenth century. French influence is also to be traced in Guantánamo (pop. 102 000), a town in the centre of the basin a good distance from the bay. At the inland end of the other basin lies the former Cuban capital of Santiago de Cuba (pop. 248 000) sharing its name with the basin (Plate 5). It was founded in 1514 by Diego Velázquez. This rapidly growing town today occupies most of the hilly district in the interior of the basin and is the second largest city in Cuba next to Greater Habana. In spite of destruction by fire and especially by earthquakes (1776, 1852, 1932 and 1947), its centre, cut in terraces from the sea, has partly preserved its colonial appearance. Santiago has various functions. The town is a very active cultural centre; its university has expanded greatly in recent years; it is a tourist centre and the second commercial port in Cuba. In addition, it is growing in importance as an industrial city: there is an oil refinery and a new power station based on mineral oil, the Bacardí rum factory which has a long tradition, and the cement factory whose capacity has doubled during the last few years. Impressive new residential areas have been built recently, e.g. 'Nueva Vista Alegre'. Nowadays Santiago airport is only served by internal flights. As the terminal of the railway and the Carretera Central, Santiago has excellent connections with all regions in Cuba.

15

Cuba before the 1959 Revolution

Agriculture

Historical foundations

Initially the Spaniards introduced the encomienda system to Cuba; however, large and extensively cultivated livestock farms (*hatos* and *corrales*) developed after the middle of the sixteenth century. Extensive cattle farming remained the most important sector of the Cuban economy until the early nineteenth century.

When tobacco cultivation was started in the seventeenth century peasant smallholdings developed in the districts surrounding Habana, and especially near Pinar del Río and Santa Clara. But, because of the Spanish mercantile trade regulations, neither the cultivation of tobacco nor of sugar cane and coffee could develop successfully during the eighteenth century. Before the Spaniards the Amerindians had cultivated tobacco and used it for cigars. Thus the cigar originated in Cuba and from there it conquered the world, representing the contribution of the now extinct Cuban Amerindians to civilization. Tobacco farming increased rapidly only when the era of free trade began in 1818. The number of tobacco farmers in the Pinar del Río province rose from 4000 in 1811 to 9500 in 1859. Tobacco cultivation requires not only laborious cultivation in the fields, but after the harvest, very careful drying of the leaves which can only be shipped to the factories for processing after a complicated process of preparation. Because of the hard labour involved the relatively small areas under tobacco in various regions of the island remained the only districts in Cuba characterized by peasant smallholdings, not counting the small mountainous areas. On the other hand, the trend towards establishing large-scale enterprises became increasingly strong in the cultivation of sugar cane.

The immigration of French refugees from St Domingue in the early nineteenth century greatly stimulated the cultivation of coffee, mainly in the Oriente. In 1827 there existed 2067 coffee plantations, 1239 of them in the Oriente. These were large-scale enterprises employing Negro slaves.

As in the US cotton belt the abolition of slavery did not result in the disintegration of the large-scale landholdings. Instead, these large economic units were operated by numerous small tenant farms. For instance, the 1052 ha of the former coffee plantation El Infierno in the Sierra de Trinidad mountains were subdivided into thirty-two tenant farms in 1950. Thus, coffee farming in the Cuban mountains is mainly a small-farming economy. Its serious decline in the early twentieth century is explained by the simultaneous boom in the sugar industry. Many coffee plantations were replaced by extensive cane areas in the Oriente Valle Central and in numerous other districts. When the sugar industry experienced its various depressions these cane fields were replaced by the cultivation of fruit and vegetables. Coffee cultivation has never regained its former position.

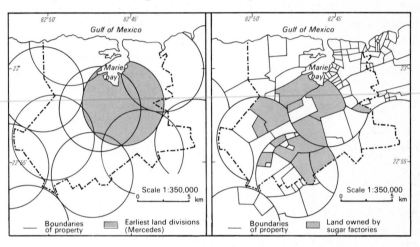

Map 28. Spanish land division and its influence on the field pattern in pre-revolutionary Cuba; Mariel, Province of Pinar del Río (after Platt).

The Spaniards introduced sugar cane to Cuba at the beginning of their colonial rule. Large-scale cultivation, however, did not develop before the nineteenth century, and Cuba only became the 'sugar island' in the twentieth century. The increase in sugar cultivation in the early nineteenth century had two causes: the 1804 slave rebellion in St Domingue led to the foundation of the independent Republic of Haiti and to the complete cessation of its supply of sugar to Europe, for which it had, until then, been the most important supplier; and final granting of free trade to Cuba in 1818 by the Madrid government. As in the Lesser Antilles and in St Domingue 100 to 150 years earlier, the establishment of the sugar cane plantation economy required an increased importation of Negro slaves causing a marked change in the racial structure of the population. Not less obvious were the changes in the landscape caused by the introduction of sugar cane cultivation. The old circular estates (*mercedes*) were now com-

147

munally owned (*haciendas comuneras*) as a result of inheritance, purchase, and other reasons. They were used exclusively for extensive livestock farming in their former size. The most important outcome of the introduction of sugar cane was the redistribution of the large *haciendas comuneras* (Map 28). This was because the size of the newly established sugar cane plantations, which both cultivated the cane and processed the sugar in their presses and boiling houses (*ingenio*), was limited by the necessity of transporting the cane and the wood required by the boiling houses to the factories in oxcarts. This shows that the latifundium does not characterize the first stage of the Cuban sugar industry. As late as 1880 the average size of sugar plantations in the Matanzas province was only 650 ha, and the area under cane averaged 311 ha. Latifundia developed only during the last thirty years of the nineteenth century and more strongly in the early twentieth century. Increasingly, the cultivation and processing of cane could only be done profitably by enterprises with sufficient financial resources to employ the improvements offered by technology. The construction of the field railway enabled plantations to allocate more extensive areas for cane cultivation, and soon only large and effective sugar factories with the most modern equipment proved able to survive the competition. Increasing numbers of the old *ingenios* were forced to give up sugar production. The number of sugar factories in Cuba decreased from 2000 to 200 between 1860 and 1890. Even before Cuba lost its colonial status the development of the latifundium within the sugar industry was accomplished, and also the separation of cultivation from processing. The large new companies produced sugar not only from cane cultivated by themselves, but also from cane supplied to them by independent planters and by tenant farms. Cane farmers became increasingly dependent on the factories. Independent planters and tenant farms (*colonos*) had no choice but to deliver the cane to the factories under conditions set by the latter. Many planters lost their independent status and became tenants. In addition, large-scale enterprises depended on a high number of factory labourers and seasonal workers. For many decades the latter were brought by car and railway from the towns to the cane fields during harvest time (*zafra*) and had practically no means of earning their living during the rest of the year.

Immediately after the end of colonial rule, and again at the time of the sugar boom during the First World War, American companies succeeded in acquiring vast stretches of land. By 1959 they possessed one million ha of sugar cane land and had invested several hundred million dollars in the sugar factories. Sugar cane cultivation was chiefly restricted to the districts surrounding Habana and the Llanura Roja in the Matanzas province until the end of the nineteenth century. Simultaneously with the developing rail network (Map 29) in the early twentieth century, and contrasting with the western provinces, the former pasture areas in the provinces of Las Villas and Camagüey and Oriente in particular became cane areas controlled to a great extent by American companies. When sugar cane mono-

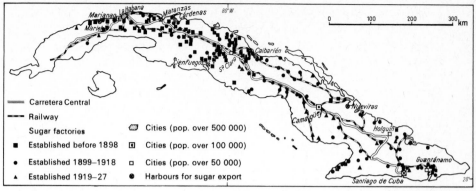

Map 29. Cuba: communications network and sugar factories.

culture spread over these districts, their scenery was changed decisively by ruthless deforestation and by the laying-out of cane fields. In addition many immigrants came from Spain and particularly from neighbouring islands because of the large labour requirements. Thus the rate of population increase was much higher here than in the western provinces. For instance, between 1900 and 1940 the increase in population was 405 per cent in the province of Camagüey and 253 per cent in the Oriente, but only 149 per cent in the provinces of Las Villas and Habana, 113 per cent in the Pinar del Río province, and not more than 84 per cent in Matanzas. In spite of this the eastern provinces still have a relatively small population. Another characteristic feature, after the expansion of cane into all areas suitable for economic production, was the trend towards concentration of ownership. As the cane area expanded, so did the number of sugar processing plants rise to 174, only to be reduced again to 161 by 1958. Until 1958 most of the sugar factories, representing modern mammoth concerns, were in the hands of companies with tenant farms cultivating a considerable part of their land.

One has to agree with the Cuban sociologist F. Ortiz who stated that the characteristic of Cuban economy and society was the dualism between sugar cane cultivation dominating most of the island in the form of large-scale enterprises, and tobacco cultivation restricted to small-scale farming areas. The unhealthy social structure, in addition to the one-sidedness and the foreign control of the Cuban economy, supplied the motives for the 1959 Revolution.

The distribution of real estate

Cuban agriculture before 1959, was dominated by large estates; 7·9 per cent of the farms, all of them of over 100 ha, occupied 71·1 per cent of the agricultural area, but 69·6 per cent of the farms cultivated only 11·2 per cent of the farmland.

149

Table 17.   Cuba: number of farms and agricultural area, according to farm size, 1945 (after *Censo Agrícola*)

Farm size ha	Agricultural area 1 000 ha	%	Number of farms 1 000	%
– 4·9	86·0	0·9	32·2	20·1
5– 9·9	210·7	2·3	30·3	19·0
10– 24·9	725·1	8·0	48·8	30·5
25– 49·9	789·7	8·7	23·9	15·0
50– 74·9	488·6	5·4	8·1	5·1
75– 99·9	329·7	3·6	3·9	2·4
100–499·9	2 193 6	24·1	10·4	6·5
> 500	4 253·6	47·0	2·3	1·4
Total	9 077·0	100·0	159·9	100·0

Large estates in Cuba were not usually managed as one unit, but were mostly divided into tenant farms of various sizes. This was the general practice with sugar cane and coffee cultivation.

Table 18.   Cuba: distribution of ownership in agriculture, 1945 (after *Censo Agrícola*)

	Agricultural area 1000 ha	%	Number of farms 1000 ha	%
Owner (*propietario*)	2 958·6	32·4	48·8	30·5
Administrator (*administrador*)	2 320·4	25·6	9·3	5·8
Tenant (*arrendatario*) with payment in money	2 713·9	30·0	46·0	28·8
Sub-tenant (*sub-arrendatario*) with payment in money	215·3	2·4	7·0	4·4
Tenant (*partidario*) with payment in kind	552·1	6·1	33·1	20·7
Squatter (*precarista*)	244·6	2·7	13·7	8·6
Others	72·1	0·8	2·0	1·2
Total	9 077·0	100·0	159·9	100·0

Table 18 shows that less than one-third of the agricultural enterprises and of the farmland was cultivated by independent farmers and that share-cropping was very common among smallholdings.

   In addition to the dominance of latifundia, the unhealthy agrarian social structure is expressed by the fact that among the 808 000 persons employed by agricultural enterprises in 1953, 70 per cent were landless farm labourers.

Production

Presentday Cuba is an agricultural state, as it was before the Revolution, and it has been dominated by sugar cane monoculture. In 1959 Cuba supplied 10·7 per cent of world sugar production and 64·5 per cent of Caribbean sugar production. The dominant position of sugar within the Cuban economy is also expressed by the fact that about 60 per cent of the farmland was under cane before the Revolution (Table 19) and that the share of sugar of Cuban exports was 80·1 per cent in 1958.

Table 19.   Cuba: distribution of farmland by crops, 1946 and 1955 (%)

	1946	1955
Sugar cane	56·0	61·0
Manioc	2·9	5·6
Other tropical tubers	4·4	5·4
Coffee	4·5	5·0
Fruit (inc. tomatoes)	4·5	5·0
Bananas	4·1	3·6
Maize	9·1	3·3
Rice	2·9	3·0
Beans	3·0	2·5
Tobacco	3·4	2·3
Vegetables	1·2	1·3
Others	4·0	2·0

Sources: After Canet (1946); White (1955).

In 1955 the farmland in Cuba totalled 9 million ha, i.e. 79·3 per cent of the entire island. Only the smaller part (25·5 per cent) was used for arable crops. Pastureland occupied 39·3 per cent and forests 14 per cent of the area. Taking into account the fact that extensive forest regions belonging to agricultural enterprises were used for cattle farming, one may assume that the area of pastureland amounted to twice as much as the area of arable cropland. But the value of cattle farming, including its various products, made up only half the value of the sugar crop in 1945 (Table 23). Nevertheless, cattle farming was second in importance in Cuban agriculture, though by a wide margin.

When new breeds of cattle were introduced, mainly Zebu and Santa Gertrudis, dairy farming gained in importance and the value of their production reached US $100 million by 1958. Before 1959, a typical latifundium raised cattle and cultivated sugar cane. Cattle farming was concentrated in the eastern provinces where pasturelands are still very extensive

Table 20.   Cuba: cattle farming, 1952

Province	Head of cattle	Number of farms with cattle
Camagüey	1 103 047	10 132
Oriente	971 602	24 827
Las Villas	970 400	25 424
Pinar del Río	407 097	9 530
Habana	303 638	11 285
Matanzas	277 901	8 736
Cuba	4 032 685	89 934

Source: After Núñez Jiménez (1959).

today (Table 20). In 1945 Camagüey province, which leads in dairy farming, had 48·1 per cent of its farmland in pasture and 16·4 per cent under arable. Several districts had extreme conditions, e.g. the Municipio Camagüey where pastures occupied 60·2 per cent, forests 8·8 per cent and arable land 9·6 per cent of the farmland. The production of meat and milk was the aim of cattle farming. The hides were supplied to the leather processing and shoe industries. An additional role was the supply of draught animals to the sugar cane enterprises.

Sugar cane clearly dominated the arable land (Table 19): 2·5 million ha of land, 27 per cent of the entire farmland, were in the possession of sugar companies by 1958. The twenty-eight largest companies had 2 million ha under cane (i.e. 83 per cent). Half this area and thirty-six sugar factories were in the hands of six companies. Among the eleven largest companies eight North American companies alone owned 1·1 million ha. The following changes regarding the number of sugar factories and the distribution of their ownership occurred between 1940 and 1958:

Table 21.   Cuba: sugar factories, 1940 and 1958

	Cuban	North American	Spanish	British	French	Dutch	Total
1940	55	77	33	4	3	2	174
1958	121	36	3	–	1	–	161

Accordingly, the US share in Cuban sugar production decreased from 55 per cent to 37 per cent in the same period. Sugar cane was cultivated throughout Cuba. Production was clearly centred on the eastern provinces where sugar cane cultivation did not develop until the twentieth century.

Table 22.   Cuba: sugar cane cultivation, 1958

Province	Number of sugar factories	Area controlled by sugar factories (ha)	Number of cane workers	utput (tonnes)
Pinar del Río	9	68 719	20 850	227 755
Habana	13	155 389	36 200	493 030
Matanzas	24	300 837	57 980	735 569
Las Villas	50	427 883	107 820	1 315 512
Camagüey	24	701 192	112 260	1 489 270
Oriente	41	816 441	136 310	1 519 437
Cuba	161	2 470 461	471 420	5 780 573

Source: After Núñez Jiménez (1959).

The Cuban sugar monoculture was able to survive for several decades only because of American subsidies. The USA paid a 2 cents per pound (lb) bonus for Cuban sugar. This subsidy was practically a gift for US citizens who were producing sugar in Cuba for export; they did not bring any advantages to the majority of the Cuban population. On the contrary, the Cuban sugar monoculture, aided by the influx of US capital and by US subsidies, was the cause of the very unbalanced structure of the island's economy with its many negative characteristics. The Cuban sugar monoculture left no room for the production of foodstuffs which consequently had to be bought and imported with the dollar profits gained from sugar exports. In addition, the Cuban economy was very dependent on the fluctuations in sugar prices on the world market. The unsound structure of rural society produced by cane monoculture is made obvious by the fact that about 3 per cent of the land owners controlled almost 60 per cent of the area under cane. Statistics record almost 500 000 employees in the sugar industry, but this figure should not obscure the fact that seasonal unemployment was the result of sugar monoculture in Cuba. The relatively short period of *zafra* (sugar cane harvest) alternated with a long dead season when a large part of the population had to live below minimum subsistence levels. Economic life in Cuba was determined by the cycle of the short period of bustling activity during harvest time, alternating with the long dead period during the growth and ripening of the cane.

Sugar production (Fig. 7) amounting to 0·2 million tonnes in 1850 totalled 1 million tonnes towards the end of colonial rule (1895). In the following years it rose rapidly and exceeded 3 million tonnes during the boom in the First World War, and 4 million tonnes in 1919. At that time Cuba supplied 25 per cent of the world's sugar. Following the boom which the Cuban sugar industry experienced during the First World War, the oversupply of the world market led to a sudden fall in price in 1920 with disastrous effects for

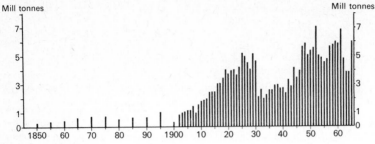

Fig. 7. Cuba: sugar production, 1850–1965.

the Cuban sugar producers: production fell drastically and exports were reduced considerably. This resulted in a further and decisive decrease in the spending power of the Cuban population. Cuban sugar production, however, experienced its greatest decline only during the international economic crisis when the USA reduced the import quota drastically and production fell to the level achieved before 1914. Less than 10 per cent of world sugar production was then supplied by Cuba, where production only regained its former volume during and especially after the Second World War. After the record-breaking crop of 7 million tonnes in 1952 production had to be curbed. Cuba's share of world sugar production, which amounted to 21 per cent immediately following the Second World War, has decreased continuously since.

Cuban sugar cane cultivation had to survive various economic crises, the first in 1920. These crises did not result in sugar monoculture being modified. After the Depression, however, the Cuban economy became slightly less dependent on sugar production insofar as sugar cane was joined

Table 23.   Cuba: agricultural products by value, 1945

	Number of farms	*Value of production US $*	%
Sugar cane	42 470	138 167 239	41·6
Beef and dairy farming	97 573	69 476 465	20·9
Tobacco	37 437	33 844 244	10·2
Grain and beans	111 875	31 159 678	9·4
Tubers	160 735	22 094 997	6·7
Vegetables	52 225	16 683 089	5·0
Coffee	18 165	8 989 154	2·7
Fruit	54 685	6 570 726	2·0
Others	16 994	4 899 650	1·5
			100·0

Source: After Núñez Jiménez (1959).

by several other export-orientated crops and locally required basic food-stuffs were produced in larger quantities.

Cuban crop cultivation has become more diversified since the 1920s. However, the three basic crops maize, rice and beans occupied an area amounting to only 21 per cent of the sugar cane area in 1958, and together with the area used for the cultivation of tropical tubers which are important in the local diet, occupied only 20 per cent of the entire arable land in 1955. Before the 1959 Revolution Cuba depended heavily on food imports. Nor had the new export crops, tomatoes, citrus, pineapples and henequén broken the dominance of sugar cane; in 1958 their value was US $14·6 million, i.e. only 5 per cent of the value of the sugar crop (US $280 million). Part of the fruit exported was canned and part fresh. On the eve of the Revolution, therefore, the predominance of sugar cane was slightly lessened but by no means broken.

Tobacco is the only cultivated plant in Cuba apart from sugar cane which has claimed an important share of the world market over a long period. The area under tobacco amounted to as little as 2·3 per cent of Cuban arable land before the Revolution, but its value totalled 6·8 per cent of Cuban exports in 1958. According to the 1946 Agricultural Census, 34 437 enter-prises cultivated tobacco but only 5000 did this exclusively. The majority of these so-called *vegas* were less than one caballería (13·4 ha) in size and were run on a family basis, sometimes with the help of a few additional labourers. The main areas of cultivation were the Vuelta Abajo in Pinar del Río pro-vince and the district of Remedios in Las Villas province. The districts of Semivuelta and Partido represented additional tobacco areas in western Cuba; the production in Oriente was comparatively low. In 1958 the area under tobacco and its yield which had shown a downward trend for a long time was distributed among the various regions as shown in Table 24.

Coffee represents the third traditional Cuban export crop. Among the 19 721 enterprises which were described as coffee farms in the 1946 Agri-

Table 24. Cuba: area under tobacco, and tobacco production, 1958

	Area under tobacco (ha)	Tobacco production (tonnes)
Vuelta Abajo	23 444	19 905
Semivuelta	4 036	2 143
Partido	1 266	675
Remedios	28 050	18 551
Oriente	863	828
Total	57 659	42 102

Source: After Núñez Jiménez (1959).

cultural Census only 9330 may be termed true coffee *fincas*. For many years, prior to the 1959 Revolution, coffee production did not meet the local demand. Cultivation was restricted to the Sierra Guaniguanico in the west, to the Sierras de Trinidad and de Sancti Spíritus in central Cuba and to the Oriente mountains including the Valle Central. The hilly and mountainous Oriente supplied 90 per cent of the Cuban coffee production. Between 1934 and 1938, the average crop was 31 000 tonnes, and was 34 000 tonnes in 1958; the area under coffee cultivation totalled about 134 000 ha, i.e. one-quarter the farmland claimed by the coffee fincas.

Mining

The colonial structure of prerevolutionary agriculture in Cuba was repeated in the island's mining industry. Cuba possesses a great wealth of mineral resources. Until 1959 exploitation was in the hands of US companies and the entire output was exported, almost exclusively to the USA. Annual production varied greatly according to the capacity of the North American market. Exceptionally high quantities of minerals were mined and exported during the two world wars and during the Korean war.

The value of nickel, copper, manganese, iron and chromiferous ore amounted to an annual average of US \$25·1 million between 1948 and 1957 (Table 25) and in 1958 its share of 3·8 per cent of Cuban exports was third by value, following sugar and tobacco. The export of nickel ore alone made up 2·7 per cent of Cuban exports (1958). In 1953, 6200 workers were employed by the mining industry, i.e. only 0·3 per cent of all employees.

Table 25.   Cuba: mining production, 1948–57

Ore	Output (tonnes)	Value (US \$ 1000)
Nickel	139 442	101 510
Copper	676 122	83 708
Manganese	1 816 641	46 858
Chromiferous ore	808 127	11 524
Iron	766 035	7 725
Total	4 206 367	251 325

The nickel ore deposits in the Sierra de Nipe and especially in the mountains of Baracoa, south of the Moa Bay, are among the richest in the world. The US-American Nicaro Nickel Company mined the lateritic iron ores in the Sierra de Nipe which contain nickel ore and enriched them for export to the USA in the Nicaro smelter built in 1942. On Moa Bay the US-American Freeport Sulphur Company started the construction of large smelting works in 1957 to extract nickel and cobalt from the lateritic minerals found in the mountains of Baracoa. Unlike nickel production, copper mining has a long tradition. All Cuban mountains contain copper deposits. The German Tetzel owned a copper mine near Cobre not far from Santiago in the Sierra Maestra; its main period of production was between 1550 and 1554. Before 1959 copper was only mined near Matahambra in Pinar del Río province and shipped from there to the USA. Manganese ores also exist in large quantities. They were mined at various places in the Valle Central and in the Sierra Maestra. Chromiferous minerals are connected with serpentinite rocks and mined chiefly near Camagüey and Holguín. The Cuban iron ore reserves, mainly the lateritic minerals in the Sierra de Nipe and the mountains of Baracoa, are estimated at 3·5 thousand million tonnes and are among the richest in the world. They were mined by the US-American Mayarí Mining Company which built efficient loading installations at Felton on the Nipe Bay from where the ore was shipped to the Bethlehem Steel Company in the USA. Cuba does not have any coal deposits, and the mineral oil resources in the provinces of Habana and Las Villas proved to be rather unproductive. Precious metals are also rare in Cuba. The Spanish conquistadores soon had to recognize the fact that the island did not offer the gold they had hoped to find. Small quantities of gold in placer deposits were mined for a few decades during early colonial rule, but the output has always been slight. Cuba's lack of precious metals turned Spanish interest away from the island and towards the mainland and is the reason for the very insignificant economic development of Cuba during the first period of colonialism.

Industry

Cuba experienced an upswing in industrial activity during the Depression and again during the 1950s, resulting in decreased dependence on imports and in the reduction of the seasonal unemployment suffered by a large proportion of the Cuban labour force. In 1958, 327 000 workers were employed in industry (Table 26), i.e. 15 per cent of all employees[1]. By 1950 industry supplied 48 per cent of the national income as against 31 per cent supplied by agriculture.

Food, beverages and tobacco

Before 1959 the food, beverages and tobacco industries led by a wide margin by value of production. The tobacco industry in particular has had a long tradition; cigars are still manufactured by hand in numerous small enterprises. The large cigar factories, where the firstrate Vuelta Abajo tobacco is processed, are situated in Habana. The high prices of the world-famous

---

[1] In 1958, all employees totalled 2·2 million. Among these 275 000 were unemployed, and 293 000 were employed in temporary or seasonal work.

Table 26.   Cuba: the industrial labour force by types of industry, 1958

Industry	Number of employees absolute	%
Sugar industry	80 000	24·4
Tobacco industry	45 000	13·8
Food industry	35 000	10·7
Mining and metallurgical industry	30 000	9·2
Textile industry	10 000	3·1
Garment and shoe industry	47 000	14·4
Other light industry	80 000	24·4
Total	327 000	100·0

Havana cigars, which result from the slow transition to mechanical processing, in addition to the general change in tobacco consumption seen in the preference for cigarettes, have seriously affected the Cuban cigar industry. The number of Cuban cigars exported fell from an annual 250 million in the early twentieth century to an average of 44 million between the years 1946 and 1957. On the other hand, the export value of raw tobacco rose. In 1958 it was three times as high as that of cigars and cigarettes taken together. Even in Cuban tobacco consumption the cigarette has surpassed the cigar. In 1958, about one-third of Cuban tobacco production was processed by fifteen cigarette factories employing 3000 workers. Nearly 23 million packets of American cigarettes were imported in 1958 in addition to a similar amount which is assumed to have entered Cuba illegally.

The sugar industry is the most important branch of Cuban export industry. About two-thirds of all industrial capital was invested here: US $ one thousand million. Until 1959 the cane was processed by 161 sugar factories which were not worked at full capacity. Only the smaller part of the raw sugar was refined. Refined sugar supplied only 12 per cent of the 1958 sugar export by value, molasses 6 per cent. Among the various by-products of the sugar industry bagasse, which is the waste from the crushing process, plays a major role. It was formerly used as fuel, more recently for paper production in Cuba and also for the production of synthetic materials outside Cuba. Bacardí rum, greatly appreciated around the world, originates in a Santiago de Cuba distillery. Before 1959 about fifty plants distilled alcohol from molasses for various industrial purposes as a byproduct of sugar production.

In addition to the sugar and tobacco industry, meat processing played an important role within the Cuban food industry before 1959. Following the Second World War numerous small and well-equipped enterprises, mainly in the cattle farming districts of the eastern provinces, were added to the large slaughterhouses in Habana and Camagüey and their modern cold storage plants. The newly developed dairy processing industry was also centred in eastern Cuba. A number of modern enterprises manufactured evaporated milk, butter and cheese. Nevertheless, the local demand could not be met.

Another young branch of Cuban industry is represented by more than 150 canning factories which handled tomatoes and pineapples, mainly for export before 1959. The large, port-orientated mill, built in 1952 in Regla near Habana, supplied 40 per cent of the Cuban flour demand, using imported grain. Before this Cuba had depended on flour imports because of the absence of flour mills. The demand for non-alcoholic drinks which is large in any warm country could be met locally even before 1959, and four recently built breweries were able to meet the greatly increased beer consumption.

Consumer goods

The production of cement is regarded as one of the most essential steps in the initial stages of industrializing an agricultural economy. The Portland cement factory built in Mariel in 1918, the only one of this type until 1955, was able to supply 70 per cent of the rising demand in Cuba. In order to satisfy the local demand which rose very steeply in the 1950s, to become independent of cement imports, and finally, to produce cement for export, two new factories were built in Santiago and in Artemisa (Pinar del Río province) after 1955. As a result, cement imports decreased drastically from 260 000 tonnes in 1955 to 22 000 tonnes in 1958. The establishment of a textile industry was another indication of the beginnings of industrialization. The Cuban textile industry is younger than cement production and originated during the Depression. Until 1927 all textiles had to be imported. Ninety very small spinning and weaving mills, most of them centred around Habana, were built by 1957 and employed 10 000 workers. A further 1000 enterprises connected with the garment industry, with 35 000 employees altogether, were scattered all over the island. The most important textile plant, the Ariguanabo cotton mill with 2500 employees, is located near Bauta, south-west of Habana. The port-orientated rayon factory in Matanzas is the second largest enterprise. US investments caused the rapid development of the textile industry which obtained nearly all the raw materials from the USA. It made textile imports largely unnecessary.

The tanning industry was also highly developed. It processed most of the 800 000 hides produced annually. About 90 per cent of the leather output was used by the 1600 enterprises of the footwear industry which met over 90 per cent of the Cuban demand, supplying more than 18 million pairs of shoes. The only imports were in the form of luxury footwear.

In spite of its mineral wealth Cuba's metallurgic industry was very poorly developed until 1959. Only small hardware articles, such as nails and screws, were manufactured and, after 1957, copper-wire. The sugar factories had their own machine shops. Larger enterprises of this kind built boilers, distilling apparatus and vacuum coppers for the sugar industry, e.g. in Sagua la Grande. The absence of metallurgical plants and a metal industry before 1959 is doubtless the result of the fact that cheap fuel and cheap electricity were available only in very small quantities. Almost the entire electrical supply depended on imported petroleum for fuel. In 1958, 1·5 thousand million kWh were produced, 90 per cent of which was supplied by a subsidiary of an American company.

Among the remaining branches of the consumer goods industry the furniture industry is important, represented by numerous small enterprises which used imported timber mainly but could not meet the local demand. The same applies to the paper industry, with three factories which only produced brown paper and which were totally dependent on imports. Paper production from bagasse did not begin until 1957. Neither could the rubber industry meet the local demand. All the raw materials required for the production of car tyres and other articles had to be imported.

The chemical industry, established with US capital and totally dependent on imports, is the newest of the consumer goods industries. It is as efficient as the sugar industry. Three large enterprises were able to satisfy the Cuban demand for fertilizers, and numerous small enterprises manufactured paint, soap, pharmaceutical and other products.

Before 1959 Cuba did not have a capital goods industry, barring the two petroleum refineries. Nevertheless, its industrial development compared favourably with that of other Caribbean and Central or South American territories. Even before 1947, national income per capita of the population amounted to US $341 in comparison with $25 in Haiti, $86 in the Dominican Republic, $123 in Jamaica and $269 in Puerto Rico (Denmark: $731; Switzerland: $870). In Cuba it had risen to $400 by 1958. It would be a mistake, however, to conclude from these figures that Cuba belongs to the richest nations of Latin America. The masses of the population, mainly in the rural districts, used to live in great poverty. The high national income is explained by the developing economy into which US companies invested more than US $1000 million. By 1958 US companies controlled about 50 per cent of the sugar industry, 90 per cent of the mines, 80 per cent of the power supply and the telephone system. The profits derived from the growing economy benefited the American entrepreneurs rather than the Cuban people. The former had invested more into Cuba than into any other Latin American territory. Cuban dependence on sugar exports and seasonal unemployment had been only slightly mitigated by industrial development after 1930. Like agriculture and mining therefore, Cuban pre-revolutionary industry also has to be termed colonial in its structure in spite of its expansion into the fields of foodstuffs and consumer goods and, not least, because of its very extensive foreign control.

Transport

Cuba possesses better transport facilities than any other Caribbean island excluding Puerto Rico. As early as 1837 a railway joined Habana with Bejucal. The eastern provinces, however, were connected to the older railway network in the west only when sugar cane cultivation developed during the twentieth century. By 1959 the Cuban railway network was 9600 km long, half of which belonged to the sugar companies. The public routes served mainly for transporting goods, 80 per cent of which were made up by sugar and sugar cane. Between 1945 and 1955 the number of passengers decreased from 15·8 million to 7 million. Car traffic played an increasingly important role as regards passenger transport. The number of motor vehicles rose from 42 000 in 1945 to 226 000 in 1955. Even before 1959 a network of bus routes covered the island, and large towns had modern bus terminals. Motor coaches offered frequent connections between such distant cities as Habana and Santiago. The arterial high-way was the Carretera Central completed in 1931 and was 1143 km long. It runs along the centre of the island from Pinar del Río to Santiago de Cuba. By 1959 the road network totalled 6000 km, 4000 km of which had an asphalt cover. On the other hand, some areas existed without any road connections: not only rather low potential districts such as the peninsulas of Guanahacabibes and Zapata, but also the coastal regions in Camagüey province as well as the Sierra Maestra and the mountains of Baracoa with its adjacent coastal strips. The busy air traffic operated by the Cubana de Aviación offered shorter travel times between the large regional centres in central and eastern Cuba and the capital, and it connected the districts not yet accessible by land transport with the remaining areas of the island. Characteristically, Oriente, where railway and road links were still very poorly developed in 1959, had more airports than any other province. In 1959, fourteen civil airports served internal air traffic in Cuba.

Most of the travellers to and from foreign countries came or went by air in 1959. Because of its geographical location, Cuba became a focus of international air traffic. There were excellent and frequent connections to North America, and good connections to the mainland of Middle and South America and Europe. The volume of air traffic through Habana international airport at Rancho Boyeros ranked second in the Caribbean, next only to San Juan in Puerto Rico. In 1959, 226 weekly scheduled flights offered 13 232 passenger seats. Proximity to the USA resulted in a large number of tourists. After 1945 an increasing percentage chose to travel to Habana by plane from Miami. Before the Second World War (1939) 63 000 tourists visited Cuba. Their number rose to 115 000 in 1946, to 187 000 in 1951, and 300 000 in 1958; 81 per cent reached the island by air. While Habana had supremacy in air traffic, this was not so as far as shipping traffic was concerned. Nevertheless, it handled 50 per cent of the transhipment of goods, 87 per cent of imports and 25 per cent of exports. Nuevitas exported most of the Cuban sugar. None of the ports along the Cuban coast which specialized in the export of either sugar or minerals had any major importance regarding imports. In spite of its extensive commercial exchange pre-revolutionary Cuba did not have its own merchant fleet. In 1954 only 40 000 gross registered tonnes were available for freight transport.

Foreign trade

Cuba's foreign trade before the Revolution had a credit balance most of the time. It mirrored the predominance of the sugar industry and the close interdependence with the USA. In 1958, sugar represented 80·1 per cent of the exports by value (Table 27). The United States received 66·9 per cent of all exports and supplied 69·8 per cent of all imports (Table 30).

Table 27.   Cuba: exports by commodities, 1958

	US $ million	%
Sugar	587·5	80·1
Tobacco	59·6	6·8
Ores	27·8	3·8
Others	69·2	9·3
Total	744·1	100·0

In accordance with its economic structure Cuba had to import mainly machines, food, and fuel (Table 28). Together they represented more than 50 per cent of the imports by value in 1958. Cuba had to import 30 per cent of its food requirements; 55 per cent of the rice and 75 per cent of the peas and beans consumed came from the USA.

The unbalanced interdependence of Cuban foreign trade with the USA was the outcome of the high value of US investments, mainly in the sugar industry. In addition, each country had preferential customs agreements

Table 28.   Cuba: imports by commodities, 1958

	US $ million	%
Machines	202·0	25·9
Food	112·2	14·4
Fuel	86·7	11·1
Iron and iron goods	73·6	9·4
Paper and timber	44·3	5·7
Textile raw materials and textiles	30·2	3·9
Oils and fats	28·9	3·8
Others	200·9	25·8
Total	778·8	100·0

between them after 1902. The USA bought the Cuban sugar for a higher price than was quoted on the world market; and Cuba allowed considerable reductions in duty on industrial goods imported from the USA.

Table 29.   Cuba: direction of foreign trade, 1859 (%)

	Exports	Imports
USA	42	28
Europe	51	63
Britain	25	19
Spain	12	28
France	8	9
Germany	6	4
Belgium	—	3

Table 30.   Cuba: direction of foreign trade, 1958

	Exports		Imports	
	US $ million	%	US $ million	%
North America	506·67	69·1	560·94	72·1
USA	490·70	66·9	542·86	69·8
Canada	15·97	2·2	18·08	2·3
Middle America	7·73	1·1	10·43	1·3
South America	6·25	0·9	70·78	9·1
Europe	114·01	15·6	107·86	13·8
EEC	34·97	4·8	60·73	7·8
EFTA	52·94	7·2	33·76	4·3
Other European countries	26·10	3·6	13·37	1·7
Communist E. European countries	15·26	2·1	1·97	0·3
Africa	12·18	1·7	0·13	0·0
Asia	51·19	7·0	17·40	2·2
Total	713·29	97·5	769·51	98·8

Source: Based on United Nations *Yearbook of International Trade Statistics.*

The role of the USA as a Cuban trading partner became increasingly important in the middle of the nineteenth century as an outcome of the effects of free trade, originally granted by Spain four decades earlier. This US participation in Cuban trade was mainly in the field of exports (Table 29). The extreme US dominance of Cuban exports, however, set in only after the Spanish-American War and the occupation of Cuba by the USA, when American investments climbed rapidly. Cuba obtained independence in 1902, but simultaneously it came under the exceptionally strong US influence which lasted until 1959 and which must be seen as the cause of the unhealthy structure of its economy.

16

Cuba after the Revolution

The 1959 Revolution affected all aspects of life in Cuba. Its aim was to change the agrarian social structure, to diversify agriculture, and to develop industry in order to raise the living standard of the population, to stabilize the economy, and to decrease the dependence on US capital. It is still very difficult to obtain an objective picture of the changes brought about by the Revolution. Nevertheless, it is possible to outline a few essential aspects of present-day Cuba which are relevant to geography.

Agriculture

Originally, the principal action of the Cuban Revolution was the law concerning agrarian reform which was drafted during the period of guerilla warfare and announced on 17 May 1959. This law provided for the following:

Any estate of more than 30 caballerías (402 ha) in size will be expropriated unless it is entirely cultivated in sugar cane or rice yielding a crop which exceeds the national average by at least 50 per cent, or is used as pasture land. In these cases the property may amount to 100 caballerías (1342 ha) if applied for. Foreigners are no longer permitted to own any landed property in Cuba. Each farm labourer has the right to claim a 'mínimo vital' of landed property (2 caballerías, 27 ha) which he will be provided with free of charge. This land may not be sold nor split up. Tenants who cultivate less than 5 caballerías will also be provided with 2 caballerías free of charge. They may acquire up to 5 caballerías (67 ha) of landed property but have to pay for the land which exceeds the mínimo vital. Any proprietor of a small or medium-sized farm of over 5 caballerías is entitled to acquire landed property up to a maximum size of 30 caballerías (402 ha). Large units of expropriated land will not necessarily be subdivided but may continue to be cultivated as units for economical reasons; however, they must be transformed into cooperatives.

165

By November 1960 a first reorganization of landed property had been accomplished, supervised by the powerful Instituto de la Reforma Agraria (INRA). During 1959 it expropriated 900 626 ha of lands cultivated by large-scale US enterprises, 349 076 ha of lands rented out by large-scale US enterprises, and 909 185 ha of large-scale Cuban enterprises. By 1960 31 425 farm labourers had received up to 27 ha of land. Almost 50 per cent of these new smallholdings (13 523) were established in Oriente. Modified in early 1961 this agrarian reform resulted in about 56 per cent of Cuban farmland being directly state-controlled. In 1961 a first consolidation was achieved before new changes were to take place. The newly established types of agricultural enterprises and their share of the Cuban farmland are listed in Table 31:

Table 31.   Cuba: farm types and their share of the farmland, 1961

Types of farm	Farmland (ha)	Share of the total farmland (%)
State farms (Granjas del Pueblo)	2 433 449	24·2
Sugar cane cooperatives (Cooperativas cañeras)	809 448	8·0
Small and medium-sized farms associated with the state-controlled Asociación de Agricultores Pequeños (ANAP)	2 416 000	24·0
Privately owned farms	4 409 193	43·8
Total	10 068 090	100·0

Most of the state farms established by 1961 were large-scale enterprises used for dairy farming and rice cultivation. Their average size was 9000 ha. Hardly any were less than 4000 ha in size, some were over 25 000 ha. In 1961 the state farms employed 96 498 labourers, 69 177 of whom were only seasonal workers. The former received $2.50 for a day (eight hours of work), the latter $3.00. The labourers did not share in the profits made by their enterprise. The central administration for all the 266 state farms was located in Habana, which, in addition to their excessive size, considerably reduced their profitability.

On the other hand the 622 sugar cane cooperatives were well organized and represented efficient large-scale enterprises each of which cultivated an area of between 1000 and 1500 ha. Their area included the most fertile regions in Cuba where the sugar factories had previously cultivated their own sugar cane (*caña de administración*). In 1961 these cooperatives employed 169 062 labourers, 46 614 of whom were only seasonal. In contrast

166

to the state farm labourers, the *cooperativistas* shared in the profits of their enterprises until 1962.

All the ANAP (*Asociación de Agricultores Pequeños*) enterprises, about 150 000 in number, were up to 67 ha (5 caballerías) in size. Sugar cane was cultivated on 40 000, tobacco and coffee each on 20 000. These enterprises participated in the steps taken by the government for the promotion of agricultural production. They received ANAP loans and various other forms of assistance, including the loan of machines.

In 1961 the only privately owned independent enterprises which remained were those between 67 and 402 ha (5 and 30 caballerías) in size. Anticipating a new wave of expropriation these enterprises were not interested in the necessary intensification of production. Most of them were between 70 and 150 ha in area. These medium-sized enterprises were in a much worse position than many of the smaller ANAP farms since only the latter benefited from the state assistance scheme. The cattle farms in particular, with sizes of 100–150 ha, could not compete with peasant smallholdings and their high yields in specialized crops like tobacco and coffee. A high percentage of the remaining privately owned farms were dairy farms. 77 per cent of the Cuban cattle was still in private hands by 1966).

Table 32.   Cuba: farmland by ownership, 1966 (after Núñez Jiménez, 1966).

	Total farmland (1000 ha)	(%)	Area under sugar cane (1000 ha)	(%)	Area under other crops (1000 ha)	(%)
Granjas Estatales	4379	57·9	1030	74·5	3349	54·2
Peasant farms	3178	42·1	353	25·5	2825	45·8
Total	7557	100·0	1383	100·0	6174	100·0

Source: After Núñez Jiménez (1966).

Further essential changes in the distribution of land ownership took place in 1963 and 1964. All farms of over 67 ha (5 caballerías) which were still privately owned were expropriated. Also the proprietors of farms of less than 67 ha are only entitled to the basic minimum 27 ha, free of charge. They have to pay for farmland which exceeds 27 ha. Tenants no longer exist since all tenant farms (more than 100 000) were transformed into independent peasant holdings. As a result of these measures Cuba has 156 217 independent farms united in the ANAP and 61 490 cooperative farms (1966). Their average size amounts to 14·6 ha.

The large-scale state agricultural enterprises were also reorganized in 1964. The distinction between *granjas del pueblo* and *cooperativas cañeras* no

167

longer exists. All agricultural large-scale enterprises are now called *granjas estatales*. There are 574 (1966) of these, with an average size of 7629 ha. They are subdivided into parcels (*lotes*) whose sizes vary according to respective farming conditions and usually do not exceed 35 caballerías (469 ha). Several *granjas estatales* are combined in *agrupaciones*. They are administered by the respective regional INRA which organizes production according to the Plan Nacional.

The steps taken in 1964 apparently indicate the end of the agrarian reform. The state now owns 57·9 per cent of Cuban farmland, and 42·1 per cent is directly controlled by the state through its influence on the ANAP and the cooperatives. The proportion of state-owned land is higher in sugar areas than in other branches of production (Table 32); 90 per cent of the tobacco, coffee and cocoa is produced on peasant farms.

The aim of the Cuban agrarian reform to establish an independent peasantry has been achieved to a large extent. The number of peasant farms of up to 67 ha has been increased from 143 300 to 217 700. Their total area rose from 2 300 000 ha to 3 178 000 ha, and their share of the farmland which had decreased by 1·5 million ha since 1945 climbed from 25·3 per cent to 42·1 per cent. In addition, their position was changed by the fact that they are not primarily cultivated by tenants but are all, without exception, owned by the peasants. Before the Revolution, enterprises of over 100 ha, i.e. the large scale properties, made up 71·1 per cent of the farmland; today the share of the *granjas estatales* has decreased to 57·9 per cent.

The Cuban government set up an enormous bureaucratic machine with headquarters in Habana to administer its huge estates. This, as well as the excessive size of the *granjas estatales* designed after the Soviet pattern (Sowchoses), probably represents an obstacle to profitable farming. The original intention to subdivide the large-scale enterprises into peasant holdings has been abandoned for the time being, apparently for economic

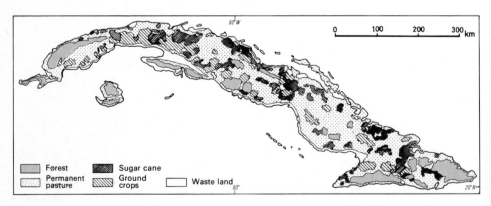

Map 30. Cuba: land use, 1964 (adapted from Núñez Jiménez).

reasons. The majority of the farm labourers have remained wage labourers; their legal and financial status, however, has improved.

The appearance of the agricultural landscape (Map 30) has been relatively untouched by agrarian reform. The vast and uniformly cultivated fields found today on the *granjas estatales* used also to characterize the field pattern of the Cuban sugar cane and cattle farming latifundia of the past. Now, as before, the difference remains between economic arrangements which are either characterized by large-scale enterprises or by peasant smallholdings. The area occupied by the latter group has expanded since agrarian reform. New features in the appearance of the agricultural landscape are the modern administrative buildings, the machine shops, and the storehouses built on many state farms and, in addition, the modern living quarters erected in some places for the labourers. The revolutionary government has greatly encouraged building activity in rural areas. At least 12 000 homes for workers were built during 1960. The new and rather attractive houses have often replaced shabby huts and they usually have running water, a lavatory, and electricity. Unemployment in rural areas, formerly rather widespread, has been abolished. In addition to rural cultural centres and so-called people's groceries many schools have been built. The new Cuba is anxious to reduce the number of illiterates. Before 1959, 43 per cent of the rural population had never attended a school.

In addition to achieving agrarian reform the Revolution made great efforts to diversify agricultural production. The data in Table 33 showing changes in the cultivated area and yields during the first three years after the Revolution indicate this effort. The yields actually obtained, however, deviate considerably from the data shown in Table 33; nevertheless, the latter indicate at least the objectives aimed at by the planned economy. After the Revolution special importance was attached to increasing the cultivation of food crops and of some valuable industrial crops in order to reduce the dependence on imports. This applied to rice, maize, and beans as well as to cotton and kenaf. These fibrous plants were not cultivated before 1958. Kenaf covered an area of 3600 ha in 1961, and cotton 28 246 ha in 1962. (Núñez Jiménez, 1966). In order to achieve diversification in agriculture large areas formerly under cane were used for other crops. Since 1964, however, all these areas have been put back to sugar cane. Starting in 1964 the cultivation of sugar cane has been given priority, and the original aim of diversifying the agricultural sector of the economy has been dropped.

Following nationalization the sugar produced by the first *zafra del pueblo* (national harvest) reached the record-breaking yield of 6·8 million tonnes in 1961. The following year, sugar production dropped rapidly (4·8 million tonnes in 1962; 3·8 million tonnes in 1963) for various reasons: endeavours to diversify agriculture; difficulties in selling the crop after the USA ceased to import Cuban sugar; and unfavourable climatic conditions (drought in 1962 and hurricane in 1963). Cuba could not even supply

169

Table 33.   Cuba: changes in cultivated area and yields, 1958–61

Crop		Area under cultivation (ha)	Yield (1000 kg)	Value (US $1000)
Sugar cane	1958	1 414 826	4235	266 020
	1961	1 273 000	5000	310 500
Tobacco	1958	57 620	903	45 150
	1961	72 615	1301	65 050
Coffee	1958	133 665	675	29 518
	1961	133 665	1125	49 196
Rice	1958	109 679	4502	34 466
	1961	212 417	9511	77 039
Maize	1958	167 500	3220	9 660
	1961	332 615	8688	26 064
Millet	1958	11 390	298	820
	1961	133 343	4030	11 082
Beans	1958	16 375	220	2 933
	1961	156 110	2446	32 605
Peanuts	1958	4 020	82	344
	1961	37 359	976	6 100
Soya bean	1958	268	6	24
	1961	14 150	370	1 572
Tomatoes	1958	2 680	1200	5 400
	1961	6 955	3374	11 303
Pineapple	1958	4 690	886	888
	1961	15 129	1860	1 646
Cotton	1958	134	4	37
	1961	40 776	1172	12 072
Henequén	1958	10 050	198	1 089
	1961	13 387	270	2 430
Kenaf	1958	—	—	—
	1961	3 082	230	2 300

Source: After Núñez Jiménez (1961).

sugar to the Communist East European countries in the quantities stipulated. After this, sugar production was again given priority within the Cuban economy, since it supplied most of the foreign exchange required to import industrial goods. The area under sugar cane was expanded to such an extent that sugar production leaped from 4·3 million tonnes in 1964 to 6·1 million tonnes in 1965. Plans provide for a yield of 10 million tonnes in 1970. The result is that sugar again dominates agricultural production completely, even more so than before the Revolution; it has assumed proportions which were experienced only during the sugar booms after the two world wars.

Even during the years of increased food production the daily food supply to the public had to be rationed. Food imports were reduced, as the foreign exchange obtained from exporting sugar had to be used to import machines, most of which were required to mechanize agriculture. Spare parts for American mechanical equipment, formerly the only machinery used, were no longer available because of the US boycott. Machinery had therefore to be replaced to a great extent, and after 1960 eight sugar factories had to terminate operation. Today (1966) they number 153. Within a three-year period US $80 million were spent on agricultural machinery; e.g. 23 094 tractors were imported between 1960 and 1965. Food production was also insufficient because of increased wages and the resulting higher demand. Finally, the desired rise in agricultural production was not achieved because of poor planning, because specialists were lacking, and because of too frequent improvizations without sufficient expert knowledge. Continuous changes in the distribution of land also obstructed an increase in production.

However, noticeable improvements have been made in supplying the population with agricultural produce, especially with meat and dairy produce. After the Revolution the cattle population was reduced by a third. By 1966 it had risen again to 6 million head of cattle because meat rationing was introduced, centres for artificial insemination had been established, and cattle were imported, e.g. 12 000 Holstein cattle from Europe and Canada. Since pastureland with poor soils cannot be improved by using Pangola grass dairy cattle and stock for fattening are fed with grain. Beef farms of this type have modern installations and are run in accordance with the latest scientific mothods, e.g. model farms like the Granja América Socialista near Santiago. Poultry farming is also run by successful modern enterprises. Between 1962 and 1965, egg production is said to have risen from 174 million to 919 million eggs per annum.

The Revolutionary government has tried to raise both agricultural productivity and the living standards of the rural population, by building agricultural experimental stations, pest control, improvement of seeds and better marketing of agricultural products. In addition, there have been improvements in schooling and social welfare work in rural areas.

Forestry and fishing

The expansion of the sugar industry had greatly reduced the forest area. Before 1959, 11 per cent of Cuba was covered by forests, all in private hands with the exception of 100 000 ha in the mountains of Baracoa. Since then the forests have passed into state owneship. An extensive afforestation programme was started in 1959. At first only the fast growing eucalyptus

(*Eucalyptus saligna*) was planted (12 000 ha in 1960), mainly in the former pine forest areas in Pinar del Río province. Various other types were added later, including *Pinus caribaea* and *Pinus cubensis*, mahogany, teak, and the *Cedrela odorata*, a deciduous tree supplying the 'cedar timber' used for cigar cases. Between 1959 and 1965, 293 million trees were planted on a total area of 145 000 ha. The former coffee plantation areas in the eastern Sierra Maestra have been the main areas reafforested.

As with forestry, and in spite of favourable conditions, fishing only developed slowly in pre-revolutionary Cuba. Fresh and canned fish had to be imported. Between 1935 and 1955, only 4500 to 9200 tonnes of fish were caught each year. After 1959 the fishermen were organized in a cooperative. Ports were dredged, a fishery school was established, nearly 200 fishing boats were built in small shipyards, and two larger fishing vessels were bought from Poland. The new fishing port of Manzanillo developed in Oriente. By 1963, 35 000 tonnes of fish were caught, the largest quantity ever. In 1963 the Soviet Union agreed to build a new harbour in Habana. It has since been completed and also serves as the base for the Russian trawlers in the Atlantic.

Industry

The problems in industry proved to be as difficult after 1959 as they were in agriculture. Industrial plants were nationalized in 1960. First the problem of spare parts emerged as a handicap, then the shortage of specialists, of raw materials and of power supplies. Thus the ambitious government industrialization programme was doomed to failure. Late in 1963 the Cuban government announced that priority was to be placed on sugar production and cattle farming within the Cuban economy for at least ten more years. Until then an attempt had been made to expand the industrial basis which had developed before the Revolution, mainly during the 1950s (cf. p. 157 f).

All the Communist East European countries have entered into agreements with Cuba according to which they not only supply food and consumer goods, chemicals, vehicles, machines and other goods, but also complete factories. Cuba supplies sugar, tobacco, fruit, tinned foods, hides and minerals in return. East European countries had built up to twenty-three factories by 1963, comprising petroleum refineries, iron works, power plants, machine and tractor works, assembly plants for trucks, paper, chemical and pharmaceutical plants, flour mills, cement, munitions, shoe and tyre factories, a radio assembly plant, factories for electrical appliances, and many more. In addition, these communist countries provide economic aid by sending hundreds of specialists to Cuba and by training thousands of Cubans.

Especially impressive industrial plants are the textile plant Alquitex in Alquizar south-west of Habana, the factory for machines and electrical appliances in Santa Clara, the chemical factories in Santa Lucía (Pinar del Río) and Matanzas, the pharmaceutical plant and the synthetic fibre and glass works in Habana, and the iron works in Cotorro (Habana) which produced 285 000 tonnes between 1962 and 1965, the gasworks in Marianao, various refineries processing mineral oil imported from the Soviet Union, and the power plant based on mineral oil. The latter raised the electricity supply to 3500 million kWh in 1965.

Plans, disclosed after the Revolution, to establish a metallurgical industry in Habana, on the Nipe Bay and in Santiago had to be abandoned when priority was given to the sugar industry and its dependent industries late in 1963. In view of the poorly developed resources for power supply and the necessarily high capital investment (see Bleckert) the construction of a Cuban metallurgical industry seems less favourable than the importing of metallurgical end-products from the industrial nations in Eastern Europe. To make these imports feasible Cuba had to expand its sugar industry greatly in the unbalanced structure mentioned above (cf. p. 169 f). As happened before the Revolution the rich mineral deposits in Cuba are being exploited at the moment mainly with the aim of exporting the minerals or the high-value concentrates. In 1961 Soviet engineers advised the temporary closure of the large American nickel smelting works on the Moa Bay. After experiments with Cuban nickel minerals had been conducted in the Klement Gottwald iron works in Mährisch Ostrau-Witkowitz (Czechoslovakia) and in Leningrad (Soviet Union) the reconstructed nickel and cobalt smelting works in Moa resumed operation in 1965.

Since the redefinition of Cuban economic priorities in 1963 the main industries to have been developed are those which process agricultural products. In addition to textile and shoe manufacturing plants which do not yet satisfy the local market, resulting in the rationing of textiles and shoes, new canning factories for meat, milk, fish and fruit were built which also produce for export. The same degree of importance is attributed to the manufacture of agricultural machines. The output of fertilizers was raised from one million tonnes between 1954 and 1958 to 2·5 million tonnes between 1961 and 1965. Special attention, however, is given to the development of the branches of the sugar industry. A large factory in Cárdenas manufactures paper from the waste materials left after the cane has been crushed. Large quantities of synthetic materials and fibres will probably also be manufactured from bagasse in the future. Cement production has also been increased considerably. Between 1961 and 1965, 4·1 million tonnes of cement were produced as against only 2·9 million tonnes between 1954 and 1958. Rural as well as urban areas have displayed intense building activity since the Revolution. For instance, the satellite city of Habana del Este has been built at high cost and includes multistorey apartment blocks amidst parks together with several kindergartens, schools, swimming pools, shopping centres and laundries. In large cities the slums have been cleared.

In contrast to Habana, a new suburb in Santiago de Cuba is made up of only single-family houses, in addition to a shopping centre, a school, a library and a stadium. It is for the labour force of the industrial plants in the neighbourhood which have been planned or recently built.

Foreign tourists, who had brought important foreign exchange, stopped visiting Cuba soon after the Revolution, and so local tourists have had to be encouraged instead. Various *centros turísticos* have been built at high cost, e.g. near Habana, and *playas populares* (public beaches) have been developed in various coastal regions, e.g. near Guardalabarca in Oriente province. Small bungalows have been built, also large tenement houses in Veradero, in addition to changing rooms and lounges, showers, and modern shops. Today (1966) Cuba possesses forty of these *playas populares* controlled by the national tourist board INIT. Between May and August 1965 they were visited by 2 495 332 persons.

In spite of the Communist aid programme and the many efforts in the industrial sector, consumer goods of any kind are very rare in Cuba, and the development of a productive processing industry is still a long way off. The very ambitious industrial development programme asked too much from Cuba which has always been an agricultural state; agricultural production experienced a crisis because of the necessary changes; and Cuba's financial status is also in a precarious situation because of the building up of an efficient army and the distribution of arms among the population.

Transport and foreign trade

The railway network developed before the Revolution is quite adequate for the present requirements of the Cuban economy. The gap in the road system which existed in Oriente province before 1959, is being filled at the moment by the Revolutionary Government. For instance, Baracoa has been connected by road with Guantánamo and Mayarí, and a road leading along the south coast from Santiago to Manzanillo via Niquero has been partly completed. A relatively dense network of air routes provided by Cubana de Aviación covers the island. Habana possesses the only international airport, but its former importance as an international air traffic centre has been lost. Cuba is the only one of the Caribbean islands which does not have any transport links with its neighbours; in addition, it is the only one where both air and shipping traffic flows are of greater volume to Europe than to the American mainland. Three regular airlines connect Habana with the European capitals, Madrid, Moscow and Prague; but only one connection exists to the American mainland, to Mexico.

Cuban ports have not changed their function because of the Revolution. Habana is the leading importing harbour where the 2·3 million tonnes of imports (1963) exceeds by seventeen times the 183 000 tonnes exported. In Santiago imports (293 000 tonnes) and exports (218 000 tonnes) almost balance each other. All the remaining ports are export harbours mainly exporting sugar. Sugar has made up 85 per cent of Cuban exports since 1961, which is more than before the Revolution. Thus Cuba's dependence on sugar exports has assumed proportions which only existed previously for a few years following the two world wars. Since 1959 the direction of foreign trade has completely changed, for political reasons. Cuban exports to Communist countries amounted to 24 per cent in 1960, but to 82 per cent by 1962; the import figures are 19 per cent and 83 per cent respectively. In 1962, 82 per cent of the Cuban foreign trade was with East European block countries; it had dropped to 70 per cent by 1964. The volume of foreign trade has risen considerably since the Revolution; however, the balance of trade is becoming increasingly unfavourable (Table 34).

Table 34.   Cuba: foreign trade, 1960–68

	1960	1961	1962	1963	1964	1966	1968
(a) Volume of foreign trade (US $1000)							
Exports	618 200	624 900	520 600	542 900	713 400	592 500	—
Imports	637 900	707 600	759 200	866 200	1 019 600	925 500	—
(b) Direction of foreign trade (%)							
Exports							
Communist E. European countries	24·2	73·3	82·0	67·4	59·2	81·4	74·7
Other countries	75·8	26·7	18·0	32·6	40·8	18·6	25·3
Imports							
Communist E. European countries	18·7	70·0	82·8	81·1	77·5	79·8	80·3
Other countries	81·3	30·0	17·2	18·9	22·5	20·2	19·7

17

Jamaica

From 1958 to 1961 Jamaica belonged to the shortlived West Indies Federation which included most of the British Caribbean island colonies. After the collapse of this Federation, caused by the withdrawal of Jamaica and Trinidad, Jamaica became an independent nation in 1962.

The island developed into a wealthy plantation colony soon after the British occupied this former Spanish colony in 1655. Until the early nineteenth century Jamaica was the most economically valuable of the British possessions in the Caribbean. The abolition of slavery in 1838 and the perpetual crises in the sugar industry during the nineteenth century led to far reaching changes in the social structure and the agricultural economy. Recent developments, especially in mining and industry, are equally important. Modern Jamaica, still associated by Europeans mainly with rum and bananas, has in fact a diversified economy and a varied land use pattern. The modern patterns no longer resemble those of the former British colony with its undiversified agricultural economy.

Physical geography

Jamaica, with an area of 11 424 sq km, is only one-tenth the size of Cuba, extending for 240 km from west to east with a maximum width of 80 km. About 150 km to the north lies Cuba, separated from Jamaica by the Cayman Trench with depths of over 7000 m; the Jamaica Channel, which reaches depths of more than 2000 m, separates it from the south-western tip of Hispaniola, almost 190 km to the east. The sea is relatively shallow only to the south of Jamaica. The Pedro Banks, constituting one part of the submarine Nicaragua Ridge, lie 70 km to the south-west. The eastern part of the island's south coast is fringed by a submarine coral limestone plateau which descends to depths of up to 40 m and on which Port Royal, the Portland Bight Cays, and many small coral sand islands have been built. Newly built coral barrier reefs are only found along this part of the Jamaican coast, contrasting with the many coral fringing reefs found elsewhere.

A flat alluvial coastal plain surrounds the island; it is only a narrow strip in the north, but is more extensive in some places along the south coast (Map 31). The rest of Jamaica is mountainous. The highest elevations are found in the eastern mountain complex, the highest point being the Blue Mountain Peak (2257 m). The mountainous interior of the island is of a rather varied nature in its geology and morphology. Almost two-thirds of the island consists of Eocene and Miocene white limestone plateaux which are over 500 m high and whose karst topography includes extensive pockets of bauxite soils (Plate 9). These limestone plateaux have an undulating or hilly relief where various types of dinaric karst features have developed, separated by numerous and sometimes quite extensive flat areas interpreted as poljes or karst plains.

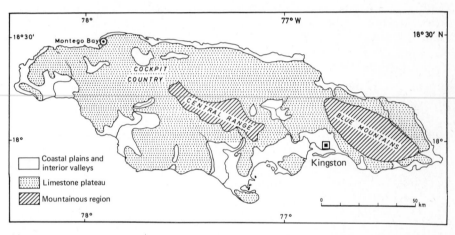

Map 31. Jamaica: regional divisions.

Among the dinaric karst landscapes one area, the Cockpit Country to the south-east of Montego Bay, is outstanding for its abundance of different forms. It is an area of tropical cone karst (*Kegelkarst*) with mostly circular and often bizarrely shaped limestone cones or haystack hills with steep slopes. They are interspersed with caves and with small, deeply imbedded, irregular but distinct hollows (*Hohlformen*) whose Jamaican name, Cockpit, is now familiar geomorphological nomenclature. In various parts of Jamaica, usually along north-west to south-east axes, the older and folded rock strata appear at the surface as a result of the uplift and warping of the white limestone formation. The main examples of this are the Central Range in the interior of the island and the lofty ridges of the Blue Mountains. These mountain ranges have a quite different relief from that of the limestone plateaux because of gully development which does not occur at all in the limestone areas where the drainage is subterranean. The erosion of the higher and very humid Blue Mountains has been so great that it is almost impossible to reconstruct former peneplains from the evidence of the very few remaining undissected erosion surfaces.

In Jamaica each physiographic region not only has different farming systems, but also varying sizes of land holdings in different regions. The pattern is like all the other islands of the Antilles with a mountainous topography: large-scale enterprises dominate the Jamaican plains and small-scale enterprises dominate the mountainous interior. This pattern, however, is now being modified.

The physiographic regions are further differentiated by climatic conditions. The contrast between the windward and leeward sides is striking and is most evident in the daily weather patterns on either side of the Blue Mountain ridge. Port Antonio on the north coast receives 3327 mm of annual rainfall, Kingston on the south coast only 762 mm. Profitable use of the southern coastal regions is not possible, therefore, without irrigation. Their location in the rainshadow of the Blue Mountains also shields them from the regular flow of the trade winds; land and sea breezes alternate rhythmically instead. The smoke from the Kingston Cement Factory shifts daily at almost the same hour in the morning when the land breeze is superseded by the sea breeze which is believed to be healthy and is therefore known locally as the 'doctor'.

Extremely heavy rainfall caused by 'northers' (cold air waves during winter) and particularly by hurricanes, cause serious landslips and landslides in the Blue Mountains. These can be disastrous where the forests have been destroyed by peasant farming systems. More serious landslides are caused by earthquakes.

In each of the different climatic regions of the island (perarid to perhumid) the flora takes a different form. Cactus savannas and dry woodland with various dyewoods (e.g. *Haematoxylon campechianum*) in the most arid part of the coastal regions in the south, together with the tropical evergreen rain forests and elfin woodlands in the Blue Mountains and the semi-evergreen seasonal and tropical deciduous forests of the Cockpit Country, can still be considered as primary cover, at least in parts. In vast areas the original forests were removed early. On the extensive white limestone plateaux they were replaced by grassland with its characteristic trees: the shady silk-cotton tree (*Ceiba pentandra*), the guango tree (*Samanea saman*), and the pimento tree (*Pimento officinalis*).

Population and settlement

Of all the states of the Greater Antilles only Puerto Rico has greater overpopulation than Jamaica, which has a population of 1·6 million (1960)[1] and a population density of 143 per sq km. The birth rate was 41 per thousand and the death rate 9 per thousand in 1962 and the population has grown rapidly, increasing by some 30 per cent between 1943 and 1960. The

---

[1] An estimated 1·972 million in 1969.

problem of overpopulation is serious in spite of a high emigration rate both past and present. At the beginning of this century thousands of Jamaicans found work in the building of the Panama Canal, and they emigrated in great numbers to the eastern coastal regions of Central America to find jobs in the newly started banana plantations and in the construction of the railways. Thousands worked on the Cuban sugar plantations and also emigrated to the USA. Between 1881 and 1921, 146 000 Jamaicans are said to have emigrated, though it is not known whether it was a permanent or only a temporary migration (Roberts, 1957). Mass emigration started again during the decade following the Second World War. Between 1953 and 1962 around 175 000 Jamaicans, more than 10 per cent of the whole population, went to Great Britain. Up to 1962 only 12 000 had returned; 1962 saw the climax of this mass emigration with 39 000 emigrants to Great Britain. The remittances sent back by the emigrants to families in Jamaica (1961 more than 60 million DM) must not be underestimated as an invisible export. In 1963 the British government curbed immigration to Great Britain drastically (in 1965 around 200 000 Jamaicans were living there), and immigration practically ceased after 1965. The possibilities of a higher emigration rate to the USA and to Canada are now the only possible outlet for Jamaica's population.

Negroes dominate the Jamaican population (76·1 per cent in 1960). Mulattoes (16·8 per cent), Asian Indians (1·8 per cent), whites (0·8 per cent), and Chinese (0·7 per cent) are small minorities. The Negroes are the descendants of slaves first brought into the country by the Spaniards and then by the English to work on the plantations. The Asian Indians, most of whom are now small farmers, came to the island as indentured labourers. The Chinese entered even more recently and work chiefly in the retail and laundry business. The most recent group of immigrants are the Lebanese who came after the First World War and who are successful businessmen.

The Amerindian population of Jamaica were Tainos, that is island Arawaks as in the other Greater Antilles, and probably numbered 40 000–60 000, but were decimated under Spanish rule. At the end of Spanish rule the island had a population of about 3000, half of it white, the other half Negro. During English colonization the population grew with economic development, and by 1788 the island had 23 000 white inhabitants and 260 000 Negroes. Among the Greater Antilles, the history of the Jamaican population finds its counterpart only in the Republic of Haiti which as a plantation colony under French rule in the eighteenth century also experienced the annual importation of a great many slaves because of the development of cane farming. The fact that Jamaica has a Negro population is therefore explained by economic developments during the eighteenth century; and the fact that, in contrast to Haiti, Asian Indians and Chinese settled in Jamaica is the result of the continuation of colonial rule in the nineteenth century when indentured labourers from Asia were brought in to remedy the crisis which evolved as a result of the abolition of slavery.

179

The present high rate of population mobility which is seen in the large numbers of emigrants is also seen within Jamaica itself. After the abolition of slavery in the nineteenth century the Negroes moved from the coastal plantation regions into the interior in order to settle as free peasants, but today there is a noticeable movement from these small farm regions to the cities on the coast, particularly to Kingston, the capital of the island, which attracts people like a magnet. The proportion of the urban population has risen from 19 per cent in 1943 to 31 per cent in 1960, but Kingston's share of the island's urban population declined from 85 per cent in 1943 to 80 per cent in 1960, because of the growth of three other cities with more than 10 000 inhabitants each. In spite of this Kingston far surpasses all the other cities (Table 35). Fourteen settlements have between 1000 and 10 000 inhabitants, though this does not necessarily imply an urban character.

Table 35.   Jamaica: towns with a population of over 10 000

	Population	
	1943	*1960*
Kingston	201 900	376 520
Montego Bay	11 500	23 610
Spanish Town	12 000	14 706
May Pen	6 000	14 085

The effects of relief and soil are clearly visible in the distribution of the rural population. The coastal plains and the basins of the limestone plateaux are thickly inhabited, as are the valleys of the Central Range and of the Blue Mountains, but considerable areas of the limestone plateaux themselves are sparsely populated. The rural settlements may be classified as those which are situated within the plantation areas and those associated with small-scale farming. In the coastal regions numerous magnificent plantation houses (some of which are more than 200 years old) are reminders of the heyday of the plantation economy. Nucleated villages have always been characteristic of this type of agricultural system which, until the nineteenth century, included all the arable land in the island, declining only after 1838 because of the growth of peasant farming. In the regions of small-scale farming the village type of settlement also dominates, but instead of nucleated villages two types of rather loose settlement are found: the linear village along the roads, founded by Christian denominations, and the dispersed and formless village which has grown more or less by chance. For the last few years the government has been favouring the dispersed type of settlement in its settlement plans for the lands of former large landholdings. Settlers are urged to build their dwellings on their holdings. Because of the smallness of these holdings the buildings, although dispersed, are still very close, so that the impression is of a dispersed village settlement. Widely scattered settlement, characteristic of Haiti, is very rare in Jamaica.

Regional divisions

Coastal plains

The southern coastal plains are much more extensive than those in the north. Following one another from west to east are the relatively small plains of Westmoreland, the Black River Plains and finally, between the May Day Mountains and Kingston, the largest of the plains and the economic heart of modern Jamaica. There is no overall name for this extensive plain; the western region is called the Clarendon Plain, the southern region near the coast is the Plain of Vere, and the easternmost part beyond the Dorothy Plain is known as the Liguanea Plain. The names for the different parts of the same plain indicate their strong regional differences.

The Liguanea Plain, which coincides with the built-up area of Kingston, was originally a huge delta built up by numerous streams coming down from the Blue Mountains. Again and again Kingston has suffered from their high flood waters. In 1963 the Sandy Gully Drainage Scheme to control the flooding of Kingston was begun.

Kingston (Map 32), the island's capital since 1872, enjoys a healthy climate in the lee of the Blue Mountains. In 1692 it was laid out in a grid pattern after an earthquake had destroyed what had been until then the most important harbour, Port Royal. Kingston itself suffered very severe damage from an earthquake and the resulting fire in 1907, as well as from various hurricanes. The city was rebuilt after 1907 so that there now remain only a very few historic buildings and some houses in the Georgian style. Near the upper edge of the plain, surrounded by beautiful gardens, lies King's House, the former residence of the British Governor and now the seat of the Governor General. It was erected in 1694 and, with its square tower, embodies the architectural style of the Queen Anne period. Since then the city has spread beyond the original town area and even across the boundary of the Parish of Kingston into the Parish of St Andrew. Half Way Tree, the old administrative centre of St Andrew, today lies at the centre of a city which has extended westward even beyond the Sandy Gully, across the Liguanea Plain, and towards the interior up to the foothills. Beyond Constant Spring the mountain slopes up to a height of 400 m are occupied by exclusive residential areas with modern and luxurious villas enjoying a pleasant climate and a splendid view of the mountains, of the sea, and of the city in between. To the east the built-up area extends beyond the botanical gardens (Hope Gardens) to the spacious campus of the University of the West Indies. Nearby there are new housing estates of detached bungalows. The city covers a wide area since private homes with gardens dominate many residential areas. Older houses are usually built of brick or white painted wood with spacious verandas. In more recent times

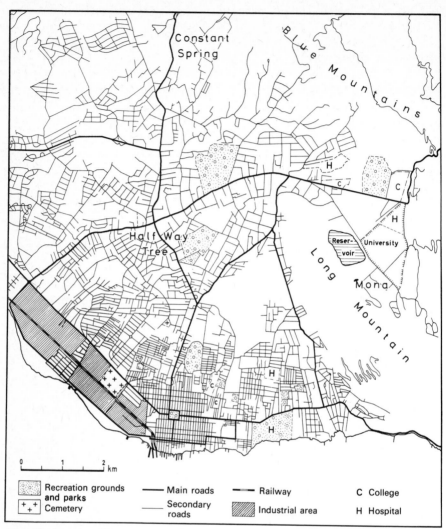

Map 32. Jamaica: Kingston street map.

concrete bungalows with flat roofs have been given preference and formerly large lots are being subdivided. The new housing schemes within the city at its northern and western edges are also concrete and are of three types: low, middle, and high income housing schemes. Each year additional modern office buildings are erected downtown. In contrast to Habana, or to San Juan de Puerto Rico, few of them are multistorey buildings.

The western part of the city houses the poor. The worst slums in the westernmost part which consisted of overcrowded shacks in terrible hygienic conditions have been cleared. Vast new housing estates under the auspices of the low income housing scheme have taken their place. Also to the west, along the Spanish Town Road, one finds the new industrial area accessible to the harbour and to the railroad system and with modern wharves at Newport West. It has been planned as an industrial estate and already contains several factories, among which is an oil-refinery.

Distinct functional zones are apparent in Kingston in the extensive socially differentiated residential areas around the city-centre, and the industrial area bordering the downtown area to the west. Within the downtown area the administrative functions are concentrated north of the central Victoria Park with the business centre to the south concentrated along King and Harbour Street where the main shops, banks, and commercial agencies are to be found, together with the famous Institute of Jamaica and its excellent library, and the spacious Myrtle Bank Hotel. Only a few paces from Harbour Street freighters are berthed at long piers and groups of cruise-ship tourists frequently disembark at Victoria Market Pier to visit the city. At the end of 1966 it was decided to redevelop completely this area adjacent to the harbour. The plan includes multistorey buildings which the city has lacked up to now.

The importance of its harbour has enabled Kingston to achieve its present size and its dominant position in Jamaica. Kingston has an excellent natural harbour which is protected by the Palisadoes, a spit connecting several Cays (coral sand islands) which stretches for 14 km across Kingston Harbour and separates it from the open sea. It is exposed to severe winds and waves during hurricanes. The international airport is built on one of the Cays and the outermost Cay which is now linked with the mainland by the spit was the site of the once wealthy town of Port Royal and Fort Charles. Port Royal used to be the base of the English buccaneers (one of whom was Henry Morgan) and it was the busiest trading centre in the British West Indies until 1692 when a severe earthquake almost completely destroyed the town.[1] Today Port Royal functions mainly as a recreation area for the population of Kingston. The gradual building up of the Palisadoes has provided Kingston Harbour with almost complete protection against the open sea but this could be destroyed at any time by another severe earthquake.[2]

Founded after the destruction of Port Royal, Kingston developed rather rapidly at first but then stagnated during the nineteenth century because of continual economic crises in Jamaica. Even the building of the railroad and the proclamation of Kingston as capital did not result in further growth until the twentieth century, when these events bore fruit. In 1871 the population of Kingston was only 29 000. Between 1921 and 1943 it grew from 88 000 to 202 000, until it reached 377 000 in 1960.

On the coastal plains west of Kingston, between the limestone plateaux in the north and limestone formations of the Hellshire Hills in the south,

[1] For detailed description of this earthquake see: D. Niddrie, 1963, p. 39ff.
[2] In 1967 it was decided to construct in Kingston Harbour two artificial islands of 90 ha each which would be connected by roads to one another and to the north as well as to the south banks.

are sugar and banana plantations. This part of the plain is the flood plain of the Rio Cobre and on its banks dykes are to be built for protection against flooding. The river contributes water for irrigation. It is hoped to minimize the heavy sedimentation of Hunts Bay, caused by this river, by building the Harkers Hall Dam which should at the same time enable the expansion of the land under irrigation. On the banks of the Rio Cobre, within the uniformly cultivated area, lies Spanish Town, founded in 1534 as Santiago de la Vega by the Spaniards and capital of Jamaica until 1872. There are no longer any buildings which date back to the Spanish period. On the whole, only the names of rivers and of some towns are reminiscent of Spanish rule. In Spanish Town the Anglican Cathedral, built in Queen Anne style, is one of the most remarkable colonial buildings; the only outstanding example of urban architecture in the island is the square and the old King's House situated in the centre of this old city with its chessboard layout. The square urgently needs restoration. After it lost its function as the capital of Jamaica, Spanish Town began to stagnate, and now only by recent developments, especially of textile and ceramic factories, has new life been brought to the city.

Farther to the west, the Dorothy Plain is mainly a small-scale tobacco and sisal farming area. This dry and, up to now, underdeveloped plain is scheduled for irrigation. The vast tropical seasonal deciduous forests of the Harris Savanna are only slightly encroached upon by small and scattered farms. Not far from Old Harbour lies the new Port Esquivel, mainly an aluminium export port which is connected by rail and road to Old Harbour. West of the Dorothy Plain, along the Rio Minho and along the lower part of the Milk River, is an irrigated area, which is the largest sugar area in Jamaica, centring on the main sugar factory at Monymusk near the coast. The main centre of this western part of the extensive southern coastal plain, the so-called Clarendon and Vere Plains, is the busy town of May Pen (pop. 14 000).

The Black River Plain, the central of three southern coastal plains, is divided by the Santa Cruz Mountains. Its upper part is a karst margin plain which is almost completely surrounded by hilly limestone country. In the south-east, where the Santa Cruz Mountains come down to the sea, lies Port Kaiser, a new bauxite exporting port. The Black River Plain is mainly a rural area of multicrop cultivation with large areas lying fallow. Following the river from the coast far into the interior is 'The Great Morass', a mangrove swamp which is to be made available for agricultural use in the future by drainage, just as the dry savannas of the Pedro Plains in the southern part of the Black River Plain are to be brought into use by irrigation.

The western part of the south coast is mainly occupied by the Westmoreland Plains. The port of Savanna-la-Mar is located there and exports sugar from the sugar plantations which make up its hinterland. They are centred on Frome, the most modern sugar factory in Jamaica. The swamp area north of Negril is now being drained. Negril's development as a tourist centre has been decided upon and in the near future several hotels will skirt the beautiful and almost unused white calcareous sand beach near Negril.

The coastal plains to the north of the island have attracted a greater share of the tourist industry than those to the south. There are two centres: Montego Bay, providing 2197 hotel beds in 1964, and Ocho Rios with 2272 beds.[1] In Montego Bay there is a distinct hotel area, whereas in Ocho Rios the hotels are scattered along the coast. Two types of hotels can be recognized: distinctive, big unit house complexes, and loosely grouped bungalow complexes. Both of these types offer every type of sport facilities on vast grounds, each hotel being a world in itself and seldom left by the average American tourist. Montego Bay, situated in the western part of the north coast, has long been an export port for the flourishing sugar plantations in this vicinity, but only since it became a holiday resort has there been any considerable growth. International flights to its airport are almost as numerous as those to Kingston airport.

The northern coastal plain is narrow except for the Queen of Spain's Valley south-west of Falmouth. Sugar cane and rice cultivation shape the landscape. From Falmouth eastward, up to a point beyond Morant Bay, a wide strip of coconut trees runs along the coast. Small drying plants are built at frequent intervals for the production of copra from the flesh of the coconuts. The bridge across the Roaring River near the limestone terraces of Dunn's River Falls west of Ocho Rios is the only structure in Jamaica dating from the Spanish period. A number of eighteenth-century stately homes are reminders of the golden age of the plantation economy; Cardiff Hall at Runaway Bay is an example. Bauxite is transported from the limestone plateaux by means of a cable way for export from Ocho Rios (Plate 8) whose harbour, like Port Kaiser, is red with bauxite dust. Port Antonio (pop. 7800), the most important banana exporting port in Jamaica until the Second World War, lost much of its importance as a result of the decline in banana production. Bananas, usually interplanted with coconuts, are the main crop in the eastern part of the coastal plain, roughly between Annotto Bay and Port Morant. There is heavy rainfall from the trade winds on the windward slope of the Blue Mountains, which are usually hidden behind clouds. The dark green of this part of the coast, its luxurious vegetation, its tree cultivations rolling endlessly across the slopes of the mountains and hiding various small townships—all this lends this area individuality and great natural beauty.

The limestone plateaux

The **Cockpit Country** (Map 33 and Plate 7), situated south-east of Montego Bay, is only one part of the limestone plateau, though the most

[1] Kingston has overnight accommodation for 1431 visitors; all the rest of the south coast has accommodation for only 52 people.

inaccessible district in Jamaica. Both the steep and often sharply pointed cones and the deeply imbedded cockpits often form remarkably straight rows which are obviously due to the strong and regular jointing of limestone. The surface of the limestone is rugged with razor-edged rock crests in places and the cockpits are rimmed by rock cliffs. As a result of the very rugged topography, together with its thick forests, the Cockpit Country is extremely hostile to transport development and settlement. As early as the Spanish period the outer parts of this cone karst area served as hideouts for runaway slaves. The escaped slaves, living in the two settlements of Trelawny Town and Accompong, preyed upon the surrounding districts and gave the British colonial government a lot of trouble. It was not until 1796 that an expeditionary force of 1520 British soldiers broke their resistance.

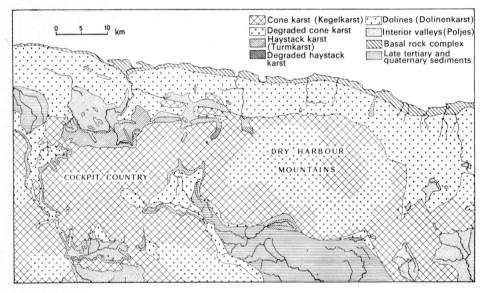

Map 33. Jamaica: Karst in the Cockpit Country (after Sweeting).

A hilly limestone country, which is an area of dinaric karst, covers the greatest part of the **white limestone plateaux**. Its height varies from almost sea-level in Westmoreland and between the Santa Cruz Mountains and May Day Mountains to 900 m in some districts; the average height is around 500 m. The strong tectonic faulting of this area is to be seen in the fault scarps between the higher and lower parts of the limestone plateau. Spur Tree Hill, the scarp between the Don Figuerero Mountains and the upper part of the Black River Plain, is most impressive. The offices of Kaiser Bauxite Co are located on its summit. Surface mining is common in the dolines of the limestone country where large excavators shovel the dark-red bauxite soil onto trucks. The bauxite is then transported to the drying installations at the new ports or to the two Canadian alumina plants in factory-owned railways or cableways. Because of the great distance to Kitimat the Canadian company does not export dried bauxite but pure aluminium.

The Jamaican government requires the rehabilitation of the mined areas for cultivation. This is done by sowing grass or by afforestation, after the previously removed native soil has been put back into the excavations. At first Guinea grass (*Panicum maximum*) was used, but this type grows in tufts and therefore does not prevent soil erosion. Today Pangola grass (*Digitaria decumbens*) which provides a continuous cover as well as quality feed is used. Various factors have helped to intensify the cattle-breeding of the Jamaican cattle and to increase the output of meat and dairy produce: the improvement of pasture through mowing and fertilizing; the fencing of pastures and the use of a rotation system; and the introduction of Santa Gertrudis cattle, a crossbreed of Shorthorn and Zebu. The bauxite companies have also established citrus plantations in various places throughout the limestone plateau. Most companies acquired their lands by buying farms of an average size of over 100 ha, but Kaiser Bauxite Company bought properties in areas of small-scale farming and has therefore had to cope with resettling the peasants. The settlements founded by the companies are far superior to those which were established by the government before 1962. Within a few years the young bauxite industry has considerably changed the landscape of the limestone plateau (Map 34) through the new agricultural settlements, the new offices and factory buildings, the new type of agriculture, and the new industrial sites.

In general, cattle farming predominates in the dry southern part and small-scale peasant farming in the more humid northern part of the limestone area. There is also a densely populated area of peasant farming in the centre of the plateau, bordering the Central Range. Starting in 1954 the Christiana Area Land Authority has tried to rehabilitate this whole area: to improve the social structure, to raise agricultural productivity, to teach new methods of farming in order to minimize erosion, and to teach market organization. Remarkable progress has been achieved. Descendants of German immigrants who came to Jamaica in the wake of the abolition of slavery live in a small town in the western part of the limestone area called Seaford Town. They adopted the way of living and the way of farming of their Negro neighbours and made their living from their smallholdings. The majority of these families succeeded in emigrating to Canada after 1950. The remaining families have been able to enlarge their farms and to improve their economic conditions.

The limestone area has few urban settlements. Mandeville (pop. 8400) on the road and railway from Kingston to Montego Bay is the centre for the southern part. Because of its altitude (600 m) it developed as a health resort even in colonial times and it retains something of the atmosphere of an English colonial settlement. Mandeville plays no role as a tourist

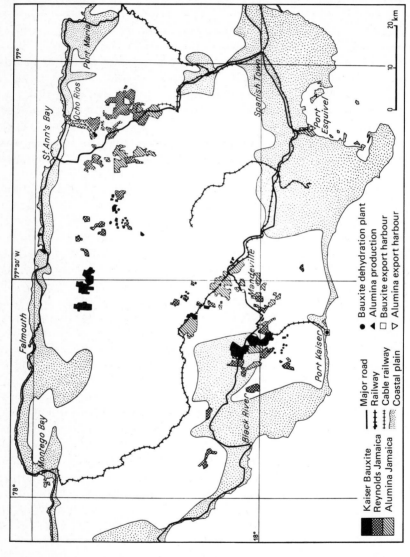

Map 34. Jamaica: land owned by bauxite companies, 1959.

centre since the tourist industry is concentrated in the coastal areas.

Karst margin plains which extend into the limestone plateaux, or the poljes enclosed within them, are called **Interior Valleys** in Jamaica. The most extensive are St Thomas in the Vale and Appleton Valley (Plate 6). In the whole area of the limestone plateau only these interior valleys have surface watercourses. The water emerges out of the limestone as a spring on one side of the basin and disappears on the other side in sinkholes. In this fashion Hector's River disappears on one side of the Hector's River Interior Valley and emerges as a karst spring, to become the Black River near Balaclava in Appleton Valley. All these interior valleys are flat, and surrounded by steep limestone slopes. The lateral solution of limestone is one of the factors which led to the formation of these basins. The fertile alluvial lands of the interior valleys were the sites of plantations in the early colonial period which are still operating today, e.g. sugar plantations in Appleton Valley and in St Thomas in the Vale. Extensive citrus cultivations supply the modern and important canning factory in Bog Walk. Small-scale farming is also present in these two interior valleys, but only on their outskirts, whereas other interior valleys are completely occupied by this type of activity.

The mountains

In contrast to the Blue Mountains the **Central Range** is not a very conspicuous mountain range and the limestone plateaux to the south (Mocho Mountains) and to the north (Dry Harbour Mountains and Vera Ma Hollis Savanna) have higher altitudes. Geologically the whole Central Range, which is formed of Cretaceous rocks at the base of the white limestone is a breach in the crest of the white limestone anticline running WNW to ESE. Geomorphologically it is an area of denudation, drained by the Rio Minho, whose numerous deeply entrenched tributaries have cut through the marls and schists of the Central Range.

Agriculture in the Central Range is part of the multicrop farming system. The majority of farms are less than 0·5 ha in size and holdings are enlarged by renting minute parcels under insecure leases, but because of the extreme fragmentation the farms are not viable. The dispersed type of settlement pattern prevails and the irregular shapes of the holdings gives the landscape a chaotic appearance. The mixed cultivation of ground crops, tubers and fruit trees is characteristic. Tubers and fruit can be harvested in small amounts throughout the year; whatever is not needed for subsistence is sold for the cash which is necessary to buy things the peasant families do not produce themselves. The Jamaican Negro small farmer has evolved a system of agriculture, which is especially typical in the Central Range. A system of marketing has developed which is closely related to the rural social structure. According to Mintz (1955), it had its origin in a time when slaves were given small parcels to cultivate themselves and used part of the crop for subsistence and sold the rest. Today, the peasants sell their small surplus to middlemen, called higglers, who are women who visit the peasants once a week in order to buy yams, paw-paws, mangos etc. and then take them to the markets. There are eighty-seven rural markets in Jamaica where this produce is sold to traders, always in very small quantities.

The only export crops produced by peasant farming in the Central Range are small quantities of coffee, cocoa, and bananas. Tree crops are found mainly on the upper slopes and ground crops on the lower. Soil erosion is a serious problem, since even the steepest slopes are cultivated and attempts to preserve the soil and its fertility are inadequate. The peasants' lack of capital forces inadequate farming methods and prohibits any progress. The multipurpose programme of the Christiana Land Authority (see p. 187) is trying to rehabilitate this area and the bordering areas of the limestone plateaux as completely as possible.

The **Blue Mountains** are very impressive, ascending abruptly from the coastal plains. They are crossed via Hardwar Gap by the countless hazardous bends of a narrow road leading from Buff Bay on the north coast to Kingston. After heavy rains the road is usually impassable because of landslides. There are only two other trails across the ridge, one via the Cuna Cuna Pass, the other via Corn Pass Gap. They wind through the dense green of a tropical mountain forest which is noted for its many tree ferns. Before the clouds hide everything at about noon one may get a commanding view from the top of Catherine's Peak (1542 m) right above Kingston, a view not only of the southern coastal plains but also of the still untouched and tree-covered mountain range to the east which reaches a height of 2257 m.

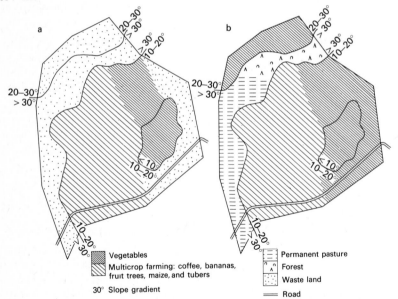

Map 35. Jamaica: Pleasant Hill.   Yallahs Valley, Blue Mountains.
a) In 1959   b) Planted

The Blue Mountains consist of the same type of rock as the Central Range. On both sides they are flanked by limestone, the most extensive area being the John Crow Mountains to the north which have a rather complex karst topography and which are therefore only penetrated with difficulty. The youthfulness of the Blue Mountains is obvious in the repeated occurrence of earthquakes and in the presence of hot springs in Bath. In spite of their relatively youthful structure the landscape is deeply dissected, a result of the high rainfall resulting from exposure to the trade winds (pp. 24 and 178). This is the only part of Jamaica where a stream network has developed. The largest river of the island is the Rio Grande flowing between the John Crow Mountains and the Blue Mountains and along which tourists may undertake romantic boating tours. Stream discharge fluctuates greatly, especially on the southern slopes of the Blue Mountains where valleys are deeply incised, and heavy damage is often caused by the flood waters of the Yallahs and Morant Rivers. The top soil has been washed away wherever cultivation has extended on to the steep slopes, whether at higher or lower altitudes. During the early period of the plantation economy coffee plantations were established in the valleys of the Blue Mountains. Today there are no large landholdings and coffee cultivation is now only carried out by peasant farmers.

A multipurpose development project is in progress in the Yallahs Valley, similar to the one in the Christiana area. Under its auspices the soil type, the slope gradient, and the extent of soil destruction of each holding has been ascertained and a utilization programme has been drawn up for each individual farmer, after taking into account the latest findings of soil and agricultural research scientists (Map 35). The farmers are advised by officials of the Yallahs Valley Land Authority. The steepest slopes are re-afforested with eucalyptus, pine trees, and juniper. Any visitor to the valley can easily detect the great damage caused by wasteful exploitation in the past and will be led to hope that the methods now being applied will be put into practice more thoroughly, not only in different parts of Jamaica, but in other islands in the Caribbean as well.

Economy

Agriculture

Farmland and area under cultivation. Although Jamaica's farmland totalled 683 000 ha in 1961 (60·5 per cent of all the island), the area actually under cultivation totals only 513 000 ha (45·5 per cent). Considerable parts of Jamaica (31·2 per cent) must be classified as wasteland either because they are naturally barren or because they have become unproductive as a result of improper farming. Neither afforestation nor renewed agricultural use is possible on 25 per cent (91 000 ha) of the unused land. The government has been trying for several years to afforest and to cultivate vast areas of former wasteland within the framework of the two multipurpose projects which include 42 000 ha of land in the Yallahs Valley in the Blue Mountains

and in the Christiana district in the Central Range. The area under cultivation is also to be enlarged and to be cultivated more intensively by means
of expanding the acreage under irrigation. So far the only irrigated land is
in the southern coastal plains: 10 000 ha in the so-called Mid-Clarendon
Scheme, 8200 ha in the Dorothy Plain, and 80 ha along the Rio Cobre.
Some projects are planned, and some have already begun, for irrigating the
following areas: 12 000 ha along the Rio Minho in the southern coastal
plain, 2400 ha in the Black River Pedro Plains in the south-west of the
island, 2000 ha in the Queen of Spain's Valley south-west of Falmouth in
the northern coastal plain. In addition, two swamp areas are to be drained:
2800 ha of the Black River Morass in the south-west, and 1800 ha of the
Negril Morass in the west of the island.

The possibilities of expanding the area under cultivation are far from
being exhausted. Expansion and increased yields are urgent, since a large
quantity of food has to be imported. The landownership pattern is definitely
the main obstacle to expansion, as large parts of the unused land belong to
large landholders. The first Five Year Plan (1963) plans for the acquisition
by the government of all those areas which belong to farms of more than
40 ha which are not used or are under-utilized. These areas are specially
taxed by the Jamaican government in order to induce the owners either to
cultivate the areas themselves or to have them cultivated by tenants. If this
is not done the government will expropriate and settle these areas.

A characteristic of the **pattern of land ownership** in Jamaica is that a
relatively large part of the farmland is in the hands of smallholders. The
abolition of slavery resulted, among other things, in the establishment of
peasant settlements. Within a hundred years not only was the pattern of
settlement changed decisively but also the agrarian social structure and
with it the appearance and functional structure of the agricultural landscape.

The development of peasant farming in Jamaica fell into three phases:
a first wave of colonization started immediately following the abolition of
slavery. It involved firstly the 'back lands' of plantations which used to be
cultivated by the slaves for their own subsistence, secondly, the unprofitable, abandoned plantations, and finally, the interior parts of the island
which at that time were Crown Lands. Improved transport and marketing
conditions which made it possible even for smallholders to cultivate for
export started the second wave of colonization (1870–1910) with the increase in banana production presenting a second incentive. The number of
smallholdings, 2114 in 1838, rose to 50 000 in 1860 and to 132 169 in 1902.
The third and final phase has been encouraged by the government settlements in former plantation areas (Map 36). This phase started in 1938.[1]

[1] Between 1938 and 1962, the so-called Land Settlement Programme was established; 193
land settlements comprising 28 000 units. In 1963 it was replaced by the Land Reform
Programme which is concerned mainly with colonizing the underutilized areas of plantations. Essentially two types of farms are planned: those with an area of 2–6 ha, and those
with 6–12 ha each; 168 dairy farms, comprising 1620 ha, and 4280 peasant farms, comprising 15 661 ha, were established between 1964 and 1968.

Table 36.   Jamaica: distribution of land ownership in colonial times
and today

	Number of farms	*Percentage of total farms*	*Farmland*	
			ha	*%*
1754				
Small farms	283	11·8	3 418	0·5
Medium-sized farms	533	22·3	26 321	4·0
Large-scale farms	1 577	65·9	638 889	95·5
Total	2 393	100·0	668 628	100·0
1954				
Small farms	192 085	96·5	301 016	39·5
Medium-sized farms	5 575	3·1	121 428	15·7
Large-scale farms	1 308	0·4	343 559	44·8
Total	198 968	100·0	766 003	100·0
1961				
Small farms	154 008	96·5	236 618	34·7
Medium-sized farms	3 803	2·8	63 980	9·4
Large-scale farms	1 130	0·7	382 026	55·9
Total	158 941	100·0	682 624	100·0

Sources:
Figures from 1754: *List of Landholders and their Holdings, 1754, Jamaica.* Public Record
Office, London, C.O.142, 31.
Figures for 1954 and 1961: *Census of Agriculture.*

In spite of this development the rural social structure is by no means sound,
since not more than 34·7 per cent of all the farmland belongs to smallholders, whilst smallholdings comprise 96·5 per cent (1961) of all agricultural enterprises (Table 36). In contrast to this only 0·7 per cent of all
enterprises (over 40 ha) own 55·9 per cent of all the farmland.

Among smallholders subdivision of property is common because of the
heavy population pressure. This leads to such a high degree of land fragmentation that the majority of smallholders cultivate an area of less than
2 ha and their farms are barely viable. Many of the government settlement
schemes are also unsuccessful since the holdings established are too small.
The Land Reform Programme has been trying since 1963 to institute
larger farms and there is also legislation to inhibit further subdivision. At
present more than half the smallholders have to depend partly on extra
work. The intense hunger for land, which cannot be satisfied since there are
no areas available for settling, is one cause of the very high mobility of the
population. An additional problem is that only second class areas as regards

193

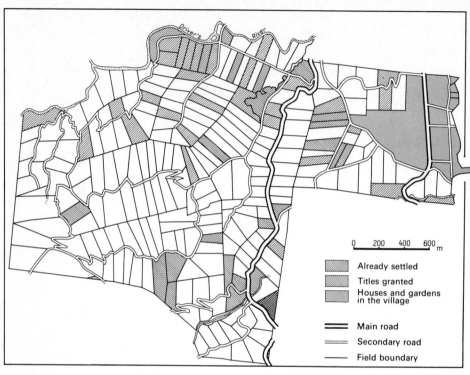

Map 36. Jamaica: Grange Hill, Portland Parish (1959).

soil, relief, and transport conditions were available for rural settlement, since more favourable districts had been claimed by plantations long before. Peasant farming could break into the stronghold of the plantation economy only where plantations were unprofitable anyway because of bad farming conditions.

Land fragmentation within the small-scale agricultural system has been going on for decades. At the same time land concentration has been the rule within the large-scale agricultural system, especially where the sugar industry is concerned. Before the abolition of slavery there were 653 sugar plantations; in 1964 the sugar output was much higher, but there are only nineteen sugar producing enterprises, all of them in the hands of companies. Recently the bauxite companies have become the largest landowners in Jamaica, acquiring vast stretches of land in the limestone plateau and becoming responsible for their agricultural development. The 1961 Census of Agriculture showed a decrease in the number of farms of all sizes (Table 36). This is not only the result of land concentration, which is beneficial in small-farming areas, but is also a result of the extremely high rate of rural depopulation. This is shown by the fact that, in the same period, the farmland fell from 766 000 ha to 683 000 ha and the number of farm hands decreased from 222 000 to 165 000, whilst the number of independent farmers and

194

their dependants decreased from 900 000 to 740 000. This development is an indication of the transformation which the Jamaican economy is undergoing at present.

As a result of the farm settlement schemes during the last hundred years the distribution of smallholdings and of plantations has a somewhat different pattern from that of other islands in the Caribbean since both agricultural systems are closely interlocked in Jamaica. In general, though, the coastal and interior plains are occupied by large-scale farms, whilst the mountainous interior is a peasant farming area.

Table 37. Jamaica: distribution of the agriculturally productive land by crops, 1967–68

	ha	%
Pastures	247 000	51·3
Sugar cane	60 000	12·5
Coconut	48 000	10·0
Bananas	38 000	7·9
Citrus	24 800	5·2
Coffee	7 000	1·4
Maize	4 000	0·8
Cocoa	5 000	1·0
Rice	1 000	0·2
Others	46 700	9·7
Total	481 500	100·0

Export-orientated production and the areas determined by it.
Sugar cane cultivation is the most important industry by acreage (Table 37 and Map 37) and by value of production (Table 38). Today, sugar cane monoculture no longer occupies all the cultivated area of the plains, as it did before the abolition of slavery. In the nineteenth century the area under sugar cane decreased considerably as a result of permanent crises in the Jamaican sugar industry, and the previously uniform sugar area disintegrated into separate areas which varied in size and cultivated different crops. This is still true of today's pattern, although sugar production has increased rapidly since the Second World War and the acreage of land under cane doubled between 1950 and 1960.

Eight dispersed sugar cultivating areas are the agricultural basis of the sugar industry. About half the area has to be irrigated. As regards cultural geography, the division of the sugar cane planting districts according to farm size is much more important than their differences in physical features. Like all districts in Jamaica which are delimited by export cultivation the sugar producing areas may be divided into two very different farming systems: the large-scale and the small-scale farming systems.

Table 38.   Jamaica: value of agricultural production, 1965 (£1000)

	1965 (£1000)	1966 (£1000)	1967/8 (tonnes)
Sugar	15 700	17 354	44 500
Bananas	5 750	6 338	153 000
Citrus	3 393	2 456	105 000
Pimento	964	1 648	1 950
Cocoa	409	271	2 000
Ginger	270	211	726
Coffee	253	215	1 400

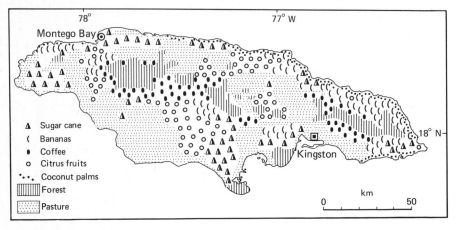

Map 37. Jamaica: land use.

Plantations occupy some 60 per cent of all the sugar cane cultivating areas and supply about 75 per cent of all the sugar produced. In 1960 two of the nineteen sugar factories in Jamaica[1] dealt with almost 50 per cent of the cane: Frome in the west, and Monymusk on the south coast, each with a capacity of 75 000 tonnes, and both belonging to the West Indies Sugar Company. The nineteen factories processed the entire Jamaican sugar cane crop. In 1950, before the sharp increase in sugar production, they cultivated 60 per cent of all the sugar cane area under their own auspices, in 1960 only 37 per cent (Table 39). This shows that during recent years the peasant farming area has expanded rapidly within the sugar cane monocultural system. Despite the decrease in area cultivated by the sugar factories their share of the sugar production only dropped from 69 per cent to 58 per cent of the entire sugar harvest within the same period. These figures express the high yield per acre achieved by more efficient methods of cultivation, and they show that plantations are far superior to smallholdings as regards profitability. In addition, the monoculture of sugar cane occupies 97·8 per

[1] In 1965 only eighteen sugar factories were in operation.

cent of the lands of the sugar factories as against only 70·6 per cent of the land in the peasant farming system.

Table 39. Jamaica: distribution and production of the area under sugar cane

		1950			1960	
		Area under cane	Cane harvest (1000)		Area under cane	Cane harvest (1000)
	Number	(ha)	tonnes	Number	(ha)	tonnes
Sugar factories	23	21 200	1 711	19	28 400	2 518
Other producers	10 000	14 000	764	21 000	46 400	1 813
Total		35 200	2 475		74 800	4 331

Banana cultivation, the second crop by export value, is, in contrast to the sugar industry, mainly in the hands of peasant farmers (68·6 per cent). Only 14·3 per cent of the total production is grown on plantations. The areas under export-orientated banana cultivation are divided into separate districts, resembling the pattern of sugar cane cultivation. One of these districts, distinguished by its coherence and size, is the entire eastern part of the island lying between the coast and Blue Mountain slopes and extending westward on the north and south coast within the perhumid area. Multicrop cultivation with coconut trees is predominant in the coastal areas of this region where small-scale farming is widespread; in the southern coastal plains where the land has to be irrigated the banana areas are on plantations. In the districts of export-orientated banana cultivation the two agricultural systems are not as closely interlocked as in the sugar cane districts. The reason for sugar cane being produced mainly on plantations and bananas mainly on smallholdings is the much higher capital requirements of sugar cane cultivation.

Table 40. Jamaica: sugar and banana exports (£ million)

	1832	1870	1890	1910	1930	1950	1961	1965	1969
Sugar, rum, molasses	1·6	0·7	0·5	0·4	0·6	7·5	16·5	17·2	32·9
Bananas	—	0·1	0·3	1·3	2·3	2·1	4·7	6·1	12·5

Banana cultivation in Jamaica did not start until the second half of the nineteenth century and it has an eventful history resembling that of sugar cane cultivation. An enormous increase in banana production took place in the late nineteenth century at a time when the sugar industry was still

197

affected by depression. Between 1910 and the start of the Second World War the value of banana exports was four times that of sugar exports (Table 40). During the years before the 1939 war Jamaica was by far the most important banana producing country in the world and banana exports totalled more than 50 per cent of all Jamaican exports. The first bananas were exported in 1870 by the American Captain Baker. His enterprise developed into the Boston Fruit Company, out of which grew the United Fruit Company in 1899, after amalgamation with the American Fruit Company. By 1937 their share in the banana export had risen to 54 per cent. To check their power the British colonial government in 1927 founded the cooperative Banana Producers' Association which controlled 34 per cent of the banana exports before the Second World War and which directed the export more and more to Britain. Before, banana exports were entirely orientated towards the USA. Until the Second World War only about 1800 ha of banana cultivation were owned by the United Fruit Company, since this company relied mainly on the produce of peasant farming. The banana boom sparked off the second wave of colonization, which was mainly directed towards the eastern part of the island causing a considerable shift in the structure of landholdings. Banana cultivation was almost brought to a standstill by the Panama Disease and Leaf Spot (*Cercospora musae*), and it was impossible to export during the Second World War. The banana industry gradually recovered after the war, until in 1951 millions of plants were destroyed by a hurricane. Then the government distributed to banana growers, the Lacatan variety, which is immune to Panama Disease. The Gros Michel banana, formerly the sole type in Jamaica, today makes up only 20 per cent of the entire crop. At present between ten and eleven million banana stems are exported annually, all to Britain where they constitute 40 per cent of British banana imports. About four to five million stems are consumed locally.

Citrus, the most recent Jamaican export fruit, takes third place by export value. Its cultivation was strongly advocated to reduce the dependence on banana and sugar exports. The land under citrus cultivation increased from 4000 ha in 1943 to 24 800 ha in 1968 and occupies various districts in the subhumid interior of the island. The most important varieties are oranges, grapefruit, and tangerines, chiefly exported as tinned fruit or as juice. The export of green fruit (to Britain and New Zealand) is low. Most of the cultivation is done by smallholders who have formed the Citrus Growers' Association.

Cocoa production, like citrus production, was stimulated by the government to diversify agricultural production. By the end of 1960 two million cocoa seedlings had been distributed. The area under cultivation has been extended, and a higher output of cocoa is to be expected in the future. Cultivated mainly by smallholders, the cocoa trees grow as part of mixed farming in various of the more humid areas of the island. Three newly built processing plants deal with the whole crop, which is harvested between

September and November and between March and May.

Ginger (*Zingiber officinale*) ranks sixth by value amongst agricultural exports and is cultivated entirely by smallholders. Pimento is also a peasant crop. The green berries of the evergreen pimento tree, which is indigenous to Jamaica and which grows wild on the pasture lands of the limestone plateau (p. 187), are collected and dried by the local population and then processed into pimento (allspice). Almost the entire world supply comes from Jamaica.

Coffee, seventh by export value, has been cultivated in Jamaica since 1728. Like sugar, it was produced on plantations, and it was the most important export product after sugar until 1814 when, after a record-breaking crop of 15 000 tonnes, it declined rapidly in the same way that the sugar industry did after the abolition of slavery. Since then coffee production has amounted to only a fraction of the production before the abolition of slavery, but Blue Mountain coffee continues to fetch the highest prices on the London market. The Blue Mountain slopes especially at heights of 900 m to 1500 m are still the main areas of cultivation. Nowadays about 80 per cent of the coffee production is from farms of less than 4 ha each. Much of the land formerly under coffee cultivation, especially on steep slopes, has suffered from heavy erosion and is now being afforested. The Coffee Industry Board, founded in 1948, was able to improve cultivating and processing methods considerably. A national coffee tree nursery which has been distributing seedlings to planters since 1962 (90 000 each year is the aim) will perhaps succeed in stimulating an increase in coffee production after 150 years of depression.

Mango production until recently was only concerned with the local market, but the export of green and tinned mangoes has now started. The demand for mangoes in the USA, Canada, and Britain was so high in 1966 that it could not be met. Peasant farming will probably play an increasingly important role within export agriculture through the production of mangoes and other tropical fruit.

Production for the domestic market. While there has been increased production in all the export crops mentioned above in recent years, production for the domestic market has not increased as was hoped; in fact, it has decreased. Maize and rice have to be imported in large quantities. Although many smallholdings and plantations have adjusted themselves to supplying the local market which has increased because of urban growth and the tourist industry, the production of export crops on all types of farms is much more important than production for the domestic market (Table 41). The local market is mainly supplied by peasant farmers, with the exception of coconut cultivation in the east of the island which is mainly in plantations. Forty-three per cent of these coconut cultivations were destroyed by a hurricane in 1944, and since 1963 they have been seriously affected by disease. Peasant farming is usually uncoordinated mixed farming. Its aim is to be self-sufficient and to supply the domestic market.

It covers extensive areas in the Central Range, at the edge of the Blue Mountains, and in the moist northern parts of the limestone plateaux. In most parts farming methods are still antiquated in spite of the improvement plans of the government and the Farmers Association. The marketing of export goods is well organized, whereas the organization of local distribution leaves much to be desired.

Table 41.   Jamaica: production for export and for the domestic market by farm size, 1961 (%)

| | | Agricultural production | |
	stock farming	export	domestic market
Small farms	5·0	56·7	38·3
Medium-sized farms	19·6	58·7	21·7
Large-scale farms	31·6	62·6	5·8
All farms	4·9	54·7	40·4

Pastureland occupies the greatest part of the land in agricultural use. The extensive, and in parts intensive, livestock industry is mainly located in the drier southern limestone plateaux of the interior. During the last few years the government and particularly the bauxite companies, which acquired vast stretches of land, have tried to improve pastures and cattle farming in order to increase meat and milk production which still cannot meet local demand. The trend seen in domestic agriculture is similar for cattle farming: between 1954 and 1961 livestock decreased from 276 000 to 240 000 head of cattle, and from 212 000 to 128 000 pigs.[1] Increased imports are therefore necessary.

The diversity of agricultural production which originated under British rule, together with the large number of small-scale farms within agriculture distinguish the young nation of Jamaica from Cuba before the Revolution. Peasant farming plays an important role in all agricultural activities except cattle farming. But since the majority of peasant farms are too small they are hardly viable. This is seen in the very strong rural exodus. The low yield per hectare also renders smallholdings unprofitable in comparison to larger farms. The increase in agricultural production necessary for viability can only be achieved through improved farming methods, by halting land fragmentation, and by establishing medium-sized farms. The most important aim concerning the agricultural economy, therefore, is for the government to put into practice the Farmers Production Programme and the Land Reform Programme. The various steps within the Land Reform Programme, started by the government in 1963, amount to an agrarian

[1] There has been a slight increase since: in 1965 there were 248 000 head of cattle and 150 000 pigs.

reform. If this can be realized a new structure of land ownership will be achieved without resort to force. This again could set an example for many states in the Caribbean and in Central as well as in South America.

Forestry

Forests cover 218 000 ha (19·3 per cent) of Jamaica. In the past they have been destroyed by ruthless exploitation, mainly by peasant clearings, and because the sugar factories demanded huge quantities of firewood. Today large areas of wasteland are being reafforested. Various types of eucalyptus, pine trees (*Pinus caribaea*), mahogany (*Swietenia Mahagoni*) and *Cedrela odorata* are the main seedlings. At the moment there are ninety-eight so-called forest reserves, designed to minimize soil erosion and to balance the fluctuating discharge of the rivers. They are also intended to be recreational areas, and felling is therefore minimal. There is an insignificant export of dyewood, and some native timber is used for manufacturing furniture, but most timber has to be imported.

Fishing industry

As in most of the other islands in the Caribbean, the fishing industry is very poorly developed, and the great demand for fish cannot be met. For several years now the government has been assisting the fishermen, and from 1955 to 1962 the catch of fish, by weight, increased by 50 per cent. In 1962 the value of imported fish equalled the value of imported cars. Dried codfish, formerly one of the basic items in the slave diet, ranks high among Jamaican food imports, as it does for all other islands in the Caribbean where the Negroes make up the majority of the population. In 1963 Jamaica joined the United Nations Fisheries Development Programme for the Caribbean. In 1967 Japan promised help for the development of the fishing industry.

Mining

Bauxite mining alone, operated by four US companies and one Canadian company through surface mining on the white limestone plateaux, is first by export value by a wide margin. The US companies have built special ports at Ocho Rios and Port Kaiser and export dried bauxite to Texas and Louisiana. The Canadian company processes aluminium in two factories in Williamsfield and Ewarton which have been extended several times. It is then shipped from the new Port Esquivel to Kitimat in British Columbia. In future aluminium is also to be produced by the American companies. Joint construction of a huge plant in the south-western part of the parish of St Elisabeth, near Port Kaiser, was decided on in 1966. Bauxite reserves in Jamaica are considered to be the largest in the world. Their exploitation, which started in 1952 and reached 8·5 million tonnes in 1965, is the basis of the North American aluminium industry, and for Jamaica it is an important source of the income, which is essential for economic development. Jamaica is the world's leading producer of bauxite.

Apart from bauxite, only limestone and gypsum mining east of Kingston is worth mentioning. While limestone is used in the manufacture of cement, most of the gypsum is exported to the USA.

Table 42. Jamaica: gross national product by economic sector (%)

	1938	1950	1962
Agriculture	38·2	30·8	12·4
Mining	—	—	8·8
Industry	6·5	11·3	13·3

Industry

Agriculture's share in the gross national product is only one-third of what it was before the Second World War, although agricultural production has increased considerably (Table 42). In contrast to this the share of industry in the gross national product has doubled during the same period. Industry has not only increased immensely but its structure has also changed very markedly. To the previously agriculturally biased economy a versatile consumer goods industry has been added, based on local as well as on imported raw material; since 1960 its production, by value, has been exceeding that of agriculture.

Industrial development began in 1952 when the Jamaica Industrial Development Corporation, with a branch in New York, was founded with the aim of following the example set by Puerto Rico where new methods of industrialization were being successfully put into practice at that time. Preferential tariffs, tax privileges, and allocation of suitable land led to foreign investments in enterprises which, as in Puerto Rico, used cheap manpower, took advantage of the nearby American market, and produced exclusively for export. Production of consumer goods for the local market has also increased steadily. With the assistance of the Industrial Development Programme eighty-five new industrial plants had been established by 1960; thirty-six more were added by the end of 1962; and in 1966 twenty-eight new factories were built. The Five Year Plan of 1963 emphasizes industrialization since unemployment is still a very serious problem. In 1960 13 per cent of all Jamaicans able to work were unemployed (19 per cent in Kingston). Most of the new industrial plants are located in Kingston. As in Puerto Rico, the construction of industrial plants in rural districts is planned but not yet satisfactorily realized.

Among the food industries the sugar industry is most important, both by value of production and numbers employed. Sugar, molasses, rum, and pure alcohol are produced at eighteen factories. Numerous canning factories are scattered throughout the island for citrus processing, the largest being at Bog Walk in the interior plain of St Thomas in the Vale. Cocoa has been processed at Richmond (St Mary), at Morgan's Valley (Clarendon), and also at Haughton Court (Hanover) since 1962. Various small plants in the Blue Mountains process coffee, which is then shipped to the central processing plant in Kingston. Copra is produced by fifty-six fairly small factories. All the margarine and essential oil processed from copra is consumed locally. The thirty rice mills and the evaporated milk plant only supply the domestic market. The branches of the food industry mentioned above rely on local agricultural production. Other sectors of the food industry, bakeries, the beverages and tobacco industries, depend entirely or partly on imported raw materials and are therefore located in Kingston, where most of the imports are landed. The food, beverages and tobacco industries produce 52 per cent of the total value of the processing industry.

The consumer goods industry is even more heavily concentrated in the Kingston-Spanish Town area than the food industry. Between 1959 and 1963 cement production in Kingston expanded noticeably and is now meeting local demand, as does tile and pipe production. In 1963 an important ceramic works began operation near Spanish Town. The Jamaican footwear industry which increased its output from 632 000 to 1·6 million pairs of shoes between 1959 and 1962 is represented by sixteen small enterprises and by the productive factory of the Bata Shoe Company in Kingston. Two-thirds of local demand is supplied. More and more footwear is exported to former British territories in the Caribbean. A new shoe factory specializes in the production of cowboy boots and exports them to the USA. The textile industry has experienced a large increase; Ariguanabo Mills, its largest plant, is located near Spanish Town. Some of the more recently constructed textile plants produce exclusively for export, e.g. the underwear factory in Port Maria. Between 1959 and 1964 the value of textile exports increased from £0·3 to 3·0 million.[1] The number of consumer goods produced in Jamaica is increasing steadily. Numerous and mostly small plants produce paint and other chemical and pharmaceutical products, paper and cardboard, synthetic materials, glass, furniture, hardware and light metal goods, electrical appliances, and the like. Alongside the waterfront in Kingston a vast industrial area with access to the railway system is under construction. The construction of a fertilizer plant (in operation since 1966), the production of synthetic materials from bagasse, and particularly the construction of an oil refinery (1963–65) are first steps towards building a capital goods industry. Still on the drawing board are plans for a steel works and a non-ferrous metal smelting works, to be built in Kingston and Spanish Town respectively.

Electricity, necessary for carrying out the Industrial Development Pro-

---

[1] Since then textile exports have been declining, for the importing countries have reduced their import quotas.

gramme, is obtained partly from hydroelectric power plants on the White and Black Rivers, but mainly from coal and oil burning plants. In 1964 the generation of current amounted to 715 million kWh, the self-supplying bauxite companies included.

The tourist industry (Table 43) is second only to the bauxite industry as a source of foreign currency. Between 1960 and 1969 the number of tourists rose from 227 000 to 407 000, 95 per cent of them coming from North America, chiefly during winter. In 1966 they spent £28 million in Jamaica. Many Jamaicans have found jobs with the tourist industry. Tourism has not only assisted in restructuring the economy, but it has also changed the country areas, especially the north coast.

Table 43.   Jamaica: number of tourist enterprises and hotel beds

	1958	1961	1969
Hotels	60	73	91
Guest houses	46	44	—
Holiday houses	92	154	—
Overnight accommodations	4700	6758	10 950

Source: The West Indies and Caribbean Year Book 1964. By 1965 the number of hotel beds had increased to 7491 and an additional 1850 beds were expected to be provided by new hotel buildings.

Transport

The total length of railway lines, operated by the Jamaica Railway Corporation, is 385 km. The main line is from Kingston to Montego Bay with a branch line from Spanish Town to Port Antonio. There are only a few other short branch lines. Only freight traffic has been profitable in recent years. A modernization programme was carried out between 1960 and 1963, and diesel coaches were introduced with the tourists in mind. The Railway Corporation hopes in this way to increase passenger traffic which has increasingly shifted to buses: 300 regular bus services operate outside Kingston. The number of motor vehicles increased from 42 000 in 1959 to 67 000 in 1968. There is an excellent network of roads in Jamaica: 4300 km of main roads, 2300 km of which are asphalted. An asphalt road almost encircles the island linking every major town. There are also four principal crossings from south to north: from Savanna-la-Mar to Lucea and Montego Bay, from Spanish Town to Ocho Rios, and from Kingston to Annotto Bay. Besides the main roads there is a close network of minor roads. Only the Cockpit Country and the Blue Mountains are still almost inaccessible to any traffic.

Since 1963 Jamaica has had its own airline, Jamaica Air Services, which operates local flights between Kingston, Montego Bay, Ocho Rios, and

Port Antonio. Air Jamaica has been flying to Miami and New York since 1966. The two international airports, Kingston (Palisadoes) and Montego Bay, are served by several foreign airlines which offer excellent connections to the Americas as well as to Europe. Their combined air traffic volume, however, is only 40 per cent of that of San Juan (Puerto Rico), which is by far the leading airport in the Caribbean. In late 1960 fifty-seven scheduled flights took off weekly from Montego Bay and sixty-one from Kingston with a seat capacity of 4095 and 4332 respectively; 37·5 per cent of all tourists came in by air, while 62·2 per cent visited Jamaica by boat. Since then the volume of air traffic and the percentage of tourists coming in by air have increased considerably. Montego Bay has now surpassed Kingston in volume of air traffic.

Kingston, having one of the best natural harbours in the Caribbean, leads in volume of international shipping. The port facilities were greatly improved by the development of the new industrial area. Kingston is mainly an importing port, handling 79 per cent of all Jamaican imports, but only 6 per cent of the exports. Bananas are exported from Port Antonio and Port Morant, sugar is exported from Savanna-la-Mar, bauxite from Ocho Rios and Port Kaiser, and aluminium from Port Esquivel. The port of Montego Bay is to be extended, starting in 1968.

Foreign trade

Among the Caribbean territories Jamaica ranks fifth in respect of foreign trade (US $389 million). In spite of its economic development, which has followed the Puerto Rican pattern, Jamaican foreign trade amounted to only one-sixth of the Puerto Rican trade in 1966. The balance of trade shows a deficit of US $36 million.

During the last ten years the export structure has changed considerably as a result of the rise in sugar production (Fig. 8), the increase in banana cultivation, and the increasingly important bauxite industry. Heading the list by value of exports in 1968 were bauxite and aluminium with 51·2, followed by sugar with 15·4 per cent and bananas with 8 per cent. Combined they account for 76·2 per cent of all exports. In spite of the changes in Jamaican exports, its export structure is still relatively unbalanced. Compared with Puerto Rico, the manufacture of industrial goods still plays an unimportant role in terms of their share of exports. However, their share of exports by value rose from 3·2 per cent in 1958 to 11·7 per cent in 1968.

In spite of the size of the textile industry and in spite of the diversity of the food industry, imported textiles amounted to 4·8 per cent and imported food, beverages and tobacco amounted to 40·5 per cent of the imports by value (1966). In view of this one of the most urgent developmental objectives will be to increase agricultural production for the home market, as well as to develop the consumer goods industry.

Jamaica's international trade associations, like its export structure, have

Jamaica

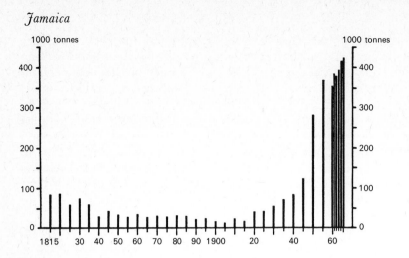

Fig. 8. Jamaica: sugar exports, 1815–1965.

changed noticeably within the last decade. Between 1953 and 1968 exports to Great Britain decreased from 62 to 27 per cent, while those to North America (USA and Canada) increased from 31 to 54 per cent. Within the same period imports from Great Britain decreased from 55 to 22 per cent, whilst those from North America increased from 33 to 47 per cent (Table 44). The changes in the direction of exports are explained by bauxite mining, since bauxite and aluminium are shipped exclusively to North America. When Cuba stopped sugar deliveries to the USA, Jamaica took its place and exports a fair amount of its sugar to the USA. Industrial products are also exported largely to the North American market. Only bananas and citrus are shipped almost exclusively to Great Britain. There has also been a considerable change in the origin of imported goods, since many US citizens are investing in hotels and industrial plants and the necessary capital equipment is imported from the USA.

The young nation of Jamaica, which is still producing mainly raw materials and agricultural products, must be thought of as a true developing country in view of the structure of its economy and trade. In contrast to the situation ten years ago the Jamaica of today can no longer be seen as a purely agricultural country. The imbalance in the agricultural sector during the period before the Second World War has, to a large extent, been overcome. In view of this, and considering the rapidly progressing industrialization programme, the outlook for economic development of Jamaica seems to be favourable. The insufficient supply of agricultural products for the domestic market, however, and the overpopulation of the island is still a serious problem, particularly the latter, since the high rate of emigration to Great Britain has been severely reduced by new British immigration laws. Only by realizing the national Land Reform Programme and by further stressing the Industrial Development Programme, which can only be achieved with the aid of foreign investments, can the problem of over-population be met and the living standard of the population be raised.

Table 44.   Direction of foreign trade, 1966

	Exports		Imports	
	£1000	*%*	*£1000*	*%*
North America	42 462	53·8	53 939	47·1
USA	30 362	38·5	41 432	36·2
Canada	12 00	15·3	12 507	10·9
Middle America	2 572	3·3	1 961	1·7
South America	390	0·5	7 768	6·8
Europe (excluding Communist E. European countries)	30 048	38·0	39 944	34·8
EEC	1 851	2·3	12 838	11·2
EFTA	28 194	35·7	27 106	23·6
Others	3(*)	0·0	—(*)	—
Communist E. European countries	345(*)	0·4	67(*)	0·1
Africa	—	—	—	—
Asia	180	0·2	3 252	2·8
Australia and New Zealand	569	0·7	4 477	3·9
	76 566	96·9	111 408	97·2

(*) Value 1965
Source: United Nations Yearbook of International Trade Statistics.

18

The Cayman Islands

The Cayman Islands rest on the submarine ridge of the same name which extends between the Cuban Sierra Maestra and British Honduras (Belize), and which forms the northern edge of the Cayman Trench demarcating the Yucatán Basin in the Caribbean Sea to the south.

Tertiary limestone formations make up the three islands Grand Cayman, Cayman Brac, and Little Cayman. The fossil cliffs of the karst plateaux, usually about 10–15 m in height, higher only in Cayman Brac, descend to coastal plains of varying width built from Pleistocene and recent coral limestone and coral sand. Long stretches of coral fringe-reefs follow the coastline.

The three Cayman Islands together make up an area of 241 sq km. They have a population of 7600 with a density of thirty-two persons per sq km. Eighty per cent of the population live on Grand Cayman; Little Cayman has less than fifty inhabitants. The proportion of the white population is relatively high, amounting to 19 per cent.[1] This is explained by the fact that fishing has always been the main means of livelihood and before the abolition of slavery it was done exclusively by whites.

Up to the eighteenth century ships of all nations called on the then uninhabited Cayman Islands for provisions especially because the large North Sound of Grand Cayman, protected by coral reefs and partly fringed by mangrove swamps, offered excellent hideouts to the buccaneers. The crews slaughtered large numbers of turtles (*Chelonia mydas*) thousands of which used to deposit their eggs on the sandy beaches. By the early nineteenth century the vast numbers of turtles had been drastically reduced. The white fishermen who had settled on these islands since 1734 (in 1670 these islands were given to Great Britain) had to turn to more distant fishing grounds, mainly to the coastal waters off Costa Rica, Nicaragua and Honduras where they still go today.

In addition to catching turtles and fish many inhabitants of the Cayman Islands earn their living as sailors. Their families are comparatively well off. Nevertheless, emigration has been high. Before 1900 most of the emigrants

[1] Negroes 17 per cent; mixed race 64 per cent.

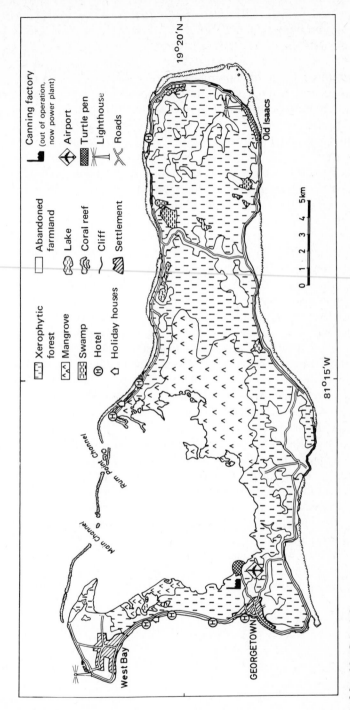

Map 38. Grand Cayman.

209

went to Central America; Cayman communities still exist in Honduras and Nicaragua; and Jacksonville on the Cuban Isle of Pines is also an English-speaking Cayman settlement. Since 1900 emigration has been mainly directed towards the USA. There is hardly any farming on the Cayman Islands. Most of the formerly cultivated areas are covered by secondary bush formations. From the palmetto leaves (*Thrinax argentea*) ropes are manufactured and exported to Jamaica.

Georgetown in the south-western part of Grand Cayman (Map 38) is the chief settlement with about 30 per cent of the entire population. All of the whitewashed wooden buildings require water tanks since neither spring nor well-water is available. On the North Sound, 3 km from Georgetown, turtle pens have been built and the live animals are exported. A former canning factory is located near to them where turtle soup was produced for a few months in 1952. But production soon had to be terminated for economic reasons. Today the building houses the electric power station.

Increasing numbers of tourists have been visiting the islands since the mid 1950s. In 1962 Grand Cayman offered accommodation for 229 tourists, Cayman Brac for twenty-eight. Two thousand tourists visited the Cayman Islands in 1962, 19 500 in 1969. This recent development has caused brisk building activity on Grand Cayman. New commercial and administrative concrete buildings have been constructed in Georgetown and hotels and holiday bungalows have been built near Georgetown and in remote areas on the north and east coast. The number of motor-vehicles has risen to 2000 (1969), and the roads near Georgetown have been asphalted. The tourist industry is made possible by the Georgetown international airport which possesses flight connections to Miami, Jamaica, and San José (Costa Rica). Seaplanes from the Cayman Brac Airways connect the three Cayman Islands.

In 1968, the value of foreign trade amounted to £506 000, not more than 1·2 per cent of which was made up by exports. Salt, crayfish, live turtles, tortoise shells, shark hides, and ropes are the only export goods. Food, textiles and building materials represent the major part of the imports.

The Cayman Islands are a British colony assigned to the colonial administration in Jamaica until 1962, but since that time directly connected to the British Colonial Office.

19

Hispaniola

Hispaniola is the second largest island in the Caribbean with an area of 76 484 sq km. The story goes that when George III inquired about the island one of his admirals took a piece of paper, crumpled it and placed it before his king saying, 'Thus looks Haiti'. Haiti means mountain country in the language of the Amerindian aborigines. None of the other Caribbean islands possesses as marked a mountainous character as Haiti.

This is not the only geographical characteristic of the island on which the Spaniards started their colonization of the New World and where more cultural influences can be clearly traced in the landscape than on the neighbouring islands. Even a casual glance detects the divergences in the cultural landscape, which originate in the political and economic developments of the past. Apart from the tiny island of St Martin, Hispaniola is the only politically divided Caribbean island. The uneasy coexistence of the Republic of Haiti in the west and the Dominican Republic in the east of the island, two extremely heterogeneous states in terms of population and economy, is evident from the contrasts between them. These contrasts in the cultural landscape are the more astonishing since the physical features are essentially similar in both the Haitian and Dominican sections of the island.

Physical geography

The very mountainous character of Hispaniola originates in the fact that the island is penetrated by two branches of the North American cordillera system, extending from the Middle American mainland. The northern branch extends from Guatemala into British Honduras (Belize), then, via the Cayman Ridge and the Cuban Sierra Maestra, into the north-west peninsula and further into Hispaniola's Cordillera Central. The southern branch stretches from the northern region of Honduras via the Nicaragua Ridge and the Jamaican Blue Mountains to Hispaniola's south-west peninsula.

The west to east or WNW–ESE axis of the mountains follows the trend of

211

the west to east extension of the island. The length of the island from Cap des Irois in the west to Cabo Engaño in the east is 660 km, with a maximum width of about 260 km. The Windward Passage, 90 km in width, separates Hispaniola from Cuba in the west, and the Jamaica Channel, 190 km, separates it from Jamaica in the south-west. Puerto Rico lies about 110 km to the east, beyond the Mona Passage.

Only a few offshore islands exist, despite the very irregular configuration of the coastline, especially in Haiti. By far the largest of the offshore islands is Gonave, 700 sq km, sharing its name with the gulf which reaches deep into the main island between the two long and narrow peninsulas which stretch out to the north-west and the south-west respectively. Off the Atlantic side of the north-west peninsula lies Tortuga Island (Ile à Tortue), and off the Caribbean side of the south-west peninsula lies Ile à Vache. The small islands of Barahona, Saona and Beata lie off the Dominican part of the south coast. Beata Island is located where the Beata Ridge begins south-ward, separating the Colombian Basin from the Venezuelan Basin in the Caribbean Sea. Otherwise, the sea bottom rapidly descends to great depths very close to the coastline. The northern Colombian Basin reaches a depth of 3000 m only 12 km off the Caribbean coast. The Cayman Trench, with depths of nearly 4000 m, continues into the Windward Passage almost as far as the Gulf of Gonave. The Puerto Rico Trench lies parallel to the north coast and 70 km off Cabo Engaño reaches a depth of 9219 m.

Both the sea bottom around Hispaniola and the island itself display a large amount of local relief. The Pico Duarte in the Dominican Cordillera Central rises to 3175 m and is the highest point in the Caribbean islands; and in the neighbouring Enriquillo Depression the land surface falls to 44 m below sea-level.

Topographically, the island is divided by four nearly parallel mountain ranges separated from each other by narrow longitudinal depressions. In addition to the flat areas in these valleys Hispaniola possesses coastal plains which are more extensive on the south coast, mainly in the Dominican part of the island near Azua and especially east of Santo Domingo. The Haitian coastal plains are comparatively small.

The complicated rugged topography of Hispaniola is not the outcome of the Late Cretaceous or Early Tertiary Alpine folding of the cordillera system; it represents Late Tertiary tectonic faulting in which some blocks were lifted and others were lowered. These post-orogenic forces began during the Pliocene era, stopped during Pleistocene times, and have been active into the present. Frequent surface and submarine earthquakes bear witness to this. The uplift of Pleistocene marine sediments for several hundreds of metres must also be seen as proof of strong and recent tectonic activity. A series of raised beaches have been formed along various coastal sectors rising to 640 m in the Plateau of Bombardopolis in north-west Haiti, i.e. higher than on the Cuban side of the Windward Passage. Recent tec-tonic activity may also be seen, both in the impressive river terraces in various transverse valleys and in frequent stream capture.

The longitudinal depressions in Hispaniola, which are very conspicuous because of their rectilinearity and their distinct limits, are faultblock depressions. Although each of them lies within a synclinorium of the fold mountains, and the mountain chains between in an anticlinorium, one may nevertheless detect considerable deviations in the direction of the fault lines and the old fold structures which determine the relief. The faults usually intersect the folds at an acute angle, sometimes greater divergence is seen. For instance, a system of fold structures turns to the south away from the Dominican Cordillera Central which runs about WNW–ESE. This is even more distinctive in the Sierra de Baoruco which is the eastern part of the southernmost mountain range. This range runs generally from west to east; the folds of the Sierra, however, follow a south-easterly direction. The distinctive fault scarp in the north bordering the Enriquillo Depression truncates the fold structures. The present relief, therefore, is to a high degree independent of the structures of the Alpine orogeny; it is clearly determined by faulting which took place after this mountain-building period. Hence, the major part of the island has to be seen topographically and structurally as a faultblock mountain.

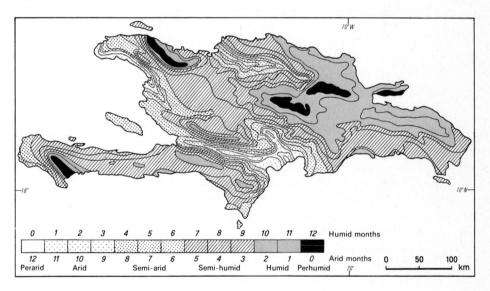

Map 39. Hispaniola: isohygromenes, Reichel's Index.

Rounded mountains characterize the range even at their highest altitudes. The prevailing relief formations are extensive erosion surfaces at various heights which have been deeply dissected in parts. The longitudinal depressions are filled with recent detritus. Vast alluvial fans occur where rivers from the mountains drop into the depressions. These alluvial fans explain the interior drainage of the salt lakes of Saumâtre and Enriquillo

213

in the southern longitudinal depression, which was still flooded by the sea during the Pleistocene.

The geomorphology of Hispaniola has hardly been examined yet, neither the development of erosion surfaces nor that of the valleys. The many karst areas are also incompletely described. Most of the karst formations are of the dinaric type, but cone karst is also rather frequent. Periglacial relief features at higher altitudes have not yet been studied systematically; boulder fields in the Dominican Cordillera Central, however, have been examined (Weyl). Only the raised beaches on the Dominican coast have been examined, mainly with regard to their dependence on tectonic movements and on eustatic changes of sea-level (Barrett).

The mountainous character of Hispaniola affects the island in various ways. It restricts settlement to very limited areas and makes transport difficult. Because of the varied relief the climatic conditions and the flora, as well as the agricultural possibilities, exhibit considerable variations in small areas both in the horizontal and in the vertical direction.

Hispaniola is the only island in the Caribbean which has all types of tropical climates. These range from arid to perhumid regions and from the tierra caliente to the tierra fría in accordance with the alternating arrangement of longitudinal valleys and mountain ranges. Increasing altitudes cause increasing amounts of rainfall in very short distances and isohyets and isohygromenes are closely spaced along the mountain slopes accordingly (Map 39). The distribution of rainfall is almost entirely determined by the relief. The plains are usually dry, the mountains wet. The windward and leeward position towards the trade winds also affects the amount of precipitation. For instance, Le Borgne on the Atlantic coast of the north-west Haitian peninsula receives an annual rainfall of 1905 mm, Gonaives on the Caribbean coast of the same peninsula only 559 mm. Of all the island's plains, barring the small Plaine des Cayes, only the eastern part of the longitudinal depression of Cibao to the north of the Cordillera Central, called Vega Real, is wet since it is accessible from the east and does not have a leeward position. Towards the west, to the lee of the Cordillera Septentrional, the Cibao quickly becomes arid. Relief also explains the extreme aridity around the Enriquillo lake in the southern longitudinal basin.

The mountainous nature and the size of Hispaniola means that the distribution of thermic-hygric climates and the resulting types of vegetation resemble the conditions which prevail on the Central American mainland, contrasting in this with the situation in the Lesser Antilles. The climatic variations caused by windward and leeward positions are expressed in the flora of the entire tierra caliente. Semidesert, dry thorn woodland, tropical deciduous and, finally, semi-evergreen seasonal forest follow each other uphill on the leeward side; tropical rain forest covers these zones on the windward. Lower montane forests grow in the tierra templada on the windward side, tropical montane forest on the leeward. Only the tierra fría has rain throughout the year both on the windward and leeward slopes

214

and has tropical elfin woodland throughout.

The northern slopes of the western and less rainy part of the Dominican Cordillera Central, west of Cotuí between 200 m and the summit region, exhibit impressive forests of *Pinus occidentalis* growing on deeply weathered and permeable soil and stretching far into the Haitian Massif du Nord. The Haitian Massif de la Selle and the Massif de la Hotte in the southern cordillera are also covered by pine forests (Plate 11). Durland believed these forests to be secondary formations created by peasants who cultivated in clearings made by burning. In view of their distribution at all altitudes, however, this theory cannot be supported. Nevertheless, the spreading of the pine might have been favoured by human cultivation at lower altitudes. On the other hand, the extent to which the large grass savannas in the upland basins, especially those in the Haitian Plateau Central, are caused by the influence of man, is still an open question. In any case, the primeval flora has to a large extent been destroyed, mainly in the Haitian part of the island. Deforestation and cultivation, even on the steepest mountain slopes, have greatly hastened soil erosion. Soil erosion and badland dissection, even of gentle slopes, have assumed alarming proportions, chiefly in the Republic of Haiti.

Taking topographical and climatic factors, together with those of plant geography, two extreme types of natural macroregions may be recognized:

Table 45.   Hispaniola: Natural macro-regions

topography	climate	Vegetation	Area
Lowland plain	arid	semi-desert; cactus and thorn scrub savanna; tropical thorn and deciduous woodland	western Cibao; north coast of the Gulf of Gonave; Azua coastal plain; Cul-de-Sac and Enriquillo Plains
	sub-humid	tropical deciduous forest; semi-evergreen seasonal forest; savanna	Plaine du Nord; coastal plain east of Santo Domingo
	humid	tropical rain forest	eastern Cibao (Vega Real); Plaine des Cayes
Upland basin	semi-arid	tropical deciduous forest; dry savanna	Valle de San Juan
	sub-humid	semi-evergreen seasonal forest; moist savanna	Plateau Central; Valle de San Juan
Mountainous country	humid	tropical rain forest; lower montane and (sub-humid) tropical montane forest; elfin woodland	all mountains

dry lowland plains covered by thorn scrub and only cultivable after irrigation; and humid mountains originally completely forest-covered (Table 45). Between these two regional types range the semi-arid to subhumid upland basins with tropical deciduous and semi-evergreen seasonal forests and the numerous savannas. Since the mountains, without exception, are humid or at least subhumid a further regional differentiation is hardly necessary. It is necessary, however, as far as the lowlands are concerned since not all of them have arid conditions. Both humid and subhumid lowland plains exist, in addition to arid plains. Humid plains, like the small Plaine des Cayes and the large Vega Real in eastern Cibao in particular, have always been the favoured areas for settlement, from the Amerindian period through all the various stages of development up to the present time. Compared with the topographically unattractive mountain areas and the climatically unattractive dry plains the humid lowland plains have always been the most important economic regions of the island.

Stages in the development of the cultural landscape
The Amerindians

Estimates concerning the number of Amerindians at the time of Hispaniola's discovery vary greatly (cf. p. 55). Oviedo, giving the number of one million, is believed to have overestimated the number of original inhabitants. The aboriginal Ciboney who at that time inhabited western Cuba seem to have been completely replaced by the Tainos (insular Arawaks) in Hispaniola except in the far south-west, and in the north-east of the island the Mazoriges, whom the Tainos considered to be intruders, seem to have come to Hispaniola only shortly before the Spaniards arrived, probably giving way to pressure by the Caribs.

At the time of discovery there were five Amerindian realms in the island which kept contact with each other only by navigation. The mountains covered by forests and hostile to any settlement represented insurmountable barriers. On the whole, only the humid plains and the adjacent mountain slopes were settled. Contemporary accounts tell of flourishing cultural landscapes. The most populated area was the Vega Real.

The Amerindians lived in populous and large villages. They went fishing, hunted small rodents and cultivated field crops. Stone axes were used for clearing the woodland, and digging sticks for working the soil. The main plants, manioc and sweet potatoes, originated in the South American homeland of the Tainos. They were cultivated in the montone pattern, i.e. the young plants were put into heaps of earth (montones). In addition, peanuts and beans were important crops, and the cultivation of tobacco and cotton was very common. The cultivation of maize which indicates some connection with Yucatán was of comparatively minor importance. Irrigated fields existed only in the Haitian Cul-de-Sac plain where the most culturally advanced Amerindian realm in Hispaniola was located.

The cultivation of plants taken over from the Amerindians is not the only effect of the earliest cultural landscape on the present. Methods of farming developed by the Amerindians are still in use on numerous peasant small-holdings, mainly by the *conuqueros* (squatters) in the Dominican mountain areas. Many place names, usually in a modified version, can be traced back to the Taino era, and some settlements have been in existence since then, e.g. Concepción de la Vega, founded by the Spaniards in the place where a *cacique* (Amerindian chief) had his seat. The complex field pattern in the Vega Real probably originates in the Amerindian period, as Credner assumed. The cultural landscape of the Amerindian period has a stronger bearing on the presentday Dominican than on the Haitian part of the island, because of their different development following the early period of Spanish colonization.

Early Spanish colonization

Spanish colonization in Hispaniola started in 1493 with the foundation of Isabela by Columbus, a settlement on the north coast half way between the present Monte Cristi and Puerto Plata. In the preceding year Columbus on his first voyage had built Fort Navidad near Cap-Haitien because he could not take all his men back to Spain on the two ships which were left to him after his flag ship was shipwrecked. When Columbus returned to Fort Navidad in 1493 none of the crew had survived; therefore the founding of Isabela represents the start of Spanish colonization in the New World. Cultivated plants and domestic animals from the Old World had been brought to Isabela. Soon, after the military resistance of the Amerindians was broken, more towns were founded in the interior of the island, e.g. in the densely populated Vega Real. Concepción de la Vega was founded in 1495, immediately followed by Santiago de los treinta Caballeros. Fifteen Spanish towns existed on the island by the very early sixteenth century, some on the coast, others in the interior; the latter were usually built in the populous areas of former cacique residences. The citizens (*vecinos*) in these newly founded towns owned both urban and rural land.

The foundation of numerous towns in Hispaniola exemplifies the peculiar Spanish method of colonization. Later it was also used on the mainland and resulted in a relatively high percentage of urban population in the former Spanish possessions, as may be seen in the Dominican Republic. In 1496 the colonial government was removed from Isabela to the newly founded Santo Domingo de Guzmán on the south coast. It developed on the left side of the Ozama mouth near the gold deposits of San Cristóbal and was transferred to the right side of the river following a hurricane in 1502. Some of the towns founded during this early period were abandoned either temporarily or permanently; some were destroyed by earthquakes and rebuilt in other places; the majority of them, however, have continued into the present, Santo Domingo being an example of the latter group. During the early colonial period it was not only the administrative centre of Hispaniola for a short time but also the seat of the viceroy who commanded all the Spanish colonies in the New World. It also served as a starting point for all Spanish expeditions into the territories adjacent to the Caribbean Sea. At that time Santo Domingo had 35 000 inhabitants and was the largest city in the New World. Numerous monuments preserve the memory of that period. Various buildings in smaller towns also date back to the early period of Spanish colonization, including the church on the hill of Santo Cerro overlooking the Vega Real where the Holy Virgin is said to have shown herself to the Spaniards in 1495 during their victorious battle against the Amerindians who were led by two caciques.

After the island had been occupied the Spanish officers and soldiers were given land as owners or as tenants. They not only controlled the land but the natives on it as well. This encomienda system, which was developed in Hispaniola and later applied on the mainland, condemned the Amerindians to serfdom. They were forced to farm the land of their landlords and, above all, to mine gold. In 1503 all Amerindians were subjected by law to forced labour. At first gold was obtained by panning; when the output decreased gold veins, which were especially rich in the Dominican Cordillera Central, were mined. As mentioned above the first settlements were established in the neighbourhood of populous villages whose inhabitants could be forced into labour; at the same time, however, they were located near to gold deposits. The Amerindians died in such numbers (partly because of imported diseases) that, despite the influx of natives from the Bahamas and the South American mainland, who had been brought to Hispaniola by force, by 1548, according to Oviedo, only 500 of them were alive. The last native village near the town of La Vega became desolate in 1544. There exist many indications, however, that Amerindian blood has survived in the Dominican population until the present day.

During the period of Spanish colonial rule gold mining, export orientated sugar cane cultivation and, finally, extensive cattle farming superseded one another as the prevailing economic activity. Gold mining terminated in Hispaniola in 1520, and that year may be regarded as the end of the early colonial rule. Minor deposits in the western part of the island were exhausted even earlier, and the Spaniards had left these areas by 1520. A first and distinctive divergence in the Hispaniolan cultural landscape developed after the end of the period of early Spanish colonization which was characterized by gold mining.

Gold mining did not leave any traces in the landscape; nevertheless the period of early Spanish colonization greatly affected the future development of the island. Probably the most important result, affecting the entire island, was the almost complete annihilation of the Amerindians. Another outcome, which also affected the entire island, was the introduction of domestic animals and cultivated plants brought by the Spaniards from the Old World to Hispaniola after 1493. Cattle and sugar cane in particular, were later to become the most important factors within the Hispaniolan economy. The end of the period of early Spanish colonial rule, with the decimation of the Amerindians and the deterioration of the cultivated land after the retreat of the Spaniards and the devastation of their settlements, turned the western part of the island into a no-man's land. As mentioned before, however, several towns in the Dominican part of the island trace their history back to the period of early Spanish colonial rule. The Vega Real and the area surrounding Santo Domingo, the two centres of Spanish colonization from the start, are still the two most economically important districts in the Dominican Republic today.

The initial phase of plantation economy and the decline of the Spanish colony of Santo Domingo

Just as the encomienda system, which was to become characteristic in all the Spanish colonies in the New World, developed in Hispaniola during the early period of Spanish colonial rule, so did the plantation economy originate in Hispaniola—later to come to full fruition in the Caribbean. The decline of gold mining initiated the beginnings of the plantation-type cultivation of sugar cane which Columbus had imported from the Canary Islands in 1493. After it had become obvious in 1517 that the Amerindians were not fit for work on plantations, Negro slaves were imported and made up the labour force.

The great house of Engombe is the only remaining evidence of these first plantations in the Caribbean islands which developed in the coastal plain of Santo Domingo, near to the seaport and to the forests which supplied the fuel. Contemporary reports list forty plantations (1550) employing up to fifty Negro slaves each. During the early sixteenth century these first plantations possessed all those characteristics which they displayed at the height of maturity 200 years later in the heyday of the sugar plantation economy in the Antilles: they had plantation houses and Negro quarters, cane presses and boiling houses, beef farming to supply draught animals, fields which served for the cultivation of both sugar cane and crops for their own consumption; they united in one enterprise both the cultivation and processing of the cane; they belonged to a financially powerful proprietor and employed slaves; they were export orientated in their production and therefore developed near seaports.

But the initially lucrative sugar cane farming in the area of Santo Domingo suffered serious setbacks during the sixteenth century. Sugar production decreased, and the fields were left uncultivated. This development symbolized the general decline of the Spanish colony at that time. When precious metals were no longer obtainable in Hispaniola, Spanish interests turned towards the mainland, and many Spaniards migrated there from Hispaniola. For navigational and military reasons Santo Domingo was no longer the most important harbour in the Antilles after the middle of the sixteenth century when it was replaced by Habana. Twenty-five ships

219

used to call at Santo Domingo annually; now it was only one ship every two or three years. The French and British privateers became increasingly active. The colonial city of Santo Domingo has never recovered from the 1586 looting by Sir Francis Drake. In order to prevent the trade with the French and British corsairs the Spanish government ordered the abandonment of the frontier towns in the north (1605) and in the west (1606). Their inhabitants were settled in the newly founded towns of Bayaguana and Monte Plata north of Santo Domingo.

The decline of the Spanish colony of Santo Domingo was also seen in the transition to extensive cattle farming. Vast forest areas (*montes*) where the wild cattle were hunted belonged to the extensive beef farms (*hatos*) which were dispersed across the plains. The densely forested mountains remained completely void of any human settlement. Cattle farming did not decrease until the second half of the eighteenth century when sugar cane plantations (*haciendas*) were developed in the coastal plain around Santo Domingo, and medium sized (*estancias*) and small peasant farms (*ranchos*), practising mixed farming, developed in the Vega Real. Squatters (*conuqueros*) cleared the forests of the marginal mountains and increasingly practised shifting agriculture. However, extensive cattle farming retained its dominant position within the economy for at least 200 years, until about 1800. During the eighteenth century it was the source of meat exports into the neighbouring, densely populated French colony of St Domingue. Towards the end of the eighteenth century only between 100 000 and 125 000 people inhabited the Spanish colony.

Rise and prosperity of the French colony of St Domingue

As mentioned above, the western part of the island had been a no-man's land since 1520. The island of Tortuga off the north coast became the stronghold of French, British and Dutch corsairs who increasingly threatened Spanish shipping and Spanish harbours in the entire Caribbean region during the sixteenth century. Starting at the end of that century the western part of Hispaniola was settled anew, first the north coast, and then the entire area which was formerly abandoned by the Spaniards. Along the coast lay the hideouts of the filibusters; the buccaneers and their white companions (*engagés*) roamed through the interior, adopting no fixed settlements and hunting wild cattle and pigs. A third group in western Hispaniola were peasant settlers (*habitants*) who lived in compact villages and cultivated tobacco and basic food crops. There was a lively interchange between these three groups. The buccaneers supplied meat and hides, the habitants tobacco and food, and the filibusters contributed a multitude of articles they had captured.

The French element was dominant among these groups in western Hispaniola even before Le Vasseur claimed the island of Tortuga as a French possession in 1640. A few years later, in 1655, the French government declared the western part of the island of Hispaniola a French colony.

In the Treaty of Rijswijk of 1697 the Spanish government had to recognize the existence of the French colony of St Domingue in Hispaniola. The French government now became anxious to call a halt to the activities of the filibusters and to induce the buccaneers to settle and to become *habitants*. By the end of the seventeenth century the period of the filibusters and the buccaneers had ended. During the last decades of the seventeenth century French colonists immigrated and started to found settlements and to expand the area under cultivation. During the eighteenth century the French St Domingue developed rapidly into the richest colony in the New World.

Table 46.   St Domingue: growth of population

	1687	*1789*
Whites	4 411	30 826
Negro slaves	3 582	465 429
Free Negroes		27 548
Total population	7 993	523 803

Source: after Ducoeurjoly and Kemp

The rapid development of St Domingue is reflected in the population figures (Table 46), which indicate the high immigration from France and the heavy importation of slaves from Africa. The change in the structure of population during the eighteenth century indicates the development of St Domingue into a plantation colony.

At first tobacco and indigo, then sugar cane, coffee and cotton were the major crops. All the suitable land was cultivated, and each crop cultivated displayed distinct regional differentiation depending on topographical factors. Sugar cane, the most important crop for the economy, was mainly restricted to the humid plains, while coffee farming occupied large areas in the mountains. Where the land was too hilly for sugar cane and too low and dry for coffee, indigo was cultivated. The dry plains were mostly used for cotton cultivation, a large-scale irrigation system enabling their agricultural utilization. The humid plains, especially the extensive Plaine du Nord and the Plaine des Cayes in the south, were the most important economic regions; they also displayed the highest density of population. Only remote regions which were not suitable for agricultural use were claimed by *hattes* (cattle farms) and *corails* (pig farms). Small peasant holdings existed, owned by whites (*petits habitants*). However, the prevailing type of enterprise was the large-scale farm which was in the hands of a financially powerful planter aristocracy (*grands habitants*) residing more and more in the home country. This latter type of farm was the plantation combining cultivation and the industrial processing of its products. The planta-

221

tions produced mainly for export. Although food crops were cultivated for the local demand, the colony had to import additional victuals.

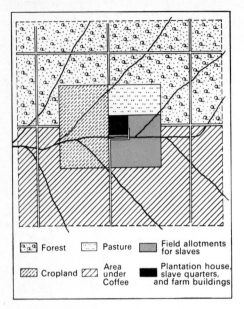

Forest	Pasture	Field allotments for slaves
Cropland	Area under Coffee	Plantation house, slave quarters, and farm buildings

Map 40. St Domingue: colonial coffee plantation (after Moral).

The settlement pattern in rural districts was determined by the plantation economy. The plantation house together with farm buildings and the village-type slave quarters usually formed one unit (Map 40). The plantation economy also expanded into areas distant from the coast since a network of roads provided good transport facilities. Since rivers were crossed by stone bridges and some of the roads were paved these could be used by carts throughout the year.

The urban settlements, with only a few exceptions, were situated along the coast and offered port and trade functions. The busiest port of the colony was Cap Français on the north coast, the present Cap-Haitien. Like all other towns it had a grid-pattern street layout. Cap Français was distinctive for its sumptuous public buildings and wide streets. Its multiple functions made this town (pop. 18 500) the economic and cultural centre of the colony.

Although French activities in St Domingue were brought to a sudden halt by the slave rebellion at the end of the eighteenth century, the period of French colonial rule has strongly influenced the region up to the present. The Haitian towns originated during that time, and the Haitian country roads follow their original French courses. Parts of the old French irrigation system are still being used today. The most important outcomes of French colonial rule in Hispaniola, however, are certainly the Negro population of the Republic of Haiti, the French language used by this nation, and the French cultural tradition, which is noticeable in the capital at least.

During the eighteenth century, when the French colony St Domingue and the Spanish colony Santo Domingo coexisted on the island, the cultural landscape of Hispaniola exhibited greater differentiation than ever before. The smaller western part of the island was densely populated, intensively used for agriculture and possessed good transport facilities; the larger eastern part of the island was still mainly characterized by an extensive pastoral economy, was only sparsely populated, and there were only a few settlements with hardly any transport facilities (Map 41).

Hispaniola during the nineteenth century

The bloody slave rebellion in St Domingue in 1791 brought about the sudden end of the French plantations; politically it led to the independent Negro Republic of Haiti in 1804, after prolonged fighting. Haiti is the second oldest republic in the New World after the USA. The political change had a number of important effects on the cultural geography. From the early nineteenth century onward small peasant holdings have increasingly come to replace the large plantations, although every effort was made to continue to operate the plantations in monarchic northern Haiti, at least in the plains then transferred to the Negro leaders. In the following period large areas of the state-owned former French plantations were sub-divided into small and minute farms, as had been done earlier in southern republican Haiti. In addition, numerous squatters settled on state-owned land. In 1930 almost 50 per cent of Haiti's territory was owned by the state, the larger portion of which was cultivated by squatter farms.

The colonial plantations had mainly produced for export; the Haitian small farms and very small smallholdings produced first of all for their own consumption and for the local market and only secondarily for export, a pattern which still persists. The output decreased greatly as compared with colonial times, and coffee became the major export crop replacing sugar cane. Coffee could only be planted in mountainous areas, as during colonial times, because of its climatic requirements. In the early nineteenth century therefore, the centres of agricultural production and settlement were trans-ferred from the plains to the mountains where the expansion of cleared lands led to serious soil erosion. Large parts of the plains have remained wasteland until today and only the ruins of former irrigation systems and plantation buildings bear witness to former intensive agricultural use. The pattern of rural settlement was also changed decisively since dispersed settlements of smallholders replaced the complex of plantation settlements.

The eastern part of the island which Spain transferred to France in 1795 was twice overrun by Haitian Negro armies and was in Haitian possession between 1801 and 1809 and between 1822 and 1844. But only the Plateau Central was permanently lost to Haiti and it still occupies a special position in the present Haitian economy. During the eighteenth century runaway

223

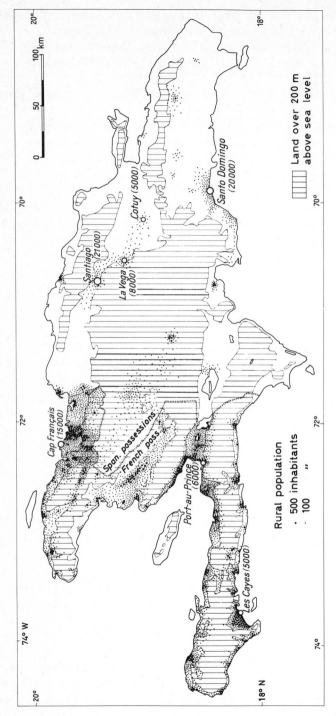

Map 41. Hispaniola: The Distribution of the population, *c* 1790.

slaves from St Domingue used to go to Santo Domingo and during the Haitian occupation large numbers of Negroes settled in the eastern part of the island. This explains the high proportion of mulattoes in the Dominican population. In addition, the negroid element in the Dominican population increased noticeably since many whites were killed or left the country because of the Haitian terror.

After the eastern part of the island had become the Dominican Republic in 1844 it submitted again to the Spanish Crown in 1861 because of the continued Haitian threat; in 1865 it finally received independence. At that time the Dominican president sought a union with the USA, but he was not successful. After 1875, however, US capital poured into the country. As happened in Cuba, this investment led to the development of large sugar cane plantations in the southern coastal plain which had already experienced plantation-type sugar cane farming in the sixteenth and eighteenth centuries. At the end of the nineteenth century, the neighbouring Republic of Haiti was exclusively characterized by small farms, mainly in mountainous areas, whereas large-scale sugar cane monocultural enterprises with huge, modern sugar factories were widespread on the coastal plain in the southern Dominican Republic. In the other central economic region, the Vega Real, the medium and small farms which until then had mainly grown produce for the home market, adjusted themselves to farming additional export-orientated crops like cocoa, coffee and tobacco. The appearance of the peasant landscape in the Vega Real still differs noticeably from the agricultural economy of Negro peasants in Haiti today. The development of the cultural landscape during the nineteenth century is characterized by the emergence of a peasantry in Haiti and by the increase in large landholdings in the Dominican Republic. This marked divergency in cultural geography still characterizes presentday Hispaniola.

Regional divisions

Cordillera Septentrional

The major landscapes in Hispaniola, that is the long mountain ranges running WNW–ESE and the longitudinal depressions, will be dealt with from north to south, the subregions within these major regions from west to east.

The northern cordillera in Hispaniola is restricted to the eastern, Dominican part of the island. The Cordillera Septentrional, also called Sierra de Monte Cristi, runs WNW–ESE for a distance of 200 km parallel to the Dominican north coast. Interrupted by the Gran Estero swamps it continues along the peninsula of Samaná which only lost its former island character since recent uplift. Without a transition zone, the Cordillera Septentrional descends in the west to the longitudinal valley of Cibao along a distinct fault; in the east the southern slopes of the range take the form of a hilly zone towards the Vega Real. The mountain range consists almost entirely of Miocene and Oligocene limestone; it exhibits distinct karst formations in parts, several erosion surfaces may be identified. It rises gradually from west to east until at Pico Diego de Ocampo, north-west of Santiago, it reaches its maximum height of 1249 m. Farther to the east the greatest heights lie between 600 and 900 m. The Samaná peninsula does not rise above 606 m; the karst region of this peninsula is flanked by uplifted marine abrasion platforms.

The entire Cordillera Septentrional and its northern foreland face the trade winds and therefore experience heavy precipitation. Sosúa on the north coast receives 2530 mm of rainfall annually, and the precipitation probably exceeds 5 m in the middle altitudes of the mountains. Tropical rain forests and semi-evergreen seasonal forests cover the lower altitudes, tropical and sometimes semi-evergreen montane forests grow at higher altitudes which still have large areas of primeval forests and land with potential for settlement.

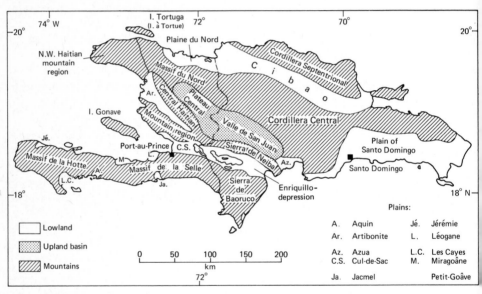

Map 42. Hispaniola: regional divisions.

The small coastal plains near Puerto Plata are occupied by sugar plantations. Two modern sugar factories process the cane, most of which they cultivate themselves. For instance, the Amistad factory near Imbert, west of Puerto Plata, controls 1500 ha of land of which 600 ha are under cane, 750 ha are in pastures, and the rest is covered by forests. Further to the east, the Dominican Government made the 9000 ha of a former banana area of the United Fruit Company available to Jewish refugees from Central Europe who founded there the Sosúa colony and have established dairy farms. Milk and cheese from the Sosúa dairy and Sosúa meat are sold throughout the Dominican Republic. A strip of coconut trees along the coast allows the production of copra in considerable amounts.

Cocoa is frequently cultivated in the lower parts of most of the valleys along the northern slopes of the Cordillera Septentrional, whereas coffee farming predominates on the entire southern slopes of that range between Santiago and Moca down to the Vega Real. This is also true of the northern slope around Puerto Plata. Coffee farms are mainly small peasant farms, not very small smallholdings as is the case in Haiti. The Dominican peasants do not usually cultivate coffee in the irregular mixed pattern which is characteristic of Jamaica and Haiti. Food crops are seldom found in coffee fields; they are cultivated in restricted areas which are dispersed along the slopes and are often shifted. In these areas bananas, tuberous plants, maize and beans are grown together side by side.

The lowland strip along the Atlantic coast and the Cordillera Septentrional are relatively accessible. A highway follows the coastline and connects the port of Puerto Plata with the ports of Sánchez and Samaná on the peninsula of the same name. Four all-weather roads cross the Cordillera Septentrional. Puerto Plata (pop. 19 000) is the largest town on the north coast. It handles 15 per cent of the Dominican exports, ranking second after Santo Domingo. The agricultural produce of the Cordillera Septentrional and the coastal area, as well as from parts of the Vega Real, is exported via Puerto Plata. The two new industrial plants of this town, where chocolate and matches are manufactured, are based on local raw materials.

Immigrants from the Canary Islands founded the small town of Samaná on the south coast of the bay of the same name in the eighteenth century. This area is remote, and there still exists in it a group of English speaking Protestant Negroes whose forefathers immigrated from the USA as free Negroes in the early nineteenth century when the present Dominican Republic belonged to Haiti.

The northern longitudinal depression

The northern longitudinal depression is divided into the Plaine du Nord in Haiti and the Cibao in the Dominican Republic.

The **Plaine du Nord**, which is chiefly composed of alluvium, stretches for 65 km, gradually gaining in width, from the town of Cap-Haitien eastward to the Massacre River, which is the border with the Dominican Republic. The precipitation decreases greatly in the same direction. Therefore, an eastern drier part may be distinguished from a wetter western region. In the more humid western part of the Plaine du Nord towards Cap-Haitien, and in the plains further to the west which stretch far into the Massif du Nord along the rivers Limbé and Grande Rivière du Nord, several ruins of former sugar factories show that these lowland plains were once occupied by numerous sugar plantations and that it used to be one of the economic centres of the French colony. Sugar cane is still cultivated in some places, e.g. around Limonade. The only sugar factory lies east of Cap-

227

Haitien. It is a small enterprise which is supplied with cane by numerous smallholders producing hardly 1000 tonnes of sugar annually. Another sugar factory built near Limonade in 1952 went bankrupt in 1958. Today, export orientated sugar cane cultivation which characterized this region in colonial times is not important in northern Haiti. Nevertheless, sugar cane is found everywhere in the peasant polyculture of the humid plain. There it is processed in the antiquated presses and boiling houses which can be found everywhere in Haiti, but nowhere else in the West Indies. An arrangement of winches is turned by cattle which rotates the vertical wooden rollers which then squeeze the cane between them (Plate 10). The juice is then boiled in a huge cauldron under a board roof. Six hundred of these antiquated boiling-houses (*guildives*) still exist in Haiti. Mainly 'clairin' is produced, a cane brandy very popular with the rural population and consumed in large quantities.

The landscape of the semi-arid eastern Plaine du Nord is characterized today by extensive sisal cultivation (Map 45). During the US occupation the Haitian Government granted foreigners the right to acquire land. Three US companies bought about 16 000 ha of land in the eastern Plaine du Nord in the 1920s. The former smallholders lost their land and are now being employed by these large-scale enterprises as workers. For instance, the Haytian American Development Corporation owns about 8000 ha of land and employs 5000 workers. Its 'Plantation Dauphin' is supposed to be the largest sisal plantation in the world. It supplies 60 per cent of the Haitian sisal production. In the surrounding parts of the plain are very extensive agave fields, the green-blue plant planted in endless parallel rows. The leaves of the sisal agave are cut for the first time four years after planting, and then again after another four years. Then the plants have to be renewed. The sisal leaves are transported from the fields by small diesel trains. Their tracks can be moved from one part of the plantation to another according to demand. The fibres are mechanically removed from the leaves in factories. Large drying grounds, where the fibres dry in the open air on wire netting or on stretched ropes, adjoin these dressing plants. Sisal dressing plants are located in Phaéton and Dérac, and the port of Fort Liberté specializes in the export of sisal. Adjacent to the sisal plantation area in the south, in the hilly and more humid foreland of the Massif du Nord, are the small fields of peasant smallholders with irregular mixed cultivation.

During the sisal boom following the Second World War even the semi-humid regions of the Plaine du Nord were taken into sisal cultivation. The sisal dressing plant in Cap-Haitien is supplied by plantations of the surrounding districts where pineapples were formerly cultivated with little success. The old pineapple canning factory has been converted into a sisal dressing and processing plant.

Cap-Haitien is the only town in the Plaine du Nord. It is also the largest in northern Haiti. Although the town was destroyed by fire during the Revolution, and again during the struggle for independence, and by an

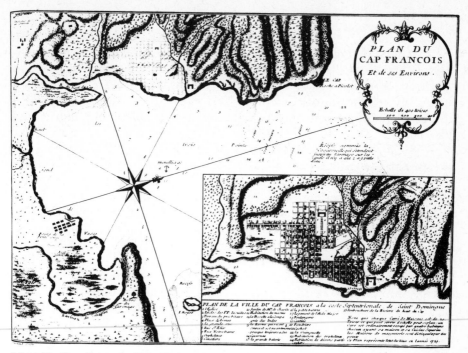

Map 43. Cap Français (Cap-Haitien) during the eighteenth century. Town map after Charlevoix (Histoire de l'Isle espagnole, Paris 1731).

earthquake in 1842, it retains a colonial atmosphere unlike any other Haitian town. Several colonial stone buildings with balconies have been preserved in addition to the fortifications along the shore and the fountain in the Place d'Armes. The cathedral was rebuilt in its original form after it was destroyed by the earthquake. The streets were built by the French in a grid pattern (Map 43) and still bear their colonial names. The ruins of the castle, Sans-Souci, 18 km south of the town and built after the plans of the castle in Potsdam, and the mighty fortress of La Ferrière at an altitude of 1000 m on the Massif du Nord, for the construction of which the dictator conscripted 200 000 people, remind one of the north Haitian kingdom of Henri Christoph. Cap-Haitien is the most important harbour after the capital. Ten per cent of Haitian exports are shipped from here, mainly coffee from the mountainous hinterland and sisal and hardwood from the Plaine du Nord. Although Cap-Haitien possesses a number of schools and various other cultural institutions, it has not regained the central cultural position which it claimed during the colonial era. However, it is the only town other than the capital to attract tourists. The tourist industry has been stimulated by the fact that the town is linked with Port-au-Prince by an asphalt road. This road continues east as far as the Dominican border. It opens the Plaine du Nord to traffic in a way that no other Haitian port hinterland is opened, except that of Port-au-Prince.

The Plaine du Nord continues eastward, beyond Manzanillo Bay and the

229

Massacre River which flows into it, as the **Cibao**. With a width of 15 to 40 km and a length of 225 km it stretches between the Cordillera Septentrional and the Cordillera Central as far east as the Samaná Bay. About halfway, near Santiago, at an altitude of 300 m, lies the watershed between the westward flowing Río Yaque del Norte and the eastward flowing Río Yuna. In the same region aridity changes to humidity within only a short distance.

The Cibao has been built up from the detritus of the neighbouring mountains, deposited there since the Miocene. Structurally it is a synclinal depression. In addition, the longitudinal fault boundaries, which are topographically distinct, show it to be a structural rift valley. In the western part of the Cibao wide river terraces covered by gravel flank the Río Yaque del Norte, and in the eastern part the Río Yuna and its tributaries have cut down into the surface of the Vega Real for 25 m. In the river channels one may observe that the bedrock is superimposed by a thick layer of black soil, 3 m in depth. It is easy to cultivate, extremely fertile and is said to be the highest yielding soil in the Antilles.

Until the twentieth century the dry western part of the Cibao was used for extensive cattle farming and had only a small population. During colonial times this Spanish region supplied draught animals to the French sugar cane plantations in the northern coastal plains of St Domingue. Today extensive areas are still covered by poor scrub savanna used for extensive cattle farming. During the last three decades, however, and especially since 1945 the landscape has changed markedly. Between 1930 and 1955 the area under irrigation in the Dominican Republic expanded from 3000 ha to 155 000 ha. The western Cibao profited most from this development. Today wet rice cultivation is characteristic of the valley floor along the Río Yaque del Norte, and newly irrigated banana plantations extend along the river terraces and are supposed to give highest yields in the Caribbean islands at the present time. Today, the western Cibao supplies the rice demand of the entire Dominican Republic. The rice is transported by trucks from the drying plants in Santiago, Valverde and Villa Isabel. New villages have developed along the Río Yaque, and the number of inhabitants in the settlements has trebled within a period of only twenty years.

Rice and banana farming is carried out almost exclusively by large-scale enterprises. A large amount of foreign capital has been invested in banana cultivation. The Grenada Company, which is affiliated to the US-American Standard Fruit Company, acquired about 74 000 ha of the scrub savanna in the Río Massacre valley at the Haitian border near Dajabón. Its extensive banana plantations are irrigated by means of overhead irrigation. The Grenada Company built the port of Puerto Libertador on the Bay of Manzanillo, today called Pepillo Salcedo, from where the first bananas were shipped in 1939. Just as Pepillo Salcedo exports bananas cultivated on American plantations, the Haitian Fort-Liberté exports sisal fibres produced by American enterprises. In this dry region of the northern longitudinal depression US companies cultivate sisal on the left bank of the Río Massacre in Haiti, on the right bank in the Dominican Republic they cultivate bananas. The Dominican government granted the Standard Fruit Company the right to establish banana plantations in these once sparsely populated areas within the framework of the *Dominicación fronteriza* policy (cf. p. 267).

In the transitional zone between the arid and the humid Cibao, where no irrigation is needed, cultivation around Santiago specializes mainly in tobacco farming. The landscape is characterized by large tobacco sheds in the open fields.

Columbus was greatly impressed by the eastern humid region, the Vega Real, with its large Amerindian population and their highly productive farming. It is the region with the highest density of population and it is one of the two oldest economic centres of the Dominican Republic. Most of the Dominican population used to live here during colonial times. Half the Dominican population, i.e. 500 000, were still concentrated in the Vega Real in 1920. Today, it supports one-third of the entire population, about one million. Credner termed the Vega Real the area with the healthiest peasant economy and, in terms of its harmony, the most beautiful cultural landscape in the Antilles. In fact, nowhere else in the Caribbean will one find more intensive and more versatile cultivation than in the Vega Real, where farming is done with extreme care by a mixed population, the majority of which is white. Cocoa fields predominate in this markedly multicrop farming region. In addition, coffee is an important export crop, and bananas, maize, sweet potatoes, manioc and dry rice are grown either for subsistence or for the home market. Usually one field contains two or three of these crops (Plate 13); however, the plants are carefully planted in rows in contrast to the extremely irregular pattern of planting characteristic of smallholders in Jamaica and Haiti. The young cocoa and coffee plants are protected against the sun first by maize, then by banana plants, and taro and sweet potatoes grow between the rows of the latter. When the cocoa trees have outgrown the shade from the banana palms fast growing trees are planted as *madres del cacao*. The crop combination and the stage in the crop sequence changes from one field to another. Again and again dispersed groups of the impressive royal palm appear in the landscape. In a changing pattern the landscape is sometimes characterized by tree cultivations, sometimes by ground crops. During the last decade, rice cultivation has greatly expanded in the eastern area, especially around Cotuí. Newly built rice mills are the landmarks of larger villages. The peasants live in compact settlements, and the roads are lined by small and also by impressive, large farm houses. Farms of various sizes adjoin each other in an extremely irregular pattern; farms of less than 20 ha are predominant. Of the farmland in the parish of Moca in the central Vega Real 62 per cent is occupied by small farms (<20 ha), 18 per cent by medium-sized farms

231

(20–75 ha), and 20 per cent by large-scale enterprises (> 75 ha). It is very probable that the extremely irregular field pattern of today is partly the outcome of the Amerindian agriculture (Map 44).

The town of La Vega (pop. 20 000), founded in 1495, Moca (pop. 14 000), and San Francisco de Macorís (pop. 26 000) are busy market-places carrying out regional functions in the Vega Real. They are all over-shadowed by Santiago (pop. 83 000), founded in 1500, which carries out supraregional functions and is located on the western border of the Vega Real on a terrace of the Río Yaque. Both the western and the eastern parts of the Cibao are orientated towards this town. Here, export merchants come to trade in the versatile food production of the entire Cibao, in addition to the coffee and cocoa from the Vega Real and the tobacco from the arid regions of the Cibao. Santiago is a friendly town with numerous modern buildings. There are only a few remnants of the early colonial period, apart from the grid pattern of the oldest parts of the city, since Santiago has been destroyed by several earthquakes in the past. Monte Cristi (pop. 5600) near the mouth of the Río Yaque is a quiet provincial capital. Salt pans cover the Icaquito Bay in its arid surrounding region.

When the Vega Real adjusted itself to export orientated farming in the late nineteenth century a British company built a railway line in 1888 to Sánchez on the Samaná Bay in order to facilitate exports. Until then Puerto Plata was the only port of the Cibao, but could only be reached from Santiago via mule tracks. A recently built road reinstated Puerto Plata as the most important harbour of the Cibao, but Santo Domingo succeeded in attracting a considerable amount of the agricultural produce after the Carretera Duarte, the first road connection across the Cordillera Central, had been completed.

The central cordillera system

The central cordillera system is divided into the north-west Haitian mountain region and the Massif du Nord in Haiti and the Cordillera Central in the Dominican Republic.

The **north-west Haitian mountain region** is composed of extrusive rock and Tertiary and Pleistocene limestone. It is relatively sparsely populated and is at a disadvantage because of its remoteness and lack of transport facilities. Its economic potential decreased decisively after the colonial era. The only road in this region, the Route du Nord, starts from Port-de-Paix and meets the Haitian main road from Cap-Haitien to Port-au-Prince at Gonaives. In the vicinity of the village Bombardopolis, in the extreme west, blue-eyed Negroes show traces of German and Swiss settlers who immigrated in the middle of the eighteenth century, some of whom soon moved on to Lousiana. During the nineteenth century squat-ters destroyed the entire forest cover of this region. Some cattle farming is done in the driest parts, otherwise small-scale mixed farming only meets local demand, with some coffee cultivation in the higher and more humid

Map 44. The Dominican Republic: field pattern in the Vega Real.

altitudes. In colonial times wealthy sugar cane plantations covered the coastal plain of Port-de-Paix and the Jean Rabel plain. Today tree and ground crops are cultivated in the former and find a ready market in the Turks and Caicos Islands and in the Bahamas. The Caicos schooners which do most of the shipping carry the dried meat of about 1·7 million sea-snails (*Strombus gigas*) annually to the ports of Port-de-Paix and Cap-Haitien. This snail meat, providing a cheap protein food, is very popular with the Haitian population.

Off the Atlantic coast of the north-west peninsula lies the mountainous island of Ile à Tortue (Tortuga). Its 220 sq km are inhabited by 12 500 people (1950) who live by mixed farming and fishing. During the seventeenth century the island was notorious for its hideouts of French free-booters. France took possession of western Hispaniola from there.

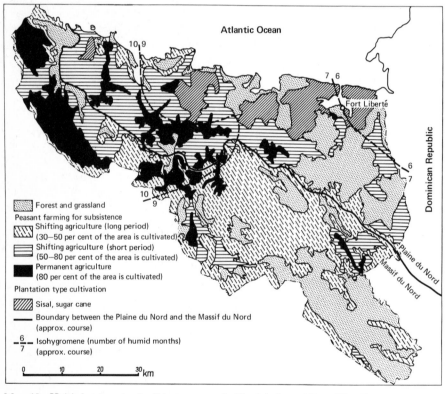

Map 45. Haiti: land use in the Département du Nord (adapted from Wood).

The **Massif du Nord** adjoining the north-west Haitian mountain region south of the Plaine du Nord consists of numerous mountain ranges which are separated from each other either by narrow, deeply incised valleys or by wide valley plains. Igneous rocks predominate; in many areas in the south, however, Cretaceous limestones can be found. The entire mountain country

234

was occupied by productive coffee plantations at the end of the colonial period. Today it is a region of peasant multicropping which is export orientated only where coffee is the main crop (Map 45). In many districts of this mountain country, mainly in those far from any transport route, the smallholders merely produce for their own consumption or for the local market. Tree cultivation is most widespread in the higher altitudes. Bananas, coffee, breadfruit, mangoes and ackees are usually intermingled in a very irregular distribution pattern. The bananas, mainly plantains, serve to shade the coffee plants. From the air the areas of tree cultivation look like forest land. The original forest, however, has been almost completely destroyed. The characteristic dispersed type of settlement cannot be recognized from the air since the buildings are hidden beneath the trees. Ground crops predominate on the lower and less humid mountain regions. Even the steepest slopes are occupied by the small irregularly shaped fields where millet, maize, upland rice and various tuberous plants are cultivated in addition to peas and beans. These fields are also characterized by an irregular intermixture of various plants. The leaves of the sweet potato creep along the ground, and the yam leaves climb up sticks or tree trunks. In between grow some maize plants, the taro spreads its large leaves, and the manioc bushes top everything. Even solitary sugar cane or banana trees may be found, sometimes entwined with beans. The trunks of the paw-paw trees extend above with fruit clusters at the top. Near the extremely dispersed, small and poorly equipped buildings grow the shady mango or breadfruit trees. In order to sell the crop which is not needed for home consumption, the peasant women often walk for hours to the market carrying the products in baskets on their head.

The **Cordillera Central** reaches a width of 130 km bordering the Massif du Nord in the south-west and sealing off the Cibao in the south. It divides into two branches. The lower branch stretches eastward across the island as far as the Cabo Engaño; it is called the mountain country of Castellanos and of Seibo, sometimes also the Cordillera Oriental. The much higher branch, which turns to the south, reaches the Caribbean coast between Santo Domingo and Azua where it is called the Sierra de Ocoa. The two branches are composed of the following major longitudinal zones which may be distinguished by their rock structure: the lower branch forms the northern sedimentary rock zone and runs eastward, while the crystalline centre and the southern sedimentary rock zone of the Cordillera Central turn to the south. A number of peaks in the last mentioned section of the mountain range exceed the altitude of 2500 m, e.g. the Alto Bandera (2834 m); the highest elevations, Pico Duarte (3175 m) and Loma la Rucilla (3045 m), rise in the central region further to the north beyond the Constanza basin. The peaks of the Cordillera Central tower above extended erosion surfaces which are dispersed widely across the mountains at various altitudes. The Cordillera Central is an obvious example of an uplifted old mountain range with accordant summits and subdued relief, in

235

spite of its remarkable height. However, the erosion surfaces are strongly dissected in parts by deeply incised valleys. The four major rivers rise in these mountains: the Río Yaque del Norte, the Río Yaque del Sur, the Río Yuna, and the Artibonite. The mountains have twelve rainy months, they receive a large amount of rainfall and are still covered by forests over wide areas. The impressive pine forests have only been utilized since the completion of a road leading from Baní into the Cibao via Constanza. Numerous woodcutters' camps have developed along this road on stretches of flat land at an altitude of 2000 m. Because of its extent, its rugged relief and its forests, the Cordillera Central acted as a decisive barrier to settlement and communication between the adjoining longitudinal valleys to the north and south from the Amerindian period until very recent times. There is still no road in the uninhabited mountain area between the Haitian border and the route Constanza–La Vega. Only the quickly exhausted gold deposits in the crystalline central zone attracted the Spaniards at the start of the colonial period.

Although the Cordillera Central possesses various ore deposits, e.g. chromiferous and nickel ores in serpentinite regions, mining still plays a minor role. After 1953 iron ore of a high grade was extracted for a short time by surface mining near Hatillo, halfway between La Vega and Santo Domingo. It was exported from Santo Domingo and Río Haina.

During the Trujillo regime a large number of agricultural colonies developed along the sparsely populated mountain slopes near the Haitian border. The agricultural development of the interior far from the border also progressed. The best example of this is the upland valley of Constanza (Plate 12). Various villages were established where the colonists settled according to their nationality and where small and clean wooden houses were built along several roads. Since 1955 Dominicans, Hungarians and Japanese have settled in Constanza. To facilitate the development of community activities, village settlements were preferred. The carefully cultivated fields of the Constanza colonists lie en bloc near the villages. Due to the altitude of the valley (1200 m) the colonists specialize in farming temperate crops. Fields with potatoes, tomatoes, cabbages, onions, beans, strawberries and many flowers which are sold in Santo Domingo, offer a rather Central European appearance. A state-owned hotel in Constanza and another in the pine forest region near Jaracaboa, 600 m high, indicate the effort made by the Dominican Government to develop a tourist industry even in the mountain regions.

Forests also cover extensive parts of the eastern lower branch of the Cordillera Central which extends towards the Cabo Engaño—the mountain country of Castellanos and mainly that of Seibo (Cordillera Oriental). These forests are untouched, especially in the inaccessible cone karst regions of Cevicos and south of the Samaná Bay (Los Haitises, Map 7). Cocoa cultivation by smallholders extends mainly along the southern edge of the mountain country of Seibo where the savannas of the coastal plain of Santo Domingo change into moist forests. The towns of Higüey, El Seibo and Hato Mayor (Plate 14) have developed as market places along the boundary between the mountain country of Seibo and the southern coastal plain.

Plains and mountains in central Hispaniola

All the regions between the central cordillera system and the southern longitudinal depression belong to this major region, e.g. the upland basins of the Plateau Central and the Valle de San Juan, the coastal plain of Azua, the central Haitian mountain country, the Sierra de Neiba, the Artibonite plain, and the island of Gonave.

The **Plateau Central** south of the main cordillera is composed of Miocene limestone and slate. Among the recent stream captures in this area that of the Artibonite is most impressive. Originally the Artibonite crossed the Valle de San Juan and flowed into the Río Yaque del Sur. The Plateau Central claims a special position within Haiti in so far as it possesses cultural geographical characteristics which point back to the time when it used to belong to the Spanish colony of Santo Domingo. Before the Haitian occupation extensive cattle farming (*hatos*) characterized the savannas of the Plateau Central. *Conuqueros* had settled in various places along the forested slopes of the valleys. The area had only a few inhabitants; it is still one of the most sparsely populated Haitian regions. Pastoral economy still predominates, but large-scale enterprises possessing vast and extensively used pastures no longer exist. Today the cattle belong to peasant farms. Surrounding the dispersed farm houses are small parcels which are cultivated in the pattern of multicropping mentioned above, serving only the home demand. According to soil and climatic conditions different plants are important, e.g. cotton and sisal in the dry areas. The grassland in the neighbourhood of the farms is used by a few head of cattle. Specialized beef farms do not exist. Hedges and fences form the boundaries between the fields and the grassland, turning the Plateau Central into a bocage landscape. The small and dispersed islands of cultivation in the arable fields and the isolated buildings scattered over the widespread grassland are clearly visible from the air. More extensive cultivated land and settlements in close proximity to each other may only be found along the rivers. Busy market places have developed mainly along the border zone of the Massif du Nord. Hinche is the largest centre, situated where a valley widens in the central region of the Plateau. Peasants farm large compact areas round the town using an irregular multicrop system. Although Hinche has a population of 4500 it does not carry out any town functions. Only one third-class road crosses the Plateau coming from the south. Absolutely no road connections exist to the north across the Massif du Nord, to the west across the Montagnes Noires, nor to the east in the direction of the Dominican border.

The **Valle de San Juan** borders the Plateau Central in the south-east between the Cordillera Central and the Sierra de Neiba. Its topographical, geological and geomorphological characteristics tally completely with those of the Haitian Plateau Central. Originally, the drainage of the entire region flowed towards the south-east. Because of recent stream capture, however, the north-western part of the drainage of the Valle de San Juan became a tributary of the present Artibonite which flows into the Gulf of Gonave. Nevertheless, the major part of the upland basin still drains towards the south-east via the Río San Juan which is a righthand tributary of the Río Yaque del Sur.

Even the climate of the Valle de San Juan corresponds with that of the Haitian Plateau Central. The relatively low precipitation is the result of its position in the lee of the Cordillera Central. The Plateau Central has a mainly semihumid climate, whereas the central region of the Valle de San Juan is arid. As in the Plateau Central, the savannas of the upland basin served for extensive cattle grazing during the Spanish colonial period, and draught animals were exported to the neighbouring French plantation colony during the eighteenth century. The farm buildings of the *hatos* are still dispersed throughout the vast and open plateaux. But the pasture areas have everywhere been interspersed with arable fields which are concentrated in the valleys cut deep into the plateaux. Irrigation enabled the expansion of the cultivated area far into the plateaux, especially around San Juan and between Elías Piña and Las Matas. Wet rice is usually cultivated by peasants on small fields in the valley floors, whereas maize and beans predominate among the irrigated cultivated plants on the plateaux. There the fields are much larger and can be ploughed. Most of these more extensive agricultural enterprises were *hatos* originally. Bee-keeping throughout the upland basin supplies large quantities of honey and beeswax. The gingerbread from Las Matas made of honey and corn meal is very popular throughout the Dominican Republic. Peasant coffee cultivation can be found in the marginal zones of the Valle de San Juan along the slopes of the mountains adjoined by the districts of the *conuqueros* with their dispersed small fields and mostly very isolated dwellings. Peasant tobacco cultivation is characteristic of the south-eastern part of the basin. The tobacco is brought to the market of Padre Las Casas in the shape of long, sausage-like rolls.

An oval stone structure from the Amerindian era near the town of San Juan de Maguana (pop. 20 000) is a reminder that San Juan was founded near the main settlement of the cacique realm of Maguana in 1504. The asphalt road Carretera Sánchez crosses the upland basin as far as the Haitian border and connects San Juan with Santo Domingo. The mountains to the north and south of the Valle de San Juan, however, are still uncrossed by any road. The provincial capital of San Juan is the central settlement of the entire upland basin which is completely given over to agriculture.

Within the framework of the *Dominicación fronteriza* a very active interior colonization programme was pursued in the province of San Rafael which

238

was only established in 1942 adjoining the Haitian border. The formerly unimportant settlement Elías Piña near the Haitian border grew rapidly after it was declared provincial capital. Today Elías Piña has wide streets, squares with trees, parks and modern public buildings and gives evidence of the successful interior colonization programme, as do the new irrigated areas in the middle section of the Artibonite and the new agricultural colonies. Several of the latter, however, which were established in remote border districts, have fallen into decay since the force exercised during the Trujillo regime has been removed. The Carretera Internacional can no longer be termed a road. It represented the national borderline between Haiti and the Dominican Republic; it was once a showpiece of Dominican interior colonization and was still listed as an asphalt road between Elías Piña and Dajabón on the road map of 1960. Between the former agricultural colony of Pedro Santana, which has now been reduced to a military camp, and the frontier in Villa Ancona the Carretera Internacional for 50 km is overgrown by shrubs and its surface has been destroyed by weathering to such an extent that it can only be used by cross-country cars. Only military patrols sometimes use the former highway. The *Dominicación fronteriza* has outlasted the Trujillo regime only in areas which have more favourable transportation: in the central region of the San Juan upland basin near Elías Piña as well as near Dajabón in the north and the Enriquillo Depression in the south.

The **coastal plain of Azua** also belongs to the longitudinal depression of the Plateau Central and the Valle de San Juan. A low watershed separates it from the latter. The Río Yaque del Sur does not follow the depression as far as the Azua plain; it turns sharply in the south-eastern Valle de San Juan and enters the Sierra de Neiba through a narrow transverse valley. Only minor rivers flow across the Azua plain, therefore, discharging no water during the dry season. The completely arid plain of Azua has extremely unfavourable conditions for irrigation. On the alluvial plains in the marginal regions of the plain one may find peasant mixed farming, depending on well water for irrigation. Economic utilization of the plain on a large scale, however, did not start until 1951 when henequén plantations were established in the districts surrounding the town of Azua (761 mm annual rainfall). Since then they have expanded mainly in a south-westerly direction. These national plantations covered an area of about 25 000 ha offering a welcome chance of employment to the population of Azua where a new sisal factory was constructed. Since 1966 these plantations lie desolate. Azua, founded in 1504, was rebuilt by the Spaniards 5 km away from its original foundations after an earthquake. The Haitians burnt down the town three times during the nineteenth century.

The **island of Gonave**, sharing its name with the surrounding gulf, is about 60 km long and 15 km wide. Its 700 sq km are inhabited by a population of 27 000, thereby representing an unparalleled low population density for Haiti (38 persons per sq km). Wide belts of mangroves, shallow waters, steep cliffs, and offshore coral reefs, make the coasts almost inaccessible. The limestone surface and karst topography, which is covered by thorn scrub savannas, and the aridity of the island only allow very limited cultivation. Quite a large portion of the population is engaged in the fishing industry. Gonave served as a sanctuary for runaway slaves during the colonial period, and during recent decades increasing numbers of landless peasants migrated from the main island. The term 'frontier' of Haiti (Hall, 1928) for this island is therefore justified to some extent.

The **Artibonite Plain** stretches from north-west to south-east between two branches of the central Haitian mountains, the Montagnes Noires in the north and the Chaine de Matheux in the south. It is completely arid near the coast. Cactus savannas cover extensive areas in the lower plain. Dams were built on either side of the river during colonial times as a protection against high floods which occur in May and October. The French inhabitants cultivated cotton for the most part; in the vicinity of Desdunes a vast cotton plantation employed 1500 slaves. Today, the Artibonite Plain is densely populated close to the river course and mixed farming on a small scale is characteristic. Smallholders cultivate rice mainly, in addition to maize, millet, tuberous plants and bananas. Until recently this cultivation depended on the flood waters of the river; 32 000 ha of irrigated land are planned in the lower section of the plain of which 10 000 ha have been made available during recent years with financial aid from the USA. The main irrigation canals have been constructed for another 10 000 ha. The Peligre Dam was built in the transverse valley of the Artibonite in the Montagnes Noires. Since control of the river has been made possible the plain is now protected against the former repeated flooding and a regular water discharge is supplied through the canals. After the network of irrigation canals had been completed, financial difficulties prevented the construction of the necessary drainage system. This resulted in soil damage for a short time through oversalination. Although experimental farms were established, new drying grounds and storage plants for rice were built, and modern machinery was supplied, and in spite of the aid of ODVA officials (Organisme de Développement de la Vallée de l'Artibonite) the government has not yet succeeded in persuading all smallholders to practise progressive farming methods. Nevertheless, the new irrigated land produced very high rice yields, giving rise to the hope that the Artibonite Plain will one day be able to provide enough food for the entire Haitian population. The Haitian main road from Port-au-Prince to Cap-Haitien crosses the lower part of the plain between St Marc and Gonaives. There are no bridges farther upstream. Only a few marketplaces exist. The only towns are St Marc and Gonaives on the Gulf of Gonave. The produce of the hinterland is exported from these towns as it was in colonial times: cotton from the surrounding districts of Gonaives, sisal fibres from the St Marc region, and coffee from the mountainous hinterland. Financial aid from the Federal Republic of

Germany was used to examine the possibilities of improving the water supply in the plain of Gonaives. New wells in the villages draw on underground water.

The **central Haitian mountain region** is divided into the Montagnes Noires between the Plateau Central and the Artibonite Depression and the Chaines des Matheux and du Trou d'Eau between the Artibonite and the Cul-de-Sac Plains. These deeply indented mountain ranges rise to heights of more than 1500 m. The Montagnes Noires, including the narrow, gorgelike transverse valley of the Artibonite, are composed of igneous rocks and Tertiary limestone. They unite with the Chaine du Trou d'Eau in the south-east and continue as the Sierra de Neiba beyond the Dominican border. The Chaine du Trou d'Eau and its continuation in the north-west, the Chaine des Matheux, are chiefly limestone mountains. Their karst plateaux are of varying sizes and are crossed by deep, canyonlike dry valleys. The central Haitian mountain region is extremely hostile to any transport because of its high degree of local relief, and its settled areas are very isolated. Numerous ruins of colonial coffee plantations are to be found there, and many peasants in these areas still wear the traditional costumes of a hundred years ago; the men, for instance, wear long blue coats, breeches and broad-brimmed hats (Moral, 1961). The mountain slopes were stripped of their former forest cover and soil erosion has assumed alarming proportions almost everywhere. The settlements with rather poor crop farming are concentrated on the steep valley sides. Tree cultivation is predominant only in the western parts of the mountains. Mixed farming on peasant smallholdings with some concentration on coffee cultivation in a few rather limited areas is found here, just as it is in the other Haitian mountains.

The long, narrow mountain range of the **Sierra de Neiba** is the continuation of the Haitian Montagnes Noires and lies between the northerly Valle de San Juan and the southerly Enriquillo Depression. The narrow water gap of the Río Yaque del Sur crosses the eastern part of the Sierra. The mountain region beyond the Río Yaque which separates the Azua plain from the Enriquillo Depression is called the Sierra Martin García. The Sierra de Neiba rises to 2249 m. Karstic features on the limestone plateaux, often steeply dipping, are very characteristic of the landscape at varying heights. Mainly semi-evergreen seasonal forests extend over the northern flanks of the mountains where some *conuqueros* cultivate their rather dispersed, small fields. Communications in the mountains are completely undeveloped, and only mixed farming by smallholders may be found. Only the small coffee production is market orientated.

The coastal plain of Santo Domingo

The coastal plain of Santo Domingo is situated south of the Cordillera Central and starts in the west at the mouth of the Río Ocoa. It stretches eastward as the Plain of Baní with a width of only 10 km, and then broadens

241

to a width of about 60 km in the Santo Domingo region, retaining this width for a distance of almost 200 km until it reaches the eastern end of the island. The eastern section is known as Llano de Seibo. The entire coastal plain is composed of Pleistocene coral limestone and has been added to the island only after several recent uplifts. Several marine terraces follow one another, the highest reaching a height of about 100 m at the foot of the mountains. The uniform plains are divided by numerous short, and sometimes deeply incised, rivers all of which originate in the mountainous hinterland which receives heavy rainfall. Karst formations are very common, especially dolines. The climate of the coastal plain of Santo Domingo consists mainly of subhumid or semi-arid conditions (1500–1000 mm of annual precipitation); there are widespread savannas with the characteristic royal palms, isolated or in groups, and Ceiba trees. This coastal plain resembles the Camagüey plains in Cuba in respect of topography and, especially, of cultural geography. The landscape is dominated by sugar cane monoculture cultivated in plantations which were established in the late nineteenth century when Cuban refugees and US capital poured into the country. Before that the plain was used for extensive cattle farming with the exception of the Santo Domingo region where the first sugar cane plantations of the New World were established in the early sixteenth century.

The coastal plains east of La Romana and the island of Saona are covered either by savannas, used exclusively for dairy farming, or by tropical deciduous and semi-evergreen seasonal forests. The major part of the plain, however, is the domain of the modern sugar economy. The most recent expansion of sugar cultivation occurred in the regions surrounding Santo Domingo: the important sugar factory of Río Haina was only established during the Trujillo regime. Vast areas of cane fields alternate with pastures, just as in central Cuba. The sugar cane plantations in the Baní Plain are less extensive than those in the Llano de Seibo where they increase in size towards the east. The cane is processed in thirteen sugar refineries, most of which are close to the coast. Sugar is the most important export item of the Dominican Republic, and in addition to Santo Domingo it is exported from Río Haina, La Romana and San Pedro de Macorís. The two last mentioned ports which only export sugar and furfurol, which is made from bagasse, together handle 30 per cent of the entire Dominican export. The Río Haina factory west of Santo Domingo with a daily capacity of 15 000 tonnes of cane is the largest in the Caribbean islands, and the La Romana factory, which is US owned and cultivates 30 000 ha of land under cane, is said to be the largest sugar cane plantation in the world. This factory centre divided its cane areas into rectangular fields of 15–30 ha each. A field railway with tracks totalling a length of 200 km transports the cane off the fields. The best cane area is found in the low-lying districts of the coastal plain on the high-yielding black earth. Cultivation is carried out without irrigation, except in the western region of the cane belt where relatively limited areas are irrigated by the Río Nizao waters. The valley floors of this river and of the Río Baní are covered by productive wet rice cultivations. Groves of coconut trees line the coast of Baní, and small-scale coffee farms are widespread in the mountainous region of San Cristóbal which borders the coastal plain. The area west of Baní cannot be used for agriculture because of the increasing aridity. Thorn scrub savannas cover the arid coastal regions as far as the Río Ocoa.

The coastal plain of Santo Domingo is relatively sparsely populated. The density of population only increases in the capital and the neighbouring districts to the west; it cannot be compared, however, with density in the Vega Real. The capital, Santo Domingo, called Ciudad Trujillo between 1935 and 1961 after the long-lived president, takes pride in being the oldest town in the New World. Founded in 1496 by Bartholomaeus Columbus, its many buildings dating from the early period of Spanish colonization make it quite unlike any other town in the Caribbean. It does not possess baroque buildings, which are very common in Cuba and other Latin American countries, since the economy of this former Spanish colony stagnated during the seventeenth and eighteenth centuries. The following buildings reflect the importance of Santo Domingo during the early Spanish colonial rule when this city was the centre of the newly created Spanish colonial empire: The Alcázar de Colón, built between 1510 and 1512, where Diego, the son of Christopher Columbus, resided as the first viceroy of the New World; the cathedral of Santa María la Menor, built between 1523 and 1541, is the oldest church of the New World and is said to contain the tomb of Christopher Columbus;[1] the ruins of the monastery of San Francisco with the tomb of the conquistador, Alonso de Hojeda; the ruins of San Nicolás de Bari, the first hospital in the New World, built with bricks between 1503 and 1508; the 'Tower of Homage' in which the viceroys swore allegiance to the Spanish Crown and in which Columbus was kept captive (Torre del Homenaje); the ruins of the old city wall at the Río Ozama and at the western end of the city (Puerta del Conde); and various others. An old ceiba tree grows on the bank of the Río Ozama to which Columbus allegedly fastened his ship. Houses in colonial style fringe the narrow streets of the city; and the Calle el Conde in the city centre is still the main shopping area. A hurricane destroyed large parts of the city in October 1930. It was rebuilt during the Trujillo regime, but suffered some damage again during the civil war in 1965.

Santo Domingo has grown rapidly only in the twentieth century. Today it has a population of 367 000 and is the fourth largest city in the Caribbean islands (Map 46). In 1920 it still had only about 30 000 inhabitants and had hardly expanded beyond the encircling walls of the old Spanish city. Car traffic is light compared with conditions in the Puerto Rican and

[1] The cathedral of Sevilla in Andalusia also claims to possess the mortal remains of Christopher Columbus. It is not known which of the two is his actual burial place.

Jamaican capitals, but its narrow streets are filled with bustling activity, especially after the midday siesta.

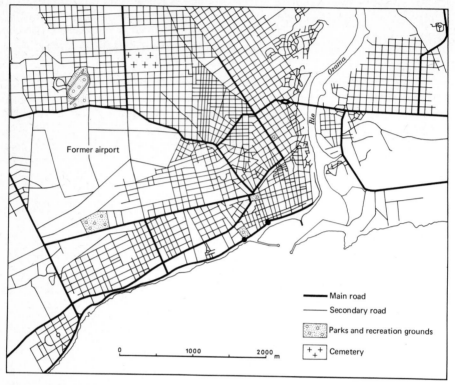

Map 46. Dominican Republic: street map of Santo Domingo.

The city developed chiefly under the government of Trujillo. Its physical and functional development is controlled by a city planning authority. The privileged residential areas, displaying impressive villas within well-kept gardens, rise steplike west of the old city along the Caribbean Sea, following the sequence of the marine terraces. This area also includes the big modern and exclusive hotels, the university campus and the government buildings constructed in 1955. The area adjoining the old airport to the north has not yet been developed (1966). Extensive residential areas, interspersed with small industrial plants, cover the northern area as far as the Río Isabela. More industrial and residential areas for workers are planned for the northern parts of the town between the Río Ozama and the Río Isabela as well as for the new suburbs on the opposite side of the Río Ozama which are connected with Santo Domingo by a highway bridge. The original city has preserved its nature as the commercial and shopping centre.

Santo Domingo did not achieve its present position because of its

244

function as the cultural and administrative centre, but because its industrial and commercial functions were systematically developed. It has no railway, and until 1930 it had no road connection with the old and important region of the Vega Real in the north. In spite of its peripheral site on the south coast it has achieved its major central position in the economy of the Dominican Republic by means of the transport network which has been developed. The construction of this road network has enabled it to handle export goods from all parts of the country. In terms of the economy the city has risen from provincial to national importance. In addition, the mouth of the Río Ozama provides an excellent harbour, with the result that today Santo Domingo handles 42 per cent of Dominican exports and nearly all the imports. Oceangoing vessels use its harbour, as well as the schooners which ship weekly loads of rice, maize and tropical fruits to the arid Dutch Islands to the Leeward. Rafts loaded with charcoal from distant parts of the plain still come down the Río Ozama to Santo Domingo. The households of the capital have an annual demand for over 6000 tonnes of charcoal. The construction of modern hotels by the government stimulated the tourist industry for a short while. The new airport for jet planes 25 km east of the city near the seaside resort of Boca Chica served the same purpose. It can easily be reached by a four-lane highway.

Under the government of Trujillo a versatile consumer goods industry was systematically developed in Santo Domingo. Its two major plants are a cement factory and a wheat mill. The construction of the Río Haina harbour only a few kilometres west of the city is intended for the development of a capital goods industry. Near to this harbour lies the large, newly established sugar factory and, since 1956, a shipyard; steel works are supposed to follow.

At the end of the last century the coastal plain of Santo Domingo joined the Vega Real in achieving outstanding economic importance after it had introduced the modern sugar economy which is the basis of the Dominican export trade. The present rapid urban growth reflects the expansion of traditional regional and supraregional functions as well as the addition of new functions. Under the government of Trujillo the plain has developed into the leading economic region of the country.

The southern longitudinal depression

The southern longitudinal depression is divided into the Haitian Cul-de-Sac Plain and the Dominican Enriquillo Depression. It is bordered by the central Haitian mountain country and the Sierra de Neiba in the north and by the southern cordillera in the south.

The **Cul-de-Sac Plain** is only 15 km wide. It stretches for 30 km from the inner coast of the Gulf of Gonave to the Dominican border. The mountains rise sharply on either side: the Chaines du Trou d'Eau and de Matheux in the north, and the Massif de la Selle in the south. Both the Cul-de-Sac Plain, which contains the salt lake of Saumâtre, and the narrow coastal

245

plain of Arcahaie, continuing towards the north-west along the Gulf of Gonave, possess a marked arid climate. The mountain slopes to the north of the plain are also arid, whereas those of the Massif de la Selle are humid. Irrigated sugar cane plantations covered large parts of the Cul-de-Sac Plain and the Arcahaie Plain during colonial times. Today parts of the northern region of both these plains are covered by sisal cultivation, but their output is smaller than that of the northern plain.

Today, as during the colonial period, sugar cane fields characterize the southern Cul-de-Sac Plain. Sugar cane cultivation disappeared in the wake of the Haitian revolution, but the Haytian American Sugar Company (HASCO), with its factories north of Port-au-Prince, reintroduced it after 1915. HASCO processes the cane which is cultivated on 9000 ha in the Cul-de-Sac Plain and on 2000 ha in the Léogane Plain. About 40 per cent of this area is farmed directly by the company on large and uniformly cultivated ractangular fields; the rest of the cane area belongs either to small-scale farms or to Haitians who own large estates and have sub-divided them into very small tenant farms. An estate of 1000 ha, for instance, is divided into 300 tenant farms, each of which cultivates cane on

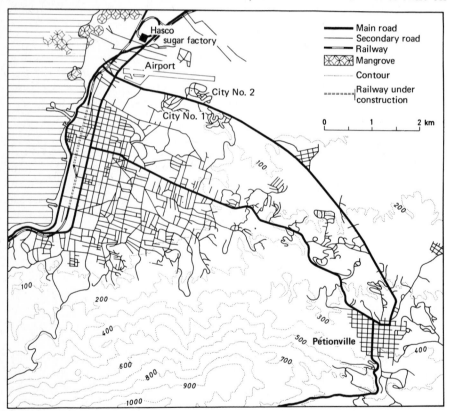

Map 47. Haiti: street map of Port-au-Prince.

0·5 ha and the usual tree and ground crops in mixed farming on the rest of it near the isolated farmhouses. Thus in this region there is a dichotomy of landscape—the monotonous areas of the sugar cane plantations on the one hand and the badly arranged, irregularly parcelled area of the peasants and tenants, living in dispersed settlements, on the other.

Port-au-Prince, the capital of Haiti, is situated at the foot of the Massif de la Selle on the inner shore of the Gulf of Gonave where the Cul-de-Sac Plain reaches the sea (Map 47). The town easily surpasses all the other towns in its population and in the centralization of various administrative, commercial and cultural functions. Founded in 1749, it suffered severe damage from several hurricanes and earthquakes, and had a population of only 9400 in 1789. Nowadays it is growing rapidly. Between 1927 and 1950 its population increased from about 60 000 to 136 000 and to an estimated 250 000 in 1965.

The grid pattern layout of the streets in the commercial section near the harbour originated during colonial times. The streets east of the extensive Champs de Mars where the town has expanded up to 100 m high are rather irregular. The villas along the slopes are arranged vertically in type according to the social status of their owners. Eight kilometres from the city centre at a height of 300 to 400 m lies Pétionville, which has become the most popular residential area because of its pleasant temperatures. Not long ago it was only the summer retreat for the wealthy inhabitants of Port-au-Prince. Today, this function is taken over by Kenscoff, a settlement at an altitude of 1500 m. Between Kenscoff and Furcy, where the mountain slopes were used for coffee cultivation during colonial times and where they are completely deforested and strongly eroded today, peasants have recently expanded their vegetable farming. Cabbage, tomatoes, lettuce, onions, carrots, artichokes and other vegetables are brought daily from Kenscoff to the urban market.

Concrete buildings have increasingly replaced the wooden structures in the commercial section of Port-au-Prince. For the city's 200th anniversary modernized harbour installations and the buildings of the international fair were erected. Four seagoing vessels can berth simultaneously alongside the 600 m long concrete pier. A little farther north the part of the town where the fishing boats and the coastal vessels berth, and where a brisk trade is done along the jetty wall near the bus terminal, is very picturesque. To the north and south of the commercial centre lie the residential areas, some of which have become slums, particularly to the north. In the hilly region east of these, two workmen's settlements were built between 1952 and 1954 (*cités ouvrières*) to improve their housing conditions. The supply of drinking water, which now serves only 30 per cent of the urban population, is to be modernized with the aid of the Inter-American Development Bank. The industrial section near the international airport expands north into the Cul-de-Sac Plain. All the important industries are found in this area: the HASCO sugar factory, a flour mill, a cement factory, a sisal dressing plant, and a sack manufacturing plant, in addition to one pharmaceutical, one shoe and one clothing factory. In spite of these few industries Port-au-Prince has so far been the only industrial location in the Haitian Republic. Trade is concentrated here, and the town is also the centre of the poorly developed transport system and of the very limited Haitian internal air service. The capital possesses a university and has an active cultural life which is very strongly influenced by the French heritage. The majority of the Haitian élite live in Port-au-Prince widely separated socially from the rural population.

The **Enriquillo Depression**, up to 20 km wide and about 100 km long, continues the Haitian Cul-de-Sac Plain to the east. It stretches between the Sierra de Neiba in the north and the Sierra de Baoruco in the south. In the recent geological past the entire southern longitudinal depression formed an inlet of the sea. The rivers entering the depression from the bordering mountains have built up impressive alluvial cones, the one by the Río Yaque del Sur being the largest. The alluvial accumulation of the Río Yaque separates the Enriquillo salt lake from Neiba Bay and is similar to the alluvial cone of the Colorado in California which separates the Salton Lake Depression from the Gulf of California. The Enriquillo salt lake lies 44 m below sea-level and has shrunk to a size of about 300 sq km because of evaporation. Rincón Lake in the marginal zone of the alluvial plain and Enriquillo Lake used to receive large quantities of additional water during high water periods of the Río Yaque. In order to protect the newly won cultivable land against the repeated floodings dykes have been built along the river banks.

The aridity of the Enriquillo Depression causes the heavy growth of bayahonda (*Prosopis julifloria*), columnar cactus and agaves which often form living hedges. Farming has only recently ventured into the thorn scrub savannas and semideserts. Oases of cultivation were created in the semidesert around the Enriquillo Lake within the framework of the *Dominicación fronteriza*. Rice and wine are now being cultivated near the settlements of Jimani, La Descubierta, Duvergé and Neiba. The population of Neiba rose from 2100 to 7300 between 1950 and 1960. With some justification Enjalbert points out the physical similarity between Jimani with its white flat-roofed houses and settlements in southern Morocco. The US-American Barahona Company has developed 10 000 ha of sugar cane in the alluvial plain of the Río Yaque in the eastern section of the Depression. Heavy financial expenditure was needed in the early 1920s to study and to employ methods of extracting the salt from the soil and how to prevent the proportion of salt from increasing again when the land was irrigated. In the midst of what was a completely useless wasteland a flourishing landscape has been created. By building dams to control the river, canals for irrigation and drainage, roads and field-railways, the Barahona sugar factory and the settlement of Batey were able to be planned and developed. Sugar cane is the predominant cultivation, interspersed with rice and lucerne fields.

Rock-salt and gypsum in the bedrock region of the Cerros de Sal south of the Enriquillo Lake can be extracted by surface mining due to the aridity of the climate. Barahona (pop. 20 000) on the Bay of Neiba, the only town in the Dominican south, exports salt and gypsum. The loading installations of its port have a capacity of 1000 tonnes per hour. The size of the deposits has been estimated at 1000 million tonnes and are believed to be the richest in Latin America.

The southern cordillera

The southern cordillera is divided into the Haitian Massif de la Hotte and the Massif de la Selle, with small coastal plains along their sides, and into the Dominican Sierra de Baoruco.

The **Massif de la Hotte** and the **Massif de la Selle** are chiefly composed of Tertiary limestone. In both massifs the limestones enclose an inner zone of basalt, andesite, and metamorphic limestones. The rivers rise within the latter zone and force their way across the limestone plateaux in deeply incised valleys. The Pic de la Selle (2680 m) is the highest point in Haiti, and the Pic de Macaya rises to an almost equal height of 2405 m in the Massif de la Hotte. The high mountain plateau of Fond-des-Nègres lies south of Miragoâne in the central region of the peninsula between these two mountain ranges. It is crossed by the road leading from Port-au-Prince to Les Cayes. Varying rock types and climatic conditions cause different karst topographies in the two ranges. Bauxite deposits are frequently found in similar situations as in the Jamaican karst plateaux. Since 1957 they have been exploited by the Reynolds Metal Company in the Rochelois Plateau south-west of Miragoâne. Dehydration plants and loading installations were constructed in Carrefour Lebrun to facilitate export to the USA. Trucks transport the bauxite from the surface mines on the plateaux to the coast on a new road built by the mining company.

The plains in southern Haiti had been deforested to such an extent that timber had to be imported from the USA. Large forests still cover the Massif de la Hotte and the Massif de la Selle. However, clearings have expanded from the valleys into the evergreen montane and semi-evergreen montane forests on a large scale. Only the pine forests (*Pinus occidentalis*) in the hardly accessible high altitude regions of the two massifs have been left untouched so far. The pine forests of the Plateau of Morne-des-Commissaires in the eastern part of the Massif de la Selle at an altitude of 1600 to 2000 m have been exploited for the last two decades. This became possible after the completion of a road which crosses the mountains. The road leads to Saltrou and may be used only by cross-country vehicles. It also stimulated the development of this remote region in south-east Haiti which had served as a sanctuary for runaway slaves during the colonial period. The Haitian government has established several settlements in this region where

249

refugees found a new home following the Dominican Negro massacres of 1937.

The mountain region in southern Haiti is of much greater economic importance than the southern Haitian coastal plains. Both the Massif de la Hotte and the Massif de la Selle are distinguished by their coffee production. During the colonial period the main coffee farming area was in the northern Haitian mountains which produced 45 per cent of the entire crop; during the nineteenth century the centre shifted to the south. In those days the mountains in southern Haiti supplied 18 per cent, today they produce 60 per cent of the Haitian coffee production. The hinterland of Petit-Goave alone produces 25 per cent of the entire Haitian coffee crop. The hilly country of Fond-des-Nègres and the surrounding mountains of the Les Cayes Plain are also important coffee regions. Among the few wealthy coffee farmers in this region are several mulattoes. They are descendants of Polish soldiers who fought with the Napoleonic army against the Haitian revolutionaries. Except for the extreme west of the peninsula between Dame Marie and Jérémie where cocoa is the main crop, almost the entire mountain country in southern Haiti is characterized by coffee cultivation, on the humid altitudes between 300 m and 800 m and sometimes up to 1200 m. Coffee can be found along the slopes, which are not too steep, and in the interfluves, wherever the top soil has been preserved on limestone as well as on volcanic rock.

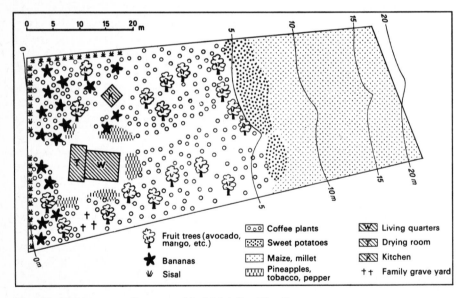

Map 48. Haiti: peasant farm near Marbial (after Moral).

Haitian coffee cultivation is not at all like that in Central and South America. It is completely different even from the Haitian pattern during the colonial period. Extensive coffee plantations do not exist; almost the entire coffee crop is produced by peasants (Map 48). In addition, coffee is not cultivated in a monocultural system but in a polycultural system. The coffee areas display the complete irregularity of a multitude of plants which is so common in Haitian agriculture. Coffee trees are shaded by high breadfruit, mango and avocado trees. The impressive trees from the *Inga* genus (Mimosaceae) are preferred since they lose their leaves at a time when the coffee enters its last stage of ripening. The coffee plants are left to their own resources in areas distant from the settlements. The plants propagate from the coffee beans which drop to the ground during the harvest and grow in a haphazard pattern. Pruning is almost unknown. Plants of any age and size grow in close proximity in a completely irregular pattern. Moral (1955) has described these coffee thickets very appropriately as *Maquis caféier*. More care is given to the coffee cultivations near the settlements, but irregularity is still the rule. Here, bananas offer protection against the sun in addition to the above mentioned trees. The foliage of the yam roots are intertwined with the banana and coffee plants. Castor-oil plants, in addition to manioc, taro and sweet potatoes are haphazardly cultivated between the coffee plants. The landscape at lower altitudes where coffee is cultivated appears somewhat different, as shade trees are often omitted and bananas are usually cultivated between the coffee plants, which are sometimes grown in straight rows.

Two different methods of coffee processing are practised. The majority of the smallholders dry the shining red coffee berries in their farmyards in the sun. At harvest time (October to December) one can often find small heaps of coffee berries lying on the steps to the living quarters or, where there is one, on the porch. After the berries have changed their colour to black they are pounded in wooden mortars. The beans, now stripped of their flesh, are sold in very small quantities to the *spéculateurs* who live in the various market-towns. During the harvest time the houses of these middlemen can easily be recognized: a pair of scales hangs just inside their door where the coffee can immediately be weighed. About 90 per cent of Haitian coffee is supplied by smallholders who do not own more than a few hundred square metres, and reaches the market through the *spéculateurs*.

In addition to the procedure described above there also exists the wet processing of the coffee done by small and sometimes modern plants which belong to more extensive estates. There the coffee berries are mechanically stripped of their flesh, and after twenty-four hours of fermentation they are first washed and then dried on an open-air concrete platform. In earlier years, the coffee from the Massif de la Hotte and the Massif de la Selle was exclusively exported from the ports in southern Haiti. Today, a large portion is brought to the capital on trucks. Port-au-Prince exports 40 per cent of the entire Haitian coffee production.

The **coastal plains in southern Haiti** adjoin both sides of the Massif de la Hotte and the Massif de la Selle. Only the more extensive among these plains are composed of fine-grained alluvial material in their coastal regions, e.g. the plains of Les Cayes, Léogane and Aquin, while the less extensive alluvial plains, and those regions of the more extensive plains which are near to the mountains, are made up of coarse-grained alluvial soils.

In the north, along the Gulf of Gonave, the plains of Léogane (205 sq km), Miragoâne—Grand Goave (195 sq km) and Jérémie (125 sq km) follow each other from east to west.

The semi-humid Léogane Plain is completely orientated towards Port-au-Prince. Here HASCO (cf. p. 246) cultivates 600 ha of sugar cane under its own management. A company-owned field railway transports the cane to the sugar factory in Port-au-Prince during harvest time, from January to June. The cane area which is cultivated by small-scale planters (1400 ha) surpasses the area cultivated by plantations, resembling in this the situation in the Cul-de-Sac Plain. The small farmers supply their cane to HASCO in addition to the small distilleries south of Léogane. Almost half this plain is covered by sugar cane. The rest is used for vegetable farming, mainly bananas and sweet potatoes which are brought to the nearby urban market of Port-au-Prince. The Léogane Plain has a special position among the plains in southern Haiti because cultivation is completely market-orientated and the sugar cane along with other plants is cultivated in a monocultural system. Mixed farming by peasants plays only a minor role.

A considerably drier coastal plain stretches further to the west between Grand Goave and Miragoâne. It is of minor economic importance. Cotton cultivation was more important than sugar cane even during the colonial period. Mixed farming by smallholders is the rule; cotton predominates in the Grand Goave region, and rice around Miragoâne Lake. A part of the large coffee production from the mountainous hinterland of this coastal plain is exported from the ports of Petit-Goave (pop. 5500) and Miragoâne (pop. 2500), which used to be very busy a few decades ago.

The Jérémie Plain reaches far into the interior along the valley of the Rivière de la Grande Anse in the extreme west of the southern Haitian peninsula. Although the eighteenth century irrigation system is still in operation only little is left of the sugar cane cultivation which used to be widespread during the colonial period. The small cane output is processed by numerous antiquated cane presses. The cane brandy from Jérémie is well-known throughout Haiti. Polyculture is characteristic of the plain. Fruit-trees are common, mainly mango and breadfruit and coconut trees. The smallholders usually own plots of land both in the plain and in the adjoining mountain region. Jérémie possesses a population of 11 000 and exports coffee and cocoa from its mountainous hinterland. Its roadstead is exposed to north winds during winter.

The plains of Les Cayes (360 sq km), Cavaillon (90 sq km), Aquin (195 sq km), and Jacmel (90 sq km) follow each other from west to east along the south coast of the southern Haitian peninsula. The humid plains of Les Cayes and Cavaillon were high-yielding sugar producing areas during the colonial period. Vast plantations developed among which the Laborde enterprise employed not less than 1400 slaves. Today, the cane area covers only about half the cultivated plain. The major part of the cane is supplied to the sugar factory which was built near the town of Les Cayes between 1948 and 1952. The regular supply of cane to the factory by the many small producers has proved to be extremely difficult. Peasant mixed farming with widespread rice-farming is very common in the narrow and marshy coastal strip. The Port Salut peninsula is especially densely populated (400 persons per sq km) resulting in an extreme fragmentation of property. In the past, this region supplied a large number of seasonal workers for the Cuban sugar harvest. Les Cayes (pop. 11 600), the capital of the Département du Sud in the interior of the bay which has the same name, used to be completely cut off from the rest of Haiti. Today it is connected with Port-au-Prince by an asphalt road. Hurricanes and earthquakes have repeatedly destroyed Les Cayes. The town played a shortlived role in the history of Latin America: it served as a refuge for Simón Bolívar, the Venezuelan national hero.

Whereas at least some of the production in the Plain of Les Cayes is export orientated, this is not so in the instances of the Plains of Aquin and Jacmel where peasants cultivate their land exclusively in a polycultural pattern and produce only for their own needs and for the domestic market. Tree cultivations in the relatively arid Aquin Plain are unimportant in comparison with the prevalent ground crops, millet and maize. Small-holders also cultivate sisal, which is processed in a small factory in Aquin. The port of Jacmel (pop. 8600) exports coffee from the Massif de la Selle. Jacmel and the other ports along the southern Haitian coast were built during the French colonial period and have hardly grown since then, except for Jérémie. The layout of their streets is a grid pattern as in Cap-Haitien and Port-au-Prince. All have a market square with a Catholic church on one side, and a small shopping centre with two- and three-storeyed buildings surrounding the square. The turnover in all of these ports has greatly decreased since the construction of a road to Port-au-Prince and after the introduction of a system of tariffs which favours the port of Port-au-Prince.

The **Sierra de Baoruco** is the continuation of the Haitian Massif de la Selle. It reaches a height of 2420 m and rises to over 1600 m in its eastern section near the coast. Its limestone plateaux exhibit karst topography and descend sharply towards the Enriquillo Depression in the north. A series of steplike erosion surfaces leads down from the mountain ridge to the Caribbean Sea, and a system of uplifted marine terraces can be recognized below 300 m. The higher altitudes of the Sierra receive rain throughout the year. The western part of the mountain range is uninhabited. Extensive forests cover this region, consisting mainly of *Pinus occidentalis*. The northern slope of the eastern mountain region is considered the most important coffee producing area in the Dominican Republic. Coffee cultivations occupy nearly 9000 ha. As in the Cordillera Septentrional, small-scale farms of sizes between 1 and 5 ha, which are larger than those in the neighbouring Haitian Massif de la Selle, are mixed with larger farms of under 20 ha. The coffee

253

is mainly processed by new plants using the wet method in contrast to the dry method practised by the Haitian peasants, and is exported from Barahona.

The Sierra de Baoruco has achieved economic importance because of its coffee production and the bauxite mining which has recently been started there. The bauxite deposits are similar to those in Jamaica. They appear near Aceitillar and Las Mercedes along the southern flanks of the western mountain region and have been exploited by the US-American Alcoa Company since 1959. The bauxite is shipped to Point Comfort in Texas.

20

Population and Economy in Hispaniola's Two Republics

Hispaniola's population is completely different in race and language in the two Republics. The distribution of population and the pattern of settlement also differ greatly, as do economy, trade and transport. Haiti and the Dominican Republic will therefore be dealt with individually in this chapter.

Haiti

Population and settlement

The Republic of Haiti emerged from the French colony of St Dominigue. Its size is 27 750 sq km. In 1950 the first census was conducted; by 1969, the population had risen to an estimated 4·8 million, The density of population in Haiti (Map 50), which amounted to 126 persons per sq km, was already considered relatively high in 1950, especially in view of the annual 3 per cent rate of increase and the mainly agricultural structure of the economy, and also in view of the mountainous nature of the Republic which does not allow any significant expansion of the agricultural acreage. The highest density of population at present, as during the colonial period, is found in the humid plains: the Plaine du Nord, the plains in the south, and especially the Plaine des Cayes. Emigration to the sugar producing areas in the Dominican Republic and Cuba, which was strong in earlier times and which did not have a mere seasonal character, is no longer possible.[1] The Haitian population is descended from African slaves who were brought to St Domingue by the French. Negroes form 95 per cent of the population. The mulattoes (5 per cent) usually constitute the urban upper class, forming the major part of the cities and above all in the capital, where they are known as the 'elite'. Opposed to it are the masses of the Negro population, divided into the small, constant, but growing social group of the urban

[1] However, 20 000 Haitian peasants worked again as cane cutters in the Dominican Republic for the first time in 1967. They were obliged to pay over part of their wages to the Haitian government.

working class and the large group of the rural population. French is the official language in Haiti. The majority of the population, however, speaks Créole which is classified either as an African language with a large element of French vocabulary, or as a Romance language with African, Indian and other elements. Ninety per cent of the population are illiterate. The Haitian population professes the Catholic belief, but the African heritage is present in the popular cult of voodoo, in which, according to Metraux, West African rites have merged with Catholic Christianity.

Haiti is a nation of peasants. Even if one designates as urban all settlements with more than 1000 inhabitants, only 11 per cent of the entire population can be described as urban. But since even the few places with a population of over 2500 have the appearance or function of villages or small marketplaces, Moral is justified in listing 93 per cent of the Haitian population as rural (Table 47).

Table 47.   Haiti: urban and rural population (%)

		Rural population	
		in	*in*
	Urban	*villages*	*dispersed*
Département	*population*	*(Bourgs)*	*settlements*
Nord	5	10	85
Nord-Ouest	4	4·5	91·5
Artibonite	4	7	89
Ouest	16	3	81
Sud	3·5	4·5	92
Haiti	7·5	5·5	87

Source: after Moral (1961)

Table 48.   Haitian towns, 1950

Town	*Inhabitants*
Port-au-Prince	135 687
Cap-Haitien	24 229
Gonaives	13 634
Les Cayes	11 608
Jérémie	11 048
Pétionville	9 477
St Marc	9 401
Jacmel	8 643
Port-de-Paix	6 405
Petit-Goave	5 378
Miragoâne	2 500
Total	238 010

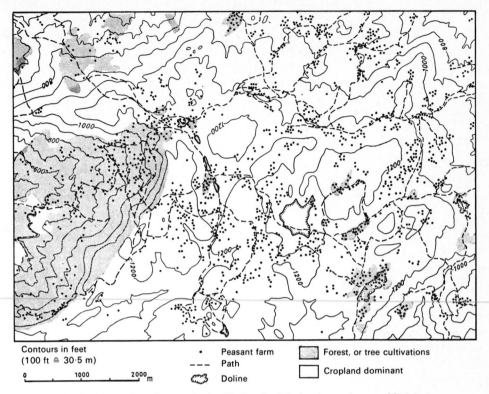

Contours in feet
(100 ft ≙ 30·5 m)

0   1000   2000 m

• Peasant farm

– – – Path

🝔 Doline

▓ Forest, or tree cultivations

☐ Cropland dominant

Map 49. Haiti: dispersed settlement in the Chaine des Matheux, south-east of St Marc.

Dispersed settlement prevails everywhere, in some regions mainly in the hamlet pattern, in others in the pattern of isolated farm houses (Map 49). Among the rural market towns in the interior of the country the following are distinguished by their large population: Hinche (pop. 4500), Petite Rivière de l'Artibonite (4400), Dessalines (3700), and Grande Rivière du Nord (3300). Only eleven towns have truly urban functions (Table 48). The major town is clearly the capital, Port-au-Prince, in the inner edge of the Gulf of Gonave concentrating in its area 57 per cent of the Haitian urban population. Second largest town is Cap-Haitien on the north coast, the former flourishing capital of St Domingue. All the eleven Haitian towns are ports except Pétionville, which today forms a residential suburb of Port-au-Prince. Their grid pattern layouts point back to their French colonial origin. These towns have scarcely increased their population since then, with the exception of the capital.

Agriculture

Seventy-five per cent of the gross national product and 80 per cent of the exports by value are supplied by agriculture, which employs more than 85 per cent of the working population. Since 70 per cent of the agricultural

257

production is supplied by smallholders the Republic of Haiti can aptly be called a nation of Negro smallholders in terms of its economy. Haiti has an agricultural acreage of about 650 000 ha. Of these, about 50 000 ha are cultivated by foreign large-scale enterprises, the majority of which developed during the American occupation between 1915 and 1934. These enterprises produce 30 per cent of the agricultural produce on 7 per cent of the agricultural acreage, demonstrating the low yield achieved by the Haitian peasant. The latter is also indicated when present agricultural production is compared with that during the French colonial period: the French plantations of St Domingue produced more for export on a smaller acreage than the Haitian Negro peasants did in the early 1960s (Table 49). The value of Haitian exports between 1960 and 1964 (an average US $38 million) amounts to only half of that during the colonial period (US $75 million in 1789).

Table 49.   Haiti: agricultural production in modern and colonial times

		Sugar	*Coffee*	*Cotton*	*Sisal*	*Agriculturally productive area* ha
Early 1960s: (average)	tonnes	15 000	30 000	1 000	24 000	650 000
	% of exports by value	8	55	1	24	
1789:	tonnes	71 000	38 500	3 500	—	500 000
	% of exports by value	48	33·6	7·7	—	

Source: After Moral (1961)

The small interest in exports shown by Haitian farmers, and the low volume of production have various causes. The prevalence of uneconomic, very small farms is probably mainly responsible for this situation. Nearly 70 per cent of all farms are less than 2 carreaux (2·6 ha), and 98 per cent of all farms are under 20 carreaux (25·7 ha). These figures apply uniformly to all subregions in Haiti in a striking way (Table 50). This situation is caused by the settlement of the former large landholdings and by increasing land fragmentation. An example of the latter is a peasant farm near Marbial, which had a size of 16 ha in 1840 and was owned by one farmer; since then, however, this farm has been divided among fifty heirs.

The percentage of tenant farms is comparatively low in all the various regions (Table 52). The majority of Haitian small peasants are believed to be the owners of the land they cultivate, although many of them cannot produce a title-deed. The farming methods applied by these family enterprises are generally very antiquated. The most important and often sole working tool is the versatile long-bladed *machette*. The lack of adequate

Table 50.   Haiti: farm sizes, 1950 (%)

Départements	< 0·65 ha < 0·5 carreaux	0·65–1·3 ha 0·5–1 carreaux	1·3–2·6 ha 1–2 carreaux	2·6–3·9 ha 2–3 carreaux	3·9–6·5 ha 3–5 carreaux	> 6·5 ha > 5 carreaux
Nord	11	24·9	33·7	14·9	9·5	4·9
Nord-Ouest	14·8	26·5	28·9	13·5	9·9	6·4
Artibonite	12·2	22·1	31·5	16·2	11·5	6·5
Ouest	18·7	23·8	28·0	13·5	9·7	5·3
Average	12·3	23·8	32·1	15·3	10·5	6·0

Source: After Moral (1961); no figures were available for the Département du Sud;
1 carreau = 1·29 ha.

farm tools means that the peasant is unable to accomplish his field work during the main working season (Table 51) in spite of the help of his family. He is dependent on the help of neighbours for clearing, tilling and harvesting. The *coumbite*, cooperative work on a neighbourly basis, is still in practice and executed to the rhythm of singing and drums. The peasant who requests the *coumbite* supplies the food and the clairin, a cane brandy spiced with aniseed. In addition to the lack of farm tools very little care is spent on cultivation and this has a negative effect on production. Methods of preventing soil erosion are almost unknown. The small plots of land very often occupy steep slopes. A few attempts have been made, without visible success, to teach modern farming methods. Cultivation is mainly to satisfy the everyday demands of the peasant family. Whatever is left of the crop is brought to the local market, sometimes in extremely small amounts. In order to get a better price in a larger market town the peasant woman will walk for hours carrying her goods in a basket on her head. A marketing system has not been developed at all, especially for the marketing of products for home demand; and without the construction of roads, the planned peasant cooperatives will also be doomed to failure. Between 93 and 94 per cent of the rural population are still illiterate, and they have to live under the worst hygienic circumstances without medical care. For instance, 92 per cent of the farm houses in the Département du Nord do not possess a toilet, and 96 per cent of the peasant families draw their drinking water from streams or irrigation canals. The diet of the Haitian peasant is inadequate, resulting in widespread malnutrition. The World Health Organization has recently (1965/6) been conducting a drive to check malaria.

Since the Second World War Haiti has received a large amount of development aid for the improvement of its agriculture, mainly for the irrigation of the Artibonite Plain. This project, as well as the reafforestation programme and the development plans for the north have not been finalized, partly because economic aid from the USA ceased in 1963. Only those projects aimed at stimulating cotton cultivation, which were carried out by the national Institut de Développement Agricole et Industriel with the aid of the Inter-American Development Bank, have proved to be successful in recent years. Between 1962 and 1964, the area in peasant cultivation in the coastal plain of Arcahaie expanded from 27 to 939 ha. On the whole one has to be resigned to the fact that so far no relief of the poverty of the Haitian population can be detected.

Table 51.   A Haitian smallholder's farm calendar

	J	F	M	A	M	J	J	A	S	O	N	D
(a) In the lower Artibonite Valley												
Work in the field (clearing by burning, weeding)	+ +	+ +				+ +	+ +	+				+ +
Sugar cane	○		× ×	× ×							○	○ ○
Cotton	○ ○	○ ○		× ×	×							○ ○
Rice	○ ○	○ ○	×	× ×	×							○ ○
Maize	× ×			○ ○								
				× ×	× ×		○ ○		○	× ×		○	○ ○
Tubers	× ×			○ ○								× ×
				× ×	× ×		○ ○	○	× ×			○ ○
Fruit trees						○	○ ○	○ ○	○ ○¹		○ ○	○ ○	○ ○²
(b) In higher altitudes of the Massif de la Selle												
Work in the field (clearing by burning, weeding)	+ +	+ +				+ +	+ +					+ +
Coffee	○ ○	○ ○	○							○ ○	○ ○
Maize			× ×	× ×	×				○ ○	○ ○	
Tubers	○ ○			× ×	× ×					○	○ ○	○ ○
Vegetables of the Tierra templada	○ ○		× ×	× ×	×		○ ○	○ ×	× ×		○	○ ○
Fruit trees						○	○ ○	○³				

+ work in the fields   × planting   ○ harvest
¹ mango and avocado   ² orange   ³ avocado
Source: After Moral.

Table 52.   Haiti: Distribution of land ownership (% of all agricultural enterprises)

Départements*	Owner	Tenants (with payments in money) state-owned land	privately owned land	Manager	Tenants (with payments in kind)
Nord	84·8	2·5	3·2	3·6	4·9
Nord-Ouest	81·2	7·0	1·9	4·7	5·2
Artibonite	87·3	2·1	3·7	3·9	3·0
Ouest	83·1	3·6	4·2	3·3	5·8
Average	84·1	3·8	3·3	3·9	4·7

* No figures were available for the Département du Sud.

The agricultural acreage, consisting of nearly 650 000 ha, is larger today than it was during the colonial period. However, it comprises only about one quarter of the entire land surface. The fact, that 50 per cent of the Haitian population live on only 17 per cent of the land surface indicates that the dry plains and the higher, or less accessible mountains are practically excluded from agricultural use. The colonial irrigation systems in the dry plains fell into decay during the nineteenth century. Nevertheless the land under irrigation has expanded from 25 000 ha to 42 000 ha during the last thirty years, not counting the Artibonite Plain where 10 000 ha of irrigated land have been newly developed since 1955 and a further 20 000 ha are planned. A slight expansion of the agricultural acreage seems possible in the Plateau Central and in the central and southern mountains. At the present, squatters move into these areas, using their own rudimentary farming methods. For instance, they destroy the entire vegetation of a slope in order to establish one smallholding. Moral (1961) justly points out that this pattern of destructive exploitation may jeopardize a more intense settlement in the future. In view of this and considering the agricultural structure of Haiti the density of population per square kilometre of the cultivated land has assumed alarming proportions. In 1950 it amounted to an average of 422 persons per sq km; it rose to at least 595 in the Département du Nord-Ouest.

It is not possible to obtain exact data about the acreage which is covered by basic food crops since these plants are nowhere cultivated singly, but as part of a mixed farming pattern and often together with commercial plants. Maize, the main food crop for the Haitian population and cultivated in very different climatic regions, occupies an estimated area of 300 000 ha. The area under millet is scarcely less extensive. Millet is cultivated mainly on the leeward mountain slopes in central Haiti. The cultivation of upland rice is restricted to the mountainous north, and the 70 000 ha of wet rice are distributed among the Artibonite Plain and the humid coastal plains. Tubers, manioc, sweet potatoes, yams and taro are common crops of the peasant mixed farming throughout the country, as well as the banana, which is no longer exported and which is cultivated on an estimated area of 78 000 ha.

The only important commercial plant for the world market is coffee. It is cultivated exclusively by mountain farmers in the polycultural system. In contrast to the colonial period, coffee is today produced mainly in the mountains of southern Haiti. It is grown over an estimated area of 140 000 ha; of the farms which produce coffee 72·8 per cent are of less than 1·3 ha, and only 1·3 per cent of them are over 6·5 ha. The first group supplies 34·4 per cent, the latter 11·1 per cent of the Haitian coffee production which decreased from 33 000 tonnes in 1957 to 29 000 tonnes in 1968 (22 500 tonnes in 1965) because of the depression of coffee prices on the world market and also because of damage by hurricanes.

Cocoa is also cultivated on smallholdings, mainly in the western part of the southern Haitian peninsula and in small areas of the Massif du Nord. It occupies only 4 700 ha. Half the entire cocoa produce of 3000–4000 tonnes is supplied by farms of under 1·3 ha. Cotton production has experienced a similar downward trend: it decreased to 1000 tonnes in 1967, and has not recovered since.

In contrast to this, most of the sugar and all the sisal are produced by foreign large-scale enterprises. Although only 1·3 per cent of the sugar producing farms have a size of more than 6·5 ha they supply 25 per cent of the total yield of about 5 million tonnes of cane. The same farm size category in sisal production constitutes 1·6 per cent and supplies 84 per cent of the entire production of 21 600 tonnes (average between 1963 and 1967). Large sisal plantations have been developed in the dry parts of the northern coastal plain and the Cul-de-Sac Plain; the irrigated sugar cane plantations cover the Plains of Cul-de-Sac and Léogane.

The chief emphasis within Haitian agriculture has shifted from the plantation to the small-scale farmer, and since coffee has replaced sugar cane as the most important crop, the main agricultural regions have shifted from the plains to the mountains.

Mining and industry

Although Haiti possesses various ore deposits and precious metals only the bauxite deposits of the Rochelois Plain in the central region of the southern peninsula are exploited at present. The US-American Reynolds Metal Company began mining in 1957. The annual loading capacity is 900 000 tonnes; the export of dehydrated bauxite, however, has only increased from 329 000 tonnes in 1958 to 359 000 tonnes in 1967 (458 000 tonnes in 1964).

Industrial development in Haiti is still in its infancy. The poorly developed road network and especially the absence of a power supply are serious handicaps for industrialization. However, it was possible to increase the power output from 18 to 70 million kWh between 1950 and 1970, of which 63 million kWh are allotted to the Département de l'Ouest with the capital. The importance of the capital, which completely overshadows all other towns, will presumably increase considerably after the completion of the power plant at the Peligre Dam in the Artibonite Valley. This plant was planned more than ten years ago, and in 1964 the Haitian government contracted an Italian company for its construction. Port-au-Prince is the only industrial site, if one disregards the processing of agricultural products, mainly of sisal in the northern coastal plain and of sugar cane in the same area and in the Les Cayes Plain. In addition to the sugar factory of the Haytian American Sugar Company with an annual capacity of 70 000 tonnes which far surpasses the small factories in Les Cayes and Cap-Haitien and which supplies the major portion of the Haitian sugar produce of 44 000 tonnes (1963), the following enterprises characterize Port-au-Prince as an industrial location: a cement factory with a capacity of 60 000 tonnes which meets the entire Haitian demand, and a flour mill completed in 1959 which also satisfies the Haitian market. The cotton spinning and weaving mill of Port-au-Prince, on the other hand, has so far not been able to satisfy the small demand for textiles. Other consumer goods industries in the capital are shoe manufacturing, sack fabrication from sisal fibres, the production of soap, pharmaceutical goods, beverages, tobacco products, vegetable oil, plastic goods, furniture and, last but not least, rum. The majority of these enterprises are very small. Less than 10 000 persons are employed in Haitian industries, including the sisal and sugar cane processing.

In view of its very limited industrialization and its insufficient agricultural production Haiti is making a great effort to promote its tourist industry. A special ministry has been established towards this end, but the results have so far been less than desired. Compared with other West Indian islands the volume of tourism in Haiti has been very limited, sometimes it has even stagnated mainly because of the unstable political conditions. New and modern hotels are available to North American tourists in the capital and more recently in Cap-Haitien. The number of foreign visitors, only 6000 in 1948, rose to 66 000 by 1956 (51 200 in 1967). The tourist industry supplied the largest amount of foreign exchange (US $10 million) in 1961 after coffee exports. Since 1962, tourism has become less significant because of the political situation. In the meantime, however, a Swiss company has received a licence to open the southern regions for tourism.

Transport

Haiti possesses only one public railway line 135 km long. It leads north from Port-au-Prince via St Marc to Verrettes in the Artibonite Plain. The passenger service was discontinued after the number of passengers had dropped from 79 000 in 1951 to 2000 in 1960. A few private narrow-gauge railway lines with a total length of 120 km transport sugar cane and sisal exclusively.

The transportation of people and goods in the interior of Haiti is by road. The roads with a total length of 3000 km, however, are insufficient for the 8400 existing motor vehicles (1962); moreover, they are in the worst imaginable condition, not excluding the only asphalt road between Port-au-Prince and Cap-Haitien. A five-year-plan provides for the improvement and construction of several roads, especially the 210 km long road leading to Les Cayes of which 40 km had been completed before American development aid ended. This road was 64 km long by mid-1971. Many regions are still without any road connections, and several roads are only passable in cross-country vehicles. Numerous roads cannot be used during periods of river flooding. The port of Jacmel, which has a population of almost 9000 is merely 40 km from Port-au-Prince, but it can only be reached over 120 km of bad roads, and several unbridged rivers have to be crossed. The transport of people and goods is to a large extent carried out by trucks. Their owners do not hesitate to use even the worst roads. Their camions, i.e. the chassis of a truck on to which a wooden body in glaring colours has been mounted, are usually in a deplorable state since they are always heavily overloaded. These vehicles have revolutionized interior transport in Haiti, and have almost destroyed the formerly busy coastwise shipping. Only about 500 old sailing boats remain, usually in a bad shape, transporting goods along the coasts. The trucks have also robbed several ports of their former important export function since most of the export goods are now taken to Port-au-Prince by land and shipped from there, encouraged by fiscal arrangements which favour the capital. The truck has also changed passenger transport, but now as before it is still common for peasant women to walk for hours in order to market their produce. In addition, the importance of the mule for transport purposes has scarcely declined. The large amount of travelling done by foot or on mules and the dispersed type of settlement which is characteristic of Haiti, have led to the development of a dense network of much frequented footpaths and mule tracks all over the country. The poor road system has probably also caused the formation of a national airline (Cohata) which offers relatively frequent flights to eight interior airports. It carried 27 800 passengers in 1958, but only 6600 in 1962.

Today, Port-au-Prince has a leading position in the handling of international trade, while at the turn of the century several ports played an important role at least in the export trade. At that time only 22 per cent of the Haitian coffee production was exported from the capital; since then it has risen to 40 per cent. Port-au-Prince handles about 70 per cent of the foreign trade in which imports exceed exports. In 1962, for instance, 95 per cent of the Haitian imports were landed here. Among the other ports only Cap-Haitien and Miragoâne handle a significant amount of foreign trade. The latter is the most important export harbour at the present because of the shipping of bauxite.

In contrast to most Caribbean islands, boats bring in more tourist traffic than do aeroplanes. The majority of visitors to Haiti come on cruises. Accordingly, the air traffic of Port-au-Prince international airport is relatively modest. It amounted to thirty-five weekly departures of regular flights with a seating capacity of 2269 (1960). The volume of air traffic has decreased continuously since then. The extension of the airport in 1964 in order to accommodate jet airliners has so far not resulted in an increase in the volume of air-traffic nor in the number of tourists.

The Dominican border is hardly ever crossed by land because of the traditionally strained relations between the two neighbouring states and also because of the bad road conditions. Of the 31 622 persons who visited the Dominican Republic in 1959, only thirty-three came by land from Haiti (0·1 per cent). In 1960 the three existing border crossing points were only opened to diplomats.

Trade

Internal trade in Haiti is extremely lively. A visitor is usually fascinated by the vivid originality and the colourful variety of a Haitian market. Several hundreds of people gather at the larger rural markets, most of them women. The harvested crop which is not needed by the family is brought regularly to the weekly market. This is the only means of obtaining the necessities which cannot be produced on the farm. One may also find a large number of pedlars who visit one market after another in a weekly rotation. Textiles and flour, pots and salt fish, hats and dried meat, in fact all kinds of commodities are offered for sale in these markets. Some of them, for example the large markets of Fond-des-Nègres and Morne-des-Commissaires (Plate 11), do not take place within the boundaries of any one place, but far away from settlement concentrations, somewhere in the open countryside. This type of market meets the demand, in particular of the people who live in the extremely dispersed types of settlement. The market on the Morne-des-Commissaires Plateau takes place each week amidst the pine forest of the Massif de la Selle at an altitude of 1600 m. In addition to the pedlars it is visited by the peasant women from all the adjoining regions—regions with different climatic conditions and therefore with varying produce. The village-type concentrations of settlements (*bourgs*) also possess their vivid markets, as do the ports. Mintz and Moral (1961) classified the Haitian markets according to their functions and areas of influence.

The volume of Haitian foreign trade (Table 53) compares very unfavourably with that of other Caribbean insular states because its agricultural production is only slightly orientated towards the world market. The volume of foreign trade amounted to US $105 million in 1952, to only $67 million in 1961 with a debit balance (exports: 32 million; imports: 35 million), and to $73 million in 1966. Coffee is the main export commodity making up an average of 54·2 per cent of the export value between 1963 and 1966, followed by sugar (5·8 per cent), sisal (5·7 per cent) and bauxite (4·9 per cent). Because of insufficient production, food imports head the list of Haitian imports, making up 18 per cent of the total. Significantly, textiles follow with 7·3 per cent since the consumer goods industry has hardly developed. The USA supply 55·4 per cent (1966) of Haitian imports, followed by the Federal Republic of Germany with 4·8 per cent. The exports are also mainly directed towards North America; in 1966, 40·4 per cent went to the USA. Italy, France, and Belgium-Luxemburg import Haitian coffee taking 40 per cent of Haitian exports. Haitian exports to the Federal Republic of Germany are negligible.

The structure of Haitian foreign trade reflects its unsound economic situation. Low production orientated towards the world market produces a small volume of trade, and low production of basic foodstuffs necessitates high food imports. The almost non-existent consumer goods industry in its turn requires the import of so many commodities that only a few capital goods can be imported. There are no indications of a change in this situation in the foreseeable future. In view of this Haiti compares very unfavourably with its neighbouring Caribbean nations. Its per capita income of only US $77 (1962) is the lowest in the entire New World, barring Bolivia.

Table 53.   Haiti: direction of foreign trade, 1957, 1962, 1964 and 1965–66 (in %)

	1957	*1962*	*1964*	*1965/6*
Exports	$32 million	$41 million	$38 million	$36 million
North America	33·8	44·6	47·4	40·4
USA	33·1	44·4	47·4	40·4
Canada	0·7	0·2	—	—
Europe	52·2	38·3	35·0	43·3
EEC	44·0	37·4	35·0	43·3
EFTA	8·2	0·9	—	—
Japan	2·6	—	6·6	5·6
Jamaica and Puerto Rico	—	—	—	4·7
Others	11·4	17·1	11·0	6·0
Imports	$38 million	$34 million	$36 million	$37 million
North America	67·8	54·0	60·8	55·4
USA	62·3	51·3	58·3	55·4
Canada	5·5	2·7	2·5	—
Dutch Antilles	5·2	3·9	3·0	—
Europe	19·7	23·5	20·1	19·8
EEC	13·2	18·6	15·4	15·9
EFTA	6·5	4·9	4·7	3·9
Japan	—	—	—	4·2
Others	7·3	18·6	16·1	20·6

The Dominican Republic

Population and settlement

The Dominican Republic emerged from the former Spanish colony of Santo Domingo and occupies the eastern part of Hispaniola, comprising two-thirds of the island's surface. Its area of 48 734 sq km makes it the second largest territory among the Caribbean islands. The population amounts to 3 million (1960),[1] showing a much lower population density (61 persons per sq km) than the neighbouring Republic of Haiti (Map 50). However, the Dominican population is growing faster than that of Haiti. Its annual rate of increase has been 4·5 per cent for the last few decades, compared with 3 per cent in Haiti. The present death rate is 10·5 per thousand, the birth-rate 39·8 per thousand (cf. p. 77 regarding age structure).

[1] Estimate for 1969: 4·2 million.

The racial structure of the Dominican population also differs from that of Haiti. Whites comprise 29 per cent, Negroes 11 per cent, and mulattoes 60 per cent. The percentage of Negroes is high mainly in the capital and in those areas which are characterized by large landholdings, especially the coastal plain of Santo Domingo. The Amerindian influence is especially obvious in the northern and central parts of the country.

The Dominicans' continuous fight against the numerical superiority of the Haitian Negroes not only helped to develop a strong national consciousness but also led to an emphasis of the Spanish cultural tradition and the general way of life, and it evoked a feeling of superiority on the part of the 'white' Dominican Republic to the neighbouring 'black' Haiti. This attitude is present in all Dominicans, irrespective of colour. Racial antagonism is therefore almost non-existent in the Dominican Republic.

Social structure in the Dominican Republic resembles that of pre-revolutionary Cuba and of many other Latin American nations in so far as it is determined by the coexistence of a small group of owners and a mass of farm workers and small peasants. The implementation of agrarian reform is considered the central problem at the present time. Only a minority of the population benefited from the economic development which took place during the Trujillo regime (1930–61). A considerable bureaucracy was established during this period but the Dominican Republic still does not possess a middle class.

Spanish is the official language, and more than two-thirds of the population belong to the Roman Catholic Church. In addition to a public health system, an educational system was developed during the Trujillo regime to such an extent that the percentage of illiterates decreased from 75 per cent (1930) to 27 per cent (1960).

Population distribution indicates two overcrowded regions. The smaller area, including the capital of Santo Domingo, is situated in the southern coastal plain, the second and much larger region is the Vega Real in the central part of the extensive northern longitudinal depression of the Cibao. The arid south-west and the frontier regions along the Haitian border are only sparsely populated. After the border had been surveyed in 1936 and in 1937, after the Haitian Negroes, who had previously infiltrated into the frontier area, had either been eradicated or driven away, the Dominican Republic established several agricultural colonies in this region in accordance with its *Dominicación fronteriza* scheme (cf. pp. 231, 236, 238). These settlements offered a new home to Spaniards, to refugees from Hungary, and to Japanese as well as to Dominican citizens. The Dominican Republic is the only Caribbean island country to have conducted this type of active settlement programme on its extensive reserves of arable land in the very recent past (Map 51).

The urban population in the Dominican Republic amounts to 30·5 per cent (1960), which is much higher than in Haiti. Almost all the towns originated during the Spanish colonial period and are among the oldest

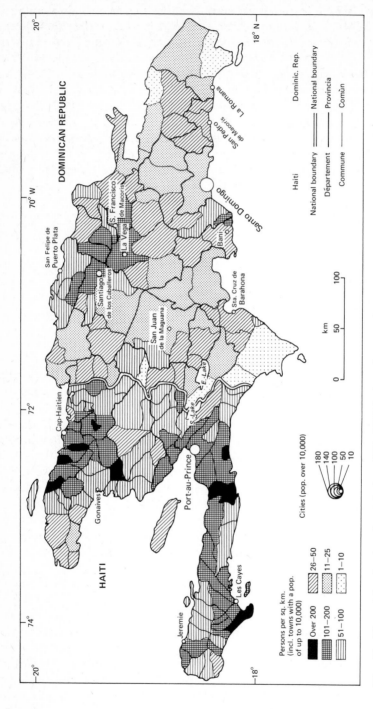

Map 50. Hispaniola: density of population, 1950 (1950 is the only year when a census was conducted in both parts of the island).

in the New World. The area which is now the Dominican Republic has always had an especially high proportion of the entire urban population. It is interesting to note that the urban population during the Spanish colonial period was far greater than the rural. The five largest towns in the eighteenth century colony (Santo Domingo, Santiago, Vega, Cotuí, Azua) together had a population of not less than 56 000, i.e. about 50 per cent of the total population. By comparison with Haiti the greater development of urbanization in the Dominican Republic at the present time is also obvious when expressed as population percentages in the two capitals: Santo Domingo has only 40 per cent of the total urban population as against 57 per cent Port-au-Prince. Sixteen Dominican towns have a population of over 10 000 (Table 54).

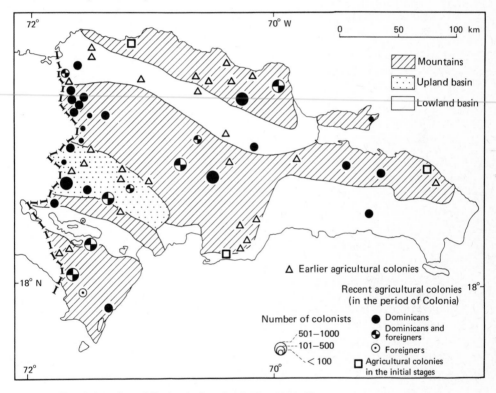

Map 51. Dominican Republic: agricultural colonies, 1930–60.

In addition to these large towns there are a large number of smaller towns and numerous marketplaces. All of them, including the larger towns, have a growing population at the moment, with rapid growth in some of them. Labour villages characterize the pattern of settlement in the regions of large landholdings. Village-type settlements are also widespread in the areas of peasant agriculture, and isolated farmhouses frequently appear.

269

The extremely dispersed type of settlement, however, which is so characteristic in Haiti is non-existent in the Dominican Republic.

Table 54.   Dominican Republic: towns with a population of over 10 000 inhabitants—1960

		Increase since 1950 %
Santo Domingo	367 053	102
Santiago de los Caballeros	83 563	48
San Francisco de Macorís	26 000	62
La Romana	24 058	71
San Pedro de Macorís	22 935	15
San Juan de la Maguana	20 449	106
Santa Cruz de Barahona	20 398	39
Concepción de la Vega	19 884	40
San Felipe de Puerto Plata	19 073	29
Valverde	17 885	171
San Cristóbal	15 525	60
Baní	14 472	42
Moca	13 829	44
Ciudad de Bonao	12 951	174
Azua de Compostela	12 350	65
Villa de Salveleón de Higüey	10 084	88

Agriculture

Farm sizes in the Dominican Republic differ considerably from those in Haiti (Table 55). Nearly half the agricultural land is in large enterprises of over 100 ha which, however, constitute only 0·7 per cent of all enterprises. Three-quarters of all agricultural enterprises are less than 5 ha, but together they possess not even 10 per cent of the entire agricultural land. The concentration of land ownership was stimulated by the development of the modern sugar industry in the late nineteenth century and increased considerably during the US occupation of the Dominican Republic between 1916 and 1922, and again during the Trujillo regime. Although the agrarian social structure is not as unbalanced as it was in pre-revolutionary Cuba, agrarian reform must still be considered very urgent. Because of this 250 000 ha of land were distributed among more than 100 000 farm workers during the Trujillo regime. At the present time plans have been made within the framework of a general agrarian reform to establish about 70 000 farms on the Trujillo lands which comprise around 440 000 ha.

Although the area occupied by agricultural enterprises has expanded from 1·7 million ha (1930) to 2·6 million ha (1960), and the land under cultivation from about 0·5 to 1·3 million ha during the same period, only one-third of the suitable land has so far been brought into cultivation. The

Table 55.   Dominican Republic: farm sizes, 1950 (%)

farm size	number of farms	agricultural area	agriculturally productive area
<5 ha	75·6	9·7	13·7
5–20 ha	18·1	21·1	20·2
20–100 ha	4·8	23·4	22·4
>100 ha	0·7	45·8	43·7

colonization of the interior under Trujillo included all the different regions; moreover, this programme is unique in the Caribbean islands. The irrigated land in the arid regions, for instance, was expanded from 3000 to 135 000 ha between 1930 and 1955. Today, the irrigation canals make up a total length of 2700 km. The western Cibao, the Valle de San Juan, the Enriquillo Depression and the Baní Plain are the major irrigated areas. The colonization of the interior was considerably increased by the agricultural colonies where foreigners were also settled (Spaniards, Hungarians, Japanese). These colonies are dispersed throughout the country, most of them being in the region along the Haitian border. Decisive changes occurred in the frontier region under Trujillo within the framework of the *Dominicación fronteriza*. Sixty-five such agricultural colonies had been established by 1959, and thirty-eight were still assisted by the Ministry of Agriculture at that time. In 1959 the latter group alone consisted of 10 421 settlers' holdings with an agricultural area of 145 000 ha, of which 42 000 ha were already under ground crops. The colonization of the interior was discontinued after the Trujillo regime. Since then the former colonies have been threatened by disintegration, partly because several of the emigrant families are returning to their homeland, and partly because rural exodus is no longer being prevented by the government. A substantial loss of cultivated land may also be observed, particularly in the remote districts along the border (cf. p. 239), but hardly any of these new settlements in the interior have been affected.

The most important export crop in the Dominican Republic is sugar cane which is mainly restricted to the coastal plain of Santo Domingo and which is cultivated by plantations in a monocultural pattern. Modern sugar production began with 18 700 tonnes of sugar in 1885 and has risen to 0·7 million tonnes by 1968. Sugar unduly dominated the economy between 1928 and 1938, making up 67 per cent of the entire exports by value. During the Trujillo regime efforts were made to diversify agriculture in order to reduce the extreme dominance of sugar. Today, sugar represents 52 per cent of the exports by value (average of 1963–67).

Coffee is the second export crop. It is cultivated mainly on peasant small-holdings which are not, however, as small as those in Haiti. The chief coffee-producing areas lie along the slopes of the Sierra de Baoruco and in the Cordillera Septentrional. Production rose from 21 300 tonnes (average of 1934–38) to 37 400 tonnes (average of 1963–67). Cocoa production, which is mainly from the Vega Real, has also experienced a great increase and amounted to 30 700 tonnes (average of 1963–67). The central part of the Cibao is the main tobacco area. The total production amounts to 19 600 tonnes (average of 1963–67). Since the expansion of the irrigated land in the western Cibao banana production has risen from 1·5 million bunches in 1950 to 22 million in 1960 (1967: 200 000 tonnes). The bananas are cultivated almost exclusively by large-scale enterprises.[1]

Both export orientated and domestic agricultural production have increased considerably. This is partly through successful interior colonization, and partly the intensification of farming which is vigorously propagated by the National Institute of Agriculture in San Cristóbal. Above all rice cultivation has expanded markedly in the irrigated regions of the Baní Plain, of the Valle de San Juan, and especially in the eastern and western Cibao. Production has risen from 7500 tonnes (1929) to 147 000 tonnes (1967). Rice imports became unnecessary in 1950. Maize production totalled 106 000 tonnes, and peanuts 52 000 tonnes in 1965. The newly introduced production of sisal, which was to provide the badly needed fibre for the manufacture of sacks for sugar, cocoa and coffee and which covered nearly 25 000 ha of state-owned land near Azua producing 2600 tonnes in 1960, has been discontinued.

Stock rearing, the most important branch of the country's economy until the end of the nineteenth century, has since greatly gained in importance. Extensive cattle farming is no longer the rule everywhere, as can be seen by the improved pastures near the Sosúa settlement of Jewish refugees where the newly imported Pangola grass has almost completely replaced Guinea and Bermuda grass. In addition, Criollo cattle have been replaced by Holstein, Zebu, Jersey and brown Swiss cattle. By 1960, the Dominican Republic had 1 million head of cattle and 1·2 million pigs; for the first time it was possible to export cattle for slaughter.

Mining and industry

A survey of mineral deposits was only started after the Second World War. For a short while after 1953 high grade iron ore was mined near Hatillo in the Cordillera Central (138 000 tonnes in 1961), and bauxite deposits in the Sierra de Baoruco have been exploited since 1959 (983 000 tonnes in 1967). Bauxite and iron ore are exported to the USA. The production of rock salt in the Enriquillo Depression amounted to an average of 77 000 tonnes between 1959 and 1962.

Industrialization in the Dominican Republic took a great step forward during the Trujillo regime. This applies to both the food and the consumer

---

[1] The production of the respective crops in 1965 amounted to: coffee 36 000 tonnes; cocoa 40 000 tonnes; tobacco 35 000 tonnes; bananas 450 000 tonnes.

goods industry which jointly employed 81 000 workers in 1962. The sugar industry clearly leads all industrial activities, employing 61 000 workers. It supplies about half the volume of industrial production and has two-thirds of the entire capital investment which totalled US $307 million in 1962. Of the sixteen sugar factories, 15 are in Dominican ownership. The chocolate factory in Puerto Plata, and the peanut oil plant, the brewery and the flour mill in Santo Domingo represent the major enterprises of the food, beverages and tobacco industry. The flour mill first went into production in 1959.

Santo Domingo is the major location for the consumer goods industry. The manufacturing of textiles, mainly from cotton, is the leading branch which, however, has so far not been able to meet the local demand. The cement factory in Santo Domingo went into operation in 1947. It produced 270 000 tonnes of cement in 1958, meeting for the first time the entire Dominican demand (298 000 tonnes in 1964). The same situation has been achieved with glass production. Industrial development has been strongly stimulated both by the production of fertilizer (since 1955) and the profitable use of bagasse, the residue from the pressing of sugar cane. In La Romana since 1956 this has been converted into furfurol, a basic material for the production of nylon. In addition, paper has been manufactured from bagasse since 1959.

The newly completed port of Río Haina, west of Santo Domingo, is to become the location of the capital goods industry. The iron ore from the Cordillera Central is shipped from here. The largest and most modern sugar factory in the Caribbean is located here, and a shipyard started operations in 1956; an iron and steel works are planned.

An essential precondition for the industrial development of the Dominican Republic is an enormous increase in the power supply. It was raised from 15 million kWh in 1937 to 979 million kWh in 1965.

The economy of the Dominican Republic has developed much faster than that of other Caribbean states since 1930, i.e. during the Trujillo regime. During the decade following the Second World War the Dominican Republic had the soundest economy in the Caribbean islands having repaid the foreign national debt in 1947 and the internal national debt in 1953, enjoying a favourable balance of trade, a stable currency and steady price levels, and carrying out an economic policy which was greatly concerned with the development of agriculture and industry and which tried to balance these two branches of economy in a reasonable way. With continued development in both the agricultural and industrial sector the annual per capita income reached US $230 in 1960 ($238 in 1968) which is four times as high as in the neighbouring Republic of Haiti. But even before the end of the Trujillo period (1961) the disadvantages of the Trujillo regime were becoming abundantly clear. The gold reserves of the Dominican Republic fell rapidly in 1961, and after the collapse of the regime the public treasury was found empty. Since 1962 numerous foreign loans have had to be raised. The conditions for a renewed growth of the temporarily stagnating economy are favourable since, in contrast to Haiti, considerable achievements had been accomplished in all economic sectors during the thirty years under Trujillo. The post-1961 political instability, however, and the several months of civil war in 1965 in particular, have prevented not only further economic development, but they have caused serious setbacks which by 1966 had led to high unemployment rates affecting principally the urban population.

The Dominican Republic is still an agricultural country in its economic structure, in spite of the industrial development before 1960. Agriculture supplied 91 per cent of the exports by value in 1960, and it employed 80 per cent of the labour force.

Transport

Railway transport is not important in the Dominican Republic. The only public line runs between La Vega and Sánchez, covering a distance of 130 km. Passengers are not transported.

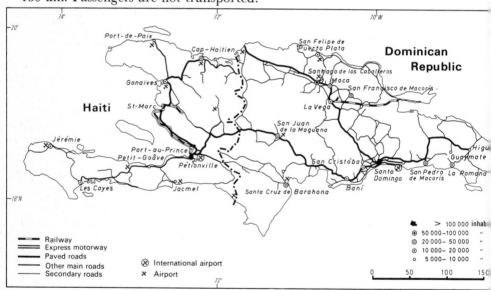

Map 52. Hispaniola: transport.

The number of motor vehicles has increased from 6000 in 1948 to more than 22 000 in 1964. The road network has been fairly well developed. About 5700 km of all-weather roads were built during the Trujillo regime connecting all parts of the country with the capital. Before that the main economic region in the north, the Cibao, could only be reached from Santo Domingo either by mule tracks or by sea. A short highway leads westward from Santo Domingo in the direction of San Cristóbal; another longer highway leads eastward to the new Punta Caucedo airport near Boca Chica. Numerous shared taxis provide a fast service from the capital into the interior. Cross-country buses are not found in the Dominican Republic in contrast to the other islands. Traffic across the Haitian border does not exist (cf. p. 264). The two countries turn their backs on each other, so to speak, as Spain and Portugal used to do in the past. The small planes of the Aerovias Quisqueyanas offer connections between Santo Domingo and the most important towns in the Dominican Republic, and the Companía Dominicana de Aviación offers flights abroad, to Puerto Rico, Curaçao, Venezuela, and the USA. Several foreign airlines serve the international Punta Caucedo airport of Santo Domingo. Nevertheless, the volume of air traffic is comparatively low. Only twenty-two weekly scheduled flights with a seating capacity of 1835 left the airport in 1960. Only 32 000 tourists visited the Dominican Republic in 1959 (20 000 by air, 10 500 on cruises). When tourists could no longer go to Cuba their number in the Dominican Republic bounced up to 295 000 in 1962. However, the 1965 civil war stopped tourism almost completely.

The port of Santo Domingo has the largest turnover in respect of international trade. It handles about 90 per cent of the imports and more than 40 per cent of the exports. Puerto Plata, La Romana and San Pedro de Macorís, on the other hand, jointly handle about 40 per cent of the exports but only 9 per cent of the imports. These figures express the differing function of the ports. All Dominican ports except Santo Domingo are export harbours, some of them very specialized, e.g. for the export of coffee or bauxite. Santo Domingo has achieved its leading position in foreign trade only since the expansion of the road network.

Trade

The volume of foreign trade in the Dominican Republic totalled US $345 million in 1968. Although it is four times as high as that of Haiti, it is still much lower than that of other independent territories in the Caribbean. However, it differed from all these in its balance of trade which was markedly favourable for the decades before 1962 (1961: US $143 million-worth of exports, $ 69 million-worth of imports). Since domestic food production has increased considerably, food imports (6·5 per cent) were much lower than in other Caribbean countries until 1961. However, they represented 20 per cent of the imports by value by 1967. Since the development of the textile industry textile imports are relatively low (2 per cent in 1967). Machinery is the second biggest item among the imports (14 per cent in 1967). In 1967, 51 per cent of the imports came from the USA, 8 per cent from the Federal Republic of Germany.

Agriculture supplies 91 per cent of the exports by value. The most important export commodities are sugar (56·4 per cent of the 1966 exports by value), coffee (15·4 per cent), cocoa (8·0 per cent), and tobacco (4·9 per cent). The considerable drop in the sugar quota during the last two decades[1]

[1] Sugar represented an average of 67 per cent of the entire exports by value between 1928 and 1938.

Table 56.   Dominican Republic: direction of foreign trade, 1966

	Exports Mill. Pesos	%	Imports Mill. Pesos	%
North America	121·50	88·9	84·30	52·4
USA	120·75	88·3	78·60	48·9
Canada	0·75	0·6	5·70	3·5
Middle America	0·53	0·4	12·41	7·7
South America	0·26	0·2	2·16	1·4
Europe (without Communist E. European countries)	12·92	9·5	42·13	26·2
EEC	8·59	6·3	26·16	16·3
EFTA	1·71	1·3	12·99	8·1
Others	2·62	1·9	2·98	1·8
E. European countries	—	—	—	—
Africa	0·63	0·4	2·30	1·4
Asia	0·25	0·2	15·71	9·8
Total	136·09	99·6	159·01	98·9

Source: United Nations Yearbook of International Trade Statistics

expresses the successfully accomplished diversification of export orientated agricultural production. The export of bauxite only started a few years ago. It amounted to 7·6 per cent of the exports by value by 1966. The chief recipient of the Dominican production is the USA (Table 56), which has always taken almost the entire coffee and cocoa harvest. Since Cuba stopped its sugar deliveries in 1961, the USA have bought nearly the entire Dominican sugar production. The proportion of exports to the USA has therefore risen from an average of 44·6 per cent between 1956 and 1958 to 88·3 per cent in 1966. The iron ore and bauxite are also shipped almost exclusively to the USA. Until 1961 Great Britain used to be the second trading partner of the Dominican Republic; however, its share of exports dropped from 27·5 per cent (1956–8) to 0·2 per cent (1966). The Federal Republic of Germany replaced Great Britain from 1962 to 1965; since 1966 Spain has become the second trading partner, and in third place is Japan.

Differences in the cultural geography of the divided island

A comparison of the various regions in Hispaniola reveals very clearly the differences between the western and the eastern part of the island in their cultural geography. The varying density of the population is most conspicuous. The smaller Haiti has more inhabitants than the larger Dominican Republic. This contrast is aggravated by the linguistic, the cultural and especially the racial differences between the Haitian and the Dominican population and has again and again led to serious confrontations between the two neighbouring nations. This contrast is aggravated by the fact that densely populated Haiti has only limited reserves of potential agricultural land as against the comparatively extensive reserves at the disposal of the only moderately populated Dominican Republic.

The rural population in both countries far outnumbers the urban though the percentage of the urban population is much higher in the Dominican Republic than in Haiti. The Dominican Republic possesses more towns than Haiti; moreover, these towns are more populous and differ in their appearance from the Haitian. The difference between the rural settlements is probably even greater. An extremely dispersed type of settlement is typical of Haiti, the village-type settlement of the Dominican Republic. Only the isolated dwelling-places of the unplanned squatter settlements in the mountain areas of the *conuqueros* resemble the isolated farm settlements in Haiti.

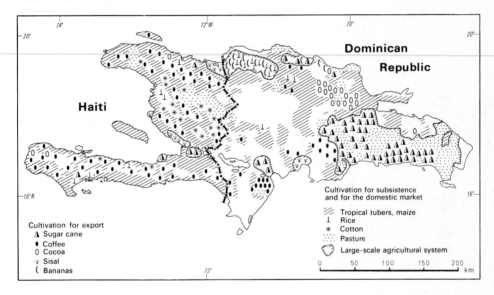

Map 53. Hispaniola: land use.

The contrast in the settlement pattern is reflected in the differences in the structure of land ownership and the types of enterprise in the two territories. Presentday Haiti is a country of small or very small farms; large landholdings, however, are the rule in the Dominican Republic, where a large number of medium-sized farms also exist, e.g. in the Vega Real. In Haiti, the main areas of agricultural production are in the mountains; in the Dominican Republic they are in the plains. The export-orientated monoculture of the large-scale enterprises covers vast regions in the plains of the Dominican Republic, but only small areas in Haiti (Map 53). There

277

could hardly be a more striking contrast in Hispaniola's basic economic landscape than that between the many latifundia found in the Dominican Republic and the numerous smallholdings farmed by peasants who cultivate both tree and ground crops, and sometimes both together, found in Haiti. Firstly, because of the completely haphazard way the plants are cultivated, and secondly, because of the small size and the dispersed pattern of smallholdings, the peasant landscape in Haiti differs essentially even from the peasant agricultural areas in the Dominican Republic; in the latter country, even if one looks at the new agricultural colonies, as well as the old peasant regions, like the Vega Real, and despite polyculture, the fields and the trees are cultivated in a geometrical pattern, the farming is done with greater care and the fields belonging to one village form a compact whole. All in all, the Dominican Republic displays an economic landscape which is thoroughly different from the Haitian.

Table 57. Hispaniola: export crops (in 1000 tonnes; average 1958–62)

	sugar	*coffee*	*cocoa*
Haiti	58·8	30·2	2·2
Dominican Republic	906·8	34·0	35·8

Dominican agricultural production meets the domestic food demand much more adequately than the Haitian and is at the same time more export-orientated and more versatile. This may be seen in the larger exports (Table 57) as well as in the distribution of the economic landscapes which can be differentiated by their prevailing type of cultivation, their farm type or size, or by their market orientation. Only the economic landscape dominated by sisal cultivated on large-scale enterprises as a single crop is more widespread in Haiti than it is in the Dominican Republic. On the other hand, the distribution of sugar cane monoculture in the Dominican Republic is very much wider than that of Haiti and on the whole banana monoculture is absent in Haiti. The pastoral economic landscape covers relatively wide areas in the Dominican Republic but only very limited areas in Haiti. The areas of peasant polyculture are unmistakably prevalent in Haiti and are present only to a small extent in the Dominican Republic.

The expansion of agricultural land in Haiti has only been slight compared with the significant results achieved by colonization of the interior in the Dominican Republic. Irrigated land in Haiti, for instance, makes up only half the irrigated area in the Dominican Republic. Because of the remarkable increase in its agricultural production the Dominican Republic today produces far more than the former Spanish colony of Santo Domingo was able to export. The agricultural output of Haiti, on the other hand, is considerably lower than that of the former French colony of St Domingue.

Although both territories possess areas which are still inaccessible, the road network has been much better developed in the Dominican Republic than in Haiti. The Dominican Republic has succeeded in establishing a fairly versatile consumer goods industry; Haiti has not. Less than 10 000 people are employed in Haitian industry; 90 000 in Dominican industries. The power supply amounts to 59 million kWh in Haiti, whereas in the Dominican Republic it totals 439 million kWh. Since its recent economic growth the Dominican Republic is less dependent on food and textile imports than Haiti. The different economic structure of the two territories is expressed in the great difference in per capita incomes which, in 1962, amounted to US $77 in Haiti and to $202 in the Dominican Republic. The contrast in educational standards is even more striking: 90 per cent of Haitians are illiterate, but only 27 per cent of the population in the Dominican Republic.

The sharp economic disparity existing between the two republics today is a complete reversal of conditions at the end of the colonial period. This reversal is partly the result of the economic progress achieved by the Dominican Republic in both agriculture and industry, and partly because the Haitian government has so far been unable to tackle the problem of poverty in its territory effectively. But the divergent characters of the two nations have even deeper roots. After the early period of Spanish colonization the eastern and the western parts of the island, both of them possessing very similar topography, have developed politically and economically in opposite directions. The cultural landscape in the two parts of the island has changed repeatedly in different ways. In the final analysis, the differences in Hispaniola's cultural geography are the outcome of its historical development.

21

Puerto Rico

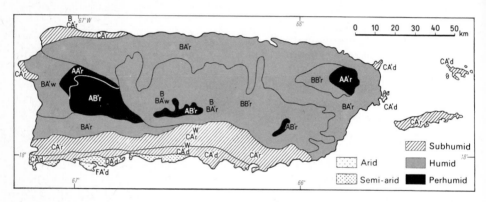

Map 54. Puerto Rico: climatic types (Thornthwaite's climatic classification, adapted by Thorp).

Puerto Rico has experienced a much greater degree of economic development during the last twenty years than any other Caribbean island. A large number of experts, mainly from developing countries in Latin America, Africa and Asia, visit Puerto Rico in order to study the remarkable changes in this island. The young Caribbean nations, such as Jamaica and Trinidad and Tobago, try to hasten their own economic development by imitating the methods used in Puerto Rico.

The recent changes in the economic structure of Puerto Rico are the more astonishing since the island was greatly neglected by the Spanish Crown during the Spanish colonial rule until its end in 1898. Although agricultural production increased greatly after the USA had taken possession, the development of sugar cane monoculture aggravated the feudal type of agrarian social structure as it did in Cuba. This development, intensified by an explosive increase of the population, caused an impoverishment of the population which assumed even more serious proportions than in Cuba. The turning-point came only in 1940. It must be attributed both to the initiative of Muñoz Marín (prime minister of Puerto Rico between

280

1948 and 1964), which was first approved of and later supported by the USA, and also to Puerto Rico's ability to exploit the advantages which result from the country's proximity to the North American continent and from its recent membership in the US free trade area.

The new constitution of 1952 made Puerto Rico an autonomous part of the USA, called the 'Commonwealth of Puerto Rico' or 'Estado Libre Asociado'.

Physical geography

Puerto Rico represents the eastern end of the island chain of the Greater Antilles and is at the same time its smallest part. It covers an area of 8897 sq km, including the three neighbouring islands of Mona (54 sq km), Vieques (132 sq km), and Culebra (28 sq km) which are administered by Puerto Rico. With its relatively little indented coastline it is roughly rectangular in shape. The island stretches for nearly 180 km from west to east with a width of 50 to 60 km.

The north coast drops over 8500 m deep into the Puerto Rico Trench, and in the south also the sea bottom falls rapidly to the 5000 m deep Venezuelan sub-basin of the Caribbean Sea. The Mona Passage in the west separates Puerto Rico from Hispaniola; it is about 120 km wide and more than 1000 m deep. A continental shelf only occurs to the east; out of it rise the islands of Vieques and Culebra both of them belonging to the Virgin Islands as regards their natural features.

Puerto Rico is a mountainous island. Its backbone is formed by the Central Cordillera and the Sierra de Luquillo, continuations of the Dominican Cordillera Central. Both mountain ranges rise to heights of more than 1000 m and represent uplifted old mountains with accordant summits in their relief form. Their fossil erosion surfaces are found at varying altitudes and of different ages, and are strongly dissected by recent erosion. Particularly on the northern slopes erosion has caused a large number of narrow and often canyonlike valleys, hostile to any traffic. Hilly regions extend north and south of the mountainous core of the island. They are chiefly built from slightly bevelled and unfolded Tertiary sedimentary rocks, with limestone the prevailing rock type. The hilly region north of the Central Cordillera forms a particularly impressive cuesta and also a karst landscape where both dinaric karst and cone karst formations are common. Very narrow coastal plains usually adjoin these hilly regions along the northern and southern slopes of the island. The coastal plain surrounds almost the entire island and is only interrupted by either mountainous or hilly areas in some places in the east and west.

This simple topographical structure gives Puerto Rico its distinct climatic division. The north coast and its hinterland are wet because of their position facing the trade winds, the south coast is dry. A comparison of the amounts of rainfall received by the weather stations of Humacao (2121 mm)

281

to the windward and of Ponce (909 mm) in the lee of the mountains illustrates the difference in precipitation. Since the watershed of the Central Cordillera is nearer to the south coast than to the north coast most of the island is perhumid (Map 54). The isohygromenes on the southern slope of the island run parallel to the ridge, almost from west to east; complete aridity is therefore experienced only at the extreme end of the small peninsula which stretches farthest south, south of Ensenada. The climatic differences within Puerto Rico are not as pronounced as in Hispaniola owing to the few topographical divisions.

Most of the former forest cover of this overpopulated island has been destroyed. Only in a few reservations, of which the nature reserve of the Sierra de Luquillo is the largest, can one get an impression of the former dense forest cover of the island. Evergreen tropical rain forest used to occupy the largest area, being replaced by montane forest at altitudes of over 400 m. Pine forests which are so very common in Cuba and Hispaniola do not exist in Puerto Rico. The montane forest is characterized by extensive areas of the palm tree *Euterpe globosa* and by tree ferns (e.g. *Nephrolepis cordifolia*). These still grow very densely in the Sierra de Luquillo, covering the mountain slopes right up to the peaks. Semi-evergreen seasonal forests are found in the southern hilly region, and dry woodland as well as thorn and cactus savannas in the southern regions near the coast.

Population and settlement

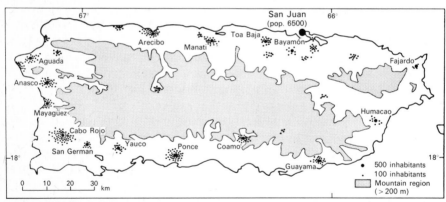

Map 55. Puerto Rice: distribution of population, 1775 (from Legajo 2396, Puerto Rico, Archivo General de Indias, Sevilla).

In 1950 79·7 per cent of the Puerto Rican population was white; the low percentage of Negroes and mulattoes in the total population, in comparison with other Caribbean islands, is explained by the fact that, as in Cuba, the plantation economy did not develop during the Spanish colonial era. For more than 200 years the Spanish Crown used the island only as a military base. At a time when the old plantation economy flourished in the British and French islands and slaves represented 90 per cent of the population in those islands, in Puerto Rico the proportion of Negroes amounted to not more than 11 per cent.[1] In contrast to almost all of the Caribbean islands at the end of the eighteenth century Puerto Rico had a population of small peasants who lived in numerous small and isolated settlements which were surrounded by virgin forests (Map 55).

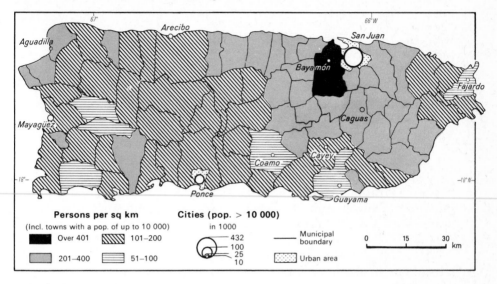

Map 56. Puerto Rico: density of population, 1960.

The population increased greatly during the nineteenth century: from 155 000 in 1800 to 953 000 in 1899. During this period the percentage of Negroes decreased continuously although, until the abolition of slavery (1873), more Negroes were needed than ever before because of the trend in agriculture towards production for export. However, whites immigrated in large numbers.

Puerto Rico experienced a population explosion in the twentieth century. The population had risen to 1·3 million by 1920 and to 2·7 million by 1970. With 302 persons per sq km (Map 56), Puerto Rico is even more over-populated than Jamaica and Haiti. The birthrate reached a maximum of 43·9 per thousand in 1947, the deathrate decreased continuously. Since then the birthrate has decreased considerably (Table 58) coinciding with the island's economic development. The present worldwide campaign for birth control with the help of contraceptive pills is based on experiments with pills which were successfully conducted in Puerto Rico. The noticeable

[1] The Puerto Rican population numbered 103 051 in 1787; percentage distribution: whites 45, Amerindians 2, free Negroes 8, free mulattoes (pardos) 34, Negro slaves 6·5, mulatto slaves 4·5.

283

Table 58.   Puerto Rican population, 1940–70

	1940	1950	1960	1970
Population	1 869 000	2 210 703	2 349 544	2 688 289
Density of population (persons per sq km)	210	248	264	302
Birth rate (per thousand)	39·0	39·6	31·5	25·5
Death rate (per thousand)	18·2	10·5	6·6	6·2
Life expectancy (in years)	46	61	68	
Annual per capita income in US $)	121	279	587	1 144*

Source: After E. P. Hanson (1962)
* 1968

decrease in the growth of the population (18·3 per cent between 1940 and 1950; but only 6·3 per cent between 1950 and 1960) was also caused by heavy emigration. Before the Second World War emigration was unimportant. Only Hawaii attracted a considerable number of Puerto Ricans in the 1890s. Of all Puerto Ricans who have emigrated to the USA 90 per cent live in New York, which had 550 Puerto Ricans in 1910, 63 000 in 1940, 275 000 in 1950, and 750 000 in 1960. Today, New York has the largest Puerto Rican community with the immigrants concentrating in certain districts. Following the Second World War thousands of Puerto Ricans left their home country each year, the maximum number of 75 000 emigrants being reached in 1953. Since then the number has slowly decreased, falling to 14 000 by 1961. Returning migrants have outnumbered emigrants since 1962. Puerto Rico had an estimated population of 2 626 000 in 1965.

Apart from emigration another characteristic of the present high mobility of the population is the rural exodus, triggered by industrialization. The urban population increased from 14·6 per cent in 1899 to 30·3 per cent in 1940 and at present (1970) represents 58·1 per cent. The number of towns[1] rose from seventeen to forty-five between 1899 and 1940, and later to eighty-four. The population of the towns increased steadily until 1950; until 1960 they have decreased, with only a few exceptions. This illustrates the fact that the rural exodus affected not only the rural population but also that of the rural towns. This was even true of most towns with a population of over 10 000. The capital of San Juan, on the other hand, was experiencing a very rapid growth coinciding with the heavy concentration of new industries (Table 59). Since 1960 there has been a steady increase in urban population affecting nearly all towns.

[1] According to the Puerto Rican census: settlements with more than 2500 inhabitants.

Table 59.   Puerto Rico: towns with a population of over 10 000 inhabitants

	1950	*1960*	*1970*
San Juan	224 767	432 377	452 749
Bayamón	20 171	15 109	147 552
Ponce	99 492	114 286	128 233
Carolina	5 041	3 075	94 271
Mayagüez	58 944	50 147	68 872
Caguas	33 759	32 015	63 215
Guayanabo	1 128	3 343	55 310
Arecibo	28 659	28 828	35 484
Cataño	9 182	8 276	26 459
Cayey	18 429	19 738	21 562
Aguadilla	18 276	15 943	21 031
Guayama	19 408	19 183	20 318
Fajardo	15 336	12 409	18 249
Levistown	—	—	17 079
Manatí	10 092	9 682	13 483
Humacao	10 851	8 005	12 411
Coamo	11 592	12 146	12 077
San Germán	8 872	7 790	11 613

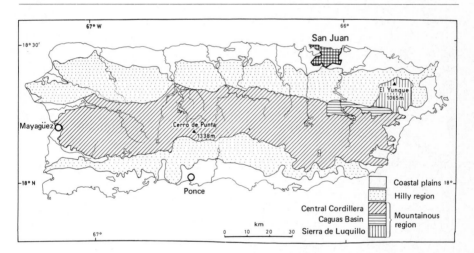

Map 57.   Puerto Rico: regional divisions.

In the past, the proportion of the urban population in Puerto Rico, as well as in the other former Spanish colonies (Cuba, Dominican Republic), was higher than in the rest of the islands. This is also demonstrated by the capital which had only 23·1 per cent of the urban population in 1899 when Spanish colonial rule ended. This percentage had increased to 41·8 per cent by 1960.

In spite of urban growth 57·4 per cent of the population still live in rural dispersed settlements (77·9 per cent in 1899). Such settlements characterize the rural areas in the hilly and mountainous regions. Nucleated settlements are prevalent only in the coastal plains, where sugar cane monoculture has developed. The villages are inhabited by workers employed in the sugar industry. However, not more than 2·1 per cent of the population (7·5 per cent in 1899) live in settlements with less than 2500 inhabitants.

Regional divisions

Coastal plains

The coastal plains of Puerto Rico have varying amounts of rainfall. The **coastal plain in the north** faces the trade winds and is therefore very wet. The amount of rainfall only decreases in the region west of Arecibo. This part of the plain is further distinguished from the rest by the fact that it is formed of limestone (Miocene Aymamón formation) while the coastal plain east of Arecibo is an alluvial plain with a width of hardly more than 10 km.

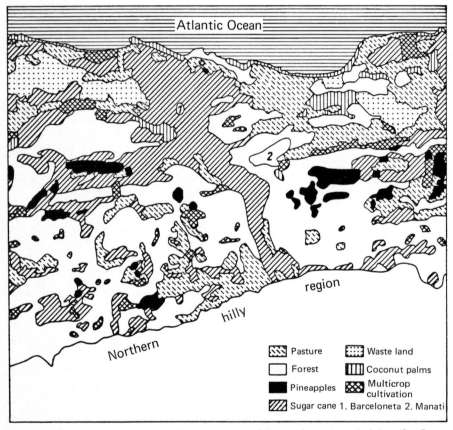

Map 58. Puerto Rico: land use in the central part of the northern coastal plain (after Jones and Picó).

Dinaric karst formations are found in the western limestone area which is, however, separated from the very wet hilly region to the south by a row of karst cones (haystacks). Sugar cane cultivation, which occupies most of the Puerto Rican coastal plains, has never assumed a major role; peasant farms, not latifundia, predominate and most of them are owned by the descendants of immigrants from the Canary Islands. The proportion made up by the white population rises to 90 per cent in some places and is therefore much higher than in other sections of the coastal plain. Sugar cane is only important in the irrigated Isabela area; otherwise, tobacco and food crops are the main crops cultivated. In various areas cotton is produced. The cultivation of vegetables for the US winter market is a very profitable source of income as well as the recently introduced dairy industry. The farms immediately west of Arecibo have specialized in dairy farming since 1950. The land use of this western section of the coastal plain is completely agricultural.

Sugar cane cultivation and, in its wake, large landholdings have developed on the fertile alluvial soils in the northern coastal plain east of Arecibo (Map 58). Ten of the thirty-five existing sugar factories are situated in the region between Arecibo and Cape San Juan. Several of the extensive, rectangular and uniformly cultivated fields of the sugar plantations stretch far into the adjoining hilly region in the south along the major rivers, e.g. the Río Grande de Arecibo and the Manatí. The plains are built from the sedimentary materials from these rivers. However, cultivation is not entirely dominated by sugar cane. Pineapples are grown over large areas today (Plate 18); many coconut trees follow the coastline and pastures have expanded greatly at the expense of the less profitable sugar cane plantations. The dairy farms on the northern coastal plain have specialized in milk production which finds a ready market because of the high concentration of Puerto Rico's townsfolk along this part of the coast.

Within the framework of agrarian reform a number of proportional profit farms (cf. p. 299) have been established in this section of the coastal plain. The landscape, already determined by large-scale enterprises, has not been changed by these alterations in the distribution of land ownership. However, a new note was added when numerous settlements were built for farm workers. These have a regular layout, a low density housing pattern and a friendly atmosphere. Each family has its own little home, built near the road, with a garden, where the owner usually produces food for his own consumption. Even when these settlements are situated in completely rural areas increasing numbers of their inhabitants are being employed by the new industries in the nearby urban centres, or by those which have been built in the rural districts. The landscape of the northern coastal plain also experienced formal and functional changes with the establishment of peasant farms within the area of former large-scale farms, especially along the hilly region where single or grouped karstic haystacks, which are cone-shaped erosional remnants of Aymamón limestone, tower above the plain, usually in long rows. These represent an obstacle to the mechanized farming used on modern large-scale enterprises.

The northern coastal plain between Arecibo and Cape San Juan is the most densely populated region in Puerto Rico. Numerous townships have developed inland, usually on rivers which cross the plain in a northerly direction. Only the two largest towns are ports: Arecibo on the mouth of the river with the same name, and San Juan, the capital.

Caparra, founded on the southern shore of the bay in 1508, was the fore-runner of San Juan. In 1521 San Juan was founded on the small island which today is connected to the main island by bridges across the inlet of Caño de San Antonio and the Laguna del Condado. The mighty Castillo del Morro, the landmark of San Juan on the tip of this island near the entrance to the harbour, together with the town wall and its fortifications, which still surround the old part of the city, demonstrate the strategic importance of San Juan during the Spanish colonial period. The vast installations of the US forces on either side of the extensive bay illustrate the fact that at the present time the possession of Puerto Rico is of no less strategic value to the USA (Map 59).

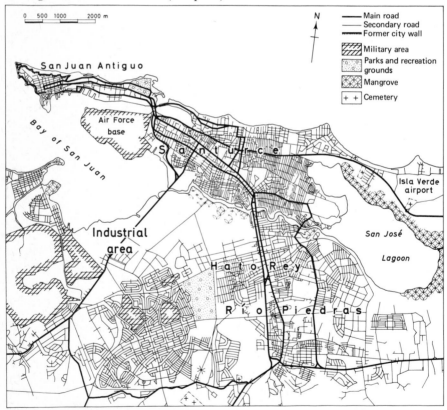

Map 59. Puerto Rico: street map of San Juan.

Only the old section of San Juan with its narrow and often steep streets, laid out in a grid-pattern around the Plaza de Armas, gives the impression of a Spanish colonial settlement. Several buildings date back to the first half of the sixteenth century, e.g. the Iglesia San José, the cathedral, the Casa Blanca built for Ponce de León, the first Spanish governor, and La Fortaleza, the present residence of the prime minister. The stepped lanes, especially the Callejon Las Monjas, are very picturesque with old and low residential buildings on either side. The older port facilities are found on the southern side of the island, with ferries leaving frequently for Cataño on the opposite shore of the bay. Most of the administrative and government buildings are centred in the area adjacent to San Juan Antigua in the east of the island. The luxury hotels Normandie and Caribe Hilton east of the Muñoz Rivera Park indicate the tourist area, which has recently expanded to the Condado peninsula beyond the bridge across the Laguna del Condado. Its beautiful sandy beach, the Condado Beach, is used by the guests of the various new hotels which have been built on either side of the broad Avenida Ashford (Plate 15).

The Santurce district is connected with San Juan Antigua by two bridges and today makes up the major part of the urban area stretching towards the interior as far as the Caño de Martín Peña and the Laguna del San José. The Avenida Ponce de León runs through this high density housing area. It covers a distance of 10 km extending from Columbus Square in the eastern part of San Juan Antigua to Río Piedras where the campus of the University of Puerto Rico has been situated since 1903 and which today is included in the city area. The continuously growing low density housing areas of Hato Rey and Martín Peña extend between Río Piedras and Santurce. The main shopping area of San Juan lies along the Avenida Ponce de León in Santurce and has busy pedestrian and car traffic, modern department stores and multistorey bank buildings. It strongly suggests a North American scene. As in the USA, modern throughways have also been built. San Juan has expanded greatly to the east on both sides of the Laguna del San José, and even further to the west. There, mass construction housing schemes for the workers cover the region immediately south of the industrial and harbour areas (Puerto Nuevo) which have also developed enormously in the recent past. These extensive and regularly laid out urban districts are characterized by small one-family houses with tiny garden lots.

San Juan's growth did not start until the twentieth century. At the end of the Spanish colonial era San Juan Antigua had 17 700 inhabitants, Santurce 5800, and Río Piedras 2200. Within the present city boundaries San Juan Antigua still had the largest population in 1920. By 1940 the overall population had risen to 189 000, and Santurce had become the major district, its population numbering 136 000, as against 36 000 in San Juan Antigua and 20 000 in Río Piedras.

The built-up area is not restricted to the metropolitan area, whose population increased between 1960 and 1970 from 648 000 to 840 000; it

289

stretches far into the coastal plain, especially towards the west. The towns of Cataño and Bayamón have been included in the metropolitan area. The commuter area stretches even further and is no longer restricted to the coastal plain west of San Juan.

Nearly half the urban population of Puerto Rico is concentrated in San Juan which has been the capital since the beginning of Spanish colonial rule. Its functions have grown and become more versatile with the economic development of the island. San Juan is the most important harbour and industrial location in the island, and the foremost cultural centre. It is also the centre of tourism, though various hotels have recently been built in other parts of the island. It possesses an excellent city transport system with a network of frequently served bus routes; in addition, the city is closely connected with all Puerto Rican towns by buses and shared taxis. The international airport of Isla Verde, east of the city between the Laguna del San José and the Atlantic, offers excellent services to all countries of the world. The rapid growth of the city is controlled by a planning board, established in 1942. The functional zoning of the metropolitan area, the solution of the transport problems, and the systematic expansion of the residential areas illustrate the excellent work done by this board. It has to a large extent succeeded in avoiding the unpleasant developments which often accompany the rapid and uncontrolled growth of Latin American cities.

Humidity in the northern coastal plain is similar to that of the flood plains at the river mouths along the east coast between Fajardo and Maunabo. These plains are of varying width and are separated from each other by mountain ridges; the Yabucoa Plain is the largest. The amount of rainfall exceeds that of the northern coastal plain and cultivation is therefore dependent on adequate drainage. On the agricultural land sugar cane is grown exclusively, cultivated by large-scale enterprises. The central sugar factory near Fajardo is one of the most important in Puerto Rico. The country towns, among which Fajardo is the largest, are all located inland, but all have a subsidiary settlement on the coast. Playa de Humacao, for instance, is the harbour of Humacao. These small harbours are no longer used for sugar export since loading at the open roadsteads has become too expensive.

Rainfall in these eastern coastal plains equals that of the west coast between Aguadilla in the north and Cabo Rojo in the south. However, the division into a summer rainy season and a winter dry season is much more distinct in the latter region. Sugar cane again predominates in the plains which are separated from each other by hilly districts. In addition to large-scale farms, however, one may find medium and small-sized farms. The entire region is focused on Mayagüez, the third largest city in the island and a busy trading and industrial centre. Like Aguadilla it was destroyed by an earthquake in 1918. Earthquakes occur particularly frequently in the western part of the island adjacent to the Mona Passage. Mayagüez is the centre of the Puerto Rican knitwear industry which was established during the Second World War and supplies the US market. Various additional industries have recently begun operations and the free port, established in 1961, will probably promote further industrial growth. In addition, the city is a cultural centre, accommodating two faculties of the University of Puerto Rico.

The **southern coastal plain**, in the lee of the mountains, has a semi-arid climate. The rainfall in its eastern section between Salinas and Patillas increases markedly towards the east. In its western section precipitation increases from south to north, i.e. towards the mountains in the interior. The isohyetes and isohygromenes, therefore, run parallel to the coast. The major part of the coastal plain, between Patillas in the east and Ponce in the west, is characterized by sugar cane cultivation (Plate 18). It replaced the extensive pastoral economy after 1914 when dams were constructed in the mountains and large areas were irrigated. The large-scale farms in this region, which require a considerable amount of capital, have hardly been affected by agrarian reform; only a few proportional profit farms were established. Only one settlement was created on the estate once belonging to the French Lafayette sugar factory, whose lands had already been bought by the Puerto Rico Reconstruction Administration in 1936. The twelve farmworker cooperatives which were established operated at a loss. This led to a redistribution of the area in 1939 when 387 farms were established with sizes ranging between 1·2 and 64 ha. In this region also most of the towns, like Guayama and Ponce, are not situated right on the coast. The latter is the second largest city in the island and has preserved the Spanish colonial atmosphere in its centre. It is growing rapidly and possesses a diversified industrial sector. Standing on the hills north of the city, where the new and luxurious hotel Ponce Intercontinental has been built, one may get a clear view of the impressive growth of this city. It has expanded from its old centre to the foothills in the north and to the coastline in the south, and it projects far into the plain both to the west and to the east.

Large landholdings are characteristic of the area west of Ponce, and sugar cane is still important, if not to the same extent as farther to the east. Nevertheless, the Guánica sugar factory is the largest in the island. These plains in the south-west are the least populated areas in Puerto Rico. Although the 10 km wide and very extensive Lajas Valley in the extreme south-west of the island has recently been irrigated and drained where necessary, other areas exist which so far have been used either as extensive grazing land (or waste land), and which still await improvement. It is true, however, that this no longer applies to such a large area of land. Cattle farming in this section of the south coastal plains is usually orientated toward meat production, but as in the north, the emphasis in recent years on dairying has led to more intensive farming. Salt pans have existed for a long time along the coast of this arid stretch of land, and the protected bays, mainly those of Boquerón and Guánica, have fishing ports. In 1898, US

291

forces landed in the Guánica Bay during the Spanish-American War. Tallaboa 20 km west of Ponce recently became the site of an oil refinery, of a petrochemical industry, and of an oil-based power plant (Plate 16). A petrochemical plant was also constructed in Guayama after 1966.

The hilly region

Adjacent to the northern and southern coastal plains towards the interior two tracts of hilly land extend from west to east: the wider northern and the slightly narrower southern region. The former is perhumid, the latter is subhumid or semi-arid.

The western part of the **northern hilly region** is made up of Tertiary limestone and marl which dip in a northerly direction. A cuesta landscape has developed owing to the stratification of the different rock types. The Lares limestone is especially impressive because of its sharp escarpment edge (Map 6). Its partial decomposition into karst stacks and cones and the existence of numerous deep depressions cause the extremely irregular topography in this section of the hilly region, which is therefore very hostile to any settlement and transport (Map 60 and Plate 19). Only a few people have settled in the cone karst areas; forest covers the greater part of the land. Sugar cane cultivation predominates on the terraces of the marl region without being associated with large-scale farms. The character of the northern hilly region changes completely east of a line from Ciales to Toa Alta. Tertiary limestone is replaced by Cretaceous argillaceous rocks. Remnants of former erosion surfaces were discovered by Meyerhoff in the hilly, sometimes mountainous relief. The large Loíza reservoir in the very wet hilly region south of San Juan serves for the generation of electricity and, most important, supplies fresh water for the capital. There are two cement factories at Guayanabo, south of San Juan, whose production, including output from the third factory at Ponce, was 35 387 000 sacks (1 sack = 94 lbs) in 1970. It is planned to reach an output of up to 45 million sacks of cement when the expansion, which was started in 1966, is completed. The eastern section of the northern hilly region is more densely populated than the western. Peasant farms are numerous, and mixed farming methods characterize the landscape. The major part of what the peasant farmers produce, mainly tropical tuberous plants and vegetables, supplies the nearby urban market. Production for subsistence is also important. In addition pineapples and grapefruit are grown for export in the peripheral areas towards the plain, and tobacco in some places. During the sugar boom after the Second World War sugar cane expanded from the plains far into the northern hilly region, but it has now disappeared.

The economic production of the **southern hilly region** cannot compete with that of the northern region. Beef farming, with the production of meat as its aim, is the most usual activity. Only in some parts of this dry hilly region could stock farming be intensified. Because of the aridity few crops are grown, in contrast to the adjacent southern coastal plain. Since there is

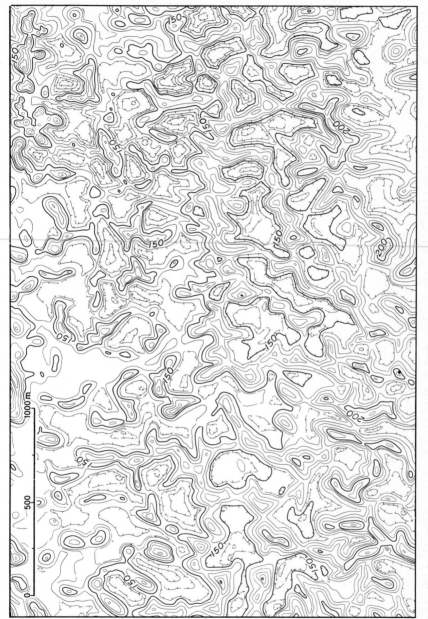

Map 60. Puerto Rico: cone karst in the northern hilly region south-east of Arecibo (after Gerstenhauer and US geological survey).

no irrigation, cultivation is restricted to the valley floors. The southern hilly region is made up of many different rocks and, like the northern, stretches from the western to the eastern part of the island. In only a few districts does it broaden to more than 10 km, especially around Coamo. Only here is the population denser and cultivation more important. Peasant polyculture with an emphasis on food crops is found in this district, though tobacco cultivation is sometimes more important.

The mountainous region

The **Central Cordillera** forms the backbone of the island. It rises steeply from the neighbouring regions to the north and to the south and is composed of folded Cretaceous sedimentary rocks and of igneous rocks, reaching its highest altitudes in its western section (Cerro de Punta, 1338 m). Rainfall increases rapidly with height. Some mountain locations have registered more than 3000 mm. This large amount of precipitation has caused strong dissection of the mountains.

Only a few remaining signs indicate the former existence of peneplanation at various heights. Numerous small and a few large dams employ the large river discharge to produce electricity. The major part of the electricity is produced in the western mountainous region. Since the drainage is mainly directed towards the north the watershed has been tunnelled in some places in order to provide the arid southern plain with water for irrigation purposes.

Because of the extremely strong local relief in the western section of the mountainous region more extensive remnants of virgin montane forest have been preserved here than anywhere else in Puerto Rico. Tree crops are characteristic of the landscape. In the late nineteenth century coffee farms flourished in the western Central Cordillera. They have repeatedly suffered heavy damage from hurricanes. Each farm possesses a *tormentera*, a low gable-roofed shed, which offers protection against hurricanes. Additional economic factors caused the stagnation of coffee production in the Central Cordillera for a time, but the improvement of farming methods, and the cultivation of better varieties led to the recovery of the coffee industry a few years ago, greatly assisted by the Puerto Rican Government. The average yield per acre increased from 200 lb to 1000 lb (1 lb = 454 g). Family-owned *haciendas* (Map 61) are the characteristic type of enterprise in the Puerto Rican coffee area. Their sizes range between only 10 ha and sometimes more than 200 ha, though the latter are rare. The Puerto Rican coffee *hacienda* is dependent on the help of landless workers, the *agregados*. Peasant farms, most of them established within the framework of the agrarian reform (Plate 20), also exist. The dispersed type of settlement is predominant. The *casas grandes* were placed irregularly in the countryside. They include the dwelling place for the planter's family and processing plants where the coffee is fermented, washed and dried. The small houses for the workers are grouped around these *casas grandes*, each with small

294

plots of land where subsistence food crops are grown. Coffee covers the major part of the *hacienda* land. Young coffee trees are shaded by banana plants. Increasingly the orange tree provides the shade, resulting in a more versatile agricultural production. Only a few winding roads cross the high mountains. Some remote haciendas cannot be reached by car after heavy rainfalls. Urban centres, which are small and have developed on the borders of the mountainous region, are very few.

Coffee cultivation has not developed in the eastern section of the Central Cordillera. Here tobacco has gained an extremely important position. The typical enterprise is the small peasant farm with an average size of about 5 ha. Tobacco plantations only developed in the La Plata Valley, and then in 1935 their lands were bought from the American Suppliers Company by the Puerto Rico Reconstruction Administration and 462 peasant farms were established. Tobacco cultivation in the eastern Central Cordillera is therefore done exclusively by smallholders, the *Jíbaros*.

The density of population in the areas of cleared land, where the settlement is dispersed, is remarkably high. It is typical to find small farmhouses surrounded by banana trees, fruit trees and vegetable gardens, and large tobacco sheds. Soil erosion has assumed serious proportions, with the deeply weathered ground standing out dark-red along the new, strongly incised gullies. Although tobacco is only planted on a quarter of the productive area during the dry winter season, through its intensive cultivation it supplies 90 per cent of the income. The urban centres are more numerous than in the western section of the Central Cordillera, and transport conditions are better. Cayey (pop. 19 700), the most important central country town, is situated on the busy highway from San Juan to Ponce. The tobacco harvest of the mountainous region is processed both in the regional towns and the Caguas Basin. A number of centres have developed into summer resorts since their temperatures are low in comparison with those in the coastal regions. However, these are frequented almost exclusively by the local population, whereas foreign tourists obviously prefer the coast. Precipitation is lower than in the western Central Cordillera; nevertheless, numerous reservoirs have been built which facilitate the generation of electricity and supply water to irrigate the southern coastal plain.

The **Caguas Basin** is located between the Central Cordillera on one side and the Sierra de Luquillo and the northern hilly region on the other. The basin does not seem to be a structural downfaulting rift valley but rather an erosional feature. It receives less rainfall (about 1500 mm) than the adjacent area since it is surrounded by hilly and mountainous country. Droughts sometimes affect the sugar cane which is the major crop grown in the basin. Milk and dairy produce are second in importance. The cultivation of vegetables for the US winter market is also considerable. Caguas (pop. 32 000), at an important crossroads on the highway from San Juan to Ponce, and connected with the latter by a fast motorway, is the largest

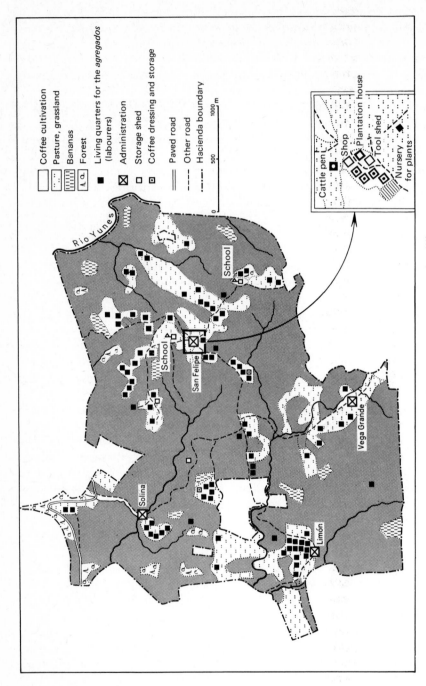

Map 61. Puerto Rico: and use on the Yunes Coffee Hacienda in the Central Cordillera (after Gulick).

town in the island's interior. Caguas is becoming increasingly important as an industrial location; it produces not only sugar, but has since 1952 what is said to be the largest cigarette factory in the world, processing the tobacco from the eastern Central Cordillera. By 1962, 54 new factories had been established in Caguas in the course of industrialization compared with 44 in Mayagüez, 63 in Ponce, and 263 in San Juan.

The **Sierra de Luquillo** is the continuation of the Central Cordillera beyond the Caguas Basin and rises to 1065 m (El Yunque). This short mountain range rises very steeply from the northern coastal plain. Its usually cloud-covered peaks are completely exposed to the trade winds and receive very heavy precipitation. La Mina at an altitude of 700 m receives an annual rainfall of 4780 mm. The beautiful montane forest covers an area of 10 000 ha which have been turned into a national park. It makes up a quarter of all the Puerto Rican forests as well as being the most extensive single forest area in the island. The Sierra de Luquillo, which is only 40 km from San Juan, has been developed for recreation. A well-constructed highway, much frequented during weekends, crosses the range, and many large car parks have been built. Improved footpaths, with shelters for protection against showers, enable the nature-lover to enjoy the montane forest of the tierra templada with its palm trees, tree ferns, bromeliaceae, and the long beardmoss of the *Tillandsia*.

Economy

Agriculture

Distribution of land ownership. In 1950 68 per cent of the entire agricultural area was owned by only 6 per cent of the farms (Table 60). The distribution of land ownership in Puerto Rico resembles the situation in the Dominican Republic, in Jamaica, and in pre-revolutionary Cuba as regards the dominance of the large landholdings. In contrast to these other countries, however, a large proportion of the Puerto Rican large-scale farms developed relatively recently.

Table 60.   Puerto Rico: distribution of land ownership, 1950

	farms		*agricultural land*	
	number	%	*ha*	%
< 4 ha	79 142	75·6	76 487	10·3
4–20 ha	19 225	18·4	159 186	21·5
20–40 ha	3 166	3·0	84 298	11·4
40–80 ha	1 483	1·4	75 205	10·2
> 80 ha	1 656	1·6	344 528	46·6
Total	104 672	100·0	739 704	100·0

Puerto Rico was characterized by peasant farming until the early nineteenth century. Export-orientated agriculture only developed during the nineteenth century when the Spanish Crown issued the Cédula de Gracias in 1815 thereby granting unrestricted trade. Large landholdings were established, mainly in the coastal regions and sugar cane monoculture expanded in these regions, relying more on white landless workers (*agregados*) than on Negro slaves. The peasants (*jíbaros*), on the other hand, held out in the mountains and at the end of Spanish colonial rule the small farms still controlled 51 per cent of the agriculturally productive land. After the USA took over the island US capital flowed into the coastal sugar cane area and resulted in an enormous concentration of land ownership, although the US Congress had ruled in 1900 that property in Puerto Rico was not to exceed 500 acres (202 ha). By 1930 four US companies controlled eleven sugar factories and owned 70 per cent of the island's total cane area.

Table 61. Puerto Rico: number of farms, 1899–1950

	1899		1940		1950	
	number	%	*number*	%	*number*	%
<4 ha	29 744	76·3	29 370	52·9	79 142	75·6
4–20 ha	7 432	19·0	19 863	35·8	19 225	18·4
20–40 ha	994	2·5	3 200	5·7	3 166	3·0
>40 ha	851	2·2	3 086	5·6	3 139	3·0
Total	39 021	100·0	55 519	100·0	104 672	100·0

The measures of agrarian reform provided for by the 1941 Land Law resulted in various alterations in the distribution of property by 1952. A comprehensive change of the agrarian social structure, however, has not been achieved. The establishment of over 50 000 farm workers' holdings, the so-called *parcelas*, with sizes up to 1·2 ha and with the previously landless *agregados* settled in village-type settlements, is without doubt the most important result. This development is the main reason for the numerical increase in very small farms seen in Table 61. In addition, various national agencies have supported settlement schemes on areas of former large-scale farms, but with limited results (Table 62). To the extent that these schemes were carried through in the region of sugar cane monoculture, only the northern coastal plain, where the latifundia tend to be smaller, was affected. This development did not take place in the southern coastal plain where cultivation can only be carried out with the help of irrigation and where the largest and financially most powerful sugar plantations have developed.

Table 62.   Puerto Rico: farm workers' holdings and small farms
established within the framework of agrarian reform

Authority	Period	Number of farms	Average size of farms	Total agricultural area
1. Homestead Commission	1921–42	2074	16 cds* 6·2 ha	24459 cds 9.539 ha
2. Puerto Rico Reconstruction Administration (PRRA)				
(a) Farm Workers' Holdings	1935–41	10026	0·25–3 cds 0·39–1·2 ha	25480 cds 9937 ha
(b) Small and Medium sized farms	1935–41	1024		24260 cds 9461 ha
3. Farm security administration (today: Farmers' home administration)	1937–59	811	43·5 acres 17·6 ha	35299 acres 15018 ha
4. Land authority				
(a) Farm Workers' Holdings	1942–59	48101 (287 communities)	1–3 cds	75000 ha appr.
(b) Small farms	1942–59	1053	5–25 cds 2–7·75 ha	18178 cds 7089 ha
(c) Proportional profit farms	1942–52	83	300–2700 cds 117–1053 ha	68238 cds 26613 ha
			Total approximately	153000 ha

Source: After Blume (1961)
* cds = cuerdas; 1 cuerda = 0·39 ha

The pattern for the establishment of small farms resembles that of the
so-called Proportional Profit Farms which are sugar farms built from
expropriated enterprises which were once over 202 ha. These Proportional
Profit Farms are also almost entirely restricted to the northern coastal plain
and are hardly ever found in the south. Eighty-three of these national farms
were established between 1941 and 1952; they are run by the National
Land Authority, and the workers and employees share in the profits. It
soon became obvious, however, that they operated less profitably than
private enterprises within the sugar industry. As a result, no further farms
of this type were created, and their number was reduced to sixty-three.
They occupy a total of 12000 ha and cultivate 8 per cent of the entire cane
area.

The distribution of small farms and Proportional Profit Farms in Puerto
Rico (Map 62) indicates that economic factors played an important role in

agrarian reform from the start; they were also responsible for bringing it to a standstill in 1952. US companies still own vast stretches of land, and the Puerto Rican plains are still cultivated by large-scale enterprises specializing in sugar cane monoculture. The political party of the Independistas which has been striving for the complete independence of the nation has reproached the Puerto Rican government with the fact that agrarian reform, so vigorously initiated, has not been carried through.

The fact is that the Puerto Rican agrarian reform remains unfinished, and not all that was carried out has been successful. It should not be overlooked, however, that its aims, namely to raise the standard of living and to overcome the island's absolute dependence on the sugar industry, have been accomplished, though in a different way: through the industrial development of the island. The complete neglect, at least up to the present, of the very urgent social aspects of agrarian reform in favour of economic factors can only be understood in this context.

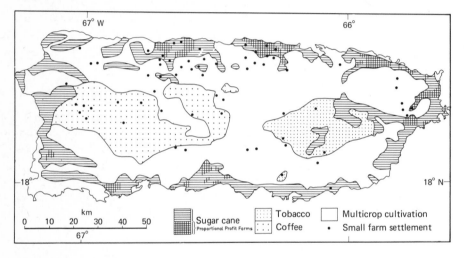

Map 62. Puerto Rico: main crops and new agricultural settlements, 1959 (after Picó and the Social Progressive Administration).

Agricultural land and its distribution. Agricultural land in Puerto Rico takes up 86·8 per cent of the island's surface, i.e. 772 200 ha (1955), of which 82·7 per cent is productive land. Owing to the island's overpopulation this includes areas, especially in the mountains, which should have remained under forest because of the steepness of the slopes. During recent years, with the aid of the Soil Conservation Service, at least 10 million trees have been planted in agricultural areas. The afforestation scheme has succeeded in extending the small and dispersed wooded areas to a total of 79 560 ha. There are a few possibilities for the expansion of the productive acreage; some irrigation has begun in the southern coastal

300

plain and by drainage some small sections of the northern coastal plain are being brought under cultivation. Agricultural land use in Puerto Rico is better known than that in any of the other Caribbean islands or, for that matter, any other countries in the tropics, owing to the Rural Land Classification Programme directed by C. F. Jones. In 1955 cropland only slightly exceeded grazing land (Table 63). Whereas pastures are dispersed among the arable cropland throughout all the regions of Puerto Rico, this arable land shows distinct regional differentiation. The island's plains are in sugar cane plantations, employing a considerable amount of capital; small tobacco farms requiring a considerable amount of labour characterize the eastern section of the hilly and mountainous country, and medium-sized coffee farms are predominant in the western section.

Sugar, tobacco and coffee represent the traditional export crops. Sugar cane heads the list as regards acreage (Table 63) and export value (US $92 million in 1967). The cane harvest is processed by thirty-two refineries quite dispersed in the northern and southern coastal plains. The latter region supplies the major part of the production and differs from the northern plain in that cultivation is dependent on irrigation developed after the USA took over the island. The cane is still cut by hand with the machete; otherwise, the entire cultivation is mechanized to the highest degree with all phases of the operation done by modern equipment and machines. The large-scale enterprises no longer require draught animals. The history of the Puerto Rican sugar industry is relatively brief. Cultivation only started to expand in the nineteenth century when, in spite of rising production, the number of small factories (*trapiches*) fell from 1552 to 553 between 1830 and 1870 as a result of land concentration which even affected the processing plants. The real boom did not develop until the USA had taken over. The expansion of the cane area from about 28 000 to 92 000 ha in only three decades and the simultaneous increase in sugar production to about one million tonnes, facilitated by modernized farming and processing methods, adversely affected not only agrarian social structure, as in Cuba at the same time, but also led to a very unbalanced export structure. In the 1930s, sugar represented more than 60 per cent of all Puerto Rican exports.

At present the annual sugar exports amount to about one million tonnes. The fixed export quota of 1·3 million tonnes has not been exploited because the sugar industry is experiencing difficulties resulting from rising production costs and a labour shortage, noticeable especially during harvest time. The cane area was reduced by about 35 000 ha between 1952 and 1962 and the number of farm workers employed by the sugar industry dropped from 85 000 to 48 000 in the same period. Today, sugar exports represent less than 14 per cent of the entire exports by value. This is the result both of industrialization and the greater diversification of export-orientated agricultural production.

Tobacco ranks next below sugar in export value which amounted to

301

Table 63.   Puerto Rico: agricultural land use, and crops, 1955

	ha	%
(*a*) agricultural area		
crop land	354 900	46·0
pastures	283 530	36·7
forests	79 560	10·3
waste land	54 210	7·0
total	772 200	100·0
(*b*) crop land		
export-orientated cultivation		
sugar cane	149 760	42·3
coffee	68 250	19·3
tobacco	14 820	4·2
citrus	6 396	1·8
coconut	5 850	1·7
pineapple	1 053	0·3
food crops		
tubers	28 977	8·2
rice	23 868	6·6
bananas	20 943	5·9
maize	390	0·1
others	34 593	9·6
total	354 900	100·0

US $43·8 million-worth of raw tobacco and $49·7 million-worth of tobacco products (1964). Tobacco production is almost exclusively from small farms from the eastern hilly and mountainous regions. Tobacco output showed considerable increases when the North American market was opened under US rule. The persistent marketing crisis which developed after 1927 because of low world market prices, of changes in smoking habits and of decreasing demand for cigar tobacco has greatly reduced cultivation. Only the recent construction of modern cigar factories has succeeded in improving the situation of the Puerto Rican tobacco growers. Production fluctuated for a long time between 11 000 and 16 000 tonnes per year, and fell to 5100 tonnes in 1968.

Although the coffee area amounts to nearly half the sugar cane area, coffee only played a minor role in exports up to 1962 (US $0·4 million in 1962). Puerto Rican coffee, which does not enjoy tariff protection, cannot be marketed in the USA and is almost exclusively consumed in Puerto Rico. Farming methods were antiquated until recently, and the yield per acre was exceptionally low. The coffee areas, which occupied mainly the western parts of the mountainous region, were rated the least progressive districts in the island and experienced the highest rural exodus. Towards the end of the nineteenth century coffee was the most important export commodity in Puerto Rico, but the industry has not recovered from the loss of the Spanish market and from damage caused by a hurricane in 1899. However, production, which at present amounts between 10 000 and 16 000 tonnes annually (1968: 11 500 tonnes) has nearly doubled since before the Second World War because of government aid programmes, and exports have increased rapidly since 1962 (US $3·2 million in 1965). It seems, therefore, that the Puerto Rican coffee industry is now firmly established after long years of crises.

The fourth place in the list of export crops is claimed by pineapple cultivation, not in terms of area, but of export value. Pineapples are only grown on the northern coastal plain, mainly by large-scale enterprises similar to sugar cane. The value of pineapple exports (not including tinned pineapples) was US $2·5 million in 1964.

Food crops for the domestic market occupy a much smaller area than export crops. They are only widespread in peasant farms in the eastern parts of the hilly and mountainous region neighbouring the tobacco areas. About half the food required by the Puerto Rican population has to be imported. Cattle farming has a special position in domestic agriculture with milk the aim of production in the northern coastal plain, and meat in the southern coastal plain and the southern hilly region, where it covers particularly large areas. Natural pastures, previously used extensively, have been improved within the framework of the Pasture Improvement Programme, and their use has been intensified. Cattle farming represents more than 30 per cent of agricultural production by value, the production of milk alone nearly 20 per cent. In spite of this, meat and milk still represent the two major items on the food import bill, after corn.

The amount of imported foodstuffs rises each year. This is largely because of growing per capita income, and is also partly because of changing consumer habits, which are subject to American influences. These statements, however, should not obscure the fact that the Puerto Rican peasant, as a supplier of food, is still very much inferior to the US farmer, although his farming methods have undoubtedly improved a great deal. But he is lacking in the financial resources required to make greater progress and to supply the market with quality products which could compete with those from the USA.

The position of agriculture within the national economy of Puerto Rico has decreased in importance after industrialization. In 1947 agriculture supplied 26 per cent of the gross national product, but only 12 per cent in 1963.

Fishery

In contrast to other Caribbean islands, Puerto Rico developed its fishing industry intensively after the Second World War. Cold storage plants were constructed in Cabo Rojo and Fajardo and in increasing number of vessels were equipped with engines. By 1962, 60 per cent of the 1100 fishing vessels were motorized. The annual catch, however, is less than 4000 tonnes, which is much less than in Cuba.

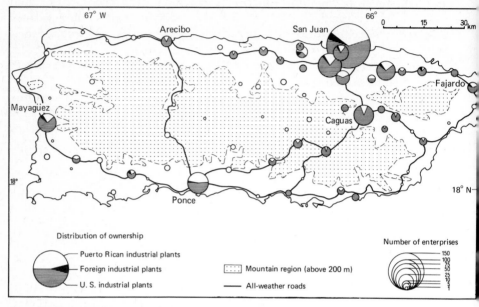

Map 63. Puerto Rico: industrial plants established with the assistance of the EDA (Economic Development Administration), 1960 (compiled from: *Directory of Fomento Promoted and Assisted Manufacturing Plants*, 1960).

Industry

Puerto Rico is the only Caribbean island which can be termed an industrial nation since the value of industrial production has exceeded agricultural since 1956. However, the number of workers in agriculture is still twice as high as those in industry. Industry increased its share in gross national product from 17 per cent in 1947 to 24 per cent in 1963. In 1965 about 120 000 workers were employed by more than 2600 industrial enterprises. Nearly 50 per cent of these plants were founded with the aid of the National Economic Development Administration (EDA) and the Puerto Rico Industrial Development Company (PRIDCO) (Map 63). By 1958, i.e. at the end of the first decade of the industrialization programme, the number of these enterprises had already exceeded 500. In the following years their number increased so rapidly that by the end of 1965 at least 1122 new factories had been established and provided over 60 000 jobs. These new industries which also offered a similar number of jobs, resulting from associated trade and public services, supply about 65 per cent of total industrial production by value, with this value doubling between 1960 and 1964. Puerto Rico experienced its highest rate of industrial growth in 1962 when a total of 275 new factories were established. At present, Puerto Rico has the highest rate of capital investment among non-communist territories. At first US capital was predominant in the investments; today 50 per cent of the capital invested in industry is supplied by Puerto Rico itself. In the course of industrialization the percentage of its labour force unemployed fell continuously from 16 per cent in 1952 to 11 per cent in 1965.

The majority of new Puerto Rican factories are either small or medium-sized enterprises, all of them operating in modern buildings. EDA has succeeded in spreading industrial enterprises throughout the island, though it has avoided the mountainous region to a great extent. On the other hand the major towns such as Ponce, Mayagüez and particularly San Juan have experienced a heavy concentration of industry.

The structure of Puerto Rican industry underwent important changes from the very start of the development programme, known by the name 'Operation Bootstrap'. The food industry with its leading sector, the sugar industry, no longer predominates: of the total industrial labour force the percentage working in the food industry decreased from 77 per cent in 1939 to 37 per cent in 1952 and 18 per cent in 1961. At the same time the percentage of the industrial labour force in the metallurgical and machine industries increased from 2 per cent to 4 per cent and to 13 per cent. At present a very diversified manufacturing sector is headed by the textile industry which employs 35 per cent of the industrial labour force. Since 1955 the consumer goods industry has been joined by a capital goods industry with oil refineries, petrochemical plants and steel works (Map 64). The capital goods industry is, in its structure, more port-orientated than the consumer goods industry and is therefore mostly concentrated in the large cities of San Juan (Cataño) and Ponce (Tallaboa).

Puerto Rico's rapid change from an agricultural country which was characterized by extreme dependence on sugar cane to an industrial nation, with a multitude of manufacturing industries, greatly interested other nations, even outside the Caribbean. This change, favoured by various factors, was achieved as a result of the thorough development policy executed by the Puerto Rican Government. At the beginning of industrialization it became obvious that the aim could be neither the supply of manufactured goods for the domestic market, because of its limited absorptive capacity, nor the supply of markets in Latin American developing countries, since these had introduced protective tariffs in order to stimulate the establishment of their own local industries. In view of the abundant and cheap local labour force, the following aim of Puerto Rico's industrialization very soon evolved: to establish labour intensive industries and to supply the US market. Furthermore, the initial practice of establishing manufacturing plants under government control was soon abandoned. The nationalized factories manufacturing cement, glass, paper, leather and pottery were sold to private industrialists even before the present indus-

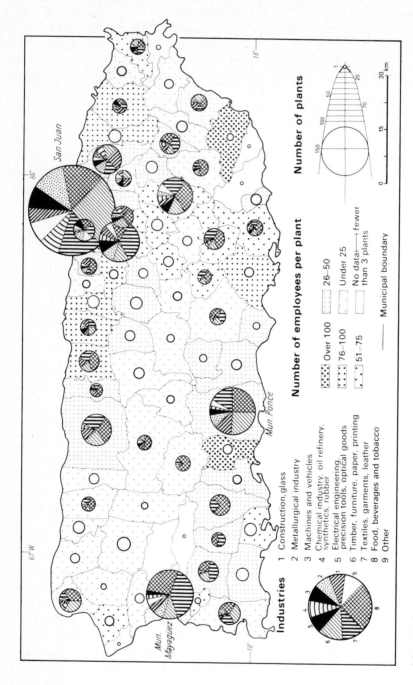

Map 64. Puerto Rico: industrialization, 1960 (from: *Censo de Industrias manufactureras de Puerto Rico,* 1960).

trialization programme began in 1950. The positive results of this programme prove the sense of the method chosen.

Since Puerto Rico is not represented in the US Congress no US income tax has to be paid in Puerto Rico and since, in addition, trade between Puerto Rico and the USA is exempted from duty, capital investment in new Puerto Rican industries is very attractive to US industrialists. This attraction is increased by various additional measures taken by the Puerto Rican government to entice US capital for industrial expansion. For instance, it grants a limited period of tax allowances to new industrial plants, provides the necessary buildings for new factories, undertakes the commercial training of the workers, grants loans at low interest, and the like. The tremendous industrial development of the island has only been possible as a result of these measures, which have been recently imitated within the Caribbean area by the governments of Jamaica and Trinidad. About sixty US corporations and other US industrialists have established branches in Puerto Rico in recent years. In addition, an increasing number of European firms have established themselves in Puerto Rico in order to gain better access to the US market. The Puerto Rican Government expects a great deal of the Mayagüez freeport, established in 1961, where extensive industrial development is planned. It hopes to attract even more European firms wishing to gain ground in the US market, and to attract US industrialists who are looking for markets in Caribbean and Latin American states. The new Puerto Rican industries import most of the raw materials and semi-manufactured goods from the USA and in return supply the USA with almost all their products, mainly textiles and electrical appliances. PRIDCO is confident that 2000 new factories will have been established by 1975 and that by then the average per capita income will have reached that of the USA. This has increased in Puerto Rico from US $121 in 1940 to $279 in 1950, to $587 in 1960 and to $1144 in 1968. Wages increased simultaneously, although they are still much lower than in the USA. The wage differential is in fact the essential factor facilitating Puerto Rican industrial progress. Especially in view of high shipping rates, Puerto Rican industrial products can only be marketed in the USA if this wage-differential continues to exist and it is therefore a necessity for Puerto Rican industry.

Other essential preconditions for industrialization have been the improvement of transport facilities and the extension of the power supply. The generation of electricity increased from 476 million kWh in 1948 to 6156 million kWh in 1969, 90 per cent supplied by thermal electric power plants and 10 per cent by hydroelectric power stations. The first nuclear power station was completed in 1964 near Rincón.

An important branch of the economy is tourism which has developed more rapidly in Puerto Rico than in the other Caribbean islands. Only 38 000 tourists visited the island in 1952, but 700 000 in 1969. In 1969, tourists spent US $229 million. Numerous new hotels have been built in various parts of the island during recent years, and more are being built in order to accommodate the constantly increasing number of tourists.

The economic development of Puerto Rico is most strongly reflected in its industrial growth. There is no doubt that the rapid change of the economic structure benefited greatly from the present political situation: Puerto Rico could not have achieved its economic boom if it had been either a US state or a completely sovereign territory. Because of this only a few people support the Independista party.[1] The methods and principles which were applied by the Puerto Rican Government to achieve changes in economic structure will undoubtedly be advantageous to many developing countries, if only in a modified form as seen in Jamaica and Trinidad. All this also explains the interest in Puerto Rico shown by the development experts and by the governments of developing countries in Latin America, Africa, and Asia.

Transport

Puerto Rico possesses an excellent road network, which has kept pace with the country's economic development; this relatively small island has 5830 km of asphalt roads (1969), used by 530 000 motor vehicles (1969; 1955: 105 400). Manufacturing plants could only be established in the small towns because most of these have good road connections. San Juan and its surrounding districts have modern express motorways, and a turnpike connects San Juan with Caguas 24 km to the south. The railway which ran round the island parallel to the coast, was discontinued in 1957 because it was running at a loss.

The major portion of the shipping traffic is handled by the modernized ports of San Juan, Ponce and Mayagüez; San Juan increased its share from 56 per cent in 1955 to 74 per cent in 1962. The tonnage of the vessels calling at Puerto Rico has also increased greatly: from 10·3 million gross registered tonnes to 27·3 million between 1951 and 1969. The rationalization of port installations is exemplified by the export of sugar: before 1939 sugar was exported from twenty ports, usually open roadsteads, seventeen of which served this purpose exclusively; today, sugar is only exported from four ports all of which possess special wharves for the loading of sugar. The entire operation is mechanized and for economic reasons sugar is no longer loaded in sacks but in bulk. The Puerto Rican ports have to an increasing extent assumed the function of transhipping goods between the US ports on the Pacific and the Atlantic coast. The advantages which result from the proximity of Puerto Rico to the North American mainland can also be seen, for example, in the fact that tuna from the Pacific is landed in Ponce

---

[1] The results of the plebiscite in July 1967 are characteristic: 60·5 per cent of the voters voted for the continuation of the present status; 38·9 per cent voted for the complete integration of Puerto Rico into the USA.

and Mayagüez where large tuna canning factories have recently been established. They supply the US Atlantic coast market more cheaply than the fish canning factories in California.

An internal Puerto Rican air service has developed in spite of the short distances. The Caribbean Airlines connect Ponce and Mayagüez with San Juan and offer numerous daily flights to the US Virgin Islands. The international Isla Verde airport near San Juan, whose traffic volume is the largest in the Caribbean islands, operates as a pivot in the air traffic of the western hemisphere. In 1960 it offered 280 scheduled flights per week with a seating capacity of about 20 500; air traffic nearly trebled by 1966. More than 90 per cent of the tourists arrive in Puerto Rico by air.

Foreign trade

Economic development has increased the volume of foreign trade from US $809 million in 1951 to $3869 million in 1969, with Puerto Rico heading the list of Caribbean island nations by a wide margin. With US $2263 million-worth of imports and $1606 million-worth of exports the economy has an unfavourable balance of trade, but this gap is closed by the revenue from tourism, by payments from the US government, by the investments of US capital, and by remittances from Puerto Rican emigrants. Puerto Rican foreign trade is completely orientated towards the USA. In 1969, 78 per cent of imports originated there, and 87 per cent of exports went there.

At present manufactured goods are the main export. Sugar exports, once the major export product, have been reduced to 8·4 per cent of the total by value (1966). Textile exports alone represented 16 per cent of the export value in 1963. The products of the electrical and machine industries rank third. The list of imports is headed by foodstuffs (22 per cent) closely followed by machinery and vehicles (19 per cent), and textiles (13 per cent) rank third.

Results of economic development

The structural change in the Puerto Rican economy, particularly the high degree of industrialization, has had various consequences. As was mentioned above, the rising standard of living led to a reduction in the birth rate and a decrease in the number of emigrants, who are now outnumbered by returning emigrants. The higher standard of living may also be seen in the rise in consumption; the products of Puerto Rican industry are to an increasing extent marketed in the island itself. Twenty-six per cent of the Puerto Rican national budget is allocated to improve the educational system for all age groups. It has made great strides forward. Only 50 per cent of all school-age children were able to attend a school in 1940; this percentage had risen to 85 per cent by 1956. Nearly 22 000 students are enrolled at the University of Puerto Rico. The government is also responsible for the commercial training of workers for the new industries. Thirty-four radio and nine television stations, the improvement of transport facilities, and the organization of agricultural marketing have freed even the smallholders in the hilly and mountainous regions from their isolation. The construction of factories is closely connected with the development of modern residential areas which have changed the settlement pattern in the urban centres just as decisively as the new farm worker settlements have altered the rural settlement pattern. All parts of the island have experienced an intense building activity for years. The improvement of hygienic conditions and of medical care has considerably lengthened the life expectancy of the population.

An Americanization of several aspects of the Puerto Rican way of life can be observed, for example in the changing habits of the consumer, in the establishment of typical American supermarkets, in the activities and the appearance of the new shopping centre in San Juan's suburb Santurce, in the large new hotels, and so on. On the other hand, only about a quarter of the population speaks English in addition to the Spanish mother tongue, and one cannot overlook the fact that the population is becoming increasingly aware of its Spanish heritage. The awareness of tradition has accompanied economic progress in Puerto Rico.

The Lesser Antilles

22
Islands to the Windward

The Islands to the Windward include all the islands of the Lesser Antilles
between the Virgin Islands in the north and Trinidad in the south. The

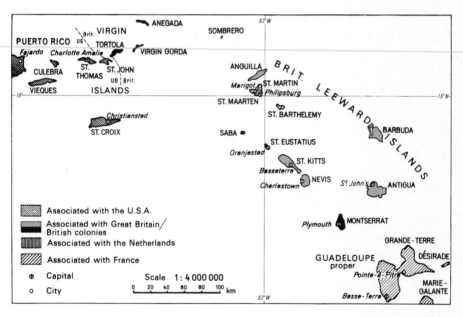

Map 65. The northern Islands to the Windward.

northernmost group, the Virgin Islands, belong to the cordillera system
of the Greater Antilles in their structure; the southernmost group, Trinidad
and Tobago, to the Venezuelan cordillera system. The islands between
these two groups are divided into an inner arc from Saba to Grenada and an
outer arc from Anguilla to Barbados. The islands of the first group are
mountainous and volcanic, those of the latter group are flat and built from
limestone. They vary also in climate, the flat islands receiving less rainfall
than the mountainous. Since rainfall increases with height, humidity

311

depends on the amount of local relief. Another regional difference in rainfall, and therefore in humidity and the possibility of agricultural use, is caused by the varying effectiveness with which the trade winds from the east are obstructed. The windward and leeward side of the islands have very different amounts of rainfall. However, both sides usually experience perhumid conditions at altitudes of more than 300 m due to the rapid increase in precipitation with height. At these altitudes tropical rain forests or montane forests cover the mountains everywhere, whilst semi-evergreen seasonal or tropical deciduous forests, and sometimes dry woodlands, are found at lower altitudes.

The political fragmentation of the Islands to the Windward is very marked. From the seventeenth century on these islands, where sugar cane was cultivated on plantations in the monocultural pattern and then processed into sugar with the help of Negro slaves, were particularly renowned as one of the wealthiest colonial regions in the world. Since then, sugar cultivation has disappeared from many islands. Today most of these formerly coveted and wealthy islands are overpopulated and possess unbalanced economies without any industry, and their people very often make a miserable living. After the traditional plantation economy had collapsed in the nineteenth century the various islands developed in divergent directions so that the present problems of these numerous islands are as varied as their colonial heritage.

Virgin Islands

The Virgin Islands which start the arc of the Lesser Antilles in the northwest constitute the eastward geological continuation of the Greater Antilles.[1] (Plate 21). They rise from a continental platform about 65 m below sea-level. Only St Croix is separated from the rest of the archipelago by greater depths: the Anegada Passage, up to 4500 m deep. The islands are composed of folded Cretaceous sedimentary rocks as well as metamorphic and volcanic rocks and have a dome-shaped or mountainous relief. The greatest heights are found in Tortola (518 m) and St Thomas (465 m); only in St Croix is there an extensive plain. All the islands have a subhumid or semi-arid climate. Perennial streams are non-existent, and droughts result in serious water shortages. Owing to the early plantation economy the former tropical deciduous or semi-evergreen seasonal forests have been everywhere replaced by a meagre growth of secondary scrub.

The island group constitutes 518 sq km. The major part of this area is US territory, the smaller part is a British Crown Colony administered by the British Leeward Islands until 1967; since then it has not formed part of a group of islands but is governed as a single unit. The Virgin Islanders elect their own legislature, and in 1970 elected their own Governor for the first time.

[1] The Puerto Rican islands of Vieques and Culebra belong geologically to the Virgin Islands.

US Virgin Islands

The largest islands of the archipelago are owned by the USA: St Croix, St Thomas, and St John. They have a total population of 32 000 (1960; 63 200 in 1970), 64 per cent of which is Negro and 17 per cent white. Their population density is 93 persons per sq km (Table 64), and more than half the population is concentrated in St Thomas where Charlotte Amalie with a population of 12 700 has developed as the only major town of the island group, its capital and always the most important harbour. After a previously eventful history St Thomas fell into Danish hands in 1677, St Croix and St John in 1733; in 1917, they were acquired by the USA for the sum of US $25 million. The Danish past is especially obvious in the small towns of Christiansted and Frederiksted in St Croix where the streets still possess their Danish names, just as they do in the old centre of Charlotte Amalie. Impressive two-storeyed commercial houses in the Droningens Gade in Charlotte Amalie and arcaded stone buildings in Christiansted (Plate 22), in yellow, pink and green colours, bear witness to the former wealth of the merchants at a time when these islands flourished. The walls of the Fort Christiansvaern at Christiansted harbour are red, the Danish national colour. The US administration has deliberately chosen to conserve the Danish tradition in the town's appearance.

Table 64.   US Virgin Islands: size and population, 1960

	Size *sq km*	*Population*	*Density of population inhabitants per sq km*
St Croix	212	14 973	71
St Thomas	83	16 201	195
St John	49	925	19
Total	344	32 099	93

All three islands were characterized by sugar plantations in the past, and numerous ruins of former cane mills point back to that time of economic prosperity. The former plantation economy (Map 66) explains the high percentage of Negroes in the islands' population. In addition, St Thomas used to be one of the important Caribbean slave markets. On the whole, the economic importance of this island group was not based on its agriculture, but rather on trade. The Danish Virgin Islands, with the large and protected natural harbour in St Thomas where the capital Charlotte Amalie developed, used to be a distributing centre and an emporium for the Antilles as well as for the Central and South American mainland. Trade experienced a rapid growth, favoured by Denmark's neutrality in the European wars and by the establishment of the St Thomas freeport in 1764. More than 2500 vessels called on St Thomas each year in the early nineteenth century.

Map 66. St Croix, US Virgin Islands: plantations in the eighteenth century (after P. L. Oxholms Kort over St Croix, 1799, Rigsarkivets Kortsamling 337, II Copenhagen).

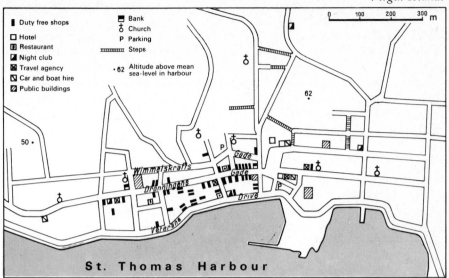

Map 67. St Thomas, US Virgin Islands: tourist facilities in the downtown area of Charlotte Amalie.

The economic prosperity of the Danish Virgin Islands ended in the middle of the nineteenth century resulting in heavy emigration, mainly to the USA. Between 1835 and 1921 the population decreased continuously from 43 000 to 26 000 and has only increased again recently. The trade of St Thomas fell victim to the development of steamships and their ability to navigate along a rhumb line; the only remaining function was to provision and to repair the trans-Atlantic ships. After 1917 the USA expanded and modernized the installations serving these purposes and developed St Thomas into a military base. In the meantime, however, St Thomas had almost completely lost even its provisioning function. In addition, the emancipation of slaves and the competition from European beet sugar ruined sugar production in the mid-nineteenth century. It disappeared completely from St John and St Thomas, because in these two islands the mountainous relief and the frequent droughts, with no possibilities for irrigation, made the economic cultivation of sugar cane impossible in these new circumstances. Sugar cane cultivation only survived in the plains of St Croix, and then only on a drastically reduced acreage, through subsidies. The national Virgin Islands Company, which runs the only sugar factory in the island, operates at a loss. In view of the frequent droughts, water shortages and, of late, manpower shortages, St Croix sugar cane cultivation does not have a bright future. An increasing proportion of the former cane area is being used for cattle farming. In 1956 L. S. Rockefeller made the major part of the island available to the US government for the establishment of a national park.

At present the most important basis for the US Virgin Islands' existence

315

is tourism, which increased quickly after the Second World War, encouraged by good air connections. Like Nassau on New Providence (Bahamas), Charlotte Amalie (Map 67) has developed into a prominent tourist centre where US tourists are greatly attracted by the possibilities of duty-free shopping for goods imported from Europe. The volume of tourism surpasses that of any other island in the Lesser Antilles: 1 107 000 visitors came in 1969 (164 000 in 1959). The per capita income rose from US $412 to $1751 between 1950 and 1963.

The British Virgin Islands

The British territory in the archipelago of the Virgin Islands comprises about forty islands with a total area of 174 sq km, inhabited by 7338 persons (1960), (10 860 in 1970), 99·5 per cent of whom are Negroes. The population density is 42 persons per sq km; but the majority of the islands are uninhabited. Tortola, the largest island with 62 sq km (101 persons per sq km), has 85 per cent of the entire population; Virgin Gorda, the third largest island with 22 sq km (26 persons per sq km), has 8 per cent of the total population, and a further 4 per cent live on the 34 sq km of Anegada.

As in the three former Danish islands, a slave-based plantation economy developed in the British Virgin Islands during the eighteenth century, in spite of their unfavourable topography. Cotton and sugar cane were cultivated. In 1798 there were 105 plantations on Tortola. Here the emancipation of the slaves and marketing difficulties led to the collapse of the plantations in the first half of the nineteenth century; also, their white owners left the islands. Agriculture and fishing have remained the means of living for the descendants of the former slaves. However, the cultivation of food crops by smallholders has decreased greatly in the recent past and the islands depend on food imports. After the Second World War cattle farming. which is more suited to the topographical conditions, became increasingly important. The produce is easily marketed in the neighbouring US Virgin Islands. The rate of emigration from the small and poor islands has been high for decades. At present there is a considerable seasonal migration to the neighbouring US islands where labourers are in demand for the cane harvest in St Croix and especially for the growing tourism of St Thomas. The various islands of the British colony are only irregularly connected to each other by sailing and motor boats, only Road Town on Tortola having daily shipping connections with Charlotte Amalie in St Thomas. The American tourists have not yet discovered the British Virgin Islands, but various hotel projects are under discussion, and there is no doubt that this remote and scenic archipelago will become a tourist attraction in the near future and will experience fundamental changes.

The relatively close economic ties between the American and the British Virgin Islands have been termed an anomaly by Augelli. Economic and transport links between neighbouring islands are in fact extremely rare in the Caribbean; connections to the outside world, to North America and

Europe are considerably stronger. These close ties with their US neighbours were the reason why the British Virgin Islands were the only British colony in the Antilles not to join the West Indies Federation when it was founded in 1958.

The Dutch Islands to the Windward

The volcanic arc of the Islands to the Windward begins with the Dutch islands of Saba and St Eustatius; Sint Maarten (Saint Martin), on the other hand, which is politically divided into a northern French and a southern Dutch part, belongs to the outer arc of the limestone islands. In spite of all the differences in their natural and cultural geography these islands have several characteristics in common: former economic prosperity as against almost complete unimportance at present; a high emigration rate, mainly to the Dutch Islands to the Leeward, and therefore no overpopulation which is typical elsewhere in the Lesser Antilles; an almost complete dependence on imported food because of the absence of cultivation; and, finally, a rather unfavourable future as regards their economy unless tourism improves the situation as is happening in Sint Maarten right now. The three islands have more connections with the Dutch Islands to the Leeward and even with the USA than with their neighbouring British and French islands. Each island has its own independent administration. Together with the Dutch Islands to the Leeward they have constituted an autonomous part of the Netherlands since 1954; jointly, however, they have only one seat out of twenty-five in the Curaçao Parliament.

Table 65.   The Dutch Islands to the Windward: size and population, 1963

	Size *sq km*	*Population*	*Density of population inhabitants per sq km*
Sint Maarten (Saint Martin)	34	3 250	96
St Eustatius	21	1 069	51
Saba	13	1 020	78
Total	68	5 339	78

Saba

Saba, a rocky ruin of a volcano, rises steeply from the sea to an altitude of 884 m. From Bottom, the main settlement 230 m above sea-level, an old flight of 500 steps leads down a ravine to the sea. A narrow, winding road has recently been built in another gully which connects the other three small settlements with Bottom and the coast. Each settlement on Saba used to be very isolated, just as the whole island still is today because of its unfriendly shores. The present population is equally divided between whites and blacks. Before the Second World War Saba used to be one of the few Caribbean islands with a predominantly white population, but the percentage of Negroes is increasing owing to their higher birth rate and to the heavy emigration of whites. The settlement of the island dates back to the seventeenth century when Dutch and Scottish immigrants arrived. Shipbuilding, shoe manufacturing and a little subsistence cultivation with the help of a few slaves was the basis of their existence. The present population of Saba lives on government subsidies and on the money earned in the Aruba oil industry. As in the Cayman Islands many men are sailors. Since the recent completion of a landing strip the island can be served by small planes.

Sint Eustatius

The vast plain of the *Cultuurvlakte* extends between the volcanic knolls in the north-west of Sint Eustatius and the beautiful 549 m high extinct volcano Quill (Plate 26). On the western shore of this plain lies Oranjestad where the entire population is concentrated. There were thirty-eight sugar cane plantations in the early nineteenth century but, as in the Virgin Islands, sugar cane cultivation disappeared and only very small quantities are now grown by smallholders. Pastures which remained in the hands of their white owners turned into wasteland several decades ago. Old sugar mills in the country and some buildings in the town are reminiscent of the heyday of the island when trade flourished even earlier and more actively than the Danish island of St Thomas. St Eustatius was probably the most important distributing centre and emporium in the entire Caribbean. In 1778 more than 3500 merchant vessels called on the island whose population at that time was 20 000 to 25 000, including Greek merchants and a strong Jewish colony. St Eustatius lost this position suddenly when the British Admiral Rodney destroyed Oranjestad in 1781. Since the plantation economy also collapsed a few decades later, St Eustatius is now without any economic importance; it is depopulated and dependent on support from the Dutch government.

Sint Maarten

Unlike Sint Eustatius, Sint Maarten has never had a trading function. This island was settled in the seventeenth century and ninety-two plantations existed at the end of the eighteenth century, equally divided between cattle farming and sugar cane cultivation. In addition to agriculture the production of salt in the Great Salt Pond has played an important role in the past. The quiet capital of Philipsburg is situated on the spit of land separating this lagoon from the open sea. The majority of the population is Negro. There is a white fishing settlement, Simson Bay Village, in the

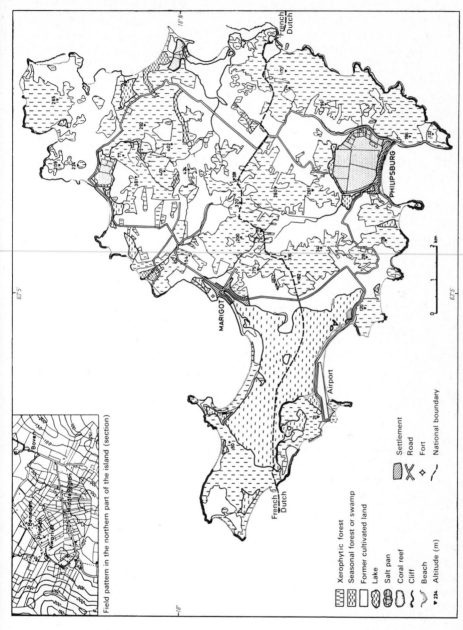

PHILIPSBURG

MARIGOT

French
Dutch

French
Dutch

Airport

2 km

0   1   2

63°5   63°5

18° N

18°

Field pattern in the northern part of the island (section)

Bover
Beacon
Prison
Mount
William
Middle Region

Xerophytic forest

Seasonal forest or swamp

Former cultivated land

Lake

Salt pan

Coral reef

Cliff

Beach

▼ 234 Altitude (m)

Settlement

Road

Fort

National boundary

Map 68. Sint Maarten (St Martin), Dutch Islands to the Windward.

western part of the island, but its inhabitants have decreased from 400 to 150 during the last fifty years. On the whole, the population decline was not as serious in Sint Maarten as in Sint Eustatius. The conspicuous increase of the population from 1600 in 1957 to 3250 in 1963 is explained by the large number of immigrants from the French part of the island owing to the developing tourist industry in Sint Maarten. The Dutch part of the island has an airport with regular flights to Curaçao, Puerto Rico, the Virgin Islands, St Kitts, Martinique and, of late, a direct flight to New York. A modern hotel exists on Little Bay near Philipsburg, and three hotels have recently been built in the town itself. It is hoped that the further development of tourism will result in an economic upswing for the island and possibly also for its handicapped neighbours. Fishing has been intensified to such an extent that a Japanese trawler, which refrigerates the catch, is berthed at the pier in Philipsburg.

The British Leeward Islands

The British Leeward Islands are divided into four administrative units: the Virgin Islands (cf. p. 312, 316), St Kitts–Nevis–Anguilla, Montserrat, and Antigua–Barbuda. The colonial status of Antigua–Barbuda as well as of St Kitts–Nevis–Anguilla was terminated in February 1967. They are now autonomous states in association with Great Britain. They are entitled to dissolve the association and to proclaim their complete independence at any time. This solution had its model in the 1964 arrangement between the Cook Islands and New Zealand.[1]

Table 66.   The British Leeward Islands: size and population, 1960*

	Size sq km	Population	Density of population inhabitants per sq km
British Virgin Islands	174	7 338	42
St Kitts–Nevis–Anguilla	399	56 644	143
Montserrat	84	12 157	143
Antigua–Barbuda	444	54 751	122
Total	1 101	130 890	119

* British Virgin Islands	10 860 (1970)
St Kitts–Nevis–Anguilla	57 617 (1966)
Montserrat	14 986 (1968)
Antigua–Barbuda	61 664 (1963)

[1] Anguilla broke away from the onion with St Kitts and Nevis in May 1967. Its political status has been open to question since then.

St Kitts–Nevis–Anguilla

The territory is composed of the volcanic islands of Nevis and St Kitts, where the capital Basseterre has developed, and the limestone islands of Anguilla and Sombrero.

Table 67. St Kitts–Nevis–Anguilla: size and population, 1966

	Size *sq km*	*Population*	*Density of population* *inhabitants per sq km*
St Kitts	176	37 150	211
Nevis	130	15 072	115
Anguilla	88	5 395	61

English as well as French colonists settled in **St Kitts**, also called St Christopher, in 1624. Together they succeeded in driving away the warlike native Caribs after a period of three years. With St Kitts as a base the neighbouring small islands were settled by the English and the French. France renounced its claim to St Kitts in 1713. Mount Misery in the north-western part of the island reaches an altitude of 1156 m. On the south-west flank of this volcano, near the coast, is Brimstone Hill, a secondary cone without a crater. It has the ruins of strong fortifications where fierce fighting took place in the eighteenth century between English and French. The mountainous St Kitts receives heavy rainfall (Map 69) except in the dry southern peninsula. The slopes, which are built from volcanic tuff and dissected by deep ravines, are cultivated up to a height of 300 m. Most of the cultivated area, 93 per cent of the entire agricultural area, is in the hands of fifty-seven large-scale enterprises (> 80 ha) whose property extends from the coastline to the mountain ridges. The monoculture of sugar cane determines cultivation as it did during the traditional plantation economy, and sugar represents 94 per cent of the St Kitts exports. Peasant farming is mainly restricted to the districts above the cane areas which are rented from the large-scale enterprises. It does not supply sufficient food for the population and one-third of the imports by value is therefore made up of foodstuffs. Sugar cane cultivation was able to survive in St Kitts because of favourable physical conditions and because of the rationalization of cane growing and processing.

A considerable concentration of land ownership has taken place during the last hundred years, and since 1910 the entire cane harvest has been processed by only one sugar factory, though the old sugar factories and cane presses are still to be seen, dispersed throughout the island. A narrow-gauge railway and a road surround the island touching each enterprise, with small farmworkers' villages situated along the road. Sugar production has increased considerably since the Second World War, with very high yields per acre giving a total of 40 000–50 000 tonnes. The production costs, however, are so high that the British government has to subsidize sugar production. The capital of Basseterre (pop. 15 900) in the lee of the island is the focus of all shipping activity and has 43 per cent of the population. Its airport has connections with Antigua, Sint Maarten, the Virgin Islands and Puerto Rico. In 1961 the completion of a hotel on Cockleshell Bay in the dry south introduced tourism to the island. In addition to the export-orientated sugar industry St Kitts has had, in Basseterre, a brewery since 1961 and a cigarette factory since 1962 which supply the local market. In order to discourage the population (97 per cent Negro) from emigrating, St Kitts is striving towards further industrialization, and in 1966 steps were also taken to expand the tourist industry, including the development of a large hotel settlement on Frigate Bay and the extension of the airport to allow jet planes to land.

The oval island of **Nevis** is a volcanic cone, which reaches a height of 985 m (Nevis Peak), with secondary cones on two of its sides. Several features resemble the landscape of St Kitts (Map 69): forests cover the higher, cultivated land the lower regions, and the capital, Charlestown, is situated in the lee. A road follows the coastline in the north and crosses the island south of the Nevis Peak. All the townships have developed along this road. The plantation economy has disappeared from Nevis, where the ruins of spacious stone buildings indicate the wealth of the former plantation owners. Owing to the much frequented hot springs in Charlestown, Nevis and its Bath Hotel served as a centre of social life during the eighteenth century boom of the sugar plantation economy. Only a small amount of sugar cane, which has to be shipped to St Kitts for processing, is cultivated by peasants. Cotton, which is cultivated on peasant farms which either developed or were established by the government on former plantations, has become the major cultivated plant as a result of the lower rainfall than in St Kitts. Large landholdings still exist on the island but their land is cultivated by numerous peasant tenants who usually make payments in kind. In addition to cotton, food crops are cultivated and exported to St Kitts. Daily shipping and air services twice weekly connect Nevis with St Kitts and the outside world. Tourism has not yet reached the island. A number of its inhabitants (99·5 per cent Negro) emigrated during recent years because of the lack of employment possibilities. The population has started to increase again only very recently.

Anguilla rises from the centre of the extensive Anguilla Bank, a continental platform at a depth of only 55 m. The island is flat and built of Tertiary limestone. It receives only little rainfall and is covered by sparse dry woodlands. The cultivation of food crops in isolated spots and extensive cattle farming supplies the domestic market. Fishery and salt making are the vital activities of the population which is mainly supported by remittances from numerous emigrants.

Sombrero is a low-lying, flat and uninhabited limestone island and the furthest to the north-west among the British Leeward Islands. It carries a lighthouse and is situated at the entrace to the Anegada Passage, only 90 km

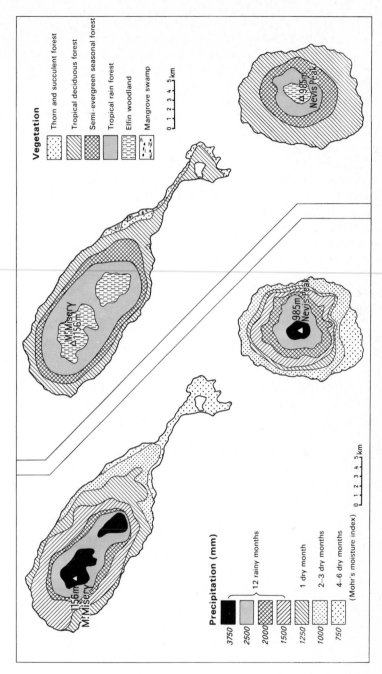

Map 69. St Kitts–Nevis: precipitation and vegetation (after Imperial College of Tropical Agriculture, Trinidad).

off Anegada (British Virgin Islands).

Montserrat

The island of Montserrat, volcanic in structure like St Kitts and Nevis, was also characterized by the sugar plantation economy in the past. Twenty-one per cent of its population emigrated between 1931 and 1960 and remittances from emigrants constitute more than a quarter of the national income, thus nearly equalling the subsidies from the British government. Owing to these invisible exports the standard of living has improved considerably in spite of the stagnation of the economy. Cotton has replaced sugar cane as the major product in Montserrat; but the Sea Island Cotton is very difficult to market and cotton cultivation also suffers from soil erosion and soil exhaustion resulting from over fifty years of cotton monoculture and the common type of tenancy whereby payments must be made in kind. Two-thirds of the agricultural area is still in farms of over 80 ha, whose owners were often unable to pay wages and could only retain the property by making their farmworkers into tenants with payments in kind. Unlike the larger islands no land was available for peasant farming following the emancipation of the slaves. In the course of agricultural diversification tomato growing for export to Canada assumed an important position. Since the shipping facilities were inadequate large amounts of tomatoes had repeatedly to be destroyed and a tomato paste factory was built in 1960 in Plymouth, the small capital in the lee of the island. A road runs from here only along the leeward coastline; another road leads across the island to the airport on the windward side which has connections to St Kitts and Antigua. Tourism has begun to reach the island, but it will hardly develop beyond the present volume until transport facilities are improved.

Antigua–Barbuda

Table 68.   Antigua–Barbuda: size and population, 1960

	Size sq km	Population	Density of population inhabitants per sq km
Antigua	280	54 534	194
Barbuda	161	1 145	7

Antigua is the only island among the British Leeward Islands with a flourishing tourist industry. This was facilitated by the large air base which the USA built on the flat limestone island after the Second World War, and which not only has connections with neighbouring islands, but offers flights to the USA, Puerto Rico and Trinidad. Like Puerto Rico, various concessions were made by the government of the island to attract foreign capital, mainly from the USA, which was invested into the hotel business.

Most of the hotels are dispersed on the bays along the coast, some of them of a very exclusive nature. In 1964, 642 hotel beds were available, and more than 46 100 tourists visited the island in the same year.

The tourist industry has undoubtedly greatly stimulated Antigua's economy: on the other hand it is all too obvious that the present type of tourism is of greater benefit to foreign investors than to the national economy. This is equally true of many of the other Caribbean islands. The hotels in Antigua receive 60 per cent of the tourist expenditure. They import almost all their food supplies and some of them even import their fresh meat and poultry by air. Up till now medium-priced hotels, whose development would probably lead to the tourist industry being a greater stimulus to the island economy, are almost non-existent in the Caribbean. On the whole, however, the formerly unbalanced agricultural economy of Antigua has been diversified by the tourist industry; the many new hotels have added another feature to the landscape; the road network has been extended, and new life put into the formerly quiet capital of St John's (pop. 13 000) in the lee of the island. The first steps towards industrialization were made in 1964 with the construction of a cement factory on Crabbs Peninsula and the establishment of an oil refinery.

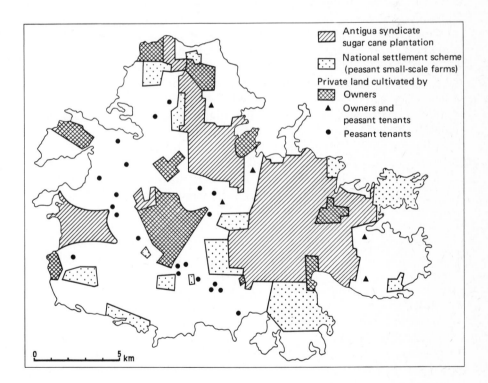

Map 70. Antigua: land ownership (after Augelli).

Agriculture is still the basis of the economy, with sugar and cotton supplying 90 per cent of the exports by value. Sugar cane has dominated the agriculture of this semi-arid island for the last 300 years. It suffered repeatedly from droughts, but it survived since no other lucrative export crop was found to replace it. The distribution of land ownership and the production of sugar have undergone fundamental changes since the heyday of the traditional sugar plantation economy: the concentration of land into large-scale enterprises was followed by the amalgamation of most of these farms into Antigua Syndicates Ltd, which in turn is controlled by the sugar factory which has been the only one in the island since 1958. Seventy-five kilometres of field railway connect nearly all the cane areas in the island with this modern factory. Plantation-type cane farming in a monocultural pattern is characteristic of the central plain, which is bordered by hilly country. The latter area, which is more extensive, is the peasant cane farming area (Map 70), but it is less carefully cultivated and fragmented into small and irregularly shaped fields and produces a much lower yield per acre. Small peasant farms have developed mainly as a result of the systematic government settlement programme started in 1917, but also because large-scale farmers have rented their lands to tenants. Cotton has become the second most important peasant export crop, mainly in the dry hilly limestone region in the east. The mountainous volcanic south-west is characterized by the peasant cultivation of food crops and arrowroot. The rural population lives in compact villages of varying sizes. The drought which lasted from 1960 to 1969 (when 1282·1 mm of rain fell) seriously threatened the island's sugar production, which dropped from 26 000 tonnes (average of the period 1956–60) to 14 000 tonnes (1965). (Annual rainfall for 1970 was 1752·4 mm. The sugar factory, which has had to be subsidized by the government for years because of its losses, was only able to operate because it received water intended to supply the population. Because of the drought the new oil refinery had to ship water in tankers from Puerto Rico. The sugar factory became insolvent in autumn 1966 and terminated its operation. It remains to be seen whether the 300 years and more of sugar cultivation in Antigua have finally come to an end or whether cultivation will persist in a different, reduced form. In any case, an improved water supply is a precondition for the continuation of cane farming and processing. In order to achieve this dams have been built since 1965 to control the surface drainage and wells have been sunk to utilize the underground water. The water situation has improved since October 1970 when a de-salination plant was opened at Crabbs peninsula supplying 1·5 million gallons of water daily.

Antigua hopes that its union with Barbados and Guyana within the Caribbean Free Trade Agreement (CARIFTA) (cf. p. 99, 103–4) of 1968 will result in an improvement of its economic situation.

The ruins of former sugar mills as well as those of the former naval base of English Harbour with its famous and recently restored Nelson's Dockyard point back to the island's golden period during the eighteenth century. Strictly speaking, Great Britain owes its victory over France in the Seven Years War in the Caribbean and the expansion and consolidation of its colonial possessions in the Islands to the Windward to Nelson's Dockyard (cf. p. 68–9).

The extremely dry limestone island of **Barbuda** in the north is a constituent part of Antigua's territory and rises to only 1–2 m above sea-level for the most part. Its 1000 inhabitants live from cattle farming, fishing, the production of charcoal and cotton cultivation.

The uninhabited rock of **Redonda** with an area of 1 sq km between Montserrat and Nevis in the inner volcanic arc of the Islands to the Windward is also part of the Antigua territory.

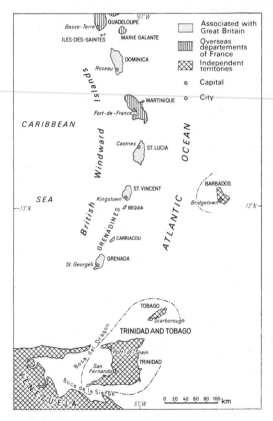

Map 71. The southern Islands to the Windward.

The French Islands to the Windward

Guadeloupe with its neighbouring islands, and Martinique are French Overseas Départements.

Guadeloupe and its neighbouring islands

The Département Guadeloupe comprises, in addition to Guadeloupe itself, the island of Marie Galante, Désirade and Les Saintes in the immediate neighbourhood of the main island, as well as the islands of St Barthélemy and St Martin further to the north-west within the region of the British Leeward Islands and the Dutch Islands to the Windward respectively (Table 70).

Table 69.   The French Islands to the Windward: size and population, 1967

	size sq km	population	density of population inhabitants per sq km
Guadeloupe	1 702	312 724	183
Martinique	1 090	320 030	293
Total	2 792	632 754	227

Table 70.   Guadeloupe: size and population, 1961, 1967

	size sq km	population 1961	population 1967	density of population inhabitants per sq km 1961	density of population inhabitants per sq km 1967
Guadeloupe proper	848	122 508	284 617	144	183
Grande Terre	586	133 332		221	
Marie Galante	150	16 341	15 867	109	100
Désirade	27	1 592	1 559	59	57
Les Saintes	14	2 772	3 269	198	233
St Martin	52	4 502	5 061	87	97
St Barthélemy	25	2 176	2 351	87	94
Total	1 702	283 223	312 724	166	183

St Martin. The northern part of the island, comprising two-thirds of its surface, belongs to France (Map 68). As in the Dutch part (cf. p. 318) the dominance of cotton during the eighteenth century was broken by the sugar plantation economy which in turn fell into decay in the second half of the nineteenth century. Cattle farming, whose produce is easily exported to the Dutch Islands to the Leeward via Philipsburg in the Dutch part of the island, is the basis of existence for the large-scale farms which still exist in the plains. Peasants used to cultivate food crops in the mountainous region for subsistence and for the local market, until the island was discovered by tourism a few years ago. Marigot, the capital on the lee of the island, is the largest market. Walls built from stones collected from the fields mark out very clearly the field boundaries of the former cultivated areas. French St Martin benefits economically from its immediate proximity to Dutch territory and from its position far from the main island of Guadeloupe. No customs barriers exist at the border between the French and the Dutch territories. As a result of this theoretical borderline trade flourishes in Marigot and is also favoured by the close proximity of British and US islands. Negroes make up the majority of the population. Their mother-tongue is English, as in the Dutch part. Tourism, which had already started in the Dutch territory in the mid-1950s and which also benefited the French population, began in the French territory in 1961, when holiday cottages were built on Terres Basses, the peninsula stretching to the west, near the Dutch airport. Hotels have also been built in Marigot.

St Barthélemy, south-east of St Martin, is mainly composed of limestone. Extensive areas of bare and karstic rocks cover the surface of this small and arid island and greatly limit its agricultural use. Plantations never existed. Peasant cultivation of tobacco, cotton and pineapples was only export-orientated for a short period in the past. The population of St Barthélemy is mainly white, similar to that of Dutch Saba before the Second World War and to the Iles des Saintes today. The inhabitants make their living from some cultivation and from sailing. The sailing boats from Saint Barth, which is the colloquial name for the island and its population, still handle the local passenger and goods traffic in the northern Islands to the Windward. The inhabitants of St Barthélemy are descendants of immigrants from Normandy; their language is not Créole, which has many African elements and is very common in the other French islands, it is pure French—a seventeenth century dialect from Normandy. The women's clothes also preserve traditional elements. Intermarriage with Negroes occurred very rarely although the Negro population has at various times in the past been more numerous than today, as from 1785 on, when France ceded St Barthélemy to Sweden. When Gustavia, the main settlement in the lee of the island, was declared a freeport trade prospered, resulting in the immigration of many merchants and their slaves. Not more than 739 persons lived on the island in 1784; their number had risen to 5492 by 1812, 3881 of them living in the town. In 1795 1568 vessels called at Gustavia harbour, but soon after the Treaty of Paris (1814) the competition of St Thomas resulted in both the stagnation of Gustavia's trade and the emigration of the merchants. The island had long become worthless to Sweden and in 1878 it changed again into French hands. Neither the economy nor the way of living of the local population was decisively affected by the short intermezzo of flourishing trade at the beginning of Swedish rule. The island, which is very isolated at present, took the first step in introducing the tourist industry when it built a small exclusive hotel, whose guests are brought from St Martin by a private plane. If the plans for further development in this direction are carried out the island and its population might soon lose the originality and independence which have until now distinguished Saint Barth from all the Caribbean islands.

Guadeloupe as a whole. Guadeloupe, called *le continent* by the inhabitants of the small neighbouring islands, basically consists of two independent islands separated from each other by the narrow inlet of Rivière Salée. The western island, Guadeloupe proper, belongs to the inner mountainous and volcanic arc of the Islands to the Windward; the eastern island, Grande Terre, belongs to the outer arc of limestone islands. This difference in geological structure and the resulting topography is reinforced by climatic variations. The eastern flat Grande Terre progresses from semi-arid to subhumid and humid from east to west; western Guadeloupe is perhumid, especially on the windward side and at higher altitudes. Agriculture reflects these differences: sugar cane is the major crop in Grande Terre and along the foothills on the eastern side of Guadeloupe proper; bananas, coffee and food crops are typical of cultivation in the humid mountainous region. Large landholdings predominate in the cane area; mainly peasant farms are found in all other cultivated areas. Mulattoes make up a high proportion of the population, especially among the peasantry. The percentage of whites and Asian Indians in the population is very small in comparison with the mulattoes and Negroes. The Asian Indians, whose ancestors were brought to the island as indentured labourers following the abolishment of slavery, constitute about 6 per cent of the entire population.

The agricultural area occupies 56 per cent of the island's surface. Peasant farms predominate, 49 per cent of the agricultural area is distributed among farms of under 5 ha, 40 per cent among those of over 100 ha. The marketing crises affecting export crops are therefore felt much less by the population in Guadeloupe than in Martinique. A considerable number of the peasant farms, especially in the cane area, are tenant farms. Sugar cane alone occupies 53 per cent of the agricultural area, i.e. 55 000 ha. Sugar cane and bananas dominate the very unbalanced export agriculture: sugar and rum made up 60 per cent of the exports by value in 1968, bananas 35 per cent. Guadeloupe has the largest volume of foreign trade among the Islands to the Windward; its balance of trade deficit, however, and its high import quotas of consumer goods and foodstuffs display the negative characteristics of an agricultural territory with unbalanced production. Except for the food processing plants, Guadeloupe shows hardly any signs of industrialization although there is a very urgent need for this in view of the rapidly increasing population and the surplus labour force. Nor has the tourist industry been developed although the airport near Pointe-à-Pitre offers good connections. The French government has recently taken steps to improve the island's infrastructure; to expand, diversify and rationalize the agriculture; to improve the transport system and the power supply; to establish industries; and to stimulate the tourist industry.

Guadeloupe proper extends for about 45 km from north to south with a width of 20 km. The mountain ridge runs parallel to the west coast reaching its highest altitude of 1467 m in Soufrière, which is an active volcano. Its last eruption occurred in 1956, terrifying the inhabitants of Basse-Terre, the capital on the south-west coast along the foothills of this volcano. The steep western slopes and the slightly less steep eastern slopes of this entirely volcanic mountain ridge, are divided into extended interfluves by numerous deeply incised ravines or narrow valleys with heavy discharges. The mountains are covered by forests except at lower altitudes. Settlements and cultivated areas fringe the periphery of the island. An old road from Basse-Terre to Pointe-à-Pitre on Grande Terre runs along the windward coast; the leeward coast was only linked by a road in 1960 thus ending its isolation, which had lasted for centuries. Guadeloupe is now entirely encircled by this well-built road. Country roads lead from it into the interior for several kilometres along some valleys and especially along the interfluves. They are usually very steep and there are more on the windward side which is more densely populated and more important for agricultural production. Small market towns have developed along the coast, usually at a distance of about 10 km from each other. Roadside villages and dispersed settlements, in particular, typify rural settlement patterns. Densely populated regions alternate with regions which are relatively sparsely populated. The cultivated land and the settlements are not found above 200 m on the windward side, whilst they extend to altitudes of up to 600 m to the leeward. Both sides include areas which are suitable for agricultural use, but have not yet been cultivated.

The main economic region lies on the windward side where sugar cane is the prevailing crop in the flat or gently sloping district to the north-east. A number of modern sugar companies, having developed factories, cultivate nearly 60 per cent of the cane area themselves. Extensive parts of this humid region are cultivated by large as well as by small farms. Crop rotation is the rule, three to five years of banana cultivation alternating with five to six years of sugar cane farming. The mixed cultivation of food crops, bananas and some coffee by peasants characterizes the higher altitudes. On the southern part of the island between Capesterre and Basse-Terre banana cultivation is most widespread. It was not introduced until the 1920s and has survived various hurricanes and the cessation of exports during the Second World War. At present it is more important than ever before. This region is not suited to modern sugar cane farming because of its extensive local relief. Small farms owned by whites have survived in this region where Asian Indians also make up a high percentage of the population. They mainly specialize in the cultivation of vegetables in the districts above Basse-Terre. Large-scale farms become less numerous here, medium-sized farms of 5 to 10 ha dominate. Their fields of single crops occupy the interfluves, whilst the polyculture of small farms occupies the slopes and changes almost imperceptibly into forest land uphill. Mango, breadfruit and coconut trees are dispersed among the banana fields, which suffered heavy hurricane damage in 1956, 1963 and 1966. Economic activity is focused on banana cultivation with harvesting throughout the year. Marketing is expertly organized with sheds for the collecting and packing of the bananas built along the road. The bunches are loaded on trucks as soon as a banana boat arrives. Boats had to anchor in the roadsteads of Basse-Terre for many years causing high loading costs until banana elevators were built for transhipment.

Gourbeyre and especially St Claude, at altitudes of 300 m and 400–600 m respectively, are the main settlements in the banana district. The latter has a pleasant climate and has attracted civil servants and merchants from Basse-Terre (pop. 14 000), which has always been the administrative centre of the Département Guadeloupe but which was surpassed in economic importance by Pointe-à-Pitre a long time ago. The old city possesses numerous colonial buildings and is bordered in the east by the new city. The slopes of Soufrière are very steep and are cultivated in places. The relief greatly limits the expansion of the urban area. Basse-Terre is the leading harbour for the export of bananas; Guadeloupe's imports, however, arrive almost exclusively via Pointe-à-Pitre.

The leeward side of the island, economically much less important, starts north of Basse-Terre. It has preserved several traditional characteristics: large-scale farms have never developed in this coastal region with its rugged relief, not even during the heyday of the colonial plantation economy and it still has the traditional peasant economy. The small and medium-sized farms are very rarely cultivated by tenants, and a large number of whites may be found among their owners. Agricultural production is clearly zoned by altitude: cattle farming and a little cultivation of food crops is carried on up to a height of 200 m, a relatively arid zone; tropical tubers, bananas and coffee are cultivated at heights of 200–400 m with this cultivation ascending to 600 m into the forest region in the hinterland of Bouillante. The leeward coast has numerous bays which offer beautiful views from the newly built winding and scenic road. Market towns, which are at the same time small fishing ports, have developed on these bays. Some of the inhabitants of the leeward coast find additional seasonal employment in the cane fields or the banana plantations on the windward side of Guadeloupe.

Grande Terre is almost entirely built from Miocene limestone; its topography, however, shows a wealth of different structures. Level plateaux are the main features, divided into cuesta topography in the north and into dolines and dry valleys in the east. The south-western part of the island, however, is characterized by bolder relief and very complex topography in the karst region of Grands Fonds (Map 72). That this is a region of dinaric karst is indicated by the pattern of compact and irregularly placed dry valleys and by the dolines on the interfluves between the valleys. Towards the swampy plain of Abymes in the west, and towards the structurally-formed elongated depression of Morne-à-l'Eau which extends far into the interior of the island in an easterly direction, the interfluves between the valleys dissolve into groups of limestone cones and in the marginal regions of these plains only isolated cones, displaying all degrees of solution, are found. The dinaric karst relief of Grands Fonds through active lateral erosion by

332

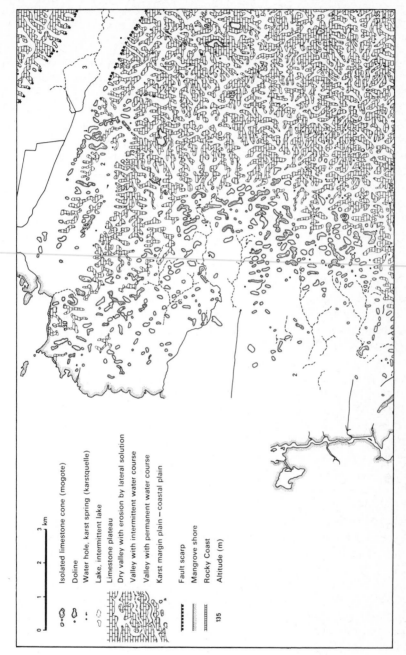

Map 72. Guadeloupe: karst on Grande Terre.

Isolated limestone cone (mogote)
Doline
Water hole, karst spring (karstquelle)
Lake, intermittent lake
Limestone plateau
Dry valley with erosion by lateral solution
Valley with intermittent water course
Valley with permanent water course
Karst margin plain – coastal plain

Fault scarp
Mangrove shore
Rocky Coast
Altitude (m)

0   1   2   3 km

333

solution is replaced by tropical cone karst at its edge. The caves west of Morne-à-l'Eau, which used to be inhabited by Caribs, are clear examples of lateral erosion by solution at the edge of the post-Pleistocene coastal plain.

Grande Terre has an agricultural economy except in the deserted swampy plain on the west coast. Peasant polyculture of food crops typifies the karst region of Grands Fonds and, together with cattle farming, the arid districts in the south-east of the island. Elsewhere sugar cane cultivation (Map 73) has prevailed since the eighteenth century, usually carried out without irrigation, but sometimes suffering from low rainfall. Large-scale farms occupy 55 per cent of the agricultural area and small farms (average of 2–3 ha) 34 per cent. Foreign ownership of the large-scale enterprises is the rule: 68·5 per cent of the main sugar factories and their land are owned by French companies, 24 per cent are in the hands of Martinique-based companies. The tenants (*colons*) of the small and medium-sized farms supply 20 per cent of the cane processed by the factories, indicating the dominance of plantation-type monoculture which has identical characteristics in all the Caribbean islands (Map 11). *Grande culture* is also preferred in Grande Terre, i.e. the harvest of the cane between January and March after eighteen instead of after twelve months (*petite culture*). Planting is therefore done between August and October in *grande culture*, and immediately following the harvest between March and May in *petite culture*. The large-scale farms prefer *grande culture* because it gives higher yields per acre. Peasant farms are widespread where the soil and climatic conditions do not favour mechanized cultivation, such as the land of former plantations which has been abandoned or which was not included in the new latifundia. A number of settlements have also developed in these districts, e.g. in the dry east. The majority of the rural population lives in villages whose simple wooden buildings, roofed nowadays with corrugated iron, and all of the same type, give these settlements a rather uniform appearance. The few market towns, connected with Pointe-à-Pitre by road, are all, but one, situated on the coast.

The karst region of Grands Fonds has hardly been penetrated by transport; only a few very winding roads lead along the ridges of the interfluves. A dispersed settlement pattern is the rule, with farmhouses scattered along these roads, but with many farms also located far away from them. Amidst the secondary forest along the slopes are small fields, where food crops are cultivated in a mixed farming system, with the rotation of fields and shifting cultivation in clearings made by burning a very common practice (Plate 23). The grassland on the valley floors is used for cattle farming. Fifty white families, the descendants of the first colonists to the island, live as small farmers among the mainly Negro population in this region. Asian Indians, who represent 20 per cent of the population in the cane area, have not settled in this region. The population of Grands Fonds supplies a large number of labourers to the sugar industry in Grande Terre.

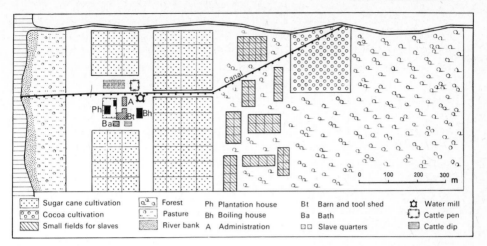

Map 73. Guadeloupe: colonial sugar plantation in Grande Terre (after Labat, from Lasserre).

Pointe-à-Pitre (pop. 28 000), which was not founded until the late eighteenth century, is situated in a marshy and unhealthy region in the south-west of Grande Terre. After a slow start it developed into the largest city in Guadeloupe only recently benefiting from its position on a large and protected bay. Pointe-à-Pitre has suffered severe damage in the past from earthquakes, hurricanes and fire; but it is developing fast now. Development plans include the whole area beyond the present administrative boundaries of the city as far as the international Raizet airport where in time a population of 60 000 can live. Beyond the extensive slum areas bordering the old city in the north, multistorey buildings have been constructed in an area which has already been cleared. These are either apartment blocks or public buildings, and are in extreme contrast to the numerous and closely packed shacks around them. The city can only expand to the north because of limestone hills to the east, the sea to the south, and the swamp to the west. Commercial enterprises and small industrial plants have developed along the road leading to the airport. The marshy districts in the north-west of the city are to become the future industrial area. Up to now Pointe-à-Pitre has lived mainly from trade. It is a busy town, contrasting with the quiet capital of Basse-Terre in its nature and function. Pointe-à-Pitre handles about 95 per cent of all imports to Guadeloupe and exports mainly sugar, turnover in its harbour has risen from 90 000 tonnes in 1913 to 0·5 million tonnes in 1961.

Marie Galante is also a limestone island. A plateau in the south, about 150 m high with a great amount of karst relief borders a uniform and low-lying platform in the north along a distinct fault scarp. Both the isolated position of the island and its aridity led to a decline of the formerly flourishing sugar cane cultivation during the nineteenth century crises of the

335

Caribbean sugar industry. Extensive cane cultivation may at present be found only in the small western coastal plain, while in all other parts cane fields alternate irregularly with pastures, secondary scrub, and small fields where food crops are grown. The cultivated area occupies 20 per cent of the island's surface, considerably less than in the past. The ruins of seventy-two former sugar mills, of old mansions, and of farm buildings are reminders of this past. Nevertheless, sugar cane is still the main crop in the cultivated area, and large landholdings still occupy two-thirds of the island, usually cultivated by tenants, so that small farms are typical. Only one of the three sugar factories which were built at the end of the nineteenth century is still in operation. In 1960 it could only process 70 per cent of the cane harvest; 30 per cent rotted in the fields uncut. The continuous deterioration of the economic situation which has lasted for decades will be halted, it is hoped, by the establishment of a new sugar factory, started in 1962 and mainly supplied by small farmers. This development, perhaps, will also curb emigration, which is directed mainly to the 'continent', i.e. to Pointe-à-Pitre and to the cane areas in Grande Terre. The capital, Grand-Bourg, has a population of less than 2000. Several impressive buildings in this quiet place testify a more lively and wealthy past. Schooners (Plate 28) and, of late, an air-service connect Grand-Bourg with Pointe-à-Pitre.

Désirade to the east of Grande Terre is, like St Barthélemy, a small, dry limestone island. For more than 200 years, until 1958, lepers were brought here from Guadeloupe. The removal of the leper colony considerably reduced the money-making opportunities of the native population. Small settlements with poor wooden buildings are restricted to the southern littoral. Steep limestone walls ascend from here to the plateau more than 200 m high which covers most of the island and which is of hardly any value to the economy. The population lives from a little cultivation and some fishing, some also work on the sailing boats which provide coastal transport around Guadeloupe. The inhabitants of Désirade, 20 per cent of whom are white, live in extremely poor conditions.

Les Saintes. This small archipelago, 10 km south of Guadeloupe proper, consists of mountainous islands which rise to heights of over 300 m. They are built from volcanic rock and are covered by tropical deciduous forest. Fort Napoleon and other military sites indicate the strategic importance of these islands during the major confrontations between France and England in the Caribbean. Only the islands of Terre-de-Haut and Terre-de-Bas are inhabited. The former has a white population of Breton descent which has been living primarily from fishing since the seventeenth century and has developed a boat called the Saintois, specially suited to this end. The entire population of Terre-de-Haut is centred in the only settlement of this island, extending along the attractive shore in the lee of an enclosed bay. Terre-de-Bas used to have more cultivation than Terre-de-Haut, but fishing now represents almost the only means of livelihood. The white population is in the minority.

336

Martinique

Martinique lies about 40 km off the British island of Dominica which separates it from Guadeloupe. It stretches for about 60 km from NNW to SSE with a maximum width of 25 km. It is volcanic, with Tertiary limestone only appearing in the extreme south-east. Bordering the wide bay of Fort-de-France alluvial deposits form the Lamentin Plain which reaches far into the interior of the island in the south-west. The highest altitudes occur in the northern part of the island. The beautifully shaped Pitons du Carbet rise to 1070 m immediately behind the capital of Fort-de-France forming landmarks which can be seen from the sea for miles. The 1397 m high Montagne Pelée (Fig. 9) in the north-west is mostly cloud-covered. In its foothills, on the lee of the island, lies the old trading town of St Pierre, all of whose 30 000 or so inhabitants, with the exception of one prisoner, perished from a volcanic eruption in 1902. Within a few minutes an explosive, burning cloud of ash and gas (*nuée ardente*) had moved down from Mt Pelée and smothered the town. Eight thousand people have resettled there. Numerous ruins and a museum of volcanology keep alive the memory of that catastrophe. The sharp andesite volcanic spire which was pushed out of the mountain for about 300 m in 1902 was destroyed again by another eruption in 1929.

The difference between the windward and leeward sides is especially distinct in the mountainous north of the island (Map 74). Marked aridity only occurs in the extreme south where the region is covered by thorn and cactus savannas. Cultivation and settlement have penetrated much further into the semi-evergreen and rain forests in the mountainous region than in Guadeloupe proper. The agricultural land, however, only takes up 65 per cent of the island's surface. Extensive and compact forest areas still cover the mountainous region especially in the north-west.

Martinique is famous for its impressive scenery, for its living Créole folklore and its eventful history. In Martinique, Père Labat developed sugar cane cultivation in the late seventeenth century. His works provide us with a clear picture of the French Antilles during the early colonial period. The future Empress Josephine, the consort of Napoleon, was born in a small village near Fort-de-France. A monument on the Savanna, the largest square in Fort-de-France, commemorates this event. Reminders of the former French–British confrontations are also found: immediately off the south-west coast lies the Rocher du Diamant which was occupied by the British for a short while in 1804 and armed with cannon like a battleship. It was known as HMS Diamond Rock.

In complete contrast to Pointe-à-Pitre, the capital, Fort-de-France, is a picturesque city, although it does not possess historic buildings except the great Fort St Louis. In earlier times the town had only military and administrative functions, but after the destruction of St Pierre it developed into the most important trading and cultural centre of the island. It is situated on a large enclosed bay in the lee of the island, which is deep enough

337

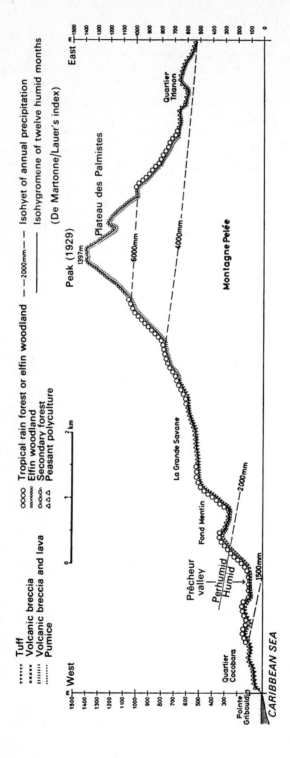

Fig. 9. Martinique: cross-section of Montagne Pelée.

338

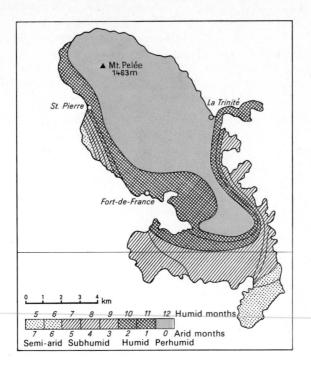

Map 74. Martinique: isohygromenes (Index Reichel).

for seagoing vessels and fulfils all the conditions required by modern shipping traffic. All exports, which are only slightly less in volume than those from Guadeloupe, are shipped from Fort-de-France. The airport, 13 km from the capital in the Lamentin Plain, offers connections to North and South America and, via Guadeloupe, to Europe. The old city lies on a narrow coastal plain with modern residential areas extending uphill. The Plateau Didier is the privileged residential area where luxurious villas lie hidden among lush vegetation. Well-built asphalt roads lead in all directions, usually very winding and very steep in parts owing to the large amount of local relief. The road network, however, is inadequate in the northern and southern parts of the island. There is no railway.

The population density is considerably higher than in Guadeloupe. Mulattoes, usually of a fairer complexion than in Guadeloupe, make up a high percentage of the population. Whites and Asian Indians make up nearly 5 per cent of the population each; the eruption of Mt Pelée greatly reduced the number of whites. The capital has 85 000 inhabitants, i.e. 25 per cent of the total population. Except for the rural market towns, which have usually developed along the coast, and the fishing villages a dispersed settlement pattern is dominant. The settlements have mainly developed along roads, but numerous farms are still very isolated, especially in the mountainous region.

As in the other Islands to the Windward the easily farmed land is owned by large-scale enterprises, mainly in the few plains and in the low-lying areas with low slopes. Small farms, usually growing food crops, may be found in the mountainous region and in the arid south, regions which, for economic reasons, are not suited to export-orientated cultivation by large farms. Continuous subdivision within the small-farming region has led to a high degree of land fragmentation, whereas the monocultural sugar cane region has experienced considerable concentration into large farms. In contrast to Guadeloupe, the main sugar factories and their lands are in the hands of old-established white families, the *békés*, who at present also control a considerable part of sugar production in Guadeloupe. Large farms (> 100 ha) occupy more than 60 per cent of the agricultural land. Tenancy on the sugar cane latifundia is less common than in Guadeloupe. Farms of less than 10 ha only cultivate about 10 per cent of the cane area, farms of more than 100 ha about 70 per cent.

The important position of sugar cane cultivation in Martinique, which had lasted since the eighteenth century, has declined since 1960. The cane area, amounting to 7800 ha in 1969 (11 400 ha in 1965), has been greatly reduced; cane fields have disappeared from the dry south and the rugged leeward side of the island and on the windward side they are restricted to low-lying areas below 200 m and are found mainly in the Lamentin Plain and its surrounding districts. The cane is transported by field railways and trucks to eleven modern sugar factories. Martinique has become famous for its production of a high quality rum. The export value of sugar has decreased considerably since the growing importance of bananas after the Second World War. The exports from banana cultivation, which only occupies 10 500 ha, had a higher value than rum and sugar together (1964, 42 against 39 per cent: 1969, 54 against 25 per cent). As in Guadeloupe, the bananas are mainly supplied by medium-sized and small farms at the edges of the mountainous region. Both types of cultivation are extremely vulnerable to hurricane winds; the entire banana crop and about half the cane fields were destroyed in September 1963. Pineapples made up 18 per cent of the exports by value in 1969. Their cultivation has been greatly expanded during recent years at altitudes of over 200 m on the moist windward slopes of Gros-Morne and at altitudes of over 500 m in the north-western mountainous region around Le Morne Rouge. Pineapple cultivation occupied an area of 820 ha in 1965. Ten factories produce tinned fruit and juice.

Sugar, bananas and pineapples supply 97 per cent of the exports by value. Food crops are only cultivated on 15 per cent of the productive land and foodstuffs therefore head the list of imports. While pineapples are exported almost exclusively to the USA, France receives the entire sugar and banana production, amounting to about 90 per cent of all exports. About 80 per cent of imports come from France. In view of these unbalanced trade relations and the unbalanced structure of the export-orientated agriculture, one can recognize that the economy of Martinique, as of

Guadeloupe, exhibits marked colonial characteristics. There is a strong drive for independence in Martinique. It is obvious, however, that this small and overpopulated island, with no industries except the processing plants for agricultural products and where the population suffers from unemployment, cannot survive on its own. The tourist industry is more strongly developed than in Guadeloupe, but so far it has not greatly improved the economic situation in Martinique.

The British Windward Islands

The group of the British Windward Islands is composed of the territories of Dominica, St Lucia, St Vincent, and Grenada (Table 71). All these islands ceased to be colonies in 1967, since when they have been autonomous territories associated with Great Britain with the right to dissociate themselves from the union at any time and proclaim complete independence (cf. p. 76). All of them are parts of the inner volcanic arc of the Islands to the Windward.

Table 71.   The British Windward Islands: size and population, 1960*

	Size *sq km*	*Population*	*Density of population* *inhabitants per sq km*
Dominica	790	59 916	76
St Lucia	603	94 718	157
St Vincent	389	80 042	206
Grenada	345	88 677	257
Total	2 127	323 353	152

```
* Dominica      70 200 (1967)
  St Lucia     100 000 (1965)
  Grenada      104 600 (1969)
```

Dominica

Dominica, situated between the French islands of Guadeloupe and Martinique, is the largest of the British Windward Islands (cf. p. 6) but has the smallest population and the lowest population density. In spite of this there used to be heavy seasonal migration during the sugar harvest in Guadeloupe and a high emigration rate to Great Britain because of the low level of economic development of the island. Today, the economic growth of Dominica is still handicapped by the island's topography. Dominica is the most mountainous of all the Islands to the Windward, and because of its large amount of local relief it receives extremely high rainfall (Map 75). Extensive areas on the leeward side are perhumid even at sea-level, receiving about 2000 mm of rainfall annually (Roseau: 1928 mm; cf. Fig. 3). The windward coast receives an annual rainfall of nearly 4000 mm, and the higher altitudes an estimated 10 000–11 000 mm. Dense tropical rain

341

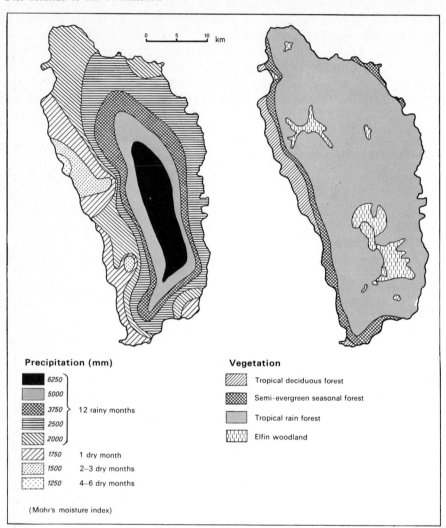

Map 75. Dominica: precipitation and vegetation (after Imperial College of Tropical Agriculture, Trinidad).

forests and montane forests still cover most of the island. Only 15 per cent of the island's surface, a narrow and often interrupted stretch of land along the coast, is used for agriculture. A road link between west and east was only completed after the Second World War, and there are still coastal districts under export-orientated cultivation without any road connections. Their only communication with the capital of Roseau (pop. 10 400) in the south-west is by coastal shipping. The special attraction of Dominica is its wild and almost undisturbed mountain nature with only a handful of paths leading into the wooded mountains which are volcanic and drained by swift flowing streams running through deep gorges. There are three mountain complexes: the northern, the central and the southern, culminating in the cone of the Morne Diablotin (1422 m) in the centre of the island. There are many fumaroles and hot springs and in the central part of the island is the famous 'Boiling Lake' in the almost inaccessible Valley of Desolation. The lake, much of whose surrounding vegetation was killed by sulphur fumes, is part of an extensive area of solfataras where a violent vapour explosion occurred in 1880. The Valley of Desolation is shaped like a large amphitheatre but as regards its morphology probably is not a crater but a widened erosional valley (Weyl).

The inaccessibility of the island, mainly on account of its unfriendly coast of steep cliffs, made Dominica a refuge for the warlike Caribs. Its settlement by French colonists only began 200 years after its discovery. The population still speaks French, although the island has belonged to England, with short interruptions, since 1763. Dominica is the only island where descendants of the Amerindian population of the Islands to the Windward have survived. The small Carib Reserve, almost in the centre of the windward coast, is inhabited by 500 Caribs, only a few of whom are pure blooded. Negroes and mulattoes make up the majority of the population in Dominica. Sixty-five per cent of the population live on farms and plantations. Peasant farms occupy a relatively large proportion (40 per cent) of the agricultural land. Large farms predominate in the south-west and north, peasant farms in the remaining coastal regions. The cultivated land is mainly restricted to the small plains at valley mouths stretching into the interior only along the valley bottoms. The higher valley slopes are usually cultivated by peasants in a field rotation system.

Export-orientated production has experienced many changes since the island was settled. By 1968 bananas had become the major export, 76 per cent of the exports by value, although their share was only one per cent in 1948. The cultivation of the Lacatán variety which is immune to Panama disease expanded considerably in the 1950s. Production is mainly by peasants, and especially in the north-east, the only region where banana plantations have developed. The main economic area used to be the south-western part of the island where for more than fifty years large-scale farms cultivated limes (*Citrus aurantifolia*), formerly Dominica's main export crop. In spite of decreases because of insect pests, lime farms are still important in this region as well as orange and grapefruit cultivation at slightly higher altitudes. Dominica is the only Island to the Windward with export-orientated citrus cultivation worth mentioning. Limes and, more important, lime juice together rank as the second most important export item making up 18 per cent of the exports by value. Copra comes third with one per cent. Eighty-six per cent of all exports (1968) are shipped to Britain, while only one-third of imports originate there. Most of the imports are foodstuffs. Roseau handles almost the entire foreign trade, although the boats have to anchor in the roadsteads. The splendid natural harbour of Portsmouth (pop. 2200) in the north-west only plays a minor role in maritime traffic. These two centres, 32 km from each other by air, are the only towns in Dominica. Since 1965 they have been linked by a road 80 km long.

With the exception of the processing of agricultural products there is hardly any industry in Dominica. Cigarettes and beverages are produced for local demand and wicker work for export. A tourist industry has not yet developed in this almost inaccessible island. As soon as hotels are available, however, and the small airport in the north-east of the island, completed in 1958, has been expanded to accommodate larger aircraft, the North American tourist will without doubt come to Dominica also.

St Lucia

St Lucia, the second largest Windward Island within sight of Martinique to the north, does not have the grandiose and wild mountain nature of Dominica. Nevertheless, Morne Gimie in the rugged coastal mountain region reaches a height of 951 m. The two Pitons right on the south-west coast of the island (Plate 24), ascend steeply to nearly 800 m. The view from the palm-lined beach of Soufrière towards these two beautifully shaped mountains is acclaimed as one of the most beautiful in the Caribbean. An extensive area of solfataras and fumaroles, where a major vapour explosion occurred in 1766, is situated near the town of Soufrière. The mountain region, covered by tropical rain and montane forests, is still not crossed by any road in its central and southern part. A road has been built only in the north where the region is composed of older volcanic rock and where local relief is less steep and mountains less high. In this region several valleys with flat, wide bottoms extend far into the mountain region: the Roseau and the Cul-de-Sac Valleys on the leeward, and the Fond d'Or (Mabouya) Valley on the windward. The only road crossing the island follows the latter two valleys over the Barre de l'Isle pass, the watershed from which numerous and deeply incised river valleys run in both directions.

The French placenames indicate the fact that St Lucia was settled by the French (Map 76). Colonization did not occur before the eighteenth century after various British attempts to settle the island had failed because of Carib resistance. The island finally became a British colony in 1803 after it had repeatedly changed from French to British hands. The population, nearly 60 per cent Negroes and 37 per cent mulattoes, still speaks the French patois containing African elements which is also common in Guadeloupe and Martinique.

Plantation-type sugar cane cultivation, mainly in the three valleys mentioned above and in others, represented St Lucia's economic basis in the early nineteenth century. The sugar industry stagnated following the abolition of slavery. Large farms amalgamated and only survived in the extensive valleys where modern sugar factories were established at the end of the nineteenth century. The higher valley slopes, however, and the mountain regions went into the hands of peasants; 46 per cent of the agricultural area is in farms of under 20 ha, and only 40 per cent in those of over 80 ha.

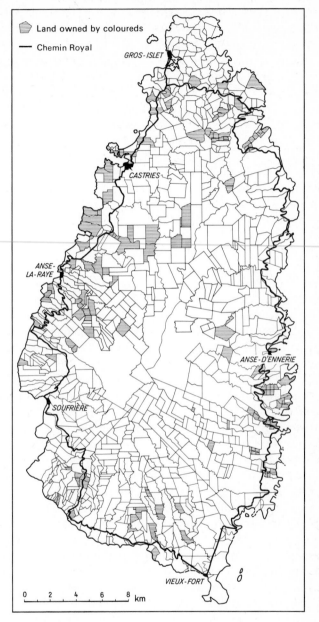

Land owned by coloureds

Chemin Royal

GROS-ISLET

CASTRIES

ANSE-
LA-RAYE

ANSE-D'ENNERIE

SOUFRIÈRE

VIEUX-FORT

0   2   4   6   8 km

Map 76. St Lucia: distribution of properties, 1787 (from M. Lefort de Latour, Description générale et particulière de l'île de Sainte Lucie, 1787; map and legend in the Public Record Office, London).

Relatively extensive areas of the agricultural land consist of so-called 'family land', where the property of the original owner is owned by all his descendants in equal parts. Thus, in extreme instances, eighty persons may own an area of 5 ha. Such land is usually left uncultivated since nobody can be certain of harvesting what he planted. For modern farming, this type of common ownership is as serious a handicap as the extreme land fragmentation and unsound tenancy conditions (payment in kind) are in other islands. The frequent rotation of fields is another unsound practice in peasant agriculture, as is the unbalanced orientation towards banana production in present peasant farming for, though it can be very profitable, it is also very risky, as was demonstrated by hurricane Abby in 1960. About half the island's surface is covered by secondary forest throughout which peasant clearings made by burning as part of a field rotation system are dispersed. Only 15 per cent of the island's surface is under permanent cultivation, mainly owned by large-scale enterprises (Plate 25).

Only one sugar factory is still in operation in the Roseau Valley, as against four before the Second World War, since cane cultivation has decreased considerably in the last fifteen years and the Roseau and Cul-de-Sac Valleys are no longer cultivated uniformly under sugar cane. As in Dominica, the reason for this development is the increased interest in bananas, which are cultivated as a single crop on former cane land both on peasant farms and by large-scale enterprises. Banana exports have exceeded sugar exports since 1956, accounting for 83 per cent of the exports by value (1964); coconut oil and copra rank second with 13 per cent. As in Dominica, the rural population has benefited greatly from the banana boom.

In the past, St Lucia had sources of income unknown to the neighbouring islands. The excellent natural harbour of Castries in the lee of the island was a coal-bunkering station for half a century after 1880. More than 1000 steamships called on St Lucia annually to bunker the coal imported from Great Britain and the USA. Since the loading was not mechanized hundreds of labourers found employment. The depression expected after bunkering ceased was offset by the establishment of two US military bases. When these were disbanded in 1948 almost the entire capital of Castries was destroyed by fire and the rebuilding of the town, facilitated by grants from the British colonial government, again employed a large labour force. At the present time the island depends on agriculture as the only source of income; however, the banana boom offers sufficient money-making opportunities. In addition, tourism reached the island a few years ago, concentrating in the scenic area around the capital. Castries is situated on a large protected bay with mountainous coasts and has 24 500 inhabitants (25 per cent of the population) and handles almost the entire trade of St Lucia. The airport, served by the British West Indian Airways, lies very near Castries. The town has been rebuilt in a rather uniform fashion with multistorey concrete apartment blocks. It has the advantage of a beautiful beach which extends beyond the Vigie peninsula for several kilometres to the north. Tourism has developed rapidly in a very short time with 17 700 tourists visiting the island in 1964, and 49 900 in 1969.

St Vincent

The volcanic island of St Vincent to the south of St Lucia possesses striking relief. In the north the impressive cone of Mount Soufrière rises to 1179 m. This geometrically-shaped composite volcano erupted violently in 1812; another eruption destroyed nearly a third of the island in 1902, when 2000 people perished. The crater walls descend almost vertically for more than 450 m and surround a lake. Richmond Peak, further to the south, rises again to 1075 m, but then altitudes finally decrease, with many ridges branching off in easterly and westerly directions from the watershed, which runs almost north to south. These ridges reach the sea as steep cliffs on both the windward and the leeward side of the island. Deeply incised valleys with flat bottoms in their lower courses meander between the ridges ending at the coast in small alluvial plains. The densely wooded mountain region receives high precipitation and is not yet crossed by any road.

Like Dominica and St Lucia, St Vincent was not settled before the eighteenth century because of the militant Caribs most of whom, partly mixed with Negroes (black Caribs), were deported to the Central American Mosquito Coast and to the Bay Islands in 1796. About 200 Caribs have survived in St Vincent; 75 per cent of the population is Negro, 20 per cent is mulatto, the rest are Asian Indians and whites. Among the latter are Portuguese from Madeira who came as indentured labourers like the Asian Indians, after the emancipation of the slaves. The island is overpopulated, and emigration has assumed large proportions. Most of the population lives in dispersed rural settlements; Kingstown, the capital, on a semicircular bay in the south-west has a population of 16 000. Its Botanical Garden, dating from 1763, is very famous. The breadfruit tree spread from here throughout the Caribbean islands. The *Bounty* under Captain Bligh was sent on her ill-fated voyage to the South Seas in 1787 in order to bring this tree and other cultivated plants from the Asiatic tropics to Kingstown's Botanical Garden.

Apart from the absence of roads in the north-west, a road follows the coastline of the island, and the cultivated areas, particularly on the windward side, have a fairly good road network which is full of bustling activity on 'banana days', when a banana boat arrives at Kingstown. The people carry their fruit to collecting points, whence gaily coloured trucks transport them to the port, which was expanded in 1964 to accommodate seagoing vessels. British West Indian Airways also serve St Vincent resulting in the development of a tourist industry which, however, has remained very moderate so far.

St Vincent depends almost entirely on its agriculture. Agricultural land occupies 57 per cent of the island's surface. Peasant farming is widespread;

only 25 per cent of the agricultural land is cultivated by large-scale farms. Land settlement on former large-scale farms was expertly conducted and the settlements are cultivated under government control. They occupy 11 per cent of the agricultural land which, in comparison with other Caribbean islands, is a relatively extensive area. Large-scale farms predominate on the windward side, peasant farms on the leeward side of the island (Map 77). Most of the peasants own the land they cultivate; they also work on plantations.

After the decline of sugar cane cultivation the large-scale farms concentrated on the cultivation of arrowroot (*Maranta arundinacea*) for export. The starch from the roots of this plant, which is used mainly for baby food and also for ice cream, was for a long time the main export from St Vincent. When the island's only sugar factory stopped production in 1962, the cultivation of arrowroot increased for a short while, but by 1964 it was only second by export value, accounting for 22 per cent (16 per cent in 1967). This was the result of the considerable increase in banana cultivation, mainly on peasant farms. The cultivation of arrowroot, like cotton cultivation, has been experiencing a crisis (1966) since the US food industry which was the main customer for St Vincent's arrowroot terminated all contracts of sale because production took a downward trend. Bananas made up 50 per cent of the exports by value in 1967. They are cultivated almost exclusively in a multicrop system and mainly on peasant farms on the lee of the island. On the windward side a strip of farmland where peasants cultivate food crops together with bananas also extends between the montane forest and the large-scale farms of arrowroot and coconut trees (copra represents 11 per cent of the exports by value). Wherever possible, the peasants try to extend their cultivation into the woodland, employing a field rotation system. Because there is extensive peasant farming, fruit and basic foodstuffs can be exported to Barbados and Trinidad, but in spite of this, foodstuffs (23 per cent), mainly grain and dairy products, head the list of imports followed by textiles (15 per cent). Thirty-one per cent of the imports originate in Britain (1967), and 56 per cent of St Vincent's exports are sent there.

Both the peasant farming and the fishing industry, too, are better and more widely developed in St Vincent than in its neighbouring islands. But above all, through its world monopoly in arrowroot production St Vincent has become quite distinctive among the Islands to the Windward. As to its landscape, one is surprised to find numerous slopes terraced to control soil erosion; the terracing of slopes is unknown in the neighbouring islands. Since there is no irrigation in St Vincent the terraces are not entirely horizontal. To a great extent these terraces are now characteristic of the lower slopes on the windward side of the island.

The northern Grenadines are administered by St Vincent (Table 72).

The Grenadines

The archipelago of the Grenadines, between St Vincent and Grenada,

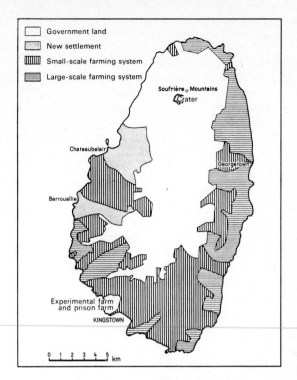

Legend:
- ☐ Government land
- ▨ New settlement
- ▥ Small-scale farming system
- ▤ Large-scale farming system

Soufrière Mountains
Crater

Chateaubelair

Georgetown

Barrouallie

Experimental farm
and prison farm

KINGSTOWN

0 1 2 3 4 5 km

Map 77. St Vincent: small- and large-scale farming systems (after J. P. Watson).

Table 72. Grenadines: size and population of the inhabited islands, 1960

	Size sq km	Population	Density of population inhabitants per sq km
St Vincent–Grenadines:			
Bequia	18	2 600	144
Union	8	1 300	163
Canouan	7	600	86
Mustique	5	100	20
Mayero	3	200	67
Baliceaux	2		
Ile de Quatre	1	25	8
All	44	4 825	110
Grenada–Grenadines			
Carriacou	34	8 100	238
Rhonde	3	100	33
Petit Martinique	2	525	263
All	39	8 725	224
Total	83	13 550	163

349

constitutes a physical and cultural unit, but is divided in its administration. The northern group of the Grenadines are administered by St Vincent, the southern group by Grenada. The 125 or so mountainous islands are mainly volcanic. Only a very few are inhabited and only two islands, Bequia in the northern and Carriacou in the southern group, are distinguished from the rest by their size and population. Low rainfall and frequent droughts with considerable fluctuations from year to year render water supply very difficult in spite of the construction of tanks and cisterns. Sometimes water has to be shipped to the islands in boats.

Although the precipitation and the topography are unfavourable for cultivation the Grenadines were plantation areas in the past, the small islands usually making up a single plantation. Carriacou, on the other hand, had fifty sugar cane and cotton plantations. The Grenadines had been settled by French colonists by the seventeenth century. Because of their former plantation economy 85 per cent of their population is Negro, 15 per cent mulatto. A French patois is spoken on all the islands, on the St Vincent Grenadines English is also increasingly spoken.

Fishing, sailing, and particularly farming form the bases of the present economy. The cultivation of maize is most common in subsistence areas; cotton is the major export-orientated cultivation: long-staple cotton on the St Vincent Grenadines and short-staple cotton on the Grenada Grenadines. The trade of the former group is orientated northwards to St Vincent, that of the latter group southwards to Grenada. Coconuts and citrus fruit, mainly limes, are produced by the few large enterprises left which have survived only in Bequia. Large farms have disappeared from Carriacou whose peasant population has a uniform culture and way of living.

The Grenadines are not served by airlines, neither do seagoing vessels call on these small islands. Only sailing and motor boats establish the link with the outside world. Bequia and Carriacou are the only islands where tourism has already started. Most of the tourists, however, come from the neighbouring larger Windward Islands, from Barbados and Trinidad, attracted by the peace and remoteness of these lonely and little known islands. In particular the main settlement, Hillsborough (pop. 500) in Carriacou, possesses old stone commercial buildings which evoke old-world reminiscences and memories of the former plantation economy and its trade. New developments are under way in the island of Canouan where the St Vincent government consented in 1966 to the construction by a US company of a harbour for oceangoing vessels. As in the island of Grand Bahama, light metal industries and hotels are to be established in Canouan.

Grenada

Grenada is the smallest territory of the British Windward Islands and the island with the highest population density (Table 71). It is the final southern island in the volcanic inner arc of the Islands to the Windward. Its mountainous region does not rise as high as those in other Windward Islands, nevertheless several peaks rise to more than 600 m, and the old Mount St Catherine volcano in the northern part of the island reaches a height of 840 m. There are no active volcanoes. Lake Antoine near the north-east coast and probably Grand Etang also at an altitude of 550 m in the central region are large and picturesque crater lakes. Numerous valleys dissect the mountain region. In the southern part of the island, where hillsides have stepped slopes, the valleys run parallel to one another. The interfluves between them stretch into the sea for several kilometres as narrow peninsulas. This coastal section, therefore, has embayments as have none of the other Windward Islands, creating a very distinct ria coast (cf. p. 36). The mountain region receives high rainfall; only the leeward south-west is semi-arid. Primeval forests, which are restricted to the almost inaccessible parts of the mountain region, still cover 15 per cent of the island's surface.

The agricultural land covers 82 per cent of the island's territory, the productive land about 65 per cent. Plantation-type sugar cane cultivation developed in the past as in St Lucia and St Vincent. At the present time, however, plantations claim little more than 50 per cent of the agricultural land. Tree crops have replaced sugar cane, cocoa trees at first, nutmeg trees later. Cocoa and nutmeg each accounted for 44 per cent of the exports by value in 1940; nutmeg 33 per cent and cocoa 23 per cent in 1968, although the new national Cocoa Rehabilitation Board had strongly supported cocoa farming. Nutmeg from Grenada represents about one-third of the world's production. It is cultivated at higher altitudes and is replaced by cocoa cultivation further downhill, whilst the coastal regions with only a little rainfall are dominated by food crops. Sugar cane only predominates in the south-west. The cultivation of tree crops occupies more than 75 per cent of the productive land and is exclusively carried out within a multicrop system. The cultivation of bananas, planted among cocoa and nutmeg trees, has increased greatly especially since the 1955 hurricane, which caused heavy damage in the tree crop areas. The number of banana plants rose from 67 000 in 1956 to 1·2 million in 1959, and in 1968 bananas made up 38 per cent of the exports by value. Whereas cocoa and bananas are mainly cultivated by large-scale enterprises small farms grow more than half of the nutmeg crop. In 1968 63 per cent of all exports went to Britain and 33 per cent of all imports came thence. Since even peasant farms are mainly interested in cultivation for export Grenada is to a great extent dependent on food imports which head the list of the imports by value by a wide margin (35 per cent).

Grenada was settled by France in the seventeenth century. The population, nearly 80 per cent Negro and about 20 per cent mulatto, speaks a French patois. English, strongly mixed with French expressions, is becoming increasingly common. White smallholders have been settled in the Mount Moritz area. Their ancestors, the so-called 'Red Legs', came to the island from Barbados as poor whites a few decades ago. About 80 per cent of the population live in dispersed rural settlements. The peasant homesteads, usually built of wood, lie hidden among the cultivated trees, with various subsistence food crops mostly planted in a very irregular pattern between fruit trees around them.

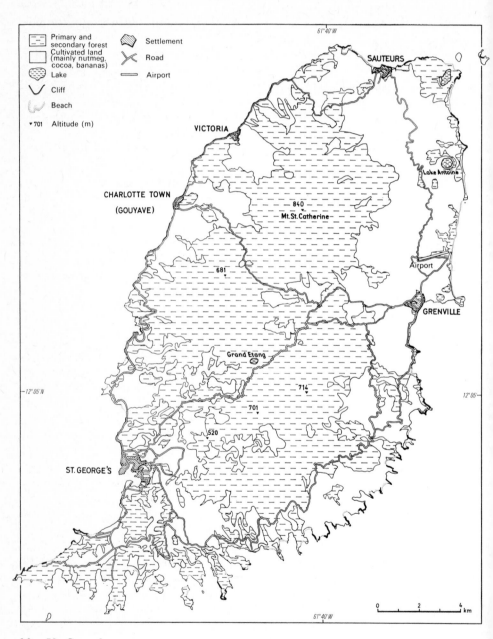

Map 78. Grenada.

St George's, the capital, on the leeward coast in the south-west, has a population of 7300. Fort George offers a unique view of what is undoubtedly the most charming town in the Windward Islands. A row of hills encircles the Carenage, the inner harbour of the bay which accommodates many schooners and even seagoing vessels. The town with its steep streets also covers the narrow peninsula between the Carenage and the open sea topped by the square tower of the Anglican church. Fort George is situated on top of the higher southern end of this peninsula which had already been tunnelled in 1889. Owing to the considerable relief only parts of the town could be built in the geometrical layout which is otherwise very common among Caribbean settlements. Urban activities are especially lively on the harbour front along the Carenage where warehouses and commercial offices are frequent and where one may find a bustling market alongside the sailing and motor boats at the jetty wall. The port installations for trans-oceanic shipping, adjacent to the Carenage, have been modernized following the damages of the 1955 hurricane.

St George's, which handles the entire export trade, is connected by roads with all parts of the island. Three roads link the windward with the leeward coast. The location of the airport, however, is disadvantageous for St George's because only the central part of the windward coast offered sufficient flat land for its construction. It is connected with St George's by 20 km of a very winding and narrow mountain road. Nevertheless, the young tourist industry is centred in and around St George's, especially to the south-west on Grand Anse Bay whose beach extends for kilometres, and where various hotels have been built. Grenada had 400 hotel beds in 1964 and was visited by 9300 tourists in 1963. By 1969 the number had risen to 29 600. The tourist industry has developed more than in most of the Windward Islands (except St Lucia), mainly owing to the better flight connections of the island which benefits from the proximity of Trinidad and Barbados.

Barbados

The island of Barbados is the topmost point of the Barbados Ridge 160 km east of the meridional arc of the Islands to the Windward and separated from these by the 2700 m deep Tobago Trench. Eighty-five per cent of the island's surface is Pleistocene coral limestone, which has been worn down only in the central part of an asymmetrical upwarping in the Scotland District which lies in the north-east of the island. Here, the limestone abuts on to the underlying folded Tertiary sedimentary rocks of the Scotland District along a distinct cuesta which, at present, is undergoing strong headward erosion. Very extensive rock slides occur frequently, as large parts of the waterlogged clay at the bottom of the limestone slide away. Furthermore, strong spring erosion is added to the effects of headward erosion of the cuesta leading to the loss of cultivated land both above and below it.

353

In order to prevent this efforts have recently been made to control the headward erosion by placing long horizontal drainage pipes along the cuesta edge at the base of the coral limestone. The coral limestone cuesta forms a very distinct regional boundary as it separates the maturely dissected area of the Scotland District from the uniform limestone plateau (Plate 27). The plateau displays a dinaric karst relief of dry valleys and dolines (Map 79). A large number of fossil cliffs, almost parallel to the coast, divide the coral limestone plateau into terraces which rise to heights of over 300 m. This increasing altitude is related to a considerable increase in annual rainfall over very short distances, ranging from 1100 mm to 2100 mm, and with an increase in humidity from six (in the north) to twelve humid months. These climatic differences are demonstrated by the existence of red earth in the moist altitudes and of dark soils in the lower and drier areas. The primary vegetation, mainly tropical deciduous and semi-evergreen seasonal forests, was soon destroyed by the expansion of sugar cane cultivation. The only remnant is the small forest (18 ha) of Turner's Hall in the northern subhumid section of the coral limestone cuesta.

Barbados experienced continuous British rule from 1625 until 1966, when it received independence. No other Caribbean island was so deeply influenced by British colonization. After the initial stage of peasant colonization plantation type sugar cane cultivation had already started by the late seventeenth century. Only twenty years after sugar cane was introduced 700 sugar cane plantations had replaced 11 000 peasant farms. The financially powerful landowners bought the land of their less wealthy or less successful neighbours, who had to find a new source of livelihood in another island or on the American mainland. The development of the plantation economy caused the rapid increase in the number of Negroes from 6000 to 82 000 within twenty years. Today, the population consists of Negroes, 90 per cent, mulattoes, 6 per cent, and whites, 4 per cent. Barbados is probably the only island with a distinct race barrier; this, however, does not result in serious tensions. Social differentiation within racial groups has developed to a greater extent than in the other islands.

Barbados was granted internal self-government in 1961 while still a British colony. The degree of overpopulation (540 persons per sq km) has assumed proportions beyond any other island in the Caribbean. Emigration has not been, either in the past or in the present, an effective escape valve for the population pressure, neither has birth-control, propagated by the government, met expectations. Bridgetown, on the south-western leeward coast, is the only urban settlement and has a population of 11 300 within its city boundaries, 5 per cent of the entire population; if the rapidly growing outskirts are included the city has 90 000 inhabitants, 38 per cent of the Barbadian population (1970: 238 000 inhabitants) Outside Bridgetown one can hardly find a place in this densely populated island where one cannot see at the same time several of the small, clean, and gaily coloured gable buildings which are also characteristic of many sections of Bridge-

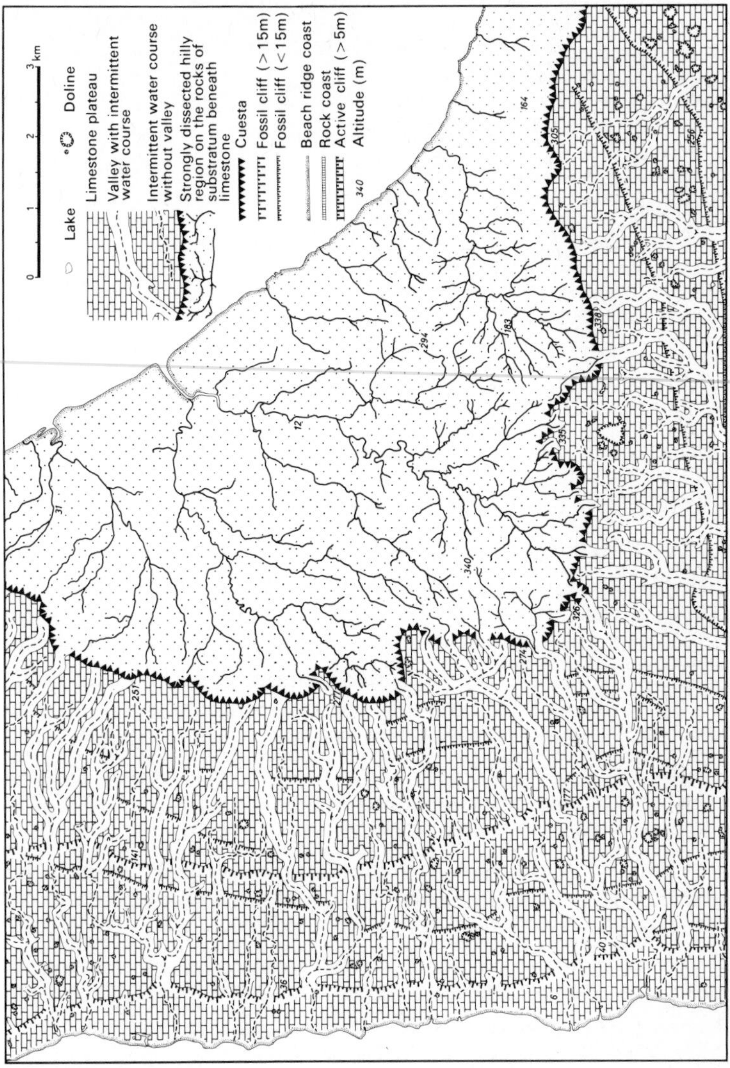
0 1 2 3 km
Lake
Doline
Limestone plateau
Valley with intermittent water course
Intermittent water course without valley
Strongly dissected hilly region on the rocks of substratum beneath limestone
Cuesta
Fossil cliff (>15m)
Fossil cliff (<15m)
Beach ridge coast
Rock coast
Active cliff (>5m)
Altitude (m)

Map 79. Barbados: karst formations.

town. The rural settlements consist of loose village-type settlements strung out along the roads with an otherwise irregular layout.

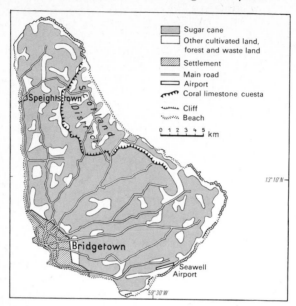

Map 80. Barbados: cane areas, settlements, and transport.

Barbados has been a 'sugar island' for the last 300 years. The agriculturally productive land occupies about 35 000 ha, i.e. 80 per cent of the island's surface, of which nearly two-thirds is under cane. Sugar, together with molasses and rum, supplied 91 per cent of the exports in 1962. By 1969 it was only 43 per cent; recently other export goods have achieved importance—shrimps and prawns, 10 per cent; textile goods, 3 per cent; electrical goods, 7 per cent. Almost 85 per cent of the sugar is produced by large-scale farms, that is the 244 farms of over 4 ha; those of 80–200 ha occupy about half the entire agricultural land and have been owned for generations by families of British descent. There are also about 4100 peasant farms of under 4 ha, and 26 500 very small farms of under 0·4 ha. The cultivation of food crops only expanded during the Second World War, when imports were impossible; farms of all sizes definitely prefer to cultivate sugar cane. Food crops, however, are not restricted to peasant farms, but on larger farms they usually occupy only the 12 per cent of the productive land required by law. In addition to cane only *Andropogon pertusus* grassland occupies extensive areas, mainly regions with a thin topsoil and the usually rocky precipices of fossil cliffs. The grass, which reaches a height of up to 75 cm, is cut several times during the year and is used as fodder and especially for the mulching of cane fields.

Sugar cane is equally characteristic of the appearance of the agricultural landscape in both the dry and humid parts of the island and even along the

356

steep slopes of the Scotland District where, in the course of a rehabilitation programme, deep ravines have been filled in and entire slopes have been levelled in recent years in order to even out the differences in relief, to prevent soil erosion and to expand the cultivated area. Barbadian cultivated land possesses distinct features of its own: carefully cultivated fields in which the land plots are smaller and more irregular than in the plantation-type sugar cane monoculture of the other Caribbean territories; narrow, winding roads leading through the cane areas; tall, slim royal palms growing either solitarily or in rows or in groups; and the casuarina often planted as a wind-shield in hedges. The aspect of this Barbadian landscape has often been compared to that of the English county of Surrey and, because of the English tradition alive in its administration, economy and cultural life, Barbados is often referred to as 'Little England'.

The cane crop is processed by twenty sugar factories which are relatively small in comparison with those in other islands. Until recently, trucks brought the sugar in sacks to the Bridgetown warehouses, and lighters shipped it to freighters anchored in the roadstead. However, the new Bridgetown harbour, opened in 1961 and accommodating seagoing vessels, has modern loading installations which, as in Puerto Rico, handle the sugar in bulk. Sugar production reached an average of 150 000 tonnes between 1959 and 1962 and is almost all exported to Britain. While 50 per cent of all exports go to Britain, only about 40 per cent of the imports come from there. Foodstuffs are the main imports totalling 30 per cent of the imports by value.

Fishing has always provided a considerable amount of food for this over-populated island. During recent years the 500 fishing boats have been equipped with engines. Another essential modernization of this industry was achieved in 1962 when a fish freezing plant was established. The majority of the catch are crustaceans and flying fish (*Exocoetus*).

The responsibility of the Barbados Development Board is to diversify the unbalanced economic structure. A higher degree of industrialization, which could reduce the seasonal unemployment and exploit the existing surplus labour more fully, seems necessary. Only small industries exist so far, all of them in Bridgetown, producing for the local market. The construction of industrial plants is planned on the raised area of the new harbour; another small industrial area already exists north of Bridgetown. The idea behind the very costly construction of the new harbour was to take advantage of the island's position out in the Atlantic by offering duty-free transit trade and bunker opportunities. A free trade agreement with Antigua and Guyana was signed in 1968 (cf. p. 99) to improve the economic situation.

The active port of Bridgetown has for a long time handled the entire foreign trade. The divided central part of the city, Bridgetown's present commercial centre, lies on either side of the old Carenage harbour, which is in fact the narrow estuary of the Constitution River which is crossed by a bridge, giving the city its name. The town has expanded, mainly along the roads, far into the interior in all directions, very irregularly in some parts, elsewhere in large, uniform settlements, which are the only areas where one finds a geometrical layout. Streets laid out in a grid pattern are not found in any other parts of Bridgetown, including the old town. The uplifted marine terraces have most often been chosen as residential areas, and along the coast, especially east of Hastings, a long row of impressive villas and a number of hotels have been built. Numerous roads lead like the spokes of a wheel from Bridgetown into the interior. They have handled all traffic since the only railway line stopped operation before the Second World War. They are, however, so narrow in many places that lorries cannot pass. After half an hour's drive in any direction one comes to the end of the road, after one has already climbed over the slopes, often steep, of fossil cliffs, and if one is driving north-east, after one has negotiated the sharp twists and turns down the steep coral limestone cuesta scarp. The roads are asphalted and there are numerous cross connections; Barbados has the most dense road network of all the Caribbean islands. The international airport in the south of the island offers excellent connections. The tourist industry is well developed and is still expanding. Many Englishmen choose Barbados as their winter resort because of its pleasant and healthy climate. In addition, the inhabitants of the neighbouring islands and of Venezuela like to spend their holidays there. It is the only Caribbean island where Americans do not make up the majority of the tourists. In 1964 20 000 of the 52 500 visitors came from Great Britain, 15 900 from the USA and 10 300 from Canada. 2000 hotel beds were available in 1964 in addition to several hundreds in private homes. The number of tourists rose to 137 600 in 1969. The central section of the west coast and the leeward section of the south coast east of Hastings are the most frequented tourist areas. The coast of the Scotland District around Bathsheba, which offers the most beautiful scenery, is not suitable for hotels because of the strong prevailing winds.

23
Trinidad and Tobago

Trinidad, the largest island of the Lesser Antilles, belonged to Spain before it became a British colony in 1797. Administratively the dissimilar islands of Trinidad and Tobago were united in 1889. After the collapse of the West Indies Federation, the Republic of Trinidad and Tobago received its independence in 1962.

Trinidad

Physical geography

The island has an area of 4828 sq km and is situated immediately off the Venezuelan coast from which it is separated by the Gulf of Paria which reaches a maximum depth of only 27 m. It is part of the South American mainland both topographically and structurally. This can also be seen by the unusually turbid sea water caused by the Orinoco sediments and by the large amount of driftwood along the shores.

Three parallel mountain ranges, running west to east and representing the continuation of the Venezuelan coastal cordillera, characterize the topography (Map 81). The Northern Range, which lies like a rampart to the north, shutting off the rest of the island, rises to 941 m in El Cerro del Aripo and to 937 m in El Tucuche. It is an almost inaccessible mountain region with deeply incised valleys and covered by tropical rain and montane forests. The mountains drop steeply to the north coast where only a very few settlements have developed, where no coastal plains exist, and which does not as yet have a road. Only two winding roads with steep gradients cross this range, offering magnificent views of the tropical green mountain world and of the sea. Narrow beaches fringed with palms exist only at Toco, Blanchisseuse and Maracas Bay.

A vast plain extends to the south of the Northern Range, made up mainly of alluvial sediments deposited by the Caroni river in the west and the northern Oropuche river in the east. Mangrove swamps stretch far into the interior along the mouth of the Caroni. The region between the Caroni and the Oropuche in the central part of the island consists of Pleistocene terraces of varying heights, which are covered by the Aripo savannas with their small, dispersed islands of woodland closely resembling the Venezuelan Llanos.

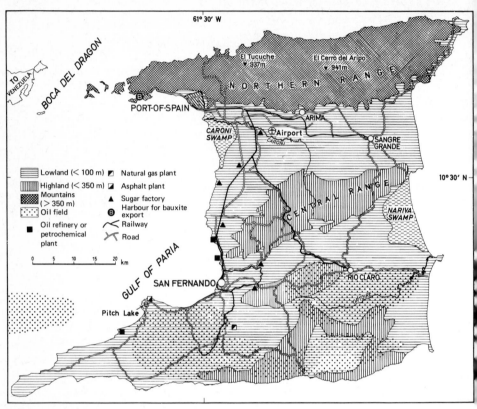

Map 81. Trinidad: regional divisions, industry and transport.

These northern plains change very slowly to the south into a wide mountain region, the Central Range, which runs south-west to north-east and has subdued relief. It hardly rises to more than 300 m and is not formed of metamorphic rock like the Northern Range, but mainly of Oligocene and Miocene limestones which were folded during the Andean orogeny. The Central Range is surrounded by hilly country, the 45 to 75 m high hillocks being remnants of the now dissected Naparima erosion surface which dates from early Pleistocene. It is very extensive, especially in the southern lowland between the Central and Southern Range. The broad valleys of the southern Oropuche river and of the Ortoire river are cut into this hilly country. The former flows to the west coast, forming the Oropuche Lagoon; the latter flows into the Nariva Swamp, the largest mangrove swamp in the island (83 sq km), which is separated from the sea by a 23 km long and completely straight beach ridge covered with coconut trees.

360

The relatively low Southern Range, built from Tertiary sedimentary rocks, is divided into several chains running south-west to north-east. Only the Trinity Hills in the southern chain reach an altitude of 303 m. Tropical rain forests cover the Southern Range which is still today very hostile to settlement and traffic. The low-lying southern peninsula which protrudes far towards the west has fossil beach ridges between Cedros and Icacos Point and represents a single compact coconut tree forest (Plate 29).

Trinidad's position between 10°N and 11°N means that the island is not touched by hurricanes so that tree cultivation does not have to withstand them as it does in most of the other islands. The position near the equator results in smaller variations of monthly average temperatures than is the case in islands further north (Port of Spain: 23·9°C in January, 25·6°C in September). Since the mountains are almost parallel to the direction of the trade winds rainfall decreases towards the west by the same amount on either side of the Northern Range. The difference in precipitation is not between the windward and leeward sides of this extensive mountain range but between its eastern and western regions, or between the eastern and western sections of its foreland. A broad tract, running north-south parallel to the coastline in eastern Trinidad, receives more than 2500 mm of rainfall annually. Even higher precipitation is experienced at higher altitudes of the Northern Range. The amount of rainfall decreases to below 1500 mm in the most western areas of the two western peninsulas (Map 82).

Semi-evergreen seasonal forests in the west, rain forests in the east and tropical montane forests in the Northern Range still cover extensive areas in Trinidad; 45 per cent of the island's surface is occupied by forests, primary forests to a large extent, where in contrast to all other Caribbean islands, South American floristic elements are dominant. 'Lastro' is also very common; this is a secondary scrub in areas cleared by burning in the course of shifting agriculture which have since reafforested themselves naturally. From the air, Trinidad looks even more forested than it really is since 62 per cent of the agricultural land is in tree crops.

Settlement and population

The Spanish colonization of the island, which was only sparsely populated by Arawak Indians, began more than three decades after its discovery by Columbus in 1498. The initially successful cocoa cultivations were so badly hit by insect pests in the early eighteenth century that many plantations were abandoned and the majority of the colonists left the island. In 1783 Trinidad had a population of only 2763 as against 14 200 people living on the neighbouring small island of Tobago. In 1790 new development occurred when French colonists arrived in the island, most of them refugees from St Domingue (Haiti). They first turned to the cultivation of coffee and, after sugar production had broken down in Haiti, to sugar cane. Plantation-type

[1] 2032 Asian Indians, 126 whites, 310 Negro slaves, and 295 free Negroes.

sugar cane cultivation expanded greatly under British colonial rule. When slavery was abolished in 1834 there were only 21 000 slaves in Trinidad. The manpower shortage on sugar cane plantations was felt even more strongly after many of the former slaves settled as smallholders in the woodland far from the coast. The sugar industry became dependent, therefore, on indentured labourers from India who were brought to the island in larger numbers after 1846. About 75 per cent of the 140 000 workers who were brought to Trinidad from India within the next seven decades remained in the island and their descendants form 40 per cent of the present population. Negroes and mulattoes together make up not more than 55 per cent. The white population, about 2 per cent, is of English, Spanish, French or Portuguese descent. Chinese make up about 1 per cent of the population, and there are more Lebanese than in other islands. Although English is the generally accepted language, French patois and Spanish are spoken in some places as well as various Hindi dialects. This colourful racial and ethnic population structure which is unique in the Caribbean produces a corresponding multitude of religions. In addition to the Catholic Church and numerous Protestant denominations a large number of Hindus and Muslims have preserved their original faith. Racial groups hardly ever mix and the relations between Negroes and Indians are sometimes tense. On the whole, they live separated from each other in different regions with the western plains—the cane areas—mainly inhabited by Asian Indians, whilst they are almost completely absent in other areas. In addition, Negroes represent a much higher percentage of the urban population than Asian Indians.

The considerable population increase from 558 000 in 1946 to 795 000 in 1960 was caused, among other reasons, by a heavy immigration from the neighbouring Islands to the Windward (1970 Census indicates population is 942 210). The density of population is high: 166 persons per sq km. Both the Northern and Southern Range as well as the extensive swamp areas are sparsely inhabited or even completely unpopulated. The population is concentrated in the western coastal regions along the Gulf of Paria where the towns of San Fernando (pop. 40 000) and Port-of-Spain (pop. 94 000) have developed at the southern and the northern corner of the Gulf respectively.

Port-of-Spain has been Trinidad's capital since 1774. It is a modern city which has achieved a major position as regards administration, trade and cultural life. It has a geometrical layout and is built on the small alluvial fan of the Maraval and St Ann's river. Its expansion is limited by the sea, the Northern Range and the Caroni swamp. Space for the jetties and the other harbour installations which were completed in 1939 and accommodate sea-going vessels could only be provided by filling in part of the Gulf of Paria. The city can only grow towards the east, and an almost continuously settled tract of varying width, including all the settlements from San Juan, St Joseph, Tunapuna and Tacarigua to Arima (pop. 11 000) 25 km away, has developed along the eastern main road at the foothills of the Northern

Range. The new industrial area, which has been under construction since 1959, has also been established in the east along the Churchill-Roosevelt Highway, a fast road connecting the city centre with Piarco airport 25 km away.

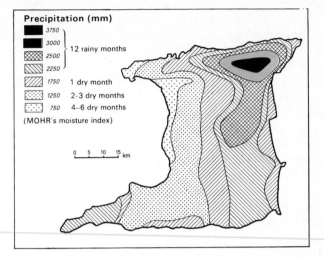

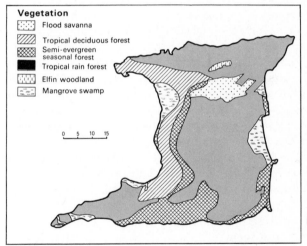

Map 82. Trinidad: precipitation and vegetation (after Imperial College of Tropical Agriculture, Trinidad).

An excellent view of the urban area may be obtained from the mountains rising to the north of the city. Privileged residential areas have developed here, Ellerslie Park and, beyond the beautiful botanical garden, St Ann's. Another comprehensive view is seen from Belmont Hill, the site of the tall Trinidad Hilton Hotel. The urban area has a planned layout with the modern commercial district occupying the old city which is centred on the spacious Woodford Square, flanked by the Anglican Cathedral, the im-

363

pressive administrative building, the Red House, and the modern town hall. Associated with the multitude of faiths, a large number of churches can be found in the urban area and its surrounding districts, among which are mosques and Hindu temples (Plate 31). The narrow streets in the centre are flanked by multistorey buildings and only allow one-way traffic. People of all races crowd the pavements, especially in Frederick Street, the main shopping street.

Adjacent to the city centre in the north lies the 80 ha Queen's Park Savannah where cricket and football are played and which includes a racecourse. To the west lies St Clair, a superior residential area, and the more densely settled New Town mainly inhabited by Chinese. West of the city centre poorer residential areas, with a mainly Negro population, stretch along the waterfront near the harbour. The St Ann's River which repeatedly flooded the city centre has been channelled into a concrete riverbed at the eastern edge of the alluvial fan. Beyond this river slums of poor wooden huts cover mountainous countryside. The poorest huts, built from boxes and cans, lie east of the city at the edge of the Caroni swamp which is much frequented by flocks of ibis. Government and administrative buildings, as well as hospitals and schools, may be found isolated or in groups in various sections of the city. St Augustine about 8 km to the east is the site of the famous Imperial College of Tropical Agriculture which has been integrated into the University of the West Indies (Kingston, Jamaica) as a Faculty of Agriculture.

Intracity transport is provided by buses and especially by shared taxis. Because of its importance as the capital city, Port-of-Spain, though on the island's periphery, has developed both as the focal point of local road and railway transport and the largest harbour for international shipping. The volume of traffic at Piarco airport is the largest of all the Lesser Antilles.

The majority of the rural population lives in nucleated settlements, especially in the sugar plantation areas where the Asian Indian labourers are usually settled in geometrically laid out villages. Terrace houses are the rule; the buildings, especially in new settlements, are concrete and rest on high stilts and are surrounded by small gardens. A number of former plantations were resettled and new settlements were also established on state land. The establishment of new settlements on 8100 ha of state land is planned for the period 1967–71. The mountain areas are only penetrated by dispersed and squatter-like settlements along the valley slopes. The oil industry added another feature to the appearance of the settlement pattern when living quarters were built for the workers and villas for the European and American employees.

Agriculture

Agricultural land covers about half the island's surface; 42 per cent is in small farms of less than 20 ha, 44 per cent in large farms of over 80 ha. The agricultural landscape may therefore be divided, as in the other islands, into two very different economic formations: peasant economy and large-scale enterprises. Export-orientated cultivation, mainly of sugar cane and cocoa, is important in both. Sugar cane characterizes the lowland in the west, cocoa the hilly and mountainous regions in the centre, with coconut trees in the numerous coastal sections (Plate 29). Thus in Trinidad, three different agricultural landscapes may be distinguished, each of which is divided into the two economic formations mentioned above (Map 83 and Plate 30). James justly interprets this distinct regional separation of different crop areas as the result of adjustment to the physical surroundings, a process which has been going on for decades and in successive stages.

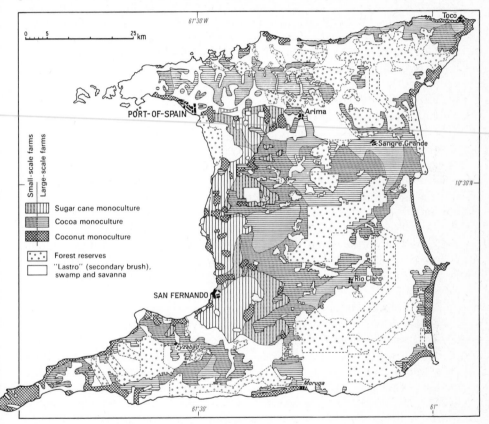

Map 83. Trinidad: land use and farming systems.

The agriculturally productive areas covers 135 000 ha, amounting to about half the total farmland. Although sugar cane is only cultivated on 33 000 ha (as against 48 500 ha under cocoa) sugar heads the list by value: six factories produced 240 000 tonnes in 1968. Between 1900 and 1920, until Trinidadian cultivation decreased because of African competition and insect pests, cocoa was the island's main export commodity; at present, it is

365

mainly cultivated in the Central Range and its surrounding hilly districts. Cocoa production has been on the increase again in recent years after state seed testing and plant breeding farms started to provide planters with one million plants annually. However, the value of cocoa exports only amounts to one-sixth of that of sugar. The harvest from coconut plantations (14 000 ha) is not exported at all, the entire crop is processed locally into oils, fats and soap. The cultivation of citrus for export (> 5000 ha), mainly grapefruit and oranges, is relatively young. Fresh fruit and juice are exported. Former cocoa valleys in the Northern Range, e.g. the Santa Cruz Valley near Port-of-Spain, are now almost entirely taken over by citrus trees. Food crops are cultivated on all peasant farms but the output is insufficient. Neither does rice production meet the local demand, although nearly 8000 ha of wet rice are cultivated by Asian Indian peasants in the western plain. Trinidad has to import more foodstuffs than Jamaica which has a population twice as large.

Mining and industry

At the present time, mining has achieved a much more important role in the economy of Trinidad than agriculture. The workable iron ore deposits in the Northern Range have not yet been developed. So far, only the production of asphalt and mineral oil are of importance.

Trinidad has the world's largest natural asphalt deposit near La Brea in the south-western part of the island near the coast; this is the famous, nearly circular, Pitch Lake with an area of about 40 ha which has been exploited for the last few decades. The asphalt is fluid in some sections but for the most part it is solid to the extent that it can be dug or dredged. A narrow-gauge railway and, recently, lorries, transport the asphalt to the processing plant in Brighton. Only half the annual production (189 200 tonnes in 1964) is exported.

The mineral oil deposits in the south of the island are Trinidad's most important resource at present. However, they only consist of dispersed and small deposits which are difficult to detect and costly to exploit. In various places the mineral oil also reaches the surface naturally, as in the Pitch Lake and, in smaller quantities, in numerous mud volcanoes where hydrocarbon penetrates through clayey layers and, together with mineral oil, appears at the surface. Numerous derricks and pumps may be seen in southern Trinidad and in the shallow waters of the Gulf of Paria. A network of pipelines covers the island. The oil companies have built roads as well as settlements in the formerly impassable Southern Range. Two large refineries have been built at Point Fortin and Pointe-à-Pierre, the former owned by the British, the latter by Americans. They not only process the output from Trinidad and the continental shelf, but also imported oil from Colombia, Venezuela and the Middle East. Both refineries were built on the coast, and their loading platforms with the pipelines protrude far into the shallow water of the Gulf of Paria. Their capacity was expanded from

5·8 to 17·3 million tonnes between 1955 and 1964. In 1963 a petrochemical industry was added to the oil refineries. More than 18 000 persons are employed by the oil and petrochemical industry which supplied 35 per cent of the inland revenue and 75 per cent of the exports by value in 1964. Oil production totalled about 6 million tonnes representing only 0·5 per cent of world production.

The Industrial Development Board, established in 1959, is endeavouring to provide a wider basis for Trinidad's economy, employing the methods used by Puerto Rico in its industrialization programme. By 1965, 116 new industrial plants had been established, employing 12 000 workers and producing various consumer goods, some for export only. At present industrial development is in full swing. The construction of a shipyard is planned for Tembladora, and of steel-works for Port-of-Spain.

Transport and trade

Trinidad has a well-developed road network supporting its economic development: 6500 km of all-weather roads exist in the island and even most of the country roads are asphalted. Extensive areas in the Southern and Northern Range, however, have not yet been opened to traffic. The absence of a road along the north coast affects tourism greatly and future planning will have to take this into consideration. The tourist industry will certainly have increased since the completion of the Scotland Bay's Hotel begun in 1967 on the Boca de Monos at the western end of the Northern Range.

The national railway network is 175 km long and connects Port-of-Spain with San Fernando, Arima, and Rio Claro (south of the central part of the Central Range). The passenger service has become unprofitable owing to the good roads and the cheap fares of buses and shared taxis.

Most tourists come to Trinidad by air. The international Piarco airport offers many connections to the neighbouring islands as well as to North and South America and to Europe. Foreign trade is not concentrated in the busy harbour of Port-of-Spain to such an extent as it is in many other Caribbean capitals. This is because oil, asphalt and much of the sugar are not exported from Port-of-Spain. The two harbours of Tembladora and Chaguaramas, both to the west of Port-of-Spain and the latter within a former US base, are transhipment ports for bauxite. Small boats carry bauxite from Surinam and Guyana across the shallow Gulf of Paria to these ports where it is either stored in warehouses or immediately transhipped on to large ore freighters to be transported to the USA, to Canada and to Norway.

The volume of Trinidad's foreign trade far surpasses that of all the Islands to the Windward and even that of several island republics in the Greater Antilles. It totalled US $757 million in 1966 showing a slight balance of trade deficit. Exports are headed by mineral oil and mineral oil products making up 79 per cent, followed by chemicals which account for 8 per cent and thirdly by sugar, about 5 per cent. Approximately half the total of imports consists of petroleum, and 11 per cent foodstuffs; 30 per cent of the imports originate in Venezuela, 17 per cent in Great Britain and 14 per cent in Saudi-Arabia. Exports are 34 per cent to the USA and 14 per cent to Great Britain.

Tobago

The narrow island of Tobago, 32 km north-east of Trinidad and extending from south-west to north-east, covers an area of only 300 sq km and is built mainly of metamorphic and volcanic rocks. The Main Ridge, nearer to the north coast, is the backbone of the island. It is covered with tropical rain and montane forests and reaches a maximum height of 572 m. Precipitation is especially high to the north-west; in the low-lying coral limestone plateaux in the south-western part of the island, however, rainfall amounts to less than 1250 mm, resulting in frequent water shortages.

Tobago's economic development has taken a completely different course to that of the large neighbouring island. Tobago repeatedly changed hands, finally becoming British in 1803. When the island was under Dutch rule for a short period in the seventeenth century sugar cane cultivation was introduced. By the end of the eighteenth century a flourishing plantation economy, based on sugar cane, had developed. Old sugar mills remain as reminders of that period. Tobago had a population of 14 200 in 1776[1], five times the size of Trinidad's, which is eighteen times the area. While Trinidad developed and expanded its modern plantation economy in the course of the nineteenth century, the plantations in Tobago fell into decay. Tree crops replaced sugar cane, and large areas of the former plantations were cultivated by peasants, either the owners of their land or tenants mostly paying in kind. A large number of old plantations have been resettled since the late nineteenth century (Map 84), but plantations still occupy the coastal strip around the island which is considerably wider on the windward side where the best land is, than on the leeward side. Peasant farming areas sometimes interrupt these coastal plains but in general they are situated at higher altitudes between the large farms near the coast and the montane forests.

Agricultural land covers about 75 per cent of the island's surface, the productive land about 40 per cent (12 000 ha). Cocoa and coconut trees are the two main crops. The landscape of coconut monoculture (copra production) surrounds the island in a narrow ribbon; cocoa monoculture follows towards the interior, with bananas and especially *Erythrina* and *Gliricidia* serving as shade trees, as in Trinidad. Tobago is an island of tree crops. Hidden among these lie the settlements hardly detectable from the air.

The large majority of the population is Negro. Only a few mulattoes and whites live here. The density of population, 116 persons per sq. km. is much lower than in Trinidad. Two major settlements have developed, the larger

---

[1] 2397 whites; 1050 free Negroes; 10 752 Negro slaves.

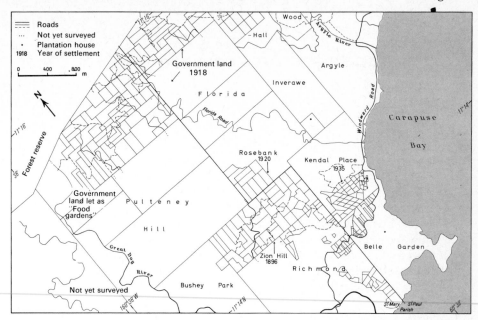

Map 84. Tobago: settlement schemes.

of the two, Scarborough, being the capital of the island with 2000 inhabitants. The road network in Tobago is still inadequate; several settlements along the north coast can only be reached by boat. Connection with the outside world is only provided via Trinidad, by a daily boat service between Scarborough and Port-of-Spain, and by the airport in the south-western part of the island which has flights from Trinidad several times a day. This has facilitated the strong development of the tourist industry in this very beautiful island with its excellent beaches in the numerous bays protected by coral reefs.

24

The Islands to the Leeward

West of Trinidad, within the South American north coast region, the climate becomes arid within a very short distance. Pronounced aridity determines the landscapes of the Islands to the Leeward off the Venezuelan mainland. The island group in the east belongs to Venezuela, the group in the west to the Netherlands.

The Venezuelan Islands to the Leeward

The Venezuelan Islands to the Leeward in the east are divided into a northern and a southern group of islands. The latter group which includes Margarita is by far the more important (Table 73).

Table 73.   The Venezuelan Islands to the Leeward

	Size sq km		Size sq km
Southern group:		Northern group:	
Los Testigos	4	Los Hermanos	4
Margarita	1150	La Blanquilla	45
Coche	43	Orchila	32
Cubagua	22	Las Roques	5
Tortuga	140	Aves Islands	2
Total	1359	Total	88

The Southern Group

Margarita

Margarita and the islands of Coche and Cubagua constitute the Venezuelan state of Nueva Esparta with a population of 89 492 in 1961 and a density of 74 persons per sq km. In view of its aridity these figures indicate overpopula-

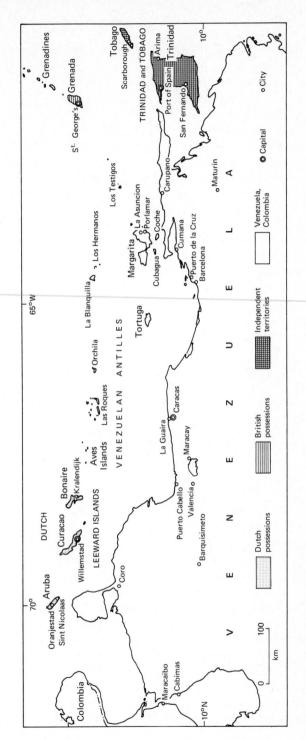

Map 85. The Islands to the Leeward.

371

tion. The inhabitants of Margarita are mestizos with a considerable number of pure-blooded Guayquerí Indians.

The vast majority of the population lives in the eastern part of the island. The western part has only one settlement, otherwise it is unpopulated. Margarita really consists of two islands, Macanao to the west and Margarita proper to the east. They are linked by a narrow isthmus (Istmo Restinga) 25 km long. The lagoon to the south of this strip, with its highly indented mangrove shores, used to serve as one of the filibusters' favourite hideouts. Mountains, built of metamorphic and intrusive rocks, rise in the centre of both parts of the island to 920 m in the Pico San Juan in the eastern part. They are fragments of the Venezuelan coastal cordillera. The lowlands are covered by cactus and thorn scrub savannas changing very quickly into tropical deciduous and semi-evergreen seasonal forests and into tropical montane forests in the mountain region which, especially in the eastern island part, receives heavy rainfall from the trade winds. The moisture of the often cloudy mountains facilitates cultivation along the foothills and especially in the valleys and their slopes. Essentially it is aridity which is responsible for the very limited amount of cultivation relative to the island's size and population; this results in overpopulation, in turn causing a high emigration rate to the Venezuelan mainland. Natural pastures occupy the greater part of the productive land offering meagre grazing, mainly for goats. The intensively used agricultural area only occupies 3·1 per cent of the island's surface and is almost equally divided between permanent and shifting agriculture. The fields of the latter, called *conucos*, are dispersed along valley slopes and are cleared by burning. Their crops depend on rainfall. The permanently used fields, called *labranzas*, occupy the valley bottoms and the flat regions, mainly alluvial fans, near the mountains. These are irrigated and used for the cultivation, mainly in peasant multi-cropping, of manioc, sweet potatoes, maize, coconuts, bananas, sugar cane, and beans. Almost every homestead possesses a garden (*solar*) where the women grow food crops for their family's needs. It remains to be seen whether the recently completed water pipeline from the mainland to Coche and Margarita will result in the expansion of the cultivated area.

The production of salt and fishing, in particular, have for a long time been the main bases of Margarita's economy. The abundance of fish in the surrounding sea is expressed by the term Paraguachoa, the name for the island formerly used by the Indians. It is very impressive to watch the hauling in of the huge nets at Pampatar beach. The fishermen seize the fish with their hands and throw them on to the beach, they are then dried in the parching sun on stones or wooden structures, some of them are salted, and most are shipped to the mainland market. Pearl fishing, practised in pre-Columban times, is again carried on in Margarita under government control.

After Columbus had discovered the island in 1498 the Spaniards were attracted by the still famous pearl banks of Cubagua where they built the

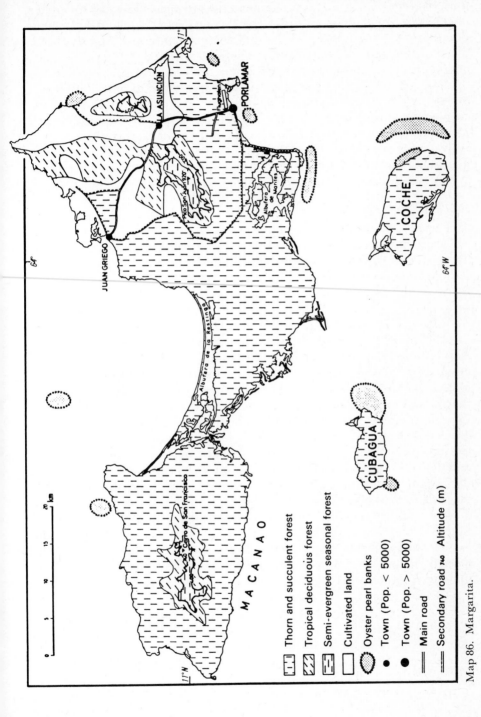

Map 86. Margarita.

Thorn and succulent forest
Tropical deciduous forest
Semi-evergreen seasonal forest
Cultivated land
Oyster pearl banks
Town (Pop. < 5000)
Town (Pop. > 5000)
Main road
Secondary road ∼ Altitude (m)

MACANAO

Cerro de San Francisco

Albufera de la Restinga

JUAN GRIEGO

Albufera de Monties

Pico San Juan 1970

LA ASUNCIÓN

PORLAMAR

COCHE

CUBAGUA

town of Nueva Cádiz. They abandoned the town in 1543 when the oyster banks were exhausted; its ruins, partly uncovered after 1954, are reminders of that early stage of Spanish colonization. On Margarita itself, the friendly capital of La Asunción (pop. 5000) at the foot of the Copey mountains in the interior possesses various architectural remains from the Spanish colonial period in its fortress, its churches and its low middle-class buildings. This town does not have a grid pattern street layout. The economic centre of the island is the port, Porlamar, on the south coast, which has regular boat services with La Guaira; its airport offers several daily flights to Maiquetía (Caracas). Porlamar is the only site of the flourishing tourist industry. The vast majority of the tourists are Venezuelans for whom Margarita is a favourite holiday resort.

Los Testigos and Tortuga

The small and mountainous island group of Los Testigos 85 km east of Margarita formed of intrusive rocks, and the much larger island of Tortuga 85 km west of Margarita, mostly flat and built from coral limestone, are not settled permanently and do not have any economic value.

The Northern Group

Most the small islands belonging to the northern group of the Venezuelan Antilles, from Los Hermanos in the east to the Aves Islands in the west, are uninhabited and usually lack water. In Table 73 they are listed from west to east. During the filibuster period, however, they provided hideouts off the Spanish mainland coast. In the middle of the nineteenth century, they were the source of guano deposits for the production of fertilizers and for a few decades, phosphate and guano were found mainly on Gran Roque and the Aves Islands. Some of them are inhabited by both sea and land birds and their dry and sun-warmed rocks swarm with lizards. The tasty meat of the *Iguana delicatissima* used to be an essential part of the filibusters' diet. Since then, most of the islands have been crowded by goats, and according to their number the vegetation has been changed to a greater or lesser degree. There is no longer any doubt that overgrazing has caused the present dominance of cactus plants in the Islands to the Leeward. The formerly extensive tropical deciduous forests have been replaced by sometimes impenetrable cactus thickets.

25

The Dutch Islands to the Leeward

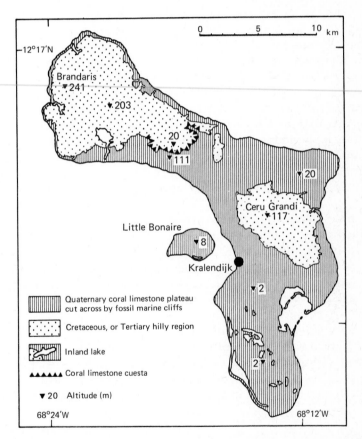

Map 87. Bonaire: geological structure (after Pijpers, Westermann, and Zonneveld).

The three Dutch Islands to the Leeward (Table 74) represent the final western parts of the Lesser Antilles. These islands resemble each other very closely in their structure. The islands' cores are formed not only of

375

various types of sedimentary rocks but also of Cretaceous rocks, mainly of volcanic origin, which provide impressive examples of hollow block weathering, especially in Aruba. Pleistocene coral limestone is deposited around the edges of these island cores. As in Barbados, the boundaries between these limestones and the underlying layers sometimes appear in the landscape as very distinct, well-developed cuestas. Erosional remnants of the coral limestone are shaped like mesas: the Curaçao Tafelberg, which is 193 m high, is an example to one of these steep-edged limestone blocks. It is visible from the sea for great distances. Coral limestone is most common in Bonaire where it makes up 70 per cent of the surface (Map 87). Stepped marine terraces have developed along the islands' coastlines (Plate 32). Alexander has made an attempt to correlate and date them. Large bays (*bocas*) which interrupt the coasts of the Dutch Islands to the Leeward, e.g. the Schottegat in Curaçao, make excellent natural harbours. Recently, they have been interpreted as fluviatile valley landscapes flooded by the postglacial rise of the sea-level (Wilhelmy). The existence of a wetter climate in the past is indicated both by the dendritic pattern of fossil valleys (*roois*) in which water flows intermittently nowadays owing to the aridity, and by the cuestas which are heavily embayed by springline erosion. In addition, red earth in the karst limestone plateaux and fossil dripstone formations and vertebrates in the limestone caves point to one or several pluvial periods. The very common cactus vegetation seems to have been caused by overgrazing here also. All of the widespread dividivis (*Caesalpinia coriaria*) in the cactus savannas exhibit a distinct wind shearing towards the west due to the strong and continuous blowing of the trade winds.

The three islands were first settled by the Spaniards. The Dutch established themselves after 1634, but the islands only came into Dutch possession in 1816. Favoured by its proximity to the mainland, Willemstad in Curaçao became the emporium and stockyard for smuggled goods. In spite of their very similar natural conditions the development of the population and the economy of the three islands showed considerable differences even during the colonial period and still does today. Although the population is very heterogeneous racially, a local language, Papiamento, developed during the eighteenth century. It is a conglomerate of Spanish, Portuguese, Dutch, English, Indian and African elements. Each of the islands has its own internal government and is represented in the Parliament of the Dutch Antilles in Curaçao according to its population size.

Bonaire

Bonaire has never achieved economic importance. Before the abolition of slavery it served exclusively as a slave market, supplying slaves to the Curaçao plantations. Negroes and mulattoes in a few villages make up the population, greatly reduced during recent decades by emigration to

Table 74.   The Dutch Islands to the Leeward: size and population,
1963

	Size sq km	Population	Density of population persons per sq km
Bonaire	288	6086	21
Curaçao	443	129676	293
Aruba	190	58506	307
Total	921	194268	211

Curaçao. Meagre farming serves the local demand, facilitated by the
so-called tanks: dams built in the dry valleys to store up the water that
drains into them after the winter rainfall. The only export crop, aloes,
does not depend on irrigation. This plant was imported from Africa and its
juice is used for pharmaceutical purposes. Extensive salt pans are situated
in the Pekelmeer Lagoon on the south-west coast of the low-lying, flat
southern part of the island which is formed entirely of coral limestone.In
their neighbourhood flocks of flamingoes can be observed on the dunes of the
lonely spit of land. The quiet town of Kralendijk is the main settlement in
this island, much of which is still untouched. There is a daily flight to
Curaçao, and tourism started with the construction of a modern hotel,
completed in 1963.

Curaçao

Curaçao developed as a plantation colony under Dutch colonial rule.
Sugar cane was cultivated in spite of the unfavourable climatic conditions
and throughout the island impressive plantations indicate that period.
Today only a very few vegetable gardens and fruit trees are to be found,
irrigated with water from water tanks and wells and forming small islands
of lush green amidst the dreary cactus and thorn scrub savannas which
cover the entire island. In the past, Curaçao exported dried bitter orange
peel to the Netherlands, where the world-famous Curaçao liqueur was
produced. The former plantation economy and the recent industrialization
which attracted many immigrants from other islands of the Lesser Antilles
explain the high proportion of Negroes (90 per cent) among the population.
Because of the early trading function of Curaçao, Sephardic Jews who
immigrated from Portugal make up a high percentage of the white population.

   The collapse of the old plantation economy in the middle of the nineteenth century caused stagnation in Curaçao's economy. Seasonal work on
sugar plantations in the Greater Antilles and the cultivation of a few ground
crops provided the population with a very modest living. However,
Curaçao benefited from the completion of the Panama Canal, which

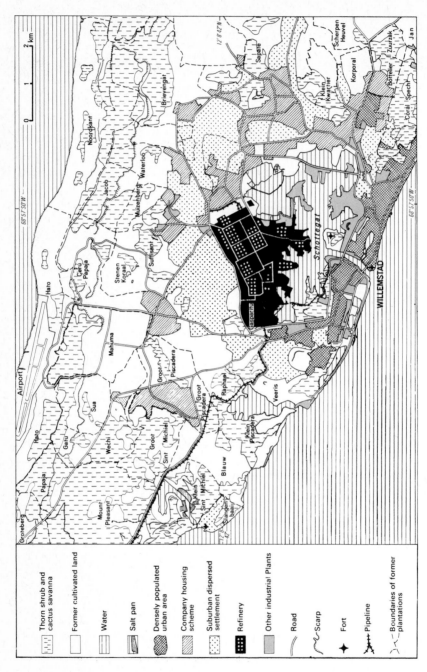

Map 88. Curaçao: Willemstad and Schottegat.

changed the island's position in regard to world shipping and led to the establishment of a bunkering station at Willemstad. Another important source of income was phosphate mining at the Tafelberg which started in the late nineteenth century. Limestone phosphate is deposited in coral limestone when rainwater dissolves the thick guano layers; 260 000 tonnes were mined in 1964, 75 per cent of which was exported to the USA. The amount of rubble (748 100 tonnes in 1964) is increasing so much that the profitability of mining has become dubious.

Curaçao's economic situation changed suddenly when the Curaçaose Petroleum Industrie Maatschappij (CPIM), today called the Shell Curaçao NV, started to construct their enormous refinery after the First World War. The population, only 43 000 in 1915, had increased to 91 000 by 1938. Proximity to the Venezuelan mainland also helped to improve Curaçao's economic situation.

The refinery on the Schottegat (Map 88) has an annual capacity of 10·5 million tonnes. It obtains crude oil from the Venezuelan oil fields and, of late, from Colombia, and exports the refined oil all over the world. The same is true of the Lago Refinery in Aruba owned by the Standard Oil Company, which has an annual capacity of 23·5 million tonnes and is among the largest in the world. Both refineries are equipped with extensive bunker facilities and are much frequented by international shipping. Owing to their oil industry the Dutch Antilles' volume of foreign trade totalled US $1426 million in 1961, only slightly less than that of Puerto Rico, and amounting to US $7239 per capita of the population as against $680 in Puerto Rico and $19 in Haiti. In 1963 mineral oil products supplied 98·5 per cent of the exports (1968: 86 per cent), and oil accounted for 84 per cent of all imports. In view of this unbalanced economic structure the necessity for industrial diversification has been realized. So far, however, next to nothing has been accomplished apart from the expanding tourist industry. Only small industrial plants for the manufacture of consumer goods have been established. The construction of an aluminium factory is planned. Nearly all the consumer goods have to be imported as well as almost the entire food demand.

Industrialization has been urgent in the 1960s since numerous workers in Curaçao and Aruba have lost their jobs through increasing automation in the refineries, but this may well be put right by the introduction of by-product industries in the future. In 1956 the oil industry employed 40 per cent of the labour force, but only 18 per cent in 1964. The Curaçao refinery employed 7000 persons in 1952, but only 4000 in 1966; 7000 and 2000 are the respective figures for the refinery in Aruba. Owing to this reduction, 25 per cent of the labour force were unemployed in 1966. The first to be dismissed were labourers from other Caribbean islands who migrated back to their home countries. A considerable number, growing every month, mainly of young people have emigrated to the Netherlands since 1965 because of the lack of employment opportunities. Light industry, mainly assembly is being developed, but there are still only a few firms, despite Government money and incentives. Clothing, transistor radios, paints, beer and cigarettes are manufactured for local consumption.

Willemstad, with the old city of Punda on the one side and the new city of Otrabanda on the other side of the narrow inlet to the Schottegat, is the only urban settlement in Curaçao. The new geometrically laid out residential areas built for the workers and employees of the refinery, interspersed with many parks and gardens, surround the wide bay. Old Fort Nassau, on a hill 58 m above Willemstad, offers a splendid view of the town, the Schottegat with its refinery and cracking plants, the oil tanks, the berths for the tankers and the bunker piers; it is an impressive view both by day and by night.

Punda, the old city on the east side of the Sint Anna Baai which is the access to the Schottegat, is the shopping centre. Sailors and visitors alike are attracted by the duty-free goods in Willemstad, and even Venezuelans are not reluctant to take the one-hour flight from Caracas in order to exploit the favourable shopping opportunities in Willemstad: 87000 tourists visited the island in 1964. The airport, which has a large volume of international traffic, was built 10 km away on the north coast. The boats of Venezuelan vendors moor along the jetty of the de Ruyter Kade offering a variety of colourful fruits and vegetables. Another attraction is the architectural design of Willemstad. The narrow multistorey buildings along the Brede and Heeren Straats (Plate 33) look as though they have been transplanted from the Netherlands. The view of the colourful façades along the Handelskade from the Koningin Emma Brug leading across the Sint Anna Baai is very famous. One is reminded of a canal in a Dutch city with its tall, slender eighteenth-century office buildings. The Governor's Palace and Fort Amsterdam at the entrance to the Sint Anna Baai have yellow and white walls and red tiled roofs, and are fine examples of Dutch colonial architecture. The large synagogue, dating from 1732, is located in the commercial district north of the Brede Straat. It demonstrates the past and present importance of the Jews in Curaçao's economic life.

Aruba

The native population of Aruba differs from that of the neighbouring islands in that it is composed of mestizos. Pure-blooded Indians were living in Aruba as late as the nineteenth century.

A plantation economy never developed, and peasant farming still predominates. Stone walls and cacti fence in the fields which are dispersed through the cactus savanna. However, industrialization, which started in 1929 when the Lago Refinery was built (cf. p. 379), is responsible for the great reduction in cultivated land. Extensive areas of formerly carefully cultivated terraced fields are now overgrown with cacti and thorn scrub. The rural population still lives in clean and attractive red and white stone

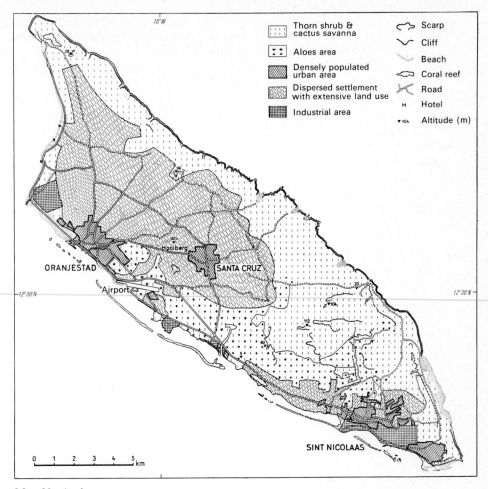

Map 89. Aruba.

buildings. Aruba still exports aloes, although cultivation is greatly reduced; it used to provide 30 per cent (Bonaire 20 per cent) of the total world production.

For a short while in the nineteenth century gold was mined in Aruba. Old adits in the island's diorite core as well as the ruins of a former processing plant on the Spaans Lagoen are relics of that period. But the oil industry alone has led to the economic boom and a considerable increase of the population (from 8000 in 1924 to 58 500 in 1963). The Lago Refinery was not built near the capital of Oranjestad; it was constructed near the south-eastern point of the island where Sint Nicolaas developed as a second town, a racially mixed settlement for workers. On the other side of the refinery an exclusive and spacious bungalow settlement was established for the American employees. Unlike Curaçao, the native labourers

381

employed by the oil industry do not live in new housing schemes near the refinery but in small settlements dispersed throughout the island. They are brought by bus to their places of work. The Lago Refinery, like the refinery in Curaçao, has much frequented bunkering installations.

The small refinery in Drūif, north-west of Oranjestad, built by Shell simultaneously with the Lago Refinery, has repeatedly closed down for several years. Since 1963 an export orientated petro-chemical plant and a fertiliser plant have been added in dependency on the big Lago Refinery of the Standard Oil Co.

The large demand for water for the industries on this arid island is met by a desalination plant which the government built in 1959 half-way between Oranjestad and Sint Nicolaas. This plant has a daily capacity of 2·2 million imperial gallons (10 000 m³). Two similar plants in Curaçao have a daily capacity of 2·75 million gallons (12 500 m³). The water shortage in Aruba has also led to the establishment of an hydroponic farm near Oranjestad where vegetables are cultivated in a nutrient fluid.

The tourist industry developed greatly during the 1960s, favoured by frequent air services mainly to North America and Venezuela. The large Aruba Caribbean Hotel, the first to be completed in 1959, and various other modern hotels benefit from the beautiful sand shore in the island's north-west. The two islands of Aruba and Curaçao have, without doubt, experienced an important economic growth as a result of the oil industry. However, their economy is up to now extremely unbalanced and entirely dependent on oil imports from the South American mainland.

Abbreviations

AAAG	*Annals of the Assocation of American Geographers*
CER	*Caribbean Economic Review*
CG	*The Canadian Geographer*
CQ	*Caribbean Quarterly*
CS	*Caribbean Studies*
EG	*Economic Geography*
JIAS	*Journal of Inter-American Studies*
MWR	*Monthly Weather Review*
	Washington
SES	*Social and Economic Studies*
	Jamaica, University of the West Indies, Institute of Social and Economic Research

2 Fourneaux   3 Formes   4 Vinaigrerie   5 Cannes   SVCRERIE   6 Gros   7 Latanir   8 Pajomirioba   9 Choux   10 Cases   11 Figuir
et Chaudieres.   de Sucre   Cocos p iic p iic   p 32   Caraibes   de Negres

1 Seventeenth century sugar factory in the French Antilles (from: Père J.-B. Du Tertre, *Histoire générale des Antilles*; Paris 1667–71, II, 122

2 Valle de Viñales in the Sierra de los Organos, Pinar del Río Province, Cuba. Steep karst haystack hills (*mogotes*) rise from the karst edge plain. Peasant tobacco fields and a tobacco shed in the centre.

3 Cuban Bohío near Viñales, Pinar del Río Province.

4 'La Rampa', the lower section of the Calle 23 near the coast in Vedado, centre of the new city of Habana. The hotel Habana Libre, formerly the Habana Hilton, in the background to the left

5 Santiago de Cuba. Numerous colonial buildings are preserved in the older part of the town where many stepped streets climb the uplifted marine terraces (foreground).

6 Jamaica. Section of an Interior Valley (polje) in the limestone plateaux in the south-western part of the island between the Nassau Mountains to the south and the Cockpit Country foothills to the north ('Me no sen you no come' District, known by the name of 'Look Behind'). The Black River meanders through the Appleton Valley (St Elizabeth parish) and is joined by the One Eye River on the left. Marginal solution created solitary limestone haystack hills (mogotes) now rising from the flat bottom of the Appleton Valley. The Kingston-Montego Bay railway line and a second class country road cross the central part of the picture. Between them lies the site of the former Raheen sugar factory which terminated operation owing to land concentration within the sugar industry. A modern sugar factory has developed at Appleton 5 km to the west. Agriculture in this plain is characterized by plantation-type sugar cane monoculture. Another farming system, peasant polyculture with small, irregular parcels small fields, can be recognized at the plain's edge towards the Nassau Mountains.
Scale: c. 1:14,000.

7 White limestone cone karst in the inaccessible Jamaican Cockpit Country. Elongated depressions (cockpits) and extended ridges divided into cones with karren flutings on the surface represent the main formations. Fault scarps or a regularly developed fault system have caused the linear pattern of the cockpits ('directed karst' after H. Lehmann). Scale c. 1:14,000.

8 Bauxite loading installations in Ocho Rios on the Jamaican north coast.

9 Bauxite resting on white limestone along a road west of Mandeville, Jamaica. The deep red bauxite earth lies in the depressions of the karst limestone plateaux.

10 Antiquated sugar cane press in the Artibonite Valley near Mirebalais, Haiti. Sugar cane in the background.

11 Market scene in Morne -des- Commissaires, Haiti. This market, far from any settlement, takes place each week amidst the pine forest of the Massif de la Selle at an altitude of 1600 m and is attended by the population of the northern and southern mountain slopes. It serves mainly the purpose of trading and exchanging smallholders' agricultural produce.

12 Constanza Valley in the upland of the Cordillera Central in the Dominican Republic at an altitude of 1200 m. This valley's agriculture has been recently developed within the framework of colonization of the interior.

13 Peasant polyculture, mainly bananas, manioc and maize, in the Vega Real near Moca, Dominican Republic.

14 Street Scene in Hato Mayor, Dominican Republic. Hato Mayor is a small, central settlement on the boundary between the coastal plain of Santo Domingo (Llano de Seibo) and the highland of the Cordillera Oriental.

15 The eastern end of the island San Juan Antigua (Puerto Rico) with a view of the Laguna del Condado and its bridges leading to the district of Santurce with Miramar (right) and Condado (left). Numerous new hotel buildings concentrate along the Atlantic coast (top left), along the lagoon and at the eastern end of San Juan Antigua. San Juan has the highest volume of tourism among the West Indian islands.

16 Petroleum based power station west of Ponce in the southern coastal plain of Puerto Rico. Oil refineries and petrochemical plants constitute a new industrial centre near Tallaboa.

17 Plantation-type sugar cane cultivation in the southern coastal plain of Puerto Rico. Lafayette sugar factory.

18 Plantation-type pineapple and (beyond) sugar cane cultivation in the northern coastal plain of Puerto Rico near Arecibo. Cone karst in the background.

9 Peasant sugar cane farming (planting) in the cone karst region of the northern mountain country near Vega Baja, Puerto Rico.

0 Peasant coffee finca (resettlement of a former plantation) near Utuado in the Puerto Rican Central Cordillera with the drying-ground in front of the living quarters. Secondary forest in the background shading the coffee plants.

21 Section of the Virgin Islands archipelago looking eastward from St Thomas across the Pillsbury Sound towards St John (US Virgin Islands) in the background right and towards Tortola (British Virgin Islands) in the background left.

22 Main street with Danish colonial merchant buildings in Christiansted, St Croix, US Virgin Islands.

23 Irregular multicrop farming by smallholders in Grande Terre, Guadeloupe. Cultivation of manioc, yams, sweet potatoes, malanga, castor oil plants, bananas etc. on a clearing made by burning.

24 The dacitic domes of the Pitons in St Lucia, British Windward Islands.

25 St Lucia. Section of the south-western part of the island between the dacitic lava dome
of the 798 m high Gros Piton, casting a large shadow (top left), and the broad alluvial
fan of Desgaitiers which is dissected by the Dorée and Balembouche rivers. Steep cliffs
dominate the entire coastal section with a flat coast only at the mouth of the Choiseul
River where the only compact settlement (Choiseul) has developed and which is the
only place where the road around the island touches the coast. The volcanic central
mountain region is drained by numerous parallel valleys. Peasant polyculture with
markedly dispersed settlements has developed among the foothills of this region, whereas
coconut monoculture (plantations Desgaitiers, Mont Lezard and Parc) typifies the
alluvial fan of Desgaitiers. Scale: *c.* 1:40 000.

26 The 549 m high Quill Volcano at the southern end of St Eustatius, Dutch Islands to the Windward. Strongly developed ravines on the volcano slope. The *Cultuurvlakte* (cultivated plain) in the background which was intensively cultivated in previous times.

27 The edge of the coral limestone plateau in Barbados bordering the Tertiary hilly region of the Scotland District. Frequent rockslides, which are caused by strong sliding movements in the underlying impermeable rocks, occur along this section (near Edge Cliff) of the relatively linear Pleistocene coral limestone cuesta. The limestone plateau divided by dolines and dry valleys is covered mainly by plantation-type sugar cane monoculture. Scale: *c.* 1:11 500.

28 Schooner in the harbour of Pointe-à-Pitre, Guadeloupe, with passengers heading for the island of Marie Galante.

29 The southern peninsula of Trinidad reaching into the Serpent's Mouth. At the bottom of the picture surf approaches the alluvial coast which shows fossil beach-ridges and swampy, extensive lowlands (Great Icacos Lagoon). Agricultural landscape of coconut monoculture with large-scale enterprises predominant. Dwelling houses and farm buildings of the Constance Plantation near Corral Point (top left). Peasant farms along the branches of the ramified Great Icacos Lagoon. Scale: *c.* 1:25 000.

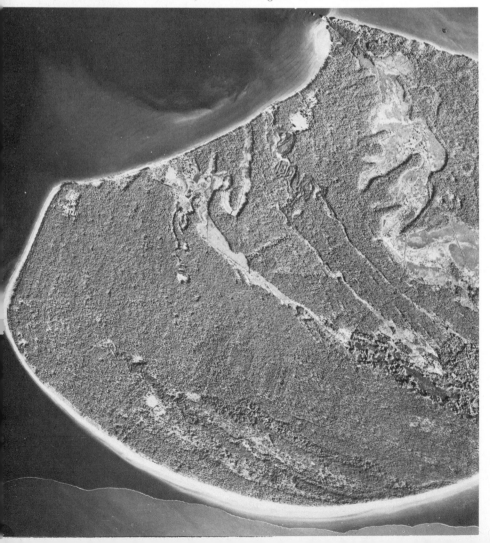

30 Trinidad. Agricultural landscape of sugar cane cultivation in the western coastal plain, south of the Caparo River (top of the picture). Large-scale farming characterizes the extensive, uniformly cultivated fields on either side of the railway line running south from Port-of-Spain to San Fernando. This line is straddled by a roadside village of Asian Indian workers (with two rows of houses in parts) in the centre of the picture. To the right of the picture small-scale farming can be seen at the eastern edge of the coastal plain with irregular plots of land, with ground crop cultivation (sugar cane) most important but also some tree crops in parts. Scale: *c.* 1:25 000.

31 Mosque and (in the background left) Anglican Church in Port-of-Spain, Trinidad.

32 Marine abrasion terraces and fossil cliffs in the Pleistocene coral limestone region of the arid island of Bonaire, Dutch Islands to the Leeward. Meagre cactus vegetation.

33 Heerenstraat, the main shopping street in Willemstad, Curaçao, Dutch Islands to the Leeward. Narrow, multistorey buildings with their gables on to the street create a Dutch atmosphere.

Bibliography (up to 1966)
The West Indies as a whole, and major subregions

Geographic Surveys

ARCINIEGAS, G. *Biografía del Caribe*, Buenos Aires 1945. Deutsch: *Karibische Rhapsodie*, Munich 1960.

AUGELLI, J., ed. *Caribbean Lands*, Grand Rapids 1965.

DEFFONTAINES, P. 'Mediterrâneo Americano e Mediterrâneo Europeu', *Bol. Paulista de Geografía* **21**, 1955, pp. 28–41.

DYER, D. R. *Lesser Antilles*, 2nd edn, Garden City 1964.

EYRE, A. *A New Geography of the Caribbean*, London 1962, 2nd edn, 1964.

GUIDES BLEUS, LES. *Antilles, Guyanes, Circuit des Caraibes*, Paris 1962.

HEPBURN, A. *Complete Guide to the Caribbean and Bahamas*, New York 1962.

HILL, R. T. *Cuba and Porto Rico with the Other Islands of the West-Indies*, London 1898.

IBERO-AMERIKA-VEREIN, ed. *Ibero-Amerika. Ein Handbuch*, ed. F. Wehner, 6th edn, Hamburg 1966.

JAMES, P. E. *Latin America*, New York 1942, 3rd edn, 1959.

JEFFERYS, TH. *The West-India Atlas*, London 1775.

KREBS, N. 'Westindien und Insulinde', in *Vergleichende Länderkunde*, Stuttgart 1951, pp. 284–97.

MACPHERSON, J. *Caribbean Lands, a geography of the West Indies*, London 1963.

MITCHELL, C. *Isles of the Caribbees*, Washington 1966.

PEARCY, G. E. *The West Indian Scene*, Princeton, NJ, 1965.

RÉVERT, E. *Les Antilles*, Paris 1954.

—— *La France d'Amérique*, Paris 1954.

—— *Entre les deux Amériques, le Monde Caraibe*, Paris 1958.

—— *Le Monde Caraibe*, Paris 1958.

SCHMIEDER, O. *Länderkunde Mittelamerikas. Westindien, Mexiko und Zentralamerika*, Leipzig and Vienna 1934.

—— *Die Neue Welt, 1. Teil Mittel- und Süd-amerika*, Heidelberg and Munich 1962.

SIEVERS, W. 'Die Inseln vor der Nordküste von Venezuela', *Globus* **74**, 1898, pp. 163–5, 291–4, 302–7.

SÖLCHER, V. *Die Antillen*, 2 vols, Stuttgart 1847.

SORRE, M. *Mexique, Amérique Centrale. Géographie Universelle*, **14**, Paris 1928.

TERMER, F. 'Mittelamerika und Westindien', in *Handbuch der Geogr. Wiss.*, ed. F. Klute, vol. *Nord- und Mittelamerika, Arktis*, Potsdam 1933, pp. 443–95.

WEST, R. C. and AUGELLI, J. *Middle America: its lands and peoples*, Englewood Cliffs, NJ, 1966.

WILGUS, A. C., ed. *The Caribbean*, Conferences on the Caribbean, School of Inter-American Studies, University of Florida, Gainesville, Fla., 1951 ff.
  1. *The Caribbean at Mid-Century* (1951)
  2. *The Caribbean: Peoples, Problems and Prospects* (1952)
  3. *The Caribbean: Contemporary Trends* (1953)

4. *The Caribbean: Its Economy* (1954)
5. *The Caribbean: Its Culture* (1955)
6. *The Caribbean: Its political Problems* (1956)
7. *The Caribbean: Contemporary international Relations* (1957)
8. *The Caribbean: British, Dutch, French, United States* (1958)
9. *The Caribbean: Natural Resources* (1959)
15. *The Caribbean: Its Health Problems* (1965)
16. *The Caribbean: Current United States Relations* (1966)

Periodicals:

Caribbean Quarterly, University of the West-Indies, Director of Extra-Mural Studies. Kingston/Jamaica.

Caribbean Monthly Bulletin, Institute of Caribbean Studies, University of Puerto Rico, Río Piedras 1963 ff.

Caribbean Studies, Institute of Caribbean Studies, University of Puerto Rico, Río Piedras 1961 ff.

Social and Economic Studies, Institute of Social and Economic Research, University of the West Indies, Jamaica 1953 ff.

The West Indies and Caribbean Year Book, London–New York–Ottawa, Annual.

Topography, Tectonics, and Morphogenesis

ANDERSON, T. 'Recent volcanic eruptions in the West Indies', *Geogrl J.*, **21**, 1903, pp. 265–81.

ANTOINE, J. W. 'Seismic studies in the Western Caribbean', *Am. Geophys. Union Trans.*, **40**, 1959, pp. 73–5.

BARR, K. W. 'The structural framework of the Caribbean region', *Caribb. Geol. Conf., Rep. 1*, Demerara 1958, pp. 30–3.

BLUME, H. 'Schichtstufen auf den Kleinen Antillen', *Verh. d. Dt. Geographentages* **33**, Wiesbaden 1962, p. 393.

—— 'Problemas de la Topografía kárstica en las Indias Occidentales, Unión Geográfica Internacional', *Conf. Reg. Latinoamericana*, vol. 3, Mexico 1966, pp. 255–66.

BUCHER, W. H. 'Problems of Earth Deformation illustrated by Caribbean Sea Basin', *Trans. N.Y. Acad. Sci.* **2**, ser. 9, 1947.

BÜDEL, J. 'Klima-genetische Geomorphologie', *Geogr. Rdsch.* **15**, 1963, pp. 269–85.

BUTTERLIN, J. *La Constitution géologique et la Structure des Antilles*, Paris 1956.

CHUBB, L. J. 'The Antillean cretaceous geosyncline', *Trans. 2nd Caribb. Geol. Conf.*, Mayagüez 1960, pp. 17–26.

CORBEL, G. 'Erosion en terrain calcaire (vitesse d'érosion et morphologie)', *Annls Géogr.* **118**, 1959, pp. 97–120.

DAVIS, W. M. *The Lesser Antilles*, New York 1926.

DECKERT, E. 'Die westindische Vulkankatastrophe und ihre Schauplätze', *Z. Ges. Erdkunde Berlin*, 1902, pp. 419–27.

DOERR, A. H. and HOY, D. R. 'Karst Landscapes of Cuba, Puerto Rico and Jamaica', *Scientific Monthly* **85**, 1957, pp. 178–87.

DONNELLY, T. W. 'Evolution of Eastern Greater Antillean Arc', *Bull. Am. Ass. Petrol. Geol.* **48**, 1964, pp. 680–96.

EARLE, K. W. *Geological Survey of the Windward and Leeward Islands*, Castries, St Lucia 1923.

EWING, M. and WORZEL, J. L. 'Gravity anomalies and structure of the West Indies', *Bull. Geol. Soc. Am.* **65**, 1954, I: pp. 165–73, II: pp. 195–9.

GERTH, H. 'Antillen-Molukken, zwei Inselbögen, ein Vergleich des geologischen Baues und der Schwereanomalie', *Geol. Rdsch.* **39**, 1951, pp. 273–84.

Bibliography

HESS, H. H. 'Gravity anomalies and island arc structures with particular reference to the West Indies', *Am. Phil. Soc. Proc.* **79**, 1938, pp. 71–96.

—— 'Outstanding problems of Caribbean geology', *Trans. 2nd Caribb. Geol. Conf.*, Mayagüez 1960, p. 11.

HOSPERS, J. 'The gravity field of northern South America and the West Indies', *Geologie en Mijnbouw*, n.s. **20**, 1958, pp. 358–65.

KUENEN, P. H. 'The negative isostatic anomalies in the West Indies', *Leidsche Geol. Mededeel.* **8**, 1936, pp. 169–214.

LEHMANN, H. 'Der tropische Kegelkarst auf den Großen Antillen', *Erdkunde* **8**, 1954, pp. 130–9.

—— 'Der tropische Kegelkarst in Westindien', *Verh. Dt. Geogr.-Tages* **29**, Wiesbaden 1955, pp. 126–31.

—— 'Las areas cársicas del Caribe', *Rev. Geogr. Habana* **30**, 1960, pp. 45–53.

MARTIN-KAYE, P. H. A. 'Note on the possible extension of the St John's peneplain of the eastern Greater Antilles into the Lesser Antilles', *Caribb. Geol. Conf., Rep. 1,* Demerara 1958, p. 37.

—— 'Accordant summit levels in the Lesser Antilles', *Caribb. Journ. Sci.* **3**, 1963, pp. 181–4.

MEYERHOFF, H. A. 'The Texture of karst topography in Cuba and Puerto Rico', *J. Geomorph.* **1**, 1938, pp. 279–95.

MITCHELL, R. C. 'Nouvelles observations à propos de la position structurale de l'arc des Petites Antilles', *Bull. Soc. géol. de France* **4**, 1954, pp. 213–24.

MOLARD, P. 'Tremblements de terre des Petites Antilles et manifestations actuelles du volcanisme de l'archipel (1936 à 1943)', *Ann. Géophys.* **3**, 1947, pp. 113–40.

—— 'Tremblements de terre des Petites Antilles (1944–1951)', *Ann. Géophys.* **8**, 1952, pp. 309–10.

ROBSON, G. R., 'Seismological and volcanological work in the eastern Caribbean', *Caribb. Geol. Conf., Rep. 1,* Demerara 1958, pp. 26.

RUSSELL, R. I. 'Caribbean Beach Rock Observations', *Z. Geomorph.,* n.s. **3**, 1959, pp. 227–36.

—— 'Origin of Beach Rock', *Z. Geomorph.*, n.s., **6**, 1962, pp. 1–16.

RUTTEN, L. 'Über den Antillenbogen', *Proc. Konink Akad. Wetensch. Amsterdam*, 1935, pp. 1046–58.

—— 'Alte Land- und Meeresverbindungen in West Indien und Zentralamerika', *Geol. Rdsch.* **26**, 1935, pp. 65–194.

SAPPER, K. 'Die vulkanischen Kleinen Antillen und die Ausbrüche der Jahre 1902 und 1903', *Neues J. Mineralogie*, 1904, pp. 39–90.

—— *In den Vulkangebieten Mittelamerikas und Westindiens. Reiseschilderungen und Studien über die Vulkanausbrüche der Jahre 1902 bis 1903, ihre geologischen, wirtschaftlichen und socialen Folgen*, Stuttgart 1905.

—— *Mittelamerka, Handbuch der Regionalen Geologie*, vol. 7, 4a, Heidelberg 1937.

SCHMEDEMAN, O. C. 'Caribbean aluminium ores', *Engineering and Mining Journ.* **149**, no. 6, 1948, pp. 78–82.

SCHUCHERT, C. *Historical Geology of the Antillean-Caribbean Region*, New York 1935.

SHURBET, G. L. and WORZEL, J. L. 'Gravity anomalies and structure of the West Indies', *Bull. Geol. Soc. Am.* **68**, 1957, pp. 263–6.

TABER, S. 'The seismic belt in the Greater Antilles', *Bull. Seism. Soc. Am.* **12**, 1922, pp. 199–219.

—— 'The great fault troughs of the Antilles', *J. Geol.* **30**, 1922, pp. 89–114.

—— 'The active fault zone of the Greater Antilles', *C.R. Congr. Géol. Intern.* **13**. sess. Belgium 1923, pp. 731–6.

VALENTIN, H. *Die Küsten der Erde, Pet. Geogr. Mitt.*, Erg.-H. 246, 2nd edn, Gotha 1954.

WEYL, R. 'Antillenbogen und Karibisches Meer', *Forsch. u. Fortschr.* **24**, 1948, pp. 281–4.

—— 'Eine neue Tiefenkarte der Caribischen See und ihre tektonische Ausdeutung', *Pet. Geogr. Mitt.* **93**, 1949, pp. 173–4.

—— 'Die geologische Geschichte des Antillenbogens unter besonderer Berücksichtigung der Cordillera Central von Santo Domingo', *Neues Jb. Geol. Paläont.*, B, **92**, Stuttgart 1950, pp. 137–242.

—— 'Die Großformen der amerikanischen Inselbögen', *Pet. Geogr. Mitt.* **95**, 1951, pp. 246–53.

—— 'Die westindischen Bauxit-Lagerstätten', *Metall* **14**, 1960, pp. 348–9.

—— 'Bau und Bild der Kleinen Antillen', *Geogr. Rdsch.* **15**, 1963, pp. 103–7.

—— 'Landschaft und Erdgeschichte der Kleinen Antillen', *Natur und Museum* **93**, 1963, pp. 12–20, 91–8, 169–76.

—— 'Geologische Forschung in Mittelamerika und Westindien', *Übersee-Rdsch.* **17**, no. 2, 1965, pp. 15–16.

—— *Erdgeschichte und Landschaftsbild in Mittelamerika*, Frankfurt 1965.

—— 'Die paläogeographische Entwicklung des mittelamerikanisch-westindischen Raumes', *Geol. Rdsch.* **54**, 1965, pp. 1213–40.

—— *Geologie der Antillen,* Berlin-Nikolassee 1966.

—— 'Tektonik, Magmatismus und Krustenbau in Mittelamerika und Westindien', *Geotekton. Forsch.* **23**, Stuttgart 1966, pp. 67–109.

WILHELMY, H. 'Die klimamorphologische und pflanzengeographische Entwicklung des Trockengebietes am Nordrand Südamerikas seit dem Pleistozän', *Die Erde*, 1954, pp. 244–73.

WOODRING, W. P. 'Caribbean Land and Sea through the Ages', *Bull. Geol. Soc. Am.* **65**, 1954, pp. 719–32.

The Sea

BRUYN, J. W. DE. 'Isogam maps of Caribbean Sea and surroundings and of South East Asia', *Proc. 3rd World Petrol. Congr.*, sec. 1, 1951, pp. 598–612.

COLÓN, F. A. *On the Heat Balance of the Troposphere and Water Body of the Caribbean Sea*, Nat. Hurricane Res. Project Report no. 41, Washington DC, 1960.

—— 'Seasonal variations in heat flux from the sea surface to the atmosphere over the Caribbean Sea', *J. Geophys. Res.* **68**, 1963, pp. 1421–30.

DEUTSCHES HYDROGRAPHISCHES INSTITUT. *Westindien-Handbuch*, I. Teil: *Die Nordküste Süd- und Mittelamerikas*, 3rd edn, Hamburg 1958.

DIETRICH, G. 'Fragen der Großformen und der Herkunft des Tiefenwassers im Amerikanischen Mittelmeer', *Ann. Hydrographie* **65**, 1937, pp. 345–7.

—— 'Das amerikanische Mittelmeer', *Z. Ges. Erdkde*, Berlin 1939, pp. 108–30.

EWING, M. and HEEZEN, B. C. 'Puerto Rico Trench, topographic and geophysical data', in *Crust of the Earth*, ed. A Poldervaart, Geol. Soc. Am., Spec. Paper 62, Baltimore 1955, pp. 255–68.

EWING, J. I. *et al.* 'Geophysical investigations in the eastern Caribbean; Trinidad Shelf, Tobago Trough, Barbados Ridge, Atlantic Ocean', *Bull. Geol. Soc. Am.* **68**, 1957, pp. 897–912.

—— 'Geophysical measurements in the western Caribbean Sea and in the Gulf of Mexico', *J. Geophys. Res.* **65**, 1960, pp. 4087–126.

FUGLISTER, F. C. 'Annual variations in current speeds in the Gulf Stream system', *J. Marine Res.* **10**, 1951, pp. 119–27.

FUKUOKA, J. 'Características de las condiciones hidrográficas del Mar Caribe', *Sociedad de Ciencias naturales de la Salle: Memoria*, **23**, no. 63, Caracas 1962, pp. 198–205.

—— 'Características de las condiciones hidrográficas del Mar Caribe (continuación)', *Sociedad de ciencias naturales de la Salle: Memoria*, **23**, no. 64, Caracas 1963, pp. 43–55.

—— 'Algunos problemas relacionados con la ocurrencia de los huracanes y la dirección de las Olas', *Sociedad de Ciencias Naturales de la Salle, Memoria* **26**, no. 73, Caracas 1966, pp. 41–52.

HEEZEN, B. C. 'Some problems of Caribbean submarine geology'. *Trans. 2nd Caribb. Geol.*

Conf., Mayagüez, Puerto Rico 1960, pp. 12–16.

—— *The Floor of the Ocean*, Geol. Soc. Am., Special Paper 65, Washington 1959.

HERSEY, J. B. 'Findings made during the June 1961 cruise of chain to the Puerto Rico Trench and Caryn Sea Mount', *J. Geophys. Res.* **67**, 1962, pp. 1109–16.

HESS, H. H. 'Caribbean Research Project: Progress Report', *Bull. Geol. Soc. Am.* **71**, 1960, pp. 235–40.

HESS, H. H. and MAXWELL, J. C. 'Caribbean research project', *Bull. Geol. Soc. Am.* **64**, 1953, pp. 1–6.

KU, T.-L. and BROECKER, W. S. 'Atlantic deep-sea stratigraphy: extension of absolute chronology to 320 000 years', *Science* **151**, no. 3709, Washington 1966, pp. 448–50.

MODEL, F., 'Pillsburys Strommessungen und der Wasserhaushalt des Amerikanischen Mittelmeers; *Dt. Hydrogr. Z.* **3**, 1950, pp. 57–61.

NORTHROP, J. 'Bathymetry of the Puerto-Rico Trench', *Trans. Am. Geophys. Union* **35**, 1954, pp. 221–5.

OFFICER, C. B. *et al.* 'Geophysical investigation in the eastern Caribbean: Venezuelan Basin, Antilles Island arc, and Puerto Rico Trench', *Bull. Geol. Soc. Am.* **68**, 1957, pp. 359–78.

—— 'Geophysical investigations: the eastern Caribbean: summary of 1955 and 1956 cruises', in *Physics and Chemistry of the Earth*, vol. 3, Oxford 1959, pp. 17–109.

PARR, A. E. 'A contribution to the hydrography of the Caribbean and Cayman Sea', *Bull. Bingham Oceanogr. Coll.* **5**, 1937, pp. 1–110.

SCHOTT, G. 'Kaltes Wasser vor der Küste von Venezuela und Kolumbien', *Ann. Hydrogr. Marit. Meteorol.* **59**, Hamburg 1931, pp. 224–7.

SCHOTT, W. and ZOBEL, B. 'Stratigraphy of deep-sea Sediments in the Caribbean', 2nd International Oceanographic Congress, *Abstract of Papers*, no. 380-S III B, Moskow 1966, pp. 323.

STURGES, W. 'Water Characteristics of the Caribbean Sea', *J. Marine Res.* **23**, 1965, pp. 147–62.

SUTTON, G. H., TALWANI, M. and WORZEL, J. L. 'West-east crustal section, through the gravity anomaly belt of the Lesser Antilles along 14° 20′ N', *J. Geophys. Res.* **65**, 1960, p. 2527.

TALWANI, M., SUTTON, G. H. and WORZEL, J. L. 'A crustal section across the Puerto Rico Trench', *J. Geophys. Res.* **64**, 1959, pp. 1545–55.

VENING MEINESZ, F. A. 'The Puerto Rico Trench: two types of deep ocean trenches', *Netherlands Geodetic Commission Publications on Geodesy*, n.s., **2**, no. 1, 1964, pp. 23–7.

WORTHINGTON, L. V. 'A new theory of Caribbean bottom-water formation', *Deep-Sea Res.* **3**, 1955, pp. 82–7.

WÜST, G. *Florida- und Antillenstrom, eine hydrodynamische Untersuchung*, Veröff. Inst. f. Meereskunde, new series vol. 12, Berlin 1924.

—— 'On the stratification and the circulation in the cold water sphere of the Antillean-Caribbean Basins', *Deep-Sea Res.* **10**, 1963, pp. 165–87.

—— *Stratification and Circulation in the Antillean- Caribbean Basins; Part 1: Spreading and Mixing of the Water Types, with an oceanographic Atlas*, Vema Research Series no. 2, New York 1964.

—— 'Wasser- und Wärmehaushalt und Zirkulation in der Warmwassersphäre des Karibischen Meeres', *Kieler Meeresforschungen* **21**, 1, Kiel 1965, pp. 3–11.

Climate

AIR MINISTRY, METEOROLOGICAL OFFICE. *Aviation Meteorology of the West Indies*, Met. Rep. no. 22, London 1959.

—— *Tables of Temperature, relative Humidity and Precipitation for the World*, II: *Central and South America, The West Indies and Bermuda*, London 1958.

BLUME, H. 'Beiträge zur Klimatologie Westindiens', *Erdkunde* **16**, 1962, pp. 271–89.

CAIN, E. E. *Cyclone 'Hattie'*, Devon 1963.

DUNN, G. E. 'Cyclogenesis in the tropical Atlantic', *Bull. Am. Met. Soc.* **21**, 1940, p. 215.
—— 'The hurricane season of 1959', *MWR* **87**, 1959, pp. 441–50.
EMILIANI, C. 'Pleistocene temperatures', *J. Geol.* **63**, 1955, pp. 538–78.
FASSIG, O. L. 'The trade-winds of the eastern Caribbean', *Trans. Am. Geophys. Union* 14th Meeting, 1933, Nat. Research Council, Washington 1933, pp. 69–78.
FISCHER, A. 'Die Hurricanes oder Drehstürme Westindiens', *Pet. Geogr. Mitt.* **159**, 1908.
FLOHN, H. 'Zur Frage der Einteilung der Klimazonen', *Erdkunde* **11**, 1957, pp. 161–75.
FROLOW, S. 'La frontologie aux Antilles', *Ann. phys. du Globe de la France d'Outre Mer* **5**, 1938, pp. 114–17.
—— 'Synoptic analysis of Caribbean weather', *Bull. Am. Met. Soc.* **22**, 1941, pp. 198–210.
GARBELL, M. A. *Tropical and Equatorial Meteorology*, New York and Chicago 1947.
GUTNICK, M., 'Climatology of the trade-wind inversion in the Caribbean', *Bull. Am. Met. Soc.* **39**, 1958, pp. 410–20.
HALL, M. 'The climate of the West Indies', *Rept. Int. Met. Congr. Chicago, Bull.* no. 11, US Weather Bureau, III, 1896, pp. 589–601.
HASTENRATH, S. 'Über den Einfluß der Massenerhebung auf den Verlauf der Klima- und Vegetationsstufen in Mittelamerika und im südlichen Mexiko', *Geografiska Annaler* **45**, 1963, pp. 76–83.
HAURWITZ, B. 'Harmonic analysis of the diurnal variations of pressure and temperature aloft in the eastern Caribbean', *Bull. Am. Met. Soc.* **28**, 1947, p. 319.
HENRY, A. J. 'The frequency of tropical cyclones (West Indian hurricanes) that closely approach and enter continental United States, 1722–1928', *MWR* **57**, 1929, pp. 328–31.
HOSLER, C. R. 'A study of easterly waves in the Gulf of Mexico', *Bull. Am. Met. Soc.* **37**, 1956, pp. 101–7.
KLOSTER, W. *Bewölkungs-, Niederschlags- und Gewitterverhältnisse der Westindischen Gewässer und der angrenzenden Landmassen*, Hamburg 1922.
KNOCH, K. 'Klimakunde von Südamerika', *Handbuch der Klimatologie*, vol. 2, sect. G, Berlin 1930.
KÖPPEN, W. *Grundriß der Klimakunde*, Berlin and Leipzig 1931.
LAUER, W. 'Humide und aride Jahreszeiten in Afrika und Südamerika und ihre Beziehung zu den Vegetationsgürteln', *Bonner Geogr.* **9**, Bonn 1952, pp. 15–98.
—— 'Klimatische und pflanzengeographische Grundzüge Zentralamerikas', *Erdkunde* **13**, 1959, pp. 344–54.
—— 'Klimadiagramme', *Erdkunde* **14**, 1960, pp. 232–42.
MARTONNE, E. DE. 'Une nouvelle fonction climatologique: l'indice d'aridité', *La Météorologie*, 1926, pp. 449–58.
—— 'Nouvelle carte mondiale de l'indice d'aridité', *La Météorologie*, 1941, pp. 3–26.
MITCHELL, C. L. 'West Indian hurricanes and other tropical cyclones of the North Atlantic Ocean', *MWR*, Suppl. no. 24, 1924.
MÖLLER, F. 'Vierteljahreskarten des Niederschlags für die ganze Erde', *Pet. Geogr. Mitt.* **95**, 1951, pp. 1–7.
PAQUEY, P. 'Un Cyclone dans la Mer Caraibe: le Cyclone Janet (Sept. 1955)', Cahiers d'Outre Mer, 1957, pp. 65–91.
—— *Centres d'Action et Vents sur l'Atlantique Nord tropical et les Antilles. Etude statistique et dynamique au Niveau de la Mer;* Actes du 25. Congrès national des Sociétés Savantes (Chambéry-Annecy 1960), Paris 1961.
POLY, A. 'A chronological table, comprising 400 cyclonic hurricanes which have occurred in the West Indies and in the North Atlantic within 362 years, from 1493–1855', *Roy. Geogr. Soc. Journ.* **25**, 1855, pp. 291–328.
'Puny Hurricane', *The Economist* **209**, London 1963, pp. 33–4.
REED, W. W. 'Climatological data for the West Indian islands', *MWR* **54**, 1926, pp. 133–60.
REICHEL, E. 'Der Trockenheitsindex, insbesondere für Deutschland, Ber. über die Tätigkeit des Preuß. Met. Inst. im Jahre 1928', *Veröff. d. Preuß. Meteorol. Inst.* no. **362**, 1929, pp. 84–105.

Bibliography

REICHS-MARINEAMT. *Westindien-Handbuch*, Berlin 1927.

RIEHL, H. *Waves in the Easterlies and the polar Front in the Tropics*, Misc. Rep. Inst. Met., Univ. Chicago no. 17, 1945.

—— 'Diurnal variation of pressure and temperature aloft in the eastern Caribbean', *Bull. Am. Met. Soc.* **28**, 1947, p. 311.

—— *Tropical Meteorology*, New York, Toronto, London 1954.

RIEHL, H. and SCHACHT, E. 'Methods of analysis in the Caribbean region', *Bull. Am. Met. Soc.* **27**, 1946, p. 569.

SARASOLA, S. *Los Huracanes de las Antillas*, Notas geofísicas meteorológicas no. 2, Bogotá 1925.

SARASOLA, S. J. *Los Huracanes de las Antillas. Segunda Edición aumentada con el Apéndice: Genesis y Evolución del Huracan de 20de Octubre de 1926 y Catálogo de Siclones en la Isla de Cuba de 1865–1926*, Madrid 1928.

SCHACHT, E. 'A mean hurricane sounding for the Caribbean area', *Bull. Am. Met. Soc.* **27**, 1946, p. 324.

SCHRÖDER, R. 'Die Verteilung der Regenzeiten im nördlichen tropischen Amerika', *Pet. Geogr. Mitt.* **99**, 1955, pp. 263–9.

SHEETE, C. C. 'West Indian hurricanes', *Trop. Agric.* **8**, 1931, pp. 178–85, 206–10.

SIMPSON, R. H. 'Synoptic aspects of the intertropical convergence near Central and South America', *Bull. Am. Met. Soc.* **28**, 1947, pp. 335–46.

TANNEHILL, I. R. *Hurricanes. Their nature and history*, London 1956.

—— *The Hurricane*, Washington, DC, 1956.

THE WEST INDIES METEOROLOGICAL SERVICE, *Climatological Summaries*, Port-of-Spain, since 1955.

THORNTHWAITE, C. W. 'The climates of North America according to a new classification', *Geogr. Rev.* **21**, 1931, pp. 633–55.

TREWARTHA, G. T. *The Earth's Problem Climates*, Madison 1961.

TROLL, C. and PAFFEN, K. H. 'Karte der Jahreszeiten-Klimate der Erde', *Erdkunde* **18**, 1964, pp. 5–28.

US DEPARTMENT OF COMMERCE, WEATHER BUREAU. *Climatological Data, West Indies and Caribbean*, vols 9–18, 1928–37.

WARD, R. DE C. and BROOKS, C. F. 'Westindien Climatology of the West Indies', *Handbuch der Klimatologie* vol 2, pt 1, Berlin 1934.

Flora and Fauna

ALLEN, G. M. 'Mammals of the West Indies', *Bull. Mus. Comp. Zool* **54**, 1911, pp. 175–263.

—— *Birds of the Caribbean*, New York 1961.

BADER, F. *Die Verbreitung borealer und subantarktischer Holzgewächse in den Gebirgen des Tropengürtels*, Nova Acta Leopoldina, Abh. d. Dt. Akad. d. Naturforscher Leopoldina, n. f., vol. 23, no. 148, 1960.

BAKER, R. H. 'The geographical distribution of terrestrial mammals in Middle America', *Am. Midland Naturalist* **52**, 1963, pp. 208–49.

BARBOUR, T. 'A contribution to the zoogeography of the West Indies, with especial reference to amphibians and reptiles', *Mem. Mus. Comp. Zool.* **44**, 1914, pp. 209–359.

—— 'Third list of Antillean reptiles and amphibians', *Bull. Mus. Comp. Zool.* **82**, 1937, pp. 75–166.

BEARD, J. S. 'Montane vegetation in the Antilles', *Caribbean Forester* **3**, 1942, pp. 61–74.

—— 'Climax vegetation in tropical America', *Ecology* **25**, 1944, pp. 127–58.

—— *The Natural Vegetation of the Windward and Leeward Islands*, Oxford Forestry Memoirs no. 21, Oxford 1949.

—— 'The savanna vegetation of northern tropical America', *Ecol. Monogr.* **23**, 1953, pp. 149–215.

BOND, J. 'Distribution and origin of the West Indian avifauna', *Proc. Am. Phil. Soc.* **73**, 1934,

pp. 341–9.

—— *Birds of the West Indies*, Philadelphia 1936.

—— *Birds of the West Indies*, London 1960.

CARIBBEAN COMMISSION, CENTRAL SECRETARIAT, *Fisheries in the Caribbean*, Port-of-Spain 1952.

CHALMERS, W. S. 'Observations on some Caribbean Forests', *Caribbean Forester* **19**, 1958, pp. 30–42.

DARLINGTON, P. J. 'The origin of the fauna of the Greater Antilles, with discussion of dispersal of animals over water and through the air', *Qt. Rev. Biol.* **13**, 1938, pp. 274–300.

—— *Zoogeography*, New York 1957.

DOMIN, K. *Florenprovinz von Westindien und Trinidad: Totius orbis flora photographica arte depicta* vol. 1, Brünn 1929.

DUNN, L. R. 'Physiography and Herpetology in the Lesser Antilles', *Copeia*, no. 3, 1934, pp. 105–11.

EKMAN, S. *Tiergeographie des Meeres*, Leipzig 1935.

FIEDLER, R. H., LOBELL, M. J. and LUCAS, C. R. *The Fisheries and Fishing Resources of the Caribbean Area*, US Dept. of the Interior, Fish and Wildlife Service, Fishery Leaflet 259, Washington 1947.

FOSBERG, F. R. 'Principal economic plants of tropical America', in *Plants and Plant Science in Latin America*, ed. F. Verdoorn, 1945, pp. 18–35.

GILL, T. *Tropical Forests of the Caribbean*, Washington 1931.

GORDON, W. A. 'Forest management in the Caribbean', *Caribbean Forester* **22**, nos. 1, 2, 1961.

GREENHALL, A. M. 'Aspects of ecology in vampire bat control in Trinidad', *Anais do Segundo Congresso Latino-Americano de Zoologia*, vol. 2, São Paulo 1962, pp. 321–5.

—— 'Trinidad and bat research', *American Naturalist*, 1965, pp. 14–21.

GRISEBACH, A. H. R. 'Systematische Untersuchungen über die Vegetation der Karaiben, insbesondere der Insel Guadeloupe', *Abh. Kgl. Ges. Wiss. Göttingen* **7**, 1857, pp. 1–138.

—— *Flora of the British West Indian Islands*, London 1864; reprinted Weinheim 1963.

GUPPY, H. B. *Plants, Seeds and Currents in the West Indies and Azores*, London 1917.

HARSHBERGER, J. W. 'Phytogeographic survey of North America', in *Die Vegetation der Erde*, ed. A. Engler and O. Drude, Leipzig 1911.

HITCHCOCK, A. S. *Manual of the Grasses of the West Indies*, USDA Misc. Publ. 243, 1936, pp. 1–439.

HOLDRIDGE, L. 'Middle America', in *A World Geography of Forest Resources*, New York 1956, pp. 183–200.

HUBBARD, F. 'Wald und Regenfall in Westindien', *Z. Österr. Ges. Meteorol.* Vienna 1876, p. 155.

KNAPP, R. *Die Vegetation von Nord- und Mittelamerika*, Stuttgart 1965.

KRAUS, O. 'Mittelamerika—Binderglied zweier Faunenreiche?', *Die Umschau in Wiss. u. Techn.* **23**, 1964, pp. 718–22.

LAMB, F. B. *Mahogany of Tropical America: its ecology and management*, Ann Arbor 1966.

LAUER, W. 'Klimatische und pflanzengeographische Grundzüge Zentralamerikas', *Erdkunde* **13**, 1959, pp. 344–54.

MATTHEW, W. D. 'Affinities and origin of the Antillean mammals', *Bull. Geol. Soc. Am.* **29**, 1918, pp. 657–66.

—— 'Affinities and origins of the Antillean mammals', in 'Climate and Evolution', *Ann. N.Y. Acad. Science* **24**, 1939, new edn 1950, pp. 171–318.

MOLE, R. R. 'The Trinidad snakes', *Proc. Zool. Soc. Lond.* 1924, pp. 235–78.

PARSONS, J. J. *The Green Turtle and Man*, Tallahassee 1962.

RICHARDS, P. W. *The Tropical Rain Forest*, Cambridge 1952.

ROSEVEARE, G. M. *The Grasslands of Latin America*, Cardiff 1948.

SAUER, C. O. 'Cultivated plants of South and Central America', in *Handbook of South American Indians*, ed. J. Steward, vol. 6, Washington 1950, pp. 487–543.

SCHWEINFURTH, G. 'Was Afrika an Kulturpflanzen Amerika zu verdanken hat und was es ihm gab', *Festschrift E. Seler*, Stuttgart 1922, pp. 503–42.

SIMPSON, G. G. *Zoogeography of West Indian Land Mammals*, American Mus. Novitates, no. 1759, New York 1956.

SMITH, F. G. W. *The Spiny Lobster Industry of the Caribbean*, Port-of-Spain and Miami 1959.

STEHLÉ, H. 'Les conditions écologiques, la végétation et les ressources agricoles de l'Archipel des Petites Antilles', in *Plants and Plant Science in Latin America*, ed. F. Verdoorn, Chronica Botanica, New Series of Plant Science Books vol. 16, New York 1945, pp. 85–100.

—— 'Forest types of the Caribbean Islands', *Caribbean Forester* **6** (Suppl.), 1945, pp. 273–408.

TROLL, C. 'Das Pflanzenkleid der Tropen in seinez Abhängigkeit von Klima, Boden und Mensch', *Verh. d. Dt. Geogr- Tages*. **30**, Remagen 1952, pp. 35–66.

—— 'Zur Physiognomik der Tropengewächse', *Jahresber. d. Ges. d. Freunde und Förderer d. Rhein*, Friedr.-Wilh.-Universität zu Bonn, 1958, pp. 1–75.

—— 'Die tropischen Gebirge. Ihre dreidimensionale klimatische und pflanzengeographische Zonierung', *Bonner Geogr*. **25**, Bonn 1959.

URBAN, I. 'Über die botanische Erforschung Westindiens', *Bot. Jb. f. Systematik, Pflanzengesch. u. Pflanzengeogr.*, ed. A. Engler, Supplement no. 73, Leipzig 1903.

VÉLEZ, I. 'Notes on the herbaceous vegetation of the Lesser Antilles', *Rapp. VIIIe Congr. Int. Bot. Paris*, sect. 7, 1954, pp. 79–81.

VESEY-FITZGERALD, D. 'Trinidad Mammals', *Tropical Agriculture* **13**, 1936, pp. 161–5.

WALTER, H. *Die Vegetation der Erde in öko-physiologischer Betrachtung. 1: Die tropischen und subtropischen Zonen*, 2nd edn, Jena 1964.

WARDLAW, C. W. and McGUIRE, L. P. *Panama Disease of Bananas. Reports on scientific Visits to the Banana growing Countries of the West Indies, Central and South America*, Empire Marketing Board no. 20, London 1929.

ZANEVELD, J. S. *The Sea Fisheries of the Netherlands Antilles*, Port-of-Spain, Trinidad, n.d.

The Amerindian Aborigines

CHARD, C. S. 'Pre-Columbin trade between North and South America', Kroeber *Anthropological Society Papers*, no. 1, Berkeley, Calif., 1950, pp. 1–27.

GEYSKES, D. C. 'Het Eerste Internationale Congres voor de Studie van de Prae-Columbiaanse Culturen in de Kleine Antillen', *Nieuwe West-Ind. Gids* **41**, 1962, pp. 272–84.

GOWER, C. D. *The Northern and Southern Affiliation of Antillean Culture*, Mem. of the Am. Anthropol. Ass. no. 35, 1927.

KROEBER, A. L. 'Native American population', *Am. Anthropol.* **36** 1934, pp. 1–25.

LALUNG, H. DE. *Les Caraibes*, Paris 1948.

LOVÉN, S. *Über die Wurzeln der Tainischen Kultur: 1 Teil, Materielle Kultur*, Göteborg 1924.

—— *Origins of the Tainan Culture, West Indies*, Göteborg 1935.

McKUSICK, M. B. *Aboriginal canoes in the West Indies* Yale Univ. Publ. in Anthropology no. 63, New Haven 1960.

REYNOSO, A. *Agricultura de las Indigenas de Cuba y Haiti*, Paris 1881.

ROUSE, J. 'Areas and periods of culture in the Greater Antilles', *Southwestern Journal of Anthropology* **7**, 1951, pp. 248–65.

—— 'Settlement Patterns in the Caribbean Area', in, *Prehistoric Settlement Patterns in the New World*, ed. Willey, Viking Fund Publications in Anthropology no. 23, New York 1956, pp. 165–72.

—— *The Entry of Man into the West Indies*, Yale University Publ. in Anthropology, no. 61, New Haven 1960.

—— 'Prehistory of the West Indies', *Science* **144**, 1964, pp. 499–513.

SAPPER, K. 'Geographie der altindianischen Landwirtschaft', *Pet. Geogr. Mitt.* **80**, 1934, pp. 41–4, 80–3, 118–21.

—— *Geographie und Geschichte der indianischen Landwirtschaft*, Ibero-Am. Studien I, Hamburg 1936.

STEWARD, J. H., ed. *Handbook of South American Indians. 4: The Circum-Caribbean Tribes*, Smithsonian Institution, Bureau of American Ethnology, Bull. 143, Washington 1948.
STURTEVANT, W. C. *The Significance of Ethnological Similarities between Southeastern North America and the Antilles*, Yale Univ. Publ. in Anthropology, no. 64, New Haven 1960.

History of Discovery, National and Economic Development, and Political Geography

ANDREWS, K. R., ed. *English Privateering Voyages to the West Indies, 1588–1595*, Cambridge 1959.
ARCHENHOLZ, J. W. v. *Die Geschichte der Flibustier*, Tübingen 1803.
ARMYTAGE, F. *The Free Port System in the British West-Indies. A study in commercial policy, 1766–1822*, London 1953.
BABCOCK, W. H. 'Antillia and the Antilles', *Geogr. Rev.* **9**, 1920, pp. 109–24.
BARRETT, W. 'Caribbean Sugar-Production Standards in the seventeenth and eighteenth Century', in *Merchants and Scholars*, ed. J. Parker, Minneapolis 1965, pp. 145–70.
BEER, G. L. *The Origins of the British Colonial System 1578–1660*, New York 1908.
BELL, W. and IVAR, O. *Decisions of Nationhood: political and social development in the British Caribbean*, Denver, Co. 1964.
BEYHAUT, G. *Süd- und Mittelamerika II, von der Unabhängigkeit bis zur Krise der Gegenwart*, Fischer Weltgeschichte vol. 23, Frankfurt 1965.
BOBB, L. E. 'The federal principle in the British West Indies: an appraisal of its Use', *SES* **15**, 1966, pp. 239–65.
BOLT, A. 'A diversity of islands: the West Indian Federation', *Geogr. Mag.* **34**, 1961, pp. 271–83.
BOXER, C. R. *The Dutch Seaborne Empire 1600–1800*, London 1965.
BRADFORD, E. *Konquistador der Meere. Sir Francis Drake—Abenteurer und Weltumsegler*, Bern 1966.
BURNEY. *History of the Buccaneers*, London 1816.
BURNS, SIR A. C. *History of the British West Indies*, 2nd edn, New York 1965.
CHECKLAND, S. G. 'American versus West Indian traders in Liverpool, 1793–1815', *J. Econ. Hist.* **18**, 1958, pp. 141–60.
CRABOT, C. 'La Fédération des Antilles britanniques', *Inform. Géogr.* **23** 1959, pp. 47–57.
DALE, E. H. 'The West Indies: a Federation in search of a capital', *CG* 5, 1961, pp. 44–52.
DANIEL, E. W. *West Indian Histories*, 3 vols, London 1936.
DESSALLES, A. *Histoire générale des Antilles*, 5 vols, Paris 1847–48.
DINEEN, J. H. 'The strategic importance of the Caribbean; U.S. military positions in this area', *Enterprise* **3**, Port-of-Spain 1964, pp. 12–17.
DRASCHER, W. *Das Vordringen der Vereinigten Staaten im westindischen Mittelmeergebiet*, Hamburg 1918.
DU TERTRE, R. P. *Histoire générale des Antilles habitées par les Français*, 4 vols, Paris 1667–71.
EDWARDS, B. *History, Civil and Commercial, of the British Colonies in the West Indies*, Dublin 1793.
EXQUEMELIN, A. O. *Die amerikanischen Seeräuber*, translated from the original Dutch edn (Amsterdam 1678), as *Der Weltkreis*, ed. H. Kauders, vol. 3, Erlangen 1926.
FAGG, J. E. *Cuba, Haiti, and the Dominican Republic*, Modern Nations in historical Perspective Series, Englewood Cliffs 1965.
FERNÁNDEZ DE OVIEDO, G. *Historia general y natural de las Indias*, Madrid 1853.
FRANCO, J. L. *La Batalla por el Domino del Caribe y el Golfo de Mexico*, 2 vols, Habana 1964 and 1965.
FRIEDERICI, G. *Der Charakter der Entdeckung und Eroberung Amerikas durch die Europäer*, 3 vols, Stuttgart and Gotha 1925–1936.
FROUDE, J. A. *The English in the West Indies*, London 1885.

Bibliography

GALINDEZ, J. DE. *Iberoamérica, su Evolución politica, socio-económica, cultural e internacional*, New York 1954.

GARCIA, A. *History of the West Indies*, London 1965.

GLUSA, R. 'Zur politischen Geographie Westindiens', dissertation, Münster 1962.

HANKE, L. *The First Social Experiments in America. A study in the development of Spanish Indian policy in the 16th century*, Cambridge, Mass. 1935.

—— *Bartolomé de las Casas, Historian*, Gainesville 1952.

HARING, C. H. *The Buccaneers in the West Indies in the XVII Century* London 1910.

—— *The Spanish Empire in America*, New York 1947.

HASENCLEVER, A. 'Die Flibustier Westindiens im 17. Jahrhundert', *Preuß. Jahrbücher* **203**, 1926, pp. 13–35.

HILL, H. C. *Roosevelt and the Caribbean*, New York 1965.

HONORÉ NABER, S. P. L. and WRIGHT, J. A. *Piet Heyn en de Zilvervloot*, Utrecht 1928.

JACOB, E. G. *Christoph Columbus. Bordbuch, Briefe, Berichte, Dokumente*, Bremen 1956.

KIRKPATRICK, F. A. *The Spanish Conquistadores*, London 1934. German trans. as *Die spanischen Konquistadoren*, Leipzig 1935.

KONETZKE, R. *Das spanische Weltreich. Grundlagen und Entstehung*, Munich 1943.

—— *Entdecker und Eroberer Amerikas*, Fischer-Bücherei 535, Frankfurt/M. 1963.

—— *Die Indianerkulturen Altamerikas und die spanisch-portugiesische Kolonialherrschaft. Süd- und Mittelamerika I*, Fischer Weltgeschichte vol. 22, Frankfurt 1965.

LEWIS, G. K. 'The Caribbean: Colonization and Culture', *Studies on the Left* **11**, no. 1, 1961, pp. 26–42.

LIER, R. A. J. VAN. *Ontwikkeling en Karakter van de Westindische Maatschappij*, The Hague 1950.

LIPSCHUTZ, A. 'La Despoblación de las Indias después de la Conquista', *América Indigena* **26** 1966, no. 3, pp. 229–47.

LOUIS, D. *Westindien und der Kontinent von Südamerika, ein historisch, statistisch und topographisches Gemälde*, Hamburg 1818.

LOWENTHAL, D. 'Two Federations', *SES* **6**, 1957, pp. 85–196.

—— 'The West Indies chooses a capital', *Geogrl. Rev.* **48**, 1958, pp. 336–64.

MAHN-LOT, M. *Les plus belles Lettres de Christophe Colomb*, Paris 1961.

MAI, W. 'Westindien und England', dissertation, Münster 1962.

MARTINEZ-HIDALGO, J. M. *Columbus' Ships*, Barre, Pa. , 1966.

MEINICKE, C. E. *Versuch einer Geschichte der europäischen Colonien in Westindien, nach den Quellen bearbeitet*, Weimar 1831.

MERRIL, G. C. 'The West Indies—the newest Federation of the Commonwealth', *Canad. Geogr. J.* **56**, 1958, pp. 60–9.

MITCHELL, SIR H. *Europe in the Caribbean; the policies of Great Britain, France and the Netherlands toward their West Indian territories in the 20th century*, Edinburgh, London 1963.

MORALES PADRÓN, F. 'Fondos relativos a las Antillas Menores en el Archivo de Indias, Sevilla, España', *CS* **6**, no. 1, 1966, pp. 41–56.

MORISON, S. E. *Admiral of the Ocean Sea*, 2 vols, Boston 1942. German trans. as *Admiral des Weltmeeres*, Bremen-Horn 1948.

MOSKOS, C. D. and BELL, W. 'Emergent Caribbean Nations face the outside World', *Social Problems* **12**, 1964, pp. 24–41.

MURRAY, D. J. *The West Indies and the Development of Colonial Government 1801–1834*, Oxford 1965.

NICOLE, C. *The West Indies: their people and history*, London 1965.

OLSCHKI, L. 'The Columbian Nomenclature of the Lesser Antilles', *Geogrl. Rev.* **33**, 1943, pp. 397–414.

OTS CAPDEQUI, J. M. *El Régimen de la Tierra en la América española durante el Período colonial*, Ciudad Trujillo 1946.

OVIEDO Y VALDÉS, G. F. DE. *Historia general y natural de las Indias, Islas y Tierra-firme del Mar Océano*, 4 vols, Madrid 1851–55.

PARES, R. *Yankees and Creoles*, London 1957.

—— *War and Trade in the West Indies, 1739–1763*, London 1965.

PARRY, J. H. *Zeitalter der Entdeckungen*, Zürich 1963.

PARRY, J. H. and SHERLOCK, P. M. *A Short History of the West Indies*, London 1960.

PLATT, D. C. M. 'British agricultural Colonization in Latin America', *Inter-American Economic Affairs* **18**, no. 3, 1964, pp. 3–38.

PLATT, R. R. *et al. The European Possessions in the Caribbean*, American Geogr. Soc., Map of Hispanic America, Publ. no. 4, New York 1941.

PROUDFOOT, M. *Britain and the United States in the Caribbean; a comparative study in methods of development*, London 1954.

RAGATZ, L. *The Fall of the Planter Class in the British Caribbean, 1763–1833*, New York and London 1928, reprinted 1963.

RAYNAL, G. T. F. *Histoire philosophique et politique des Etablissements et du Commerce européen dans les deux Indes*, 6 vols, Amsterdam 1770.

RÉVERT, K. 'Géographie politique du Monde Caraibe', *Ann. Géogr.* **63**, 1954, pp. 34–47.

RIPPY, J. F. *Latin America. A modern history*, Ann Arbor 1958.

ROEMER, H. *Die Einmischungen der USA in die Revolutionen und Bürgerkriege der westindischen und zentralamerikanischen Republiken*, Essen 1943.

SAPPER, K. 'Mittelamerika und Westindien', *Z. Geopolitik* **3**, 1927, pp. 334–44, 448–61, 534–39.

SAUER, C. *The Early Spanish Main*, Berkeley and Los Angeles 1966.

SCHÄFER, E. 'Der Verkehr Spaniens mit und in seinen amerikanischen Kolonien', *Ibero-Amerika-Archiv* **11**, 1937/38, pp. 435–55.

SCHOEN, W. FREIHERR VON. *Geschichte Mittel- und Südamerikas, Weltgeschichte in Einzeldarstellungen*, vol. 9, Munich 1953.

SERRANO Y SANZ, M. *Orígenes de la Dominación española*, Madrid 1918.

SHERIDAN, R. B. 'The West Indian Sugar crisis and British slave emancipation, *1830–1833*', J. Econ. Hist. **21**, 1961, pp. 539–51.

SIMPSON, L. B. *The Encomienda in New Spain*, Berkeley 1950.

SPRINGER, H. W. 'Federation in the Caribbean; an attempt that failed', *International Organization* **16**, 1962, pp. 758–75.

—— *Reflections on the Failure of the first West Indian Federation*, Center for International Affairs, Harvard Univ., Cambridge Mass. 1962.

TAYLOR PARKS, E. 'European possessions in the Americas', *JIAS* **4**, 1962, pp. 395–405.

VERLINDEN, C. *Christoph Columbus*, Göttingen 1962.

WAUGH, A. *A Family of Islands: a history of the West Indies*, London 1964.

WEHLER, H.-U. 'Stützpunkte in der Karibischen See. Die Anfänge des amerikanischen Imperialismus auf Hispaniola', *Jb. f. Geschichte von Staat, Wirtschaft und Gesellschaft Lateinamerikas* **2**, 1965, pp. 399–428.

WILHELMY, H. 'Südamerika im Spiegel seiner Städte', Hamburger Romanistische Studien, Ibero-Amerikanische Reihe vol. 23, Hamburg 1952.

WILLIAMSON, J. A. *The Age of Drake*, London 1938.

—— *Short History of British Expansion*, 2 vols, London 1951–53.

Population, Settlement, and Social Structure

ABBOTT, G. C. 'Estimates of the growth of the population of the West Indies to 1975: two projections', *SES* **12**, 1963, pp. 236–45.

ANDIC, F. M. and MATHEWS, T. G., eds. *The Caribbean in Transition*, Second Caribbean Scholars' Conference 1964, Río Piedras 1965.

AUGELLI, J. P. 'The country-to-town movement in the West Indies', *Proc. 17th Int. Geogr. Congr.*, Washington 1952, pp. 719–23.

—— 'The Rimland-Mainland concept of culture areas in Middle America', *AAAG* **52**, 1962, pp. 119–29.

Bibliography

BASIL, M. D. *Crisis of the West Indian Family. A sample study*, Extra-Mural Dept. of the Univ. College of the West Indies, Trinidad 1953.

BASTIEN, R. 'Procesos de aculturación en las Antillas', *Revista de Indias* **24**, Madrid 1964, pp. 177–96.

BEAUREGARD, C. F. *A Study of the Caribbean, its People, their Social, Political and Economic Life and Educational Problem; general aspects of the culture of the Caribbean area and more especially international cooperation within the Caribbean*, Hato Rey, Puerto Rico, 1963.

BENNETT, J. H. Jr 'The problems of slave labor supply at the Codrington plantations', *J. Negro History* **26**, 1951, pp. 406–41; **27**, 1952, pp. 115–41.

BROOM, L. 'Urban research in the British Caribbean: a prospectus', *SES* **1**, 1953, pp. 113–19.

BRUNSCHWIG, H. 'Le Négro hors d'Afrique: planteurs et esclaves: Indes Occidentales, Mascareignes, Madagascar', *Revue Historique* **87**, vol. 230, Paris 1963, pp. 149–70.

CARIBBEAN COMMISSION, *Caribbean Land Tenure Symposium*, Washington, DC, 1946/47.

—— 'Historical Account of Land Tenure Systems in the Caribbean', *CER* **1**, 1949, pp. 133–52.

—— 'Land Tenure in the Caribbean', *CER* **2**, no. 2, 1950.

—— *Aspects of Housing in the Caribbean*, Port-of-Spain, Trinidad 1951.

—— *Cooperatives in the Caribbean*, Port-of-Spain, Trinidad 1954.

CUMPER, G. E. *The Social Structure of the British Caribbean (excluding Jamaica)*, Extra-Mural Dept., Univ. College of the West Indies, Caribbean Affairs Series, Kingston, n.d.

DALE, E. H. 'The demographic problem of the British West Indies', *Scott. Geogr. Mag.* **79**, 1963, pp. 23–31.

DAVISON, R. B. *West Indian Migrants*, London 1962.

DEBIEN, G. 'Les Origines des esclaves des Antilles', *Bull. Inst. Fr. Afr. Noire* **23**, Dakar 1961, pp. 363–87; and **24**, 1963, pp. 1–38.

DORAN, E. 'The West Indian hip-roofed cottage', *California Geographer* **3**, 1962.

ERICKSEN, E. G. *The West Indies Population Problem; dimensions for action*, Lawrence 1962.

FOERSTER, R. F. *The Racial Problems Involved in Immigration from Latin America and the West Indies to the United States*, A Report submitted to the Secretary of Labor, US Dept. of Labor, Washington 1925.

FURLEY, O. W. 'Protestant Missionaries in the West Indies: Pioneers of a non-racial Society', *Race* **6**, no. 3, 1965, pp. 232–42.

—— 'Moravian Missionaries and Slaves in the West Indies', *CS* **5**, no. 2, 1965, pp. 3–16.

GILLIN, J. 'Is there a modern Caribbean culture?', in *The Caribbean at Mid-Century*, ed. A. C. Wilgus, Gainesville 1962, pp. 129–35.

GUÉRIN, D. *The West Indies and their Future*, London 1961.

HAREWOOD, J. 'La surpopulation et le sousemploi dans la Fédération des Antilles', *Revue Internationale du Travail* **82**, 1960, pp. 117–55.

HEIDE, H. TER. 'West Indian migration to Great Britain: a review article', *Nieuwe West-Indische Gids* **43**, 1963, pp. 75–88.

HELWIG, G. V. 'Society in the British West Indies', in *The Caribbean: British, Dutch, French, United States*, ed. A. C. Wilgus, Gainesville 1958, pp. 27–38.

HERSKOVITS, M. *The Myth of the Negro Past*, New York 1941.

HILLS, T. 'Land settlement schemes: lessons from the British Caribbean', *Rev. Geogr. Inst. Pan-Am.* **63–5**, no. 2, Rio de Janeiro 1965, pp. 67–82.

HOCKEY, S. W. 'An emerging culture in the British West Indies', in *The Caribbean: British, Dutch, French, United States*, ed. A. C. Wilgus, Gainesville 1958, pp. 39–50.

HOETINK, H. 'Enkele sociaal-geographische Kenmerken van het Caribische Gebied', *Geogr. Tijdschr.* **14**, 1961, pp. 145–56.

—— *De gespleten Samenleving in het Caribisch Gebied*, Assen 1962.

—— 'Change in prejudice; some notes on the minority problem, with reference to the West Indies and Latin America', *Bijdragen tot de Taal-, Land- en Volkenkunde* **119**, no. 1, The Hague, 1963.

LEWIS, G. K. 'El Fondo histórico de la Sociedad del Caribe', *La Torre* **11**, 43, Río Piedras

1963, pp. 31–55.

LIER, R. A. J. VAN. *The Development and Nature of Society in the West Indies*, Royal Inst. for the Indies, Report no. 92. Department of Cultural and Physical Anthropology, no. 37, Amsterdam 1950.

LOWENTHAL, D. 'The range and variation of Caribbean societies', *in* 'Social and cultural pluralism in the Caribbean', ed. V. Rubin, *Annls. NY Acad. Sci.* **83**, Art. 5, 1960, pp. 786–95.

—— 'Caribbean views of Caribbean Land', *CG* **5**, 1961, pp. 1–9.

MERRILL, G. C. 'The historical record of man as an ecological dominant in the Lesser Antilles', *CG* **11**, 1958, pp. 17–22.

MINTZ, S. A. and RICHARD, B. S. 'The Caribbean: Puerto Rico, Cuba, Haiti, the Dominican Republic', *Lands and Peoples* **7**, New York 1964, pp. 22–49.

NAIPAUL, V. S. *The Middle Passage: impression of five societies—British, French and Dutch—in the West Indies and South America*, London 1962.

NIDDRIE, D. L. 'Eighteenth-Century Settlement in the British Caribbean', *Trans. Inst. Br. Geogr.* **40**, 1966, pp. 67–80.

PELLIER, J. 'La region des Caraibes: problèmes de population', *Études et Conjoncture*, Institut national de la Statistique et des Études économiques, **13**, 1958, pp. 973–84.

PICÓ, R. 'Comparisons and Contrasts in the Greater Antilles', *Hispanic American Studies* **2**, 1941, pp. 132–42 and *Caribe* **1**, 3, Río Piedras 1942, pp. 29–33.

—— 'Problems of Land Tenure Reform in Latin America', *JIAS* **6**, 1964, pp. 143–56.

POPULATION RESEARCH CENTER, Univ. of Texas, Bureau of Business Research. *International Population Census Bibliography: Latin America and the Caribbean*, Austin 1965.

PRICE, A. G. *White Settlers in the Tropics*, Am. Geogr. Soc., Spec. Publ. 23, New York 1939.

PROCTOR, J. H. 'East Indians and the Federation of the British West Indies', *India Quarterly* **17**, 1961, pp. 370–95.

PROUDFOOT, M. J. *Population Movements in the Caribbean*, Port-of-Spain 1950.

QUELLE, O. 'Der islamische Kulturkreis in Iberoamerika', *Pet. Geogr. Mitt.* **89**, 1943, pp. 257–60.

RAMOS, E. 'The population crisis and sugar cane', *Sugar y Azúcar* **60**, 1965, pp. 130–4.

REUBENS, E. P. 'Migration and Development in the West Indies', *SES* **10** (suppl.), 1961.

ROBERTS, G. 'The demographic position of the Caribbean', *Population Bull.* **19**, Washington 1963, pp. 184–9.

ROBERTS, G. W. and BYRNE, J. 'Summary statistics on indenture and associated migration affecting the West Indies, 1834–1918', *Population Studies* **20**, 1966, pp. 125–34.

RUBIN, V., ed. 'Social and cultural pluralism in the Caribbean', *Annls. NY Acad. Sci.* **83**, Art. 5, 1960, pp. 761–916.

—— *Caribbean Studies: a symposium*, Seattle 1957, 2nd edn, 1960.

SAPPER, K., VAN BLOM D. and NEDERBURGH, J. A. *Die Ansiedlungen der Europäer in den Tropen*, vol. 2: *Mittelamerika, Kleine Antillen, Niederländisch-West- und Ostindien*, Schr. des Vereins für Sozialpolitik, vol. 147, II, Munich, Leipzig 1912.

SMITH, M. G. *West Indian Family Structure*, Seattle 1962.

—— *The Plural Society in the British West Indies*, Berkeley and Los Angeles 1965.

SMITH, R. T. 'Culture and social structure in the Caribbean: some recent work on family and kinship studies', *Comparative Studies in Society and History* **6**, 1963, pp. 24–46.

STEVENS, P. H. M. 'Planning in the West Indies', *Town and Country Planning* **25**, 1957, pp. 503–8.

TANNENBAUM, F. *Slave and Citizen, the Negro in the Americas*, New York 1947.

VRIES, E. DE, ed. *Social Research and rural Life in Central America, Mexico and the Caribbean Region*, Proc. of a Seminar, organized by Unesco, Mexico City 1962, Unesco 1966.

WAGLEY, C. and HARRIS, M. 'A typology of Latin American subcultures', *Am. Anthropol.* **57**, 1955, pp. 428–51.

WILLIAMS, E. *The Negro in the Caribbean*, Washington DC, 1942.

—— *Capitalism and Slavery*, Chapel Hill 1944, 2nd edn, London 1964.

WOLF, E. R. and MINTZ, S. W. 'Haciendas and plantations in Middle America and the

Antilles', *SES* **6**, 1957, pp. 380–412.

ZELINSKY, W. 'The historical geography of the Negro population of Latin America', *J. Negro History* **34**, 1949, pp. 153–221.

—— 'Population growth in Central America and the West Indies: prospects and problems', *Mineral Industries* **35**, no. 6, 1966, pp. 1–2, 4–7.

Economy

ABBOTT, G. C. 'The future of economic cooperation in the West Indies in the light of the break-up of the Federation', *SES* **12**, 1963, pp. 160–78.

—— 'Stabilisation policies in the West Indies sugar industry', *CQ* **9**, 1963, pp. 53–66.

—— 'The West Indian sugar industry, with some long term projections of supply to 1975', *SES* **13**, 1964, pp. 1–37.

—— 'The collapse of the sea island cotton industry in the West Indies', *SES* **13**, 1964, pp. 157–87.

ALLEN, R. L. *El Aspecto ecónomico de la Influencia soviética en la América Latina*, México 1964.

ANDIC, F. M. and GUTIERREZ, E. 'Inter-Caribbean Trade Pattern', *CS* **6**, no. 2, 1966, pp. 46–58.

BAZIN, H. 'L'Economie de la région caraibe est-elle harmonisable?' *Développement et Civilisation* **20**, Paris 1964, pp. 54–72.

BEACHEY, R. W. *The British West Indies Sugar Industry in the late 19th Century*, Oxford 1957.

BELLET, D. *Les Grandes Antilles. Etude de géographie économique*, Paris 1909.

BLUME, H. 'Die britischen Inseln über dem Winde (Kleine Antillen). Grundbesitz und Betriebsformen in ihrem Einfluß auf das Bild der Kulturlandschaft', *Erdkunde* **15**, 1961, pp. 265–87.

—— 'Die gegenwärtigen Wandlungen in der Verbreitung von Groß- und Kleinbetrieben auf den Großen Antillen', *Beiträge zur Geographie der Neuen Welt*, Schr. d. Geogr. Inst. d. Univ. Kiel, vol. 20, Kiel 1961, pp. 75–123.

—— 'Westindien als Fremdenverkehrsgebiet', *Die Erde* **94**, 1963, pp. 47–72.

BOER, C. N. *Promotion of Intra-Caribbean Trade, Fruits and Vegetables*, Ministry of Foreign Affairs, Netherlands Bureau for International Technical Assistance, The Hague 1963.

CAMPBELL, L. 'Production Methods in West Indies Agriculture', *CQ* **8**, 1962, pp. 94–104.

CARIBBEAN COMMISSION, *The Sugar Industry of the Caribbean*, Washington, DC, 1947.

—— *Statistical Abstract to the joint Conference on Education and Small Scale Farming* **2**: *Caribbean Small Scale Farming*, Port-of-Spain, Trinidad 1954.

CARLE, B. 'The tourist potential of the Caribbean', *The Caribbean* **13**, 1959, pp. 50–5.

CHAPMAN, C. P. 'A new development in the agronomy of Pimento', *CQ* **11**, nos 3/4, 1965, pp. 3–9.

COLONIAL OFFICE, *An Economic Survey of the Colonial Territories 1951*, vol 4: *The West Indian and American Territories*, London 1953.

COULTER, J. K. 'Soil and land use problems in the West Indies', *World Crops* **15**, London 1963, 349–54.

COURTENAY, P. P. *Plantation Agriculture*, London 1965.

CREDNER, W. 'Probleme der Landnutzung auf den Grossen Antillen', *Z. Ges. Erdkunde Berlin*, 1940, pp. 287–302.

—— 'Typen der Wirtschaftslandschaft auf den Großen Antillen', *Pet. Geogr. Mitt.* **89**, 1943, pp. 1–23.

CUMPER, G. E., ed. *The Economy of the West Indies*, Kingston, Jamaica, 1960.

—— 'Labour and Development in the West Indies, Part 1', *SES* **10**, 1961, pp. 278–305.

—— 'Labour and Development in the West Indies, Part 2', *SES* **11**, 1962, pp. 1–33.

—— 'The Differentiation of economic groups in the West Indies', *SES* **11**, 1964, pp. 319–32.

DEFFONTAINES, P. 'L'introduction du bétail en Amérique latine', *Cahiers d'Outre Mer* **10**, 1957, pp. 5–22.

DEMAS, W. G. *The Economics of Development in Small Countries, with special reference to the Caribbean*, Montreal 1965.

FAULKNER, O. T. and SHEPHARD, C. Y. 'Mixed farming. The basis of a system for West Indian peasants', *Tropical Agriculture* **20**, 1943, pp. 136–42.

FAUVEL, C. D. *Report on Industrial Development in the Caribbean Area*, 2 vols, Caribbean Commission, Port-of-Spain 1952.

FINKEL, H. J. 'Patterns of land tenure in the Leeward and Windward Islands and their relevance to problems of agricultural development in the West Indies', *EG* **40**, 1964, pp. 163–72.

—— 'Attitudes toward work as a factor in agricultural planning in the West Indies', *CS* **4**, 1964, pp. 49–53.

FIRTH, R. and YAMEY, B. S. *Capital, Saving and Credit in Peasant Societies: Studies from Asia, Oceania, the Caribbean and Middle America*, London 1964.

FRASER, D. G. L. 'Canada's role in the West Indies', Canadian Institute of International Affairs, *Behind the Headlines* **23**, no. 3, Toronto 1964.

GERLING, W. *Wirtschaftsentwicklung und Landschaftswandel auf den westindischen Inseln Jamaika, Haiti und Puerto Rico*, Freiburg i. Br. 1938.

—— 'Die Plantagenwirtschaft des Rohrzuckers auf den Großen Antillen', *Würzberger Geogr. Arbeiten*, vol. 2, Würzburg 1954.

GUERRA SÁNCHEZ, R. 'Problemas de la economía antillana', *Revista bimestre cubana* **75**, 1958, pp. 5–91.

HALL, D. 'Incalculability as a feature of sugar production during the eighteenth century', *SES* **10**, 1961, pp. 340–52.

HARRIS, E. 'The role of government in industrial development in the Caribbean', *CER* **5**, 1955, pp. 118–26.

HERNÁNDEZ, F. J. 'Tourist travel and economic development in the Caribbean', in *The Caribbean 7, Contemporary International Relations*, ed. A. C. Wilgus, Gainesville 1957, pp. 166–74.

HILL, O. M. 'Canada's trade with the West Indies', *Canad. Geogr. J.* **58**, 1959, pp. 2–9.

HINCKLEY, T. M. 'The decline of Caribbean smuggling', *JIAS* **5**, 1963, pp. 107–21.

HODNETT, G. E. and NANTON, W. R. E. 'Definitions of a farm and a farmer in agricultural statistics in the West Indies', *SES* **8**, 1959, pp. 190–6.

HOY, D. R. 'Trends in the banana export industry of tropical America', *J. Geogr.* **63**, 1964, pp. 108–16.

HUGGINS, H. D. *Aluminium in Changing Communities*, London 1965.

ISSA, A. E. *A Survey of the Tourist Potential of the Eastern Caribbean*, Port-of-Spain 1959.

JOLLY, A. L. 'Small-scale farm management problems', in Caribbean Commission, *Small Scale Farming in the Caribbean*, Port-of-Spain, Trinidad 1954, pp. 15–24.

—— *Readings in Small Scale Farming*, St Augustine, Trinidad 1957.

KUNDU, A. 'Rice in the British Caribbean islands and British Guiana, 1950–1975', *SES* **13**, 1964, pp. 243–81.

LEWIS, W. A. 'The industrialisation of the British West Indies', *CER* **2**, no. 1, 1950, pp. 1–61.

—— 'Issues in Land Settlement Policy', *CER* **3**, 1951, pp. 58–92.

LOWENTHAL, D. 'Economic tribulations in the Caribbean: a case study in the British West Indies', *Inter-American Economic Affairs* **9**, 1955, pp. 67–81.

LUKE, S. *Development and Welfare in the West Indies*, London 1955.

MACFARLANE, D. 'The future of the banana industry in the West Indies', *SES* **13**, 1964, pp. 38–93.

—— 'The foundations for future production and export of West Indian citrus, *SES* **13**, 1964, pp. 118–56.

MANTEL, P. 'Pêche de la langouste aux Antilles par les pêcheurs bretons', *Bull. Soc. Océanogr.*, 1936, pp. 1515–20, 1528–30.

MARTIN-KAYE, P. H. A. *Salt in the Leeward Islands*, St John's, Antigua, 1954.

MATHEWS, T. G. *et al.*, *Politics and Economics in the Caribbean. A contemporary Analysis of the*

Bibliography

Dutch, French and British Caribbean, Río Piedras 1966.

McIntyre, A. 'Aspects of development and trade in the Commonwealth Caribbean', *Economic Bulletin for Latin America* **10**, no. 2, 1965, pp. 163–87.

Mejia-Ricart, M. A. 'Crisis of a small state in the present economic world. A study of the problems of small underdeveloped states, with special reference to Central America and the Caribbean Area, dissertation, Freiburg (Switzerland) 1958; London 1960.

Mikusch, G. *Kuba, Haiti und Louisiana als Zuckerländer*, Ber. üb. Landwirtsch., new series, sp. publ. 21, Berlin 1930.

Miller, T. M. 'Growth and development of air transportation in the Caribbean', in *The Caribbean 72 Contemporary International Relations*, ed. A. C. Wilgus, Gainesville 1957, pp. 184–95.

Niddrie, D. L. 'The Caribbean islands today', *J. Inst. Bankers*, June 1963, pp. 1–11.

Odell, P. R. 'The development of the Middle Eastern and Caribbean refining industries 1939–63', *Tijdschr, voor Econ. en Soc. Geogr.* **54**, 1963, pp. 202–13.

O'Loughlin, C. 'Economic problems of the smaller West Indies islands', *SES* **11**, 1962, pp. 44–56.

Paget, E. 'Value, Valuation, and Use of Land in the West Indies', *Geogrl. J.* **127**, 1961, pp. 493–8.

Palmer, J. J. 'The banana in the Caribbean Trade', *EG* **8**, 1932, pp. 262–73.

Pan-American Union. *Plantation Systems of the New World*, Social Science Monographs no. 7, Washington 1959.

Percival, D. A. 'Industrialization a historical background, existing industries and industrial potential of the Caribbean area', *CER* **5**, 1953, pp. 5–19.

Perronnette, H. 'Alimentation et problèmes nutritionelles en Caraibes', *Caraibe Medical* **1**, no. 1, 1965, pp. 27–8.

Peter, J. 'Étude comparative des industries des Antilles françaises, de Trinidad et de Barbade', *Bulletin de la Chambre de Commerce et d'Industrie de la Martinique* no. 4, Fort-de-France 1965, pp. 25–37.

Pitman, F. W. 'The settlement and financing of British West Indian plantations in the eighteenth century', in *Essays in Colonial History*, New Haven, Conn., 1931, pp. 252–83.

Poole, B. L. 'Economic trends in the British West Indies', in *The Caribbean: British, Dutch, French, United States*, ed. A. C. Wilgus, Gainesville 1958, pp. 11–26.

Price, R. 'Caribbean fishing and fishermen: a historical sketch', *American Anthropologist* **68**, no. 6, 1966, pp. 1363–83.

Rees, P. W. *Air Transport in the Lesser Antilles*, University of California, Department of Geography, Berkeley 1964.

Sapper, K. 'Die wirtschaftlichen Verhältnisse der Kleinen Antillen', *Pet. Geogr. Mitt.* **57**, 1911, pp. 125–7; 180–4.

Sauer, C. O. 'Economic prospects of the Caribbean', in *The Caribbean: its economy*, ed. A. C. Wilgus, Gainesville 1954, pp. 15–27.

Shephard, C. Y. 'The sugar industry of the British West Indies and British Guiana with special reference to Trinidad', *EG* **5**, 1929, pp. 149–75.

—— *Peasant Agriculture in the Leeward and Windward Islands*, St Augustine, Trinidad 1945.

Simmonds, N. W. 'The growth of post-war West Indian banana trades', *Tropical Agriculture* **37**, 1960, pp. 79–85.

Starkey, O. P. *Commercial Geography of the Eastern British Caribbean*, Technical Report no. 12, Dept. of Geography, Indiana University, Bloomington 1961.

Taxacher, H. 'Entwicklungsgeschichte der deutschwestindischen Wirtschaftsbeziehungen', Dissertation, Cologne 1929.

Tempany, H. A., *Agriculture in the West Indies*, Colonial Office no. 182, London 1942.

Tjon A-Ten, E. R. *A Study of Cooperatives in Jamaica and Puerto Rico*, Department van Landbouw, Paramaribo 1961.

Waibel, L. *Probleme der Landwirtschaftsgeographie*, Breslau 1933.

Wilhelms, C. and Almeida Sedas, J. G. de. *Quellenverzeichnis zur Wirtschaftsstatistik Ibero-*

amerikas, Bibliographie und Dokumentation 10, Hamburg 1966.

WILLIAMS, C. H. B. *Peasant Farming in the British Caribbean*, Dept. of Agriculture, Port-of-Spain, 1954, and *J. Agr. Soc. Trinidad and Tobago* **54**, 1954, pp. 226–36.

—— 'Small-scale farming in the Caribbean', *J. Agr. Soc. Trinidad and Tobago* **55**, 1955, pp. 244–9.

WILLIAMS, E. 'The importance of small-scale farming in the Caribbean, in Caribbean Commission, *Small Scale Farming in the Caribbean*, Port-of-Spain, Trinidad 1954, pp. 1–14.

WILLIAMS, G. *The Economics of Everyday Life in the West Indies*, University College of the West Indies, Extramural Dept., Mona 1953.

WOLFF, R. P. and VOYLES, R. *Tourist Trends in the Caribbean 1951–1955*, Coral Gables, Fla., 1956.

THE ISLANDS

Bahama Islands

AGASSIZ, A. 'A reconnaissance of the Bahamas and of the elevated reefs of Cuba in the Steam Yacht "Wild Duck", January to April, 1893', *Bull. Mus. Comp. Zool. Harvard College* **26**, Cambridge, Mass., 1894–95, pp. 1–204.

ATHEARN, W. D. 'Bathymetry of the Straits of Florida and the Bahama Islands', 2: Bathymetry of the tongue of the ocean, Bahamas', *Bull. Marine Science of the Gulf and Caribbean* **13**, no. 3, 1963, pp. 365–77.

BARCLAYS BANK. *The Bahamas; an economic survey*, London 1961.

BOOY, T. DE. 'The Turks and Caicos Islands, British West Indies', *Geogr. Rev.* **6**, 1918, pp. 37–51.

BOUNDS, J. H. 'Land use in the Bahamas', Dissertation, Knoxville 1966.

BRITTON, N. L. and MILLSPAUGH, C. F. *The Bahama Flora*, New York 1920, reprinted 1962.

BROOKS, C. E. P. 'The meteorology of Nassau, Bahamas, 1852–1919', *Quart. Journ. Royal Met. Soc.* **47**, 1921, pp. 59–62.

COLLINS, D. 'The Turks and Caicos Islands. Some impressions of an English visitor', *CQ* **7**, 1961, pp. 163–7.

COLONIAL OFFICE REPORT. *Bahamas 1960 and 1961*, London 1963.

DORAN, E. *Land Forms of the Southeast Bahamas*, Univ. of Texas. Publ. no. 5509, Austin 1955.

—— *The Caicos conch trade'*, *Geogr. Rev.* **48**, 1958, pp. 388–401.

FIELD, R. M., *et al.* 'Geology of the Bahamas', *Bull. Geol. Soc. Am.* **42**, 1931, pp. 759–84.

GRANBERRY, J. 'The cultural position of the Bahamas in Caribbaan archaeology', *American Antiquity* **22**, 1956, pp. 128–34.

ILLING, L. V. 'Bahamian calcareous sands', *Bull. Am. Ass. Petrol. Geologists* **38**, 1954, pp. 1–95.

LONG, E. *Bahamas*, Garden City 1964.

NEWELL, N. D. 'Bahamian platforms', in *Crust of the Earth*, ed. A. Poldervaart; Geol. Soc. Am., Spec. paper 62, Baltimore 1955, pp. 303–15.

OTTERBEIN, K. F. *The Andros Islanders. A study of family organization in the Bahamas*, Kansas City 1966.

SEIBOLD, E. 'Untersuchungen zur Kalkfällung und Kalklösung am Westrand der Great Bahama Bank', *Sedimentology* **1**, 1962, pp. 50–74.

SEVER, B. B. *Basic Data on the Economy of the Bahama Islands*, US Bureau of International Commerce, OBR 64–38, Washington 1964.

SHATTUCK, G. B. *The Bahama Islands*, New York 1905.

STEWART, G. 'San Salvador Island to Cuba: a cruise in the track of Columbus', *Geogr. Rev.* **21**, 1931, pp. 124–30.

TALWANI, M., WORZEL, J. L. and EWING, M. 'Gravity anomalies and structure of the Bahamas', *Trans. Second Caribb. Geol. Conf.*, Mayagüez 1959, pp. 156–61.

Cuba

ACADEMIA DE CIENCIAS DE CUBA, Instituto de Geografía. *Area de Cuba*, Habana 1965.

ADAMOVICH, A. and CHEJOVICH, A. 'Sobre el relieve premaestrichtiano del Norte de Oriente y sus relaciones con la geomorfología contemporánea', *Rev. tecnológica* **3**, no. 2, Habana 1965, pp. 29–34.

ALLEMANN, F. R. *Fidel Castro. Die Revolution der Bärte*, Hamburg 1961.

BATCHELDER, R. B. 'The evolution of Cuban land tenure and its relation to certain agro-economic problems', *South Western Social Science Quarterly* **33**, 1952/53, pp. 239–46.

BECKFORD, G. L. F. 'A note on agricultural organization and planning in Cuba', *CS* **6**, no. 3, 1966, pp. 45–51.

BELLOWS, I. 'Economic aspects of the Cuban Revolution', *Political Affairs* **43**, no. 1, 1964, pp. 14–29; no. 2, 1964, pp. 43–51.

BENNETT, H. H. and ALLISON, R. V. *The Soils of Cuba*, Washington 1928.

BIANCHI, A. *Land Reform in Cuba*, London 1963.

BLECKERT, H. 'Beiträge zur ökonomischen Geographie der Republik Kuba', *Pet. Geogr. Mitt.* **110**, 1966, pp. 36–41, 116–23, 200–5.

BLOCH, P. 'Kuba 1963', *Geogr. Rdsch.* **15**, 1963, pp. 291–7.

BOYER, H. M. 'Distribution of sugar cane production in Cuba', *EG* **15**, 1939, pp. 311–25.

BOYTEL, JAMBÚ, F. *Restauración de un Cafetal de los Colonos franceses in la Sierra Maestra*, Habana 1962.

BRÖNNIMANN, P. and RIGASS, D. 'Contribution to the geology and paleontology of the area of the city of La Habana, Cuba, and its surroundings', *Ecl. Geol. Helvetiae* **56**, 1963, pp. 193–480.

BRÜMMER, A. 'Zur Entwicklung auf Kuba', *Wirtschaftswissenschaft* **9**, 1961, pp. 572–80.

CALVACHE, A. *Bosquejo histórico del Conocimiento de la Geología de Cuba*, Habana 1965.

CANET, G. *Atlas de Cuba*, Cambridge, Mass., 1949.

CARABIA, J. P. 'The vegetation of the Sierra de Nipe, Cuba', *Ecol. Monogr.* **15**, 1945, pp. 321–41.

CEPERO BOUILLA, R. *Azúcar y Abolición*, Habana 1960.

CHAMBERLIN, T. W. 'Rainfall maps of Cuba', *MWR* **68**, 1940, pp. 4–10.

CHEN, C.-S. *Land Use and Sugar Industry in Cuba*; Research Report no. 43, Inst. of Agric. Geography, Taipei, Taiwan 1954.

CHONCHOL, J. 'Análisis crítico de la Reforma agraria Cubana', *El Trimestre económico* **30**, Mexico 1963, pp. 69–143.

CREMER, W. 'Die Bevölkerungsentwicklung der Insel Kuba', *Erdkunde* **6**, 1952, pp. 180–3.

CRIST, R. E. 'Some notes on recent trends in rice production in Cuba', *EG* **32**, 1956, pp. 126–31.

CUBAN ECONOMIC RESEARCH PROJECT. *A Study on Cuba*, Coral Gables 1965.

DAMBAUGH, L. N. 'Tobacco production: Vuelta Abajo region, Cuba', *J. Geogr.* **55**, 1956, pp. 442–6.

DAVITAJA, F. F., MAŠBIC, J. G. and RJABČIKOV, A. M. 'Sostojame geografii Kube (Der Stand der Geographie in Kuba)', *Izv. Akad. Nauk SSSR*, Ser. geogr. 2, Moskow 1966, pp. 111–4.

DEBIEN, G. 'De Saint-Domingue à Cuba avec une famille de réfugiés (1800–1809)', *Revue de la Faculté d'Ethnologie, Port-au-Prince* **8**, 1964, pp. 7–31.

DECKERT, E. *Cuba*, Bielefeld and Leipzig 1899.

DESPORTS, F. 'L'agriculture dans l'économie cubaine', *Economie et Politique* **109**, 1963, pp. 66–75.

DEUTSCH-SUDAMERIKANISCHE BANK. *Wirtschaftsbericht Kuba*, Hamburg 1954.

DUCLOZ, C. 'Étude géomorphologique de la région de Matanzas, Cuba', *Archives des Sciences* **16**, Geneva 1963, pp. 351–402.

DUMONT, R. *Cuba, Socialisme et Développement*, Paris 1964.

DUMONT, R. and COLEOU. J. *La Réforme agraire à Cuba: ses Conditions de Réussite*, Etudes 'Tiers

Monde', Problèmes des Pays sous-développés, Paris 1962.

DYER, D. R. 'Sugar regions of Cuba', *EG* **32**, 1956, pp. 177–84.

—— 'Urbanism in Cuba', *Geogr. Rev.* **47**, 1957, pp. 224–33.

EGGERT, K. 'Ein Beitrag zur politischen und ökonomischen Geographie Cubas', *Z. Erkundeunterricht* **12**, 1960, pp. 220–7.

ELY, R. T. 'The old Cuba trade: highlights and case studies of Cuban-American inter-dependence during the nineteenth century', *Business History Review* **38**, Boston 1964, pp. 456–78.

FITZGIBBON, R. H. *Cuba and the United States, 1900–1935*, New York 1964.

FOSCUE, E. J. 'Rainfall maps of Cuba', *MWR* **56**, 1928, pp. 170–3.

FRIEDLAENDER, H. E. *Historia económica de Cuba*, Habana 1944.

FURRAZOLA-BERMÚDEZ, G. and NÚÑEZ JIMÉNEZ, A. *et al.* *Geología de Cuba*, Habana 1964.

—— 'Comentarios sobre el nuevo mapa de Yacimientos minerales de Cuba, Escala 1:500 000, *Rev. tecnológica* **3**, no. 6, 1965, pp. 20–3.

GERLING, W. *Die wirtschaftsgeographische Entwicklung der Insel Kuba unter besonderer Berucksichti-gung der Zuckerwirtschaft und des Problems Kapitalismus und Landwirtschaft*, Solingen-Ohligs 1935.

GRADZINSKI, R. and RADOMSKI, A. 'Types of Cuban caves and their dependence on factors controlling karst development', *Bull. Acad. Pol. Sci.*, Sér. Geol. Géogr. **11**, no. 3, 1963, pp. 151–60.

—— 'Origin and development of internal poljes 'hoyos' in the Sierra de los Organos (Cuba)', *Bull. Acad. Pol. Sci.*, Sér. Géol. Géogr. **13**, no. 2, 1965, pp. 181–6.

GUERRA Y SÁNCHEZ, R. *Azúcar y Población en las Antillas*, Habana 1927. English trans. as *Sugar and Society in the Caribbean*, New Haven and London 1964.

GUTELMAN, M. 'L'agriculture cubaine', *Etudes rurales* **8**, 1963, pp. 62–83.

HILDÉN, K. 'Cuba som Sockerproducent', *Ekonomiskgeografiska Studier Handelshögskolans Göteborg*, no. 1, Göteborg 1959, pp. 98–104.

HILL, P. A. 'Geology and structure of the northwest Trinidad mountains, Las Villas Province, Cuba', *Bull. Geol. Soc. Am.* **70**, 1959, pp. 1459–78.

HOWELL, W. E. 'A study of the rainfall of central Cuba', *J. Meteorol.* **10**, 1953, pp. 270–8.

HUGUET, L. 'Forêts et économie forestière de Cuba', *Annales de l'Ecole nationale des Eaux et Forêts et de la Station de Recherches et Expériences* **18**, Nancy 1961, pp. 533–616.

HUMBOLDT, A. VON. *Essai politique sur l'Isle de Cuba*, 2 vols, Paris 1826.

INTERNATIONAL BANK FOR RECONSTRUCTION AND DEVELOPMENT, in collaboration with the Government of Cuba. *Report on Cuba. Findings and Recommendations of an economic and technical Mission*, Washington 1951.

KEIJZER, F. G. *Outline of the Geology of the eastern Part of the Province of Oriente, Cuba (E of 76° WL) with notes on the geology of other parts of the island;* Geogr. en Geol. Med., Phys.-Geol. Reeks, Ser. 2, no. 6, Utrecht 1945.

KLEIN, H. S. *Slavery in the Americas. A comparative study of Cuba and Virginia*, Chicago 1966.

KRÖMMELBEIN, K. 'Beiträge zur geologischen Kenntnis der Sierra de los Organos (Cuba)', *Z. Dt. Geol. Ges.* **114**, no. 1, 1962, pp. 92–120.

KUMAN, V. E. and GAVILÁN, R. R. 'Geología de la Isla de Pinos', *Rev. technológica* **3**, no. 4, Havana 1965, pp. 20–38.

LEHMANN, H. *Internationaler Karstaltlas*, sheet 1: *Sierra de los Organos, Cuba;* no place of publication (1959)

LEHMANN, H., KRÖMMELBEIN, K. and LÖTSCHERT, W. 'Karstmorphologische, geologische und botanische Studien in der Sierra de los Organos auf Cuba', *Erdkunde* **10**, 1956, pp. 185–204.

LEWIS, G. E. and STRACZEK, J. A. *Geology of South-central Oriente, Cuba*, US Geol. Surv. Bull. **975**-D, Washington 1955.

LEWIS, J. W. 'Geology of Cuba', *Bull. Am. Ass. Petrol. Geol.* **16**, 1932, pp. 533–55.

LÖTSCHERT, W. 'Die Übereinstimmung von geologischer Unterlage und Vegetation in der Sierra de los Organos (Westcuba), *Ber. dt. bot. Ges.* **71**, 1958, pp. 55–70.

403

LUTZ, O. 'Kuba. Eindrücke von einer Antillenreise', *Mitt. Ges. f. Erdkunde Leipzig 1923–25*, 1926, pp. 58–86.

MACGAFFEY, W. and BARNETT, C. R. *Cuba. Its people, its society, its culture*, New Haven 1962.

MARIE-VICTORIN, F. and LÉON, F., *Itinéraires botaniques dans l'Ile de Cuba*. Contribution de l'Institut botanique de l'Université de Montréal no. 68, Montreal 1956.

MARRERO, L. *Geografía de Cuba* 3rd edn, Habana 1957.

—— *Histori económica de Cuba*, Guí de Estudio y Documentación, Habana 1956.

MARTINEZ SAENZ, J. 'Política agraria cubana', in *Caribbean Land Tenure Symposium*, ed. Car. Comm., Washington 1947, pp. 247–71.

MASSIP, S., *La Ciudad de la Habana; Comptes Rendus C. I. G. Amsterdam 1938*, vol. 1, Leiden 1938, pp. 469–73.

—— 'La Revolución y la geografía aplicada en Cuba', Unión Geográfica Internacional, *Trans. Conferencia Regional Latinoamericana*, vol. 2, Mexico 1966, pp. 219–27.

MASSIP, S. and ISALQUÉ, S. E. *Introducción a la Geografía de Cuba*, Havana 1942.

MASSIP VALDÉS, S. 'El Atlas Nacional de Cuba', Unión Geográfica Internacional, *Trans. Conferencia Regional Latinoamericana*, vol. 3, Mexico 1966, pp. 561–72.

MATHEWS, T. 'The agrarian reform in Cuba and Puerto Rico', *Revista de Ciencias Sociales* **4**, Río Piedras 1960, pp. 107–23.

MATTHEWS, H. L. *Cuba*, New York 1964.

MEARS, L. G. *Agriculture and Food Situation in Cuba*, US Dept. of Agriculture, Economic Research Service, Washington 1962.

MIKUSCH, G. *Kuba, Haiti und Louisiana als Zuckerländer;* Ber. über Landwirtschaft, n. f., sp. publ. 21, Berlin 1930.

MILLARES, M. 'Problemas del comercio interior en Cuba', *Cuba Socialista* **6**, no. 61, 1966, pp. 21–39.

MINNEMAN, P. G. *The Agriculture of Cuba*, Foreign Agriculture Bull., no. 2, Washington, DC, 1942.

MONZÓN, M. A. and SANTOS RIOS, E. *Estudio económico social de la Isla de Pinos*, Havana 1952.

MOULIN, J. DU, et al., 'Monocultivo y proletarización, dos ejemplos de Las Villas', *Ciencias Sociales Contemporáneas* **1**, no. 1, Havana 1965, pp. 119–44.

NELSON, L. *Rural Cuba*, Minneapolis 1950.

NÚÑEZ JIMÉNEZ, A. *Geografía de Cuba;* 2nd edn, Havana 1959, 3rd edn, n.d. (1966).

—— *In the 2nd Year of the Cuban Agrarian Reform*, Havana 1961.

—— *La Reforma agraria de Cuba*, Havana 1966.

NÚÑEZ JIMÉNEZ, A., PANOS, V. and STELCL, O. *Investigaciones carsológicas en Cuba*, Academia de Ciencias de Cuba, Habana 1966.

O'CONNOR, J. 'The labour force, employment and unemployment in Cuba, 1957–1961', *SES* **15**, 1966, pp. 85–91.

ORTIZ, F. *Contrapunto Cubano de Tabaco y el Azúcar*, Havana 1940. English trans. as *Cuban Counterpoint: tobacco and sugar*, New York 1947.

PALMER, R. H. 'Outline of the geology of Cuba', *J. Geol.* **53**, 1945, pp. 1–34.

PERAZA SARAUSA, F., ed. *Bibliografía cubana*, 2nd edn, Gainesville 1966.

—— *Bibliografía cubana, Complementos: 1937–1961*, Gainesville 1966.

PÉREZ DE LA RIVA, J. 'La población actual de la Gran Habana', *Boletín de la Escuela de Geografía* **1**, no. 2–3, Habana 1964, pp. 29–32

PLANK, J. N., ed. *Cuba and the United States*, Washington 1966.

PLATT, R. S. 'Geography of a sugar district: Mariel, Cuba', *Geogr. Rev.* **19**, 1929, pp. 603–12.

PRADO PÉREZ, L. *Clasificación ocupacional de Cuba*, Habana 1955.

REGALADO, A. 'Credits for small farmers in Cuba', *World Marxist Review*, **8**, no. 3, Toronto 1965, pp. 29–32.

RIGASSI-STUDER, D. 'Sur la géologie de la Sierra de los Organos, Cuba', *Archives des Sciences* **16**, Geneva 1963 pp. 339–50.

RITZHAUPT, H. *Las Pesquerías de Cuba y algunas Recomendaciones para su Intensificación*, Instituto Nacional de la Pesca, Havana 1965.

RIVERO MUNIZ, J. *Tabaco; su Historia en Cuba*. vol 1: *desde 'su Descubrimiento en 1492 hasta la Implantación de la segunda Factoría de Tabacos en La Habana en 1761*, Instituto de Historia, Comisión Nacional de la Academia de Ciencias de la República de Cuba, Habana 1964.

RODRIGUEZ-CABRERA, M. 'Land tenure and land distribution in Cuba', in *Land Tenure*, ed. K. H. Parsons, R. J. Penn and P. M. Raup, Madison 1956, pp. 323–8.

ROIG DE LEUCHSENRING, E. *Historia de la Habana*, Habana 1938, reprinted 1963.

RUTTEN, L. 'Enkele morfologische Opmerkingen over Cuba', *Tijdscher. Ned. Aardr. Gen.* **58**, 1941, pp. 992–1001.

SAGRA, R. DE LA. *Cuba: 1860; selección de artículos sobre agricultura cubana*, Habana 1963.

SCHERF, K. 'Ökonomisch-geographische Strukturwandlungen der Republik Kuba', *Geogr. Berichte* **9**, 1964, pp. 149–77.

SEERS, D., ed. *Cuba: the Economic and Social Revolution*, Chapel Hill 1964.

SEIFRIZ, W. 'Pflanzengeographie von Kuba', *Botan. Jahrbücher* **70**, 1940, pp. 441–62.

—— 'The plant life of Cuba', *Ecol. Monogr.* **13**, 1943, pp. 375–426.

SEMEVSKIY, B. N. 'Basic national-economic problems of the Republic of Cuba', *Soviet Geography; Review and translation*, **7**, no. 2, 1966, pp. 36–43; trans. from *Izvestiya Vsesoyuznogo Geograficheskogo Obshchestva* **97**, no. 6, Leningrad 1965, pp. 527–33.

SIMONS, F. S. and STRACZEK, J. A. *Geology of the Manganese Deposits of Cuba*, Washington 1958.

SMITH, E. E. *The Forests of Cuba;* Maria Moors Cabot Foundation Publ. no. 2 Harvard Forest, Petersham, Mass. and Atkins Research Laboratory, Cienfuegos 1954.

SMITH, R. F. *The United States and Cuba, Business and Diplomacy, 1917–1960*, New York 1960.

SOLSONA, J. B. and JUDOLEY, C. M. 'Esquema tectónico e Historia de la Evolución geológica de la Isla de Cuba', *Rev. tecnológica* **1**, Habana 1964, pp 4–13.

SPITZE, R. G. F. and GREGORIO ALFARO, A. 'Property rights, tenancy laws of Cuba, and economic power of renters', *Land Economics* **35**, 1959, pp. 277–83.

STATISTICHES BUNDESAMT. *Der Außenhandel der Bundesrepublik Deutschland*, Ergänzungsreihe: Der Außenhandel des Auslandes, no. 104, Cuba; Stuttgart, Mainz 1959.

STRODE, H. *Kampf um Kuba*, Munich 1938.

TABER, S. 'The Sierra Maestra of Cuba, part of the northern rim of the Bartlett Trough', *Bull. Geol. Soc. Am.* **45**, 1934, pp. 567–619.

TEICHERT, P. C. M. 'Die wirtschaftspolitischen und soziologischen Auswirkungen der kubanischen Revolution auf Lateinamerika', *Wirtschaftsdienst* **41**, 1961, pp. 211–18.

—— 'Latin America and the socio-economic impact of the Cuban Revolution', *JIAS* **4**, 1962, pp. 105–20.

TORRE, C. DE LA, AGUAYO, A. M. and MARRERO, L. *Geografía de Cuba*, 12th edn. n.d.

TORRENTE, J. *Un Tema de Geografía histórica: El Desbordamiento del Rio Almendares en 1791 y Cambio del Cauce en una Zona de su Curso*, Instituto de Geografía, Academia de Ciencias, Habana 1966.

TRAPPEN, F. 'Die Agrarreform in Kuba', *Deutsche Außenpolitik* **6**, 1961, pp. 183–93.

—— 'Entwicklungsprobleme des sozialistischen Kuba', *Einheit* **18**, 1963, pp. 127–35.

UPHOF, J. C. T. 'The plant formations on the coral reefs along the northern coast of Cuba', *Am. J. Bot.* **11**, 1924, pp. 409–16.

VALDES, A. J. *Historia de la Isla de Cuba y en especial de La Habana*, Habana 1964.

VOGT, J. 'Quelques aspects de l'agriculture cubaine d'après le Censo Agricola de 1946', *Information géographique* **18**, Paris 1954, pp. 85–93.

WAGNER, M. L. 'Habana', *Dt. Rdsch. Geogr.* **37**, 1914/15, pp. 193–200.

WAIBEL, L., 'Place names as an aid in the reconstruction of the original vegetation of Cuba', *Geogr. Rev.* **33**, 1943, pp. 376–96.

WERNER, T. G. 'Das Kupferhüttenwerk des Hans Tetzel aus Nürnberg auf Kuba und seine Finanzierung durch europäisches Finanzkapital', *Viertelj.-Schr. Sozial- u. Wirtschaftsges.* **48**, 1961, pp. 289–328 and 444–502.

WHITBECK, R. H. 'Geographical relations in the development of Cuban agriculture', *Geogr. Rev.* **12**, 1922, pp. 223–40.

WHITE, B. *Azúcar amargo; un estudio de la economía Cubana*, Havana 1954.

405

Bibliography

Whittlesey, D. S. 'Geographic factors in the relations of the United States and Cuba', *Geogr. Rev.* **12**, 1922, pp. 241–56.
Winsberg, M. D. 'The rise and decline of the American grapefruit industry on the Isle of Pines, Cuba', *Am. J. Econ. Sociol.* **20**, 1961, pp. 543–8.
Ysalqué de Massip, S. E. 'Las regiones geomorfológicas de Cuba', Unión Geográfica Internacional, *Trans. Conferencia Regional Latinoamericana*, vol. 3, Mexico 1966, pp. 106–14.

Jamaica

Aley, T. *Origin and Hydrology of Caves in the White Limestone of north central Jamaica*, Department of Geography, University of California, Berkeley 1961.
Asprey, G. F. and Robbins, R. G. 'The vegetation of Jamaica', *Ecol. Monogr.* **23** 1953, pp. 359–412.
Barclays Bank. *Jamaica, an Economic Survey*, London 1959.
Beau, K. and McKinnon, R. 'Jamaika. Insel im Zeichen des wirtschaftlichen Fortschritts', *Z. Wirtschaftsgeogr.* **6**, 1962, pp. 175–7.
Bigelow, J. *Jamaica in 1850*, New York and London 1851.
Biscoe, J. S. 'Tyndale. The Jamaican Arawak—his origin, history and culture', *Jamaican Historical Review*, Kingston, **3**, no. 3, 1962, pp. 1–9.
Black, C. C. de Brosse. *The Story of Jamaica, from Prehistory to the Present*, London 1965.
Blake, J. *Family Structure in Jamaica*, New York 1961.
Blaut, J. M. 'Jamaican farming systems in Nicaragua, Costa Rica and Panamá', *AAAG* **50**, 1960, pp. 304–5.
Blaut, J. M. *et al.* 'A study of cultural determinants of soil erosion and conservation in the Blue Mountains of Jamaica, *SES* **8**, 1959, pp. 403–20.
Blume, H. 'Der Bauxitbergbau auf Jamaika', *Geogr. Rdsch.* **14**, 1962, pp. 227–35.
Brennau, J. F. *Meteorology of Jamaica*, Kingston, Jamaica, 1936.
—— *The Rainfall of Jamaica from about 1870 to end of 1939*, Kingston 1943.
Brockmann-Jerosch, H. and M. *Jamaika, Vegetationsbilder* **16**, nos. 5/6, Jena 1924/26.
Burns, D. J. 'Some chemical aspects of bauxite genesis in Jamaica', *Economic Geology* **7**, 1961, pp. 1297–1303.
Callender, C. V. 'The development of the capital market institutions of Jamaica', *SES* **14**, no. 3, Suppl., 1965.
Carley, M. M. *Jamaica, the Old and the New*, London 1963.
Central Planning Unit, Government of Jamaica. *Economic Survey, Jamaica 1958*, Kingston 1959.
Chapman, V. J. 'The botany of the Jamaica shoreline', *Geogrl J.* **96**, 1940, pp. 312–23.
Chubb, L. J. *A Subsidence in the Mountains of Jamaica*, Geol. Survey Dept. Jamaica, Short Paper no. 2, London 1953.
Clarke, C. G. 'Problemas de Planeación urbana en Kingston, Jamaica', Unión Geográfica Internacional, *Trans. Conferencia Regional Latinoamericana*, vol. 1, Mexico 1966, pp. 411–31.
—— 'Population pressure in Kingston: Jamaica; a study of unemployment and overcrowding', *Trans. Inst. Br. Geogr.* **38**, 1966, pp. 165–82.
Clarke, E. 'Land tenure and the family in four communities in Jamaica, *SES* **1**, no. 4, 1953, pp. 81–116.
—— *My Mother Who Fathered Me. A study of the family in three selected communities in Jamaica*, London 1957.
Clarke, O. M. 'The formation of bauxite on karst topography in Eufaula district, Alabama and Jamaica, West Indies', *Economic Geology* **61**, 1966, pp. 903–16.
Cumper, G. *The Social Structure of Jamaica*, Caribbean Affairs, Extra-Mural Department, University College of the West Indies, Kingston. n.d.
—— 'Labour demand and supply in the Jamaican sugar industry 1830–1950', *SES* **2**, no. 4, 1953, pp. 1–50.

—— 'A modern Jamaican sugar estate', *SES* **3**, Kingston 1954, pp. 119–60.

—— 'Population movements in Jamaica, 1830–1950', *SES* **5**, 1956, pp. 261–80.

—— 'The Jamaican family: village and estate', *SES* **7**, 1958, pp. 76–108.

—— 'Tourist expenditure in Jamaica, 1958', *SES* **8**, 1959, pp. 287–310.

—— 'Preliminary analysis of population growth and social characteristics in Jamaica, 1943–60;', *SES* **12**, 1963, pp. 393–431.

DALLAS, R. C. *The History of the Maroons*, 2 vols, London 1803. German trans. *Geschichte der Maronen-Neger auf Jamaika*, Weimar 1805.

DAMBAUGH, L. N., 'Jamaica: an island in transition', *J. Geogr.* **52**, 1953, pp. 45–57.

DANEŠ, J. V. 'Karststudien in Jamaika', *Sitz. Ber. d. Kgl. Böhm. Ges. d. Wiss., Math.-naturw. Kl., Jg.* 1914, no. 20, Prague 1914, pp. 1–72.

DAVENPORT, C. B. and STEGGERDA, M. *Race Crossing in Jamaica*, Carnegie Institution Publication no. 395, Washington 1929.

DAVENPORT, W. *Jamaican Fishing*, Yale Univ. Publ. in Anthropology no. 59, New Haven 1960.

—— 'The family system of Jamaica', *SES* **10**, 1961, pp. 420–54.

DELATRE, R. *A Guide to Jamaican Reference Material in the West India Reference Library*, Kingston 1965.

DEPARTMENT OF STATISTICS, JAMAICA. *Agricultural Statistics 1954, 1955*, Kingston 1957.

—— *Agricultural Census 1961–1962*, Bull. no. 3, Kingston 1963.

—— *Industrial Activity 1960*, Report on a Survey of Establishments, Kingston 1963.

DRASCHER, W., 'Deutsche Siedlungen auf Jamaika', *Ibero.-Am. Archiv* **6**, 1932, pp. 84–90.

EDWARDS, D. T. 'An economic study of agriculture in the Yallahs Valley area of Jamaica', *SES* **4**, 1955, pp. 316–41.

—— *An Economic Study of Small Farming in Jamaica*, Institute of Social and Economic Research, University College of the West Indies, Kingston 1961.

—— 'An economic view of agricultural research in Jamaica', *SES* **10**, 1961, pp. 306–39.

EISNER, G. *Jamaica, 1830–1930. A study in economic growth*, Manchester 1961.

Five Year Independence Plan 1963–1968: A long-term development programme for Jamaica, Kingston 1963.

FRANCIS, O. C. *The People of Modern Jamaica*, Dept. of Statistics, Kingston 1963.

FURNESS, A. 'The Jamaican coffee boom and Jack Mackeson; a Blue Mountain coffee planter, 1807–1819', *Jamaican Hist. Rev.* **3**, no. 3, 1964, pp. 10–21.

GORDON, H. 'A note on Jamaica's fisheries', *CQ* **10**, no. 3, 1964, pp. 41–50.

GORDON, W. E. 'Imperial policy decisions in the economic history of Jamaica, 1664–1934', *SES* **6**, 1957, pp. 1–28.

GOREAU, T. F. 'The ecology of Jamaican coral reefs', *Ecology* **40**, 1959, pp. 67–90.

HALL, D. *Free Jamaica, 1838–1865*, New Haven 1959.

HALL, M. 'Storms and hurricanes in Jamaica, 1655 to 1915', *MWR* **43**, 1915, p. 620.

HART, C. W. J. 'A contribution to the limnology of Jamaica and Puerto Rico', *Car. J. Sci.* **4**, nos 2–3, 1964, pp. 331–4.

HILL, R. T. 'The geology and physical geography of Jamaica', *Bull. Mus. Comp. Zoology at Harvard College* **34**, Cambridge, Mass., 1899, pp. 1–256.

HOPPÉ, O. F. *Blaue Berge von Jamaika*, Berlin 1956.

HOSE, H. R. 'The geology and mineral resources of Jamaica', *Colon. Geol. and Min. Resources* **1**, 1950, pp. 11–36.

HOY, H. E. 'Blue Mountain coffee of Jamaica', *EG* **14**, 1938, pp. 409–12.

HOYTE, C., ed. *The Yearbook of Industry and Agriculture in Jamaica 1957*, Kingston 1957.

INNIS, D. Q. 'The efficiency of Jamaican peasant land use', *CG* **5**, 1961, pp. 19–23.

—— 'The economic geography of Jamaica', *Rev. Canad. Géogr.* **17**, 1963, pp. 26–30.

INTERNATIONAL BANK FOR RECONSTRUCTION AND DEVELOPMENT. *The Economic Development of Jamaica*, Baltimore 1952.

JACOBS, R., 'Jamaica, seine physikalisch-politische Geographie und wirtschaftliche Bedeutung', dissertation, Erlangen 1916.

JAMAICA AGRICULTURAL SOCIETY. *The Farmer's Guide*, 2nd edn, Glasgow 1962.

JAMAICA, CENTRAL PLANNING UNIT, *Planning Survey, Jamaica 1963*, Kingston 1964.

JAMAICA INDUSTRIAL DEVELOPMENT CORPORATION. *Annual Report*, Kingston.

KATZIN, M. 'The Jamaican country higgler', *SES* **8**, 1959, pp. 421–35.

KNOWLES, W. H. 'Social consequences of economic change in Jamaica', *in* 'Agrarian Societies in Transition', ed. B. Hoselitz, *Ann. Am. Acad. Polit. Soc. Sci.* **305**, Philadelphia 1956, pp. 134–44.

KRUIJER, G. J. 'The Impact of Poverty and Undernourishment on Man and Society in rural Jamaica', *Mens en Maatschappij* **32**, 1957, pp. 284–290

—— 'Het Christianagebied: Een Landhervormingsproject in Jamaica', *Tijdschr. Kon. Ned. Aardr. Gen.* (Journal of the Royal Dutch Geographical Society) **75**, 1958, pp. 252–69.

KÜCHLER, A. W. 'Jamaica, eine Passatinsel', in *Amerikanische Landschaft*, ed. E. von Drygalski, Berlin–Leipzig 1936, pp. 347–459.

LONG, E. *History of Jamaica*, 3 vols, London 1744.

McGRATH, B. R. G. and ZANS, V. A. 'Dunn's Hole Sink', *Geonotes* **1**, 1958, pp. 89–99.

McMORRIS, C. S. 'Small-farm financing in Jamaica', *SES* **6**, no. 3 (Suppl.), 1957.

MATLEY, C. A. *et al. Geology and Physiography of the Kingston-District, Jamaica*, London 1951.

MAUNDER, W. F. 'The significance of transport in the Jamaican economy: an estimate of gross expenditure in internal transport', *SES* **3**, 1954, pp. 39–63.

—— 'The new Jamaican emigration', *SES* **4**, 1955, pp. 38–63.

—— *Employment in an Underdeveloped Area: a sample survey of Kingston, Jamaica*, New Haven 1960.

MINTZ, S. W. 'The Jamaican internal marketing pattern', *SES* **4**, 1955, pp. 95–109.

MINTZ, S. W. and HALL, D. *The Origins of the Jamaican internal Marketing System*, Yale Univ. Publ. in Anthropology no. 57, New Haven 1960.

MINTZ, S. W. and RICHARD, B. S. 'The wealth of Jamaica in the eighteenth century', *Econo. Hist. Rev.*, 2nd ser., **17**, 1965, pp. 292–311.

MOES, J. E. 'The Creation of full Employment in Jamaica', *CQ* **12**, no. 2, 1966, pp. 8–21.

MOORE, E. A. *Flood Control and Drainage Problems of Western Expansion of Kingston*, Kingston 1962.

MOORHEAD, G. A. 'Bauxite mining in Jamaica', *Mine and Quarry Engineering*, June 1961, pp. 2–11.

MOSER, C. A. *The Measurement of Levels of Living with Special Reference to Jamaica*, London 1957.

NETTLEFORD, R. 'National identity and attitudes to race in Jamaica', *Race* **7**, 1965, pp. 59–72.

NORTON, A. V. and CUMPER, G. E. '"Peasant", "plantation" and "urban" communities in rural Jamaica; a test of the validity of the classification', *SES* **15**, 1966, pp. 338–52.

O'LOUGHLIN, C. 'Long-term growth of the economy of Jamaica', *SES* **12**, 1963, pp. 246–82.

PAGET, E. 'Land use and settlement in Jamaica', in *Geographical Essays on British Tropical Lands*, ed. R. W. Steel and C. A. Fisher, London 1956.

PAGET, H. 'The free village system in Jamaica', *CQ* **10**, no. 1, 1964, pp. 38–51.

PEARSON, R. 'The geography of recreation on a tropical island: Jamaica', *J. Geogr.* **56**, 1957, pp. 12–22.

—— 'The Jamaica Bauxite Industry', *J. Geogr.* **56**, 1957, pp. 377–85.

PECK, H. A. 'Economic planning in Jamaica', *SES* **7**, 1958, pp. 141–63.

REID, M. *The Maroon: or Planter Life in Jamaica*, New York 1964.

ROBERTS G. W. *The Population of Jamaica*, Cambridge 1957.

—— 'Provisional assessment of growth of the Kingston- St Andrew area, 1960–70', *SES* **12**, 1963, pp. 432–41.

ROBERTS, G. W. and MILLS, D. O. 'Study of external migration affecting Jamaica, 1953–55', *SES* **7** (Suppl.), 1958.

ROBINSON, E. 'Observations on the elevated and modern reef formations of the St Ann Coast', *Geonotes* **3**, 1960, pp. 18–22.

ROBINSON, E., VERSEY, H. R. and WILLIAMS, J. B. 'The Jamaica earthquake of March 1, 1957', *Trans. 2nd Caribb. Geol. Conf.*, Mayagüez 1960, pp. 50–57.

Salas, G. P. *Los Depósitos de Bauxite en Haiti y Jamaica y Posibilidades de que exista Bauxita en Mexico*, Universidad Nacional Autonoma de Mexico, Bol. no. 59 del Instituto de Geología, Mexico, D F, 1959.

Sangster, D. B. 'Le développement économique de la Jamaique', *Bull. Soc. belge Et. et Expans.* **211**, 1964, pp. 419–26.

Senior, C. and Manley, D. *A Report on Jamaican Migration to Great Britain*, Kingston 1955.

Sheridan, R. B. 'The wealth of Jamaica in the eighteenth century', *Econ. Hist. Rev.*, 2nd ser., **18**, no. 2, Utrecht 1966, pp. 292–312.

Shreve, F. *A Montane Rain-Forest. A Contribution to the Physiological Plant Geography of Jamaica*, Carnegie Institution Publ. no. 199, Washington 1914.

Sires, R. V. 'Negro labor in Jamaica in the years following emancipation', *J. Negro History* **25**, 1940, pp. 484–97.

Smith, G. W. *The Irrigation Needs of Jamaica*, Regional Research Centre, Imperial College of Tropical Agriculture, St Augustine, Trinidad 1959.

Smith, M. G. 'Community organization in rural Jamaica', *SES* **5**, 1956, pp. 295–314.

—— *A Report on Labour Supply in Rural Jamaica*, Kingston 1956.

—— 'The plural framework of Jamaican society', *Br. J. Sociol.* **12**, 1961, pp. 249–62.

Soil and Land Use Surveys, Jamaica, Regional Research Centre of the British Caribbean, Imperial College of Tropical Agriculture, St Augustine, Trinidad 1958 ff.

Stark, J. *Jamaica. Parish of St Elisabeth, Soil and Land Use*, Trinidad Regional Research Centre, Imper. Coll. Trop. Agric., Soils Research and Survey Section no. 14, 1963.

Steers, J. A. 'The coral cays of Jamaica', *Geogrl J.* **95**, 1940, pp. 30–42.

Steers, J. A. *et al.* 'Sand cays and mangroves in Jamaica', *Geogrl. J.* **96**, 1940, pp. 305–28.

Stycos, J. M. and Back, K. W. *The Control of human Fertility in Jamaica*, Ithaca, N. Y. 1964.

Sweeting, M. M. *Hydrogeological Observations in Parts of the White Limestone Areas in Jamaica, B. W. I.*, Geol. Survey Dept. Jamaica, Bull. no. 2, Kingston 1956.

—— 'The karstlands of Jamaica', *Geogrl J.* **124**, 1958, pp. 184–99.

Taylor, S. A. G. 'The water resources of the Clarendon Plains', *SES* **4**, 1955, pp. 216–30.

Taylor, S. A. G. and Chubb, L. J. 'The hydrogeology of the Clarendon Plains, Jamaica', *Proc. Geol. Assoc.* **68**, 1957, pp. 204–10.

Thomas, C. Y. 'Coffee production in Jamaica', *SES* **13**, 1964, pp. 188–217.

Thompson, R. 'The role of capitalism in Jamaica's development', *CQ* **12**, no. 2, 1966, pp. 22–8.

Thorne, A. P. 'Size, structure and growth of the economy of Jamaica', *SES* **4** (Suppl.), 1955.

Tidrick, G. 'Some aspects of Jamaican emigration to the United Kingdom, *1953–1962*', *SES* **15**, 1966, pp. 22–39.

Urquhart, A. W. *The Landforms of the Cockpit Country and its Borderlands, Jamaica*, Dept. of Geography, Univ. of California, Berkeley 1958.

Versey, H. R. and Prescott, G. C. *Progress Report on the Geology and Ground Water Resources of the Clarendon Plains, Jamaica, B. W. I.*, Geol. Survey Dept., Jamaica, Kingston 1958.

Versey, H. R., Williams, J. B. and Robinson, E. 'The earthquake of March 1, 1957', *Geonotes* **1**, 1958, pp. 54–65.

Whitbeck, H. R. 'Agricultural geography of Jamaica', *AAAG* **22**, 1932, pp. 13–27.

Williams, J. B. 'The structure, scenery and stratigraphy of the central inlier', *Geonotes* **2**, 1957, pp. 7–17.

Wünsche, B. 'Die wirtschaftliche Entwicklung und Gliederung der Insel Jamaika', dissertation, Hamburg 1936.

Yin Lee, T., ed. *The Chinese in Jamaica*, Kingston 1957.

Young, B. S. 'Jamaica's bauxite and alumina industries', *AAAG* **55**, no. 3, 1965, pp. 449–64.

Zans, V. A. *Economic Geology and Mineral Resources of Jamaica*, Geol. Survey Dept., Jamaica, B. W. I., Bull. no. 1, Kingston 1951.

—— 'Bauxite resources of Jamaica and their development', *Colon. Geol. Min. Resources* **3**, 1953, pp. 307–33.

—— 'Geology and mineral deposits of Jamaica', *Handbook of Jamaica*, Kingston 1957,

409

pp. 12–18.
—— 'Recent coral reefs and reef environments of Jamaica', *Geonotes* **1**, 1958, pp. 18–25.
—— *The Pedro Cays and Pedro Bank*, Geol. Survey Dept., Jamaica, Bull. no. 3, Kingston 1958.
—— 'Judgment Cliff landslide in the Yallahs Valley', *Geonotes* **2**, 1959, pp. 43–8.
—— 'Caves and cave exploration in Jamaica', *Geonotes* **2**, 1959, pp. 59–69.
—— *Geology and Mineral Deposits of Jamaica*, Geol. Survey Dept., Jamaica, Publ. no. 72, Kingston 1961.
ZANS, V. A., *et al. Synopsis of the Geology of Jamaica. An explanation of the 1958 Provisional Geological Map of Jamaica*, Geol. Survey Dept., Bull. no. 4, Kingston 1962.

Cayman Islands

BILLMYER, J. H. S. 'The Cayman Islands', *Geogr. Rev.* **36**, 1946, pp. 29–43.
BUCHLER, I. R. 'Shifting Cultivation in the Cayman Islands', *Antropologica*, no. **12**, 1963, pp. 1–5.
DORAN, E. 'Land forms of Grand Cayman Island, British West Indies', *Texas J. Sci.* **6**, 1954, pp. 360–77.
DOUGLAS, A. J. A. 'The Cayman Islands', *Geogrl J.* **95**, 1940, pp. 126–31.
MATLEY, C. A. 'The geology of the Cayman Islands, (British West Indies) and their relation to the Bartlett Trough', *Q. J. Geol. Soc. London* **82**, 1926, pp. 352–87.

Hispaniola

ALPERT, L. 'The areal distribution of mean annual rainfall over the island of Hispaniola', *MWR* **69**, 1941, pp. 201–4.
CIFERRI, R. *Studio geobotanico dell'Isola Hispaniola (Antille)*; Atti dell'Instituto Botanico dell' Università di Pavia, serie iv, vol. 8, Pavia 1936.
CRIST, R. E. 'Cultural dichotomy in the island of Hispaniola', *EG* **28**, 1952, pp. 105–21.
DEUTSCH-SÜDAMERIKANISCHE BANK, *Wirstschaftsbericht Dominikanische Republic-Haiti*, Hamburg 1955.
DYER, D. R. 'Distribution of population on Hispaniola', *EG* **30**, 1954, pp. 337–46.
FASSIG, O. L. 'A tentative chart of annual rainfall over the island of Haiti – Santo Domingo', *MWR* **57**, 1929, pp. 296–7.
GUERRA PEÑA, F. 'Las regiones fisiográficas de la Isla de Santo Domingo', Unión Geográfica Internacional, *Trans Conferencia Regional Latinoamericana*, vol. 3, Mexico 1966, pp. 209–25.
HOLDRIDGE, L. R. 'A brief sketch of the flora of Hispaniola', in *Plants and Plant Science in Latin America*, ed. F. Verdoorn, 1945, pp. 76–78.
LOGAN, R. W. *Haiti and the Dominican Republic*, London 1963.
STUART, R. 'Haiti or Hispaniola', *Royal Geogr. Soc. J.* **48**, 1878, pp. 234–74.
TERMER, F. 'Hispaniola oder Haiti?', *Pet. Geogr. Mitt.* **80**, 1934, pp. 334–5.
TIPPENHAUER, C. G. *Die Insel Haiti*, Leipzig 1893.
URBAN, I. 'Zur Pflanzengeographie von Hispaniola', *Symb. Antill.* **9**, 1923, pp. 1–54.

Haiti

ARISTIDE, A. 'Aspects et conditions de l'urbanisme en Haiti', in *Problèmes haitiens*, Port-au-Prince 1958, pp. 45–74.
AUBOURG, M. 'Introduction à la géographie sociale d'Haiti', *Revue de la Faculté d'Ethnologie*, **11**, Port-au-Prince 1966, pp. 38–43.
BARKER, H. D. and DARDEAU, W. S. *Flore d'Haiti*, Port-au-Prince 1930.

BASTIEN, R. 'Haitian rural family organization', *SES* **10**, 1961, pp. 478–510.

BEGHIN, I. 'Le problème de l'alimentation et de la nutrition en Haiti', *Bull. de l'Institut français d'Haiti*, **99**, Port-au-Prince 1965, pp. 40–57.

BELLEGARDE, D. *Haiti et son Peuple*, Paris 1953.

—— *Histoire du Peuple haitien, 1492–1952*, Port-au-Prince 1953.

BENDRAT, T. A. 'Physiogeographie der Küste von Haiti', *Pet. Geogr. Mitt.* **75**, 1929, pp. 248–9.

BENOIT, P. *Cent cinquante Ans de Commerce extérieur d'Haiti, 1804–1954*, Port-au-Prince 1953.

—— *Évolution budgetaire et Développement économique d'Haiti*, Port-au-Prince 1954.

BIN, M. 'Le problème de l'alimentation et de la nutrition en Haiti', *Conjonction 99*, Port-au-Prince 1965, pp. 40–57.

BOUCHEREAU, M. S. 'La classe moyenne en Haiti', *Materiales para el Estudio de la Clase media en la América latina*, vol. 5, Unión Panamericana, Washington 1951, pp. 50–67.

—— *Haiti. Porträt eines freien Landes*, Frankfurt 1954.

BUTTERLIN, J. *Géologie générale et régionale de la République d'Haiti*, Paris 1960.

CASIMIR, J. 'Aperçu sur la structure économique d'Haiti', *América Latina* **7**, no. 3. Rio de Janeiro 1964, pp. 37–56.

—— 'Aperçu sur la structure sociale d'Haiti', *América Latina* **8**, no. 3, Rio de Janeiro 1965, pp. 40–61.

COMHAIRE-SYLVAIN, S. and J. 'La alimentación en la región de Kenscoff, Haiti', *América Indigena* **12**, Mexico 1952, pp. 117–203.

—— 'Urban stratification in Haiti', *SES* **8**, 1959, pp. 179–89.

—— 'A statistical note on the Kenscoff market system, Haiti', *SES* **13**, 1964, pp. 397–404.

CURTIS, J. T. 'The Palo Verde forest type near Gonaives, Haiti, and its relation to the surrounding vegetation, *Caribbean Forester* **8**, 1947, pp. 1–26.

DARTIQUE, J. 'Quelques données sur la situation agraire dans la République d'Haiti', *Car. Land Tenure Symposium*, ed. Car. Comm., Washington 1947, pp. 315–33.

DEBIEN, G. *Une Plantation de Saint-Domingue: la Sucrerie Galbaut du Fort: 1690–1802*, Les Presses de l'Institut français d'Archéologie orientale du Caire, Cairo 1941.

—— *Etudes Antillaises XVIIIᵉ Siècle*, Paris 1956.

—— *Plantation et Esclaves à Saint-Domingue*, Fac. Lett. et Sc. hum., Univ. Publ. Section d'Hist., no. 3, Dakar 1962.

—— 'Une cafetière-résidence aux Grand-Bois', *Revue de la Faculté d'Ethnologie*, **6**, Port-au-Prince 1963, pp. 3–21.

DEPARTMENT OF ECONOMIC AFFAIRS, *Annotated Index of aerial photographic Coverage and Mapping of Topography and natural Resources, Haiti*, Pan American Union 1964.

DESPOIS, J. 'Une étude sur la vie rurale en Haiti', *Ann. Géogr.* **81**, 1962, pp. 426–7.

DEVAUGES, R. 'Une capitale antillaise: Port-au-Prince (Haiti)', *Cahiers d'Outre Mer* **7**, 1954, pp. 105–36.

DORSINVILLE, I. 'La Plaine des Vases à Haiti', *Géographie* **54**, Paris 1930, pp. 182–5.

DUCOEURJOLY, S. J. *Manuel des Habitans de Saint-Domingue*, 2 vols, Paris 1802.

EATON, F. M. *Land Development of the Artibonite Plain of Haiti*, UN, New York 1952.

EDWARDS, B. *An Historical Survey of the French Colony in the Island of Santo Domingo*, London 1797.

EKMAN, 'A botanical excursion in La Hotte, Haiti', *Svensk Botanisk Tidskr.* **22**, 1928, pp. 200–19.

'Enquête agricole et démographique dans la Vallée de l'Artibonite', *Bull. trimestriel de Statistique* **7**, Port-au-Prince 1952, pp. 7–48.

'Enquête agricole de démographique dans le sud est (région Grand-Gosier-Anse-à-Pitre)', *Bull. trimestriel de Statistique* **8**, Port-au-Prince 1953, pp. 7–58.

GATZ, W. 'Haitis industrielle Grundlagen und Entwicklungsmöglichkeiten', *Weltwirtsch. Archiv* **83**, 1959, pp. 99–126.

HALL, R. B. 'The island of Gonave: a study in karst landscape', *Papers Michigan Acad. Sci.* **10**, 1928, pp. 161–8.

—— 'The geography of the Republic of Haiti', *Scott. Geogr. Mag.* **46**, 1930, pp. 140–52.

411

Bibliography

HALL, R. B. and KENDALL, H. M. 'The climates of the Republic of Haiti', *Papers Michigan Acad. of Science, Arts and Letters* **14**, Ann Arbor, Mich., 1931, pp. 351–66.

HARDOUIN, A. C. 'Haiti: a study in regression', *Mexico Quart. Rev.*, Mexico City, October 1963, pp. 77–86.

HERSKOVITS, M. J. *Life in a Haitian Valley*, New York an London 1937.

HOETINK, H. 'Over de sociaal-raciale structuur van Haiti', *Tijdschr. Kon. Ned. Aardr. Gen.*, 2nd series, **78**, 1961, pp. 146–56.

HOLLY, M. A. *Agriculture in Haiti*, New York 1955.

HOUDAILLE, J. 'Trois paroisses de Saint-Domingue au XVIIIe siècle', *Population* **18**, 1963, pp. 93–110.

HUBERT, G. A. 'Some problems of a colonial economy: a study of economic dualism in Haiti', *Inter-American Economic Affairs* **3**, no. 4, Washington 1949, pp. 3–29.

INSTITUT HAITIEN DE STATISTIQUE. *Guide économique de la République d'Haiti*, Port-au-Prince 1964.

INTER-AMERICAN COMMITTEE FOR AGRICULTURAL DEVELOPMENT (CIDA) HAITI. *Inventory of Information basic to the Planning of Agricultural Development in Latin America*, Pan American Union, Washington 1963.

JEAN-MICHEL, M. S. 'Die Bedeutung des Kapitals für den Fortschritt der Landwirtschaft in Haiti', dissertation, Bonn 1960.

JOSEPH, R. *Haiti*, 2nd edn, Garden City 1964.

KEMP, K. 'Die wirtschaftlichen Verhältnisse der Republik Haiti einst und jetzt', dissertation, Bonn 1909.

KOBLINSKI-SIEMENS, G. VON. 'Zur agrargeographischen Gliederung von Haiti', *Erdkunde* **8**, 1954, pp. 194–8.

KOCH, W. 'Beiträge zur Landschaftskunde und zur Geschichte der Landschaftsumwandlungen der Republik Haiti', dissertation, Hamburg 1937.

KRIEGER, H. W. 'Culture sequences in Haiti', *Explorations and Field-Work of the Smithsonian Institution in 1931*, Publications 3134, Washington 1932, pp. 113–24.

LAROCHE, R. 'Situation de l'agriculture paysanne haitienne: perspective d'avenir', *Revista de Ciencias Sociales* **4**, 1960 pp. 151–69.

LAURENT, G. and ALPHONSE, D. *Etude socio-économique de la Vallée de Camp-Perrin, Plaine des Cayes*, Port-au-Prince 1956.

LEYBURN, J. G. *The Haitian People*, New Haven 1941, reprinted 1966.

LOBB, J. 'Caste and class in Haiti', *Am. J. Sociol.* **56**, 1940/41, pp. 23–34.

LUBIN, M. A. 'Quelques aspects de l'économie haitienne', *JIAS* **1**, 1959, pp. 425–47.

—— 'Quelques aspects des communautés rurales d'Haiti', *América Latina* **5**, nos. 1–2, Rio de Janeiro 1962, pp. 3–22.

LÜTGENS, R. 'Land, Leute, Reisen in der Republik Haiti', *Z. Ges. f. Erdkunde Berlin*, 1914, pp. 771–80.

—— 'Geographische und geologische Beobachtungen in Nordwest-Haiti', *Mitt. Geogr. Ges. Hamburg* **32**, 1919, pp. 41–90.

—— 'Grundzüge der wirtschaftsgeographischen Entwicklung und Gliederung Haitis', *Mitt. Geogr. Ges. Hamburg* **38**, 1927, pp. 375–4 4.

MANIGAT, L. *Haiti of the Sixties, object of international concern*, Washington 1964.

MARIE-VICTORIN, F. 'Les hautes Pinedes d'Haiti', *Contr. Inst. Bot. Univ. Montréal* **48**, 1943, pp. 47–60.

Marktinformationsdienst der Bundesstelle für Außenhandelsinformation, *Haitianische Agrarwirtschaft*, Cologne 1955.

MÉTRAUX, A. 'Etude sur l'agriculture paysanne dans une vallée haitienne', *Acta Americana* **6**, 1948, pp. 173–91.

—— *L'Homme et la Terre dans la Vallée de Marbial*, Unesco, Paris 1952.

—— *Voodoo. A complete study of the colorful practices and traditions of Voodoo within the social framework of present-day Haiti*, London 1959.

—— *Haiti: Black Peasants and their Religion*, London 1960.

412

MINTZ, S. 'A tentative typology of eight Haitian marketplaces', *Revista de Ciencias Sociales* **4**, Río Piedras 1960, pp. 15–57.

MINTZ, S. and CARROL, V. 'A selective social science bibliography of the Republic of Haiti', *Revista interamericana de Ciencias sociales* **2**, 1963, pp. 405–19.

MINTZ, S. W. 'Living fences in the Fond-des-Nègres region, Haiti', *Econ. Bot.* **16**, 1962, pp. 101–5.

MONTAGUE, L. L. *Haiti and the United States, 1714–1938*, New York 1940, reprinted 1966.

MORAL, P. 'La culture du café en Haiti', *Cahiers d'Outre Mer* **8**, 1955, pp. 233–56.

—— 'La Maison rurale en Haiti', *Cahiers d'Outre Mer* **10**, 1957, pp. 117–30.

—— *L'Economie haitienne*, Port-au-Prince 1959.

—— *Le Paysan haitien. Etude sur la Vie rurale en Haiti*, Paris 1961.

MOREAU DE SAINT-MÉRY, M. L. E. *Description topographique, physique, civile, politique et historique de la Partie française de l'Isle Saint-Domingue*, Philadelphia 1797, new edn, ed. B. Maurel and E. Taillemite, 3 vols, Paris 1958.

PARET-LIMARDO DE VELA, L. 'Quelques aspects des problèmes de la main-d'œuvre haitienne', *JIAS* **4**, 1962, pp. 121–44.

PATTEE, R. *Haiti, Pueblo afroantillano*, Madrid 1956.

PIERRE-CHARLES, G. *La Economia haitiana y su Via de Desarollo*, Cuadernos Americanos, Mexico, DF, 1965.

PRICE-MARS, D. J. 'Aspectos generales del sistema de explotación rural en el Nuevo Mundo; la colonización de Saint-Domingue y el Desarrollo de las plantaciones en la parte occidental de la isla', *Rev. Geogr.* **28**, no. 54, Rio de Janeiro 1961, pp. 101–20.

PRICE-MARS, S. 'La Position d'Haiti et de la Culture française en Amérique', *JIAS* **8**, no. 1, 1966, pp. 44–53.

Récensement général de la République d'Haiti, Août 1950, 5 vols, Port-au-Prince, Haiti.

RÜSCH, E. *Die Revolution von Saint Domingue*, Hamburg 1930.

SALGADO, J. M. 'Survivance des cultes africains et Syncrétisme en Haiti', *Revue de l'Université d'Ottawa* **32**, 1962, pp. 431–67.

SIMPSON, G. E. 'Haitian peasant economy', *J. Negro Hist.* **25**, 1940, pp. 498–519.

STATISCHES BUNDESAMT. *Der Außenhandel der BR Deutschland*, Supplement: *Der Außenhandel des Auslandes, no. 114, Haiti*, Stuttgart, Mainz 1959.

—— *Allgemeine Statistik des Auslandes, Länderberichte, Haiti*, Stuttgart and Mainz 1965.

STREET, J. M. *Historical and Economic Geography of the Southwest Peninsula of Haiti*, Dept. of Geogr., Univ. of California, Berkeley 1960.

STREITBERG, T. DE. 'La République d'Haiti', *Bull. Soc. Belge d'Études Col.* **26**, 1919, pp. 309–77.

TALMAN, C. F. 'Climatology of Haiti in the eighteenth century', *MWR* **34**, 1906, pp. 64–73.

TIPPENHAUER, L. G. 'Geologische Studien in Haiti', *Pet. Geogr. Mitt.* **45**, 1899, pp. 25–9, 153–5, 201–4; **47**, 1901, pp. 121–7, 169–78, 193–9.

—— 'Neuer Beitrag zur Topographie, Bevölkerungskunde und Geologie von Haiti', *Pet. Geogr. Mitt.* **55**, 1909, pp. 49–57.

TROUILLOT, H. 'Economie et finances de Saint-Domingue', *Rev. Soc. haitienne d'Hist. Géogr., Géol.*, Port-au-Prince **33**, 1965, pp. 1–139.

UNDERWOOD, F. W. *The Marketing System in Peasant Haiti*, Yale Univ. Publ. in Anthropology no. 60, New Haven 1960.

UNITED NATIONS. *Mission to Haiti*, Report of the United Nations Mission of Technical Assistance to the Republic of Haiti, New York 1949.

WILSON, E. *Red, Black, Blond and Olive; studies in four civilizations: Zuni, Haiti, Soviet Russia, Israel*, London 1956.

WINGFIELD, R. and PARENTON, V. J. 'Class structure and class conflict in Haitian society', *Social Forces* **43**, no. 3, 1965, pp. 338–47.

WOOD, H. A. 'Stream piracy in the central plateau of Hispaniola', *CG*, no. 8, 1956, pp. 46–54.

—— 'Physical influences on peasant agriculture in Northern Haiti', *CG* **5**, no. 2, 1961, pp. 10–18.

Bibliography

—— *Northern Haiti: Land, land use, and settlement, a geographical investigation of the Département du Nord*, Toronto 1963.
WOODRING, W. P., BROWN, J. S. and BURBANK, W. S. *Geology of the Republic of Haiti*, Baltimore 1924.
YOUNG, M. DE. *Man and Land in the Haitian Economy*, Latin American Monographs 3, Gainesville 1958.
—— 'Class parameters in Haitian society', *JIAS* **1**, 1959, pp. 449–58.

The Dominican Republic

AGUIRRE, J. A. and McPHERSON, W. W. 'Desarollo económico de la industria avícola dominicana: problemas y potenciales', *Turrialba* **15**, no. 2, 1965, pp. 88–98.
AUGELLI, J. P. 'The Dominican Republic', *Focus* **10**, no. 6, New York 1960.
—— 'Agricultural colonization in the Dominican Republic', *EG* **38**, 1962, pp. 15–27.
—— 'The Dominican Republic', *Focus* **15**, no. 9, New York 1965.
—— 'Aspectos de la colonización agrícola y del desarollo económico en la República. Dominicana', Unión Geográfica Internacional, *Trans. Conferencia Regional Latinoamericana*, vol. 1, Mexico 1966, pp. 278–90.
BARRETT, W. 'Emerged and submerged shorelines of the Dominican Republic', *Revista Geográfica*, **56**, Rio de Janeiro 1962, pp. 51–77.
BARTELS, W. 'Beiträge zur Kenntnis der Bodenschätze der Dominikanischen Republik, *Metall und Erz* **38**, 1941, pp. 45–50, 75–8.
BAUM, F. *Bericht über Lagerstätten und Mineralvorkommen in der Dominikanischen Republik*, Bundesanstalt für Bodenforschung, Hannover 1963.
BLOCH, P. 'Kleine Landeskunde der Dominikanischen Republik', *Geogr. Rdsch.* **12**, 1960, pp. 351–9.
BOSCH, J. *et al. The Dominican Republic*, Inter-American Center for the Study of Contemporary Latin America, San Juan, PR, 1964.
CASTELLANI, E. 'Impression di un agronomo nella Republica Dominicana', *Ann. Acad. Agricolt.* **102**, Torino 1959–60, pp 267–88.
CHARDON, F. E. 'Los Pinares de la República Dominicana', *Caribb. Forester* **2**, 1941, pp. 120–31.
CONSEJO ADMINISTRATIVO, REPÚBLICA DOMINICANA, DISTRITO NACIONAL. *Evolución urbanística de Ciudad Trujillo*, Ciudad Trujillo 1956.
CORDERO MICHEL, J. R. 'Datos sobre la reforma agraria en la República Dominicana', *CS* **2**, no. 1, 1962, pp. 23–33.
CUCURULLO, O. *La Hoya de Enriquillo*, Universidad de Santo Domingo, Instituto geográfico y geológico Publ. no. 3, Ciudad Trujillo 1949.
—— 'Rasgos sobre la orogénesis y la topografía de Santo Domingo', *Ann. Univ. de Santo Domingo*, **53/56**, 1950, pp. 163–76.
—— 'Un capítulo sobre la geografía de Santo Domingo', *Panta Rhei* **1**, Santo Domingo 1961, pp. 3–10.
DEPARTMENT OF ECONOMIC AFFAIRS. *Annotated Index of Aerial Photographic Coverage and Mapping of Topography and natural Resources, República Dominicana*, Pan American Union, 1964.
DUPUY, R. J. 'Les Etats-Unis, l'O.E.A. et l'O.N.U. à Saint-Domingue', *Ann. fra. Droit internat.*, Paris 1965, pp. 71–110.
DURLAND, W. D. 'The forests of the Dominican Republic', *Geogr. Rev.* **12**, 1922, pp. 206–22.
ENJALBERT, H. 'La renaissance économique de la République Dominicaine', *Cahiers d'Outre Mer*, **5**, 1952, pp. 330–56; **6**, 1953, pp. 61–87.
ESPAILLAT, R. 'Política agraria dominicana', in *Caribbean Land Tenure Symposium*, ed. Caribb. Comm., Washington 1947, pp. 273–314.
FAIRCHILD, F. R. 'The problem of Santo Domingo', *Geogr. Rev.* **10**, 1920, pp. 121–38.
GARCIA AYBAR, J. E. *El Presente y Futuro de la Industria azucarera dominicana*, Santo Domingo

414

1965

HARTWELL, F. E. 'The Santo Domingo hurricane of September 1 to 5, 1930', *MWR* **34**, 1930, pp. 362–4.

HEINRICH, K. 'Erfolgreiche Wirtschaftspolitik der Dominikanischen Republik', *Ubersee-Rdsch.* **7**, no. 11, 1955, pp. 7–9.

HOETINK, H. ' "Americans" in Samaná', *C* **2**, no. 1, 1962, pp. 3–22.

—— 'Materiales para el estudio de la República Dominicana en la segunda mitad del siglo XIX. I. Cambios en la estructura agraria', *CS* **5**, no. 3, 1965, pp. 3–21.

INCHÁUSTEGUI CABRAL, J. M. *Geografía descriptiva de la República Dominicana*, 10th edn, Ciudad Trujillo 1957.

INTER-AMERICAN COMMITTEE FOR AGRICULTURAL DEVELOPMENT. *Inventario de la Información básica para la propagación del Desarrollo agrícola en la América Latina: República Dominicana*, Pan-American Union, Washington 1963.

'La Loi de Réforme agraire dans la République Dominicaine', *Revue Internationale du Travail* **88**, no. 1, Geneva 1963, pp. 83–6

LOWENTHAL, A. F. *Hydraulic Resource Development in the Dominican Republic; an historical Review*, Santiago de los Caballeros, RD, 1965.

Marktinformationsdienst der Bundesstelle für Außenhandelsinformation, no. A/22, *Stand der Wirtschaftsentwicklung in der Dominikanischen Republik*, Cologne 1955.

MEARS, L. G. *The Dominican Republic—Agriculture and Trade*, US Dept. of Agriculture, Economic Research Service, Regional Analysis Divisions, ERS–Foreign 51, Washington 1963.

NORRIS, O. *Situation et Perspectives de la Démographie dominicaine*, Centre d'Etudes Régionales Antilles-Guyane, Cahiers no. 5, Fort-de-France 1964.

ORTIZ, A. *Basic Data on the Economy of the Dominican Republic*, US Bureau of International Commerce, Overseas Business Reports, Washington 1964.

OSORIO LIZARAZO, J. A. *La Isla iluminada*, Santiago, Dom. Rep., 1947.

PALM, E. W. *The Pocket Guide to Ciudad Trujillo*, Ciudad Trujillo 1951.

—— *Los Monumentos arquitectónicos de la Española*, 2 vols, Ciudad Trujillo 1955.

'Plano piloto de la República Dominica. Plano del Levantamento regional do Valle del Yaque del Norte', *Rev. Inst. Geogr. Panam.* 62–34, Rio de Janeiro 1965, pp. 121–2.

RATEKIN, M. 'The early sugar industry in Española', *Hispanic Am. Hist. Rev.* **34**, 1954, pp. 1–19.

RODMAN, S. *Quisqueya: a History of the Dominican Republic*, Seattle 1964.

ROGERS, G. E. *Human Resources of the Dominican Republic*, Santo Domingo 1962.

—— *Land Tenure in the Dominican Republic and Cadastral Descriptions of known State-owned Lands*, 3 vols, Santo Domingo 1963.

ROYEN, W. VAN, 'A geographical reconnaissance of the Cibao of Santo Domingo', *Geogrl. Rev.* **28**, 1938, pp. 556–72.

STATIST, THE. *Economic Survey, Dominican Republic*, London 1960.

STATISTICHES BUNDESAMT. *Der Außenhandel der Bundesrepublik Deutschland*. Ergänzungsreihe: *Der Außenhandel des Auslandes, no. 113: Dominikanische Republik*, Stuttgart, Mainz 1959.

STATISTICHES BUNDESAMT. *Allgemeine Statistik des Auslandes, Länderberichte: Dominikanische Republik*, Stuttgart, Mainz 1965.

TOLENTINO ROJAS, V. *Reseña geográfica, histórica y estadística de la República Dominicana*, 3rd edn. Ciudad Trujillo 1954.

TRONCOSO DE LA CONCHA, M. DE J. 'La clase media en Santo Domingo', *Materiales para estudio de la clase media en la América latina*, vol. 6, Unión Panamericana, Washington 1951, pp. 57–67.

US BUREAU OF INTERNATIONAL COMMERCE. *Economic Development in the Dominican Republic*, OBR–63–72, Washington, DC, 1963.

VALVERDE, A. S. *Idea del Valor de la Isla Española, y Utilidades, que de ella pueda sacar su Monarquía*, Madrid 1785.

VAUGHAN, T. W. *et al. A Geological Reconnaissance of the Dominican Republic*, Domin. Republ.

415

Bibliography

Geol. Survey Mem., vol. 1, 1921.

VEALE, P. T. 'Characteristics of certain soils in the Dominican Republic', *Proc. Soil Sci. Soc. Am.* **17**, 1953, pp. 391–5.

VEGA, B. *La República Dominicana ante el Proceso de Integración económica en Latinoamérica*, Santo Domingo 1966.

WESTBROOK, J. T. 'Socio-economic factors related to success and failure in agrarian reform: the "Caracol" project. República Dominicana', in *The Caribbean in Transition*, ed. F. M. Andic and T. G. Mathews; Río Piedras 1965, pp. 293–325.

WEYL, R. 'Blockmeere in der Cordillera Central von Santo Domingo (Westindien)', *Z. Dt. Geol. Ges.* **92**, 1940, pp. 173–9.

—— *Bau und Geschichte der Cordillera Central von Santo Domingo (Westindien)*, Veröff. d. Dt. Dominikanischen Tropenforschungsinstitutes Hamburg, vol. 2, Jena 1941.

—— 'Die Sierra de Bahoruco von Santo Domingo und ihre Stellung im Antillenbogen', *Neues Jb. f. Geol. u. Paläont.*, Abh. B, **98**, 1953, pp. 1–27.

Puerto Rico

ACOSTA VELARDE, J. 'The Land Authority of Puerto Rico', in *Caribbean Land Tenure Symposium*, ed. Caribb. Comm., Washington 1946, pp. 203–22.

ALEGRIA, J. S. 'Del San Juna morisco: Callejones', *Revista del Instituto de Cultura Puertorriqueña* **6**, no. 18, 1963, pp. 33–5.

ALEXANDER, W. H. 'Climatology of Puerto Rico from 1867 to 1905', *MWR* **34**, 1906, pp. 315–24.

ANDIC, F. M. *El Desarrollo económico y la distribución del ingreso en Puerto Rico*, San Juan 1964.

ANDIC, F. M. and ANDIC, S. 'Concentration in the external trade of Puerto Rico', *CS* **4**, 1964, pp. 3–13.

ARCENEAUX, G. 'Producción de Azúcar en Puerto Rico: pasado, presente y futuro', *Sugar y Azúcar* **59**, 1964, pp. 109–18.

AUGELLI, J. P. 'San Lorenzo, a case study of recent migrations in interior Puerto Rico', *Am. J. Econ. Sociol.* **11**, 1951–52, pp. 155–60.

BABIN, M. T. *Panorama de la Cultura puertorriqueña*, New York 1958.

BADILLO, E. *Efectos de la Emigración en la Composición de la Población puertorriqueña y algunas de sus Implicaciones para el Desarrollo económico de Puerto Rico*, Río Piedras 1963.

BAER, W. 'Puerto Rico: an evaluation of a successful development program', *Q. Jl Econ.* **73**, 1959, pp. 645–71.

—— *The Puerto Rican Economy and United States economic Fluctuations*, Río Piedras, PR, 1963.

BALCHIN, W. G. and COLEMAN, A. 'Puerto Rico', *Geography* **50**, 1965, pp. 274–86.

BARANANO, E. *Regional Plan: San Juan metropolitan area*, Puerto Rico Planning Board, Santurce, PR, 1956.

BERBUSSE, E. J. *The United States in Puerto Rico, 1898–1900*, Chapel Hill 1966.

BERRYHILL, H. L. *Geology of the Ciales Quadrangle, Puerto Rico*, Washington 1965.

BIROT, P. 'Observations sur le relief de deux petits batholites de granodiorite à Porto Rico et à la Jamaique', *Earth and Moon. Studies presented in Homage to J. B. Bakker*, Leiden 1966, pp. 220–6.

BLANTON, J. H. *et al.* 'A dietary study of men residing in urban and rural areas of Puerto Rico', *Am. J. clin. Nutr.* **18**, no. 3, 1966, pp. 169–75.

BLOCH, P. 'Kleine Landeskunde von Puerto Rico', *Geogr. Rdsch.* **11**, 1959, pp. 152–7.

—— 'Wirtschaftsgeographie von Puerto Rico', *Z. Wirtschaftsgeogr.* **5**, 1961, pp. 14–22.

BOGART, D. B. *et al. Water Resources of Puerto Rico*, San Juan 1964.

BONNET, J. A. 'Latosols of Puerto Rico', *Trans. Fourth Internat. Congress of Soil Science*, vol 1, Groningen 1950, pp. 281–5.

—— 'Soil salinity studies as related to sugarcane growing in southwestern Puerto Rico', *J. Agric., Univ. of PR.* **37**, 1953, pp. 103–13.

416

—— 'A guide to the soils of Puerto Rico', *Sugar y Azúcar* **59**, 1964, pp. 100–2.

BRIGGS, R. P. 'Laterization in East Puerto Rico', *Trans. 2nd Caribb. Geol. Conf.*, Mayagüez 1960, pp. 103–19.

—— *Provisional Geologic Map of Puerto Rico and Adjacent Islands 1: 240 000*, US. Geol. Surv. Dept. Misc. Geol. Invest., Map 1–392, Washington 1964.

BRIGGS, R. P. and AKERS, R. P. *Hydrologic Map of Puerto Rico and adjacent Islands*, Washington 1965.

CALERO, R. *Análisis de algunos Cambios recientes en la Población de Puerto Rico*, Rió Piedras 1964.

CAPLOW, T. *et al. The Urban Ambience; a study of San Juan, Puerto Rico*, University of Puerto Rico, College of Social Sciences, Río Piedras 1964.

CAPLOW, T. and WALLACE, E. 'Ecología social del Area urbana de San Juan', *América Latina* **8**, no. 3, Rio de Janeiro 1965, pp. 97–111.

CARRIÓN, A. M. 'The historical roots and political significance of Puerto Rico', in *The Caribbean: British, Dutch, French, United States*, ed. A. C. Wilgus, Gainesville 1958, pp. 139–69.

CASTELLANOS, I. 'Los viajes del sabio naturalista alemán Don Juan Gundlach a Puerto Rico', *Atenea* **2**, no. 2, Mayagüez 1965, pp. 45–60.

CHARDON, F. *La Perspectiva de la Industria azucarera en Puerto Rico*, Río Piedras 1963.

—— 'Puerto Rico's sugar industry in the 16th century', *Sugar y Azúcar* **60**, New York 1965, pp. 117–20.

CHAVES, A. F. *La Distribución de la Población en Puerto Rico*, Río Piedras 1949.

CIFRE DE LOUBRIEL, E. *La Immigración a Puerto Rico durante el Siglo XIX*, San Juan 1964.

CLARK, V. S. *et al. Porto Rico and its Problems*, Washington 1930.

COLÓN, E. D. *Datos sobre la Agricultura de Puerto Rico antes de 1898*, San Juan 1930.

—— *La Gestión agrícola después de 1898*, San Juan 1948.

CRIST, R. 'Sugar cane and coffee in Puerto Rico', *Am. J. Econ. Sociol.* **7**, 1947/48, pp. 173–84, 321–37, 469–74.

DAMBAUGH, L. N. 'Puerto Rico's ambition', *J. Geogr.* 50, 1951, pp. 89–98.

DARLING, H. D. and RAY, R. S. *Manufacturing Occupations in Puerto Rico*, Río Piedras 1954.

DEPARTAMENTO DEL TRABAJO, ESTADO LIBRE ASOCIADO DE PUERTO RICO. *Censo de Industrias manufactureras de Puerto Rico, Octubre 1960*, San Juan n.d.

DESCARTES, S. L. 'Land reform in Puerto Rico', *J. Land and Public Utility Econ.* **19**, 1943, pp. 397–417.

—— 'Land reform in Puerto Rico's program of economic advancement', in: *Family Farm Policy*, ed. J. Ackerman and M. Harris, Chicago 1947, pp. 285–305.

—— 'Historical account of recent land reform in Puerto Rico, in *Caribbean Land Tenure Symposium*, ed. Caribb. Comm., Washington 1947, pp. 129–62.

DIAZ SOLER, L. M. *Historia de la Esclavitud negra en Puerto Rico*, 2nd edn, Río Piedras 1965.

DOERR, A. H. 'The salt industry of southwestern Puerto Rico', *J. Geogr.* **52**, 1953, pp. 335–9.

ECONOMIC DEVELOPMENT ADMINISTRATION, Office of Economic Research, General Economics Division, *Directory of Fomento promoted and assisted manufacturing Plants*, San Juan, half-yearly.

EDEL, M. 'Land reform in Puerto Rico, 1940–1959', *CS*, **2**, 1963, no. 3, pp. 26–60; no. 4, pp. 28–50.

ESTEVES, G. 'Activities of the Puerto Rico reconstruction administration in connection with the agrarian reforms in Puerto Rico', in *Caribbean Land Tenure Symposium*, ed. Caribb. Comm. Washington 1947, pp. 163–77.

FASSIG, O. L. 'Average annual rainfall of Puerto Rico, W. I.', *MWR* **37**, 1909, pp. 982–6.

—— 'The Trade Winds in Porto Rico', *MWR* **39**, 1911, pp. 796–99.

—— 'The climate of Porto Rico', *AAAG* **1**, 1911, pp. 127–34.

FERNANDEZ, N. A. 'Nutritional status of people in isolated areas of Puerto Rico; survey of Barrio Naranjo, Moca, Puerto Rico', *Am. J. Clin. Nutr.* **19**, no. 4, 1966, pp. 269–84.

FERNÁNDEZ MÉNDEZ, E., ed. *Portrait of a Society; a book of readings on Puerto Rican sociology*, Río Piedras 1956.

Bibliography

—— *The Sources on Puerto Rican Culture History: a critical appraisal*, Río Piedras 1961.

FLEISHER, B. M. 'Some economic aspects of Puerto Rican migration to the United States', *Rev. Econ. Stat.* **45**, 1963, pp. 245–53.

FOXWORTH, D. M. 'The San Juan metropolitan area transportation study. A comparison', *Revista del Colegio de Ingenieros, Arquitectos y Agrimensores de Puerto Rico* **14**, 1964, pp. 50–9.

GARCIA-MOLINARI, O. *Grasslands and Grasses of Puerto Rico*, Río Piedras 1952.

GAYER, A. D., HOMAN, P. T. and JAMES, E. K. *The Sugar Economy of Puerto Rico*, New York 1938.

GERSTENHAUER, A. 'Nord-Puerto Rico', Internationaler Karst-Atlas sheet 3, *Beilage zu Erdkunde*, vol. 18, 1964.

GLEASON, H. A. and COOK, M. T. *Plant Ecology of Porto Rico; Scientific Survey of Porto Rico and the Virgin Islands*, vol. 7, New York Academy of Science, New York 1927.

GLYNN, P. W., ALMO D'OVAR, L. R. and GONZALES, J. G. 'Effects of hurricane Edith on marine life in La Parguera, Puerto Rico', *Caribb. J. Sci.* **4**, no. 2–3, 1964, pp. 335–46.

GOMEZ CHAPEL, A. *Plantificación e implementación de un programa de desarrollo agricola en el Valle de Lajas*, Estación Experimental Agrícola, Universidad de Puerto Rico, Bol. 192, Río Piedras 1965.

GONZÁLES, A. J. 'La economía y el status político de Puerto Rico', *Revista de Ciencias sociales*, **10**, no. 1, 1966, pp. 5–49.

GUERRA-MONDRAGON, M. 'The legal background of agrarian reform in Puerto Rico', in *Caribbean Land Tenure Symposium*, ed. Caribb. Comm., Washington 1947, pp. 99–127.

GUILLOU, R. B. and GLAS, J. J. 'A reconnaissance study of the beach sands of Puerto Rico', *US Geol. Survey Bull.* 1042–1, Washington 1957, pp. 273–305.

GULICK, L. H. *Rural Occupance in Utuado and Jayuya Municipios, Puerto Rico*, Univ. of Chicago Research Paper no. 23, Chicago 1952.

—— 'A Puerto Rican Coffee Hacienda', *Oriental Geographer* **4**, Dacca 1960, pp. 118–26.

GUZMAN, R. M. 'Rural water supply in Puerto Rico', *J. Am. Water Works Assoc.* **58**, 1966, pp. 989–94.

HAAS, W. H. 'Puerto Rican agriculture a century ago', *Agricultural History* **10**, 1936, pp. 97–110.

HADSWORTH, F. H. and BONNET, J. R. 'Soil as a factor in the occurrence of two types of montane forest in Puerto Rico', *Caribb. Forester* **12**, 1951, pp. 67–74.

HANCOCK, R. *Puerto Rico, a Success Story*, Toronto, London, New York 1960.

HANDLIN, O. *The Newcomers: Negroes and Puerto Ricans in a Changing Metropolis*, New York Metropolitan Region Study, vol. 3, Cambridge, Mass., 1959.

HANSON, E. P. *Transformation. The story of modern Puerto Rico*, New York 1955.

—— *Puerto Rico. Ally for Progress*, New York 1962.

—— *The Commonwealth of Puerto Rico*, Garden City 1962.

HARTZELL, C. R. 'The hurricane of September 1928 in Porto Rico', *Bull. Am. Met. Soc.* **10**, 1929, pp. 43–6.

HIBBEN, T. and PICÓ, R. *Industrial Development of Puerto Rico and the Virgin Islands of the United States*, Report of US Section, Caribb. Comm., Port-of-Spain, Trinidad 1948.

HILL, R., STYCOS, J. M. and BACK, K. W. *The Family and Population Control. A Puerto Rican Experiment in social Change*, Chapel Hill 1959.

HOLDRIDGE, L. R. 'Some notes on the mangrove swamps of Puerto Rico', *Caribb. Forester* **1**, 1940, pp. 19–29.

—— 'A brief sketch of the Puerto Rico flora', in *Plants and Plant Science in Latin America*, ed. F. Verdoorn, 1945, pp. 81–3.

HOWELL, B. 'The planning system of Puerto Rico', *Town Planning Rev.* **23**, 1952, pp. 211–22.

HUBBARD, B. 'The geology of the Lares district, Porto Rico', NY Acad. Sci., *Scient. Porto Rico and The Virgin Islands*, vol. 2, Washington 1923, pp. 1–115.

IRIZARRY, G. *El Agricultor de Puerto Rico y los Servicios agrícolas*, Servicio de Compra y Suministro, División de Imprenta, San Juan 1962.

JAFFE, A. J. *People, Jobs and Economic Development. A case history of Puerto Rico*, Glencoe, Ill.,

1959.

JONES, C. T. 'Significant nickpoint levels of seven rivers draining western Puerto Rico', *Caribb. J. Sci.* **4**, 1964, pp. 255–60.

—— ed. *The Rural Land Classification Program of Puerto Rico*, Northwestern University Studies in Geography no. 1, Evanston, Ill., 1952.

JONES, C. T. and PICÓ, R. *Symposium on the Geography of Puerto Rico*, Río Piedras 1955.

JUNTA DE PLANIFICACIÓN. *Estatísticas Municipales*, San Juan n. d.

KAYE, C. A. *Geology of the San Juan Metropolitan Area, Puerto Rico*, Geol. Survey Profess. Paper 317 A, Washington 1959.

—— *Shoreline Features and Quaternary Shoreline Changes, Puerto Rico*, Geol. Survey Profess. Paper 317 B, Washington 1959.

—— *Geology of Isla Mona, Puerto Rico and Notes on Age of Mona Passage*, Geol. Survey Profess. Paper 317 C, Washington 1959.

KOENIG, N. *A Comprehensive Agricultural Program for Puerto Rico*, Washington, DC, 1953.

KUMME, K. W. O. and BRISCOE, C. B. 'Forest formations of Puerto Rico', *Caribb. Forester* **24**, no. 2, Río Piedras 1963, pp. 57–65.

LEOPOLD, N. *Checklist of Birds of Puerto Rico and the Virgin Islands*, Río Piedras 1963.

LITTLE, E. L. and WADSWORTH, F. H. *Common Trees of Puerto Rico and the Virgin Islands*, US Department of Agriculture, Forest Service, Agriculture Handbook 249, Washington, DC, 1964.

LLORENS, A. A. and GONZALES, R. P. 'El mercado de la piña en Puerto Rico', *Bol. Estac. Exp. Agr., Univ. Puerto Rico* **175**, 1963, pp. 1–35.

LOBECK, A. K. 'The physiography of Porto Rico', NY Acad. Sci., *Scient. Surv. Porto Rico and the Virgin Islands*, vol. 1, Washington 1922, pp. 301–79.

LOUNDSBURY, J. F. 'Economic development in Latin America; Puerto Rico as a case study', *Revista geográfica* **34**, no. 60, 1964, pp. 27–32.

LUGO LOPEZ, M. A. and MARTINEZ, M. B. 'Drainage of sugar cane fields in east-central Puerto Rico', *Sugar J.* **15**, no. 5, 1952, pp. 14–20.

MACPHAIL, D. D. 'Puerto Rican dairying: a revolution in tropical agriculture', *Geogr. Rev.* **53**, 1963, pp. 224–46.

MANNERS, R. A. and STEWARD, J. H. 'The cultural study of contemporary societies: Puerto Rico', *Am. J. Sociol.* **59**, 1953, pp. 123–30.

MARVEL, T. S. 'Hato Rey, the new center of San Juan', *San Juan Review* **1**, no. 7, 1964, pp. 9–13.

MATHEWS, T. 'The agrarian reform in Cuba and Puerto Rico', *Revista de Ciencias Sociales* **4**, Río Piedras 1960, pp. 107–23.

MATTSON, P. H. 'Geology of the Mayagüez area, Puerto Rico', *Bull. Geol. Soc. Am.* **71**, 1960, pp. 319–62.

MAYNE, A., ed. *Puerto Rico Planning Board: Proceedings of the Seminar on the Contribution of Puerto Rico*, Univ. of Puerto Rico, Agric. Exp. Stat. Bull. no. 40, Río Piedras 1935.

McCORD, J. E., DESCARTES, S. L. *A Farm Management Study of small Farms in three Areas of Puerto Rico*, Univ. of Puerto Rico, Agric. Exp. Stat. Bull. no. 40, Río Piedras 1935.

McCORD, J. E., DESCARTES, S. L. and HUGHE, R. A. *Farm Management Study of small Farms in two Areas of Puerto Rico*, Univ. of Puerto Rico, Agric. Exp. Stat. Bull. no. 43, Río Piedras 1936.

McCORD, J. E. SERRALLES, JR. J. J. and PICÓ, R. *Types of Farming in Puerto Rico*, Univ. of Puerto Rico, Agric. Exp. Stat. Bull. no. 41, Río Piedras 1935.

MEYERHOFF, H. A. *Geology of Puerto Rico*, Monogr. of the Univ. of Puerto Rico, Series B, no. 1, San Juan 1933.

—— 'The texture of karst topography in Cuba and Puerto Rico', *J. Geomorph.* **1**, 1938, pp. 279–95.

MEYERS, F. I. *The Puerto Rico Sugar Manual including Data on Dominican Republic, Haiti and Virgin Islands*, New Orleans, La., 1956.

MINTZ, S. W. 'The culture history of a Puerto Rican sugar plantation: 1876–1949', *Hispanic*

Bibliography

Am. Hist. Rev. **33**, 1953, pp. 224–51.

—— 'Puerto Rican emigration: a threefold comparison', *SES* 4, 1955, pp. 311–25.

MITCHELL, R. C. *A Survey of the Geology of Puerto Rico*, Río Piedras 1954.

—— 'Die geologische Bedeutung von Schwereuntersuchungen auf Puerto Rico', *Neues Jb. Geol. Paläont.*, Stuttgart 1957, pp. 206–15.

MONROE, W. H. 'Sinkholes and towers in the karst area of north-central Puerto Rico', *US Geol. Surv. Profess. Paper* 400-B, 1960, pp. 356–60.

—— 'Large retrogressive landslides in north central Puerto Rico, US Geol. Survey, Profess. Paper 501 B, Washington 1964, pp. 123–5.

—— 'The Zanjón, a solution-feature of tropical karst topography in Puerto Rico', US Geol. Survey, Profess. Paper 501 B, Washington 1964, pp. 126–9.

—— 'Dominio litológico en la Formación de algunas Formas de Relieve en Puerto Rico', Unión Geográfica Internacional, *Trans. Conf. Reg. Latinoamericana* vol. 2, Mexico 1966, pp. 286–91.

—— 'Formation of tropical karst topography by limestone solution and reprecipitation', *Caribb. J. Sci.* **6**, no. 1–2, 1966, pp. 1–7.

MORALES, J. O. and DESCARTES, S. L. *A Credit Study on 167 Tobacco Farms (Puerto Rico 1939–40)*; Univ. of Puerto Rico, Agric. Exp. Stat. Bull. no. 69, Río Piedras 1946.

MORSE, R. 'The sociology of San Juan: an exegesis of urban mythology', *CS* 5, no. 2, 1965, pp. 45–55.

MOSCOSO, T. and ECHENIQUE, M. 'Le développement industriel à Porto Rico. Base et développement du processus', in *Méthodes de Développement industriel*, Paris 1962, pp. 93–125.

MYERS, G. C. and MORRIS, E. W. 'Migration and fertility in Puerto Rico', *Population Studies* **20**, 1966, pp. 85–96.

NEGRÓN RAMOS, P. and VAZQUEZ CALCERRADA, P. B. 'Notes on increasing the economic supply of land in Puerto Rico', *in* 'Redistribution of Farmland in seven Countries', *Internat. J. Agrarian Affairs* **2**, no. 1, London 1955, pp. 64–9.

NELSON, A. E. and MONROE, W. H. *Geology of the Florida Quadrangle, Puerto Rico*, US Geol. Surv. Bull. 1221-C, Washington 1966.

NIDDRIE, D. L. 'The problems of population growth in Puerto Rico', *J. Trop. Geogr.* **20**, 1965, pp. 26–33.

NOVAK, R. T. 'Distribution of Puerto Ricans on Manhattan Island', *Geogr. Rev.* **46**, 1956, pp. 182–6.

OLIVERAS, C. 'The economy of Puerto Rico', in *The Caribbean: British, Dutch, French, United States*, ed. A. Wilgus, Gainesville 1958, pp. 170–9.

OTERO, J. I., TORO, R. A. and PAGÁN DE OTERO, L. *Catálogo de los Nombres vulgares y científicos de algunas Plantas puertorriqueñas*, Río Piedras 1945.

PAGÁN DE COLÓN, P. 'Puerto Rican society in transition', in *The Caribbean: British, Dutch, French, United States*, ed. A. C. Wilgus, Gainesville 1958, pp. 180–9.

PERKINS, M. F. *et al. Credit and Related Problems in the Agriculture of Puerto Rico*, 2 vols, Río Piedras 1956.

PICÓ, R. 'Factores geográficos y económicos que influyen en la Agricultura de Puerto Rico', *Summer School Rev.* **14**, no. 6, Río Piedras 1936, pp. 6–12.

—— 'Land tenure in the leading types of farming of Puerto Rico', *EG* **15**, 1939, pp. 135–45.

—— *The Geographic Regions of Puerto Rico*, Río Piedras 1950.

—— 'Puerto Rico: its problems and its program', *Town Planning Rev.* **24**, 1953.

—— *Geografía de Puerto Rico*, vol. 1: *Geografía Física*, vol. 2: *Geografía Económica*, Río Piedras 1954, 1964.

—— *Economic Growth in Puerto Rico*, San Juan, PR, 1959.

—— *The Government Development Bank and Puerto Rico's economic Program*, San Juan 1959

—— *Puerto Rico: Planificación y Acción*, San Juan 1962.

—— 'The Commonwealth of Puerto Rico', *Focus* **14**, no. 2, New York 1963.

—— *El Banco Gubernamental de Fomento y la Economía puertorriqueña*, San Juan 1964.

—— *Cartography in Puerto Rico*, San Juan 1964.

420

Rios, J. M. *et al.* 'Aspectos sociales de la Industria del Café en Puerto Rico', *Revista de Agricultura de Puerto Rico* **44**, No. 2, 1965, pp. 156–61.

Rivera Guzman, M. 'La industria del turismo en Puerto Rico y la influencia ejercida sobre ella el gobierno de Puerto Rico', *Rivista del Colegio de Comercio* **1**, no. 1, Río Piedras 1966, pp. 119–47.

Rivera Santos, L. 'Tenure Innovations and agricultural Production in Puerto Rico', in *Land Tenure*, ed. K. H. Parsons, R. J. Penn and P. M. Raup, Madison 1956, pp. 328–37.

Roberts, R. C. *Soil Survey of Puerto Rico*, Washington 1942.

Rodriguez Cruz, J. 'Las Relaciones raciales en Puerto Rico', *Revista de Ciencias sociales* **9**, 1965, pp. 373–86.

Roosevelt, T. 'Land Problems in Puerto Rico and the Philippine Islands', *Geogrl Rev.* **24**, 1934, pp. 182–204.

Rosario, J. C. 'The Porto Rican Peasant and his historical Antecedents', in *Porto Rico and its Problems*, ed. V. S. Clark *et al.*, Washington 1930, pp. 537–75.

Ross, D. F. 'The costs and benefits of Puerto Rico's Fomento programmes', *SES* **6**, 1957, pp. 329–62.

Rossen, K. S. 'Puerto Rican land reform: the history of an instructive experiment', *Revista Juridica de la Universidad de Puerto Rico* **33**, Río Piedras 1964, pp. 189–215.

Safa, H. I. 'From shanty town to public housing: a comparison of family structure in two urban neighborhoods in Puerto Rico', *CS* **4**, no. 1, 1964, pp. 3–12.

Senior, C. *Puerto Rican Emigration*, Río Piedras 1947.

Serra, G. and Piñero, M. *An Economic Study of Family sized Farms in Puerto Rico, San José Farm Security Administration Project, 1943–1944, 1944 to 1945*, Univ. of Puerto Rico, Agr. Exp. Stat. Bull. no. 77, Río Piedras 1948.

Shurbet, G. L. and Ewing, M. 'Gravity reconnaissance survey of Puerto Rico', *Bull. Geol. Soc. Am.* **67**, 1956, pp. 511–34.

Stead, W. H. *Fomento: el Desarrollo económico de Puerto Rico*, Mexico 1963.

Steward, J. H., ed. *The People of Puerto Rico. A study in social anthropology*, Univ. of Illinois Press, 1956, 2nd edn, 1966.

Stone, L. O. 'Population redistribution and economic development in Puerto Rico, 1950–1960', *SES* **14**, 1965, pp. 264–71.

Strassmann, W. P. 'Is Puerto Rican economic development a special case?' *Inter-American Economic Affairs* **18**, no. 1, Washington 1964, pp. 61–76.

Stycos, J. M. *Family and Fertility in Puerto Rico: a study of the lower income group*, New York 1955.

Taylor, M. C. 'Tax exemption and new industry in Puerto Rico', *SES* **4**, 1955, pp. 121–32.

Thieme, F. P. *The Puerto Rican Population. A study in human biology*, Anthropological Papers no. 13, Ann Arbor 1959.

Thorp, J. 'Climate and settlement in Puerto Rico and the Hawaiian islands', in *Climate and Man; Yearbook of Agriculture 1941*, US Dept. of Agr., Washington 1941, pp. 217–26.

Tió, A. *Fundación de San Germán y su Significación en el Desarollo político, económico, social y cultural de Puerto Rico*, San Juan 1956.

Toro Lucchetti, H. 'Breve reseña sobre los sistemas de riego público en Puerto Rico', *Revista de Agricultura de Puerto Rico* **50**, no. 2, 1963, pp. 66–87.

Tumin, M. M. *Social Class and social Change in Puerto Rico*, Princeton, New Jersey, 1961.

Valladares de Sotomayor, A. *Historia geográfica civil y política de la Isla de San Juan Bautista de Puerto Rico*, Madrid 1788.

Vázquez Calcerrada, P. B. *The study of a Planned Rural Community in Puerto Rico, Castañer*, Agr. Exp. Stat. Bull. no. 109, Río Piedras 1953.

Váquez Calzada, J. L. 'La emigración puertorriqueña, solución o problema?' *Revista de Ciencias Sociales* **7**, no. 4, 1963, pp. 323–32; also in *Bienestar Público* **19**, no. 74, San Juan 1963, pp. 50–6.

Velarde, J. A. 'The Land Authority of Puerto Rico', in *Caribbean, Land Tenure Symposium*, ed. Caribb. Comm., Washington 1947, pp. 203–31.

Velazquez, G. *Anuario bibliográfico puertorriqueño; Indice alfabético de Libros, Folletos, Revistas y*

421

Periódicos publicados en Puerto Rico durante 1957–1958, San Juan 1964.
WEAVER, J. D. 'Note on higher level erosion surfaces of Puerto Rico', *Trans. 2nd Caribb. Geol. Conf.*, Mayagüez 1960, pp. 96–7.
WILL, R. R. 'Activities of the Farm Security Administration in Puerto Rico', in *Caribb. Land Tenure Symposium*, ed. Caribb. Comm., Washington 1947, pp. 179–202.
WILLARDSON, L. S. *Lajas Valley Drainage Problems*, Univ. of Puerto Rico, Agric. Exp. Stat. Bull. no. 143, Río Piedras 1958.

Virgin Islands

AUGELLI, J. P. 'The British Virgin Islands: a West Indian anomaly', *Geogr. Rev.* **46**, 1956, pp. 43–58.
BOOY, T. DE. 'The Virgin Islands of the United States', *Geogr. Rev.* **4**, 1917, pp. 359–73.
BÖRGESEN, F. 'Notes on the shore vegetation of the Danish West Indian islands', *Bot Tidskr.* **29**, 1909, pp. 201–59.
BRADY, E. F. *The Economy of the U.S. Virgin Islands*, Río Piedras 1963.
CHILES, K. 'Manufacturing industry comes to St Thomas', *Employment Security Rev.* **28**, no. 4, 1961, pp. 3–7.
COMELLA, L. J. *Basic Data on the Economy of the British Virgin Islands*, US-Bureau of International Commerce, OBR 64–110, Washington 1964.
CREQUE, D. and GOEGGEL, H. *A Study of the Tourist Industry in the U.S. Virgin Islands*, St Thomas 1964.
'Danish Building in the Virgin Islands', *J. Am. Inst. Architects* **39**, no. 1, 1962, pp. 27–32.
DONNELLY, T. W. 'The geology of St Thomas and St John, Virgin Islands', *Trans. 2nd Caribb. Geol. Conf.*, Mayagüez 1960, pp. 153–5.
EARLE, K. W. 'The geology of the British Virgin Islands', *Geol. Mag.* **61**, 1924, pp. 339–51.
EGGLESTON, G. T. *Virgin Islands*, London, New York 1959.
HENDRICKSON, G. E. *Ground Water for Public Supply in St Croix, Virgin Islands*, US Geological Survey, Water-Supply Paper 1663-D, Washington 1963.
HUMLUM, J. 'St Croix, St Thomas og St Jan', *Kulturgeografi* **16**, no. 89, 1964, pp. 53–80.
KINGSBURY, R. C. *Commercial Geography of the British Virgin Islands*, Technical Report no. 2, Dept. of Geography, Indiana University, Bloomington, Ind., 1960.
—— 'The Virgin Islands', *Focus* **11**, no. 7, New York 1961.
KINGSBURY, R. and P. *The Virgin Islands*, Garden City 1963.
MARTIN-KAYE, P. H. A. *Water Supplies of the British Virgin Islands*, Georgetown, B. G., 1954.
MENTZE, E. *Danmarks sidste Tropeland: St Thomas, St Croix og St Jan. Oerne i det Caraibiske Hav som blev Solgt til U.S.A. 1916*, Copenhagen 1965.
MEYERHOFF, H. A. 'The Physiography of the Virgin Islands, Culebra and Vieques', NY Acad. Sci., *Scient. Survey of Porto Rico and the Virgin Islands*, vol. 4, 1926/27, pp. 71–219.
MORRILL, W. T. and BENNET, D. 'A French community on St Thomas. Research Commentary', *CS* **5**, no. 4, 1966, pp. 39–47.
MULLINS, T. *An Economic Survey of Family Farms on St Croix, Virgin Islands, 1953*, US Dept. of Agriculture, Agricultural Research Service, Territorial Experiment Station Division, ARS 24–2, Washington 1954.
O'LOUGHLIN, C. 'A survey of economic potential, fiscal structure and capital requirements of the British Virgin Islands', *SES* **11** (Suppl.), 1962.
ROSE, F. 'Landeskundliche Untersuchung der Jungfern-Inseln (Virgin Islands)', dissertation, Leipzig 1930.
SHAW, E. B. 'St Croix: A marginal sugar-producing island', *Geogr. Rev.* **23**, 1933, pp. 414–22.
—— 'The balanced economy of St John Island', *EG* **9**, 1933, pp. 160–6.
—— 'St Thomas: The Keystone of the Antilles', *J. Geogr.* **32**, 1934, pp. 131–9.
—— 'The Chachas of St Thomas', *Scientific Monthly* **38**, 1934, pp. 136–45.
—— Population adjustments in our Virgin Islands', *EG* **11**, 1935, pp. 267–79.

Svensson, O., ed. *Three Towns, Conservation and Renewal of Charlotte Amalie, Christiansted and Frederiksted of the U.S. Virgin Islands*, Copenhagen 1965.

US Dept. of Agriculture, Agricultural Research Service, Territorial Experiment Station Division, *Appraisal of Virgin Islands Agricultural Production and Marketing*, ARS 24–1, Washington 1954.

Virgin Islands of the United States, Econ. Development Board, *Overall Economic Development Program of the Economic Development Board*, Charlotte Amalie, St Thomas 1962.

Westergaard, W. *The Danish West Indies under Company Rule (1671–1754)*, New York 1917.

The Dutch Islands to the Windward

Hartog, J. *SSS: St Maarten, Saba, St Eustatius*, Oranjestad 1965.

Keur, J. Y. and D. L. *Windward Children. A study in human ecology of the three Dutch Windward Islands in the Caribbean*, Assen 1960.

Kruythoff, S. J. *Netherlands Windward Islands*, 3rd edn, Oranjestad 1964.

Molengraaff, G. A. F. 'Saba, St Eustatius (Statia) und St Martin', in *Leidsche Geol. Mededeel. 5 (Feestbundel* K. Martin), Leiden 1931, pp. 715–39.

Price, A. G. 'White settlement in Saba Island, Dutch West Indies', *Geogr. Rev.* **24**, 1934, pp. 42–60.

Veenenbos, J. S. *A Soil and Land Capability Survey of St. Maarten, St Eustatius and Saba*, Publ. of the Foundation for Scientific Research in Surinam and the Netherlands Antilles, Utrecht, no. 11, Utrecht 1955.

Westermann, J. H. 'De geologische Geschiedenis der drie Bovenwindse Eilanden St Martin, Saba en St Eustatius', *De West-Indische Gids* **37**, 1956/57, pp. 127–68.

Westermann, J. H. and Kiel, H. *The Geology of Saba and St Eustatius*, Publ. of the Foundation for Scientific Research in Surinam and the Netherlands Antilles, no. 24, Utrecht 1961.

Winsemius, J. 'Some Notes on St Maarten, Bonaire and Saba (Netherlands Antilles)', *Tijdschr. Econ. Soc. Geogr.* **54**, 1963, pp. 202–8.

Zonneveld, J. I. S. 'St Eustatius', *Tijdschr. Kon. Ned. Aardr. Gen.* (second series) **78**, 1961, pp. 53–6.

—— 'Kustvormen op Sint Maarten', *Tijdschr. Kon. Ned. Aardr. Gen.* (second series) **78**, 1961, pp. 379–84.

The British Leeward Islands

Alexander, W. H. 'Climatology of St Kitts', *MWR* **27**, 1899, pp. 583–7.

—— 'Rainfall on the Island of St Kitts, W.I.', *MWR* **28**, 1900, pp. 487–8.

—— 'The climatology of Antigua', *MWR* **29**, 1901, pp. 165–7.

—— 'Reforestation and Rainfall in the Leeward Islands', *MWR* **29**, 1901, pp. 254–6.

Auchinleck, G. G. *The Rainfall of Antigua and Barbuda*, St John's, Antigua, 1956.

Augelli, J. P. 'Patterns and Problems of Land Tenure in the Lesser Antilles: Antigua, B.W.I.', *EG* **29**, 1953, pp. 362–7.

Baker, E. C. *A Guide to the Records in the Leeward Islands*, Oxford 1965.

Barclays Bank. *Leeward Islands. An economic survey*, London 1958.

Brown, A. P. 'Notes on the Geology of the Island of Antigua', *Proc. Acad. Nat. Sci. Philadelphia* **65**, 1914, pp. 584–616.

Campbell, L. G. and Edwards, D. *Agriculture in Antigua's Economy: Possibilities and Problems of Adjustment*, Agricultural Series no. 1, University of the West Indies, Barbados 1965.

Crist, R. 'Static and emerging cultural landscape on the islands of St Kitts and Nevis, B. W. I.', *EG* **25**, 1949, pp. 134–45.

—— 'Changing cultural Landscapes in Antigua, B. W. I.', *Am. J. Econ. Sociol.* **13**, 1954, pp. 225–32.

423

Bibliography

EARLE, K. W. *Report on the Geology of St Kitts–Nevis, B. W. I. and the Geology of Anguilla, B. W. I.*, London 1923.

—— *Report on the Geology of Antigua*, St John's, Antigua 1923.

FENTEM, A. D. *Commercial Geography of Antigua*, Technical Report no. 11, Dept. of Geography, Indiana University, Bloomington 1961.

GIFFIN, J. *Basic Data on the British Leeward Islands*, US Bur. Comm. OBR 64–16, Washington 1964.

GOVEIA, E. V. *Slave Society in the British Leeward Islands at the End of the Eighteenth Century*, New Haven 1965.

GUPPY, R. S. L. 'On the geology of Antigua and other West Indian Islands', *Q. J. Geol. Soc.* **67**, 1911, pp. 681–700.

HARRIS, D. R. 'The invasion of oceanic islands by alien plants: an example from the Leeward Islands, West Indies', *Trans. and Papers Inst. Br. Geogr.*, no. 31, 1962, pp. 67–82.

—— *Plants, Animals and Man in the outer Leeward Islands, West Indies; an ecological Study of Antigua, Barbuda, and Anguilla*, California Univ. Publications in Geography no. 18, Berkeley, Los Angeles 1965.

JULIEN, A. J. 'On the Geology of the Key of Sombrero, W. I.', *Ann. Lyc. Nat. Hist. NY* **8**, 1867, pp. 251–78.

KIMBALL, H. H. 'The seasonal Variations in the Climate of Antigua, W. I.', *MWR* **29**, 1901, pp. 168–73.

LOVELESS, A. R. 'The vegetation of Antigua, W. Indies', *J. Ecol.* **48**, 1960, pp. 495–527.

LOWENTHAL, D. and COMITAS, L. 'Emigration and Depopulation', *Geogr. Rev.* **52**, 1962, pp. 195–210; (205 ff. Montserrat).

LUFFMAN, J. *Brief Account of the Island of Antigua*, 2nd edn, London 1789.

MACGREGOR, A. G. 'The Royal Society expedition to Montserrat, B. W. I.; the volcanic history and petrology of Montserrat, with observation on Mt Pelé, in Martinique, *Phil. Trans. Roy. Soc.*, B. **229**, 557, London 1938, pp. 1–90.

MARTIN-KAYE, P. H. A. *Reports on the Geology of the Leeward and British Virgin Islands*, Castries, St Lucia 1959.

MERRILL, G. C. *The Historical Geography of St Kitts and Nevis, the West Indies*, Inst. Panamericano de Geogr. e Histor. Publ. no. 232, Mexico 1958.

NIDDRIE, D. L. 'An Attempt at Planned Settlement in St Kitts in the Early Eighteenth Century', *CS* **5**, no. 4, 1966, pp. 3–11.

OLIVER, V. L. *The History of the Island of Antigua*, 3 vols, London 1894, 1896, 1899.

O'LOUGHLIN, C. 'The economy of Montserrat', *SES* **8**, 1959, pp. 147–78.

—— 'The economy of Antigua', *SES* **8**, 1959, pp. 229–64.

—— 'The economy of St Kitts–Nevis–Anguilla', *SES* **8**, 1959, pp. 377–402.

—— 'Problems in the economic development of Antigua', *SES* **10**, 1961, pp. 237–77.

PERRET, F. A. *The Volcano-seismic Crisis at Montserrat 1933–37*, Carnegie Inst. Publ. no. 512, Washington 1939.

POWELL, C. F. 'The Royal Society Expedition to Montserrat, B. W. I., Final Report', *Phil. Trans. Roy. Soc.*, A **237**, London 1938, pp. 1–34.

ROBSON, G. R., BARR, K. G. and SMITH, G. W. 'Earthquake Series in St Kitts–Nevis, 1961–62', *Nature* **195**, 1962, pp. 972–4.

RUSSELL, R. J. and McINTIRE, W. G. *Barbuda Reconnaissance*, Louisiana State University Studies. Coastal Studies Series no. 16, Baton Rouge, La., 1966.

SHERIDAN, R. B. 'The rise of the colonial gentry: a case study of Antigua 1730–1775', *Econ. Hist. Rev.*, ser. 2, **13**, Utrecht 1961, pp. 342–57.

SMITH, G. W. *The Irrigation Needs of Antigua, W. I.*, St Augustine, Trinidad, 1959.

SPENCER, J. W. W. 'On the geological and physical development of Anguilla, St Martin, St Bartholomew, and Sombrero', *Q. Jl Geol. Soc.* **57**, 1901, pp. 520–33.

STARKEY, O. P. *Commercial Geography of Montserrat*, Technical Report no. 6, Dept. of Geography, Indiana University, Bloomington 1960.

—— *Commercial Geography of St Kitts–Nevis*, Technical Report no. 7, Dept. of Geography,

Indiana University, Bloomington 1961.

TRECHMANN, C. T. 'Notes on Brimstone Hill, St Kitts', *Geol. Mag.* **69**, 1932, pp. 241–58.

—— 'Some Observations on the Geology of Antigua, West Indies', *Geol. Mag.* **78**, 1941, pp. 113–24.

TURNER, P. E. *Progress in Sugar-Cane Agriculture in Antigua during the Period 1933–1940*, Port-of-Spain, Trinidad 1940.

—— *Sugar Estate Agriculture in Antigua*, St John's, Antigua 1957.

VAUGHAN, T. W. 'Notes on the igneous rocks of the north-east West Indies and on the geology of the island of Anguilla', *J. Washington Acad. Sci.* **16**, 1926, pp. 345–58.

WILLMORE, P. L. 'The Earthquake Series in St Kitts–Nevis', *Nature* **169**, 1952, pp. 770–2.

The French Islands to the Windward

BANBUCK, N. *Histoire politique, économique et sociale de la Martinique sous l'Ancien Régime 1635 jusque 1789*, Paris 1935.

BARRABÉ, L. 'Observations sur la Constitution géologique de la Désirade (Guadeloupe)', *Bull. Soc. géol. de France*, ser. 6, **3**, 1954, pp. 613–26.

BARRABÉ, L. and JOLIVET, J. 'Les récentes manifestations d'activité de la Guadeloupe (Petites Antilles)', *Bull. Volc.* ser. 2, **19**, Naples 1958, pp. 143–57.

BESNARD, J.-L. *Situation et Perspectives de la Démographie martiniquaise*, Cahiers du Centre d'Etudes Régionales Antilles-Guyane no. 2, Cayenne 1964.

BOISMERY, A. 'Les relations commerciales entre Marseille et les Antilles', *Cahiers d'Outre Mer* **17**, 1964, pp. 386–413.

BRÉTA, F. *Les Saintes* (*Dépendances de la Guadeloupe*), Paris 1939.

BRUET, E. 'La Soufrière de la Guadeloupe. Contribution à l'étude des edifices volcaniques péléens', *Ann. Géophys.* **6**, 1950, pp. 51–64.

—— 'Recherches géologiques dans la Guadeloupe volcanique', *Cahiers géol.* no. 5, Thoiry 1951, pp. 41–7.

—— 'Etudes volcanologiques dans l'Archipel des Saintes (Antilles françaises)', *Bull. Soc. géol. de France*, ser. 6, **2**, 1952, pp. 485–90.

—— 'L'âge absolu de la dernière grande éruption péléenne de la Soufrière de la Guadeloupe', *Bull. Volc.*, ser. 2, **13**, Naples 1953, pp. 105–7.

BYAS, V. W. 'Ethnologic aspects of the Martinique Créole', *J. Negro Hist.* **28**, 1943, pp. 261–83.

CAMPAN, G. *Note sur la Climatologie des Antilles et de la Guyane française*, Monographies de la Météorologie nationale no. 15, Direction météor. nationale, Paris 1959.

CHRISTMANN, R. A. 'Geology of St Bartholomew, St Martin and Anguilla, Lesser Antilles', *Bull. Geol. Soc. Am.* **64**, 1953, pp. 65–96.

COINTET, A. 'Le surpeuplement des Antilles françaises, en particulier de la Guadeloupe', *Rév. des Etudes Coopératives* **26**, 1954, pp. 111–24.

COULTHARD, G. R. 'The French West Indian background of "Négritude"', *CQ* **7**, 1961, pp. 128–36.

DARDET, V. *Etude sur l'écononomie agricole des Antilles françaises*, Marseille 1939.

DEBIEN, G. 'Destinées d'esclaves à la Martinique (1746–1778)', *Bull. Inst. Fr. Afr. Noire*, ser. B, **22**, Dakar 1960, pp. 1–91.

—— 'Les origines des esclaves des Antilles', *Bull. Inst. Fr. Afr. Noire*, ser. B, **23**, Dakar 1961, pp. 363–87.

—— 'Informaciones bibliográficas americanas: "Antillas Francesas"', Anuario de Estudios Americanos **21**, Sevilla 1964, pp. 669–89.

—— 'Antillas de Lengua francesa: bibliografía 1965', *Escuela de Estudios Hispanoamericanos*, Sevilla 1965, pp. 129–51.

—— 'Le marronage aux Antilles françaises au XVIIIe siècle', *CS* **6**, no. 3, 1966, pp. 3–43.

DELAUNEY-BELLEVILLE, A. *Choses et gens de la Martinique*, Paris 1963.

Bibliography

Delawarde, J. B. *Les Défricheurs et les petits colons de la Martinique au XVIIe Siècle*, Paris 1935.
—— *Essai sur l'Installation humaine dans les Mornes de la Martinique*, Fort-de-France 1935.
—— *La Vie paysanne à la Martinique*, Fort-de-France 1937.
Delobez, A. 'La population et l'économie de la Martinique en 1960', *Inform. géogr.* no. 1, Paris 1964, pp. 22–6.
La Documentation Française. Notes et études documentaires, no. 1633, *La Situation économique des Départements d'Outre Mer, Martinique et Guadeloupe*, Paris 1952.
Ekman, E. 'St Barthélemy and the French Revolution', *CS* **3**, no. 4, Río Piedras 1964, pp. 17–29.
Faugères, M. L. 'Observations sur le modèle des versants dans la région des Pitons du Carbet (Martinique)', *Bull. Ass. Géogr. Fr.* **342**–3, 1966, pp. 52–63.
Gisler, A. *L'Eslavage aux Antilles françaises XVIIe à XIXe Siècle*, Studia Friburgensia, NF **42**, Fribourg 1965.
Gottmann, J. 'The isles of Guadeloupe', *Geogr. Rev.* **35**, 1945, pp. 182–203.
Grébert, R., 'Les forêts de la Guadeloupe', *Bull. Agence écon. des Colonies autonomes et des Territoires Africains sous Mandat* **27**, Paris 1934, pp. 639–702, 765–875, 941–1015.
Grunevald, H. *Carte géologique de la Martinique. Notice explicative*, Paris 1961.
Guillaume, J. *La Canne à Sucre aux Antilles françaises; Culture et Fabrication*, Gembloux and Paris 1933.
Heilprin, A. *The Tower of Pelée*, Philadelphia and London 1904.
Hildebrand, I. *Den svenska Kolonin St Barthélemy och Västindiska Kompaniet fram till 1796*, Lund 1951.
Horowitz, M. M. and Klass, M. 'The Martiniquan East Indian cult of Maldevidan', *SES* **10**, 1961, pp. 93–100.
Houdaille, J. *et al.* 'Les origines des esclaves des Antilles', *Bull. Inst. Fr. Afr. Noire*, ser. B, **25**, no. 3–4, Dakar 1963, pp. 215–65.
Hoy, D. R. 'Changing agricultural Land Use on Guadeloupe, French West Indies', *AAAG* **52**, 1962, pp. 441–54.
—— 'The banana industry of Guadeloupe, French West Indies', *SES* **11**, 1962, pp. 260–6.
Jackson, M. H. 'The economy of the French Caribbean', in *The Caribbean: British, Dutch, French, United States*, ed. A. C. Wilgus, Gainesville 1958, pp. 105–24.
Jefferys, T. *The natural and civil History of the French Dominions in North and South America*, 2 vols, London 1761.
Jesse, C. 'Du Tertre and Labat on 17th Century slave life in the French Antilles', *CQ* **7**, 1961, pp. 137–57.
Jolivet, J. 'La crise volcanique de 1956 à la Soufrière de la Guadeloupe', *Ann. Géophys.* **14**, 1958, pp. 305–22.
Koerfer, H. 'Der Guadeloupe-Archipel und seine wirtschaftliche Bedeutung', dissertation Bonn 1910.
Kopp, A. 'L'agriculture à la Guadeloupe', *Ann. Géogr.* **38**, 1929, pp. 480–500.
Labat, R. P. *Nouveau Voyage aux Isles de l'Amérique*, 6 vols, Paris 1722.
Lacour, A. *Histoire de la Guadeloupe Basse-Terre 1855–1860*, reprint, 4 vols, Basse-Terre 1960.
Lacroix, A. *La Montagne Pelée et ses Eruptions*, Paris 1904.
—— *La Montagne Pelée après ses Eruptions*, Paris 1908.
Lasserre, G. 'Marie-Galante', *Cahiers d'Outre-Mer* **3**, 1950, pp. 123–52.
—— 'Une plantation de canne aux Antilles: la sucrerie Beauport (Guadeloupe)', *Cahiers d'Outre-Mer* **5**, 1952, pp. 297–329.
—— 'Les "Indiens" de la Guadeloupe', *Cahiers d'Outre-Mer* **6**, 1953, pp. 128–58.
—— 'Notes sur le karst de la Guadeloupe', *Erdkunde* **8**, 1954, pp. 115–18.
—— 'Evolution des versants calcaires de Grande-Terre et Marie-Galante (Guadeloupe)', *1er Rapport Comm. Et. Versants, I. G. U.*, Amsterdam 1956, pp. 134–6.
—— *La Guadeloupe, Etude géographique*, 2 vols, Bordeaux 1961.
—— 'El uso del suelo en las Antillas francesas Martinica y Guadeloupe', Unión Geográfica Internacional, *Trans. Conferencia Regional Latinoamericana*, vol. 2, Mexico 1966, pp. 316–36.

Leiris, M. *Contacts des Civilisations en Martinique et en Guadeloupe*, Paris 1955.

Lokke, C. L. 'Society in the French Caribbean', in *The Caribbean: British, Dutch, French, United States*, ed. A. C. Wilgus, Gainesville 1958, pp. 125–36.

Martin, G. *Histoire de l'Esclavage dans les Colonies françaises*, Paris 1948.

May, L.-P. *Histoire économique de la Martinique (1635–1763)*, Paris 1930.

Martineau, A. and May, L.-P. *Trois Siècles d'Histoire antillaise; Martinique et Guadeloupe*, Paris 1935.

Maurice, J. 'L'expansion de l'economie agricole de la Martinique', *Rev. Econ. Fr.* **85**, no. 1, 1963, pp. 23–8.

McCloy, S. T. *The Negro in the French West Indies*, Lexington, Kentucky, 1966.

Pagney, P. 'Mouvements marins d'origine cyclonique. Leurs manifestations dans la Mer Caraibe spécialement sur les côtes de la Martinique', *Bull. Ass. Géogr. Fr.* no. **276/7**, 1958, pp. 61–72.

Pailler, G. 'La vitalité démographique du Département de la Martinique', *Norois* **12**, no. 46, Poitiers 1965, pp. 217–23.

Péron, Y. 'La Population des Départements français d'Outre-Mer', *Population* **21**, 1966, pp. 99–132.

Perret, F. A. *The Eruption of Mt Pelée 1929–1932*, Carnegie Institution of Washington Publ. no. 458, Washington 1935.

—— 'Peuplement et population de la Guadeloupe', *Population* **18**, no. 1, Paris 1963, pp. 137–40.

Pouquet, J. *Les Antilles françaises*, Paris 1952.

Price, R. 'Magie et pêche à la Martinique', *Homme* **4**, no. 2, Paris 1964, pp. 84–113.

Questel, A. *La Flore de la Guadeloupe (Antilles françaises)*, Paris 1951.

Rennard, J. *La Martinique historique des Paroisses des Origines à la Séparation*, Thonon-les-Bains 1951.

Révert, E. 'La Montagne Pelée et ses dernières éruptions', *Ann. Géogr.* **40**, 1931, pp. 275–91.

—— 'L'economie martiniquaise', *Cahiers d'Outre Mer* **1**, 1948, pp. 28–39.

—— *La Martinique*, Paris 1949.

—— 'Problèmes de géographie antillaise', *Cahiers d'Outre Mer* **3**, 1950, pp. 1–27.

—— *La France d'Amérique*, Paris 1955.

Reynal, A. de. *Carte géologique de la France, Département de la Guadeloupe, 1: 50 000. Feuille de Grande Terre et Notice explicative*, Paris 1961.

Robequain, C. 'Saint-Barthélemy, terre française', *Cahiers d'Outre Mer* **2**, 1949, pp. 14–37.

—— *Madagascar et les Bases dispersées de l'Union française*, Paris 1958.

Robert, G. *Les Travaux publics de la Guadeloupe*, Paris 1935.

Roberts, W. A. *The French in the West Indies*, Indianapolis 1942.

Salandre, H. and Chessac, R. *Histoire et Civilisation des Antilles françaises: Guadeloupe et Martinique*, Paris 1962.

Sanderson, A. *French West Indies: agricultural Production and Trade*, Department of Agriculture, economic Research Service, Regional Analysis Division, Washington, DC, 1964.

Satineau, M. *Histoire de la Guadeloupe sous l'Ancien Régime 1635–1789*, Paris 1928.

Stehlé, H. *Flore de la Guadeloupe et Dépendances. Essai d'Ecologie et de Géographie botanique*, Basse-Terre, Guadeloupe, 1935.

—— 'Les associations végétales de la Guadeloupe et leur intérêt dans la valorisation rationelle', *Rev. Bot. appliquée et Agric. trop.* **17**, 1937, pp. 98–109, 188–95.

—— 'Esquisse des Associations végétales de la Martinique', *Bull. Agr. Martinique* **6**, 1937, pp. 194–204.

—— *Les principaux Types de Pâtures et Savanes naturelles et les Mélanges fourragers dans l'Archipel caraibe*, Centre des Recherches agronomiques des Antilles et Guyane françaises, Etude no. 36, Basse-Terre 1955.

—— *Essai de Détermination du Micro-Climat de l'Archipel des Saintes d'après le Relief, les Affinités floristico-sociologiques de sa Végétation et les Cultures*, Basse-Terre, Guadeloupe, n.d.

Stehlé, H. and Stehlé, M. *Monographies des Antilles françaises: une excursion à la Soufrière*,

Basse-Terre 1958.

WERNER, P. 'Martinique nach Geschichte, Natur und wirtschaftlicher Entwicklung seit seiner Entdeckung', dissertation, Bonn 1910.

The British Windward Islands

ANDERSON, R. M. *Handbook of St Vincent*, Kingstown 1909.

ANDERSON, T. and FLETT, J. S. 'Report on the eruptions of the Soufrière in St Vincent in 1902, and a visit to Montagne Pelée, in Martinique', *Phil. Trans. Roy. Soc. London* A **200**, 1903, pp. 353–553; A **208**, 1908, pp. 275–332.

ANDRÉ, E. 'The volcanic eruption at St Vincent', *Geogrl J.* **20**, 1902, pp. 60–8.

AUCHINLECK, G. C. 'Peasant agriculture in Grenada: suggestions for its control and improvement', *WI Bull.* **13**, 1912, pp. 83–94.

BANKS, E. P. 'A Carib village in Dominica', *SES* **5**, 1956, pp. 74–86.

BAROME, J. 'Spain and Dominica 1493–1647', *CQ* **12**, no. 4, 1966, pp. 30–46.

BELLAMY, C. V. 'The rainfall of Dominica', *Roy. J. Met.* **23**, 1897, pp. 261–73.

—— 'The rainfall of Dominica', *Roy. J. Met.* **29**, 1903, pp. 23–8.

BREEN, H. H. *St Lucia: historical, statistical and descriptive*, London 1844.

BULLEN, R. P. *The Archaeology of Grenada, West Indies*, Contributions of the Florida State Museum, Social Sciences, no. 11, Gainesville 1964.

—— 'The first English settlement on St Lucia', *CQ* **12**, no. 2, 1966, pp. 29–35.

CLARKE, W. C. *Notes on the Geography and History of Dominica*, Univ. of California, Dept. of Geogr., Berkeley 1962.

DEVAS, R. P. *The History of the Island of Grenada, 1850–1950*, Barbados 1965.

EARLE, K. W. *The Geology of St. Vincent and the neighbouring Grenadines*, Kingstown, St. Vincent, 1924.

—— *Geological Survey of Grenada and the Grenadines*, St. Georges, Grenada, 1924.

—— 'Geological notes on the island of Dominica', *Geol. Mag.* **65**, 1928, pp. 169–87.

FENTEM, A. D. *Commercial Geography of Dominica*. Technical Report No. 5, Dept. of Geography, Indiana University, Bloomington, Ind., 1960.

—— *Commercial Geography of St Vincent*, Technical Report no. 10, Dept. of Geography, Indiana University, Bloomington, Ind., 1961.

FOREMAN, R. A. *Land Settlement Scheme for Saint Lucia*, Castries, St Lucia, 1958.

HAREWOOD, J. 'Population growth in Grenada in the twentieth century', *SES* **15**, 1966, pp. 61–84.

—— 'Employment in Grenada in 1960', *SES* **15**, 1966, pp. 203–38.

HARRISON, L. C. 'Dominica: a wet tropical human habitat', *EG* **11**, 1935, pp. 62–76.

HAY, R. L. 'Origin and weathering of late pleistocene ash deposits on St Vincent, B.W.I.', *J. Geol.* **67**, 1959, pp. 65–87.

HILL, O. M. 'St Vincent in the Windwards', *Canad. Geogrl J.* **59**, 1959, pp. 162–7.

HODGE, W. H. 'The vegetation of Dominica', *Geogr. Rev.* **33**, 1943, pp. 349–75.

HODGE, W. H. and TAYLOR, D. 'The ethnobotany of the island Caribs of Dominica', Webbia 12, Florence 1957, pp. 513–644.

HOWARD, R. A. *The Vegetation of the Grenadines Windward Isles, B. W. I.*, Gray Herb., Harvard Univ., Contr. no. 174, 1952.

KERSHAW, M. 'The banana industry in the Windward Islands', *Tropical Science* **8**, 1966, pp. 115–27.

KINGSBURY, R. C. *Commercial Geography of the Grenadines*, Technical Report no. 1, Dept. of Geography, Indiana University, Bloomington, Ind., 1960.

—— *Commercial Geography of Grenada*, Technical Report no. 3, Dept. of Geography, Indiana University, Bloomington, Ind., 1960.

LASSERRE, G. 'La Dominique et les derniers Caraibes insulaires', *Cahiers d'Outre Mer* **6**, 1953, pp. 37–60.

LEHNER, E. *Artesian Water Supply of Carriacou*, St George's, Grenada, 1935.

LEIGH FERMOR, P. 'The Caribs of Dominica', *Geogrl Mag.* **23**, 1950, pp. 256–64.

MARSHALL, W. K. 'Metayage in the sugar industry of the British Windward Islands, 1838–1865', *Jamaican Hist. Rev.* **5**, no. 1, 1965, pp. 28–55.

—— 'Social and economic problems in the Windward Islands 1835–65', in *The Caribbean in Transition*, ed. F. M. Andic and T. G. Mathews, Río Piedras 1965, pp. 234–57.

MARTIN-KAYE, P. H. 'The geology of Carriacou', *Bull. Am. Paleont.* **38**, no. 175, Ithaca, New York 1958.

MILSTEAD, H. P. 'Cacao industry of Grenada', *EG* **16**, 1940, pp. 195–203.

O'NEALE, H. W. 'The economy of St Lucia', *SES* **13**, 1964, pp. 440–70.

PINCHON, R. P. 'Description de l'Ile de Saint-Vincent', *Bull. Soc. Hist. Martinique*, no. 9, Fort-de-France 1961, pp. 31–81.

PUGNET, J. F. X. *Essai sur la Topographie de l'Ile de Sainte-Lucie*, Paris 1804.

ROSE, J. C. and LEWIS, A. C. *The New Plan for Castries, St Lucia*, Office of the Executive Architect, Windward Islands, BWI, Castries 1949.

SAPPER, K. 'Ein besuch der insel Grenada', *Centralbl. Min. Geol. Paläont.*, 1903, pp. 182–6.

—— 'Bericht über einen Besuch von St Vincent', *Centralbl. Min. Geol. Paläont.*, 1903, pp. 248–58.

—— Zur Kenntnis der Insel St Lucia in Westindien', *Centralbl. Min. Geol. Paläont.*, 1903, pp. 273–8.

—— 'Ein Besuch von Dominica', *Centralbl. Min. Geol. Paläont.*, 1903, pp. 305–14.

SMITH, M. G. 'The transformation of land rights by transmission in Carriacou', *SES* **5**, 1956, pp. 103–38.

—— 'Kinship and household in Carriacou', *SES* **10**, 1961, pp. 455–77.

—— *Kinship and Community in Carriacou*, New Haven and London 1963.

—— *Stratification in Grenada*, Berkeley, Los Angeles 1965.

STARKEY, O. P. *Commerical Geography of St Lucia*, Technical Report no. 8, Dept. of Geography, Indiana University, Bloomington, Ind., 1961.

TAYLOR, D. 'The Caribs of Dominica', Bureau of *Am. Ethnol. Bull.* **119**, 1937, pp. 103–59.

TRECHMANN, C. T. 'The pitons of St Lucia, B. W. I.', *Nat. Hist. Mag.* **5**, 1935, pp. 134–5.

VÉRIN, P. 'Sainte-Lucie et ses derniers Caraibes', *Cahiers d'Outre Mer* **12**, 1959, pp. 349–61.

—— 'Les Caraibes à Sainte Lucie depuis les contacts coloniaux', *Nieuwe West-Indische Gids* **41**, 1961, pp. 66–82.

WALKER, F. 'Economic progress of St Vincent, B. W. I., since 1927, *EG* **13**, 1937, pp. 217–34.

WATSON, J. P. *et al.*, *Soil and Land Use Surveys*, no. 3: *St Vincent*, St Augustine, Trinidad, 1958.

Barbados

BETHEL, J. 'A national accounts study of the economy of Barbados', *SES* **9**, 1960, pp. 123–252.

CHANDLER, M. J. *A Guide to Records in Barbados*, Oxford 1965.

CUMPER, G. E. 'Employment in Barbados', *SES* **8**, 1959, pp. 105–46.

—— 'Household and occupation in Barbados', *SES* **10**, 1961, pp. 386–419.

FONAROFF, L. S. 'Geographic notes of the Barbados malaria epidemic', *Prof. Geogr.* **18**, 1966, pp. 155–63.

GALLOWAY, J. H. 'The sugar industry in Barbados during the seventeenth century', *J. Trop. Geogra.* **19**, 1964, pp. 35–41.

GOODING, E. G. B., LOVELACE, A. R. and PROCTOR, G. R. *Flora of Barbados*, Great Britain, Ministry of Overseas Development, Research Publication no. 7, London 1965.

HALCROW, M. and CAVE, J. M. *Peasant Agriculture in Barbados*, Dept. of Science and Agriculture, Bull. no. 11, new series, Bridgetown, Barbados, 1947.

HANDLER, J. 'Some aspects of work organization on sugar plantations in Barbados', *Ethnology* **4**, Pittsburgh 1965, pp. 16–38.

—— 'Small-scale sugar cane farming in Barbados', *Ethnology* **5**, 1966, pp. 264–83.

HARLOW, V. T. *A History of Barbados*, Oxford 1926.

HARRISON, J. B. and BROWNE, A. J. J. 'The geology of Barbados', *Geol. Mag.* **4**, 1902, pp. 550–4.

HENSHALL, J. D. 'The demographic factor in the structure of Agriculture in Barbados', *Trans. Inst. Br. Geogr.* **38**, 1966, pp. 183–95.

HENSHALL, J. D. and KING, L. S. 'Some structural characteristics of peasant agriculture in Barbados', *EG* **42**, 1966, pp. 74–84.

HUNTE, G. 'Barbados in the federal tourist picture', *The Caribbean* **13**, 1959, pp. 231–3, 243.

INNES, F. C. 'Desarollo planeado en un continuo de tendancias establecidas, Barbados', Unión Geográfica Internacional, *Trans. Conf. Reg. Latinoamericana* vol. 2, Mexico 1966, pp. 76–82.

JUKES-BROWNE, A. J. and HARRISON, J. B. 'The geology of Barbados. I. The coral-rocks of Barbados and other West-Indian islands', *Q. Jl Geol. Soc.* **47**, 1891, pp. 197–250.

—— 'The geology of Barbados. II. The oceanic deposits', *Q. Jl Geol. Soc.* **48**, 1892, pp. 170–226.

KUGLER, H. G. 'Tertiary of Barbados', *Geol. Mag.* **98**, 1961, pp. 348–50.

LEWIS, J. B. 'The coral reefs and coral communities of Barbados, W. I.', *Canad. J. Zool.* **38**, 1960, pp. 1133–45.

LIGON, R. *A True and Exact History of the Island of Barbados*, London 1657.

LOWENTHAL, D. 'The population of Barbados', *SES* **6**, 1957, pp. 445–501.

MAKINSON, D. H. *Barbados, a Study of North American–West Indian Relations, 1739–1789*, Studies in American History, no. 3, The Hague 1964.

MARTIN-KAYE, P. and BADCOCK, J. 'Geological background to soil conservation and land rehabilitation measures in Barbados, W. I.', *Trans. 3rd Caribbean Geol. Conference*, Mayagüez 1962.

OGUNTOYINBO, J. S. 'Evapotranspiration and sugar cane yields in Barbados', *J. Trop. Geogr.* **22**, 1966, pp. 38–48.

OYELESE, J. O. 'Some aspects of food crop cultivation in the plantations of Barbados, W. I.', *Nigerian Geogrl J.* **9**, 1966, pp. 55–70.

PAN AMERICAN INSTITUTE OF GEOGRAPHY AND HISTORY, Commission of History. *Barbados, Guía de los Documentos microfotografiados por la Unidad Movil de Microfilm de la Unesco*, Instituto Panamericano de Geografía e Historia, Publicación 270, Mexico 1965.

PEETERS, L. 'Erosion et glissements de terrain à la Barbade', *Rev. Belge Géogr* **87**, no. 2, 1963, pp. 211–25.

POYER, J. *The History of Barbados from the first Discovery in the Year 1605 till the Accession of Lord Seaforth, 1801*, London 1808.

PRICE, E. T. *Notes on the Geography of Barbados*, Dept. of Geogr., University of California, Berkeley 1958.

ROBERTS, G. W. 'Emigration from Barbados', *SES* **4**, 1955, pp. 245–88.

ROBINSON, J. B. D. 'A comparative study of some soil nutrients in the coralline sugar cane soils of Barbados', *J. Soil Sci.* **3**, 1952, pp. 182–9.

ROUSE, W. R. *The Moisture Balance of Barbados and its Influence on Sugar Cane Yield*, McGill University, Dept. of Geography, Climatol. Research, Ser. 1, A, Montreal 1966.

RUSSEL, J. 'Coral cap of Barbados', *Tijdskr. Kon. Ned. Aardr. Gen.* **83**, 1966, pp. 298–302.

SAINT, S. J. 'The coral limestone soils of Barbados', *Agric. J.* **3**, no. 3, Dept. of Science and Agriculture, Bridgetown, Barbados, 1934, pp. 1–37.

SCHOMBURGK, SIR R. H. *The History of Barbados*, London 1847.

SENN, A. 'Paleogene of Barbados and its bearing on history and structure of Antillean-Caribbean region', *Am. Ass. Petr. Geol. Bull.* **24**, 1940, pp. 1548–1610.

—— *Inventory of the Barbados Rocks and their possible Utilization*, Bull. no. 1, new series, Dept. of Science and Agriculture, Bridgetown, Barbados, 1944.

—— *Report of the British Union Oil Company Limited on geological Investigations of the Ground-Water Resources of Barbados, B. W. I.*, Bridgetown, Barbados, 1946.

—— 'Die Geologie der Insel Barbados, B. W. I. (Kleine Antillen) und die Morphogenese der umliegenden marinen Großformen', *Eclogae Geologicae Helvetiae* **40**, 1947, pp. 199–222.

SEVER, B. *Basic Data on the Economy of Barbados*, US Bureau of Internat. Commerce OBR 64–68, Washington 1964.

SKEETE, C. C. *The Condition of Peasant Agriculture in Barbados*, Dept. of Science and Agriculture, Bridgetown, Barbados, 1930.

—— 'Barbados rainfall', Dept. of Science and Agriculture, pamphlet no. 9, Bridgetown 1931, pp. 5–18.

SPENCER, J. W. W. 'On the geological and physical development of Barbados, with notes on Trinidad', *Q. Jl Geol. Soc.* **58**, 1902, pp. 354–67.

STARKEY, O. P. *The Economic Geography of Barbados*, New York 1939.

—— *Commercial Geography of Barbados*, Technical Report no. 9, Dept. of Geography, Indiana Univ., Bloomington 1961.

STRAW, K. H. 'Some preliminary results of a survey of income and consumption patterns in a sample of households in Barbados', *SES* **1**, no. 4, 1953, pp. 5–40.

TRECHMANN, C. T. 'The uplift of Barbados', *Geol. Mag.* **70**, 1933, pp. 19–47.

—— 'The base and top of the coral-rock in Barbados', *Geol. Mag.* **74**, 1937, pp. 337–59.

VERNON, K. C. and CARROLL, D. M. *Barbados*. Soil and Land-Use Surveys no. 18; St Augustine, Trinidad, 1966.

WATTS, D. 'Algunos aspectos del desarrollo agrícola moderno en Barbados, Antillas', Unión Geográfica Internacional, *Trans. Conferencia Regional Latinoamericana*, vol. 2, Mexico 1966, pp. 574–85.

—— *Evapotranspiration and Energy Relationships at Waterford, Barbados, 1960*, McGill University. Dept. of Geography, Climatol. Research ser. 1, B, Montreal 1966.

—— *Man's Influence on the Vegetation of Barbados, 1627 to 1800*, Hull. Univ. Occasional Papers in Geography no. 4, Hull, 1966.

Trinidad and Tobago

AHIRAM, E. 'Distribution of income in Trinidad-Tobago, and comparison with distribution of income in Jamaica', *SES* **15**, no. 2, 1966, pp. 103–20.

AHSAN, S. R. *East Indian Agricultural Settlements in Trinidad; a study in cultural geography*, Gainesville 1963.

ARMSTRONG, E. 'Projections of the growth of the economy of Trinidad and Tobago', *SES* **12**, 1963, pp. 283–306.

ARNOLD, R., MacREADY, G. A. and BARRINGTON, T. W. *The First Big Oil Hunt, Venezuela 1911 to 1916*, New York 1960.

AUGELLI, J. P. and TAYLOR, H. W. 'Race and population patterns in Trinidad', *AAAG* **50**, 1960, pp. 123–38.

BAIN, F. M. *The Rainfall of Trinidad*, Dept. of Agriculture, Port-of-Spain n. d.

BARDENS, D. 'Trinidads wirtschaftliche Aussichten', *Z. Wirtschaftsgeogr.* **7**, 1963, pp. 89–91.

BEARD, J. S. *The Natural Vegetation of Trinidad*, Oxford Forestry Memoirs no. 19, Oxford 1946.

BECKFORD, G. L. F. 'Agriculture in the development of Trinidad and Tobago; a comment', *SES* **14**, 1965, pp. 217–20.

CAMPBELL, J. S. and GOODING, H. J. 'Recent developments in the production of food crops in Trinidad', *Trop. Agric.* **39**, 1962, pp. 261–70.

CARMICHAEL, G. *The History of the West Indian Islands of Trinidad and Tobago, 1498–1900*, London 1961.

CHARTER, C. F. *A Preliminary Survey of Soil-Types of Sugar Estates of Trinidad*, Trinidad 1939.

CHENERY, E. M. *The Soils of Central Trinidad*, Port-of-Spain, Trinidad, 1952.

DEY, M. K. 'The Indian population in Trinidad and Tobago', *Internat. Jl Comp. Sociol.* **2**, Dharwar 1962, pp. 245–53.

Bibliography

Dyson, A. 'Land use in the Maracas-St Joseph Basin, Trinidad', in *Geographers and the Tropics: Liverpool Essays*, ed. R. W. Steel and R. M. Prothero, London 1964, pp. 261–76.

Fenwick, D. W. 'The problem of rehabilitation of coconuts in Tobago; (1) Production of planting material), *J. Agric. Soc.* **64**, no. 1, Port-of-Spain 1964, pp 75–95.

Fonraoff, L. S. *Biogeographic Aspects of Malaria in Trinidad*, Univ. of California Dept. of Geography, Berkeley 1966.

Frost, R. 'Exceptional rainfall of Trinidad, 1951', *Met. Mag.* **81**, 1952, pp. 107–12.

Fukuoka, J. 'Observaciones oceanográficas cerca de la Isla de Trinidad y en las Afueras de la Desembocadura del Rio Orinoco, *Memoria, Sociedad de Ciencias naturales de la Salle* **24**, no. 67, Caracas 1964, pp. 91–7.

Green, H. B. 'Socialization values in the Negro and East Indian subcultures of Trinidad', *J. Soc. Psychol.* **64**, 1964, pp. 1–20.

Hardy, F. 'The chief soil types of Trinidad', *Proc. Agric. Soc. Trinidad–Tobago* **35**, 1934, pp. 443–458.

—— 'Soil erosion in Trinidad and Tobago', *Trop. Agric.* **19**, 1942, pp. 29–35.

—— 'Effective rainfall and soil moisture in Trinidad', *Trop. Agric.* **25**, 1947, pp. 45–51.

Hardy, F. and Jordan, J. W. 'Soil fertility of some peasant lands in Trinidad', Tropical Agriculture **23**, 1946, pp. 12–19.

Harewood, J. *Employment in Trinidad and Tobago, 1960*, Univ. of the West Indies, Kingston, Jam., n.d.

—— 'Population growth in Trinidad and Tobago in the twentieth century', *SES* **12**, 1963, pp. 1–26.

—— 'Labour force in Trinidad and Tobago', in *The Caribbean in Transition*, Río Piedras 1965, pp. 128–40.

Herklots, G. A. C. *The Birds of Trinidad and Tobago*, London 1965.

Herskovits, M. J. and Herskovits, F. S. *Trinidad Village*, New York 1947.

Hill, I. D. *Micromorphological Studies in some Soils of Tobago*, St Augustine, Trinidad, 1964.

Ibbotson, P. *Indians in Fiji, Trinidad and Mauritius, Asia and Africa Review* **2**, no. 4, London 1962.

Illing, V. C. and Kugler, H. G. *Eastern Venezuela and Trinidad. The science of petroleum*, Oxford 1938.

James, P. E. 'The climate of Trinidad, B. W. I.', *MWR* **53**, 1925, pp. 71–5.

—— 'Geographic factors in the Trinidad coconut industry', *EG* **2**, 1926, pp. 108–25.

—— 'A geographic reconnaissance of Trinidad., *EG* **3**, 1927, pp. 87–109.

—— 'Changes in the geography of Trinidad', *Scott. Geogr. Mag.* **73**, 1957, pp. 158–66.

Jolly, A. L. 'Peasant farming in the Bejucal area of Trinidad', *Trop. Agric.* **22**, 1945, pp. 83–8.

—— 'Peasant agriculture. An economic survey on the La Pastora land settlement, Trinidad, May 1944 to 1945', *Trop. Agric.* **23**, 1946, pp. 117–22.

—— 'Peasant farming in two districts of the Oropouche Lagoon—June 1944–45', *Trop. Agric.* **25**, 1949, pp. 23–32.

Kingsbury, R. C. *Commercial Geography of Trinidad and Tobago*, Technical Report no. 4, Dept. of Geography, Indiana University, Bloomington, Ind., 1960.

Klass, M. *East Indians in Trinidad: a study of cultural persistence*, New York and London 1961.

Koldewijn, B. W. *Sediments of the Paria-Trinidad-Shelf*, Publicaties van het fysisch-geografisch Laboratorium van de Universiteit van Amsterdam, no. 1, Amsterdam 1958.

Kugler, H. C. 'Summary digest of geology of Trinidad', *Bull. Am. Ass. Petr. Geol.* **20**, 1936, pp. 1439–53.

—— 'Jurassic to recent sedimentary environments in Trinidad', *Bull. Ass. Suisse Géol. Ing. Pétrole* **20**, no. 59, 1953, pp. 27–60.

Laurence, K. O. 'The settlement of free Negroes in Trinidad before emancipation', *CQ* **9**, no. 1–2, Port-of-Spain 1963, pp. 26–52.

Lehner, M. E. *Introduction à la Géologie dr Trinidad*, Paris 1935.

Marshall, R. C. *The Physiography and Vegetation of Trinidad and Tobago*, Oxford Forestry

Memoirs no. 17, Oxford 1934.

MAXWELL, J. C. 'Geology of Tobago, B. W. I.', *Bull. Geol. Soc. Am.* **59**, 1948, pp. 801–54.

NARDIN, J. C. 'Sur le Nom de l'Ile de Tobago', *CS* **2**, no. 2, 1962, pp. 31–4

NIDDRIE, D. L. *Land Use and Population in Tobago. An environmental study*, London 1961.

OTTLEY, C. R. *History of Tobago*, Trinidad 1946.

—— *The Story of Port-of-Spain, Capital of Trinidad, West Indies, from the earliest Times to the present Day*, Port-of-Spain 1962.

PASSARGE, S. 'Der asphaltsee in Trinidad im Jahre 1901', *Jb. Geogr. Ges. Hannover*, 1930, pp. 94–6.

RAMPERSAD, F. B. 'Some aspects of the external trade and payments of Trinidad and Tobago, 1951 to 1959', *SES* **12**, 1963, pp. 101–40.

—— 'Growth and structural change in the economy of Trinidad and Tobago, 1951–1961', *SES* **13**, (Suppl.) 1964.

RICHARDSON, W. D. 'Observations on the vegetation and ecology of the Aripo Savannas, Trinidad', *J. Ecol.* **51**, 1963, pp. 295–313.

ROSE, P. 'Teak in Trinidad', *Econ. Bot.* **13**, 1959, pp. 30–40.

SCHWARTZ, M. M. 'Pattern of East Indian family organization in Trinidad', *CS* **5**, 1965 pp. 23–36.

SHEPHARD, C. Y. 'Economic survey of the cacao industry of Trinidad, B. W. I.', *EG* **3**, 1927, pp. 239–58.

—— Some economic aspects of cacao production in Trinidad with special reference to the Montserrat district', *Trop. Agric.* **13**, 1936, pp. 85–90.

—— *The Cacao Industry of Trinidad*, Part 4, *Historical 1870 to 1920, Port-of-Spain*, Trinidad 1932.

—— 'Agricultural labour in Trinidad', *Trop. Agric.* **12**, no. 1–7, 1936.

SIMPSON, G. 'The Shango cult in Nigeria and in Trinidad', *American Anthropologist* **64**, 1962, pp. 1204–19.

SKUTSCH, J. 'Die Inseln Trinidad und Tobago. Landeskundliche Darstellung einer britischen Kolonie', dissertation, Leipzig 1929.

SPETH, W. W. *Notes on the coastal Geography of Trinidad*, Dept. of Geography, Univ. of California, Berkeley 1962.

SUZE, J. A. DE. *The New Trinidad and Tobago; a descriptive account of the geography and history of Trinidad and Tobago*, 14th edn, London and Glasgow 1965.

TRECHMANN, C. T. 'Tertiary and quaternary beds of Tobago, W. I.', *Geol. Mag.* **71**, 1934, pp. 481–93.

VERTEUIL, L. A. A. DE. *Trinidad, its Geography, Natural Resources, Administration, Present Condition, and Prospects*, London 1858.

—— *Essai sur l'Agriculture de la Trinidad*, Beauvais 1896.

WARRING, G. A. *The Geology of the Island of Trinidad, B. W. I.*, John Hopkins Univ. Stud. in Geol., no. 7, Baltimore 1926.

WEHEKIND, L. and SMITH, G. W. *Trinidad Rainfall, 1933–1952, and Rainfall Reliability in Trinidad*, Port-of-Spain 1955.

WILLIAMS, E. *History of the People of Trinidad and Tobago*, Port-of-Spain 1962, New York 1964.

WILSON, P. N. 'Observations in the grazing behaviour of cross bred Zebu-Holstein-cattle managed on Pangola pasture in Trinidad', *Turrialba* **11**, 1961, pp. 57–71.

WILSON, T. B. 'The economics of peasant farming in Trinidad', *World Crops* **6**, 1954 pp. 135–40.

WOODCOCK, H. I. *A History of Tobago*, Ayr 1867.

The Venezuelan Antilles

ALEXANDER, C. S. *The Geography of Margarita and adjacent Islands, Venezuela*, Berkeley and Los Angeles 1958.

Bibliography

—— 'Margarita Island, exporter of people', *JIAS* **3**, 1961, pp. 549–57.
BUDOWSKI, G. *La Isla de Margarita y sus Problemas*, Ministerio de Agricultura y Cría Departamento de Divulgación agropecuaria, Caracas 1949.
DEPARTMENT OF ECONOMIC AFFAIRS. *Annotated Index of aerial photographic Coverage and Mapping of Topography and natural Resources, Venezuela*, Pan American Union 1964.
GHAVES, L. F. *Margarita y su Región seca*, Universidad Central de Venezuela, Caracas 1964.
GOLDBRUNNER, A. W. 'El clima de la Isla de Margarita', *Memoria de la Sociedad de Ciencias Naturales de la Salle* **22**, no. 62, Caracas 1962.
HESS, H. H. and MAXWELL, J. C. 'Geological reconnaissance of the island of Margarita', *Bull. Geol. Soc. Am.* **60**, 1949, pp. 1857–68.
JAM, L. P. and MENDEZ AROCHA, M. 'Geología de las islas de Margarita, Coche y Cubagua', *Memoria de la Sociedad de Ciencias Naturales de la Salle 22*, Caracas 1962, pp. 51–93.
KUGLER, H. G. 'Contribution to the geology of the islands Margarita and Cubagua, Venezuela', *Bull. Geol. Soc. Am.* **68**, 1957, pp. 555–66.
LOPEZ, J. E. 'Tendencias de la Población Venezolana', *Revista Geográfica* **6**, nos. 14/15, Mérida, Venezuela, 1965, pp. 5–44.
MARCHAND, B. 'Etude géographique de la population du Vénézuela', *Ann. Géogr.* **72**, 1963, pp. 734–45.
MARRERO, L. *Venezuela y sus Recursos*, Caracas 1964.
MURPHY, R. C. 'Bird islands of Venezuela', *Geogr. Rev.* **42**, 1952, pp. 551–61.
OJER, P. 'Los comienzos de la administración española en Margarita', *Revista de Historia* **4**, no. 24, Caracas 1965, pp. 11–30.
ROST, M. 'Die venezuelanischen Inseln Las Aves, Los Roques, Las Orchilas und die Phosphatlagerstätte von Gran Roque', *Z. Dt. Geol. Ges.* **90**, 1938, pp. 577–96.
RUTTEN, L. 'New data on the smaller islands north of Venezuela. On the geology of Margarita. Cubagua and Coche (Venezuela)', *Proc. Kon. Akad. Wetensch.* **43**, Amsterdam 1940, pp. 820–41.
TAYLOR, G. C. 'Geología de la Isla de Margarita, Venezuela', *Mem. 3 Congr. Geol. Venezolano*, vol. 2, Caracas 1960, pp. 838–93.
VILA, M.-A. *Aspectos geográficos de Nueva Esparta*, Corporación venezolana de Fomento. Monografías económicas estadales, Caracas 1958.
WAGENAAR HUMMELINCK, P. 'Islote Aves, een Vogeleiland in de Caraibische Zee', *De West-Indische Gids* **33**, 1952, pp. 23–34.

The Dutch Islands to the Leeward

ALEXANDER, C. S. 'The marine terraces of Aruba, Bonaire, and Curaçao, Netherlands Antilles', *AAAG* **51**, 1961, pp. 102–23.
Aruba and its Industries, Aruba 1963.
ASSENDERP, A. L. VAN. 'Some aspects of society in the Netherlands Antilles and Surinam', in *The Caribbean: British, Dutch, French, United States*, ed. A. C. Wilgus, Gainesville 1958, pp. 86–94.
BRAAK, C. *Het Klimaat van Nederlandsch West-Indie*, Kon. Ned. Met. Instituut no. 102, Med. en Verh. 36, The Hague 1935.
BÚISONJÉ, P. H. DE. 'Marine terraces and subaeric sediments on the Netherlands Leeward Islands, Curaçao, Aruba and Bonaire, and indications of quaternary changes on sea level and climate', *Proc. Kon. Ned. Akad. Wetensch.*, ser. B. **67**, Amsterdam 1964, pp. 60–79.
BÚISONJÉ, P. H. DE and ZONNEVELD, J. I. S. *De Kustvormen van Curaçao, Aruba en Bonaire*, Curaçao 1960.
HAMILTON, R. and SESSELER, W. M. *Bijdrage tot de bodemkundige Kennis van (Nederlandsch) West-Indie*, Mededeeling Indisch Instituut no. 63, Kon. Vereeniging, Afd. Handelsmuseum no. 29, Amsterdam 1945.
HARTOG, J. *Bonaire van Indianen tot Toeristen*, Aruba 1957.

—— *Aruba past and present. From the Time of the Indians until today*, trans. from Dutch, *De geschied. van de Nederl. Antillen 1*, The Hague 1962.

HENRIQUEZ, P. C. 'Problems relating to hydrology, water conservation, erosion control, reforestation and agriculture in Curaçao', *Pub. Nat. Sci. Study Group of the Neth. Ant.*, *Nieuwe West Indische Gids* **42**, 1962, pp. 1–54.

HISS, P. H. *Netherlands America: the Dutch territories in the west*, New York 1943.

HOETINK, H. *Diferencias de Relaciones raciales entre Curazao y Surinam, Revista de Ciencias Sociales* **5**, 1961.

—— *Het Patroon van de oude Curaçaosche Samenleving*, 2nd edn, Amba 1966.

HOUKEN, P. H. J. M. *De Associative van Suriname en de Nederlandse Antillen met de Europese Economische Gemeenschap*, Leiden 1965.

HOYER, W. M. *A Brief Historical Description of the Island of Curaçao*, Curaçao 1948.

KUIP, E. J. VAN DER. *An Investigation into the Occurrence of Trypanosomiasis cruzi in Aruba*, Utrecht 1966.

LAGAAIJ, R. A. *Rapport over de radiometrische Opname in 1962 van Curaçao, Aruba en Bonaire*, Utrecht 1963.

MARTIN, K. *Bericht über eine Reise nach Niederländisch West-Indien und darauf gegründete Studien*, 2 vols, Leiden 1888.

MOLENGRAAFF, G. J. H. *Geologie en Geohydrologie van het Eiland Curaçao*, Delft 1929.

—— 'Curaçao', *Feestbundel für K. Martin, Leidsche Geol. Med.*, Part 5, Leiden 1931, pp. 673–89. 1931, pp. 673–89.

NORDLOHNE, E. 'The Netherlands Antilles', *Tijdschr. voor Econ. en Soc. Geogr.* **47**, 1956, pp. 167–70.

OCHSE, J. J. 'Economic factors in the Netherlands Antilles and Surinam', in *The Caribbean: British, Dutch, French, United States*, ed. A. C. Wilgus, Gainesville 1958, pp. 73–85.

PIJPERS, P. J. 'Bonaire', *Feestbundel für K. Martin, Leidsche Geol. Med.*, Part 5, Leiden 1931, pp. 704–8.

—— *Geology and Paleontology of Bonaire (D. W. I.)*, Geogr. en geol. Med., Physiographisch-geologische Reeks, no. 8, Utrecht 1933.

POLL, W. VAN DE. *De Nederlandse Antillen*, The Hague 1950.

ROBBINS, J. and BLAIR, L. F. *The Distinctive Architecture of Willemstad; its conservation and enhancement*, New York 1961.

ROMER, R. A. *Ons Semenzijn in sociologisch Perspectief; een Introductie in de curaçaose Samenleving*, Curaçao 1964.

ROOS, P. J. *The Distribution of Reef Corals in Curaçao*, vol. 20, *Studies on the Fauna of Curaçao and other Caribbean Islands*, ed. P. Wagenaar Hummelinck, The Hague 1964.

RUTTEN, L. 'De geologische Geschiedenis der drie Nederlandsche Benedenwindsche Eilanden', *West-ind. Gids* **13**, 1932.

SCHAUB, H. P. 'Geological observations on Curaçao (N. W. I.)', *Am. Ass. Petr. Geol. Bull.* **32**, 1948, pp. 1275–91.

STEENMEIJER, F. *Food and Nutrition of Arubans*, Utrecht 1957.

STOFFERS, A. L. *The Vegetation of the Netherlands Antilles*, Utrecht 1956.

VERMEULEN, L. P. 'De Bevolkningsstructuur der Nederlandse Antillen', *Tijdschr. Kon. Ned. Aardr. Gen.* **79**, 1962, pp. 34–58.

—— 'De Volkstelling 1960 in de Nederlandse Antillen', *Tijdschrift Kon. Ned. Aardr. Gen.* **80**, 1963, pp. 186–92.

VERMUNT, L. W. J. and RUTTEN, M. G. 'Geology of Central-Curaçao', *Proc. Kon. Ned. Akad. Wetenschr.*, **34**, 1931, pp. 271–6.

—— 'Some remarks on the geology of N. Curaçao', *Proc. Kon. Ned. Akad. Wetensch.*, **34**, 1931, pp. 1028–31.

WAGENAAR HUMMELINCK, P. 'Zoologische Erhebnisse einer Reise nach Bonaire, Curaçao und Aruba im Jahre 1930; no. 1, Reisebericht', *Zool. Jahrb.* (Abt. f. Systematik etc.) **64**, 1933, pp. 289–326.

—— 'Over Verweeringsholten in Diorietblokken op Aruba', *West-Indische Gids* **20**, 1938,

pp. 364–9.

—— 'Studies on the fauna of Curaçao, Aruba, Bonaire and the Venezuelan Islands I', dissertation, Utrecht 1940.

—— 'Zoogeografische Opmerkingen over de Nederlandsche Benedenwindsche Eilanden', *West-Ind. Gids* **25**, 1943, pp. 168–80.

—— 'Over Grotten en Grottenvorming op Curaçao, Aruba en Bonaire', *West-Ind. Gids* **25**, 1943, pp. 365–75.

—— 'En Luchtreiziger over het Landschap van de Nederlandse Benedenwindse Eilanden', *Tijdschr. Kon. Ned. Aardr. Gen.* **65**, 1948, pp. 683–91.

—— *Roststekeningen van Curaçao, Aruba en Bonaire*, 3 parts, Curaçao 1953, 1957, 1961.

WESTERMANN, J. H. *The Geology of Aruba*, Geogr. en Geol. Med., Physiogr. Geol. Reeks 7, Utrecht 1932.

—— *Overzicht van de geologische en mijnbouwkundige Kennis der Nederlandse Antillen*, Mededeeling Indisch Instituut Amsterdam 85, Afd. Trop. Producten no. 35, Amsterdam 1949.

WESTERMANN, J. H. and ZONNEVELD, J. I. S. *Photo-geological Observations and Land Capability and Land Use Survey of the Island of Bonaire (Netherlands Antilles)*, Kon. Inst. voor de Tropen, Mededeeling 123, Afd. Trop. Producten no. 47, Amsterdam 1956.

WILHELMY, H. 'Die klimamorphologische und pflanzengeographische Entwicklung des Trockengebietes am Nordrand Südamerikas seit dem Pleistozän', *Die Erde*, 1954, pp. 244–73.

—— 'Curaçao, Aruba, Maracaibo—eine ölwirtschaftliche Symbiose', *Festschr. f. H. Mortensen*, Bremen 1954, pp. 275–302.

WINKLER, O. 'Niederländisch-Westindien', *Mitt. Ges. f. Erdkunde Leipzig, 1923/25*, Leipzig 1926, pp. 87–137.

ZANEVELD, J. S. *The Sea Fisheries of the Netherlands Antilles*, Trinidad 1960.

ZONNEVELD, J. I. S. 'Een Luchtfoto-Onderzoek op de Benedenwindse Eilanden', *Tijdschr. Kon. Ned. Aardr. Gen.* **77**, 1960, pp. 389–400.

ZUYLEN, G. F. A. VAN. 'De Neerslag op de Nederlandse Antillen', *Geogr. Tijdschr.* **15**, 1962, pp. 203–8.

Supplement 1967–1970

ABRAHAMS, R. D. 'The shaping of folklore traditions in the British West Indies', *JIAS* 1967, pp. 456–80.

ACADEMIA DE CIENCIAS DE CUBA, *Atlas Nacional de Cuba*, Habana 1970.

ADAMS, N. A. 'An analysis of food consumption and food import trends in Jamaica 1950–1963, *SES* **17**, no. 1, 1968, pp. 1–22.

—— Internal migration in Jamaica: an economic analysis, *SES* **18**, no. 2, 1969, pp. 137–51.

ADELAIDE, J. 'La Colonisation française aux Antilles à la Fin du 17ème Siècle d'après les "Voyages aux Isles d'Amérique" du R. P. Labat', *Bull. Soc. Hist. de le Guadeloupe*, **1**, 1964, pp. 12–17, **3–4**, 1965, pp. 22–8.

ALCEDO, A. DE. *Diccionario geográfico de las Indias Occidentales o América*, Madrid 1967.

ALEXANDER, M., ed. *Proceedings of the First West Indian Agricultural Economics Conference*, St Augustine, Trinidad, 1967.

AMIAMA CASTRO. O. *Santo Domingo en la Cartografía Antigua*, Universidad autónoma de Santo Domingo, Santo Domingo 1966.

ANDIC, F. M. and ANDIC, S. *Government Finance and planned Development; fiscal Surveys of Surinam and Netherlands Antilles*, Institute of Caribbean Studies, Río Piedras 1968.

ANDREW, E. M. *et al. Gravity Anomalies in the Lesser Antilles*, London 1970.

ARANDA, S. *La Revolución agraria en Cuba*, Mexico 1968.

ARCHAMBAULT, J. *Un Village de Pêcheurs, Deshaies en Guadeloupe*. Montreal 1967.

ASHCROFT, M. 'Caves of Jamaica', *Jamaica Journal* **3**, no. 2, Inst. Jamaica, Kingston, Jamaica, 1969, pp. 32–6.

AUGELLI, J. P. 'Nationalization of Frontiers: the Dominican Borderlands under Trujillo' (Abstract), *AAAG* **57**, 1967, p. 166.

AUGIER, F. R. *et al. The Making of the West Indies*, London 1967.

BADÍA, R. M. 'Puerto Rico', *World Atlas of Agriculture*, Monographs, vol. 3, Americas, Novara 1969, pp. 388–95.

BAIR, A. *The Barbados Fishing Industry*, McGill Univ., Dept. of Geogr., Publ. no. 6, Montreal 1962.

BAKER, E. C. *A Guide to Records in the Windward Islands*, Oxford 1968.

BARITEAU, C. *Organisation économique et Organisations familiales dans une Ile antillaise: La Désirade*, Montreal 1968.

BARKIN, D. 'Agricultura: El Sector Clave del Desarrollo de Cuba', *Comercio Exterior*, Banco Nacional de Comercio Exterior, Mexico, DF 1970, pp. 224–36.

BARROS, J. 'Une analyse de l'économie haitienne', *Cahiers d'Outre-Mer* **21**, no. 84, 1968, pp. 421–4.

BASSEREAU, D. 'Mécanisation de la culture de la canne aux Antilles', *Agron. trop.* **21**, no. 10, 1966, pp. 1155–61.

BASTIDE, R. *Les Amériques noires: les civilisations africaines dans le Nouveau Monde*, Paris 1967.

BAYITCH, S. A. *Latin America and the Caribbean: a bibliographical guide to works in English*,

437

Miami 1967.

BAYO, A. *Puerto Rico*, Habana 1966.

BEAUREGARD, C. F. 'Tourisme et Développement', *Bull. Chamb. Comm. et Ind. Martinique*, no. 1–6, Fort-de-France 1967, pp. 88–105.

BECKFORD, G. *The West Indian Banana Industry: Studies in regional economic Integration, vol. 2*, no. 3, Kingston 1967.

BECKFORD, G. and BROWN, E. A. 'Economic aspects of food availability in Jamaica', *CQ* **14**, no. 4, 1968, pp. 61–8.

BECKFORD, G. and GUSCOTT, M. *Intra-Caribbean agricultural Trade: Studies in regional economic Integration*, vol. 2, no. 2, Kingston 1967.

BEINROTH, F. H. *An Outline of the Geology of Puerto Rico*, Agr. Exper. Station, University of Puerto Rico, Bull. 213, Río Piedras 1969.

BENOIST, J. 'Types de plantations et groupes sociaux à la Martinique', *Cahiers des Amériques Latines* **2**, 1968, pp. 130–59.

BENSON, M. *Non-cooperation in a Trinidad Land Settlement Project*, Brandeis Univ., Waltham, Mass., 1968.

BENSON, J. *Urban Countryside: the external relations of a Trinidad Land Development Project*, Brandeis Univ., Waltham, Mass., 1968.

BENT, R. M. and BENT-GOLDING, E. L. *A Complete Geography of Jamaica*, London 1966.

BENTLEY, G. *Some Preliminary Observations on the Chinese in Trinidad*, Montreal 1968.

BERG, C. A. VAN DEN. 'The Caribbean; battle field for weathermen', *Weather* **23**, no. 11, 1968, pp. 462–8.

BERINGUIER, C. 'L'Espace régional martiniquais', *Cahiers d'Outre Mer* **20**, 1967, pp. 150–84. 150–84.

BEST, L. *et al. West Indies-Canada Economic Relations*, Jamaica Inst. of Social and Econ. Res., Univ. of the West Indies, Kingston 1967.

BHARATH, S. A. 'Note on the cultivation of soybeans and groundnuts with special reference to Trinidad and Tobago', *J. Agr. Soc. Trinidad–Tobago* **66**, no. 2, 1966, pp. 171–82.

BIROT, P., CORBEL, J. and MUXART, R. 'Morphologie des Régions calcaires à la Jamaique et à Puerto Rico', *Mém. et Doc.*, NS, no. 4, Centre de Recherches et Documentation cartographiques et géographiques, Paris 1968, pp. 335–92.

BLUME, H. 'Barbados, jüngste und kleinste Republik der Neuen Welt', *Ubersee-Rundschau* **19**, no. 4, 1967, pp. 17–18.

—— 'Wirtschaftslandschaften und Agrarsozialstruktur in Westindien', *Geogr. Rundsch.* **19**, 1967, pp. 449–57.

—— 'Types of agricultural regions and land tenure in the West Indies', *Revista Geográfica* **67**, Rio de Janeiro 1967, pp. 7–20.

—— 'Agrarlandschaft und Agrarsozialstruktur in Kuba', *Geogr. Z.* **56**, 1968, pp. 1–17.

—— 'Zur Problematik des Schichtstufenreliefs auf den Antillen', *Geol. Rundsch.* **58**, 1968, pp. 82–97.

—— 'Kulturgeographische Divergenzen im LandschaftsbildeHispaniolas', In Memoriam H. Smeds, *Acta Geographica* **19**, no. 3, Helsinki 1968, pp. 31–45.

—— 'Karstmorphologische Beobachtungen auf den Inseln über dem Winde', in Beitr. z. Geogr. der Tropen und Subtropen, Festschr. f. H. Wilhelmy, *Tübinger Geogr. Studien H.* **34**, Tübingen 1970, pp. 33–42.

—— 'Besonderheiten des Schichtstufenreliefs auf Puerto Rico', *Deutsche geographische Forschung von heute, Festschr, f. E. Gentz*, Kiel 1970, pp. 167–79.

—— Die Inselwelt der Antillen, *Bild der Wissenschaft*, **10**, 1970, pp. 998–1005.

—— 'Die kulturräumliche und wirtschaftsgeographische Gliederung der Antillen', *Wirstschafts und Kulturräume der aussereuropäischen Welt, Festschr. f. A. Kolb*, Hamburg 1971, pp. 335–47.

BONUZZI, V. 'Bahamas', *World Atlas of Agriculture, Monographs*, vol. 3, *Americas*, Novara 1969, p. 65.

—— 'Cayman Islands', *World Atlas of Agriculture, Monographs*, vol. 3, *Americas*, Novara 1969,

p. 163.

—— 'Netherlands Antilles', *World Atlas of Agriculture, Monographs*, vol. 3, *Americas*, Novara 1969, p. 345.

—— 'Turks and Caicos Islands', *World Atlas of Agriculture, Monographs*, vol. 3, *Americas*, Novara 1969, p. 408.

—— 'Virgin Islands', *World Atlas of Agriculture, Monographs*, vol. 3, *Americas*, Novara 1969, p. 497.

BOORSTEIN, E. *The Economic Transformation of Cuba, a first-hand account*, New York, London 1969.

BORROTO MORA, A. 'Descentralización del Mercado único de La Habana', *Academia de Ciencias de Cuba*, Habana, **4**, 1967, pp. 79–98.

BOSTON, R. A. S. *Social and Physical Factors affecting Farming in two Areas of the Oropouche Lagoon*, St Augustine, Trinidad, 1967.

BOUNDS, J. H. 'The Bahamas', *Focus* **19**, no. 9, 1969.

BOURNE, D. D. and R. *Thirty Years of Change in Puerto Rico. A case study of ten selected rural areas*, New York 1967.

BOWDEN, M. J. *et al. Water Balance of a dry Island: the Hydroclimatology of St Croix, Virgin Islands, and Potential for Agriculture and urban Growth*, Worcester, Mass., 1968.

BREWSTER, H. and THOMAS, C. Y. 'Dynamics of West Indian economic integration', *Caribbean Integration* **1**, Kingston 1967.

BROWN, W. H. *Marine Fisheries of the British West Indies*, Univ. of Calif. Dept. of Geogr., Berkeley 1967.

BYRNE, J. 'Population growth in St Vincent', *SES* **18**, no. 2, 1969, pp. 152–88.

CAMPBELL, L. G. 'Some considerations for sprinkler irrigation in Trinidad and Tobago', *J. Agr. Soc. Trinidad–Tobago* **65**, no. 1, 1965, pp. 34–46, 185–92.

—— 'The development of natural resources in Dominica', *Agr. Ser., Univ. West Indies* **3**, 1965, pp. 1–34.

—— 'Production on small farms in St Vincent: prospects for increasing efficiency', *Agr. Ser., Univ. West Indies* **4**, 1966, pp. 1–32.

CARIBBEAN ISLANDS. *World Atlas of Agriculture*. Novara 1969, Plate 48.

CARLOZZI, C. A. and CARLOZZI, A. A. *Conservation and Caribbean Regional Progress*. Yellow Springs, Ohio, 1968.

CARRINGTON, E. 'Industrialization in Trinidad and Tobago since 1950', *New World Quarterly. New World Group* **4**, no. 2, Kingston, Jamaica 1968, pp. 37–43.

—— 'The post-war political economy of Trinidad and Tobago', *New World Quarterly. New World Group* **4**, no. 2, Kingston, Jamaica 1968, pp. 45–67.

CASTRO, S. DE. *Problems of the Caribbean Air Transport Industry*, Studies in Regional Economic Integration 2, no. 6, Inst. of Social and Economic Research. Univ. of the West Indies, Mona, Jamaica, 1967.

CASTRO, S. DE and LAURITZ, S. 'Some steps towards an optimal foodstuffs consumption, production and importation programme for Trinidad and Tobago', *SES* **16**, 1967, pp. 349–64.

CAZES, G. 'Le Développement du tourisme à la Martinique', *Cahiers d'Outre Mer* **21**, no. 83, 1968, pp. 225–56.

CENTRAL PLANNING UNIT, GOVERNMENT OF JAMAICA. *Economic Survey, Jamaica*, Kingston 1967.

CERRUTTI, J. and NEBBIA, T. 'Jamaica goes it alone', *National Geographic Magazine* **132**, no. 6, 1967, pp. 843–73.

CHEN-YOUNG, P. L. 'The cost of location of the apparel industry in Puerto Rico and Jamaica', *CS* **8**, no. 1, 1968, pp. 3–31.

CHIA, L.-S. 'Albedos of natural surfaces in Barbados', *Qt. Jl Roy. Nat. Soc.* **93**, 1967, pp. 116–20.

CLARKE, C. G. 'An overcrowded metropolis: Kingston, Jamaica', in *Geography and a crowding World*, ed. R. M. Prothero, L. Kosinski and W. Zelinsky, New York 1970.

439

Bibliography: supplement

COLE, H. *Henry Christophe: King of Haiti*, New York 1967.

COMITAS, L. *Caribbeana 1900–1965. A topical bibliography*, Seattle 1968.

CÓRDOVA, E. 'La encomienda y la desaparición de los Indios en las Antillas Mayores', *CS* **8**, no. 3, 1968, pp. 23–49.

CORTEN, A. and CORTEN, A. *Cambio social en Santo Domingo*. Estudio Especial no. 5, Inst. d. Estudios del Caribe, Río Piedras 1968.

CORWIN, A. F. *Spain and the Abolition of Slavery in Cuba, 1817–1886*, Austin 1967.

CREQUE, D. D. *The US Virgins and the Eastern Caribbean*, Philadelphia 1968.

CROCKER, J. *The Centaur Guide to Bermuda, the Bahamas, Hispaniola, Puerto Rico and the Virgin Islands*, Fontwell 1968.

CRIST, R. E. and POPENOE, H. 'Jamaica and Martinique: contrasting aspects of folk, agriculture and non-folk agriculture' (abstract), *AAAG* **57**, 1967, pp. 169–70.

CROUSE, N. M. *The French Struggle for the West Indies. 1665–1713*, New York 1966.

CUMPER, G. 'New pattern for Kingston', *Geogrl Mag.* **10**, 1967, pp. 588–98.

CURTIS, T. D. *Land Reform, Democracy and Economy Interest in Puerto Rico*, Tucson, Arizona, 1966.

—— 'Democratic land reform in Puerto Rico', *Arizona Review* **16**, no. 1, 1967, pp. 1–6.

DACEY, M. F. 'An empirical study of the areal distribution of houses in Puerto Rico', *Trans. Inst. Br. Geogr.* **45**, 1968, pp. 51–70.

DAGENAIS, H. *Le Système de grandes plantations à la Guadeloupe*, Montreal 1968.

DANSEREAU, P. *Studies on the Vegetation of Puerto Rico*, Mayagüez 1966.

DAVIDSON, R. B. *Labour Shortage and Productivity in the Jamaican Sugar Industry*, Institute of Social and Economic Research. University of West Indies, Mona 1968.

DAVITAYA, F. F., MASHBITS, Y. G. and RYABCHIKOV, A. 'The status of geography in Cuba', *Soviet Geography: Review and Translation* **8**, no. 1, 1967, pp. 33–40; trans. from *Izvestiya Akademii Nauk SSSR, Seriya geograficheskaya*, no. 2, 1966, pp. 111–3.

DEBIEN, G. 'Plantations à la Guadeloupe: la Caféière et la Sucrerie Bologne au Baillif (1787)', *Bull. Soc. Hist. Guadeloupe* no. 3–4, 1965, pp. 11–21.

—— 'Antilles de Langue française, bibliographie', *CS* **7**, no. 2, 1967, pp. 249–61.

DEBIEN, G. 'Plantations à la Guadeloupe: la Caféière et la Sucrerie Bologne au Baillif

DEMAS, W. G. *The Economics of Development in Small Countries with special Reference to the Caribbean*, Montreal 1965.

DEYMIER, R. 'La culture de la canne à sucre à Porto-Rico', *Agron. trop.* **22**, no. 11, 1967, pp. 1106–20.

DIAZ DE ACIN, N. *La Participación de la Estación experimental agrícola de la Universidad en el Desarrollo agrícola de Puerto Rico*, Río Piedras 1967.

DIRECTION DÉPARTEMENTALE DE L'AGRICULTURE: 'GUADELOUPE', *World Atlas of Agriculture, Monographs*, vol. 3, *Americas*. Novara 1969, pp. 266–8.

DIRECTION DÉPARTEMENTALE DE L'AGRICULTURE DE MARTINIQUE: 'MARTINIQUE', *World Atlas of Agriculture, Monographs*, vol. 3, *Americas*. Novara 1969, p. 318.

DODGE, P. 'Comparative racial systems in the Greater Caribbean', *SES* **16**, 1967, pp. 249–61.

DORAN, E. 'The demise of the tortola boat', *AAAG* **57**, 1967, p. 787.

DOSSICK, J. J. 'Doctoral research on the Caribbean and Circum-Caribbean accepted by American, British and Caribbean Universities, 1966–1967', *CS* **8**, no. 2, 1968, pp. 89–96.

DOUGLAS, E. *Continuity and Change in a Jamaica suburban Housing Estate*, Univ. West Indies, Inst. Soc. and Econ. Res., Mona 1968.

DUKE, K. S. *et al. Development of Tourism in the Commonwealth of Puerto Rico*, prepared for: Economic Development Administration of Puerto Rico. Stanford Research Institute. South Pasadena, Calif., 1968.

DUPUIS, J. 'Les paradoxes de Curaçao: a travers les provinces de l'empire Shell', *Cahiers d'Outre Mer* **22**, no. 85, 1969, pp. 63–74.

DYER, D. R. 'Cuban sugar regions', *Revista geográfica (Rio de Janeiro)* **67**, 1967, pp. 21–30.

DYSON, A. Population Trends in the eastern Caribbean, in *Liverpool Essays in Geography: a Jubilee Collection*, ed. R. W. Steel and R. Lawton, London 1967, pp. 380–405.

440

EBANKS, G. E. 'Differential internal migration in Jamaica, 1943–60', *SES* **17**, no. 2, 1968, pp. 197–228.

EDEL, M. 'Jamaican fishermen: two approaches in economic anthropology', *SES* **16**, 1967, pp. 432–9.

EDWARDS, D. T. 'The development of the dairy industry in Jamaica and Barbados', *CQ* **14**, no. 3, 1968, pp. 50–5.

EGOROV, S. V. and LUEGE, J. R. *Hidrogeología de Cuba*, Habana 1967.

ELY, R. T. 'Cuba and sugar—four centuries of evolution', *CS* **7**, no. 3, 1967, pp. 65–76.

ERB, D. K. 'Geomorphology of Jamaica', *Photogrammetric Engineering* **34**, no. 11, 1968, pp. 1148–60.

EVANS, F. C. *A First Geography of Jamaica*, Cambridge 1968.

—— *A First Geography of Trinidad and Tobago*, Cambridge 1968.

EYRE, L. A. *Land and Population in the Sugar Belt of Jamaica*, Univ. of the West Indies. Dept. of Geography, Occasional Publication no. 1, Kingston 1966.

FERMER, J. *Northers and Weather at Kingston, Jamaica*, Univ. of the West Indies, Dept. of Geography, Research Notes no. 2, Kingston 1970.

FERNÁNDEZ MÉNDEZ, E. *Las Encomiendas y la Esclavitud de los Indios de Puerto Rico, 1505–1550*, Sevilla 1966.

FLOYD, B. 'Jamaica', *Focus* **19**, no. 2, 1968.

—— *Agricultural Innovation in Jamaica: The Yallahs Valley Land Authority*, Univ. of the West Indies, Dept. of Geography, Occasional Paper no. 4, Kingston 1969; also in: *Econ. Geogr.* **46**, 1970, pp. 63–77.

—— *Undergraduate Research Papers in Geography at U. W. I. 1968–1970*, Univ. of the West Indies, Dept. of Geography, Research Note no. 4, Kingston 1970.

FOCHLER-HAUKE, G. 'Kuba: wirtschaftsgeographische Aspekte und Wirtschaftsprobleme', in *Geogr. Taschenbuch und Jahrweiser für Landeskunde*, 1966/69, ed. E. Meynen, Bad Godesberg 1968, pp. 191–8.

FONAROFF L. S. *Biogeographic Aspects of Malaria in Trinidad*, Berkeley 1966.

—— 'Man and malaria in Trinidad: ecological perspectives of a changing health hazard', *AAAG* **58**, 1968, pp. 526–56.

FOSTER, P. and CREYKE, P. *The Structure of Plantation Agriculture in Jamaica*, College Park, Md, 1968.

FOUCHARD, J. and DEBIEN, G. 'Aspects de l'esclavage aux Antilles françaises; le petit Marronage à Saint-Domingue autour du Cap (1790–1791)', *Cahiers des Ameriques Latines* **3**, 1969, pp. 31–67.

FOUND, W. C. 'A multivariate analysis of farm output in selected land-reform areas of Jamaica', *CG* **12**, no. 1, 1968, pp. 41–52.

FRANCO, F. J. *Los Negros, los Mulatos y la Nación Dominicana*, Santo Domingo 1969.

FROSTIN, C. 'Les colons de Saint-Domingue et la Métropole', *Revue Historique*, 1967, pp. 381–414.

FRUCHT, R. 'A Caribbean social type: neither "Peasant" nor "Proletarian"', *SES* **16**, 1967, pp. 295–300.

FUKUOKA, J. 'Condiciones meteorológicas e hidrográficas de los Mares adyacentes a Venezuela 1962–1963', *Sociedad de Ciencias Naturales de la Salle. Mem.* **25**, no. 70–72, 1965, pp. 11–38.

GARNIER, B. J. 'Recent developments in the McGill University climatology programme in Barbados', *Climatol. Bull.* **3**, 1968, pp. 18–22.

GARNIER, B. J. and OHMURA, A. *Estimating the Topographic Variation of Short-Wave Radiation: the example of Barbados*, Climate Res. Series 6, Montreal 1968.

GARNIER, B. L. 'The McGill University climatology programme in Barbados', *Bull. Am. Nat. Soc.* **49**, 1968, pp. 636–9.

GERLING, W. *Die Vereinigten Staaten von Amerika im karibischen Raum*, Vorgänge und Probleme der Amerikanisierung, Würzburg 1969.

GERSTENHAUER, A. 'Diskussionsbemerkungen zu "Physiographic and Geological Control in Development of Cuban Mogotes" von V. Panos and O. Stelcl', *Ž. Geomorphol.*, NF, **12**, 1968, pp. 165–8.

GIACOTTINO, J.-C. 'La Barbade indépendante', *Cahiers d'Outre Mer* **20**, 1967, pp. 209–27.

—— 'L'économie trinidadienne', *Cahiers d'Outre Mer* **22**, no. 86, 1969, pp. 113–60.

—— 'Les petites Antilles britanniques', *Cahiers d'Outre Mer* **23**, no. 91, 1970, pp. 307–34.

GILDEA, R. Y. 'Haiti', *Focus* **17**, no. 9, 1967.

GIRALT, R. J. M. 'Size of sugarcane farms. A factor in the decline of Puerto Rican sugar production', *Sugar J.* **29**, no. 2, 1966, pp. 16–17.

GIRVAN, N. *The Caribbean Bauxite Industry.* Studies in regional economic Integration, vol. 2, no. 4, Kingston 1967.

GONZALES VILLAFANE, E. and CAPO, B. G. *Produción comercial de Azúcar de diferentes Variedades de Caña, por Zonas de Produción*, Puerto Rico. Río Piedras 1967.

GOODING, E. G. B. 'Crop diversification in Barbados', *World Crops* **20**, no. 1, 1968, pp. 34–9.

GOODWIN, G. D. W. 'Economic ideas in the development of Jamaica', *South Atlantic Quarterly* **1**, no. 2, 1968, pp. 338–69.

GORDON, A. L. 'Circulation of the Caribbean Sea', *J. Geophys. Res.* **72**, no. 24, 1967, pp. 6207–23.

GREEN, B. *Basic Data on the Economy of Jamaica*, US Bureau of International Commerce, *OBR* 67–38, Washington 1967.

GUTELMAN, M. 'L'Agriculture cubaine en 1964', *Études rurales*, no. 19, 1965, pp. 5–31.

—— *L'Agriculture socialisée à Cuba*, Paris 1967.

HANDLER, J. S. 'Slave population of Barbados in the seventeenth and early eighteenth centuries', *CS* **8**, no. 4, 1969, pp. 38–64.

HANNAH, R. *et al. Fomento, the Dynamics of Economic Development in Puerto Rico*, Waukesha, Wisconsin, 1968.

HARDING, V. ed. *Origins of Afro-Americans*, New York 1970.

HARRIS, R. N. S. and STEER, E. S. 'Demographic-resource push in rural migration: a Jamaican case study', *SES* **17**, no. 4, 1968, pp. 398–406.

HENDRICKS, G. *Acculturation and Assimilation Processes in a Group of West Indian Negro Migrants: Puerto Plata, Dominican Republic*, New York 1968.

HERMIDA, A. G. and MORERA, A. *La Explotación minera del Cobre en Puerto Rico: Factores legales, económicos y de Contaminación*, Río Piedras 1969.

HERNÁNDEZ, A. S. *Return Migration to Puerto Rico*, Univ. of Calif., Inst. of Internat. Studies, Berkeley 1967.

HESS, H. H. ed. 'Caribbean geological Investigations', *Geol. Soc. Am.*, no. 98, 1966.

HILL, I. D. *Antigua, Soil Land-Use Survey of British Caribbean*, World Land Use Surv., no. 19, Ebbingford, Bude 1966.

HIRSCH, G. P. 'Jamaica: a regional approach', *Regional studies* **1**, 1967, pp. 47–63.

HITT, D. S. and WILSON, L. C. *Bibliography of the Dominican Republic: A Century after the Restoration of Independence*, US Dept. of Commerce, Clearing House for Federal Scientific and Technical Information, Washington 1968.

HOETINK, H. *The Two Variants in Caribbean Race Relations. A contribution to the sociology of segmented societies*, London 1967.

—— 'Materiales para el Estudio de la República Dominicana en la segunda Mitad del Siglo XIX. Parte II. Cambios en la Estructura demográfica y en la Distribución geográfica de la Población', *CS* **7**, no. 3, 1967, pp. 3–34.

—— 'Materiales para el Estudio de la República Dominicana en la segunda Mitad del Siglo XIX. Parte III. Cambios en la Estructura de las Comunicaciones', *CS* **8**, no. 3, 1968, pp. 3–22.

—— 'Materiales para el Estudio de la República Dominicana en la segunda Mitad del Siglo XIX. Parte V. Cambios en la Estructura de los Aparatos de Sanción', *CS* **9**, no. 2, pp. 3–37.

—— 'Materiales para el Estudio de la República Dominicana en la segunda Mitad del Siglo XIX. Parte V. Cambios en la estructura de los Aparatos de Sanción', *CS* **9**, no. 2,

1969, pp. 5–26.

—— ed. *Encyclopedie van de Nederlandse Antillen*, Amsterdam-Elsevier-Brussel 1969.

HOLBROOK, S. *The American West Indies: Puerto Rico and the Virgin Islands*, New York 1969.

HOROWITZ, M. M. *Morne Paysan: Peasant Village in Martinique*, New York 1967.

HUDSON, G. I. *The unspoiled Cayman Islands*, Grand Cayman 1966.

HUETZ DE LEMPS, C. 'L'homme et la végetation à la Barbade', *Cahiers d'Outre Mer* **20**, 1967, pp. 406–9.

INGHAM, M. C. and MAHNKEN, C. V. W. 'Turbulence and productivity near St Vincent Island, B. W. I., a preliminary report', *Caribb. J. Sci.* **6**, no. 3–4, 1966.

JAMES, P. E. 'Middle America: a natural resources survey of the Dominican Republic', *Geogr. Rev.* **59**, no. 2, 1969, pp. 287–9.

JIMÉNEZ, R. 'La cultura negra en Cuba, Origenes y División de los Afrocubanos, Aspectos religiosos, Teologia y Magia fetichista', *Universidad de la Habana* **19**, 211, 1968, pp. 9–15.

JOHANNESSEN, O. M. *Preliminary Results of Some Oceanographical Observations carried out between Barbados and Tobago*, Montreal 1968.

JOHNSON, I. E. and MORGAN REES, A. M. 'Jamaica', *World Atlas of Agriculture, Monographs*, vol. 3, *Americas*. Novara 1969, pp. 307–16.

JOLLY, A. L. 'Trinidad and Tobago', *World Atlas of Agriculture, Monographs*, vol. 3, *Americas*. Novara 1969, pp. 403–8.

JOLLY, A. L. and NANTON, W. R. E. 'Barbados, the Windward and Leeward Islands', *World Atlas of Agriculture, Monographs*, vol. 3, *Americas*. Novara 1969, pp. 66–9.

JONES, M. R. *The Approach to Cocoa Rehabilitation in Trinidad and Grenada*, Univ. West Indies, St Augustine, Trinidad, 1968.

JOROND, A. V. *La Guadeloupe et ses Iles; guide practique du visiteur*, Basse-Terre 1965.

KANTROWITZ, N. *Negro and Puerto Rican Populations of New York City in the Twentieth Century*, New York 1969.

KELLENBENZ, H. 'Von den Karibischen Inseln. Archive und neuere Literatur, insbes. zur Geschichte von der Mitte des 17. bis zur Mitte des 19. Jh', *Jb. f. Geschichte v. Staat, Wirtschaft und Gesellschaft Lateinamerikas*, 1. Part **5**, 1968, pp. 378–404; 2 Part **6**, 1969, pp. 452–69; 3. Part **7**, 1970, pp. 381–410.

KESHISHEV, V. N. 'The runoff in eastern Cuba', *Soviet Geography: Review and translation* **8**, no. 1, 1967, pp. 1–12, trans. from *Vestnik Moskovskogo Universiteta*, Seriya geografiya no. 2, 1966, pp. 71–8.

KERSHAW, M. 'The banana industry in the Windward Islands', *Trop. Sci.* **8**, no. 3, 1966, pp. 115–27.

KIMBER, C. 'Dooryard gardens of Martinique', *Yearbook of the Assoc. of Pacific Coast Geographers* **28**, 1966, pp. 97–118.

KIRKWOOD, R. *A Farm Production Policy for Jamaica. The Sugar Manufacturers Association of Jamaica*, Kingston 1968.

KLEIN, H. S. *Slavery in the Americas; a comparative study of Cuba and Virginia*, Chicago 1967.

KNÜBEL, H. 'Kuba bleibt eine Zuckerinsel', *Geogr. Rundsch.* **19**, 1967, pp. 149–52.

KONETZKE, R. Neuere Kolumbusforschung. *Jb. f. Geschichte v. Staat, Wirtschaft und Gesellschaft Lateinamericas* **5**, 1968, pp. 366–77.

KRUIJER, G. J. *Cuba, Voorbeeld en Uitdaging*, Amsterdam 1968.

KRUYTHOFF, S. 'The Netherlands Windward Islands or the Windward Group of the Netherlands Antilles; a Handbook of useful information for Visitors as well as Residents', 3rd edn. Oranjestad, Aruba, 1964.

LAGAAY, R. A. *Geophysical Investigations of the Netherlands Leeward Antilles*, Utrecht 1968.

LAMORE, J. 'Cuba', *Que sais-je?* no. 1395, Paris 1970.

LANG, D. M. and CARRED, D. M. *St Kitts and Nevis*. The Regional Research Centre, Imperial College of Tropical Agriculture, St Augustine, Trinidad, 1966.

LARRAZÁBAL BLANCO, C. *Los Negros y la Esclavitud en Santo Domingo*, Santo Domingo 1967.

LASSERRE, G. 'Petite propriété et réforme foncière aux Antilles françaises', *Les Problèmes agraires des Amériques latines*. Centre National de la Recherche Scientifique, Paris 1967, pp 109–24.

LATEEF, M. A. 'Vertical motion, divergence, and vorticity in the troposphere over the Caribbean, August 3–5, 1963', *MWR* **95**, no. 11, 1967, pp. 778–90.

LAURENCE, K. M. 'Notes of Leres, the Amerindian name for Trinidad', *CQ* **13**, no. 3, 1967, pp. 45–51.

LEEMANN, A. 'Trinidad', *Z. Wirtschaftsgeographie* **12**, no. 4, 1968, pp. 114–17.

—— 'Curaçao', *Z. Wirstschaftsgeographie* **12**, no. 8, 1968, pp. 229–32.

—— 'Trinidad', *Geographica Helvetica* **24**, no. 4, 1969, pp. 191–4.

—— 'Barbados', *Z. Wirtschaftsgeographie* **14**, no. 1, 1970, pp. 17–20.

—— 'Barbados', *Geographica Helvetica* **25**, no. 3, 1970, pp. 130–5.

—— 'Curaçao', *Geographica Helvetica* **25**, no. 3, 1970, pp. 136–40.

LETOURNEAU, G. *La Relation Homme-Sol en Milieu traditionnel. Carel-Calebassier, Marie Galante*, Montreal 1968.

LEWIS, G. K. 'British colonism in the West Indies: the political legacy', *CS* **7**, no. 1, 1967, pp. 3–22.

LEWIS, J. B. *et al. Comparative Growth Rates of some Reef Corals in the Caribbean*, Montreal 1968.

LEWIS, L. A. 'Some pluvial geomorphic characteristics of the Manatí Basin, Puerto Rico', *AAAG* **59**, no. 2, 1969, pp. 280–93.

—— 'The spatial properties of population mobility within Puerto Rico', *J. Trop. Geogr.* **29**, 1969, pp. 33–8.

LEWIS, S. and MATHEWS, T., eds. *Caribbean Integration*, Río Piedras 1967.

LIMA, C. 'Cuba and its ports', *Cuba For. Trade* 1966, no. 2. pp. 26–35; no. 3, pp. 2–11.

LIND, A. O. *Coastal Landforms of Cat Island, Bahamas*, Univ. of Chicago, Dept. of Geogr., Research Paper no. 122, 1969.

LOGAN, R. W. *Haiti and the Dominican Republic*, New York 1968.

LONG, E. J. *Jamaica*, rev. edn, Garden City, NY, 1967.

LORENZETTI, S. 'Dominican Republic', *World Atlas of Agriculture, Monographs*, vol. 3, *Americas*. Novara 1969, pp. 230–41.

LOWE, A. J. 'Trinidad and Tobago', *Americas* **19**, no. 5, 1967, pp. 1–10.

LOWENTHAL, D. 'Race and color in the West Indies', *Daedalus: J. Am. Acad. Arts and Sciences*, 1967, pp. 580–626.

LUBIN, M. A. 'Les premiers rapports de la nation haitienne, avec l'étranger', *JIAS* **10**, no. 2, 1968, pp. 277–305.

LUCIA, F. J. 'Recent sediments and diagenesis of South Bonaire, Netherland Antilles', *J. Sedim. Petr.* **38**, 1968, pp. 845–58.

L'VOV, J. A. 'Torfjanya bolota Kuby (Die Torfmoore in Kuba)', *Izv. Akad. Nauk SSSR*, ser. geogr., no. 3, Moscow 1967, pp. 23–32.

MACK, R. W. 'Race, class and power in Barbados. A study of stratification as an integrating force in a democratic revolution', in *Social Change in Developing Areas*, Cambridge, Mass., 1965, pp. 131–54.

MAHADEVAN, P. 'The future for dairying in the West Indies', *Trop. Sci.* **9**, no. 1, 1967, pp. 5–12.

MAILLARD, J.-C. 'Élements pour une Histoire de l'Industrie bananière en Guadeloupe et aux Antilles françaises', *Bull. Soc. Hist. Guadeloupe* **8**, 1961, pp. 42–59.

—— 'La banane en Jamaique et dans les Windward Islands', *Cahiers d'Outre Mer* **22**, no. 87, 1969, pp. 313–24.

MALAVE GONZÁLES, L. *La Corporación de Desarrollo económico del Caribe, hacia el Logro de un Desarrollo integrado y acelerado del Area del Caribe*, Río Piedras 1967.

MALIGNAC, G. 'La situation démographique des quatre départements d'Outre Mer: Martinique, Guadeloupe, Réunion, Guyane', *Études et Conjonctures* **22**, no. 11, 1967, pp. 103–45.

MARRERO, I. *Geografía de Cuba*, New York 1967.

MARSHALL, W. K. 'Peasants development in the West Indies since 1838', *SES* **17**, no. 3, 1968, pp. 252–64.

MASSIP, S. YSALGUÉ DE MASSIP, S. E. 'Applied geography in Cuba: the Isle of Pines Plan', *Colloque International de Géographie Appliquée, Comptes Rendus,* Liège 1967, pp. 377–83.

MATHEWS, T. G., *et al. Politics and Economics in the Caribbean. A contemporary analysis of the Dutch, French and British Caribbean,* Puerto Rico, Inst. Caribb. Stud., Río Piedras 1966.

MAU, J. A. *Social Change and Relief in Progress: a study of images of the future in Jamaica,* Ann Arbor, Michigan, 1967.

MAYNES, P. M. 'The development of a commercial system of yam production in Trinidad', *Trop. Agric.* **44**, no. 3, 1967, pp. 215–21.

MCALPINE, J. D. *Agricultural Production and Trade of Puerto Rico,* Economic Research Series, US Dept. Agric., Washington, DC, 1968.

MESSENGER, J. C. 'The influence of the Irish in Montserrat', *CR* **13**, no. 2, 1967, pp. 3–26.

MILLÁS, J. C. *Hurricanes of the Caribbean and adjacent Regions, 1492–1800,* Acad. Arts and Sciences of the Americas, Washington 1968.

MINGS, R. C. 'Puerto Rico and tourism', *CQ* **14**, no. 3, 1968, pp. 7–21.

MINTZ, S. W. 'Petits cultivateurs et prolétaires ruraux dans la région des Caraibes', in *Les Problèmes agraires des Amériques latines.* Centre National de la Recherche scientifique, Paris 1967, pp. 93–100.

MITCHELL, C. 'A fresh breeze stirs the Leewards', *Nat. Geogr. Mag.* **130**, no. 4, 1966, pp. 488–537.

—— 'The Bahamas: more of sea than of land', *Nat. Geogr. Mag.* **131**, no. 2, 1967, pp. 218–67.

MITCHELL, H. 'L'agriculture aux Antilles', in *Les problèmes agraires des Amériques latines.* Centre National de la Recherche scientifique, Paris 1967, pp. 83–91.

MITCHELL, SIR H. *Caribbean Patterns. A political and economic Study of the contemporary Caribbean,* Edinburgh and London 1967.

MONROE, W. H. 'The karst features of northern Puerto Rico', *Nat. Speleol. Soc. Bull.* **30**, Washington 1968, pp. 75–86.

—— 'Evidence of subterranean sheet solution under weathered detrital cover in Puerto Rico', in *Problems of the Karst Denudation,* Brno 1969, pp. 111–21.

MORAL, P. 'Essai de comparaison entre l'Afrique de l'Ouest et l'Amérique Latine', *Ann. Géogr.* **76**, 1967, pp. 680–703.

—— 'Le "Faciès agraire" haïtien: définition—problèmes', in *Les Problèmes agraires des Ameriques latines,* Centre National de la Recherche scientifique, Paris 1967, pp. 101–8.

MORDECAI, J. *Federation of the West Indies,* Evanston, Ill., 1968.

MÖRNER, M. 'Das vergleichende Studium der Negersklaverei in Anglo—und Lateinamerika: ein Literaturbericht', *Jb. f. Geschichte v. Staat, Wirtschaft und Gesellschaft Lateinamerikas* **5**, 1968, pp. 405–21.

—— 'Einige Endrücke von der Situation und der Möglichkeiten der historischen Forschung auf Kuba', *Jb. f. Geschichte v. Staat, Wirtschaft und Gesellschaft Lateinamerikas* **7**, 1970, pp. 432–50.

MULCHANSINGH, V. C. *CARIFTA, New Horizons in the West Indies,* University of the West Indies, Dept. of Geogr., Occas. Publ. no. 3, Kingston, Jamaica, 1968.

—— *Trends in the Industrialisation of Jamaica,* Univ. of the West Indies, Dept. of Geography, Occasional Paper no. 6, Kingston 1970.

MURRAY, D. B. 'The role of the crops in West Indian agriculture', *J. Agric. Soc.* **67**, no. 3, Port-of-Spain 1967, pp. 379–84.

MYERS, G. C. 'Migration and modernization: the case of Puerto Rico, 1950–1960', *SES* **16**, 1967, pp. 425–31.

NELLESSEN, B. Die Wirtschaft Cubas ist todkrank. *Ubersee-Rundsch.* **19**, H. 6, 1967, pp. 16–17. pp. 16–17.

NELSON, A. E. *Geologic Map of the Utuado Quadrangle,* Puerto Rico, US Geol. Survey, Misc. Geol. Investigations, Map I–480, Washington 1967.

NELSON, A. E. and TOBISCH, O. T. *Geologic Map of the Bayaney Quadrangle, Puerto Rico,* US Geol. Survey, Misc. Geol. Investigations, Map I–525, Washington 1968.

NEWTON, A. P. *The European Nations in the West Indies 1493–1688,* London 1933, reprinted

New York 1967.

NIDDRIE, D. *Wenn die Erde bebt*, Munich 1963.

NORTON, A. *A Bibliography of the Caribbean for Geographers*, Univ. of the West Indies, Dept. of Geography, Occasional Paper no. 7, Kingston 1970.

NORTON, A., ed. *Essays on Jamaica*, University of the West Indies, Dept, of Geography, Kingston 1970.

NORTON, G. 'Islands of Sunshine (Trinidad)', *Geogrl Mag.* **40**, no. 6, 1967, pp. 491–502.

—— 'People of the Out Islands, Bahamas', *Geogrl Mag.* **40**, no. 8, 1967, pp. 704–14.

NORVELL, D. G. and THOMPSON, M. K. 'Higglering in Jamaica, and the mystique of pure competition', *SES* **17**, no. 4, 1968, pp. 407–16.

NÚÑEZ JIMÉNEZ, A. 'Poznámky o Krasu na Kube (on the Cuban karst landscapes)', *Acta Univ. Carolinae Geographica* **2**, Prague 1967, pp. 27–47.

—— *Cuevas y Pictografías; Estudios espeleológicos y arqueológicos*, Habana 1967.

—— 'Cuba', *World Atlas of Agriculture, Monographs*, vol. 3, *Americas*. Novara 1969, pp. 221–9.

OBIOLS, A. and PERDOMO, R. *Atlas de Información básica existente y Lineamientos para la Planificación del Desarrollo integral de la República Dominicana*, Guatemala 1966.

O'CONNOR, J. 'The labour force, employment and unemployment in Cuba 1957–1961', *SES* **15**, no. 2, 1966, pp. 85–91.

O'LOUGHLIN, C. *Economic and Political Change in the Leeward and Windward Islands*, New Haven 1968.

ORTIZ, F. 'Alejandro Humboldt, su Obra cubanófila', *Casa de las Américas*, Habana 1969, pp. 216–33.

OXTOBY, F. E. 'The role of political factors in the Virgin Islands Watch industry', *Geogr. Rev.* **60**, no. 4, 1970, pp. 463–74.

PAGNEY, P. *Climat des Antilles*, 2 vols, Paris 1966.

PALMER, R. W. *The Jamaican Economy*, New York 1968.

PANIN Y. 'La population des départements français d'Outre Mer', *Population* **21**, no. 1, 1966, pp. 97–130.

PANOŠ, V. and ŠTELCL, O. 'Physiographic and geological control in development of Cuban mogotes', *Z. Geomorphol.*, NF, **12**, 1968, pp. 117–65, 168–710 with discussion by H. Lehmann, pp. 171–3.

PAQUETTE, R. 'Une cité planifiée et une cité spontanée, (Fort-de-France, Martinique)', *Cahiers de Géographie de Québec*, no. **29**, 1969, pp. 169–86.

PASTNER, S. L. *Process and Value in a Trinidad Mountain Community*, New York 1967.

PATTEE, R. *La República Dominicana*, Madrid 1967.

PATTERSON, H. O. 'Slavery, acculturation and social change: the Jamaican case', *Brit. J. Sociol.*, 1966, pp. 151–63.

PATTERSON, O. *The Sociology of Slavery: an analysis of the origins, development and structure of Negro slave society in Jamaica*, London 1967.

PEACH, C. *West Indian Migration to Britain: a social geography*, London 1968.

PEACH, G. C. K. 'Factors affecting the distribution of West Indians in Great Britain', *Trans. Geogr. Inst. Br.* **38**, 1966, pp. 151–63.

PEREZ DE LA RIVA, J. 'La population de Cuba et ses problèmes', *Population* **22**, no. 1, 1967, pp. 99–110.

PERKINS, D. *The United States and the Caribbean*, 2nd edn, Cambridge 1967.

PERSAUD, B. 'A banana costing study in St Lucia: the first report', *Agricultural Series, Univ. West Indies* **2**, 1965, pp. 1–46.

PERSAUD, B., et al. 'Impact of agricultural diversification in Barbados', *SES* **17**, no. 3, 1968, pp. 353–65.

PFEFFER, K.-H. 'Neue Beobachtungen im Kegelkarst von Jamaica', *Verhandl. d. Dt. Geographentages* **36**, Wiesbaden 1969, pp. 345–58.

PICÓ, R. 'La estrategia de la planificación en Puerto Rico', *Rev. Soc. Interamericana de Planificación*, Cali, Colombia, 1968, pp. 50–6.

446

PIERRE-CHARLES, G. *L'Economie haitienne et sa voie de développement,* Paris 1967.

PIPPAN, T. 'Geographische Skizze über Puerto Rico', *Mitt. Osterr. Geogr. Ges.* **110**, no. 213, 1968, pp. 245–56.

—— 'Characteristics of valley sections in a moderate relief controlled by fluvial erosion (Puerto Rico) compared with such influenced by both fluvial and glacial erosion (Alpine Flysch Zone and Bohemian Forest)', *Z. Geomorphol.,* Suppl. no. 9, 1970, pp. 119–26.

PLANK, J. *Cuba and the United States long range perspectives,* Washington 1967.

POCTHIER, G. 'Observations effectuées sur des Plantes fourragères en Grande Terre (Guadeloupe)', *Agronomie tropicale* **21**, no. 2, 1966, pp. 171–90.

POLLAK-ELTZ, A. 'Woher stammen die Neger Südamerikas', *Umschau Wiss. Tech.* **67**, 1967, pp. 244–9.

—— 'Kulturwandel bei Negern der Neuen Welt', *Umschau Wiss. Tech.* **67**, 1967, pp. 623–6.

POPE-HENNESSY, J. *Sins of the Fathers: a study of the Atlantic slave traders 1441–1807,* London 1967.

PREISWERK, R., ed. *Regionalism and the Commonwealth Caribbean,* Institute of International Relations, University of the West Indies, St Augustine, Trinidad, 1969.

PRICE, R. 'Caribbean fishing and fishermen: a historical sketch', *Am. Anthropol.* **68**, no. 6, 1966, pp. 1363–83.

PUSHCHAROVSKII, Y. M. *Geology and Mineral Resources of Cuba,* Aeronautive and chart information Center, St Louis 1968.

PY, C. and BARBIER, M. 'Nouvelles techniques dans la culture de l'ananas aux Antilles', *Fruits* **21**, no. 5, 1966, pp. 229–30.

RANDALL, R. E. 'Measurements of aerial salt on the coast of Barbados', *Climatol. Bull.* **3**, Montreal 1968, pp. 23–35.

RAYMOND, N. 'Cane fires on a British West Indian island', *SES* **16**, 1967, pp. 280–8.

REED, A. J. *The Geology of the Bog Walk Quadrangle Kingston,* Bull. Jam. Geol. Surv. Dept., no. 6, 1966.

RIVERO, W. 'La Producción azucarera en Cuba', Universidad de la Habana **19**: 211, 1968, pp. 35–8.

ROBERTS, G. W. 'Demographic aspects of rural development; the Jamaican experience', *SES* **17**, no. 3, 1968, pp. 276–82.

ROBERTS, T. E., *et al. Area Handbook for the Dominican Republic,* American University Foreign Area Studies Division, Washington 1966.

ROCHON, L. 'La Sociedad agropecuaria "Jesús Feliú". Un Caso de Cambio en el Medio rural, bajo un Régimen socialista de Transición', *Academia de Ciencias de Cuba,* no. 4, Habana 1967, pp. 23–38.

RODRIGUEZ CRUZ, J. and MATHEWS, T. G. 'Race Relations in Puerto Rico', *Race, J. Inst. Race Relations,* London 1968, pp. 339–41.

RUSSELL, R. J. and MCINTIRE, W. G. *Barbuda Reconnaissance,* Baton Rouge 1966.

SANDERSON, A. G. 'Notes on the agricultural economies of dependent Territories in the Western Hemisphere and Puerto Rico', Economic Research Service, US Department of Agriculture, **145**, 1965, pp. 1–68.

SAXE, A. *Study of urban Squatters in Port-of-Spain,* Brandeis Univ., Waltham, Mass., 1968.

SCHAEFFER, J. A. *Field Report Dajabon, Dominican Republic,* Teachers College, Columbia Univ., New York 1968.

SCHENKEL, P. '10 Jahre cubanische Revolution', *Übersee-Rundsch.* **21**, no. 2, 1969, pp. 8–10.

SCHNAKENBOURG, C. 'L'industrie sucrière dans la partie française de Saint-Martin au XVIIIème siècle', *Bull. Soc. Hist. Guadeloupe,* **8**, 1967, pp. 12–25.

SCHUBIN, W. 'Die Intensivierung der Landwirtschaft Kubas', *Int. Z. der Landwirtschaft* **2**, 1966, pp. 217–19.

SEDA BONILLA, E. 'Toro Bravo: una comunidad tradicional de pequeños agricultores en el centro montañoso de Puerto Rico', *Revista de Ciencias sociales* **12**, no. 2, 1968, pp. 239–53.

SEGAL, A. 'El Desarrollo económico de Barbados', *Comercio Exterior* **17**, no. 6, México 1967, pp. 476–80.

447

Bibliography: supplement

—— *Politics and Population in the Caribbean*, Inst. Carib. Stud., Río Piedras 1968.

—— *The Politics of Integration in the Caribbean*, Inst. Carib. Stud., Río Piedras 1968.

—— 'Economic integration and, preferential trade: the Caribbean experience', *The World Today* **25**, no. 10, Royal Institute of International Affairs, London 1969, pp. 415–47.

SELDEN, R. *The Caribbean*, New York 1968.

SEMEVSKIY, B. N. 'Social and natural conditions of Cuban agriculture', *Soviet Geography: Review and Translations* **8**, no. 1, 1967, pp. 12–25; trans. from *Vestnik Geograficheskogo Universiteta* (Seriya Geologii i Geografii) no. 18, 1965, pp. 59–71.

—— 'The problems of Cuba's energy supplies', *Soviet Geography: Review and Translations* **8**, no. 1, 1967, pp. 25–33; trans. from *Vestnik Leningradskogo Universiteta* (Seriya Geologii i Geografii) no. 6, 1966, pp. 72–9.

SHERIDAN, R. B. 'The plantation revolution, 1625–1775', *CS* **9**, no. 3, 1969, pp. 5–26.

SIEUCHAND, A. C. *A Junior Geography of Trinidad and Tobago*, London 1967.

SIGURET, R. 'Esclaves d'indigoteries et de caféières au quartier de Jacmel, Saint-Domingue 1757–1759', *Rev. Fr. Hist. d'Outre Mer* **2**, 1968, pp. 190–230.

SIMMONDS, W. A. 'Barbados, twenty-third member state of the OAS', *Américas* **19**, no. 12, 1967, pp. 3–12.

SINCLAIR, I. G. L. 'Bauxite genesis in Jamaica: new evidence from trade element distribution', *Econ. Geol.* **62**, 1967.

SLATER, M. *The Caribbean Islands*, London 1968.

SMITH, D. 'Farm and labor problems squeeze Puerto Rican factories', *Sugar y Azúcar* **71**, no. 2, 1966, pp. 47–8.

SMITH, H. *Study of the Cost and Structure of Distribution in Grenada and St Lucia*, University of the West Indies, Institute of Social and Economic Research, Mona, Kingston, 1967.

SMITH, R. V. 'Industrial development in Puerto Rico: locational factors and distributional patterns', *Southampton Research Series in Geography*, no. 5, 1969, pp. 31–58.

SPRINGER, H. W. 'Barbados as a sovereign state', *J. Roy. Soc. Arts* **115**, no. 5132, 1967, pp. 627–41.

STELCL, J. and PANOS, V. 'Výzkum krasu kubánských nízin (Karstuntersuchungen in den kubanischen Tiefebenen)', *Zpr. geogr. Ustavu CSAV, Opava* **2**, 1967, pp. 1–4.

STONE, D. H. F. *Industrial Relations in Jamaica and Trinidad*, Kingston 1968.

TABIO, E. E. and PAYARES, R. *Sobre los Cafetales coloniales de la Sierra del Rosario*, Habana 1968.

THEVENEAU, A. *Le Climat de la Guadeloupe*, Monogr. Mét, Nat., no. 50, 1965.

THOMAS, C. Y. 'A model of pure plantation economy: comment', *SES* **17**, no. 3, 1968. pp. 339–48.

THOMAS, R. P. 'The sugar colonies of the old Empire: profit or loss for Great Britain?', *Econ. Hist. Rev.*, 2nd ser. **21**, no. 1, 1968, pp. 30–45.

TORTELLA CASARES, G. 'La industria azucarera cubana: 1868–1895', *Moneda y Créd.* **96**, 1966, pp. 15–31.

TOUT, D. G. 'The climate of Barbados', *Climatol. Bull.* **3**, Montreal 1968, pp. 1–17.

—— 'An analysis of the 1964 solar radiation record at the Brace Experiment Station, St James, Barbados', *Climatol. Bull.* **2**, Montreal 1967, pp. 29–44.

ULLMAN, J. R. and DINHOFER, A. *Caribbean Here and Now: the complete vacation guide to 52 sunny islands in the Caribbean Sea*, New York 1968.

VALENCIÈRE, P. 'Die überseeischen Départements und Gebiete Frankreichs', *Z. f. Wirtschaftsgeogr.* **11**, 1967, pp. 79–84.

VALLEE, L. *The Negro Family in St Thomas*, Ann Arbor, Michigan, 1967.

VALLES, M. T. *Les Idéologies coopérativistes et leur applicabilité en Haiti*, Paris 1967.

VAZQUEZ CALZADA, J. 'El cremimiento poblacional en Puerto Rico: 1943 al presente', *Rev. Ciencias Soc.* **13**, no. 1, 1968, pp. 5–22.

VÉLIZ, C. *Latin America and the Caribbean: a handbook*, London 1968.

VERNON, K. C. and CARROLL, D. M. 'Barbados', *Soil Landuse Survey, Brit. Caribbean*, 1966, pp. 1–38.

VILLAR ROCES, M. *Puerto Rico y su Reforma agraria*, Río Piedras 1968.

448

VITERITTI, A. 'Haiti', *World Atlas of Agriculture, Monographs*, vol. 3, *Americas*. Novara 1969, pp. 289–95.

VOLKOVA, Y. D. 'Basic trends in the population geography of contemporary Cuba', *Soviet Geogr. Review and Translation*, Dec. 1969, pp. 612–7; trans. from *Vestnik Moskoskogo Universiteta, Geografiya*, no. 3, 1969, pp. 78–83.

VRIES, E. DE and GONZALES, C. P. 'Social research and rural life in central America, Mexico and the Caribbean region', *Z. ausländ. Landwirtschaft* **8**, no. 1, 1969, pp. 89–90.

WALKER, M. *Social, Economic and Political Life in the Valley of Constanza, Dominican Republic; a preliminary report*, Teachers College, Columbia Univ., New York 1968.

WARFORD, J. J. 'A pricing and investment policy for Antigua's water supply', *SES* **16**, 1967, pp. 127–55.

WATTS, D. *Evapotranspiration and Energy Relationships at Waterford, Barbados, 1960*, McGill Univ. Dept. of Geogr., Climatol. Res. Ser. **1**, 1966.

WEHLER, H.-U. ' "Cuba-Libre" und amerikanische Intervention. Der kubanische Aufstand seit dem Februar 1895 und drei Phasen der amerikanischen Kubapolitik bis zum September 1897', *Jb. f. Geschichte v. Staat, Wirtschaft und Gesellschaft Lateinamerikas* **5**, 1968, pp. 303–46.

WEINER, J. *The Jewish Migrant Settlement of Sosua, Dominican Republic, Report*, Teachers' College, Columbia Univ., New York 1968.

WELCH, B. 'Population density and emigration in Dominica', *Geogrl J.* **134**, no. 2, 1968, pp. 227–35.

WELLER, J. A. *The East Indian Indenture in Trinidad*, Inst. Carib. Stud., Río Piedras 1968.

WESTPHALEN, J. 'Cuba—elf Jahre nach der Revolution', *Ubersee-Rdsch.* **22**, no. 6, 1970, p. 10.

WHITEHEAD, R. A. 'Some notes on dwarf coconut palms in Jamaica', *Trop. Agric.* **43**, 1966, pp. 277–94.

WIARDA, H. *The Dominican Republic, a Nation in Transition*, New York 1969.

WINTERS, H. F. and MISKIMEN, W. *Vegetable Gardening in the Caribbean Area*, US Dept. of Agric., Agric. Ser., Washington 1967.

WITTHAUER, K. 'Cuba (Länderbericht)', *Pet. Geogr. Mitt.* **112**, 1968, pp. 143–7.

WOOD, D. *Trinidad in Transition, the Years After Slavery*, London 1968.

WOODLEY, J. D. 'A history of the Jamaican fauna', *Jamaican Journal* **2**, no. 3, Institute of Jamaica, Kingston 1968, pp. 14–20.

WORTH, C. B. *A Naturalist in Trinidad*, Philadelphia and New York 1967.

ZONNEVELD, J. I. S. 'Quaternary climatic changes in the Caribbean and N. South-America', *Eiszeitalter und Gegenwart* **19**, 1968, pp. 203–8.

ZONN, S. V. 'O lateritach i lateritoobrazovanii na Kube. (On laterite and lateritic formation in Cuba)', Izv. Akad. Nauk. SSSR., Ser. geogr. **2**, Moscow 1968, pp. 5–11.

Topographical Maps

			number of sheets
Cuba	1 :	250,000[1]	19
single sheets	1 :	50,000[1]	
Jamaica	1 :	50,000	12
Haiti	1 :	50,000[1]	
Dominican Republic	1 :	50,000[1]	
Puerto Rico	1 :	20,000	65
Bahama Islands			
Abaco	1 :	25,000	20
Grand Bahama	1 :	25,000	13
Eleuthera	1 :	25,000	8
Cat Island	1 :	25,000	6
New Providence	1 :	25,000	
US Virgin Islands			
St Croix	1 :	24,000	3
St Thomas	1 :	24,000	3
St John	1 :	24,000	3
British Virgin Islands	1 :	25,000	6
Dutch Islands to the Windward			
St Eustatius	1 :	20,000	1
St Maarten	1 :	20,000	2
Saba	1 :	20,000	1
British Leeward Islands			
St Kitts–Nevis–Anguilla	1 :	25,000	3
Montserrat	1 :	25,000	1
Antigua	1 :	25,000	2
French Islands to the Windward			
Guadeloupe	1 :	20,000	32

[1] restricted distribution

450

(with neighbouring islands)	1 :	50,000	6
Martinique	1 :	20,000	23
	1 :	50,000	4

British Windward Islands
Dominica	1 :	25,000	3
St Lucia	1 :	25,000	3
St Vincent	1 :	25,000	2
Grenada	1 :	25,000	2

| *Barbados* | 1 : | 10,000 | 18 |
| | 1 : | 50,000 | 1 |

Trinidad and Tobago
Tobago	1 :	10,000	21
	1 :	25,000	3
Trinidad	1 :	50,000	9

Dutch Islands to the Leeward
Bonaire	1 :	25,000	6
Curaçao	1 :	25,000	8
Aruba	1 :	25,000	4

Place Index

italicized numbers indicate maps and diagrams

(NB: only those names are listed below which differ in German)

452

German	English

Puerto Rico-
  Graben
	Puerto Rico
	  Trench

Roque-Kanal Roseau-Tal	Roque Canal Roseau Valley

Samaná-Bucht
Samaná-Halbinsel
Saumâtre-See
Schlangensund etc.
Silber-Bank-
  Rucken
	Samaná Bay
	Samaná Peninsula
	Saumâtre Lake
	Serpent's Mouth
	Silver Bank
	  Ridge

Tobago-Becken Tobago-Rinne Turks-Inseln	Tobago Basin Tobago Trench Turks Islands

Venezolanisches
  Becken
Vigie-Halbinsel
	Venezuelan
	  Basin
	Vigie Peninsula

Yucatán-Becken Yucatán-Strasse Yucatán-Strom	Yucatán Basin Yucatán Channel Yucatán Current

Subject Index

456

457

458

460

461

462

463